DICTIONARY OF SOCIOLOGY

EDITORIAL BOARD

DICTIONARY OF
SOCIOLOGY

Edited by

HENRY PRATT FAIRCHILD, PH.D., LL.D.

1965

LITTLEFIELD, ADAMS & CO.

TOTOWA, NEW JERSEY

1965 Edition

By Littlefield, Adams & Co.

Copyright 1944
By Philosophical Library, Inc.

PREFACE

Every science must have its special vocabulary or terminology. Sciences deal with ideas, thoughts, and concepts, and these must be expressed in words. Even the facts which are the groundwork of science must be set forth largely in words. No science, therefore, can have any more precision and exactitude than the words or other symbols, such as mathematical or chemical formulae, in which it is embodied. Quite generally, this situation calls for a special dictionary or glossary for each particular science.

The foregoing is perhaps even more true for sociology than for many other sciences. Since sociology deals with matters of commonplace· experience, the thoughts, ideas, and concepts which it must express are, with relatively few exceptions, included in any standard general dictionary, and most of the really important terms are already to some degree familiar even to the immature members of society, and are frequently used in everyday speech. Scientific accuracy demands that precise and limited meanings should be assigned to these terms, in order that they may be used uniformly alike by specialists, students, and amateurs in the field. In the case of some words, a sufficiently precise sociological definition may be found in a general dictionary, and what is needed is an underscoring of this particular interpretation. In other cases, the requirements of the science call for specialized definitions which do not occur in the precise form in any ordinary dictionary. For both these purposes, a special volume is indispensable. If this process occasionally appears to do violence to the preconceptions already held by users of a given word there seems to be no escape, and one who wishes to deal scientifically with sociology must resign himself to the effort of accommodating his use to standardized practice. The only alternative that has suggested itself is to invent artificial and arbitrary words, probably derived from some classic roots, which will be given as exact a significance as possible by the inventor. This has never had any wide success, as the use of strange, artificial terms creates an impression of pedanticism and remoteness, and destroys the sense of human reality which is needed to give life and acceptability to the science. There is hardly a score of words in this Dictionary which were deliberately created to cover sociological concepts.

A dictionary has two main purposes, first to consolidate and standardize the existing uniformities of linguistic usage, and second, to establish new uniformities and precisions by selecting for authoritative support one or more of various meanings currently assigned to a given word or phrase. In the Dictionary of Sociology, exceptional emphasis is laid upon the latter task, because of the conditions already mentioned. The usefulness of such a dictionary in helping to develop a genuine science must depend largely upon the extent to which sociologists are content to accept the definitions given in the Dictionary, and use them consistently and scrupulously in accordance with the meanings indicated.

A good definition, likewise, has two main aspects. It should give the uninformed person a clear and adequate notion of the character of the object, even though he may never encounter it in his experience, and it should enable a person correctly to identify the object the first time he does meet it in his experience. A good definition must be something more than either a classification or a recipe, although both of those factors may be embodied in it. Since definitions are couched in words (and sometimes in other symbols), if a definition is to be precise and clear every word used in it must be equally precise and clear. In a general dictionary, every word used in any definition is presumably defined in its own appropriate place. While there is, therefore, a sort of an endless circle, nevertheless it is a real circle and there should be no breaks in it. In a sociological dictionary, most of the words used in defining are not themselves defined in this particular volume, but they are taken from everyday usage, and their definitions are to be looked for in a standard dictionary. This creates a regrettable, but inescapable, element of indefiniteness. But there is also a great gain in the use of certain definitely sociological words in defining other sociological terms. In this respect a dictionary can be consistent and constructive.

A special difficulty arises from the fact that, partly because of the situation just described, a very large proportion of sociological terms are not single words, but phrases of two or more words. This introduces peculiar technical problems in preparing a Dictionary of Sociology. The question of primary and secondary listings is almost unanswerable. To adopt the uniform rule of putting the substantive first and the modifier afterwards would produce such absurdities as "ladder, agricultural" and "chaser, ambulance." The expedient of putting the more distinctly sociological word first and the more general word second has logic on its side, but also presents no solution in the case of terms where both words are equally sociological, as for example, "antagonistic cooperation." It has not been possible to discover any comprehensive formulae that could be applied unvaryingly to this and related problems. The best procedure has seemed to be to deal with each case or type of cases on the basis of its own characteristics, following the guidance of common sense, practicality, and minimum violence to the expectation of the user. As an example there may be cited the procedure of giving all terms beginning with the word "social" primary listing under that head, even though in some cases it might have seemed more logical to treat them as subdivisions of some other important sociological concept. Having done this with "social," it seemed only reasonable to follow the same practice for the terms beginning with the word "individual." As for the rest, each particular term has been handled in accordance with its apparently most reasonable and practical place in the entire scheme.

One additional problem arises from the fact that sociology, as a comprehensive science, must necessarily overlap several more specialized fields, such as those of anthropology, economics, psychology, political science, statistics, and history. It is not possible to set up any rigid dividing lines, nor to work out an inclusive formula that will prescribe exactly how far into each of these domains it is expedient to go. In this case, some guidance is to be found in the degree of sociological character of various specific terms. Thus "amulet" is definitely an anthropological term, and yet it has genuine sociological significance. On the other hand "blow-gun" is a little too specialized to belong in a Dictionary of Sociology.

The preparation of this Dictionary has rested with a staff composed of an Editor, an Associate Editor, three Advisory Editors and ninety-three Contributing Editors, whose names are listed on a preceding page. The large bulk of the definitions has been supplied individually by the members of the Board of Contributing Editors. Such contributions are identified by appropriate initials. In a few cases, it seemed expedient to assign certain rather specialized fields to one individual, who would act as Coordinator, and consolidate the offerings of the group of Contributing Editors working in each respective area. Thus Dwight Sanderson accepted this function for Agricultural Sociology, Walter C. Reckless for Criminology, Clyde V. Kiser for

Population, and E. A. Hoebel and George P. Murdock for Anthropology. Definitions which are not identified by initials have been derived from three main sources: 1) They have been prepared, either individually or collectively, by the Editor, Associate Editor, or Advisory Editors. 2) They have been derived from other works from which permission to quote verbatim has courteously been granted, such as Young's Social Worker's Dictionary, and the Glossary of Housing Terms mentioned below. 3) In a few cases they have been submitted at special request by individuals who were not members of the Board of Editors, but graciously consented to cover certain concepts with which they were particularly familiar. In the last analysis, by virtue of his official position, the Editor must take the final responsibility for every definition as printed. But as a matter of fact the great majority of the definitions submitted by others has been very little, if at all, modified. As a unit, the Dictionary stands as a unique representation of the precise thinking of the American sociological fraternity as a whole.

In the conduct of the work, much use has been made of certain other reference works, particularly Merriam's Webster's New International Dictionary of the English Language, Seligman and Johnson's Encyclopaedia of the Social Sciences, Erle Fiske Young's The New Social Worker's Dictionary, E. B. Reuter's Handbook of Sociology, Earle Edward Eubank's The Concepts of Sociology, Harold A. Phelps' Principles and Laws of Sociology, Edgerton's Statistical Dictionary of Terms and Symbols, Constantine Panunzio's Major Social Institutions, and Building Materials and Structures, A Glossary of Housing Terms compiled by Subcommittee on Definitions, Central Housing Committee on Research, Design, and Construction, of the United States Department of Commerce and the National Bureau of Standards. Grateful acknowledgment of this use is tendered herewith.

Finally, the Editor cannot refrain from becoming personal sufficiently to express his deep gratitude and appreciation to all who have helped to make the book what it is. In the face of extraordinary difficulties and complications arising out of the war period, which struck the United States after the book was planned, there has been a uniformly high level of cooperation and promptness, and patience with the many demands made necessary by the expediting of the work. To the publisher, also, the Editor extends with pleasure his thanks for generous, competent, and sympathetic support and guidance.

A

abandoned child. Cf. child, abandoned.

abduct. In general, to take away a human being by stealth and often with violence; to kidnap. In more frequent usage the word signifies to seize and take away unlawfully a young woman for purposes of marriage or rape. w.g.

abnormal. (1) Out of adjustment with the general structure of a particular system. Prejudicial to the efficient functioning of a system as a whole. Contrary to social expectation. (2) Deviating from the customary, the usual, or the average.

abnormality. Absence of, or deviation from, normality.

abnormality, social. Cf. social abnormality.

abolition. The agitation carried on in the U. S. by Wendell Phillips, William Lloyd Garrison and others against manhood slavery between 1832 and 1862. The means advocated ranged from the aiding of runaway slaves, and the use of force by private parties, to legal enactments and compensation for emancipated slaves by the State. g.m.f.

abortion. In lay, inaccurate language, a criminal interruption of pregnancy, in the early months. In more accurate medical terminology abortion is any detachment or expulsion, or both, from any cause of the fertilized ovum or fetus before it is capable of independent life (i.e., first 26 or 28 weeks). After this period, and up to the normal conclusion of pregnancy, expulsion is called premature birth (q.v.). Abortion is medically classified as (a) spontaneous, (b) induced, (c) legal or illegal. A spontaneous abortion is the detachment or expulsion of the previable fetus by conditions or states not under the control of normal physiological functions (e.g., some pathology in the woman or an accident). An induced abortion is an artificial interruption of pregnancy, usually by an operation. Our confused laws make it impossible to define legal abortion briefly, but, generally speaking, a legal abortion is one induced by a physician, with the corroboratory consent of a medical colleague in good standing, for adequate and generally accepted medical indications (e.g., to save the life or preserve the health of the pregnant woman). Otherwise abortion is illegal in the U.S.A. The laws of one or two states do not permit even the above, but medical custom accepts the principle just stated. n.e.h.

abortion, criminal. The unlawful destruction of a fetus by the use of drugs, instruments, or manipulation. Cf. abortion e.r.g.

absolute divorce. The legal dissolving of a marriage permitting one or both members of the former union to remarry. e.r.g.

absolutism. The form of national government in which the supreme power is exercised by a monarch, or a small group, either with or without a constitution. By a figure of speech, the term is applied to autocratic control exercised over any social group by one or a few persons. g.m.f.

abstinence. Voluntary total avoidance of satisfaction of an appetite, because of taboo or moral restraint as in the avoidance of meat on fast days, or of alcoholic liquors. f.h.h.

abstinence, marital. (*general*) The refraining from indulging the sexual appetite in

1

marriage. (*specific*) 1. The postponement of marriage until one can support a family on a decent standard of living. This is Malthus' theory of "moral restraint." 2. The refraining from sexual intercourse in marriage (a) completely, or (b) except for procreation.

abstract collectivity. That kind of plurel (q.v.) characterized by the highest degree of abstractness. Such plurels are ideological, for they are not simple summations of social processes, but abstract products of simpler plurels (crowds, organized groups, etc.) which themselves are products of directly observable social processes. In other words, abstract collectivities are constructs (q.v.), although rarely if ever scientific constructs; folk language usually has much to do with them. They are almost always results of "social animism", although they can be scientifically observed and their recurrence predicted. Churches, nations, classes, parties, etc., are abstract collectivities. Related terms are associations, large social structures, and corporate bodies.   H.B.

abundance. A supply of material necessaries, comforts, and simple luxuries adequate to provide the physical basis for "a good life." The term has come into vogue in recent years, particularly in connection with the concept of "an economy of abundance," as a contrast to the actual scarcity and its supporting philosophy, which have prevailed, even in countries of advanced economic culture.

abundance, economy of. Cf. economy of abundance.

academic freedom. Cf. freedom, academic.

acceleration. Increase in momentum of a moving object, applicable to a social movement or a process involving rate of change.   N.A.

acceleration of social change. Acceleration is the speeding up of the time rate of social change. It is the time rate of increase in the velocity of a process. "Deceleration" is the slowing down of the rate of change. "Celeration" denotes either acceleration or deceleration, either positive or negative changing rate of the rate of a process. These terms are measurable and therefore operationally definable, by the difference between two periods in the rate of a social change, divided by the time interval between the mid-dates of the two periods.   S.C.D.

accident insurance. Cf. insurance, accident.

acclimatization. The process whereby migrants become organically adjusted to a new climate, or the state of such adjustment. Also, figuratively, mental and social adjustment to a new social environment.   F.H.H.

accommodation. (1) Any social process, whether conscious or unconscious, which consists in the alteration of functional relations between personalities and groups so as to avoid, reduce or eliminate conflict and to promote reciprocal adjustment (q.v.), provided that the altered behavior pattern is transmitted by social learning rather than by biological heredity; and (2) the social relationships which result from this process. Among the varieties (or methods) of accommodation most often mentioned are arbitration, compromise, conciliation, conversion, subordination, and toleration.   H.H.

accommodation, creative. That conscious and deliberate form of accommodation in which a solution for conflict is sought through discovering and developing potential areas of agreement, whereby the underlying needs, interests and motives of all those involved may be fulfilled to the maximum possible degree. As contrasted with compromise, creative accommodation seeks to avoid the sacrifice of any important underlying interest on either side; as contrasted with legalistic justice, creative accommodation seeks emergent, voluntarily acceptable solutions.   H.H.

accommodation, group. The process in which interacting groups modify their organization, rôle, or status to conform to the requirements set up by the situation or by the inclusive social unit.   J.P.E.

accordance. A phase of human association of personal-social or common-human type, most clearly exemplified in the pair or dyad, but also occurring within and between plurels of every other variety, and characterized by a low degree of social distance. If the emphasis on the common-human aspect is retained, synonyms and/ or related terms are agreement, conformity, accommodation, assimilation, acculturation, harmony, concord, etc. When association reaches the intensity of accordance, mutual participation in emotions, memories, and habitual attitudes ensues; conduct becomes more and more in accord, grows more and more similar. Nevertheless, accordance marks only the phase of similarity, not of identity; although in many respects very close to concepts such as social amalgamation, fusion, unification, solidarity, etc., it does not signify the maximum degree of association.   H.B.

accouchement. Child delivery.   E.R.G.

accountability (*financial*). A situation in which a person can be "held to account", i.e., legally made financially responsible for damage, loss, or results of neglect; (*criminological*) a situation in which an offender, whether or not "guilty" or "morally responsible", is considered to have committed without duress an act injurious to others, so that organized society through legal measures must so treat him as to minimize repetition of the act or continuation of "criminal behavior". Cf. responsibility.   T.D.E.

acculturation. (1) A process of conditioning: (a) a child in the behavior patterns —overt and covert—of his in-groups, or (b) a member of an out-group for assimilation into, accommodation to, or imitation of the pattern of the in-group.   D.E.W.
   (2) The assumption of culture through contact, especially with a people of higher civilization. Cf. diffusion.   G.P.M.

accumulation. The process or act of collecting or amassing culture traits such as ideas, artifacts, or techniques.   J.P.E.

achievement. Progress toward a desired objective. While generally used in the sense of conscious improvement of society, it may be used as attaining a goal, whether or not that attainment has been beneficial to anyone.   M.C.E.

achievement, social. Cf. social achievement.

acquired. Received from some outside source; not innate. Cf. acquired characteristic.   J.P.E.

acquired character. Cf. character, acquired.

acquired characteristic. Cf. characteristic, acquired.

acquired pattern. Cf. pattern, acquired.

acquisitive. Having a strong desire to receive or possess.   J.P.E.

acquisitiveness. The quality of having a strong desire to receive or possess. J.P.E.

acquisitiveness, social. Cf. social acquisitiveness.

Act of God. An event or situation the cause of which may be explained in terms of human or natural action, but which is not attributable to the carelessness or the forethought of anyone in particular. N.A.

action. A process involving change as well as progressive alteration of status. M.C.E.

action, corporate. Action engaged in by individuals so united as to react to the environment as though they were parts of the same living organism.   M.S.

action, direct. The resort to such non-political methods as strikes, sabotage, violence or non-violent resistance to government in order to accomplish political, social or economic changes; in contrast to political action (q.v.)   R.N.B.

action, impulsive. Action without foresight of goal or voluntary direction. M.S.

action, individual. Cf. individual action.

action, political. The use of political machinery to accomplish changes in the social and economic order, as contrasted with direct action (q.v.).   R.N.B.

action, reciprocal. Action in which each of a plural number of participants matches the action of each of the others.   M.S.

action, serial. Action in which the first participant initiates activity, and in which the second, and each subsequent, participant in turn responds to the action of a predecessor and stimulates another participant.　　　　M.S.

action, social. Cf. social action.

action pattern. An arrangement of social actions (q.v.) in social space and/or time; it may therefore have both static and dynamic aspects. Social processes are action patterns in which the stress is on the dynamic; social structures or plurels are action patterns in which the stress is on the static. Whether an action pattern "exists" at any given time or place is strictly a matter of greater or lesser probability.　　　　H.B.

active ideationalism. Cf. ideationalism, active.

activity, subversive. Cf. subversive activity.

actuality (*philosophical, methodological*). A situation in which an object or "gestalt" is considered to exist, or to have existed, in the external, verifiable and communicable world. (Cf. reality, with which actuality is often confused and from which it is usefully distinguished.)　　　　T.D.E.

adapt. To fit an organism to environmental conditions by processes of selection, natural or artificial, resulting in organic modifications. Similarly, to fit a cultural trait, especially a material trait, to new uses or to a new cultural medium. F.H.H.

adaptation. The process of acquiring fitness to live in a given environment. Commonly, and most correctly, the term is applicable to changes in morphological traits of the physical body. By inference, under contextual safeguards, it may also be used to indicate cultural modification to suit a particular human environment. Cf. assimilation.

adaptation, social. Cf. social adaptation.

adapté. The subject of the adaptive process; the individual, group or mass undergoing this process.　　　　F.E.L.

adaptive culture. Cf. culture, adaptive.

adaptive growth. Cf. growth, adaptive.

addict. A victim of a drug or of a pernicious habit.　　　　F.W.K.

additive. Capable of being treated by the mathematical process of addition.

adelphic polyandry. Cf. polyandry, adelphic.

adequate sample. Cf. sample, adequate.

adjust. To modify personal behavior, as through accommodation, into harmonious and effective relationship with the cultural environment.　　　　F.H.H.

adjustment. Cf. social adjustment.

adjustment, individual. Cf. individual adjustment.

adjustment, institutional. Modification of the customary functions and relationships of an institution. The mass-movement character of institutional adjustment makes it usually take place in an unplanned and largely unpredicted fashion, beyond the immediate foresight of individuals. Institutional adjustment is occasioned by changed life-conditions, especially technological and ecological changes. It takes place more readily in institutions closely associated with societal self-maintenance and least readily in general in the religious institution, removed as it is from the immediate and constant check of economic and political experience. A.M'C.L.

adjustment, personal. A condition or state of being in which the individual is in harmonious relationship with a given social situation. The process of attaining such a state.　　　　W.E.G.

adjustment, social. Cf. social adjustment.

adjustment, vocational social. The preparation and adaptation of young people to their occupational and economic status, in such a way that their social and domestic needs are also met. Such adjustment includes both a subjective and an objective aspect in that it gives to the individual a thorough knowledge of his inborn aptitudes and acquired trends of the more important occupational fields. Specific training in skills and scientific placement are involved. Cf. vocational guidance; vocational rehabilitation; vocational training.   A.E.W.

adjustment of personality. (1) Those types of relationship between the parts of a personality (q.v.) which promote the long-run interests of the personality and the requirements of the social groups on which the interests of the personality depend. (2) Those processes which tend to produce such relationships; social processes (q.v.) when analyzed from the standpoint of the changes which occur in the individual and the effects of those changes upon the long-run interests of the individual.   H.H.

administration, household. Cf. household administration.

administrative regulation. An order issued by an administrative officer of government in pursuance of an act of legislature which delegates either general or restrictive authority to the administrator to modify or amplify the provisions of the original act. The regulation has the status of law and is enforceable by the courts; it may be challenged in the court as exceeding the powers or purpose of the law (ultra vires). Administrative orders are becoming increasingly important in fields such as public health, immigration, public welfare, social insurance, and regulation of business.   J.W.M'C.

adolescence. A period in the development of the human individual between puberty, the beginning of greatly accelerated sex development, and full maturity. Commonly used as a synonym for youth.   E.R.G.

adolescent court. Cf. court, adolescent.

adoption. Voluntary acceptance, confirmed usually by recognized court or other legal action, of a child of other parents to be the same as one's own natural child.   A.J.T.

adult education. Cf. education, adult.

adult probation. Cf. probation, adult.

adultery. Socially unsanctioned sexual relations on the part of a married person with a person other than the spouse. G.P.M.

advance. The first tentative, incipient stages of association occurring after social contact in one or another form has been established. Synonyms and/or related terms are: to make overtures, to establish relations, to "break the ice," etc. From the social-psychological standpoint it may be said that, in advance, there always remains some feeling of hesitation; the incipient association is regarded as a more or less doubtful experiment. Usually one of the two participants (advance is a common-human process most clearly exemplified in the pair) manifests greater indecision and is less desirous of closer approach than the other. The conscious or unconscious resolve to break the reserve holding them apart falls to the latter, who then carries out an act of advance or, as it were, makes advances or overtures. Exceptions are fairly numerous, however; oftentimes advance on both sides takes place because mutual desire for it is latent or manifest.   H.B..

advertising. A display of the presumed values of consumption goods, or of production goods when offered for sale, ranging all the way from dignified restraint to lying ostentation, and using any means of communication. Disvalues are never mentioned.   F.E.L.

aesthetic ideationalism. Cf. ideationalism, aesthetic.

affiance. To solemnly pledge oneself or (in the case of parents) another, in marriage; to betroth.   W.G.

affiliation. 1. A state of legal, formal or cooperative relationship between two or more organized social groups; the process of establishing same. 2. A legal action or process whereby an illegitimate child is declared the offspring of a designated man.   F.H.H.

affinity. Relationship by marriage, as with the consanguine relative of a spouse or the spouse of a consanguine relative. Cf. consanguinity.   G.P.M.

after care. Usually, social case work services rendered a client after his discharge from a hospital or institution. Also used in nursing and allied fields.   W.P.

agamogenesis. Asexual reproduction; reproduction by virgin females by means of eggs which develop without being fertilized by spermatozoa; syn. parthenogenesis. On subhuman level found chiefly among certain crustaceans, insects and worms; in human culture history so-called "virgin birth."   A.J.T.

age, gang. Cf. gang age.

age,' power. Cf. power age.

age-area concept. The theory that the extent of distribution of an element of culture is directly proportionate to its age, i.e., that of two comparable culture traits (q.v.) the more widely diffused is the older.   G.P.M.

age-class. An age-grade (q.v.).

age of consent. In popular interpretation this phrase refers to that minimum age at which an individual's agreement to marry is legally valid. This meaning, however, is not technically correct. More accurately, age of consent is that lowest age at which a girl may give her consent to sexual intercourse without making the man liable to a charge of rape. Prior to the twentieth century in the United States the ages of ten and twelve years were generally acknowledged as the age of consent by common law. However, as late as 1885 the State of Delaware recognized the age of seven as legally sufficient. In most of the States today the common law rule has been changed by statute to provide for higher age limits; sixteen years of age is a common "age of consent" on State statutes at present. The States of California and Colorado have set this limit at eighteen.   J.H.E.

age distribution. (1) The classification or composition of a population by age of its members. (2) A quantitative description of the actual or proportionate importance of specific ages or age-groups within a population.   C.V.K.

age-grade. A social group, admission to which and promotion from which are largely dependent upon age, in a society whose members, or more commonly male members, are organized into a graduated hierarchy of such groups.   G.P.M.

age of maximum criminality. That chronological age period in a person's life during which, judging from criminal statistics, he is most likely to get into conflict with the criminal law. In the case of serious offenses against property (robbery, burglary, larceny) the 16-20 year age span seems to fall in this category, a slightly higher age group leading in offenses against the person. Offenses against public order are most common in the third decade of life. The uneven quality of American statistics makes positive assertions difficult. However, in some foreign countries, England for instance, the highest offense rates for serious crimes seem to lie in the early adolescent period. Generally speaking, crime rates decline after the age of twenty and very rapidly after the age of forty.   T.S.

age pyramid. A graphic portrayal of the age-sex composition of a population, so named because of its characteristic shape. In structure, the age pyramid consists of a central vertical line of origin from which a horizontal scale is extended toward the left for males and one toward the right for females. On the basis of the number in each age-sex group, bars are drawn to the appropriate length along these horizontal scales and are placed in ascending order with increasing age. When percentages rather than actual numbers are used, each age-sex group is expressed as a per cent of the total population rather than as a per cent of the total for the given sex.   C.V.K.

agent, business. Cf. business agent.

agent, county. Cf. county agent.

agent provocateur. An undercover agent who uses the method of inciting individuals to overt acts in order to compromise them. Best known is the agent employed to work within trade unions, radical political parties and similar labor groups, for the purpose of disruption, by provoking individuals to violence or similar unlawful acts, which will involve them with police and courts, create internal dissension, and bring discredit on their organization.   K.DP.L.

agglomeration. The process or result of

people gathering together indiscriminately.

M.S.

aggregate. Cf. social aggregate. The process of bringing units together into an unorganized body or mass, without any permanently significant binding consensus.

aggregate, genetic. A group of kindred persons who have lived together from birth in one place; a settled group recruited exclusively by its own birth rate; a group whose members are of one blood through in-group marriage.

N.L.S.

aggregate, social. Cf. social aggregate.

aggregation. Cf. aggregate. In matrix algebra and in dimensional sociology, a list of separately recorded entities. Thus a calendar of a month is an aggregation of days, a map is an aggregation of regions, a roll call is an aggregation of persons and a scale is an aggregation of units.

S.C.D.

aggression. Action directed toward controlling the person, action or possessions of one or more others against their will, for the primary benefit of the controlling agent, but also with the purpose of producing suffering or discontent on the part of those controlled.

M.S.

agitator. (1) A person who by voice and pen expresses the grievances of disadvantaged classes and groups and attempts to organize radical reforms.

R.N.B.

(2) One who attempts to produce discontent, restlessness or rebellious behavior in others.

M.S.

agnate. A consanguine relative in the patrilineal (q.v.) or male line. Cf. cognate.

G.P.M.

agnation. The kinship system, prevailing in ancient Rome, whereby relationship was traced exclusively through males. Relatives having a common male ancestor, traced through male descent, were called *agnati*.

W.G.

agoraphobia. Neurotic fear of open places, especially of crossing them; in some cases possibly the result of social isolation Cf. ghetto

J.H.B.

agrarian movement. Widespread collective action for the establishment of new values for the improvement of agriculture both as an industry and as a mode of life; e.g., the Granger Movement of the 1870's and the Non-Partisan League in the Dakotas after the first World War.

D.S.

agreement (*political*). An international agreement for which, in the United States, the advice and consent of the Senate is solicited and obtained is called a treaty. The name "Agreement" or "Executive Agreement" has come to be attributed to the many agreements signed by the Executive with foreign Powers—over 1200 in number—without submission for the approval of the Senate. These agreements cover a wide range, all the way from postal agreements to such important documents as the Lansing-Ishii Agreement of 1917 and the Roosevelt-Litvinoff Agreement of 1933. Some have had congressional approval; others have not. Based on the premise that the Constitution does not specify the subject-matter of treaties, and on certain dicta in the Supreme Court's decision in the Curtiss-Wright Export Corporation case, 299 U. S. 304, there has in recent years been a strong effort to demonstrate that in the interests of "democracy" the two-thirds requirement of Senate approval is and should be deemed outmoded and the Executive Agreement, with or without congressional approval, should be substituted. Its opponents regard this as a dangerous encroachment of the Executive power on the United States Constitution and Government.

E.M.B.

agricultural extension service. A cooperative adult educational enterprise, supported by federal and state and county funds, to assist farmers and their wives in improving farm and home practices, and the farm population in improving and enriching rural life.

E.des.B.

agricultural ladder. An expression used in rural sociology and agricultural economics to denote the vertical social mobility between the agricultural social classes, and more specifically the process by which a farm youth commences as a hired hand and passes successively through the stages of renter and part-owner or mortgaged owner ultimately to attain the ownership of a farm.   T.L.S.

agricultural parity, parity prices, parity income: The term "parity" as used in agricultural programs and legislation refers to *prices* which will give each agricultural commodity a purchasing power per unit relative to articles that farmers buy, interest, and taxes equivalent to the purchasing power of such commodity in the base period, August 1909 to July 1914; and to *incomes* which will give a per capita net income to individuals on farms from farm operations that bears the same relation to the per capita net income of individuals not on farms as prevailed during the period from August 1909 to July 1914.

agricultural planning. Cf. planning, agricultural.

agriculture. The utilization of the fertility of the land for the production of humanly useful plants and animals. The term includes all forms of crop raising and animal husbandry. It depends upon the extraction from the land of materials which are at least theoretically replaceable, either by the slow processes of nature or by artificial fertilization. Therefore, it does not necessarily deplete the land. The hunting and fishing of wild creatures lies in the border zone between agriculture and mining. (q.v.)

ahimsa. The doctrine of nonviolence, as practised in India by Gandhi and his followers in their civil disobedience campaigns. The term includes all nonviolent forms of resistance, but excludes rioting, which often accompanies such campaigns. Cf. satyagraha.   S.C.M.

aid, mutual. Cf. mutual aid.

aided-recall technique. A research device which consists in presenting the informant with a printed list of items from which he is asked to select those which apply. E.g., surveys of radio listening habits supply a list of programs which were on the air at the time in question, and the informant is asked to choose the ones to which he listened.   M.Pt.

aim. The goal or purpose toward which human behavior is directed. The term usually implies activity over a period of time.   J.P.E.

albinism. A variable hereditary trait, found among both white and colored races, indicated by marked deficiency of pigment in skin, hair, and eyes. In complete albinism the eyes are pink, the hair is white and the skin is milk white with no pigment. In partial albinism these conditions are only approximated. It is due to a gene substitution, inherited in many cases as an autosomal recessive. Among partial albinos are usually included persons with piebald or white-spotted skin.   F.H.H.

alcoholism. Abnormal addiction to alcohol. The basis of all malted and distilled liquors is ethyl alcohol which is a poison when taken in excess. According to Freudian theory the psychological craving for alcohol has its basis in repressed homosexuality. More generally, however, alcoholism is an escape from conflict and is often associated with inferiority feelings. Undoubtedly alcoholism is indirectly associated with crimes against the person. Intemperance and poverty are also associated. The evil effects of alcoholism often fall heavily upon the non-drinking members of the alcoholic's family. Alcoholism is a problem of a narcotic indulged in to escape depressing psychological or social conditions.   N.F.C.

aleatory element. The element in life of the inexplicable, unpredictable. The luck element. Chance.   A.G.K.

alibi. A legal defense whereby an accused person pleads that he was present at another place than the place where the crime or offense was committed at the time when it was committed and, therefore, that he could not have committed the crime or offense of which he is accused.   F.W.K.

alien. A foreign born resident of a country of which he is not a citizen. In the verb form (to alienate) the word has two possible meanings important in sociology: (1) to cause the withdrawal or affection from another; (2) to convey or transfer property.   J.W.M'C.

alienation. (1) The state of estrangement of one spouse from the other. (2) A condition of mental derangement or lapse from normal state of mind.   F.W.K.

alienist. A semi-legal word meaning a specialist in mental diseases who appears in court to testify as to a person's mental state at present or during the act of committing a crime.   J.W.M'C.

alley dwelling. An intra-block dwelling fronting on an alley. These often constitute hidden slums behind respectable facades.   S.S.

alimony. An allowance required by a court to be paid out of the estate or earnings of a husband to his wife or by a former husband to his former wife, or by a wife to a husband. In about one-third of our states alimony is allowed to the former husband out of the former wife's estate. Temporary alimony (pendente lite) is an allowance required from the husband to the wife before a divorce is granted. Permanent alimony is an allowance after divorce. The amount of alimony and the length of time it must be paid vary according to the financial circumstances, health, age, social position and other factors decided by the court. The court frequently revises the amount and methods of payment to meet new circumstances.   O.W.

allotment. A share of land set apart for the benefit of a person or group for immediate possession or use, formerly for cultivation.   F.W.K.

allrightnick. A returned immigrant, ordinarily from the United States, who brings with him a superficial veneer of the culture of the land in which he has temporarily resided, including a smattering of its language and a glib smartness and affectation of superiority.

almoner. One commissioned or authorized to distribute alms. The office of almoner was originally instituted by the church, and once performed a much more important function than now.   J.M.R.

almonry. (1) A place where alms are officially distributed. (2) Place where almoner resides.   J.M.R.

alms. The pittance of charity, generally given by individuals to beggars, but in the traditions of charity extolled as blessings to the giver Cf. dole.   N.A.

almshouse. An institution housing the publicly supported poor of an administrative unit. (Variously known as "poor farm," "county farm" and "poor house".)   W.P.

almsman. (1) A recipient of alms. (2) In the past, also a giver of alms.   J.M.R.

altruism. Regard for others, devotion to others, usually implying some self-sacrifice. The opposite of egoism.   O.W.

altruistic. Not egoistic; unselfish; marked by altruism; having primary regard for the interests and welfare of others or of the social group; especially having such regard with respect to others in the intimate personal relations of social life. Interested more in the total amount of happiness than in its distribution.   F.H.H.

amalgamate. To participate in, or experience, the process of amalgamation. (q.v.)

amalgamation. (1) The biological process whereby two or more racial types are fused into a homogenous blend by means of interbreeding and progressive combination of the respective germ plasms. (2) By analogy, the union into a functional group of two or more separate persons or groups, differing in minor characteristics but sufficiently similar in fundamental traits so that the result of the combination is a smooth and homogeneous blend

ambil-anak. A special exception to the usual marriage customs in the case of a daughter, frequently occurring in patrilineal (q.v.), patrilocal (q.v.) societies when a family has no sons, whereby for one generation residence is matrilocal (q.v.), descent is matrilineal (q.v.), and the customary bride-price (q.v.) is omitted or reduced.   G.P.M.

ambulance chaser. A lawyer, or a person on behalf of a lawyer, who solicits legal business contrary to the standards of professional ethics; sometimes generally applied to persons who fail to observe professional standards of behavior in any professional field.   F.W.K.

ameliorate. To improve or to make more tolerable; for example, to ameliorate the living conditions of the share cropper, or of the slum dweller. (A relative term which, strictly speaking, might correctly be applied to any situation or condition capable of improvement, but actually applied chiefly to situations or conditions widely recognized as being definitely in need of improvement.)   R.E.B.

ameliorative. Bettering, remedial, curative, making for improvement; (*social work*): applied to measures or treatment considered as raising a personal or social situation toward accepted standards of living or social normality (q.v.), whether or not actually achieving that plane.   T.D.E.

amenities. Decorative structural elements, open spaces, parks, playgrounds, plantings and all other natural or artificial characteristics of an area which add to its pleasantness or attractiveness as a place to live or which protect it against unpleasant sights, noises, or other nuisances.   S.S.

amentia. (1) Mental deficiency. (2) In certain parts of Europe, particularly Germany, Austria, Holland, and Norway, amentia is applied to psychotic conditions characterized by an acute organic syndrome in which there is loss of memory, clouding, confusion, perplexity, bewilderment, disorientation, and emotional disorders.   C.F.S.

Americanism. The spirit and traditions of American democratic institutions, often perverted in common usage to mean adherence to a particular interest, such as "free private enterprise."   R.N.B.

Americanization. The process by which people of alien culture acquire American ways, standards of living, and national allegiance; the assimilation of American culture by people of foreign birth or heritage.   N.L.S.

amitate. A conventional relationship of especial importance between a person and his paternal aunt. Cf. avunculate.

amok (amuck). Among Malay peoples, a condition of psychic depression which culminates in a brief outburst of homicidal mania. Coll., to run amuck, any irresponsible, unrestrained behavior. Cf. berserk.   E.A.H.

amoral. Wholly lacking in a sense of moral responsibility, as an amoral criminal, or imbecile.   F.H.H.

amorality. The state or quality of being not subject to judgment by a moral code; outside the bounds of moral standards; also, the condition of individuals who are incapable of making moral judgments or discerning moral distinctions.

amulet. An object or ornament worn as a magical or fetishistic protection against disease, witchcraft, or other evils. Cf. fetish; talisman.   G.P.M.

amusement, commercial. A relatively passive entertainment provided for spectators by a concern organized for profit, as contrasted with active recreation. Cf. recreation.   M.H.N.

anabolism, social. Cf. social anabolism.

analysis, social. Cf. social analysis.

anaphrodisiac. A food or drug designed to lessen sexual desire.   E.R.G.

anarchism. A social philosophy or a form of social organization which implies the absence of the state and formal government. It rests upon the doctrine that an ideal society could administer its affairs without any use of force, and therefore without the necessity of any agents officially authorized and equipped to use force. In its basic assumptions it is practically the opposite of socialism and communism.

anarchy. Absence of centralized government; a state or condition of human interactions and relationships without or in defiance of a traditionally accepted ultimate authority. A state of chaos or disorder.   F.E.L.

anatomy, social. Cf. social anatomy.

ancestor cult. Cf. cult, ancestor.

ancestor worship. Cf. worship, ancestor.

anchorite. A religious hermit.   L.P.E.

androcracy. A social condition of masculine supremacy, especially when based primarily on brute strength. Cf. father-right; patriarchate.   G.P.M.

angel. One who supports a cause or activity, a contributor or benefactor who supplies the money for an activity or work, perhaps making the gift anonymously.   N.A.

animals, family life of. Care by one or both parents most common among mammalians, but found more or less among birds, and occasionally among certain fish. Facts are so contradictory that no general principle except vague "parental instinct" can be derived from animal life for human family forms or contributions to social evolution.   A.J.T.

animatism (*anthropological*). Belief that all or certain important objects are alive, or contain communicable energy (mana). If sufficiently powerful to be objects of magic or worship, they are respected as vehicles of impersonal power or as being themselves personal in motivation. Contrasted with animism, which conceives certain objects as inhabited by personalized spirits, detachable like human shoots from the body or object in question. Cf. mana; fetishism; animism.   T.D.E.

animism. The belief that all things, animate and inanimate, are endowed with personal indwelling souls, or the theory that the belief in spiritual beings, i.e., souls (q.v.), ghosts (q.v.), and spirits (q.v.). is the original and basic element in religion. Cf. animatism; preanimism.   G.P.M.

anomalies. Abnormalities associated with criminal constitutions and believed to be causal correlates.   J.P.S.

anomalies, physical. The physical stigmata which Cesare Lombroso held would identify the criminal. It was Lombroso's contention that criminals were born, not made, and evidence of criminality could be seen in the peculiar shape of various parts of the face and head particularly. Although the theory has been discredited,

it has been revived in recent years by a small group of physical anthropologists.   J.W.M'C.

anomie. A French word meaning normlessness (q.v.), social and personal disorganization, demoralization, etc.   H.B.

anonymity. The state of being anonymous, disclosing no name, not known.   O.W.

anonymous. Characterized by being unnamed, and thus undefined and unclassified or unlocated. Examples are unknown benefactors and writers—and criminals.   F.E.L.

anonymousness. The state or condition of being without a name; undesignated and therefore unknown. Anonymity has the same meaning   F.E.L.

antagonism. Active opposition to, or interference with, another object, personal or abstract. One of the overt manifestations of antipathy. Antagonism may be directed against a person, a group, an idea, or a movement.

antagonistic. Acting or feeling in opposition or in contravention.   F.H.H.

antagonistic co-operation. Cf. co-operation, antagonistic.

antagonistic effort. Cf. effort, antagonistic.

antagonize. To act in opposition, or so as to produce opposition.   F.H.H.

antecedents. Events preceding a situation and having some causal relation to it. Consideration of antecedents involves the assumption of a continuity relation between events in a series.   N.A.

anthropic. Pertaining to precultural man, the life of genus homo as animals among other competing species. Distinguished from anthropoid (q.v.), human (q.v.), cultural (q.v.).   T.D.E.

anthropocentrism. That view which assumes man to be the central fact of the universe, to which all other facts have reference.   J.G.L.

anthropogeography. The scientific study of man, his history and culture in their relation to the geographical environment. Cf. ecology.   G.P.M.

anthropoid. A primate family consisting of man and the tailless apes. Traits or characteristics similar to those found in man.   E.A.H.

anthropology. The study of man and his works. The discipline has two fundamental aspects: one, the study of man as an organism (physical anthropology) and its sub-divisions—human biology, primatology, anthropometry and biometrics; and two, the study of human behavior (ethnology), social anthropology, cultural anthropology, archaeology, ethnography and race psychology.
Anthropology is therefore both a natural science and a social science. Historically it has tended to limit its area of study to prehistoric and primitive man and cultures. To some extent it has also concerned itself with the study of the men and cultures of non-occidental civilized society. Recently, there has become manifest an increasing tendency to expand anthropology to include the study of contemporary American and European cultures as well.   E.A.H.

anthropology, criminal. Measurement and enumeration of bodily characteristics to determine their relationship to criminality.   J.P.S.

anthropology, cultural. The study of the social behavior of man. In its fullest sense the term is synonymous with sociology (q.v.). In its more restricted meaning it applies to the social life of primitive man. Cf. anthropology, somatic; archaeology; ethnography.   E.A.H.

anthropology, physical. Cf. anthropology, somatic.

anthropology, social. Cf. social anthropology.

anthropology, somatic. That branch of anthropology, also termed "physical anthropology," which concerns itself with the study of the human organism, especially with its evolution or phylogeny, its individual life cycle or ontogeny, and its variations in different racial stocks and their measurement, i.e., anthropometry (q.v.). Cf. anthropology, cultural.   G.P.M.

anthropometry. The scientific and precise measurement of significant features of the human body, and their arrangement into classificatory systems.

anthropometry, social. Cf. social anthropometry.

anthropomorphism. That type of religious thought which ascribes human attributes, both physical and psychic, to deity.   J.H.E.

anthropophagy. Cannibalism (q.v.).

anticipate. To act or respond in advance to the stimulus that would normally elicit such response. Behavior in relation to an expected stimulus. It may be habitual behavior.   N.A.

antipathetic. Having antipathy, or a deep-seated, largely organic, attitude of opposition or repugnance toward a person or object, as in the common reaction to snakes. Sometimes used to describe feelings of race difference.   F.H.H.

antipathy. A feeling against a particular object, personal or abstract. The opposite of sympathy. The attitude that leads to various forms of negative association, all the way from withdrawal to opposition or conflict.

anti-Semitism. Opposition by word and deed to the equal participation of Jewish people in the social and legal rights which a nation affords to its people generally. Also denouncement in speech or writing of Jewish culture, traditions and attitudes as being inimicable to a nation's welfare. Personal withdrawal from and resentment for members of the Jewish race. J.W.M'C.

anti-social. Cf. social, anti-.

anti-social action. Action by a person or persons which places the interest of certain individuals or of minority groups above the general welfare of the community or population affected.   G.M.F.

anti-social grudge. A deep-seated resentment against society in general or social regulations in particular which may in turn lead to delinquent or criminal conduct as a "grievance reaction."   M.A.E.

apartment. A living unit or a suite of rooms in a building containing three or more living units having some common services or facilities, or both, and served by a common entrance hall.

apartment house. (1) A building containing three or more living units having common services or facilities, or both, and served by a common entrance hall. (2) A structure two or more stories in height under one roof, designed for the accommodation of two or more families.

aphrodisiac. A food or drug designed to originate or increase sexual desire or potency.   E.R.G.

applicant. In social work, a person who seeks the services of a social agency. W.P.

application blank. A form for recording data furnished by one who applies for service, relief, employment, etc.   W.P.

application interview. A part of the application process, usually the more formal or complete interview in which the client's request for assistance is explored.   W.P.

applied sociology. Cf. sociology, applied.

approach. A category of attitudes contrasted with those of withdrawal, when all attitudes are classified as attitudes of approach, withdrawal, indifference, ambivalence or combinations thereof.   T.D.E.

approach, conceptual Cf. conceptual approach.

approach, objective. An attitude toward a situation in which cultural or group evaluations and personal interest or bias are either absent or so controlled as to reduce their effects to a minimum. Approach is objective to the degree that personal tensions productive of biassed observation or interpretation are relaxed or frankly recognized but dissociated from the process of inquiry.   T.D.E.

approach, subjective. An attitude toward a situation in which cultural, group or personal valuations are permitted to affect observation and judgment; an attitude acceptable in our culture when taken by a practitioner, a poet or artist, or in the appraisals of every day life, but considered inconsistent with strict scientific method.   T.D.E.

aptitude test. A method of measuring present performance as a means of estimating future potentialities of the one tested for success in a contemplated course of training or study. The estimate based on such a test is necessarily in terms of probabilities only, e.g., scholastic aptitude test, tests for aptitudes for skilled trades, clerical occupations, executive positions, learned professions, and artistic pursuits.   F.D.W.

arbitration. The process of submitting a matter in dispute to one or more disinterested persons called arbitrators, whose decision, called the award, is binding upon the parties. Arbitration is now generally recognized by law as a method of settling disputes without legal action and awards are frequently enforcible by the courts. In certain trades and occupations having elaborate codes and customs arbitration is the method almost invariably resorted to for the settlement of disputes and detailed provisions are set up defining its use.   F.W.K.

arbitration, industrial. The process of referring disputes between employers and employees to the decision of "impartial adjudicators." Arbitration may be either voluntary or compulsory. The former exists whenever a collective labor agreement provides for the machinery of impartial adjudication. The latter exists when the state requires both parties to submit their disputes to arbitration, whether a labor agreement provides for it or not. The term is to be contrasted with international arbitration which covers disputes between nations which concern their political relations, and with commercial arbitration which is concerned with the settlement of disputes arising out of business contracts, under which commerce and trade are carried on.   F.D.W.

archaeology. The scientific study of early or primitive cultures, particularly as manifested by their artifacts.

archive. A place for the safe keeping of documents and records especially having public or historic interest; also applied to the documents or records deposited in a designated place for safe keeping especially because of public or historic interest. F.W.K.

area. A geographical region having specific boundaries; a set of phenomena having some common, unifying characteristic. P.F.C.

area, blighted. An area usually but not necessarily residential which has lost use value to such an extent that it can no longer return economic rents, pay fair taxes, and provide for fundamental repairs. Because of the resulting deterioration it tends to fall at an accelerating rate toward slum status but is not properly a slum until it has passed the point of economical rehabilitation without extensive demolition and clearance. S.S.

area, building. Cf. coverage.

area, culture. Any portion of humanity that is connected by similarity in the culture of its constituent groups, or one through which any cultural trait will be diffused readily and quickly.

area, cut over. Cf. cut over area.

area, delinquency. An area of a city marked by an abnormal delinquency rate as compared to other areas of the city of similar size and population. Such areas are often located in zones of transition, and are marked by industrial buildings, waterfronts and railroad yards, deteriorated buildings and population of mixed nationalities. Cf. ecology, human. J.W.M'C.

area, industrial. A district, of a town, city, county, state, or region, devoted predominantly to manufacturing.

area, interest. A set of phenomena around which the attention of a group of individuals tends to focus. P.F.C.

area, interstitial. An area between two use districts, such as retail and wholesale, which partakes of the characteristics of the adjacent use districts, or which may be distinguished by another, generally lower, use, as in the case of a rooming house area between a declining residential and an encroaching business district. Cf. zone of transition. E.E.M.

area, marginal. 1. (*anthropology*) Territory adjacent to two culture areas in which a mixed type of culture prevails. 2. (*human ecology*) Frequently used interchangeably with "area of transition" or "transitional area" (q.v.). C.F.S.

area, metropolitan. A region including a large concentration of population together with the surrounding areas where the daily economic and social life is predominantly influenced by the central city.

area, natural. Any particular extent of surface that has become differentiated as the result of unplanned ecological and/or social processes rather than as the result of conscious planning and/or administrative control. J.A.Q.

area, registration. A section of a country designated for the collection and consolidated tabulation of a particular group of data. The components of such an area are not necessarily contiguous, but are included on the basis of the acceptability of the methods used. In the United States, the two most important registration areas are the death registration area, established in 1880, and the birth registration area, established in 1915.

area, rural problem. Cf. rural problem area.

area, second-settlement. A section of the community to which any particular ethnic group, generally an immigrant group, has tended to move upon leaving the place of original settlement. E.E.M.

area, trade. That territory surrounding a trade center, and immediately tributary to it, from which the center draws its rural trade. The trade area is of uncertain shape, and in size is somewhat proportional to the size of the trade center. It has no fixed or definite boundary, but rather a transitional fringe which varies with inter-trade center competition and its differential growth or decline. C.E.L.

area, transitional. Cf. area of transition.

area, urban. Limited geographical area inhabited by a relatively dense population; officially, in the United States, 2500 or more population.   E.E.M.

area of characterization. That region or section of the earth's surface in which any group develops its distinctive traits. As generally used, the term refers to the geographical region in which any particular section of the human species, as a result of physical adaptation and sex selection operating under conditions of isolation and segregation, develops into a race with distinctive traits or characters.

area of deterioration. Cf. zone of deterioration.

area of sympathy. A set of phenomena about which a common emotional concern is shared by a group of individuals.   P.F.C.

area of transition. That territory in which a different form of land usage is becoming established. The term refers to the area in a city between the business district and the surrounding zone of working men's homes. Cf. zone of transition.   J.P.E.

area of understanding. A set of phenomena concerning which a group of individuals share mutual information or have a common universe of discourse.   P.F.C.

areas, social and economic. Cf. social and economic areas.

areas, vice. Localities which have a concentration of houses of prostitution and/or soliciting prostitutes on the streets sufficient to characterize them. They develop usually under favorable conditions, especially in districts which cannot contest their existence. They are to be found in or on the fringe of urban communities. But they also display a mushroom growth in non-urban areas where unusual aggregation of unattached men (i.e. non-family men) abounds, such as in a boom town, a mining camp, army camp, and so forth.   W.C.R.

argot. The so-called "slanguage" of any group; particularly the ungrammatical and unfamiliar characteristic jargon of a nonconformist group, such as tramps, gypsies or a gang. It is a distinguishing feature of a social type.   F.E.L.

argot, criminal. Cf. criminal argot.

aristocracy. The socially superior, the commonly recognized "best families." Those set apart by highest social esteem, most cultivated manners, greatest dominance in social, and frequently political, affairs. Strictly speaking, the upper nobility whose rank and powers are hereditary and legally established above those of other socio-political strata. The patricians were an aristocracy, par excellence. The FFV's were de facto aristocrats.   W.C.H.

arrest, liability to. Cf. liability to arrest.

arson. In common law, the willful and malicious burning of the house or outhouse belonging to, or in possession of, another man. Its felonious or heinous character reflects the sacredness that was attached to the habitations of men. Statutory law has enlarged upon the common law meaning of arson so as to make it include maliciously setting fire to buildings other than dwelling houses, or even other kinds of inflammable property. Under the statutes of many states and of the Federal government arson may be punished by death.   A.E.W.

art. (1) One of the primary social institutions attempting to answer symbolically the riddle of life, as religion does spiritually. This quest man pursues constantly in the desire to alleviate his ever-present fear of death. The sociological importance of art and artworks lies in their evidence of a collective mind (q.v.) which unites the creating artist through the artwork with the receptive audience. Art by means of conscious irrationalization effects the eternalization of a given culture. Cf. beauty; religion; value .   J.H.B.

(2) Skill, technique, manipulation, organized, communicable, culturally transmitted. Practical or applied arts are distinguished from the fine arts (dance, drama, poetry, architecture, painting, sculpture, music) which have in common the extension of human experience through the sharing of imagination and of feeling. Art is distinct from ritual in that the latter undertakes the work of

changing the course of "nature" directly by magic or indirectly by influencing supernatural persons supposed to be in control of the relevant phenomena. Art is distinct from games in virtue of its objectives of aesthetic communication and its canons or conventions.　　　　T.D.E.

art, sociology of. Cf. sociology of art.

artel. A group banded together for work or other common ends. A type of cooperative. Specifically the collectivized Russian village where land and productive capital are pooled under a common management.
　　　　N.L.S.

articulated street pattern. The design and construction of streets and walks to serve particular functions such as through traffic, local traffic, service lanes, pedestrian walks, etc., resulting in economical paving and utilities costs, and yielding privacy to residential areas and freedom from traffic hazards.　　　　S.S.

artifact. A material object fashioned by human workmanship; an element of material culture (q.v.).　　　　G.P.M.

artificial. Having existence because of the application of human intelligence; the antonym of artificial is natural (q.v.).

arts, fine. The deep appreciation and powerful expressions of values in human life, such expressions taking the forms of play, dancing, drama, drawing, painting, sculpture, architecture, other plastics, literary prose, poetry and music; using the finer more developed techniques of line, color, form, tone and words; and giving rise to social vocations and institutions in developing them.　　　　C.J.B.

arts, social. Cf. social arts.

ascendancy. Superiority of power, influence or position.　　　　M.S.

ascendancy, individual. Cf. individual ascendancy.

ascendancy, personal. Cf. personal ascendancy.

ascendancy, social. Cf. social ascendancy.

ascetic ideationalism. Cf. ideationalism, ascetic.

asceticism. Extreme rigor and self denial practised for an ideal.　　　　L.P.E.

asexual. Having no sex.

assault. A civil wrong or *tort* for the commission of which damages at law are recoverable (in the Anglo-American legal system), consisting of a threat to strike or to harm another.　　　　F.W.K.

assessment. (1) The process of evaluating property for general taxation purposes; also the value so assigned — usually called "the assessed valuation." (2) Special assessment. A charge imposed by a government upon a restricted group or class of properties to defray part or all the costs of specific improvements or services presumed to be of special (but not necessarily exclusive) benefit to such properties.

assimilation. Cf. social assimilation.

assimilation, social. Cf. social assimilation.

assistance, old age. Cf. old age assistance.

assistance, public. Cf. public assistance.

associate. Broadly, to engage in any form of social interaction with others, whether of opposition or co-operation. More narrowly, to join with one or more other persons in common action, regardless of the psychological motivations leading thereto. Specifically, to form an association. One who is so related to another, or others.　　　　F.H.H.

association. (1) The fundamental relationship which unites individuals into groups or societies. A comprehensive term for the relationships of interstimulation and response, usually of a somewhat enduring nature in contrast to mere contact. (2) An organized group formed in pursuit of some common interest with its own self-contained administrative structure and functionaries. E.g. The National Manufacturers Association, Association of American Colleges, Association of Junior Leagues of America, etc.

association, cooperative. Cf. cooperative (2).

association, criminal. 1. A group organized expressly for the pursuit of criminal interests. 2. A process of intimate and friendly communication with criminals which tends to result in the assimilation of criminal behavior-patterns.   E.H.S.

association, differential. The distribution of a person's associations in a manner different from those of other persons; generally stated as an hypothesis of criminal behavior, namely, that a person who develops criminal behavior differs from those who do not develop criminal behavior in the quantity and quality of his associations with criminal patterns and in his relative isolation from anti-criminal patterns, and that differential association with these criminal and anti-criminal patterns is therefore the cause of criminal behavior. According to this hypothesis, either the techniques, motives, rationalizations, and other elements are learned exclusively in association with criminal patterns, or, if learned in part in other kinds of association, are combined and organized in association with criminal patterns.   E.H.S.

association, voluntary. A group freely organized by citizens for the pursuit of some interests in contrast to a state established agency.

assortative (assortive) mating. The mating of persons of similar genetic traits, as tall with tall, or blond with blond; the opposite of random mating. Although sometimes used to describe the mating of persons of similar social traits, such as similarity in education or religious belief, strict usage limits this term to the mating of persons who are similar in one or more hereditary traits.   F.H.H.

asthenic physique. Cf. physique, asthenic.

astrology. Divination (q.v.) by interpreting the influence of the stars upon human affairs.   G.P.M.

asylum. (1) A sacred and inviolable sanctuary (q.v.), e.g., a temple, from which a criminal or other fugitive, seeking refuge there, may not be forcibly removed; or the right of a fugitive to remain inviolate in such a place. Cf. city of refuge.   G.P.M.

(2) An institution (q.v.) for the organized care, protection, or support of some needy element in the population, such as orphans, insane, or feeble-minded.

asylum, right of. The recognition by law or custom of entry to and protection in a country, or institution, of persons escaping from political, religious or racial persecution. Applied also in medieval times to religious refuges open to criminals and debtors from which they could not be removed without sacrilege. Cf. sanctuary.
        R.N.B.

atavism. The reappearance of a trait which appeared in an ancestor more remote than the parent. Atavism and reversion are frequently used synonymously although atavism refers to the reappearance of a specific trait while reversion refers to a type or a combination of less specific traits.   O.W.

atavistic. Pertaining to atavism. (q.v.).
        O.W.

athletic physique. Cf. physique, athletic.

atomism. The theory or belief that a group is to be explained or understood in terms of its individual members or units rather than in terms of a collective whole; the denial that society or any group has any existence or meaning apart from that of its individual members.

atomize. The type of social process by which social groups are broken into fragments or larger social patterns are reduced to smaller ones.   N.A.

atrophy. The disappearance of a part of the body by disuse, pressure or disease; a wasting or withering of any part of the body.   O.W.

attack. That aspect of social conflict in which one personality or group seeks to damage the physical, psychological, or social structures, or to thwart the purposes, of another personality or group.
        H.H.

attention, focus of. That area in the content of consciousness of which the individual is most aware at a given moment.
        P.H.F.

17

attitude. An acquired, or learned, and established tendency to react toward or against something or somebody. It is evidenced by either approaching or withdrawing types of behavior, and the object of the reaction becomes thereby either a positive or a negative value, respectively, from the subject's viewpoint. An attitude may be largely latent, subjective, unexpressed, or it may represent any degree between two extremes. An attitude may be characteristic of a person, and as such relate to the given person, or to other persons, or to social groups, or to society or the universe. An attitude may be social in the sense that is characteristic of a homogeneous group of persons.

attitude, experiential. Attitude derived from the personal experience of its possessor.   M.S.

attitude, indoctrinated. Attitude acquired in response to the influence of another.
                                              M.S.

attitude, social. Cf. social attitude.

attitude, typical. (1) An attitude which is most frequently found in an individual or group, or (2) is characteristic of or predominates in the individual or group; therefore, a representative attitude. F.E.L.

attitude scale. A series of indices of attitudes, each of which has been given a quantitative value relative to that of each other. The usual indices are propositions which are ranked or rated in reference to the degree of antagonism or protagonism expressed toward some object of thought. The indices may be selected so that the interval between each two consecutive ones appears equal to that between each other two consecutive ones.
                                              M.S.

attitudinal. Of or relating to a mental set or disposition which is known as an attitude.   M.Pt.

Auburn System. The system of imprisonment originating in the New York prison at Auburn in 1821 and fully developed in 1823, in which the prisoners were kept in separate cells at night and worked in association in the shops during the day, but were kept from communicating with each other at all times by the "rule of silence" enforced by severe disciplinary measures.
                                              J.L.G.

audimeter. Instrument attached to radios in private homes to detect every time the set is turned on and off and to indicate the station to which the radio is tuned. Used as a measure of radio listening habits of population.   M.Pt.

audition. A trial or test of fitness for some dramatic, musical, or other artistic activity. Although originally practically synonymous with "hearing," the term is used in connection with dancing.

augury. Divination (q.v.) by omens or auspices, e.g., by observing the flight of birds.   G.P.M.

authoritative. Having authority (q.v.).

authority. Power, rule, or command in a social or political group, e.g., in a household, where it is said to be "patripotestal" (q.v.) if wielded by the father or paternal grandfather, "matripotestal" (q.v.) if wielded by the mother or maternal grandmother, "avuncular" if wielded by the maternal uncle. Cf. avunculate; succession.
                                              G.P.M.

authority, charismatic. Cf. charismatic authority.

authority, individual. Cf. individual authority.

authority, social. Cf. social authority.

autistic thinking. An egoistic type of thought with a minimum of relationship to external stimulation. The term, which is of Freudian origin, includes daydreaming and the relatively undirected thought of small children and insane persons.
                                              S.C.M.

autocracy. Rule by arbitrary authority, usually in the hands of one man or a small group or party, thus including various forms of arbitrary rule such as despotism, oligarchy and dictatorship; the opposite of democracy.   R.N.B.

autoerotism. Self-induced sexual satisfaction. Frequently used as a synonym for masturbation but rightly a more inclusive term.   E.R.G.

autointoxication. State of an individual suffering from absorption of uneliminated endogogenous toxin in the intestinal tract. The presence of the toxin is caused by intestinal stasis (constipation).   J.M.R.

automatic selection. Cf. selection, automatic.

autonomic. Referring to that part of the human organism which is concerned with carrying on the vital processes. It includes the viscera with their involuntary muscles and nervous system (the physiological basis of the emotions) as distinct from the higher brain centers and striped muscles having to do with reasoning and movement. The latter is sometimes called the projicent system as contrasted with the former or autonomic system.   F.D.W.

autonomous. Characteristic of a political organ, a social institution, or a social group which possesses the right and power to determine its own course of action.   G.M.F.

autonomy. A state or condition in which self-direction is enjoyed; this self-direction being the property of the group or a people within a geographical area, or even of a scattered group.   N.A.

average. A device for representing as accurately as possible in a single symbolic unit the occurrence and distribution of a trait or character in a series of units. Cf. mean; median; mode.

average, moving. A method of smoothing to show the trend in a series of numerical items. It consists in replacing the items by a succession of averages each of which is based upon a set number of adjacent items which overlap those contributing to the net average.   M.Pt.

aversion, individual. Cf. individual aversion.

aversion, social. Cf. social aversion.

avocation. A leisure activity that is followed regularly and seriously, and that has recreational and other useful values. An interest pursued consistently with specific time devoted to it. It is unlike a vocation or regular employment in that the main drive is the interest in the activity; not engaged in chiefly for financial gain, nor pursued for any reward beyond itself. Cf. hobby.   M.H.N.

avoidance. Evasion or warding off of ill by practical, magical, and religious methods.   J.G.L.

avoidance relationship. A special relationship between particular relatives, e.g., between a man and his mother-in-law, according to which each avoids physical contact or familiarity with the other. Cf. joking relationship.   G.P.M.

avunculate. A special relationship between maternal uncle and sister's son, particularly where the former exercises authority (q.v.) over his nephew and where the latter inherits from or succeeds him.
                                              G.P.M.

avunculocal. Pertaining to customary or preferential residence, on the part of a married couple, at the home of the husband's maternal uncle. Cf. matrilocal; patrilocal.   G.P.M.

B

bad nigger. A Negro who violates the community's concept of the "Negro's place." He characteristically treats the penalty for such violations with contempt. This is an America-wide concept varying in content.   w.r.c.

bail. Stated consideration imposed by the court permitting accused to remain in the community while awaiting trial. Security required to guarantee appearance for trial at a later date.   j.p.s.

balance, social. Cf. social balance.

balanced population. Cf. population, balanced.

ballistics (*forensic*). The use of guns, shells, bullets, powder marks, etc. as a means of criminal identification. It has been found that no two guns even of the same make have identical rifling, nor does the firing pin on any two guns make identical marks on the shell. Consequently by means of the microscope-camera it is possible to compare the markings on bullet and shell found in connection with a crime with those made by a gun found on the person of the accused or found under conditions that make it probable that he had it in his possession. Forensic ballistics is only a special subdivision of general ballistics which has to do with guns of all kinds.   j.l.g.

band. A local group or community of associated families who reside together and otherwise maintain face-to-face relations, especially under nomadic or semi-nomadic conditions.   g.p.m.

banditry. Consistent and organized robbery and other forms of theft with violence; especially, such behavior when committed by persons who reside in mountainous or other sparsely settled regions.   e.h.s.

banishment. An alternative to capital punishment practiced both by tribally organized and civil societies. The culprit was ordered to leave the society on pain of death. Among the tribal societies those banished were known as "kin-wrecked" men. It was practiced in ancient Greece and Rome, in England, Turkey and Russia.   j.l.g.

bare rent. Cf. rent.

bargaining, collective. Cf. collective bargaining.

barrelhouse. A saloon of the pre-prohibition period, usually one where liquor was sold in ample quantities at low price and where service was rough and ready. Perhaps free lunch was served.   n.a.

barrow. An earth-covered dolmen (q.v.). Syn. tumulus.   e.a.h.

barter. A form of exchange or trade in which goods are exchanged directly for other goods without the use of a recognized medium of exchange. Cf. dumb barter.   g.p.m.

barter, dumb. Cf. dumb barter.

base map. A type of map used in sociological research which portrays certain ecologically significant facts of the geographical and cultural environments such as rivers, lakes, ravines, prominent hills and other topographical features, railroads, canals, boulevards, industrial areas, commercial sections, vacant property, heavily travelled thoroughfares, parks, schools, and cemeteries. Maps of this kind provide an important background or framework for superimposing primary and other data, thus facilitating the location of specific problems, the verification of hypotheses, the analysis of data, and the discovery of hidden facts and relationships.   C.F.S.

bastard. A person born out of wedlock; an illegitimate person; a person who under the English common law, and except where otherwise provided by law, has no claim to succeed to property of his parents or to the name of either.   F.W.R.

bastardy. The state of being a bastard; illegitimacy; the legal offense of begetting a bastard child.   F.W.K.

battery. The unlawful use of force by one person upon another; beating, wounding, including every touching however trifling of another's person or clothes, in an angry, insolent or hostile manner; legally, the offense may be a civil wrong, a tort, or a criminal offense. Cf. assault.   F.W.K.

Baumes laws. The restrictive penal legislation sponsored by a committee of the New York State Senate of which Senator Caleb H. Baumes was chairman. These laws, enacted in 1926, provided an increase in penalty with each successive offense and an automatic life sentence for the fourth offense whether known at the time of conviction or discovered after sentence. The term "Baumes laws" has been widely applied to similar habitual offender laws subsequently enacted in other states.
                                          M.A.E.

beauty. That quality which brings intense appreciation of values or inspiring ideals. Beauty is composed of harmonies and contrasts of line, color, form, tone and words; suggesting or presenting nature's appeals, human conditions, achievements, anticipations or dreams. These, as beautiful, are enjoyed, not merely technically as means, but finally as ends, for their intrinsic worth, immediately and without question. Beauty is the central theme or consideration in the social function of the fine arts.   C.J.B.

beggar. One who habitually solicits money

or other goods from those not socially responsible for his maintenance, without offering anything of equivalent value in return.

behavior. The manner of acting in a given situation.   J.P.E.

behavior, acquired. Behavior resulting from factors modified through previous action of the organism or through the influence of the environment.   M.S.

behavior, collective. The behavior of a group when it is of such a nature as to give the appearance of arising from unity of attitude, feeling, and motivation. The type of behavior consistent with the analogical concept of the group as an organism.

behavior, covert. Behavior not observable to another through any process of sensation; behavior known to another only by inference from other behavior.   M.S.

behavior, criminal. Cf. criminal behavior.

behavior, customary. Conduct in conformity to traditional patterns; modes of action in harmony with long-standing and accepted standards; habitual observance of the folkways and mores.   N.L.S.

behavior, familial. The interactions of members of a family as expressed in conduct.   E.R.G.

behavior, family. The activities of an individual family, or the interactions within a family of its various members.   E.R.G.

behavior, group. Cf. group behavior.

behavior, human. The acquired manner in which a human being acts in a given situation as a result of his previous human association. Contrasted with any innate activity which is common to other forms of animal life.   J.P.E.

behavior, individual. Cf. individual behavior.

behavior, native. Behavior resulting from factors that were present in the organism from its beginning.   M.S.

behavior, organismic. Behavior carried out by the organism as a whole.   M.S.

behavior, overt. Behavior that can be detected by another through sensation.   M.S.

behavior, pluralistic. (1) Observable similarities of conduct generally occurring amongst individuals in the same locality. (2) Conduct performed in the name of the group.   B.M.

behavior, reciprocal. Behavior in which each of a plural number of participants reciprocates the behavior of each of the others. Cf. action, reciprocal.   M.S.

behavior, sympathetic. A vaguely inclusive term with wide range of denotation and connotation. At least six distinguishable sets of phenomena, many of these classifiable into sub-varieties, can be isolated. Adam Smith, for example, dealt at great length with a kind of "sympathy" in which the spectator, in order to relieve his own discomfort, induced by a sort of emotional contagion, gave relief to the sufferer. Other writers, among the most prominent of whom was Max Scheler, treated this transference phenomenon as what we may here term mere (1) transpathy. Obviously this is strikingly different from the emotional solidarity experienced by persons who together mourn, let us say, the loss of the same love-object. They experience in solidarity not only the same value-complex but also the same emotional susceptibility in relation thereto; consequently we here term their emotion (2) compathy. Quite different from this again is the emotional participation which appears when A experiences the sorrow of B as belonging to B. Upon the understood content of this sorrow the pity of A is directed; i.e., A's pity and B's sorrow are, phenomenologically speaking, two different facts rather than one fact as in the case of compathy. Following this lead, as well as the idiomatic hints contained in phrases such as "rejoice with them that rejoice," "feel for them in their sorrow," we here term this emotional participation (3) propathy. There are, of course, other kinds of emotion in which self and other are separately experienced; among them is the kind of emotional relation with a character which may be felt by the actor depicting that character, or by a novelist with his subject, or by the biographer with the person, living or dead, whose life he is writing. This emotional reduplication is sometimes designated "feeling one's way into the role," "living oneself into the hero's experience," and so on. Because of the importance of such emotional capacities in the art of the actor, in the mimetic art, we here place them under the head of (4) mimpathy, even though they function in many spheres of "real life" rather than only on the stage. Still another variety of sympathetic behavior is to be found in what is perhaps best designated as emotional introjection or (5) empathy. Originally developed in conjunction with esthetic theory, it was there used to explain why, for example, the observer might take pleasure in a sinuously curving line; the graceful movements introjected and kinesthetically apprehended at the sight of the line give rise to pleasurable sensation and emotion. The current use of empathy in the United States, however, takes it far beyond this esthetic context; social workers, for example, are often told that they "should empathize with the client, but need not always "sympathize with him." In terms of the present set of definitions, the social worker is being told that mimpathy is necessary for case study, but that propathy, compathy, transpathy, or unipathy should be regarded as superfluous in the social worker's professional role. Mention of (6) unipathy or emotional identification in the foregoing comment should not lead to its being confused with other varieties of sympathetic behavior, for it is quite distinct. To be sure, it may be regarded as closely akin to transpathy, in particular, especially when emotional contagion occurs in a highly suggestible personality. Hypnotic rapport may be the result. Nevertheless, it differs from transpathy in that it is usually bound up integrally with verbalizations or other symbolic manifestations. Moslem and Christian mysticism, for example, are of unipathetic character. There are several other types, of course: many euphoric and ecstatic states are based on unipathy; it is clearly evident in the mental-social development of the child; the love-suffused sex act, with its phenomenon of "mutual emotional fusion" is unipathetic.

Any definition of sympathetic behavior which does not take account of at least the six main varieties noted is patently inadequate.   H.B.

behavior clinic. Psychiatric and/or psychological clinic dealing with child and adult behavior problems. The clinics, for the most part, render diagnostic service and receive their intake from courts, schools, social agencies, and state institutions. Some clinics, however, undertake treatment of cases as well as diagnosis. In many instances, behavior clinics are connected with hospitals and state institutions which give out-patient service. Separately housed child guidance clinics have been established in American cities since 1920 and these have operated primarily as social agencies, drawing their support from private funds. Some states have provided mobile behavior clinics to be accessible for referrals of children's cases from smaller towns. Behavior clinics, whether for children or adults or both, are an important cog in the mental hygiene movement.   W.C.R.

behavior pattern. Cf. pattern, behavior.

behavior patterning. A socio-psychological process in which behavior is definitely shaped by the models to which the person responds. In its simplest form, behavior patterning is the acquisition of easy modes of behavior—say a gesture or a new slang expression. In its complicated aspects, it involves the progressive acquisition of special skills, attitudes, and philosophies of life, such as characterize a circus clown, a professional wrestler, a nurse, a professional soldier, a gangster, a case worker. It is presumed that behavior patterning takes place in association. It is something more than learning, imitation, and suggestion, although it involves all of these to some extent. At the complicated level, it is a processing of personality by experience and association, affecting habits, attitudes, and values. At this level, it produces social types.   W.C.R.

behavior problem. Any conduct which is sufficiently abnormal to merit help from a social organization, a psychiatrist, a psychologist, etc.   W.P.

behavior process. Cf. process, behavior.

behaviorism. A school of psychology holding that scientific psychology studies only behavior. Consciousness, objects of consciousness, and conscious processes are considered as not subject to scientific investigation, or are interpreted as covert language activity. The introspective method is discarded or given only minor attention. Behaviorism is not necessarily identified with the philosophy of mechanism; nor is it correctly confined to the study of partial or isolated actions, such as conditioned reflexes or habits.   M.S.

behavioristic. (1) Referring to any view of psychology as predominantly interested in behavior.
(2) A term sometimes applied by psychologists to the tendency to define psychology as the study of active relations between organisms and their environments. Such a psychology is a modified form of behaviorism.   M.S.

being (*sein*). Generally, the totality of everything which exists; specifically all processes of which this totality consists; more particularly the definite form in which such processes persist. (Non-being, *nicht sein*).   J.H.B.

being, human. Man in his pure general quality; the definite form of crystallization of life processes into an organism endowed with spiritual attitudes, the lack of which characterizes sub-human beings. By way of a value system which eventually becomes independent, man creates a super-human being.   J.H.B.

being, non-social. Man viewed as an isolated phenomenon.   J.H.B.

being, social. Cf. social being.

belief. (1) The acceptance of any given proposition as true. Such acceptance is essentially intellectual, although it may be strongly colored by emotion. In any case, it establishes a mental condition in the individual which may serve as the basis for voluntary action. The reality of belief is not dependent upon the intrinsic, objective truth of the particular proposition. There are false beliefs and true beliefs. A particular belief may be based on sound factual evidence or upon prejudice, intuition, or misleading appearances. There can, accordingly, be scientific belief, superstitious belief, whimsical belief. The nature of its derivation does not affect the potency of belief itself. People will act just as energetically, determinedly, fanatically upon the basis of false beliefs as of true beliefs. Intelligent action must always be based upon belief, but intelligence itself can be utilized to test beliefs and check the validity of their foundations.

(2) The acceptance as true of a proposition which has not been, or cannot be, proved by the scientific method.

bench parole. A term sometimes used to cover what is properly termed probation. Cf. probation.   J.L.G.

benefit of clergy. Medieval privilege permitting members of religious bodies (and, later, persons of rank and all who could read or had clerical tonsure) to be tried in ecclesiastical courts before ecclesiastical judges rather than by the secular authorities for violations of the law.   J.P.S.

benevolence. Literally "willing or wishing well" to others. Act of kindness or gift of money or goods. Formerly considered a natural human quality leading to altruistic behavior. In early American theology, the supreme virtue from which all morality flows. In special sense, gifts extorted by various English kings from their subjects. Cf. charity.   W.P.

berdache. A person who adopts the dress and lives the life of a member of the opposite sex.   G.P.M.

berserk. A wild, furious fighter. One given to furious fighting. Cf. amok.   E.A.H.

Bertillon method of identification. A system of determining whether an individual under investigation is the same individual as one whose anthropometric measurements are on record. It was invented by Alphonse Bertillon and applied to the identification of criminals when he was made head of the Paris police department in 1883. It consisted of a series of measurements of certain parts of the body, of standardizing the photograph, of noting

peculiar markings, and of so classifying the data as to make easy the location of thousands of records. His method is based on the observation that physical maturity fixes the skeletal dimensions for life.

It has been widely superseded by the fingerprint method, because Bertillon's method is not adapted to immature persons, is often unreliable for adult women, marks can be altered, and facial expression in the photograph changes often with age.   J.L.G.

betrothal. A mutual promise or contract made by a man and woman to marry at some future time. The power to arrange betrothals remained in the hands of parents from ancient to modern times. In large parts of Japan, China, and India betrothal and marriage are still arranged by parents.   W.G.

beweddung. During the early Middle Ages beweddung was the first step in contracting marriage among all Teutonic peoples. At first beweddung was a contract between the father and the suitor to give the girl to the man on payment of certain valuables, such as cattle, arms or money. In early times, no doubt, the goods were paid and the girl handed over at one and the same time. But as the centuries passed the interval between beweddung and *gifta*, or handing over the girl, lengthened under Roman influence. The crude contract or *wed* between the father and the suitor was changed to a contract between the girl and the man; and the payment of goods to the father was transformed into a contract to provide for the widow in case of her husband's death.   W.G.

bias. A conditioned tendency to favor and support a certain point of view or conclusion despite the absence of adequate or even any evidence; a disposition to reject evidence that conflicts with a preconceived conviction. It is frequently used as a synonym for prejudice.   F.E.L.

biased. Erring in one direction; statistical values which tend to be consistently on one side of the true value. A prejudiced attitude or procedure.   M.Pt.

biased sample. Cf. sample, biased.

bifurcation. The distinguishing, in kinship terminology, of relatives through males from like relatives through females, e.g., between a paternal and a maternal uncle.
G.P.M.

big brother plan. A plan for reducing juvenile delinquency by securing the co-operation of recognized community leaders to act as "big brothers" to boys who appear before the juvenile court. The plan aims to organize the economic and social resources of the community to assist boys who need a helping hand and a little practical guidance in growing into self-respecting manhood. The service is entirely voluntary on the part of the men of the community, but the success of the plan is almost impossible to determine since adequate records of their work are seldom maintained.
J.W.M'C.

bilateral. Reckoning descent (q.v.) or inheritance (q.v.) equally in both the male and the female lines, or indifferently in either. Cf. unilinear.
G.P.M.

bill of rights. Cf. rights, bill of.

biological heredity. Cf. heredity, biological.

biological mutation. Cf. mutation, biological.

biological sociology. Cf. sociology, biological.

biology, criminal. Cf. criminal biology.

bird of passage. A temporary immigrant, who oscillates between his own land and some other country, ordinarily following the economic fluctuations in the country of destination (q.v.).

birth. In demographic studies and reports, an infant born. Births are of two categories, live, or showing signs of life after being born, and still, or dead when delivery is completed.
F.H.H.

birth, premature. Detachment or expulsion of the fetus after independent viability (e.g., after 26-28 weeks) but before completion of normal gestation.
N.E.H.

birth control. Behavior designed to prevent conception as a result of coitus, or of a social relationship within which coitus is normal and sanctioned, specifically marriage. The term includes contraception (q.v.), and also marital abstinence or continence (q.v.). It does not include celibacy (q.v.) or deferred marriage, the preventive checks which were approved by Malthus, and against which the precursor of the Birth Control movement, Neo-Malthusianism, was a direct reaction, if not revolt.

The term Birth Control is theoretically inappropriate, and practically unfortunate —inappropriate because it lays emphasis upon birth instead of fertilization, and unfortunate because it opens the way to the ignorant or deliberately false assumption that it includes abortion (q.v.), to which it is diametrically opposed in spirit and practice. However, the term is established in customary usage, and there is no present likelihood that it will be discarded.

birth rate. Cf. rate, birth.

birth rites. Cf. rites, birth.

Black Death, the. A violent epidemic of bubonic plague, probably concurrent with pneumonic plague, appearing in southeast Europe in 1346 and reaching England in 1348. Especially fatal among the lower classes, it is variously estimated to have killed thirty to fifty per cent of the English population, the percentages varying from none to seventy-five in different areas. Some authorities claim that it hastened the decline of villeinage, greatly disturbed the balance of wages and prices and led to the Peasants' Revolt of 1381, but all these claims are disputed by others. It seems clearly to have led to the Statutes of Labourers, 1350.
F.H.H.

blight. Deterioration resulting from a decline in the use value of real estate. Cf. blighted area.
S.S.

blighted area. Cf. area, blighted.

block. An urban area bounded on all sides by public streets or by streets and a river, park, railroad right of way or similar barrier. The customary unit in real property surveys.
S.S.

block sampling. Cf. sampling, block.

blood groups. The four types of human blood determined by the presence or absence of two chemical elements, called A and B: (1) Group I or O, which contains neither A nor B, which coagulates or agglutinates the cells of blood of the other three groups when mixed therewith, but which is not itself agglutinated by an admixture of other types of blood, and whose owners are consequently known as "universal recipients" in blood transfusion; (2) Group II or A, which contains A but not B, agglutinates groups III and IV, and is agglutinated by groups I and III; (3) Group III or B, which contains B but not A, agglutinates groups II and IV, and is agglutinated by groups I and II; (4) Group IV or AB, which contains both A and B, which, although agglutinated by all the other groups, itself agglutinates none of them, and whose owners are consequently known as "universal donors" in blood transfusion.

With respect to these four types, the various races and biological stocks of the human species differ in the distinctive percentages according to which the types are represented. There is no difference in the blood composition of individuals of each particular type, whatever their racial affiliation. That is, while Nordics and Negroes differ in the percentages of the various blood types each group possesses, a Nordic individual with type A and a Negro with type A are not differentiated in the chemistry of their blood.

blood money. A payment in composition of blood vengeance (q.v.). Cf. composition; wergild.   G.P.M.

blood revenge. Blood vengeance (q.v.).

blood sacrifice. Cf. sacrifice, blood.

blood vengeance. The obligatory act or practice of avenging the slaying of a relative by killing the culpable party or one of his kinsmen. Cf. composition.
                                    G.P.M.

boarder. One who secures his meals at a specified place, in return for payment, ordinarily on a basis at least as permanent as weekly or monthly. In common usage, the term frequently includes also the relationship of roomer (q.v.).

boarding boss. An individual who combines the economic processes of supplying groups of workers to employers and providing the meals, and usually also living quarters, to the workers. This is a social pattern which developed in the United States particularly in connection with unskilled immigrant groups, unfamiliar with the English language or American customs, without normal social contacts, and in need of an intermediary between themselves and the problems of self-maintenance in the United States.

Bolshevik. The etymological origin *bolshinstvo* (meaning majority) refers to the vote taken at the Second Congress of the Russian Social Democratic Party held in Brussels and London, 1903, when the radical wing won a majority. The Bolsheviks under the leadership of Lenin favored revolutionary policies, discontinuation of cooperation with bourgeois parties, and the creation of a centralized party organization with exclusive acceptance for membership of professional revolutionaries. This political body may be regarded as a first appearance of the modern totalitarian party.

The doctrine of Bolshevism before the victorious seizure of power in November, 1917, represented an extension of the Marxian interpretation of capitalism, its basic discrepancies, and its inevitable breakdown adjusting this theory to the patterns of the capitalism of the monopoly state. Imperialism—the monopolistic period of capitalism and its necessary outcome, the fight over colonial markets in imperialistic wars—was regarded as a precondition for a successful proletarian revolution in the defeated nation which, contrary to Marx, would not have to be the most highly industrialized country. The final seizure and retention of power by the Bolsheviks is partly a result of the masterful strategy of Lenin, his successful combination of three revolutions (the liquidation of the war, the peasants' fight against the big landowners, Bolshevist control of industrial production), and his realistic evaluation of the predominant forces (i.e. his NEP policy).

Victorious Bolshevism before and after the death of Lenin has undergone a revolutionary process passing through different and often divergent stages. Even after a quarter of a century Soviet Russia is still far from any definite structure and form. National characteristics, historical circumstances, and strategy of leadership have created in Bolshevism a specifically Russian phenomenon which cannot simply be identified with or transplanted into the Communist movements of other countries. For one thing, the early upheavals, social revolutions and the attempt at westernization in Russia were so strikingly blended and inextricably mixed that their attack seemed to become only a two-fold advance of one and the same movement (Lenin—the Peter the Great of the twentieth century). The industrialization of agrarian Russia, the emancipation of women and the family, the advancements in health and education are as much a genuine part of the revolution as are the destruction of the old ruling class, the dictatorship of the proletariat and the socialization of rural Russia.

The historical struggle between Trotsky and Stalin and the final victory of the latter have further led to far-flung changes in policy. "Socialism in a single country" seems to have won the upper hand though the idea of a possible "world revolution" was nurtured and directed by the Third International.

Finally, the international situation, especially the threatening rise of National Socialism and its expected and final assault in the Soviet fatherland, has shaped the structure of Bolshevism. It may be safely stated that Bolshevism in addition to its undoubtedly revolutionary character has taken on many elements of genuine Russian nationalism. Cf. Menshevik.   S.N.

Bolshevo. The modern Soviet Commune for the special training of young offenders, located not far from Moscow. The institution provides normal community life and excellent academic and vocational instruction. Only selected persons are admitted. These are 16 to 24 at time of admission now although originally the institution was for 13 to 17 year olds, chiefly for the so-called "Wild Children" following the Revolution. Persons admitted must show evidence of ability to profit from the training. Life partakes of a village nature with industries, school

and sports. Married offenders bring their families and are given apartments. Unmarried persons live in dormitory fashion.   M.A.E.

bond, mutual. Cf. mutual bond.

bootlegging. The production of, or trading in, commodities in a manner prohibited by law; especially, such production of, or trading in, alcoholic drinks.   E.H.S.

born criminal. Cf. criminal, born.

Borstals. The English institutions which are organized for the treatment and treasuring of youthful offenders. Eleven in number, these institutions provide special care for the varying types of offenders. Four of the Borstals are walled, four are open, one is for boys who have broken parole (designated as "revokees") and one for the especially difficult problem cases.   M.A.E.

bourgeois. A member of the bourgeoisie (q.v.) As an adjective it describes the traits and attitudes of the bourgeoisie. Through its control of education, the press, the church, and government, this class extends its influence over much of the proletariat. Typical are the white collar workers who, though essentially wage earners, emulate the manner of life and ideology of the bourgeoisie. This is especially true of the labor movement in the United States. Though it nominally represents the proletariat and is often engaged in controversies with the capitalists, it has sought in the main for a larger share in the partition of wealth currently produced. It has not attempted to overthrow the present system of production for profit in behalf of a system of production for use. From the borderline groups there is movement toward both of the two main classes. The bourgeois ideology characterizes not only the dominant bourgeoisie and the borderline groups, but extends far down into the proletariat.   M.Pm.

bourgeoisie. During the French Revolution this term acquired political and social significance as the name of the middle class between the nobility and the working class. With the rise of modern capitalism and the rapid disappearance of an hereditary aristocracy it has acquired a much wider meaning. It now designates collectively all those whose interests are allied with the owners of the means of production. As such it is distinguished from the proletarian class. It includes not only the capitalists themselves, but also their henchmen, retainers and dependents. Among the capitalists are not only the large landowners, big industrialists and merchants, and bankers and financiers who exercise an extensive control over industry, commerce and agriculture, but also the small farm owners and the petty business enterprisers. In the higher ranks of the henchmen and retainers are the corporation attorneys, executive and factory managers, consulting engineers and technicians, public relations counselors and advertising agents. In the lower ranks are most of the lawyers, the store and plant managers and foremen, the smaller technicians. Belonging in the main to the higher or lower ranks of the henchmen are the professors and teachers, writers and journalists, ministers of religion and physicians, and politicians. Whether or not hired by the owners of the means of production, these professions consciously or unconsciously share their interests and work for the maintenance of their economic system. On the borderline between the bourgeoisie and the proletariat are the tenant farmers who hope to become farm owners, and many of the white collar retainers, such as accountants, bookkeepers and clerks, who hope to climb into the capitalistic group.   M.Pm.

box-heading. A title which extends over more than one column in a statistical table.   M.Pt.

brachycephalic. Characterized by a relatively broad head, with a cephalic index (q.v.) of 82 or higher.   G.P.M.

brand tillage. A type of shifting agriculture in which new land is periodically cleared by slashing and burning, while old fields are abandoned and allowed to regain their natural cover.   G.P.M.

branding. Sometimes referred to as a method of punishment, but in reality it was a method of identifying slaves, captives of war, and those who had been adjudged guilty of crime. It consisted of burning an identifying symbol deeply enough into the flesh of some part of the body exposed to sight to produce a scar. Sometimes when applied to criminals the symbol indicated the type of crime of which the individual had been guilty, as T for theft.   J.L.G.

brank. A harness made to fit over the head and fastened under the chin with a gag attached to fit into the mouth in order to keep the prisoner from talking. Originally it was designed to punish a common scold. Colloquially referred to as the "gossip's bridle."   J.L.G.

breeding. (1) Improvement of the hereditary qualities by selective mating. (2) Training in the approved folkways and mores.   F.H.H.

bride-price. A payment made, in securing a wife, by the groom or his kinsman to the father or other kinsmen of the bride. A bride-price is seldom regarded as an actual purchase price. On the contrary, its usual functions are to stabilize the union and to compensate the bride's relatives for the loss of her services.   G.P.M.

bride-service. A mode of marriage whereby a man obtains a wife by working for or serving his prospective parents-in-law, often in lieu of a bride-price. (q.v.).   G.P.M.

bride-wealth. Bride-price (q.v.).

bridewell. A House of Correction for the confinement of disorderly persons. By Act of 1576 the English Parliament directed each county to establish a House of Correction. The most notorious of this type was located at Blackfriars, London, at a site called St. Bridget's Well. Here was an old palace given to the city of London by Edward VI and converted into a lodging house for beggars. It provided the dual functions of jail and workhouse, and, hence, may be regarded as a forerunner of the modern prison.   A.E.W.

broadcast. The transmission of a program by radio intended to be received by the public. Music, spoken words, and sound effects are the three aspects of a broadcast program.   M.H.N.

broadcasting. The term originally meant scattering seeds on the ground. Now applied to the dissemination of communication by radio, the broadcasts being intended for public reception. Organized broadcasting has reference to the production and transmission of programs by standard stations for public consumption. A broadcasting station is a place where radio programs originate and from which these programs are transmitted through the air. M.H.N.

broken home. Cf. home, broken.

Buddhism. A comprehensive name for the various religious systems which developed historically from the teachings of Gautama Buddha (most probable dates, 563-483 B. C.). P.H.F.

budgetary studies. The scientific method of gathering data (derived either from questionnaires or actual records) as to the expenditures of family income in all levels of society. The method was first developed by Frederic LePlay (French economist) in the middle of the 19th century for the purpose of determining standards of living. It has been widely used and developed since that time in both the United States and elsewhere. A.E.W.

building area. Cf. area, building.

bureaucracy. A graded hierarchy of officials each of whom is responsible to his superiors. Ordinarily applied to governmental organization in its executive branches, but existing also in business, industry, commerce, labor unions, social institutions, churches, and other forms of social organization. Bureaucratism is usually characterized by adherence to routine, more or less inflexible rules, red tape, procrastination, unwillingness to assume responsibility, and refusal to experiment. M.Pm.

burglary. Breaking and entering the dwelling place or place of business of another with the intent to commit theft. Traditionally the common law defined the term as breaking and entering the dwelling place of another, in the night time, with felonious intent. Statutes of the various states have modified the meaning

of the term to meet modern conditions. J.W.M'C.

burial. Inhumation (q.v.), and also other methods of disposing of a dead body, such as canoe burial, cremation, exposure, mummification, ossuary, platform burial, second funeral, tower of silence, urn burial, water burial. G.P.M.

burial, urn. The practice of disposing of corpses, or of the ashes of cremation (q.v.), in urns or vessels. G.P.M.

burial, water. The practice of disposing of the corpses of the dead by throwing them into the sea or another body of water or setting them adrift in boats. G.P.M.

business. A situation-process devoted to the conduct of self-maintenance activities. In practice it is often differentiated from professions on the one hand and finance on the other. It involves the assumption of ownership and/or management, and is therefore sharply contrasted to the contribution made by labor, or the passive participation of the landlord or simple capitalist. More specifically, a business is a productive unit, organized according to whatever pattern is characteristic of any particular culture, or permitted by its mores.

business agent. The paid head of a local trade union who acts as executive officer, employment officer, and representative of the local in all dealings with the employers of members of the local. Although in theory the business agent is appointed democratically from among the bona fide members of the local, many business agents are autocrats wielding tremendous power over union members and employers alike. In fact the position of business agent has frequently lent itself to large scale racketeering. On the other hand, to curtail the power of the business agent is tantamount to curtailing the power of the union in bargaining with the employer. J.W.M'C.

business cycle. The alternation of prosperity and depression characteristic of the capitalistic system, and apparently inseparable from it in its present development. The figure of the cycle is inappropriate and unfortunate, as economic conditions never return precisely to any previous point. Analogy to a roller-coaster would be much more accurate.

business district. An area in a city or town given to commercial purposes, often limited and defined by use and zoning laws.

business organization. The systematic forms of human cooperation for producing and exchanging economic goods. As now developed in the countries having the more advanced industrial methods, it is the system of economic activities organized by leaders interested in managing the transformation of the raw resources of the earth by modern efficient processes into finished products for the use of the people who can pay for them at a price sufficient to cover the costs of production and leave a profit for the producers. In this system today the resources and capital goods are extensively and mainly in private ownership and the center of attention is on production and securing of profit. The present leading features or functional parts of the current system of business include (1) profits to owners, (2) wages to labor, (3) salaries to middle class workers, (4) specialized investment finance, (5) legal assistance and governmental protection, (6) banking services, (7) accounting systems, (8) insurance, (9) experimental laboratories, (10) machine techniques, (11) specialized buying, (12) specialized producing, (13) specialized advertising, (14) specialized selling, and (15) use of specialized and often "invisible" government agencies to secure private favors.   C.J.B.

C

ca'canny. In ordinary usage in Scotland and England to ca-canny is to go cautiously, carefully, or warily. But more particularly this word is applied to the willful restriction of industrial production by British workmen. It is the "slow-down strike" of this country. Ca'canny strategy is directed against labor-saving machinery, bonus system of remuneration, and other devices and techniques for raising industrial efficiency. Its methods are based upon the assumption that increased industrial output will result in wage reductions and unemployment.   J.H.E.

cadet. In social literature dealing with vice conditions the term is applied to a person who solicits trade for a prostitute. Also called a pimp or procurer. He may be identified with various related vices such as gambling or robbery.   N.A.

caisse de compensation. A fund first collected by certain large industrialists in France with the object of paying workingmen with families according to the number of their dependent children under thirteen. To avoid the probable discrimination by employers against married men the plan was devised of inducing the owners to pool the total cost of family allowances and set up a general compensation fund (caisse de compensation). According to this scheme the expense of family allowances was divided among all cooperating employers in proportion to the number of their employees or the size of their wage bill. Compensation funds, paying family allowances, were also organized in Belgium and Austria after 1920. In 1932 France provided by law for a national compulsory system of compensation funds paying family allowances.   W.G.

cajolery. A form of pressure put on others, consisting of amusing chatter, fair and often deceptive flatteries, intended to win favor. Wheedling, flattery, coaxing and entrapping are terms very similar in meaning.   F.E.L.

cake of custom. Cf. custom, cake of.

caliphate. See kalifate.

calling. Cf. vocation.

camorra. An underworld, secret, criminal organization which arose in the city of Naples, in 1830 and continued to thrive until about 1922. While the Camorra was identified with the underworld of Neapolitan life it also had contacts with civil, political, and religious authorities during its varied career. It represented a nineteenth century version of an entrenched "racket" protected by civil and political authorities.   N.F.C.

cannibalism. The practice of eating human flesh, occasionally as an ordinary article of food, but more commonly in order to wreak vengeance upon an enemy, to incorporate in oneself the spiritual qualities of the victim, or to fulfill a religious or ceremonial requirement. G.P.M.

canon law. Cf. law, canon.

canonical court. Cf. court, canonical.

capillarity, social. Cf. social capillarity.

capital. Material objects used in the production of wealth or in the rendering of economic services. Capital is one of the four factors commonly recognized in economics as necessary for a productive unit, or business (q.v.), the other three being land, labor, and organization. It is the least essential of the four, land and labor both being indispensable, as well as that infinitesimal degree of organization needed even by the primitive man to enable him to apply his labor to the land. Social evolution has been marked by a continuous increase in the relative importance of capital in the characteristic business unit. Its sudden emergence into a dominating position in the last few generations has caused the resulting economic system to be called "capitalism" (q.v.). The term capital is subject to many loose and vague usages, such as applying it to all forms of invested wealth. In strict analysis it should be confined to tangible instruments, apart from land, used in the productive process. Cf. capitalism; production goods; production.

capitalism. The general economic system giving characteristic form to the present social order of the industrially advanced countries of the world. Leading features include: (1) private ownership of land and capital resources by individuals, partnerships and corporations, (2) operation in competition primarily for private profit for the owners, (3) much stimulation of enterprise, (4) increase of inventions, (5) improvement of technical processes, (6) high specialization of finance in particular, (7) rapid enlargement of production, (8) world-wide extension of commerce, (9) growth of large powerful corporate organizations, producing (10) some private control of government, (11) periodic depressions and (12) increasingly powerful labor organizations that are securing improved status and influence of the workers. The stinting of market purchasing power by excessive capitalist concentration of incomes, technological unemployment and limitation of wages is making it impossible to maintain the abundant production without also abundant consumption. This is resulting in extensive transfer of economic control to government agencies, responsible to the public for making public consumer service the dominant motive of industry. Cf. business organization.   C.J.B.
A more precise and severe definition limits the application of the term simply to the predominant position held by the factor of capital in the typical business structure of any economic system, regardless

of the incidental or associated features. Thus capitalism would be just as characteristic of the Union of Soviet Socialist Republics as of the United States of America.

capital crime. Cf. crime, capital.

capital punishment. Cf. punishment, capital.

capitulations. The provisions, by treaty, for the government of secular strangers within the Ottoman Empire, the subjects of the Sultans being under sacred law (the Seriat). Under the capitulations, foreign nationals living in the Ottoman Empire (1299-1922), and in Egypt until 1937, were subject to the laws and consular courts of their respective states, much as native non-Muslims were governed by millets, (q.v.).   D.E.W.

caption. The heading of a column in a statistical table; title placed at the top of a table to refer to the columns of data in the body of the table.   M.Pt.

care, custodial. Cf. custodial care.

case. In social work, an individual or family under the care of a social agency. Cf. case record.   W.P.

case history, case record (community, family, group, social). The information which has been recorded about an individual, family, group, or community. The term is constantly used in social work agencies, and also in sociological, medical and psychiatric studies. Cf. case study method.   W.P.

case load. In work with individuals or families the number of such individuals or families with whom the social worker is working at any one time or period of time.   W.P.

case record. Cf. case history.

case study method. The method used in social research whereby data are collected and studied which depict any phase of a, or an entire, life process of a unit in its various interrelationships and in its cultural setting. The unit studied may be a person, a family, a social group, a so-

cial institution, a community or a nation. In contrast to the statistical method, the case study method gives a more or less continuous picture through time of the experiences, social forces and influences to which the unit has been subjected.
A.E.W.

case work. The function of professional social workers in assisting disadvantaged individuals and families to secure the greatest possible measure of normal living. Cf. social case work; case study method.
R.N.B.

case work, social. Cf. social case work.

case worker. One who practices social case work. Cf. social case work. W.P.

cash tenant. Cf. tenant, cash.

caste. In India, a homogeneous, endogamous, social control organization with distinctive rituals, especially those pertaining to a religious purity. Cf. caste system in India; caste society. Each caste and sub-caste is given an official status rating, high or low according to the date of its origin, its supposed one-time occupation, and the strictness of its moral and religious codes. Also, as in Europe, a minority with separate community life; e.g., the gypsies and Jews. In the United States, the white race which enforces social separatism and the Negroes who accommodate by following codes and rituals of deferential behavior. Caste has been freely used, as in describing the Byzantine Empire, to denote hereditary occupations, per se. Caste has also been, in a very loose manner, used synonymously with social class.
W.C.H.

caste society. A population with a common general culture, divided by social barriers into endogamous units, each of which possesses cultural specialties. Cf. caste system in India. Kinship and social control organizations split the people into segments, separated by differences in rituals, morals, and canons of exclusiveness. These units (sub-caste organizations) are usually hierarchized according to their "purity" or "holiness" rank. Some—especially out-caste groups—are also characterized by their social status. W.C.H.

caste system in India. Society in India is broken up into about 8,000 endogamous units, which are best thought of as social control (q.v.) organizations, each group with distinctive rules and rites concerning worship, food, marriage, and contamination. Most of these groups are Hindu (twice-born) sub-castes, some are "scheduled", i.e., depressed caste groupings, some are isolated tribes, some even Christian or Mohammedan groups. Caste groups are somewhat similar in Indian civilization to clans among primitives, except that they are always endogamous. "Traditional occupation" is of caste significance only among scavengers, laundrymen, and priests. Other occupations are engaged in by persons of many different caste groups. Economic and social class homogeneity characterizes only some of the depressed castes, the so-called untouchables. All other castes contain diverse economic and social class elements, even in their local units. W.C.H.

castration. The removal of the testicles from a male, or the ovaries from a female, though the term is usually applied to the former. R.E.B.

catastrophic change. Cf. change, catastrophic.

catchword, catch phrase. A word or phrase that has gained currency and is used as if its meaning were perfectly simple, clear, and unambiguous. It is defined, however, only vaguely and with protean connotations. Such words are familiar, unquestioned, popular, and shrouded in pathos. They coerce and overwhelm people who are not trained in propaganda analysis. They are particularly useful to propagandists for the purpose of substituting a precise appeal to emotion, sentiment, and tradition for a more rational review of facts. Wide ranges of special-interest proposals are "packaged" for popular consumption in such catchword "cartons" as "Democracy", "Americanism", "The People", and other glittering generalities. Proposals are also branded as undesirable by the use of such name-calling words as "Wall Street", "Slave", "Fascist", and "Nazi". A.M'C.L.

categoric. Applied to the word judgment to distinguish it from personal or sympathetic judgment of a person or group or situation. A categoric judgment places a previously unknown person in a definite preconceived category and pre-judges him (prejudice) as possessing all traits in the stereotype of that category. Categoric contacts are contacts on the basis of group membership or stereotypes rather than on a person-to-person basis. Cf. prejudice.   T.D.E.

categorical contact. Cf. contact, categorical.

category. A class, group or type in a classified series. The term is in frequent use in the classification of needy persons in order to administer programs of work, rehabilitation, relief, pensions, etc. Cf. classification.   N.A.

catharsis, theory of. A theory that holds that witnessing the expression of an emotion (e.g., in drama), or expressing it verbally or imitatively by gestures, induces a sufficient release of similar tensions and feelings repressed or suppressed in the subject to relax him and thus rid him of the need of overt expression of such emotions in actual life; a theory that partial release of tensions (such as those of sex in "dating", "dancing", "petting") relaxes rather than rouses them, or sublimates rather than fixates or intensifies the habitual cravings; a theory that confessional (religious, psychoanalytic, or informal) relaxes tensions, guilts, and other conflicts, "gets them off one's chest." Cf. sublimation; substitution.   T.D.E.

Caucasio-centrism. That form of ethnocentrism which considers the Caucasian, or white, race-conscious group as possessing the most desirable physical, mental, social, and moral qualities of all peoples. The major content of the ideology which it symbolizes is the "divine right" to rule the human race.   W.R.C.

causal. Relating to cause, or being in the relation of a cause.   F.H.H.

causality. The quality of inherent relation implied in the necessary connection of cause and effect, or of antecedent and consequence.   F.H.H.

causation. The relation between the anterior and posterior elements in a behavior sequence, which is of such a character that it can be stated as a scientific law. In any particular case, a statement of causation is an enumeration of the factors which in a given combination may be expected to be followed by a specified phenomenon. The ultimate "why" of causation lies beyond the scope of science, and belongs in the field of philosophy, religion, or intuition. . . .

In operational terms, if B denotes the effect and if A denotes the set of antecedent events, all events being measured either in present-or-absent form or in more accurately graded form, then complete causation of unity RaB equals 1.0, and partial causation is measured by the multiple correlation of less than unity.
                                    S.C.D.

causation, multiple, theory of. The theory that no one "cause" in any process leading to a given event is the sole cause thereof; a further theory that many factors have interacted to produce the actual result at any given moment; that at a given moment many factors in any given situation are interacting in a field from which the succeeding situation-process will be derived, and that many separable factors may be indispensable to a given effect but produce their unique resultant situation-process only when thus combined in this particular and unique configuration. Cf. causation; gestalt.   T.D.E.

causation, social. Cf. social causation.

causative. Of such nature that a given phenomenon may be expected to appear as a consequence. Cf. causal.

cause. That which results in an effect, or in any movement or change; the condition, or the conditions, necessarily antecedent to an event.   F.H.H.

cause, initial. A purely hypothetical or imaginary factor or set of factors which will regularly be followed by a particular consequence, but which itself has no antecedent. Such a concept lies entirely outside the field of science since in every causative sequence nothing comes from nothing, and every antecedent must con-

tain the full potentialities of its consequence, and no consequence contains anything which is not comprehended in its
antecedent.

cause, single. A factor separable logically or actually from other factors in a
process leading to an observed resultant
situation. In actual operation no single
cause acts independently of multiple
causes in a field. "Causes" and "factors"
have reality (q.v.) on a useful level of
abstraction, but in actuality (q.v.) there
is a total, interacting situation-process in
which an observer analyzes and abstracts
observable units which he denominates
"single causes" or "factors". Cf. causation; causation, multiple.   T.D.E.

cause, social. Cf. social cause.

cause of crime. Cf. crime, cause of.

caveat emptor. (Latin, let the buyer be-
ware.) The use of this formula under
certain legally qualified conditions enables
the seller to decline legal responsibility
for the quality or quantity of his ware. It
does not, however, apply to the question
of the title of property.   J.H.B.

ceiling, (*statistical*). The upper limit of
the highest class in a series of classes.
Used in contradistinction to floor or cellar.
          M.Pt.

celibacy. State of being unmarried; applied especially to one who has taken a
vow not to marry.   O.W.

cell (*statistical*). The compartment formed
by the intersection of a column and a row
in a statistical table. The number of
cases in a cell is referred to as the cell
frequency.   M.Pt.

cenotaph. An empty tomb commemorat-
ing a person buried elsewhere.   G.P.M.

censorship. The function exercised by
public officials,—and also the authorities
in certain private organizations,—of controlling, ordinarily in advance of publication, performance or receipt by the public, the content of publications, plays,
films, or radio programs. The function
of control after publication or perform-

ance, by prosecution, injunction or summary police action, is an exercise of the
police power over alleged offenses, to be
distinguished from the advance control
of censorship to prevent presumed offenses.   R.N.B.

census. A periodic enumeration of the
population of a political unit. The data
secured ordinarily include not only the
simple number of persons, but also facts
concerning sex, age, race, and a variety
of other characteristics which may be
very inclusive. The oldest continuous
genuine census in the world is that of the
United States, which was inaugurated at
the beginning of its independent national
life in 1790, and has been conducted regularly at ten-year intervals ever since.

census household. Cf. household, census.

census tract. A relatively small, permanent, homogeneous area, having a population usually between 3,000 and 6,000,
into which certain large cities (and sometimes their adjacent areas) have been
subdivided for statistical and local administrative purposes through the cooperation
of a local committee and with the approval
of the United States Bureau of the Census. In 1940 there were 60 American
cities with census tract systems.   C.F.S.

census tract street coding guide. Cf.
census tract street index.   C.F.S.

census tract street index. Cf. index, census tract street.

center, culture. That place within a culture area where a particular culture trait
or culture complex is found in its most
characteristic and least modified form.
This is usually, although not necessarily,
its place of origin.   J.P.E.

center, recreation. Cf. recreation center.

center, trade. Cf. trade center.

central index. Cf. social service exchange.

centralization. A process or situation in
which control has become in some degree
concentrated in the hands of fewer and

fewer persons considered as central to a concentric structure of power, and emanating from a single center toward the periphery; accompanied by a reduction of independence of decision or of local autonomy in subordinate groups and persons. Concentration of inhabitants, or of activities and land use, at centers of community areas or structures. T.D.E.

In rural sociology it involves either the concentration of the equipment or personnel of an institution at a central point in space with the abolition or subordination of minor units, as in the central or consolidated rural school, or it may consist of centralization of authority, as in the taking over of functions of the township by the county and those of the county by the state. This tendency exists in all large organizations where strong control is important for success. D.S.

centralization, urban. Cf. urban centralization.

centrism, ego-. The tendency of an individual to judge everything in relation to himself. P.F.C.

centrism, group. The tendency of a group of individuals to consider all human experience in relation to their own group, generally considering their own group superior to all others. P.F.C.

centrogram. Cf. centrography. C.F.S.

centrography. A body of statistical techniques used in the analysis of geographical distributions. These techniques are specifically concerned with centers of population, median centers, median points, and related procedures. The terms centrography and centrogram are applied interchangeably and were first used by the Mendelew Centrographical Laboratory in Leningrad, U.S.S.R. C.F.S.

cephalic index. Cf. index, cephalic.

ceremonial. Having the quality of ceremony; the term may apply to minor acts or conventions such as a hand shake or greeting, for which the noun ceremony would seldom be used; when occasionally used as a noun, it is the equivalent of ceremony (q.v.). T.D.E.

ceremonial license. Socially sanctioned sexual license on ceremonial occasions, e.g., at corroborees (q.v.), agricultural fertility rites, or initiation ceremonies. Cf. ritual union. G.P.M.

ceremony. A series of acts organized in a recognized pattern, having as definite purpose the group's recognition and signalization of some special event, person, or value, and the reinforcement of its meanings and sentiments for the group. Participants may go through the motions without realization of this original purpose, or may get from the experience different meanings from that recognized in the cultural heritage or advertised for the occasion. Cf. rite; ritual; etiquette. T.D.E.

chain gang. Cf. gang, chain.

chance. The mode of occurence of phenomena uncontrolled by human capacity or purpose. Cf. luck; aleatory element.

chancery procedure. Formerly the procedure in Chancery Courts where the King's representative (the chancellor) presided in cases in which were involved certain persons, usually women or children, who were unable under existing laws to protect themselves. Today such procedure has been adopted by the juvenile court in assuming the guardianship of the delinquent child and a protective interest in his welfare. M.A.E.

change. Change involves motion, modification, becoming, not merely a difference through time, in the object to which this is applied. A change is said to have taken place when an object or member of a system of moving things has been positionally shifted in such a way that the structural arrangement of the system is different. A causal relationship exists between two objects or entities when a change in the one has resulted in a change in the other. Cf. causation. S.J.

change, catastrophic. The violent, sudden upheaval or change in the social scene quickly followed by conditions of imbalance, instability and disorganization, generally described as disaster. Catastrophies may be sub-socially or socially determined. Sub-social types are either physical-social, those arising wholly outside the social order, such as earthquakes, floods, cyclones, tornadoes; or bio-social, such as pestilences or epidemics, plagues or invasions of pests, and perhaps famines; arising wholly within the social sphere are wars, revolutions and economic crises. Catastrophies may create a temporary interference with social equilibrium, or on the other hand, make for vital and enduring changes of the social order. As against the great, immediate destruction of life and property as, in the long run, not wholly unmixed evils; often unexpected socially advantageous changes have resulted or the period of cultural lag shortened. With the growth of science and technology and improved social control, man has set up increasingly adequate cultural protective and preventive devices in the physical-social and bio-social fields of disaster. In the control of major socially determined catastrophies, such as wars and revolutions, social technology has made relatively little advance, owing to the complexity of the factors involved.   S.J.

change, evolutionary. Cf. evolutionary change.

change, genetic. Cf. genetic change.

change, population. Cf. population change.

change, revolutionary. Cf. revolutionary change.

change, social. Cf. social change.

change, technological. Cf. technological change.

change, telic. Any purposive or planned alteration of group structure, relations or functions; change directed toward some end or ideal.   N.C.S.

change of life. The common term for the climacteric, the gradual passing of the reproductive function. It is also used as a synonym for the menopause, which is incidental to the climacteric.   E.R.G.

changes, cultural. Cf. cultural changes.

character. A quality, trait or sum of traits, attributes or characteristics which serve to indicate the essential nature of a person or a thing. As a moral quality, the sum and organization of traits, attitudes, and habits oriented with reference to an objective standard of conduct. The life-organization of a person; the motives, attitudes, habits, sentiments, ideals, and values that condition or determine the course of action in a situation requiring choices of conduct. The character of a person ranges from exemplary conduct or standard of conduct, deserving imitation, to misconduct and socially tabooed forms of behavior or plane of living. As a mark of distinction, the attributes and qualities of a person which serve to indicate his essential intrinsic nature; the sum of traits conferring distinctiveness and uniqueness; the peculiarities, the exemplary or notable traits. The degree of subjective organization of traits, whether strong or weak.   M.H.N.

Personality (q.v.) viewed from the standpoint of the predictability of its reactions, and thus of its capacity to be fitted into the behavioral requirements of the social groups to which the individual is related.   H.H.

A trait considered as separately heritable or traceable in the process of biological intermixture. Cf. trait.   T.D.E.

character, acquired. That attribute of an object (especially a person) which has been derived or developed from some source other than itself. A trait brought from or by contact with the environment, either physical or social. Cf. characteristic, acquired.   J.P.E.

character, individual. Cf. personality.

character training. The process of developing personal habits, attitudes, moral values, ideals, and behavior patterns through instruction, guidance, precept and example, and by providing experiences in situations in which moral decisions are made.   M.H.N.

characteristic. That trait, property, or attribute of an individual, group, or culture which distinguishes it from others.   J.P.E.

characteristic, acquired. A trait, quality or property of an individual, group or type added after the process of fertilization has occurred either before or after birth. This term is almost inseparably connected with the theories of Jean Lamarck (1744-1829) and August Weismann (1834-1912). Lamarck taught that characteristics acquired during the lifetime of an individual may be transmitted through heredity to the succeeding generation. He thought that such a characteristic as the webbed feet of birds was acquired because of the stretching of their toes in attempts to swim and the long neck of the giraffe in response to its use in reaching more food, and that such characteristics were transmitted by heredity to the next generation. Weismann challenged Lamarck's theory by showing that germ cells are separate from somatic cells and are therefore unaffected by any characteristic acquired after fertilization.   o.w.

characterization. The process of taking on distinctive traits, either through heredity or environment, or a combination of the two. Specifically, the process whereby an isolated and segregated human group achieves racial differentiation.

characterization, area of. Cf. area of characterization.

charisma. A spiritual gift. This term, long used in theological literature and in church history, was introduced into sociological theory by Max Weber to designate extraordinary merit, grace, genius, or power in a personality. Such uncommon qualification is the basis of the influence exerted by those individuals who come to be regarded as exemplary superhuman and divinely conditioned and hence are accepted as leaders in the capacity of rulers, party chiefs, prophets, founders of religion, etc. Ultimately charisma is at the root of all mass movements by virtue of the attraction exerted by creative personalities. Their authority or domination is based on the direct personal allegiance of their followers as contrasted with traditional or legal control where the personal element has been superseded by the institutional. Particular problems in the distribution of power arise at the aging or death of the leader when routinization has set in and provision has to be made for the institutionalization and per-

petuation of the movement and apparatus crystallized around the charismatic personality. Historically the divine right of kings and cult of genius and the *Fuehrerprinzip* constitute diverse recognitions of the unequal distribution of charisma. E.F.

charismatic authority. Personal ascendency based on presumed capacity for preternatural experience.   P.H.F.

charity. Charity has two aspects in common usage: (1) An attitude, or quality of feeling, toward those who are suffering from misfortunes. (2) The method of dealing with the unfortunate. Both have been closely related historically to religion (see 1st Cor., XIII). Toward the end of the last century there came into the concept of charity an emphasis on the rights of the individual. The Charity Organization Movement, originating in London was based on this newer concept, out of which has developed much of modern social work. Charity is frequently applied to a single deed; philanthropy helps the individual because of his membership in the group or race, or refers to activity providing for large numbers. Charity, as applied to an organization, has come to mean a more definite program and a greater interest in specific individual problems than would be indicated by philanthropic association. Benevolence is a term less limited than charity, while philanthropy usually applies to wide schemes of human welfare. Cf. benevolence. W.P.

charity girl. A term coined during World War I to denote girls who had sex intercourse with soldiers without asking for pay (as opposed to the regular prostitutes who were driven from the vicinity of army camps.)   R.E.B.

charity organization society. A social work organization privately supported, originally intended to cordinate the various philanthropic activities of a community; an organization carrying a social case work program and frequently other social and health activities.   W.P.

check-interviewer. One who re-interviews informants to check upon work of initial interviewer.   M.Pt.

checks, positive. Cf. positive checks.

checks, preventive. Cf. preventive checks.

chief. The leader or head of a tribe, clan or other social group, especially when his position and authority are institutionalized.   **G.P.M.**

child. A young person variously defined as to age in different states. In general, Child Welfare Services handle children only up to 18. In New York State the Juvenile Court has three ages for children —16 for delinquency, 17 for truancy, and 21 for crippled children. The Aid to Dependent Children Section of the Social Security Act was amended in 1939 to include children up to 18 years of age who are attending school.   **W.P.**

child, abandoned. A child (q.v.) who is abandoned or deserted in any place by both parents or by the parent having its custody, or by any other person or persons lawfully charged with its care or custody and left (a) in destitute circumstances or (b) without proper food, shelter, or clothing, or (c) without being visited or having payments made toward its support, for a period of at least one year, by its parents, guardian or other lawful custodian without good reason.   **W.P.**

child, neglected. A child (q.v.) who is not receiving from its parents or guardian such care, education, and upbringing as is in conformity to the expectation of society for the class to which it belongs. The concept is variously defined legally in the different states of the U. S. The tendency of recent years has been to make it more severe and comprehensive.

child care. Cf. welfare, child.

child guidance. The process by which persons trained in mental hygiene work with children who show behavior difficulties which call for a knowledge of social work, psychology, psychiatry, pediatrics or education.   **W.P.**

child guidance clinics. Clinics first established by Dr. William Healy, in connection with the juvenile court in Chicago in 1909 to diagnose the nature and the causes of delinquency in the individual, and to prescribe a remedial program on the basis of the accumulated information. The emphasis was at first upon the physical and psychological analysis, but in recent years environmental factors have been given more recognition. Aside from the original clinic in Chicago the most famous clinic is that established by Dr. Healy in Boston in 1917 under the Judge Baker Foundation. Approximately 100,000 cases annually are handled by such clinics.   **J.W.M'C.**

child labor. Cf. labor, child.

child welfare. Cf. welfare, child.

childrens court. Cf. court, juvenile.

chivalry. The knightly class of feudal times; also, the ideals of honor, the usages and manners of knights. In modern times the term has come to mean courtesy toward women and the weak and helpless. In mediaeval English law chivalry meant the tenure of land by knights' service in war, rendered to an overlord or to the king. Chivalry had an important influence in softening manners in the rude centuries of the Middle Ages; first the manners of knights and ladies in the castles and later those of the middle class burghers and their wives.   **W.G.**

choice. Conscious selection of an alternative act or object; used without implying any theory of free will, determinism, etc. In personal choice the person feels that his selection is not imposed upon him from without by persons alien to his interests. Social choice is better called deliberate social selection, in which a group after discussion and development of consensus selects its own members, policy, or course of action. Cf. will; free-will theory; social selection.   **T.D.E.**

choice, multiple. A method of (1) examining students and (2) conducting research into attitudes and opinions, wherein the student or investigatee is required to select the correct answer from a list of three or more proposed or possible answers.   **F.E.L.**

Christian ethics. Cf. ethics, Christian.

Christianity. The religion of the fatherhood of God and brotherhood of man as taught by Jesus. It is significant to sociology, not only as historically increasing the public understanding and practices of organic social union, but also, in this development, as spreading the democratic recognition of the personal possibilities, intrinsic worth and social rights of the common man. Considered as an ideal way of living, Christianity may be regarded as thorough democracy, defined as voluntary, intelligent and happy team work for the common welfare maintained by universal good will. In pursuit of this ideal Christianity has developed a vast complex of institutions: churches, missions, schools, etc., and has exerted a positive influence on behalf of many social reforms.   C.J.B.

chromosome. One of the definite bodies into which the chromatin of a cell nucleus divides during mitotic cell division. Chromosomes usually exist in pairs, are of characteristic size and shape for each species, and are visible during cell division. The human body cells each contain 24 pairs. The mature germ cells (gametes) normally contain only one from each pair of chromosomes.   F.H.H.

church. (1) An outward organization of an association, or associations, of believers in a common, dogmatically set, religious ideal. (2) A building in which Christ is worshipped and Christianity taught, notably Protestant, the Roman Catholic being called also Cathedral and Chapel. (3) An institution which, through symbolic acts and/or ethical prescriptions, purposes to keep its members constantly aware of the necessity of religion and its promise—in the Christian church specifically of redemption through grace and salvation; which also administers the religious life of the community and distributes means of healing and comfort.   J.H.B.

church, community. One of the several types of Protestant churches which are solely responsible for religious ministry to a given community.   E.des.B.

church, institutional. A Protestant church which features social services to its members and the people of the neighborhood, to such an extent as to become essentially a non-sectarian community center. In the United States such a church is ordinarily located in a rapidly changing neighborhood, characterized by the fact that its original members have moved to the suburbs, giving place to a low income immigrant population. The old membership continue their support and occasionally attend regular services, but the activities of the church tend to become more social, cultural, and recreational, and to operate primarily for the benefit of the new population.   J.W.M′C.

church attendance. The average number, age, sex, residence and occupational distribution of the persons attending the chief public services of worship and preaching in one or more church parishes, recorded and analyzed in order either to ascertain the strength and adaptation to its constituency of the religious ministry under examination, or to form a basis of comparison among individual churches or an array of churches.   G.M.F.

church social. A friendly gathering arranged by a religious unit for its members and attendants and their friends, usually for the purpose of combining pleasurable contacts with the promotion of institutional unity, and frequently also to secure money or other contributions for some religious cause.

cicatrization. Scarification (q.v.).

cicisbeism. The practice whereby a married woman is permitted to have a recognized lover or lovers. Cf. concubinage; polygamy.   G.P.M.

cihat. Turkish spelling of Jihad (q.v.).

circular reaction. Cf. reaction, circular.

circulation, class. Cf. class circulation.

circulation, social. Cf. social circulation.

circulation of élites. Cf. élites, circulation of.

circumcision. A genital mutilation consisting in the excision of the prepuce or foreskin in males, and, by extension, of the labia minora in females. Cf. clitoridectomy; subincision; supercision.   G.P.M.

circumvention. The act of avoiding an issue or situation for the purpose of reaching another, and possibly contrary, objective.   N.A.

cities, ancient. Urban communities of the early civilizations of Babylonia, Egypt, Greece, etc.   E.E.M.

city. A more or less permanently settled general population (adults and children of both sexes) living in a relatively compact area wherein are carried on the customary social or family life, political organization as a rule, and economic activities or occupations. (*legal*) A community with classification and status of city as granted by charter issued by state authority.   E.E.M.

city, garden. Cf. garden city.

city, industrial. An urban community of city proportions in which industry and production are the predominant occupational activities of the inhabitants. E.E.M.

city planning. Cf. planning, city.

city of refuge. A specially designated city, particularly among the ancient Hebrews, recognized by the mores during the transitional period between private vengeance and state punishment of criminals, wherein an individual guilty of an unintentional injury to another might find sanctuary from the pursuing avenger. Once safely within the walls of the city of refuge the accused individual passed out of the conventionally approved power of the injured party and came under the jurisdiction of the authorized representatives of society. Cf. sanctuary.

civic center. A quarter in a town where the principal public buildings such as the town hall, library, and auditorium are grouped according to a pre-arranged plan. Cf. community center.   S.S.

civil liberties. Cf. liberties, civil.

civil rights. Cf. rights, civil.

civil service. A system providing for and regulating the impartial selection by examination or with regard to fitness, ability and experience, the tenure, advancement, compensation and conditions of employment of governmental employees; an agency of the government to administer civil services usually presided over by commissioners. In the United States the civil service systems were established during the latter part of the nineteenth century in order to overcome the evil effects of the spoils system, to give government employees the security of a career and to supply the government with properly trained and experienced workers and to meet the growing need for technically trained personnel.   F.W.K.
In a more general sense, the term may be used to distinguish non-military from military activities under government.

civilization. Cultural development. The distinctly human attributes and attainments of a particular society. In ordinary usage, the term implies a fairly high stage on the culture evolutionary scale. Reference is made to "civilized peoples" in contrast to "uncivilized" or "non-civilized peoples." More accurate usage would refer to more highly and less highly civilized peoples, the determinative characteristics being intellectual, aesthetic, technological, and spiritual attainments.

civilization, dynamic. Society at the upper cultural level which is characterized by constant change or cultural alteration.   N.L.S.

civilization, ideal. A condition of human society conforming to any ideal pattern.

civilization, static. Society at the upper cultural level in proximate equilibrium; one not subject to significant cultural change.   N.L.S.

clan. A unilinear and usually exogamous kin-group, especially in former American usage, one characterized by matrilineal descent. Often used synonymously with "sib" (q.v.), but preferably reserved for a localized sib, i.e., for the group consisting of the adult members of a sib who reside together and of the spouses and children of these members. Cf. descent; exogamy; gens; sept.   G.P.M.

clandestine marriage. Cf. marriage, clandestine.

class. A totality of persons having one or more common characteristics; a homogeneous unit within a population; one category in a series by which persons may be classified. Class may or may not signify the existence of a hierarchical scale of social power. There are age, nativity, occupational, industrial, social, ideo-politico-economic, and income classes. However, races and nationalities, which may also divide the population, are not properly referred to as classes. Class legislation (tariffs, soldiers' bonuses, AAA allotments) is a revealing and proper use of class, denoting category but not rank. Cf. caste; class struggle; social class.   w.c.h.

class, leisure. Cf. leisure class.

class, marriage. Cf. marriage class.

class, middle. Cf. middle class.

class, social. Cf. social class.

class, working. Cf. working class.

class circulation. (1) Movement of individuals from one social class to another; vertical social mobility. (2) Circulation of élites.   a.m'c.l.

class conflict. Cf. conflict, class.

class consciousness. (1) An awareness of one's class position. Fundamentally, an awareness of the difference existing between one's class position and that of some other individual or individuals. This awareness is also generally accompanied by certain attitudes towards those occupying other class positions. These attitudes may be a feeling of superiority or inferiority towards those who occupy respectively a lower or higher rank; or a feeling of opposition or hostility where a situation of class conflict exists; or merely a feeling of aloofness or strangeness because of the difference in folkways, mores and ideologies of the different classes. (2) The attitude of shame because of, and disloyalty to, one's own social class (q.v.) and the desire, especially on the part of social climbers (q.v.), to desert their own cliques and be admitted into socially higher groups. This form of class consciousness is characterized by the open aping and envying of the higher social classes. Aspirational social class consciousness is as old as social stratification. (3) The spirit of group loyalty in the rivalry, scorn, and conflict between capitalists and workers, according to the Marxian formula of politico-economic struggle for power. In such a conflict man's loyalty is to his class; theoretically men rise or fall together as capitalists or workers. This form of social conflict received its specific character in the nineteenth century, and in the Soviet Union it ended in final victory for the workers' organizations. In fascist Germany and Italy the class struggle was suppressed by the State.   w.c.h.

class differences. Distinguished and differentiating characteristics of the several social, economic, and occupational strata, especially those pertaining to their associative behavior, manners, morals, canons of exclusiveness and respectability, standards of consumption, interests, and attitudes.   w.c.h.

class interest. Cf. interest, class.

class interval. The width between the upper and lower limits of a class into which quantitative data are grouped. Used synonymously with class, step-interval, class size, group interval.   m.pt.

class-interval script. The class-interval script, or pre-subscript, s^1, is used in dimensional Sociology to denote the statistical class-intervals, or grouped units, of a quantitative variable.   s.c.d.

class mind. The ideologies, attitudes, beliefs and standards which characterize the members of a given social class.

class morality. Cf. morality, class.

class prejudice. Cf. prejudice, class.

class script. The class script or post-subscript, ^1s is used in dimensional sociology to denote the number and kind of logical classes.   s.c.d.

class structure. The hierarchical organization of individual behavior responses to key stimuli of rank, title or privilege; accompanying gradations of superiority and inferiority response patterns above or below equalitarian patterns of response; with such responses part of a semi-rigid framework of prestige and social esteem. F.S.C.

class struggle. Cf. struggle, class.

class thought. Cf. thought, class.

classical. Based upon the accurate subdivision of data into classes or categories, and to that extent systematic and scientific.

classical penal theory. The theory advanced by eighteenth century jurists and philosophers, notably Beccaria (Italian), Bentham (English), and Feuerbach (German) holding that punishments for crimes should be meted in an exact fashion according to the degree of seriousness of the offense. This theory was widely incorporated in penal laws and still operates in Europe and America in the majority of the provisions for convicting and sentencing criminals adjudged guilty. M.A.E.

classical school of penology. Cf. classical penal theory.

classification. The act of sorting items or types of a series in some orderly arrangement to one another. The process normally calls for a systematic description of the items in the series by uniform standards and in uniform terminology in so far as this is possible due to likeness. Another quality in classification is the identification of differences. A correct classification must always be based upon some logical and recognized principle of likeness or difference. N.A.

classification of prisoners. The process through which the social background of the offender is studied and his individual aptitudes and needs are examined and appraised so that the treatment he may receive can be based on factual data and related to his special requirements. N.S.H.

classificatory system. A kinship system (q.v.) in which the terms of relationship are normally applied to more than one category of relatives each. Today it is recognized that most kinship systems are of this type, and the word "classificatory" is usually reserved for particular terms that are applied to relatives of different categories, e.g., "uncle" or "cousin" in English. G.P.M.

claustrophobia. A morbid fear or dread of being shut in or enclosed; opposite of agoraphobia. W.E.G.

clear and present danger. A phrase adopted by the U. S. Supreme Court in World War I, by which to measure the degree of probability of unlawful acts flowing from speech or publication; and used to uphold the constitutionality of war-time statutes penalizing certain utterances, despite the apparent prohibition of the First Amendment. R.N.B.

clearance, slum. Cf. slum clearance.

clemency. A blanket term used to cover all types of reduction of sentence of a prisoner exercised by the authority having the pardoning power: absolute pardon, conditional pardon, and commutation of sentence. J.L.G.

climate. General or average meteorological conditions of an area, manifest in temperature, moisture, sunshine and air movement. Figuratively, as in "social climate", to indicate the general character of public attitudes, especially the relatively permanent attitudes registered in mores and law. F.H.H.

clinic. A division of a dispensary in which a specified group of related diseases are treated; e.g., dental, neurological, ophalmological, cardiac clinics. (The terms dispensary and clinic are often used interchangeably and without distinction.) E.E.M.

clinic, behavior. Cf. behavior clinic.

clinical sociology. Cf. sociology, clinical.

clique, social. Cf. social clique.

clitoridectomy. A genital mutilation of the female consisting in the excision of the clitoris. Cf. circumcision. G.P.M.

close custody. Cf. custody, close.

closed shop. Cf. shop, closed.

closed systems. Groups of limited membership and to which additions are received only as determined from within; labor unions, professional societies or social sets may be of the type. A characteristic of such is their resistance to new thought or any influence from without that might threaten the thought pattern or practices within. Also applied to organized bodies of thought or doctrine. N.A.

club. A form of voluntary association, in which the members are organized around certain specific common objectives. Such objectives are often recreational or cultural in character, but may involve also religious, political, social, or economic purposes. Clubs are usually self-governed and determine their own membership by election. Generally the term is used for organizations in which a social bond or a desire for sociability exists between the members as well as the formal agreement on the common purpose. G.L.C.

co-adaptation. The process of bringing the activities of the members of a group to unity of objective aim. This process is also called by some sociologists "social adaptation", or "social coordination." As it is the process which makes group action or group behavior possible, this is a very important concept in sociological theory. Individuals in order to form a functioning group of any sort, and especially to carry on a common life, have to co-adapt or coordinate their activities so that they work toward a common objective aim. As a human social group has unity only through this mutual adjustment of the activities of its members, this coordination or co-adaptation makes the group and its life. In a football team, for example, the coordinated activities of the members of the team make the behavior of the team. This is true of all human groups. If the form of co-adaption, or coordination, is to change there must be in human groups exchange of ideas or sentiments, at least mental stimulation and response, until a new form of adjustment is reached. Thus the conscious life of all human groups centers about this process of social adaptation or coordination, just as the conscious life of the individual centers about the process of individual adaptation. The social process within the group

consists largely of various forms of communication which bring about the adjustment of individuals to one another so that the group can act as a unit. Cf. group behavior. It should be pointed out that social adaptation or coordination has many degrees. Not all social adaptation is cooperative, at least not in the popular sense. Toleration, for example, is a form of social adaptation, but is not usually regarded as cooperation. Modified hostility, or regulated conflict, may also be considered a form of social adaptation, though hardly cooperative. Coordination or co-adaptation between the members of a group is therefore a wider concept than cooperation. Social cooperation is to be regarded from the standpoint of group stability and efficiency, as simply the highest and most harmonious form of co-adaptation or coordination. C.A.E.

coalition. A combination of persons or groups into a body or integrated group. Frequently used for relatively temporary governmental and military combinations for the purpose of concerted action in crisis. M.S.

code. A socially recognized and enforced body of prescriptions and prohibitions. (*legal*)—A systematic arrangement of formulated mores (e.g., Manu, Mosaic, Lycurgus) or of legislation dealing with some special aspect of law such as civil or criminal procedure, criminal law, administration, city government, children, labor; (*moral*)—a systematic arrangement of mores or moral precepts, formulated for greater effectiveness in social control; (*ethical, professional*)—a systematic arrangement of principles, standards and rules set up by and for a professional or quasi-professional group for the control and guidance of "ethical" conduct of and among its membership. T.D.E.

code, moral. Those rules or principles of morality that are commonly understood and generally accepted by the members of a given social group, and subject to social sanctions of varying degrees of severity. F.H.H.

code, social. Cf. social code.

codification. A process (or its completion) by which mores, rules, or statutes previously in effect but without system or consistency are classified, arranged in some logical order, reconciled and perhaps filled in symmetrically where gaps appear. The net product is a code (q.v.). T.D.E.

coding. Assignment of class symbols to the various categories or combinations of categories of qualitative variables preparatory to tabulation. Codes may be numbers, letters, words, or other symbols. M.Pt.

coemptio. A form of marriage in use in ancient Rome, in which the services of priests were not employed. The essential rite consisted in a symbolical sale of the woman to her betrothed. A coin of small value was used and the "sale" was purely symbolic of the fact that by this rite the wife was brought under the *manus* (hand) or power of the husband. W.G.

coerce. To force another person against his will to move or act in a way desired. T.D.E.

coercion. The process of forcing, often by the use of fear, a person to move or act contrary to his free choice. That method of exploitation (q.v.) or domination (q.v.) in which the purposes of the exploiter or dominator are imposed on the exploited or dominated in conflict with their own long-run purposes, by means of direct physical force or psychologically, by means of intimidation, threats, or torture. A psychologically coerced action is always undertaken (or a psychologically coerced state accepted) in order to escape some alternative penalty believed by the coerced to be worse. Rewards, payments, and bribes induce but do not coerce. Cf. fraud; freedom. H.H.

coercion, non-violent. The exercise of moral compulsion by an individual or group by refusal to cooperate, always without the use of physical violence. (More common term, non-violent resistance. Civil disobedience is the term used when resistance is against a civil authority.) A.E.W.

cognate. A consanguine relative in the matrilineal (q.v.) or female line. G.P.M.

cohabitation. The living together of husband and wife. Sexual intercourse is usually presumed, but in law this is not necessary for the husband and wife status. E.R.G.

cohort. (*demographic usage.*) A group of persons starting life together. Thus, hypothetical cohorts are established in the construction of life tables and in the computation of other indices in which the principles of the life table are followed. Cf. life table; reproduction, gross rate of; reproduction, net rate of. C.V.K.

coition. Cf. coitus.

coitus. Entry of the penis in the vagina. While movements and ejaculation are the usual consequence, they are not essential to the definition. N.E.H.

coitus interruptus. Coitus followed by withdrawal of the penis usually just before ejaculation, which commonly takes place outside the vagina. Widely used as a birth-control measure before the invention of modern mechanical and chemical methods. A very old method, it is still widely used by the less well informed. Statistics show coitus interruptus to be one of the three most common methods of birth control used prior to clinical instruction. Medical opinions differ on its reliability and physical effects. Though it has been known to cause nervous ailments, these have frequently been exaggerated by modern writers on birth control (q.v.). N.E.H.

coitus reservatus. Coitus without ejaculation. Movements and contact may endure much longer than in ordinary coitus. Sometimes classified as a non-mechanical birth-control method. Perhaps most extensively practiced in the Oneida Community (New York State). N.E.H.

collecting economy. A mode of life based primarily upon the gathering of wild plant foods, as contrasted with a hunting, fishing, pastoral, or agricultural economy. G.P.M.

collection culture. The lowest stage of human culture, upon which men carry on their self-maintenance activities with no tools, implements, or artifacts of any kind. For their livelihood they depended upon the supplies furnished them by nature, on essentially the same basis as the sub-human species. The invention or discovery of basic implements and weapons marks the transition to hunting culture. Cf. collecting economy.

collective. As an adjective, the word is opposed to individual; it is approximately identical with groupal, organizational, and communal. It refers to the structure or action of any collectivity composed of two or more individuals. As a noun, it means, in general, any such unit. According to a more restricted usage, a collective is an undertaking or service owned by a group or association as such, not by individual persons. Collectives in this sense include not only publicly owned enterprises, but a great variety of voluntary collectives ranging in size from families or clubs owning their capital equipment to large mutual companies and religious bodies. Usage of the term collective is so diverse that specific definition for the purpose in hand is essential. Cf. cooperative.   S.E.

collective action. Goal-diretced mutual and simultaneous effort of persons or groups of persons to change the state of a subject or object, temporarily or permanently.   J.H.B.

collective bargaining. The right and process of negotiation between an employer, or a group or association of employers, and representatives of workers organized in a union. The National Industrial Recovery Act established this right in the United States by providing that "employees shall have the right to organize and bargain collectively through representatives of their own choosing." (73rd Congress, Public No. 67, H. R. 5755, approved June 16, 1933, Section 7 (a).) The right was further defined as follows in the act creating a National Labor Relations Board: "Employees shall have the right to self-organization, to form, join, or assist labor organizations, to bargain collectively through representatives of their own choosing, and to engage in concerted activities, for the purpose of collective bargaining or other mutual aid or protection." (74th Congress, Public No. 198, S. 1958, approved July 5, 1935, Section 7.) The National Labor Relations Act established the National Labor Relations Board. "Collective bargaining" differs from employees' representation, or so-called company unions, in that it is self-organization by workers, usually including workers in more than one establishment, while employees' representation is limited to one company. The phrase "collective bargaining" was first used by Beatrice Webb in her writings on trade unions in England.   M.VK.

collective behavior. Cf. behavior, collective.

collective egoism. A belief in the superiority of interests which associates have in common, manifest in either an exclusive preference for what concerns their welfare or in a patronizing attitude toward outsiders.   B.M.

collective egotism. Self-centered satisfaction with the character and achievements of one's own group, analogous to the feelings of an egotistical individual with respect to himself. An easy variant of patriotism (q.v.), sanctioned and even commended in many societies. For example, the social conventions of the United States do not permit a citizen to say, "I am the finest individual in the world," but they do endorse the sentiment, "The American nation is the finest nation in the world, and I am an American."

collective feeling. Cf. feeling, collective.

collective mind. Sum total of reactions, rational or irrational, of two or more persons confronted with a single phenomenon or process of phenomena.   J.H.B.

collective opinion. Cf. opinion, collective.

collective product. Any achievement or result which is traceable to collective behavior (q.v.) or joint effort of a group, at any level of coordination, organization or cooperation. Strictly speaking, this excludes results due merely to like responses to like stimuli, as the kill of a pack, or a bank panic. Collective product implies a collectivity (q.v.).   T.D.E.

collective psychology. Cf. psychology, collective.

collective representation. Cf. representation, collective.

collective response. Cf. response, collective.

collective security. A plan for stabilizing international relations through multilateral treaties guaranteeing the territorial integrity of the signers of the treaties against aggression of other nations, by force of arms if necessary. In the days just prior to World War II, France and Russia urged England and the United States to participate with them in such a plan of collective security, but the plan was rejected because it infringed upon the traditional isolationism of the United States and because it was allegedly sponsored by the Communist International.
           J.W.M'C.

collective telesis. Cf. telesis.

collective unity. The aspect of a functional group in which its behavior appears to be that of a unit larger than any subgroup or person comprised within it. T.D.E.

collectivism. The theory or practice of collective enterprise, collective action, or collective control in any of their manifold forms. The word is commonly used as a general term for various "isms" advocating a collective economy or denoting such an economy in operation. Included are syndicalism, Fabian socialism, guild socialism, Marxian socialism, and soviet communism (a variety of Marxism), besides a home-grown variety of collectivism identifying it simply with collective ownership, both public and voluntary. Contrary to some definitions collectivisms are not all authoritative in the sense of being non-representative or undemocratic in the basic controls. The word collectivism is often used somewhat loosely to designate non-ownership controls by the state or other collective unit, or even the corporate organization of business. Obviously, the term needs precise definition for the purpose in hand. Cf. communism; socialism.   S.E.

collectivity, human. A unity of interacting personalities in which those participating possess awareness of more or less homogeneity of composition, of interests or of joint action. It ranges from the pair to a league of nations. T.D.E.

colonization. A form of population movement characterized specifically by the establishment, by a state, of political control over outlying territory and a definite movement of settlers from the home state to that territory. Colonization differs from imperial expansion in the relative importance of the actual permanent transfer of population from the dominant country, and in the preponderance of these settlers over the natives in the outlying area. It differs from immigration (q.v.) in that both the areas involved in colonization are under the same political jurisdiction, while true immigration always crosses a political boundary. Colonization is an ancient device, and has been utilized by many powers from the early Chinese through the classical Greeks down to contemporary states. In all true colonization the native peoples are either so few in number or so inferior in culture as to impose no serious obstacle. While there may be, and usually is, an initial period of forcible suppression of the native population, colonization is not essentially a warlike movement. Historically, practically all great colonizing powers have been located in the temperate zones, mainly the north temperate. Colonization itself has taken two main forms, one where the subject territory is located in the tropics, the other where it also is located in the temperate zones. The type of administration and the social and economic life of the two classes differ greatly. The tropical colony is likely to remain in subjection indefinitely while the manifest destiny of a temperate zone colony is to become an independent state.

colonize. To engage in the process of colonization (q.v.), either as the dominant power or as a settler.

colony. A minor subdivision of a state, settled by migrants from the homeland in varying proportions to the native population. These settlers remain subject to the central power, but ordinarily with an inferior political status to those who remain at home. Cf. colonization.

colony, penal. A secluded area, generally a distant island outside the nation proper, or occasionally a remote part of the nation, where criminals are sent upon conviction of crimes, usually those within special categories. In effect, sentence to a penal colony involves virtual banishment. M.A.E.

(*Historical note*) The system originated in England as a phase of penal transportation after the American Revolution had ended penal transportation to the American Colonies, and England diverted the transportees to Australia. Since there were too few free colonists in Australia to absorb the transportees as laborers, as had been possible in the American Colonies, England had to place these transportees to Australia in settlements or colonies. The first was established in 1787-1788 at Botany Bay near Sydney. Other countries tried these colonies—Russia, France, India, Mexico, etc. A few still remain—France at Cayenne, French Guiana; Mexico at Tres Maria Islands, Brazil; and the Philippines. J.L.G.

commensalism. (*ecological, biological.*) A form of symbiosis in which two species sharing the same gross habitat do not compete for its resources in so far as their demands upon it, like those of Jack Sprat and his wife, are different. There may also be no mutual aid, but merely juxtaposition; (*social-ecological*) sometimes used to describe non-competing persons or groups dwelling in the same community area having independent rôles, needs and interests, without conflict or mutual aid. Cf. symbiosis; mutual aid. T.D.E.

commerce. As applied to economic relationships, the term has reference to transactions in trade or barter. The term also has reference to social intercourse, the exchange of communications, etc. N.A.

commercial amusement. Cf. amusement, commercial.

commercial recreation. Cf. recreation, commercial.

commercial rent. Cf. rent.

commercial revolution. Cf. revolution, commercial.

commercialization. The ordering of any institution or activity solely or chiefly through the motive of private profits, especially in cases where this seems to involve the leaving out of account of other motives and values which might be accorded an important part in ordering the activity. F.N.H.

commercialize. To set the ideals, habits and methods of a person, association or community in the forms or terms predominately of bargaining and exchanging for profit advantage; usually as necessitated by current commercial conditions without definite responsibility or concern for the general welfare of the other party to the transaction. The term refers especially to the tendency of the current competitive struggle for private profit to extend its motives into the methods of the other social functions besides those of production and exchange (viz., sustenance, healing, publicity, education, religious and moral control, politics, fellowship, recreation, and art) thus distorting their functions into private profit seeking exchange, in place of their normal services. C.J.B.

commercialized amusement. Cf. amusement, commercial.

commercialized vice. Cf. vice, commercialized.

commissar, (*Russian, Komissar*). A commissioner or head of a department of government. Used especially in the U.S.S.R. to designate heads of commisariats or the governmental departments in the separate Republics of the Soviet Union or the members of the national cabinet. N.L.S.

commitment. (1) A warrant or order by which a court or magistrate directs an administrative officer to take a person to some type of custodial institution, a prison or reformatory, a mental hospital, a correctional institution for juveniles, or some other type of custodial institution. It must be made in writing under the hand and seal of the magistrate, indicating his authority, and the time and place of making it. In the case of a commitment to prison the warrant for custody is directed to the keeper or warden of the particular prison to which the person is sent, stating that he has been charged on oath, indicating the offense for which he has been convicted, and the length of sentence to be served. In American states sentences are either for definite periods of time, or indefinite, but providing maximum and minimum limits. Commitments may be made for further examination or final. If the latter, the warden of the prison is directed to keep the prisoner until he is discharged by due process of law. If a prisoner during his trial is found "not guilty on account of insanity", he may in some states be committed directly, without further examination, to a hospital for the criminal insane. A few states take cognizance of certain delinquent or criminal types for whom commitments may be made for an entirely indeterminate period of time, without maximum or minimum limits. Such types are principally so-called defective-delinquents and sexual psychopaths. Coommitments to industrial schools, made from the juvenile court, are for an indefinite period, but not exceeding the age of twenty-one years. Finally, in case of a commitment to an institution for the civil insane, or for some other afflicted type, it is made by a civil rather than a criminal court.   A.E.W.

(2) A pledge, involving or binding oneself to the support of, or participation in, a program, cause, or some form of social activity, and binding within the moral or ethical code.   F.W.K.

common. Shared by more than one person; or shared by all or most of a given group.   T.D.E.

common carrier. A person or agency who, as his or its regular business, receives goods for hire or convey from one place to another and who by law possesses a lien for such services.   F.W.K.

common law. Cf. law, common.

common-law marriage. Cf. marriage, common-law.

common sense. The equipment of the average socius to deal with the everyday problems of life, independent of any special education or unusual knowledge. Native intelligence developed and fortified by the everyday experiences of the ordinary citizen.

communal. (1) Relating to, characteristic of, or belonging to the commune; or, more generally, to the community.

(2) Relating to the hypothetical marriage of all brothers, sisters and cousins of a given age grade or generation as a promiscuous group, believed by some to have been the necessary cultural antecedent of the classificatory system of relationships.   F.H.H.

communalism. (1) A system of collective or communal, as opposed to private or individual, ownership of land, food stores, or other property.   G.P.M.

(2) A theory of government based on a maximum of autonomy for all local minority groups. As commonly used in India, the term refers (a) to the practice of assigning a certain number of seats in the legislatures of the eleven British provinces to each sizeable religious group, and (b) to the struggle for power (in the form of additional seats) which results.   S.C.M.

commune. In medieval social organization, a body politic, guild, corporation, or association, representing the growing artisan-merchant classes and providing the necessary public defense, internal order and other public services—exhibition halls, quays, etc.—for a trading center or an incipient urban community. In its earlier form, it was usually a purely personal group for the promotion and protection of common interests in trade; later it developed into a chartered territorial political unit, culminating in the "free" city. F.H.H.

Commune, The. Term used to designate one of several insurrectionary governments of radical revolutionary type, chosen through excited mass action. Thus the government that usurped power during the French Revolution from 1792 to 1794 and carried out the "Reign of Terror" is called The Commune, or the first commune. Usually the term refers to The Commune of Paris, March 18-May 29, 1871, or the second commune. While the first was essentially a bourgeois (q.v.) uprising, the second was essentially proletarian (q.v.), advocating revolutionary socialistic or communistic policies. The term is also applied to the government set up under Bela Kun in Hungary, which sought to spread the Bolshevist revolution to that country.   F.H.H.

communication. The process of making common or exchanging subjective states such as ideas, sentiments, beliefs, usually by means of language, though also by visual representation, imitation and suggestion. The process of social interaction in human groups is largely a process of communication usually through articulate speech or language. The lower forms of communication through emotional cries, bodily movements, and other forms of signals are common in the animals below man; but so far as is known, man alone possesses articulate speech, although articulate speech is unquestionably derived from emotional cries. As this higher form of communication which we call language has become the chief form of social interaction between the members of human groups, it has enabled man not only to share his experiences with the members of his group but to record and preserve these experiences and their accompanying ideas, sentiments, and beliefs. Hence, human groups have been able to share ideas, sentiments, and beliefs among all their members and to attain in this way like-mindedness and common activities. Communication in human groups becomes the chief factor in their unity and continuity and the vehicle of culture. It is accordingly not too much to say that, as the higher forms of communication, particularly language, have enabled groups to accumulate, pass on, and preserve the culture of a group, communication is the very basis of human society. Concretely, the term is commonly applied to such instrumentalities as the mail, telegraph, telephone, and radio.   C.A.E.

communication, mechanism of. 1. (*physiological.*) The organs with which human beings transmit messages to others in the form of words, gestures, facial expressions. 2. (*societal*) The devices through which an individual's messages are transmitted to a broad social audience, includ-

ing the societal ramifications of an individual's communications. Examples: gossip, public speeches, town meetings, picketing, handbill distribution, newspaper publication, radio broadcasting, etc. To be more detailed, the newspaper segment of the societal mechanism of communication involves local reporting and newsprocessing arrangements, national and world-wide news gathering organizations (working through functionaries, cables, radio, etc.), and printing, publishing, and distributing facilities. This whole segment is integrated with all other segments of the societal communications mechanism.
A.M'C.L.

communism. A social philosophy or a system of social organization based upon the principle of the public ownership of the material instruments of production and economic service, associated with doctrines as to the means by which such a system is to be established and maintained. In its fundamental philosophy, communism is practically identical with socialism (q.v.). Like socialism, it derives much of its support and its theoretical formulation from the works of Karl Marx and Friedrich Engels, although it has given its own special emphasis to certain stereotypes and slogans, such as the "dictatorship of the proletariat." Communism differs from socialism in its repudiation of the philosophy of gradualism and its insistence that slow, piecemeal measures can never be adequate to introduce the new type of society. It may even go so far as to deny the possibility of introducing a collectivized economy by constitutional means, even in states where political democracy exists. Consequently, it is committed to the justifiability, and quite probably the necessity, of forcible or even violent means of breaking down the capitalistic system and introducing the new order. The second important divergence of communism from socialism has to do with the system of compensation of the worker. Both agree that "ownership income" must disappear and only "doership income" remain. But while socialism is content to allow incomes to be adjusted on the basis of personal ability or social service competitively appraised within the collective system, communism would eliminate even the competition of individual quality. The familiar communist slogan, "From each according to his ability and to each according to his need" seems to contest the field with the doctrine of equal pay for all workers.

Like socialism, communism is primarily an economic, rather than a political, system. The political implications which seem to infuse communism even more strongly than socialism probably stem from the doctrine, mentioned above, that communism cannot be achieved through the authorized use of political methods even in state systems that have a free electorate. There is no adequate ground, in communist theory or practice, for the assumption that communism is committed to the overthrow of government in general, or of any particular government. No doubt communists would endorse the doctrine that any people whose government has become tyrannical, oppressive, or unresponsive to the popular will, and which cannot be displaced by peaceful means, can be legitimately ousted by forcible means. But in this communists do not differ from any other school which accepts the doctrine of the occasional necessity and justifiability of revolution. It was in keeping with this doctrine that the Union of Soviet Socialist Republics was established in 1917, and the United States of America in 1776. In this connection, it may be noted that communism, in certain periods of its development at least, has been more concerned with world revolution than has socialism.

The Union of Soviet Socialist Republics, while unquestionably instituted as the result of communist agitation and in the spirit of communism, is not at present a communistic society. Its own leaders proclaim this fact emphatically, and insist that while they may have a communistic objective in mind, they are still a long way from it, and are at present in the socialist phase. This contention is supported by the great differences in personal incomes that prevail today in the Soviet Union. This country is very far from being a classless society in so far as questions of status, levels of living, and recognition are concerned.

In the United States, communism has had a somewhat checkered career. It has existed mainly as a philosophy, never having been established as an economic system on a sufficiently large scale to be significant. There have been several groups using the name and claiming to be the authentic representatives of the doctrine. The Communist Party, as far as any one group can lay exclusive claim to that title, is numerically a very small body. As a group, probably as a result of the vigorous opposition of its opponents, it has a social potential far out of proportion to its numerical strength or to the social potential of its individual members.

Before the relative standardization of the concept which followed the work of Marx and Engels, communism frequently had a vaguer but more inclusive connotation. It was considered to involve the common ownership, not only of the material means of production, but of all material instruments, including consumption goods. On account of the strong property implications of the marriage institution, this doctrine frequently led to sweeping modifications in the mores of marriage and the family, involving at least the theoretical implications of communal sex relations. It was on this rock, perhaps as much as any other, that some of the early adventures of Utopian communism eventually foundered. One of the oldest records of a group with definitely communistic features relates to the early Christian church, of which it is said: "Neither said any of them that aught of the things which he possessed was his own; but they had all things common."

communism, sexual. Permissible freedom in sexual relations within a group of men and women, apart from the prevailing marriage institution. Cf. group marriage; pirrauru.   G.P.M.

communist. One who adheres to the doctrines of communism, or advocates and works for the establishment of a communistic order. The term can have no more precision than that of "communism" itself. Aside from membership in a group that officially labels itself communist, or self-adoption of the label, the application of this term to any individual can have little precision or scientific validity. The use of the word as an opprobrious epithet, while common, has no definitive significance.

community. (1) A sub-group having many of the characteristics of society, but on a smaller scale, and with less extensive and coordinated common interests. Implicit in the concept of "community" is a territorial area, a considerable degree of interpersonal acquaintance and contact, and some special basis of coherence that separates it from neighboring groups. The community has more limited self-sufficiency than society, but within those limits has closer association and deeper sympathy. There may be some special bond of unity, such as race, national origin, or religious affiliation. (2) The totality of feelings and attitudes that binds individuals into such a group as described in (1).

community, moral. The sharing of ultimate values among a number of persons so as to produce in them a sense of common orientation and striving. Moral community may be present in as small a group as a family and as large a group as a nation. R.C.A.

community, planned. A community designed and organized according to some plan or ideal; distinguished from one that has grown spontaneously without benefit of prearrangement. N.L.S.

community, prison. Cf. prison community.

community, rural. Cf. rural community.

community, rural industrial. Cf. rural industrial community.

community, satellite. A subordinate center, in a metropolitan area or within the zone of influence of a large city. It is usually a separate political entity.

community, village. A term applied to the typical agricultural community of medieval Europe and still surviving in modified form in parts of the Orient. The village community consists of families engaged in agriculture whose houses are aggregated in a village and of their lands which surround the village and consist of intermixed holdings and of lands which are held in common. The whole area has a definite boundary and various officials and institutions for its control, but is more of a socio-economic than a political unit. D.S.

community center. An organization which provides a meeting place and equipment for recreational and other groups, usually from a neighborhood or with similar occupational or racial backgrounds. W.P.

community chest — federated financing. (1) A fund collected by an organization, frequently a federation of agencies, for the purpose of supporting private social work agencies. (2) The organization for the collection of such funds. W.P.

community church. Cf. church, community.

community coordination. A process whereby the forces, organized groups, agencies and institutions, and individuals of an area are integrated and function in a cooperative manner to achieve common objectives. Cf. community organization; coordinating council. M.H.N.

community facilities. Common social, transportation, recreational, or convenience facilities available to residents of a housing project or other neighborhood, including social halls, public utilities, street cars and buses, stores, restaurants, shops, churches, schools, community laundry equipment, parks and playgrounds, and other educational, domestic, health, or welfare equipment. S.S.

community organization. A process whereby people living in a contiguous geographic area build up common centers of interest and activities and function together in the chief concerns of life. It is a basic way in which groups of persons become integrated in making collective adjustments directed toward common ends. In a technical and administrative sense, as used by social workers, it is a method of coordinating institutions, agencies, groups, and individual persons of an area to make collective adjustments to social needs and resources, to create and maintain facilities and services, and to integrate activities for common welfare. Cf. coordinating council. M.H.N.

community organization, rural. Cf. rural community organization.

community property. In various civil law systems (as the French and the Spanish) this term refers to the partnership, or joint holding of property between husband and wife, by virtue of the marriage itself. The idea originated in the Middle Ages but was rejected by English law. The extent and nature of ownership varies in different legal systems. Sometimes the community property includes all property held before marriage by the spouses as well as that acquired after marriage; in other systems the community property comprises only the property acquired after marriage. In the United States there are eight commonwealths acquired by purchase or conquest from France and Spain, namely, Louisiana, Texas, Arizona, New Mexico, Nevada, Idaho, California and Washington. In these states all property acquired after marriage by the joint efforts of husband and wife is held to be community property. It is controlled, however, by the husband who receives and invests the proceeds. This control holds true even of the wife's earnings.

W.G.

community recreation. Services and activities provided for the benefit of the people of a region; particularly, public (tax-supported) and semi-public (privately supported for public use), including play, games, sports, athletics, entertainments, amusements, and certain art forms, as contrasted with commercially supported amusements or informal private leisure pursuits.   M.H.N.

commutation. (1) The practice of travelling to and fro between a suburban or rural residence and a city center, ordinarily for business or professional, but sometimes for recreational and other social, purposes.
(2) A change of punishment from one of greater to one of less severity. It may be granted only by the authority in which the pardoning power resides. This power in American states being a perogative of the Governors, it is they who grant commutations, acting with or without an advisory board of some sort.   A.E.W.

commuter's zone. A peripheral area surrounding large cities from which residents travel regularly to and from work in the city, generally via public transportation systems.   E.E.M.

compacts, interstate. Cf. interstate compacts.

companion, rejected. An individual who is not accepted as a participant in the group activities of those with whom he comes into social contact.   P.H.F.

companion, tolerated. A member of a play group who is usually allowed by the others to take part in group activities but whose participation is seldom requested by them.   P.H.F.

companionate crime. Cf. crime, companionate.

companionate marriage. Cf. marriage, companionate.

company housing. Dwelling units, appurtenances and community facilities supplied by an industrial concern to its employees.   S.S.

company town. A community inhabited solely or chiefly by employees of a single industrial concern or group of concerns under one management. Part or all of the housing is usually owned by the company and the community is, as a rule, unincorporated. Frequently used invidiously to imply political and economic domination of the community by the company.   S.S.

comparative method. Cf. culture case study; typology, constructive.

comparative religion. Cf. religion, comparative.

compensate (*financial*). To give a quid pro quo payment for service, sacrifice, loss or sale; (*sociological*) to offset recognized but undesired social trends by counteraction; (*psychological*) to strive to maintain mental and emotional balance or status by offsetting or making up for a shortcoming, directly by correcting it, or indirectly by seeking recognition, security, power, etc., through some other skill or talent; (*physiological*) to react organically so as to avoid or offset tensions, frustrations, felt needs, defects of function, either directly or by use of other organs. To overcompensate is to continue the special compensatory behavior beyond the demands of the need-situation which originally stimulated it.   T.D.E.

compensating error. An error which exhibits positive and negative variations or fluctuations and which tends to cancel out on the average and in the long run. Synonymous with chance error, accidental error, or variable error.   M.Pt.

compensation. (*financial*) Payment for goods, services, sacrifice, or loss; (*physiological*) organic reaction to avoid or offset defect, felt need or tension, frustration or danger and to restore organismic balance; (*psychological*) personal reaction to restore equanimity or complacency by correcting defects or avoiding threats or frustrations of wishes; (*sociological*) a reaction to threatened status, an avoiding or offsetting of recognized but unfavorable trend of social events; (*insurance and legal*) amount specified by policy, law, or court as payment for loss incurred by accident, illness, or other insurable risk.   T.D.E.

compensation, mechanism of. (1) A process, movement or action which restores a part of the organization to its normal or neutral position or which restores the equilibrium of the organization. (2) Action which makes amends for some lack or loss, including instances of attempts to overcome a handicap by strong effort, attempts to gain self-esteem by developing some other quality than that in which the person feels a lack, and attempts to justify the self by denying the importance of the quality that is lacking.   M.S.

compensation, unemployment. Cf. unemployment compensation.

compensation, workmen's. Cf. workmen's compensation.

compensatory. Balancing, offsetting, repaying, corrective. Compensatory behavior is behavior to offset or avoid an undesired condition of personality or situation.   T.D.E.

compensatory principle. (*physics*) The theory that action and reaction are equal and opposite; (*biological*) the theory that living matter maintains equilibrium by its capacity to offset the shocks and strains placed upon it by its environment, and to maintain balance of energies (metabolism, q.v.) within an organism; (*psychological*) the theory that emotional tensions, being also of organic basis, also produce organic reactions so as to regain normal relaxation and stable personal equilibrium.   T.D.E.

compete. To seek either consciously or unconsciously the same objective as another is seeking; the objective (food, status, security, wealth or other goods) being something which both cannot have, at least in equal degree. One may compete consciously without conflict, as in a game or other friendly or indifferent situation. Cf. conflict.   T.D.E.

competency, social. Cf. social competency.

competent. Competing, able to compete, able to earn one's living, to carry on one's affairs with sufficient skill and intelligence to maintain status and self-support; recognized as trained and qualified to perform a given social function.   T.D.E.

competition. The struggle for the possession or use of limited goods. These goods may be physical or material objects, or matters of social esteem, rank, and immaterial reward. The essence of competition is a clash of interests of such a sort that gratification on the part of one individual or unit precludes gratification on the part of another individual or unit. The basis of competition is found in the finite character of the earth, and in the limited emotional and aesthetical resources of society.

competition, causative. The striving against others for a scarce desideratum. Operationally, it is that antecedent behavior which correlates reliably and positively with gains of the desideratum among the competitors. Thus advertising expenditure, because it correlates with subsequent increase of business, is an item of causative competition.   S.C.D.

competition, cooperative. Cf. cooperative competition.

competition, cultural. Cf. cultural competition.

competition, ecological. That form of ecological interaction in which two or more organisms, each striving to obtain some limited supply of an environmental resource, decrease the amount of that supply obtained by others. J.A.Q.

competition, effective. The redistributing of a limited desideratum among those desiring it. Effective competition is measurable, and therefore operationally definable. S.C.D.

competition, institutional. The process of social interaction which determines that some institutions shall continue to exist, and perhaps grow by gaining adherents and supporters, or become more elaborate in their organization, while other institutions decline through loss of supporters, and perhaps eventually cease to exist. Institutional competition results from the fact that institutions exist only through individuals' support; and individuals cannot support an indefinitely large number of separate institutions; furthermore, some institutions are inherently opposed to others, so that both of such a pair cannot very well continue to exist in the same society. F.N.H.

competition, social. Cf. social competition.

competitive contact. Cf. contact, competitive.

competitive cooperation. Cf. antagonistic cooperation.

complex. (*psychological*) A constellation or system of impulses, or of ideas with emotional tones; a set of memories, beliefs, ideas, words, attitudes, emotional dispositions, wishes, etc., related to each other by association with some nuclear memory, emotion, interest, or goal; (*psychiatric*) the same when dissociated, repressed, illusory or obsessive; (*ethnological*) a configuration of culture traits related by association with some nuclear objectives, idea, belief, or custom shared by the group. Normal psychological complexes correspond approximately to relevant complexes in the culture. When there is sharp discrepancy or absence of a corresponding culture complex the personal complex is considered an eccentricity or possible pathological symptom. T.D.E.

complex, culture. Cf. culture complex.

complex, trait. A number of culture traits interrelated in a functional way; the smallest unit of culture capable of functioning. For example, a bow is capable of existing but not of functioning as a unit of culture until it becomes associated with an arrow or a shaft as a hunting weapon or a fire drill. The former are traits; the latter are trait complexes. H.E.J.

component group. Cf. group, component.

component society. Cf. society, component.

composite family. Cf. family, composite.

composition. The settlement, by agreement between the parties concerned, of an injury or claim by some form of compensation, e.g., the composition of murder by the payment of blood money (q.v.) or wergild (q.v.). G.P.M.

composition, demotic. The make-up of a population in respect to density, proportions of the sexes, age groups, race, etc. T.D.E.

composition, social. Cf. social composition.

compound. To make a composition of a debt; to settle or discharge a debt for less than the sum due. F.W.K.

compound a felony. To enter into an agreement for a valuable consideration not to prosecute a felon, an act which is in itself a felony. F.W.K.

compound group. Cf. group, compound.

compromise. An agreement reached by mutual concession; a conciliatory process consisting of the exchange of values until all parties are more or less satisfied—at least more of them are more satisfied than before the exchange. The characteristic procedure in democratic legislation and administration.   F.E.L.

compulsion. (*social control*) A situation process in which a person (or group) feels forced by external threat or danger to act against what has previously been his interest and will; the act or process of coercing or otherwise compelling a recalcitrant or reluctant person; (*psychiatric*) a sense of being driven by some element (complex) within the personality or by some weird alien "force", to perform acts which the ego or super-ego rebels against. Cf. coercion.   T.D.E.

compurgation. A primitive form of defense against an accusation of crime, whereby the accused tried to establish innocence by bringing into court a sufficient number of persons who by oath testified to their belief in the innocence of the defendant. It used to be commonly assumed that the jury system arose out of this procedure.   T.S.

conation. Social effort or striving under the stimulus of desire or "the feelings", the objectives sought being "the ends of conation."   F.H.H.

concentration. The process in which people tend to come together in limited areas for social purposes such as living, working, recreation, or fighting.   J.P.E.

concentration, ecological. Cf. ecological concentration.

conception control. Cf. birth control.

concepts, ecological. Those distinctive terms, taken largely from plant ecology and sociology, which have assumed distinctive meanings when applied to the distribution of populations and institutions within an area. Society refers to the regulatory aspects of regional or city life, for instance, while community pertains to the naturalistic actions of individuals struggling for place in space. Other strictly ecological concepts include; natural order, zones, gradients, biotic relationships, ecological concentration, centralization, segregation, invasion, dominance, succession.   W.C.H.

concepts, sociological. The distinctive verbal symbols which have been given to the generalized ideas abstracted from the scientific perception of society.   J.P.E.

conceptual approach. The method of study of a science which gives primary emphasis to the clarification of its basic concepts, afterwards using them as "tools" for the further analysis, organization, amplification, and interpretation of its materials. Distinguished from other approaches, such as the historical or problem, each of which makes its own contribution to scientific understanding.

conceptual pattern. Cf. pattern, conceptual.

conciliate. To conduct negotiations between parties to a dispute by reconciling them to a position laid down for guidance of behavior in a particular field; unlike mediation, moral suasion and ethics are used to sanction the position advanced by the conciliator.   F.W.K.

conciliation. One of the methods of restoring peaceful relations between employers and employees. Cf. arbitration, industrial. When the negotiations between employer and employees are conducted entirely between the two parties to the dispute or their representatives, and the procedure consists only of discussion and mutual concession between the two, the process is known as conciliation. F.D.W.

concubinage. The practice whereby a man is permitted to take a concubine (q.v.) or concubines. Cf. cicisbeism; polygyny.
                                    G.P.M.

concubine. A woman who becomes the socially-recognized sexual partner of a man, by custom or law, usually being taken into his household (a) in lieu of a legal wife or (b) in addition to a legal wife or wives. The status of the concubine varies greatly in different cultures, but most commonly she has the right of support, her children are legitimate, but she and her children have no inheritance rights and the children may or may not be allowed to take the father's name. The legal wife and her children have rights both in name and inheritance.   R.E.B.

condemnation. (1) The exercise of the right of eminent domain to secure legal title to private property required for public use. (2) A declaration by a duly constituted authority that a property or structure is unfit for use or habitation or dangerous to persons or other property. S.S.

conditional curse. A curse (q.v.) uttered with a conditional qualification. I.e., the curse is to become operative only on condition of certain stated facts or circumstances. E.g., "If this be false, may God smite me." E.A.H.

conditioned. An organism is said to be conditioned when a conditioned response has been established, or more generally, when a response to some situation has been acquired or learned. M.Pt.

conditioned participation. Incomplete access to the culture of a region by a subordinate group, the degree of access depending upon the rôle assigned to and accepted by such partically excluded groups. Thus Negroes and some other ethnic groups are denied full participation in American culture, the degree of exclusion being limited by the status awarded such groups, the reaction to such status by the subordinate group and the accompanying attitudes on the parts of both dominant and subordinate groups; these elements making a conditioning process applying to both groups. Basic factors in terms of which this conditioning process operates seem to be ease of identification of members of the subordinate group through biological or cultural differences and traditions which define the appropriate rôle for members of each group. The groups conditionally participating may or may not possess foreign culture traits with which to supplement their partial participation; Negroes do not; other ethnic groups do. Cf. marginal group. H.E.M.

conditioned reflex (conditioned response). A simple automatic behavior pattern as compared to innate or inborn automatic behavior patterns which are termed unconditioned reflexes or responses. The learning process is brought about by substituting a biologically inadequate stimulus for a biologically adequate stimulus to produce an original response. To use I. P. Pavlov's famous example, the flow of saliva in a dog's mouth when food is presented is an unconditioned reflex or response; the flow of saliva when a bell is sounded, when water is dropped on the dog's skin or when it is pricked with an electric needle is a conditioned reflex or response built up by the experimenter (teacher) associating these stimuli with food. P.H.L.

conditioning. (1) The process of developing a conditional response. (2) Causing the organism to form an association or learn; similar to teaching. M.Pt.

conditioning, negative. Process of adaptation to unpleasant stimuli with a resultant tendency on the part of an organism to inhibit the response associated with the unpleasant stimulus. M.S.

conduct. Behavior appraised or guided in the light of mores, moral rules or ethical or aesthetic norms and principles; self-conscious, free behavior, characteristic of human beings as contrasted with other animals. T.D.E.

confarreatio. A form of religious marriage used in ancient Rome chiefly by patricians. The formal consensus or consent to the marriage by the parties concerned, which was the essential act in marriage, took place in the home of the bride. Then the girl was carried in the evening in torchlight procession to the home of her husband who lifted her over the threshold. Immediately there followed the ceremony of confarreatio which consisted in the eating by the bride and groom of a sacred cake made of the ancient grain "far" This simple rite was performed in the presence of the Pontifex Maximus, chief of the college of priests, the Flamen Dialis, or priest of Jupiter, and ten other witnesses. W.G.

confederate. To join together in loose political alliance. A person closely associated with and aiding another in achieving a given result. F.W.K.

confederation. A league of autonomous associations for action on matters of common interest, intermediate between a federation and an alliance. F.H.H.

confidence game. A method of swindling which involves elaborate psychological preparation of the victim over a period of time, sometimes as much as several weeks. During this time the victim's confidence in his swindler associates is carefully built up to the point where he is willing to join with them in a shady financial enterprise which seems to promise big returns in easy money. It usually involves betting on races or investing in the stock market. Fake gambling establishments or brokerage offices, known as "the big store" or "the joint," are utilized. The victim, commonly known as the "mark" or "sucker", is sent home to raise as much money as he can, or whatever he can be induced to risk. In a carefully staged series of transactions the victim is deprived of his money and then gotten rid of in what is known as the "blow-off." A type of confidence game, known as the short con, requires less time and fewer operators. The aim is to deprive the victim of whatever money he has on his person at the time.   A.R.L.

configuration. That combination of the various traits and complexes composing the cultural pattern of an area at a given time, based upon the presence or absence of cultural elements and the manner in which these elements are united, i.e., the set of interrelationships existing between them and the interpretation given these facts by the folk occupying the region; the social gestalt. This concept fixes attention on cultures as wholes, the parts of which are interlocked so that whatever affects one will also affect all others. Thus the region is seen as a configuration of institutions, folkways, mores, traditions, transportation facilities, all of which are found within a certain geographic area and all of which take part of their character from that of all the others. The church, the school, the political institutions, the economic arrangements, the family structure are each affected by each of the others; the unit for study is the configuration. Such configurations are more or less well integrated and cohesive if the culture is able to function at all; the degree of integration being positively correlated with the efficiency of the functioning of the society. Thus, the concept of configuration demands a functional

view of a society with emphasis on what the cultural elements do rather than upon the structure of the social order. Since the configuration is a functional whole composed of interacting parts, a culture is not to be understood by mere mathematical addition of the elements of which it is composed; there is in addition a remainder made up of the products of that interaction. Thus a configuration will possess characteristics not to be discovered by separate examination of its separated parts; in interaction the parts will perform functions not inherent in their composition. Configurations operate as wholes; they must be seen as wholes, by means of synthesis of the parts rather than by analysis into parts, if they are to be understood.   H.E.M.

confinement, congregate. A method of imprisonment characterizing the early jails of Europe and of this country before the reforms introduced into the Walnut Street Jail of Philadelphia in 1790. Before this change was undertaken the prisoners were allowed to associate day and night. Owing to serious abuses the change in the Walnut Street Jail consisted of keeping the more hardened inmates in separate cells without work, but allowing the others to be lodged in dormitories and to work together in common workshops. Afterwards the term was applied to the Auburn system in contrast with the Pennsylvania or separate system.   J.L.G.

confinement, solitary. The most severe measure of prison discipline now current in most prisons. It consists of placing the prisoner in a special cell with little light, usually with only a board or the floor on which to sleep, a ration of bread and water, and sometimes a chain upon the prisoner to restrict his movements. Sometimes numerous variations are introduced to increase the discomfort of the prisoner, such as chaining by the wrists to the bars of the door at such a height that the prisoner's feet barely touch the floor. But such measures are becoming less common as prison discipline becomes better understood.   J.L.G.

conflict. A process-situation in which two or more human beings or groups seek actively to thwart each other's purposes, to prevent satisfaction of each other's interests, even to the extent of injuring or destroying the other. Conflict arises out of the principle of limitation inherent in a finite universe. The wishes and interests of sentient beings run counter to each other, and the quality of egoism impels each party to seek to eliminate the other to the extent necessary for the satisfaction of his own desires. By analogy, the term may be extended to include the struggle with inanimate or subhuman objects(Cf. struggle for existence), but in its sociological meaning all the parties involved must be human. Conflict may exist in varying degrees of intensity and severity, and with reference to objects of varying degrees of importance. It may be organized or unorganized, transitory or enduring, physical, intellectual, or spiritual.

conflict, class. (1) Violent opposition between groups of persons; the groups being more or less stably associated and publicly recognized as different in their training, privileges and status; as indicated by differences of educational experience, wealth, political influence, leisure, style, or aesthetic taste. They are divided usually into two general, opposed sides or parties: the conservatives and the progressives. Being historically and mainly a minority of more highly favored persons with vested interests in resources which are not sufficiently available for public needs, the conservatives are generally compelled or accustomed to restrict the use of available goods and services, by the older autocratic methods of reserving them for the few. The progressives, on the other hand, being historically and mainly the majority, less favored, more helpless and without large vested interests, have been generally compelled or accustomed to try to widen the use of the available goods and services, by the newer democratic methods of extending them to the many.   c.j.b.
(2) The assumed inherent opposition of the interests of the working class and their employers, and the struggles which result from it; and more generally,   R.N.B.
(3) The historic struggles of the lower and restive economic groups (whether or not "class conscious") to free themselves from domination or "exploitation" by the upper or "privileged" classes, and of the latter to maintain their domination and privileged position; supposedly to continue until the latter are permanently eliminated.
(4) A process or situation in which one social class (q.v.) is trying to injure or destroy another.   T.D.E.

conflict, constructive. A mental or moral struggle or clash between seemingly incompatible desires or aims, which however are gradually harmonized and integrated so that the end result is one of growth and development. Contrast with destructive conflict where the desires prove impossible of integration, and the conflict can not be resolved.   A.E.W.

conflict, cooperative. Cf. cooperative conflict.

conflict, covert. Before or after overt conflict, it proceeds in the form of attitudes, or secret sabotage (conscious or unconscious), during situations of unrest, truce, conquest, domination, captivity, slavery, frustration, suppression, supersocial control, unwilling accommodation.   T.D.E.

conflict, cultural. Conflict in which members of two groups in contact, each fairly homogeneous culturally, and in competition, identify certain of their own cultural elements with the solidarity and continuity of the group's ethos; and in which, the corresponding traits of the "enemy" or "competing" culture being considered dangerous, efforts are made to overcome, suppress, or eliminate them. Often used to include or describe cultural competition (q.v.), in which, without true conflict, alternate traits from the two cultures present choices for imitation and one or the other pattern is selected for survival. Also called "conflict of values."   T.D.E.

conflict, mental. The process in which two or more opposing ideas or wishes strive for the conscious control of the individual's behavior.   J.P.E.

conflict, race. Cf. race conflict.

conflict, revolutionary. A relatively rapid oppositional process which may be variously defined: (*politically*) as a total change of the government of a people, or as a translocation of sovereignty from one class or group to another, or as a reconstitution of the State; (*socially*) as social change brought about by elements other than by the ruling class, or as the strain toward adventure breaking the strain toward consistency, or as a rupture of the cake of custom entailing a new social ritual, or as a social movement seeking to establish a new way of life politically and socially; (*philosophically*) as a total transvaluation of values, or as social idealism moving through the violence of social waste to achieve a new direction of the human mind; (*psychologically*) as a radical change in social attitude toward the institutional structure of society, or as an operation of the human mind demanding both destruction and reconstruction, or as a societal protest against frustration of basic motivations and institutional relations induced by cultural lag. It is denoted by the scope of its projected reconstruction (revolution vs. reform), by its speed (revolution vs. evolution), by the apparent violence of its methods (revolution vs. parliamentarism), by its progressive character (revolution vs. "counter-revolution" or "counter-evolution").

conflict, social. Cf. social conflict.

conflict situation. Cf. situation, conflict.

conform. To acquiesce in one's behavior to some rule or pattern of behavior which may or may not involve agreement with the pattern. N.A.

conformity. Correspondence of behavior or condition to some recognized pattern, norm or standard; compliance to a cultural or other dominant standard or relatively rigid model. A policy of conformity, in social control, means a pattern of controls obviously or deliberately directed at bringing variants into line with the mode, or with some criterion, or at keeping in line those already conforming. T.D.E.

Confucianism. The philosophical and quasi-religious system founded by Confucius (K'ung Fu Tsu, traditional dates, 551-479 B.C.) and considerably modified by later followers; the variety of Confucianism de-

veloped under the Sung Dynasty, chiefly by Chu Hsi (1130-1200), is often distinguished as Neo-Confucianism. P.H.F.

congenital. Existing at or dating from birth; e.g., a congenital deformity. This term is not to be confused with hereditary which should be used only to refer to those qualities which are fixed at the moment of conception. Since the normal period of gestation in human beings is nine months, the unborn baby has a pre-natal environment from which it may acquire certain characteristics; e.g., congenital syphilis. F.D.W.

congeries. Agglomerations of culture traits lacking logical or functional cohesiveness and based on mere spacial adjacency; characterized by heterogeneity. In congeries one observes an assortment, not an association of units; there is a lack of causal interconnections and of functional interdependence. Hence units of congeries may change without producing changes in meaning or function of other units, though not without producing changes in the configuration (q.v.). United on the basis of no observable principle known to the observer. The term is also used to describe the lack of mutuality, of dependence or of interdependence between clusters of traits in culture patterns. H.E.M.

congested district. An area of highly concentrated occupation or use, crowded with people, vehicles, or buildings.

congestion. (1) Circulatory: Interference with necessary circulation of pedestrian and vehicular traffic arising from excessive population density and inadequate street layouts. (2) Land: Excessive population densities accompanied by crowding of land and extreme lot coverages resulting in a lack of sufficient light, air, and play space. S.S.

Housing congestion has been divided into (1) area congestion, where so high a proportion of land is occupied by houses that inadequate space is left for light, air and play or garden; and (2) room congestion (roughly, more than one person per room in a household), where persons rather than buildings are involved. T.D.E.

congestion, housing. Cf. housing congestion.

congregate. To assemble together into a crowd, an audience or a body of worshippers.   F.H.H.

congregate confinement. Cf. confinement, congregate.

conjugal. Belonging to marriage; appropriate to married persons or the marriage state, as conjugal affection or conjugal rights.   W.G.

conjuncture. The combination of forces or circumstances of a given social situation; especially, the complication of circumstances in a critical or accidental situation.   F.H.H.

conjuncture of the markets. The comparative conditions of supply and demand at the opposite ends of a trade relation.

conquest. A population movement essentially the opposite of invasion (q.v.). Here, too, there are two political units involved but in the case of conquest the initiative and aggression are taken by the people with the higher culture and ordinarily more than one inferior people is involved. Conquest is more an extension of political domination and economic exploitation than an actual transfer of population. The end product of conquest is empire (q.v.).

conquest of nature. Term referring to civilized man's successful efforts at circumventing the factors of the physical environment which impede his efforts to attain satisfactions through working within limits imposed by nature. Thus man's understanding of the laws of aerodynamics has enabled him to construct airplanes and man is said to have "conquered" the air. Much of our culture gives us a better understanding of such natural forces so that the effects of limitations upon civilized man are much less direct and startling. Obviously the term applies only in a figurative sense.   H.E.M.

consanguine. Related by blood or consanguinity (q.v.).   G.P.M.

consanguine group. Cf. group, consanguine.

consanguineous. Based on blood relationship. Cf. group, consanguine.   E.A.H.

consanguinity. Blood relationship; being descended from a common ancestor (civil, canon, and common law all reckon the degree of lineal consanguinity as one degree for each person in the line of descent, exclusive of the one for whom the computation is being made.) The degree of consanguinity of a male and female is almost universally a major determinant in their right to marry.   R.E.B.

conscience. The system of thought and feeling with which a person meets problems of conduct; conscience is moral in the sense that it determines what is right or wrong for the particular person in a particular situation but not in the sense that it is always a mere reflection of the mores.   R.C.A.

conscious. Aware. Cf. consciousness.

conscious experience. Cf. experience, conscious.

consciousness. Consciousness as such cannot be defined. "Self", "alter ego", and "we" presuppose consciousness, but represent only components or fields of it. Indirect descriptions of consciousness depend upon particular philosophical theories. According to recent interpretations, consciousness must be regarded as a "process of opening", "a direction to" something transcending consciousness, in opposition to the old theories of consciousness as a closed circle. In sociology, the term has been at the center of several controversies: (a) behaviorism denied its usefulness and tried to replace it with "stimuli" and "responses"; but many behaviorists were forced to introduce into their sociological analyses the concepts of "reflective responses" and "reflective behavior", as well as of specific "social stimuli", which terms imply the reintroduction of consciousness and communication among consciousnesses; (b) different theories of "group mind" and of "collective consciousness" denied the limitation of consciousness to individuals; some of them even regarded "collective consciousness" as the only reality, with individual consciousness as wholly subordinated to the former or only reverberating it; (c) certain newer doctrines stress "the reciprocity of prospectives" between individual and group consciousness, and their mutual immanence. According to this interpretation, the aforementioned terms are only abstractions from the same concrete stream of mental life but in different directions (e.g., the direction to self, alter ego, and we). The exact meaning of the terms would be: mental interdependence (individual consciousness, signifying orientation to self and alter ego) and mental interpenetration (collective consciousness, signifying the direction to the we). The discussion of consciousness as a sociological term is of considerable significance because it is related to the problem of the rôle of cultural patterns, symbols, values, ideals, in social life. Both behavioristic doctrines, as well as their opposites, the doctrines which limit consciousness to individuals, are inclined to reduce the rôle of the aforementioned elements in social life. On the other hand, theories of the "group mind" and "collective consciousness" incline to confuse the social as fact and the social as an idea. The newer conception of the "reciprocity of perspectives" appears best fitted to reveal the exact rôle of symbols, values, and ideas in social reality.   G.G.

consciousness, class. Cf. class consciousness.

consciousness, ethnic. Awareness of membership in, and affiliation with, an ethnos (q.v.). Sympathy that arises out of both racial and cultural connections with a particular group.

consciousness, focus of. That which says "I" within a personality (q.v.); that which pays attention; the personality as observer and operator.   H.H.

consciousness, public. General recognition of social trends or movements which concern the entire group over and above the effect upon individual members or units. It involves freedom in the choice of action by the general social group, or public, in which the needs or desires of sta-

the individuals are submerged into a general mobilization for collective or corporate understanding or action.   M.C.E.

consciousness, race. Cf. race consciousness.

consciousness, social. .Cf. social consciousness.

consciousness of kind. Recognition of similarities of behavior of other persons to that of the observer plus the fellow-feeling and sympathy which accompany such recognition. This consciousness is not limited to overt physical activities, but in mankind at least, extends also to the purposes and motives and becomes the basis for cooperation and competition. It is this, in the opinion of Giddings, which converts gregariousness into society. Consciousness of kind is subjective, or psychological, in its nature, whereas pluralistic behavior (q.v.) is objective and external.   H.E.M.

consciousness of likeness. Cf. consciousness of kind.

consensus. Group decisions in which all members consciously or rationally participate; a sentiment held in common; the sharing by a given group of (approximately) the same definition of a given situation; awareness (in members of a group) of shared sentiments, traditions, ethos, beliefs, opinions, ideas, and definitions of situations. Expressed in solidarity (q.v.) and symbolized by collective representations (q.v.).   T.D.E.

consent, age of. Cf. age of consent.

conservation. Saving for future or more efficient use; applied chiefly to natural resources, and by extension to raw materials, sources of energy, manpower, health, talent, leisure, cultural heritage. Using an organismic analogy, conservation is to efficiency in social economy as anabolism (q.v.) is to katabolism (q.v.) in bodily economy.   T.D.E.

conservatism. The social philosophy or attitude which tends to resist change, and to adhere to and support the established order. The basic source of social stability. It has been long recognized that there is a sort of philosophical antagonistic cooperation (q.v.) between stability and progress, permanence and change. Conservatism represents the valuation of the old, the tried, the familiar, the dependable. Liberalism or radicalism represents the recognition of the necessity of movement, experimentation, and the acceptance of the new and untried. Without conservatism there could be no social institutions. With complete conservatism, social institutions become stereotyped and eventually decay and break down. As ordinarily used, the term "conservatism" frequently carries an implication of development to the degree that it becomes an obstacle to social progress.

conservative. (1) a person who clings to the status quo, opposing all but inconsequential changes, on the assumption that anything new is likely to be worse.   R.N.B.

(2) Characterized by conservatism (q.v.); cautious, moderate; resistant or reluctant to act. As a noun: a person who reveres the past, who is conservative, who has attitudes of conservatism; "one who believes that nothing should ever be tried for the first time", "who learns nothing and forgets nothing". A spectrum of attitudes toward the desirability of social change, the speed of special change and the means and ends of social change, would read from left to right: radical, liberal, progressive, conservative, reactionary.   T.D.E.

conserve. To save or protect a possession. The thing to be conserved may be a tangible property or it may be a social institution.   N.A.

consistency. A characteristic of the parts of a culture pattern to the whole. Culture is so described because it is an equilibrium of stable elements and of constant or repetitive changes.   H.A.P.

consolidated school. Cf. school, consolidated.

conspiracy, seditious. Cf. seditious conspiracy.

conspirital society. Cf. society, conspirital.

constant. A factor in any causative sequence which is, or is assumed to be, unchanging. Used particularly in statistical analyses.

constant error (*statistical*). An error due to observational, instrumental, or other bias which persists in one direction and so can not cancel out like a chance error. Synonymous with persistent error, systematic error, biased error.   M.Pt.

constituent society. Cf. society, constituent.

constitution, criminal. Cf. criminal constitution.

constitution, social. Cf. social constitution.

constitutional inferiority. Subnormality arising from an organic or physiological basis.   M.S.

constraint, social. Cf. social constraint.

construct. Man selects the data which he organizes into his perceptual as well as his conceptual world. In view of this, both percepts and concepts can be regarded as constructs. Ordinarily, however, we think of the construct as something like the Bohr atom or the economist's "rational man"—namely, as a kind of model utilizable in the scientific explanation of phenomena. Such usage restricts "construct" to the model constructed planfully, with full awareness of the means employed and the end to be served. It is probably wise to adhere to this limited meaning. Cf. typology, constructive; prediction; culture case study; and typology, sociological. H.B.

constructive typology. Cf. typology, constructive.

consumer. One who enjoys the final use of an économic good or service.   E.E.M.

consumer credit. Credit extended to finance the purchase of consumer goods by the ultimate consumer. While open accounts at retail stores have existed for unknown decades, installment buying and the personal finance business are new forms and largely responsible for the tremendous expansion of consumer credit. The use of consumer credit is so important in modern economic transactions that not a few economists claim that business cycles are caused or at least aggravated by the over-expansion or manipulation of consumer credit.   J.W.M'C.

consumer goods. Cf. goods, consumption.

consumers' cooperation. A social procedure whereby people organize to meet particular needs of life by establishing and managing a business on the basis of one vote only per member and of distributing the net earnings to the members prorated according to patronage participation. Cf. Rochdale principles.

consummation. The completion of the marriage relationship by coitus.

consummation, deferred. Ritual continence (q.v.) on the part of a newly married couple during a period immediately following their wedding.   G.P.M.

consumption. The final use of goods or services in the satisfaction of human wants.   E.E.M.

consumption goods. Cf. goods, consumption.

contact. The primary or elemental stage in the associative process. It involves a minimum of conscious relationship, and may be momentary or continuing.

contact, categorical. A social contact characterized by adjustment of participants on the basis of group or category membership. Cf. contact, secondary.   M.S.

contact, competitive. Relatively temporary interaction involving rivalry.   P.F.C.

contact, cooperative. Relatively temporary interaction involving mutual effort toward some common goal.   P.F.C.

contact, direct. Relatively temporary interaction involving close physical relationship.   P.F.C.

contact, group. Interpersonal contact within a group, between group and person, or between groups as such.   T.D.E.

contact, indirect. Communication via messenger or other third party; by mechanical or electrical devices.   T.D.E.

contact, individual. Cf. individual contact.

contact, primary. A social contact characterized by face-to-face, personal, and intimate relationships of participants.

Such contacts are the ones first experienced by the child in the family, play group and neighborhood. Cf. contact, sympathetic.   M.S.

contact, race. Cf. race contact.

contact, secondary. A social contact characterized by lack of intimacy and adjustment of participants on the basis of only a limited part of the personality. Such contacts may occur in indirect relationshpis. Cf. contact, categorical.   M.S.

contact, social. Cf. social contact.

contact, symbolic. Contact through the use of significant objects, gestures, or devices, including language. Most social contact, other than coercion or physical intercourse, is symbolic.   T.D.E.

contact, sympathetic. A social contact characterized by mutually apprecative relations of participants. Cf. contact, primary.   M.S.

contact, tertiary. Transmission of influence without personal contact, as by means of radio or printing; the situation in which one person, the recipient, reacts to another person, the actor, without possibility of immediate interaction. The originator of the contact may, at a later time, react to the recipient if the latter uses similar indirect means to establish contact, as through "fan mail," book reviews, etc. Cf. contact, symbolic.   H.E.M.

contacts of (historical) continuity. Contacts in which stored stimuli (q.v.) are transmitted from the past, making for continuity of culture and tradition. Distinguished from contacts of mobility (q. v.), though there are situations involving both features.   T.D.E.

contacts of mobility. Contacts occurring through transportation and circulation of contemporary persons or news, messages, novelties, from place to place. Contrasted with contacts of (historical) continuity (q. v.); custom upon contacts of continuity.   T.D.E.

contagion, social. Cf. social contagion.

contagious magic. Cf. magic, contagious.

content, social. Cf. social content.

continence. Abstinence from sexual intercourse whether by the married or unmarried. Frequently referred to as an old, simple, natural birth-control measure. Marital continence (q.v.) is to be considered a form of birth-control. Cf. birth control.   N.E.H.

continence, marital. Self-restraint in refraining from sexual intercourse in marriage, except for procreation.   R.E.B.

continence, ritual. Abstention from sexual intercourse on the part of a married couple for magical, ceremonial, or kindred reasons, e.g., during pregnancy, lactation, mourning, or periods of economic or social crisis. Cf. deferred consummation.   G.P.M.

continence in marriage. Renouncement of coitus by a married couple. A custom which grew up among the early Christians, under the influence of asceticism, whereby husband and wife refrained from marital intercourse as a sacrifice pleasing to God. It often happened that one spouse only renounced intercourse after marriage, which naturally caused bitterness and alienation on the part of the other mate. These one-sided resolves to remain virgin after marriage finally resulted in so much unhappiness that the Church Fathers later ordained that the abstinence of married couples from sexual intercourse, in accordance with the ascetic ideal, should be only by mutual consent. Cf. birth control; abstinence, marital; continence, marital.   W.G.

continuation, social. Cf. social continuation.

continuity, social. Cf. social continuity.

contraception. Modification of, or interference with, coitus in such a way as to prevent the fertilization of the ovum by the sperm and with that purpose in view.

contraceptor. One who practices contraception.   N.E.H.

contract. A relationship between persons, or between persons and society, in which there are assumed to be certain obligations binding on each to conform to the conditions of the agreement.   N.A.

contract, marriage. Cf. marriage contract.

contract, parole. Cf. parole contract.

contract, social. Cf. social contract.

contract, yellow dog. Cf. yellow dog contract.

contract labor. Cf. labor, contract.

contract system. A system of employment of prison labor in which an employer contracts for the use of prisoners at or near the prison but food, clothing and general supervision are provided by the prison. The system began at the end of the 18th century and for a time was the most popular form of prison labor. Opposition of the labor unions and of private manufacturers and the obvious abuses caused by unscrupulous prison officials led to the rapid decline of the system. Less than 1% of all prisoners are now employed under this system. In spite of all objections no other system of prison labor has succeeded in providing such a large volume of work under disciplined conditions as the contract system. A return to it, however, is improbable.   J.W.M'C.

contractual. Pertaining to the social and economic results of the process of conscious agreement between or among two or more parties; denoting those conditions or relations springing from the process of conscious agreement as distinguished from those derived from law or from inheritance.   F.W.K.

contra-suggestion. Cf. suggestion, contra-.

contravention. (1) A process of social interaction midway between competition and conflict, consisting of a wide range of activities from mere withholding of cooperation to reproaching, disparaging, thwarting, betraying or conniving against another, but always falling short of the use of violence or the threat of violence. . . .
(2) In the French penal code offenses are divided into crimes, delits and contraventions in the order of their diminishing seriousness. This classification does not correspond exactly with that of the English common law—treason, felony and

misdemeanor. Under French law contraventions are violations of police regulations.   J.L.G.

contributory negligence. Lack of ordinary or reasonable precaution to prevent an injury by another when set up as a defense to an action seeking compensation for an alleged injury. Contributory negligence exists in a legal sense where the defense is able to show in a court action that failure to exercise reasonable care on the part of the injured person (or another to whom negligence may be imputed) contributed to the injury.   J.M.R.

control. A restraint, or inhibition, or prohibition; a check, a guidance, a manipulation; an influence, positive or negative. As a verb: to check, to restrain, to guide, to manipulate, to influence, to modify behavior.   T.D.E.
The process by which one order modifies, regulates, or directs the behavior of another order existing within the same functional system.   J.P.E.

control, birth. Cf. birth control.

control, conception. Cf. conception control.

control, culture. Often used synonymously with "social control." Strictly speaking culture control refers specifically to the regulation of behavior through the imposition of impersonal, institutionalized patterns, and excludes control exercised by means of specific inter-personal relationships. It may also mean the control of culture change as e.g. in social planning.   A.R.L.

control, formal. Types of social control (q.v.) which are exerted by the more concrete manifestations of society, such as established institutions and the law. Such controls are ordinarily embodied in definite codes, usually written.

control, informal. Those forms of social control (q.v.) which are exerted in less concrete and tangible ways, as through the folkways, mores, conventions, and public sentiment.

control, institutional. The restraint placed upon some individual or group behavior,

and the eliciting or compelling of other behavior, by social institutions. Regulatory pressures are exerted through the various physical and psychical implementing agencies and procedures (administrative bodies, standardized rôles, group opinion, etc.) of institutions which tend to produce a considerable degree of conformity to their codes and standards. All institutions exercise a high degree of effective social control over all of the associative activities of human beings. Under the influence of each institution we regulate our actions in relation to others along a given line according to the rules and established practices of that institution. Some institutions such as the communicative and aesthetic, control only in the sense that they provide ordered means of expression. But the great mass—religious, economic, political, domestic, educational—are definitely means of regularizing and standardizing individual and group conduct, and of establishing and compelling socially necessary or, at least socially acceptable, behavior. This results in social order and group maintenance. Cf. social institutions.   J.O.H.

control, psycho-social.   Cf. psycho-social control.

control, rational. Regulation for foreseen, calculated and reasonable ends by means appropriate and adequate to such ends.
                                                 A.R.L.

control, representative. Control of members of a group by and through persons of their own choosing. The elected symbol of repreesntative control can be approached, convinced of the rightness of a proposal, and then motivated to transmit and advocate his decision to his followers. A proposal thus gains acceptance to a degree and with a facility in many cases not possible through more direct means. Cf. control; control, social; control, culture.   A.M'C.L.

control, self-. Control that for convenience is said to be the regulation of his own behavior by a person's conscious, voluntary effort. It involves a choice among alternative courses of action. It is a useful term, although a person never entirely controls his behavior, even temporarily;

and as a rule what is explained by self-control in one set of circumstances is partially the result of social influence or control on some previous occasion. Cf. will.   M.S.

control, social. Cf. social control.

control, societal. Cf. societal control.

control, sub-social. Control in which an individual or group is physically coerced without any responding behavior in the victim. Shanghaiing sailors would be sub-social control; so would pushing conscientious objectors into torture.   T.D.E.

control, super-social. Social control situations in which a person or group in power, but threatened in that power, utilizes any and every means to maintain status and position. The foisting upon society of means of social control by some scheming group. In addition to intensification of ordinary controls, super-social control situations develop other more characteristic techniques, such as purges, packing, privileges, suppression, persecution, inquisition, terror, espionage, provocateurs, concentration camps.   T.D.E.

controlled sampling. Cf. sampling, controlled.

controls, subhuman. Social controls operating among animals, especially among gregarious animals.   T.D.E.

convention. (*social*) A general practice or usage current in the social group.   W.E.G. (*political*) Cf. treaty.

conventional. Conforming to the folkways or mores of the group; characterized by uncritical conformity to the attitudes and behavior most common in society.   P.H.F.

conventional imitation. Cf. imitation, conventional.

conventionality. Conformity to convention (q.v.). In conventionality there is, by contrast with morality, a minimum of connection between the usage and any meaning attaching to it. Cf. ceremonial.   T.D.E.
    A mechanism employed in the interactional process of accommodation where-

by an otherwise unacceptable form of behavior may become acceptable or permissible under certain circumstances. Gradually the usage may become general and common without regard to special circumstances.   W.E.G.
    A tacit agreement to deny the existence of certain situations, usually those threatening social solidarity.   M.K.

convergence. Parallelism, or the independent development of similar traits, whether racial or cultural, in different areas. Parallel or convergent evolution, as hairiness of Ainu and Caucasian or similar copper ax-heads in Peru and Egypt.   F.H.H.

convergence, cultural. Cultural parallelism (q.v.).

conversion. (1) (*social-psychological*). The relatively sudden emergence of a new rôle or character in a personality: a complex or attitude previously latent comes into dominance, and the individual is a new person. Often associated with a new outlook, vision, or belief, at a time of personal or social crisis. The former self may be dissociated, with or without amnesia or repression, permanently or temporarily. Most typically observed in religious revivals, whence the term; but by extension the word applies also to other personal "mutations" or metamorphoses resulting from shock, drug, disease, crisis, marriage, bereavement, etc.   T.D.E.
    (2) (a) A process of acculturation in which an individual voluntarily adopts the pattern and ethos of an out-group, and/or
    (b) a process of personality adjustment from divergent, atypical behavior or demoralized individuation to the customary, approved patterns regarded by the dominant collectivity as normal.
    In either case a period of conditioning is necessary. In its initial stages this conditioning may be acquired voluntarily or involuntarily, not infrequently the latter due to the play of ambivalence. This conditioning involves change in one or more of the following aspects of culture (hence acculturation): approved habits, rôle assumption, stereotypes, group membership (of whatever degree of activity), loyalties.   D.E.W.
    (3) A mechanism employed in the interactional process of accommodation where-

by one attitude and value system is abandoned and a new attitude and corresponding value complex is taken on and made the focus of attention and center of activity. W.E.G.

convert. One who accepts the beliefs, tenets, doctrines, and practices of a particular system of thought having previously adhered to those of a competing system. J.P.E.

convict. Any person confined to a state or federal prison under sentence of more than a year for the commission of crime. The term does not apply to persons confined in city and county jails. J.W.M'C.

convict lease system. The system of prison labor in which a private party contracts with the prison for the labor of prisoners at so much a head, but in contrast with the contract labor system, undertakes to house, feed, clothe, guard, and otherwise care for the prisoners, and thus relieve the prison of every financial responsibility. Under this system the most terrible abuses occurred. It has now been abandoned by every state in the United States. Cf. contract labor. J.L.G.

cooperating companion. A member of a play group who is accepted as a participant in all the activities of the group; his suggestions are given respectful attention and he may occasionally act as temporary leader of the group. P.H.F.

cooperation. Any form of social interaction (q.v.) in which personalities or groups combine their activities, or work together with mutual aid, in a more or less organized way, for the promotion of common ends or objectives, in such a way that, the greater the success of one party to the interaction, the greater the success of the other party or parties; the opposite of opposition (q.v.). H.H.

cooperation, antagonistic. Cooperation where inevitable antagonisms are suppressed in view of the actually experienced, or forecasted, superior expediency of making common cause. A.G.K.

cooperation, coerced. A distorted semblance of cooperation in which the pur-

poses promoted are not shared by all th individuals or groups whose activities ar combined, but where one or more of th individuals or groups join activities witl the others in order to escape punishmen rather than for the sake of the activit itself or of its direct results. H.E

cooperation, competitive. Cf. competitiv cooperation.

cooperation, consumers. Cf. consumers co operation.

cooperation, ecological. That form of eco logical interaction in which two or more organisms either (a) reciprocally increase limited supplies of environment on which one or all depend, or (b) reciprocally decrease the environmental dangers which threaten one or all. J.A.Q.

cooperation, voluntary. That species of cooperation in which the purposes promoted are common to all of the individuals or groups whose activities are combined. Under such conditions, the greater the immediate or direct success of one personality or group, the greater the immediate or direct success of the others. Voluntary cooperation is thus the antithesis of opposition (q.v.). H.H.

cooperative. (1) Willing to work, or actually working, together to achieve a common end or purpose. J.P.E.
(2) A group of people organized to achieve a common end or purpose. Frequently found among consumers or producers of economic goods where the purpose is to secure the economic benefits derived to all the members of the group. Cf. Rochdale principles. J.P.E.

cooperative, health. (a) A non-profit organization of laymen under their own control to provide health care for themselves at low cost on a periodic prepayment plan, with physicians being employed on salaries, with a central office and varied equipment being maintained, with specialists on the medical staff, and with the director of the medical staff having charge of the medical policies.
(b) A limited form of type (a) in which physicians are in control and in which

laymen participate on a low cost periodic prepayment plan as long as they are satisfied with the medical care they receive.

cooperative, housing. (1) A non-profit organization of persons who pool their financial resources in buying a piece of land and in building their homes, which when completed become the individual property in each case of the members. Sometimes known as a home-building cooperative.

(2) A non-profit organization of persons for the ownership as well as the building of homes. Individuals hold membership shares equivalent in value to the value of their respective homes. They pay their association monthly sums prorated according to the costs of upkeep, taxes, insurance, depreciation, amortization, and they sell their memberships only to the association or on the association's approval.

(3) Housing owned and maintained by a cooperative association the shares of which are purchased by the occupants and which cannot be sold at a profit. Title remains in the association which rents the dwelling units to members so as to cover all charges including amortization.   S.S.

cooperative competition. Rivalry which is restricted or limited by a desire of the participants to work together for some common goals. Cf. cooperative conflict.
     P.F.C.

cooperative conflict. Strife in which hostility is limited by the existence of some common goals, mutually desired by the participants. Cf. antagonistic cooperation.
     P.F.C.

cooperative contact. Cf. contact, cooperative.

cooperative farmers' association. An economic agency through which farmers unite to market their produce or purchase their supplies jointly; characterized by the principle of one man (member) one vote without regard to the number of shares held, and by dividends based on the amount of patronage each member gives.
     E.des.B.

cooperative movement. (a) A widespread development of societies known as consumers' cooperatives, producers' cooperatives, welfare and utility cooperatives, credit unions, operating in many lands during the past several decades, on a non-profit basis, by democratic voting, and in the spirit of mutual aid.

(b) A more limited development of consumers' cooperatives with emphasis on one member, one vote, on patronage refunds, and on educational programs for the cultivation of the spirit of mutual aid and of democracy in all phases of life.

cooperative response. Activity engaged in by a number of individuals responding together to a common stimulus.   P.F.C.

coordinate. To place together things of similar rank or order; to organize activities, parts, or ideas so that they form an orderly arrangement or structure-function.
     T.D.E.

coordinating council. An organization composed of representatives of governmental departments, private social agencies, civic organizations, religious and educational institutions, and other groups and services, as well as interested citizens, to promote cooperation among them, to integrate their efforts and functions, to study conditions and resources, to inform the public regarding conditions, and to secure democratic action in meeting local needs. As a community or neighborhood council, with activities built around geographic and area problems and interests, it has a degree of formal organization, composed of representatives of a wide range of groups, yet it functions informally, being a coordinating rather than a functional agency.

In basic purposes and organization coordinating councils differ widely, centering attention of the community on plans designed to prevent or reduce delinquency; to promote protection of children and youth and to meet their physical, recreational, cultural, and social requirements; to develop citizenship and to provide civilian protection; to improve family life; and to plan all welfare services of the community through coordinated effort designed to make the region a better place in which to live.   M.H.N.

coordination. The working together of groups and individuals in an organized and integrated way.   M.H.N.

coordination, community. Cf. community coordination.

coordination council. Cf. coordinating council.

coquetry. The gestural and verbal artifices employed by females to attract the attention and possibly induce the love-making of males.   F.E.L.

corporal punishment. Cf. punishment, corporal.

corporation. A socio-economic organization composed of individuals and born of legal sanction for the purpose of manipulating property rights and other interests to the benefit of those who compose it. If the function is primarily to create and distribute profits to a relatively limited membership it is a private corporation. On the other extreme, if the dominant purpose relates to politically organized general welfare it is a public corporation. Virtually all corporations in some degree partake of both functions.

There is little doubt that the most successful method to date of aggregating capital is the private or business corporation. But it is more than a mere method of holding property. The modern business corporation has become the prevailing method of organizing economic effort.

With all of its advantages over simpler organizations in increasing production many new social changes have occurred. The tremendous growth in size is one consideration. The assets of a few business corporations even exceed the assessed valuation of some States of the U. S. This concentration and control of capital has restricted the area of competition as it existed in the earlier stages of a free-pricing economy. A further factor is the growth of two classes: a managerial class to replace the old type of entrepreneur and an absentee-ownership class. Control is thus separated from ownership.   J.H.E.

corporative. The corporative state (*il stao corporativo*) of Italian fascism is in theory based upon the corporations (*corporazione*) or guilds composed of employ ers and of their employees respectively in industry, agriculture, commerce, finance, transportation, etc. The parliament (*camera corporativa*) is composed mainly of representatives of these corporations, but it is anticipated that it will be succeeded by a council of the corporations. Higher in the fascist hierarchy is the grand council (*gran consiglio fascista*), and above all is the fascist leader (*duce del fascismo*) who is the chief of the state and government (*capo di stato e del governo*). Through this form of the state, not yet fully realized, the fascists propose to bring economic processes under the control of the government.   M.Pm.

correction, house of. Cf. house of correction.

correctional institutions. Cf. institutions, correctional.

correlate. To compare two or more phenomena or situation-processes in such a way as to bring out concomitant relationships. Recent statistical usage has given the word a special narrower meaning, based upon a formula for calculating coefficients of correlation (q.v.) between measurable phenomena.   T.D.E.

correlate function. Cf. function, correlate.

correlation. (1) The degree to which change in one variable is accompanied by corresponding change in another variable; the relationship may be either direct or inverse. (2) Measurement of the degree to which paired items or measures of two (or more) variables vary concomitantly.

correlation, coefficient of. A numerical index of closeness of relationship or association between series of paired measures which represent variables under comparison. Frequently used is the Pearson product-moment correlation coefficient (r) which is a decimal fraction ranging in value from minus 1 through zero to plus 1 and capable of indicating all degrees of relationship from perfect negative or inverse to perfect positive.   M.Pt.

correlation, multiple. The maximum correlation possible between one variable and any weighted sum or average of two or more other specified variables.   P.H.F.

correlation, partial. The estimated correlation between two variables, the influence of one or more other variables being eliminated.   P.H.F.

correlation, social. Cf. social correlation.

corroborate. To prove true some statement or prediction, fear or hope. Certain predictions or epithets, slogans, etc. which imply or assume predictions (whether desirable or undesirable) tend to corroborate theselves by inspiring confidence or fear, by releasing energies (or to offset themselves by stimulating compensatory activities).   T.D.E.

corroboration. The act or process or result of corroborating. Cf. corroborate.   T.D.E.

corroboree. A tribal dance or ceremony of the aboriginal Tasmanians and Australians.   E.A.H.

corvée. An obligation to give specified services to the lord or sovereign (*feudal*) ; forced labor, chiefly on public works, frequently required of primitive peoples by colonizing nations (*modern*).   E.E.M.

council of community agencies, council of social agencies, welfare council, federation. A federation of social work agencies, sometimes including educational, industrial, civic, labor, business, government, and religious agencies and programs, to continuously study, plan and develop co-ordination and expansion of services of public and private agencies, to prevent overlapping programs or neglecting social problems and to secure intelligent participation of citizens. Cf. coordinating council.   W.P.

counterselection. Survival of inferior social foms, values, or people. Syn. dysgenic selection. Ant. eugenics; euthenics; eudemics.   H.A.P.

country life movement. The country life movement is the working out of the desire to make rural civilization as effective and satisfying as other forms of civilization. Its inception in this country may be dated from the work of the Country Life Commission appointed by President Theodore Roosevelt in 1908.   D.S.

country of destination. A country to which an immigration stream directs itself.

country of origin. A country from which an emigration stream flows.

country weekly. A newspaper published in a community of rural characteristics for distribution through the mail as second class matter on a stated day of the week to the residents of the town and the surounding open country as a medium of local information, intercommunication, and co-ordination of town and country activities, in which is reflected the life, customs and institutions of the people who constitute its readership.   C.E.L.

county agent. A person employed jointly by the state and federal governments and by the county government or local co-operating group under the provisions of the Smith-Lever Act of Congress approved May 8, 1914. This cooperative employee has his office at the county seat and serves to aid in diffusing among the people useful and practical information on subjects relating to agriculture and home economics, and to encourage the application of such knowledge. Men are known as county agricultural agents and women as home demonstration agents, or for brevity, county agent and home agent.   C.E.L.

county library. A tax-supported library serving all of a county through central headquarters, branches and depositories.   E.des.B.

court, adolescent. An experimental court designed to deal with persons between the age of sixteen (when the jurisdiction of the juvenile court ends) and eighteen or twenty-one when moral responsibility seems to have matured. The procedure follows the same infomal pattern as the juvenile court, and probation and other protective services are used extensively. Chicago and New York have experimented with this type of court but opinions differ as to its value.   J.W.M'C.

court, canonical. The ecclesiastical court of the Middle Ages to which criminal cases and cases involving domestic and marital law were referred.   M.A.E.

court, domestic relations. A court having jurisdiction over cases involving strained relations between husband and wife, such as desertion and neglect as well as cases of juvenile delinquency. In the latter cases, parent-child relationships are recognized as basically important in producing the delinquency and similarly significant in working out any effective adjustment or plan of treatment for the child. The general philosophy underlying the organization of such courts for dealing with delinquency is to the effect that the family is a unit and that the adjustment is frequently a family rather than an individual problem. Domestic Relations Courts exist only in our larger cities where sufficient cases arise to warrant a separate court.   M.A.E.

court, juvenile. A court dealing with youthful offenders or juvenile dependents and with adults who contribute to the delinquency of children. In most states the jurisdiction of such courts is limited to children under sixteen; a few have jurisdiction over cases under eighteen, and California has jurisidction over young persons under twenty-one. In general capital offenses of juveniles may be transferred to the regular criminal court, however. Juvenile delinquents are considered wards of the court and are presumed to be treated as children needing help rather than as guilty persons requiring punishment. Hearings are usually private, and there is generally no trial, although a number of states paradoxically allow a trial if demanded by the child's parents or his "next friend."   M.A.E.

court, magistrates. In most cities, the lowest court of original jurisdiction in criminal cases. Suspects apprehended by the police are first arraigned in magistrates court. Here evidence is examined. If in the mind of the magistrate the evidence is sufficient the suspect is bound over for the grand jury or some other specialized court, and bail is set to insure the suspect's appearance at trial. If the offense is a minor one such as violation of a city ordinance the magistrate may have the power to make a judgment and set the penalty.   J.W.M'C.

court, specialized. A court which has jurisdiction over special types of criminal civil suits. For example the Morals Court, the Juvenile Court, the District Court, the Appellate Court, are specialized courts.   M.A.E.

Court, World. The popular name for Permanent Court of International Justice. This was created by article 14 of the Treaty of Versailles, and was to be a permanent bench of fifteen judges, with provision for substitute judges. It was conceived as having compulsory jurisdiction, but in the debates to frame the Statute of the Court, this was changed to voluntary jurisdiction in special types of cases. In practically all cases the parties must agree to submit the case. The Council and Assembly of the League also had power to request advisory opinions from the Court, a provision which deterred the United States Senate from ratifying the protocol of adherence to the Court. Altogether it decided about seventy cases, divided between regular judgments and advisory opinions. The judges were elected by Council and Assembly for nine years, with provision for re-election. In 1939, with the outbreak of war, the Court ceased to function. Many of its cases arose out of the interpretation of the peace treaties of 1919.   E.M.B.

courtship. The association of an (normally) unmarried man and woman mutually attracted; an explorative comradeship revealing the strength of the allurement each has for the other. In the United States, the common and approved method of finding one's mate.   E.R.G.

couvade. The customary simulation of childbirth by the father, or his confinement at parturition, and the observance by him of taboos designed to promote the welfare of the child.   G.P.M.

coverage. That percentage of the area of a site occupied by buildings.

craft union. A trade union (q.v.) consisting of persons following the same craft or skill regardless of the industry or business in which they may be working. The object of such a union is to bargain collectively with the employer for favorable conditions of employment for members of the craft. The power of the craft union comes from its monopoly of a particular skill which is made possible by control over apprenticeship and licensing. It is obvious that a craft union organization could offer but little to the great masses of unskilled workers. In opposition to the craft principle of trade union organization is the idea of industrial organization (q.v.) which aims to incorporate into one union all workers in a given industry regardless of skill or craft differences. J.W.M'C.

cranial capacity. The cubic capacity of the interior cavity of the skull, usually measured in cubic centimeters. G.P.M.

cranial deformation. Artificial modification of the shape of the head, effected during infancy by tight bandaging, the application of flat boards, etc. G.P.M.

cranial index. Cf. index, cranial.

craniometry. The branch of osteometry concerned with measurements of the skull. G.P.M.

creative accommodation. Cf. accommodation, creative.

creative activity. Effort directed to the production of desired objects or values and containing an element of design or invention. It stands in contrast with automatic or "mechanized" effort. Individual, group, or societal activity may be of this nature. Degrees and levels of creative activity are as significant as the activity itself. These are exemplified in the realm of production, ranging from unskilled labor or work on an assembly line, at one extremes, to the work of the inventor or executive at the other extreme. Creative activity is directed to the modification of prsonality—one's own or another's—no less than to the production of material objects. Development of understanding or cultivation of attitudes, for example, is a process of creation. S.E.

creative evolution. Purposive or planned social change in which the particular development is a part of universal evolution. Cf. élan vital. M.C.E.

creative synthesis. The mental process in which existing unitary ideas are combined into a whole which has not previously been recognized as an existing concept. J.P.E.

credit, consumer. Cf. consumer credit.

creed. A definite statement of belief. Especially characteristic of Western religious groups. L.P.E.

cremation. The practice of disposing of the corpses of the dead by burning them. Cf. burial. G.P.M.

cretinism. A physical condition appearing in early childhood of stunted development, often with goiter or defective thyroid gland which secretes insufficient iodine, resulting in scaly skin, brittle hair, dwarf stature and low mentality. A type of feebleemindedness resulting from this malfunctioning of the thyroid gland.

crime. A violation of the criminal law, i.e. a breach of the conduct code specifically sanctioned by the state, which through its legislative agencies defines crimes and their penalties, and through its administrative agencies prosecutes offenders and imposes and aministers punishments. The term crime is often carelessly and erroneously used to designate any kind of behavior as injurious to society, even though not defined by the criminal law. T.S.

crime, capital. An offense where the punishment may be death, regardless of whether or not the death penalty is actually inflicted. It remains so even where juries are given the option of imposing life imprisonment instead of death as the penalty. Capital crimes are usually not bailable. The number of offenses regarded as capital has been sharply reduced in modern times. A.E.W.

crime, causes of. Imputed agents or forces determining violations of law. The causes of crime have never been satisfactorily isolated. When used to explain the incidence of crime in general or of certain classes of crimes, the imputed causes of crime are more likely to describe factors of greater or lesser risk for individuals getting acted upon officially. When used to explain the behavior of a single individual, causes represent the attempts to factorize individual cases by ordinary qualitative analysis or clinical diagnosis. The search for causes of crime or of criminal behavior has been fraught with the difficulty of isolating the differential impact of situational factors on varying mental and physical constitutions. It has also been fraught with the difficulty of demonstrating that such and such combination of factors apply to delinquents rather than to non-delinquents or to delinquent behavior rather than to non-delinquent behavior.   W.C.R.

crime, companionate. A crime committed jointly by two, or occasionally more than two, persons against a third party. Companionate crime is differentiated from organized crime, in that the former is occasional and generally involves only one offense, while the latter is consistent and habitual behavior. It is differentiated also from such behavior as fornication or gambling in that it has a victim, while fornication and gambling have no third party who is a direct victim.   E.H.S.

crime. etiology of. The study of the causes of criminal behavior by the case study or clinical method, usually proceeding from the study of individual cases. Isolation of a factor connected with crime in general, by statistical or observational methods, would be conceived as contributing to a study of general causes rather than to etiology of crime.   W.C.R.

crime, multiple causes of. Opposed to the conception of a single cause of crime, such as heredity, feeblemindedness, poverty, and so on, multiple causes imply that several factors are at work cumulatively to produce crime. The efficaciousness of the conception of multiple causes of crime becomes more apparent in the study of individual cases than in the study of crime in general. Multiple causes can include one dominant factor and two or three minor factors, or they can merely include several reinforcing factors without reference as to which plays the major rôle. There are limits to the multiplicity of causes. In the clinical or individual case approach, insistence that there are more than four or five causative factors in any case usually means that the clini-

cian or researcher has seized upon factors not fundamentally or directly related to the course of behavior. In the study of general causes of crime by mass statistics or general observation, the inclusion of almost any and all kinds of causes is almost as bad as the fixation on one cause. Everything under the sun cannot be included under multiple causes, unless we desire to discover some very remote and very indirect connections with crime which are not at all causative. Many of the indirect factors related to crime by contingency methods are likely to be risk factors rather than causative factors.   W.C.R.

crime, organized. Crime which involves the cooperative effort of two or more criminals in the broadest sense of the term. All degrees of organization may be involved, from the loose informal type to a rather strict institutionalized kind like that of any business organization, or from an organization involving only a few persons to one involving hundreds.   A.R.L.

crime gradient. A concept adopted by some criminologists in the study of the ecological distribution of crime. It designates the profile of a curve based on the crime rates of consecutive geographic areas located along a straight line.   T.S.

crime index. Cf. index, crime.

crime rate. Cf. rate, crime.

crime surveys. Surveys made with reference to the nature and extent of crime, penal law enforcement, and the administration of criminal courts. The Report of the National Commission on Law Observance and Enforcement is the most notable survey made in the U. S. Other surveys include the Missouri Crime Survey and the Illinois Crime Survey.   M.A.E.

crimes known to the police. Reports to police that crimes have been committed. Index currently in use to determine the amount and rates of crime in the United States.   J.P.S.

criminal. A person who has committed a crime. Statistically, a person who has been convicted of a crime. The attempt to include in the concept of "criminal" only those who have committed crimes of a more serious nature, or crimes involving extreme moral turpitude, or persons whose motives are distinctly evil has no basis in science and can lead only to confusion.

criminal, born. A concept formulated by Lombroso in accordance with which certain persons are biologically so constituted that they must of necessity be criminals. A hereditary criminal.   J.P.S.

criminal, endogenic. A term used by European criminologists to denote a type of offender whose criminality is determined mainly by hereditary and constitutional (both physical and mental) factors. W.C.R.

criminal, exogenic. Used by European criminologists to designate a type of offender whose etiology is determined primarily by situational factors.   W.C.R.

criminal, habitual. A person who has adopted a criminal mode of life to such an extent that it hase become an established personality pattern. He may or may not be a professional criminal (q.v.) but at least a considerable part of his activity is of a criminal character. Cf. recidivism.

criminal, pathological. A criminal who deviates from the mentally normal type. There are no generally accepted classifications of the mentally abnormal types. The following simple classification, however, is frequently used; mental defective or feebleminded, psychotic or insane, and psychopathic. The latter is the most difficult to define. It includes those criminals who are neurotic, epileptic and who are judged to possess either a post-encephalitic or a psychopathic personality. Encephalitis is a disease resulting from lesions in the central nervous system. It makes for lethargic and irritable behavior. It also retards learning. The chief characteristic of a psychopathic personality is the deeply disturbed emotional life. There is no standard method of diagnosing a personality as psychopathic. A comparison of psychiatric reports on the psychopathy of criminals shows wide variations in the conclusions as to the proportion of criminals so characterized.   N.F.C.

criminal, professional. One who participates regularly and as a business in a developed criminal culture, with a body of specialized skills and knowledge. The professional criminal is differentiated from the habitual criminal who engages regularly in crimes but does not have a developed and specialized skill, and from the amateur criminal who neither engages regularly in crime nor has specialized skill.   E.H.S.

criminal, white-collar. A person of the upper socio-economic class who violates the criminal law in the course of his occupational or professional activities; the state, in so far as it reacts against white collar crimes, generally does so through bureaus and commissions rather than through the police and the criminal courts. A wealthy confidence man, who is a part of the underworld, would not be a white-collar criminal, because he does not have the esteem of the law-abiding community. A wealthy and esteemed business man who commits murder in connection with a "love-triangle" would not be a white-collar criminal.   E.H.S.

criminal abortion. Cf. abortion, criminal.

criminal anthropology. Cf. anthropology, criminal.

criminal argot. The special jargon or slang which criminals use in conversation with each other. In general, criminal argot is known only to the initiated. Thus "cannon" is criminal argot for pickpocket; "taking the rap" is receiving a prison sentence; "heel" is a sneak thief.   M.A.E.

criminal association. Cf. association, criminal.

criminal behavior. Usually synonymous with crime or violation of criminal code. However, usage places the emphasis on violating behavior whether known or unknown to authorities. As a form of violation, it is akin to violations of all codes or rules: those of family, church, school, labor union, and various associations. The thing which makes behavior criminal is that the offense against code becomes reportable to the governmental or state authorities.   W.C.R.

criminal biology. The scientific study of the relation of hereditary physical traits to criminal character, i.e. to innate tendencies to commit crime in general or crimes of any particular type.

criminal career. A career involving habitual crime or devoted to crime as a means of livelihood.   A.R.L.

criminal constitution. The innate traits of an individual that predispose him to criminal conduct or a life of crime.

criminal culture. An integrated set of overt practices and ideas characteristic of a group of people and in conflict with the criminal law; a particular criminal act may be supported by, and be a part of, the criminal culture, which would include similar acts by other members of the group, and for all of these acts rationalizations, evaluations, and codes of behavior in agreement with the criminal acts; in contrast, embezzlement and murder are often committed without the support of any such criminal culture. E.H.S.

criminal fence. A person or firm that makes a business of trading in stolen commodities, either exclusively or more often in connection with a legitimate business. A receiver of stolen goods may make trade in such goods a business, in which case he would be a fence, or he may receive a stolen commodity and use it for his own purposes, in which case he would not be a fence; every fence is a receiver, but not every receiver is a fence.   E.H.S.

criminal gang. Cf. gang, criminal.

criminal insane. The legal term for the state of mental derangement which accompanies or induces the commission of a crime and prevents the criminal from knowing the criminal nature of the act committed. The basic test of insanity is the knowledge of right and wrong; thus mental defect is often confused with mental deficiency. Greater interest in the mental processes of those who commit crimes led to a direct challenge of the traditional legal interpretations of insanity as a defense in criminal cases.
     J.W.M'C.

criminal intent. The mental element in crime, a concomitant of the physical act. It is a state of mind which precedes or accompanies the offense. It is not capable of direct proof, but may be derived by just or reasonable deductions from acts and facts that are proved. Intent is an aspect of the consciousness of wrong doing which is an indispensable element in crime.
     A.E.W.

criminal justice. In the broad meaning of the phrase criminal justice refers to the machinery, procedures, personnel, and purposes, which have to do with the content of the criminal law and with the arrest, trial, conviction and disposition of offenders. The administration of criminal justice thus involves the penal code, the police system, the prosecutor's office, courts, penal institutions, probation, parole, and the officials charged with administering their defined duties.   N.F.C.

criminal justice, mortality of. Surveys, in the form of statstical data, which serve as guides in the anlysis of procedural and administrative steps in the administration of criminal justice. Such data on crime cases and prison population reveal the strength or weakness in the various agencies of justice.   N.F.C.

criminal man. The conception of the criminal as an individual possessing distinctive physical or psychical characteristics.
     M.A.E.

criminal maturation. The development of a criminal in the established techniques, atttiudes, and ideology of criminal behavior; this phrase is based on the assumption that development in criminal behavior follows a standardized pattern analogous to physiological development with advancing age.   E.H.S.

criminal organization. The structure of relationships between persons and groups which makes the commission of crime possible and which facilitates avoidance of the legal penalties. This structure may be loose, informal and decentralized, or it may be explicitly institutionalized and centralized. Also, any group of persons who systematically devote themselves, as a collective unit, to the commission of crime.   A.R.L.

criminal responsibility. Criminal liability for an offense. To be so liable the person commiting the act must have done so of his own free will and volition; he must have the capacity for distinguishing right from wrong; and he must have the ability to foresee the evil consequences of his act. The presence of these conditions constitutes responsibility; hence, liability and punishability. On the other hand, certain circumstances may negate responsibility under the criminal law. These are principally:

(a) Infancy. Under the common law children under seven years of age are regarded as not being responsible. A like presumption holds for children between seven and fourteen years of age, except that in such cases the presumption may be overcome by evidenece. At fourteen years of age under the common law a child becomes fully responsible for his acts. However, it may be added that in most states statutory provisions have given to the juvenile courts jurisdiction over the criminal or delinquent acts of children including those who are beyond the age of fourteeen. The maximum age for such juvenile court jurisdiction varies among the states from fifteen to twenty-one years. But it is to be noted that in most states for grave crimes the juvenile courts may waive jurisdiction, thus making children liable to the penalties imposed in the criminal courts.

(b) Insantiy. A second exemption from criminal responsibility, and hence from liability, is on grounds of insanity. This is interpreted by the courts to mean that the person on trial is of such a mind that he is incapable of making moral distinctions between right and wrong, or of knowing the evil consequences of his acts. The existence or non-existence of insanity is a matter of evidence at the time of trial, and the issue is determined by the trial jury. If an insanity plea is sustained, the accused person is held not responsible and therefore not liable to punishment.

(c) Intoxication. Ordinarily, intoxication provides no exemption from criminal liability, though it may reduce the degree of responsibility which a drunken person may be assumed to have had at the time of his offense, and, hence, lessen the severity of his punishment.   A.E.W.

criminal saturation, law of. A theory developed by the Italian criminologist, Ferri. The gist of it was that each society has the number of criminals which the particular conditions in that society produce. "As a given volume of water at a definite temperature will dissolve a fixed quantity of chemical substance and not an atom more or less; so in a given social environment with definite individual and physical conditions, a fixed number of delicts, no more and no less, can be committed."   J.L.G.

criminal statistics. The tabulated numerical data found in the official reports of agencies which deal with the apprehension, prevention, and treatment of offenders against the criminal law. The unit of tabulation may be the case, the offender, or the offense. A common classification of criminal statistics distinguishes between police, judicial, and penal statistics. In the United States the term is generally inclusive; on the continent of Europe it is ordinarily used to designate only the tabulations based on the characteristics of the offender, as distinguished from statistics of criminal justice, and statistics of penal institutions.   T.S.

criminal syndicalism. A legal phrase of American law to describe the advocating of the unlawful destruction of property, or an unlawful change in its ownership; a doctrine and practice attributed to the Industrial Workers of the World, a labor organization, and embodied in many state statutes aimed to curb their activities, adopted from 1917 to 1924. Cf. syndicalism.   R.N.B.

criminal tendencies. Classifiable behavior tendencies which, if not recognized or checked, may end in the ultimate commission of a criminal act or acts; behavior tendencies which under certain conditions can be expected to develop into a delinquent or criminal pattern; tendencies toward criminal behavior.   F.W.K.

criminal tribes. Tribes with a culture which sanctions behavior toward nonmembers of the tribe which is prohibited by the laws of the state to which those tribes are subject; especially certain tribes in India with tribal culture which sanctions violence toward non-members which is prohibited by the laws of India. E.H.S.

criminality. The sum total of offenses against the criminal law in a geographic area, a population group, or a person. T.S.

criminality, inheritance of. A theory once held before the biological mechanism of heredity was worked out, which assumed that because crime sometimes runs in families it was therefore handed down by heredity from father to son, etc. Careful students of the genesis of criminals admit that certain biological and psychological traits, which under favorable social conditions may contribute to the making of the criminal, are passed by heredity from parent or ancestor to descendant. But crime is conduct, and as such cannot be inherited, any more than politeness, boorishness, stinginess, or extravagance. J.L.G.

criminality, maximum, age of. Cf. age of maximum criminality.

criminally insane. Persons who have committed crimes, usually of a serious nature, but who are not held responsible for their offenses by virtue of being adjudged "insane." Cf. criminal responsibility. M.A.E.

crisis. Any interruption of the regular and expected succession of events; a disturbance of habit or custom which requires conscious attention on the part of the individual or the group in order either to reestablish the disturbed equilibrium or to establish new and more adequate habits or customs. Crises which occur repeatedly and with some regularity in the life history of the individual or the group, such as birth, puberty, marriage, death, seasonal changes, phases of the moon, etc., are said to be recurrent. Crises which occur relatively infrequenlty and irregularly, such as earthquakes, floods, defeat in war, etc., are said to be singular. H.E.J.

crisis, precipitating. A crisis severe enough to result in that degree of personal or social disorganization which requires some social action to be taken either to protect society or to rehabilitate the person or group affected, or to secure both such protection and rehabilitation. Thus, the loss of a job on the part of an already emotionally unstable person may constitute the precipitating crisis which requires social intervention to stabilize the personality and to protect both him and society from the consequence of neurotic or psychotic behavior. H.E.J.

crisis, social. Cf. social crisis.

criteria. Standards, indexes, rules. Syn. measurements; norms. H.A.P.

critical moment. The turning point in a crisis; or (by analogy with critical points in physics or of visual insight) a historic moment in which a new or revolutionary definition of a cultural situation is perceived as a revelation of "a new heaven and a new earth," and societal transmutation or metamorphosis emerges. Disorganization or dissolution may also follow the critical moment. T.D.E.

cross cousins. Cousins who are the children of a brother and a sister. Among some primitive peoples cross cousins were allowed to marry each other while parallel cousins (children of two brothers or two sisters) were forbidden to marry each other. O.W.

cross-cultural. Pertaining to different cultures; comparative, as used in ethnology (q.v.). G.P.M.

cross fertilization of cultures. Fusion or welding of traits or complexes from fundamentally different cultures to produce new traits or complexes having characteristics not observed in the originals. Thus, for example, the Chinese art of carving type, when united with the Phoenician alphabet, the European cider press, and other traits resulted in the printing complex which has done much to revolutionize Western culture; a result which was not possible in any of the three original cultures alone. As in cross pollination of plants new and seemingly new specimens are often obtained, so in cross fertilization of cultures new inventions often result, some of which may change the course of the society adopting them. This idea is used to support the theory that most inventions are merely new combinations of existing traits. H.E.M.

cross reference. A term in general use in connection with cataloging or recording information. In the recording of one item attention is called to related items in connection with which pertinent information may be found.   N.A.

crowd. A temporary aggregation of human beings at a particular spot, whether called together or responding spontaneously to like stimulus; more specifically, such an aggregation in which the members, aware of a common emotional interest, have their attention concentrated in that direction, physically and mentally; are in rapport or consensus, and tending to reinforce each other in behavior, so that the complex representing that interest is in the ascendant in each member, and the ordinary and "rational" controls of personality are relaxed or in abeyance, making a crowd subject to suggestion and to hysterical or mob behaviors. The word crowd has also occasionally been used to denote a psychosis or a state of mind: a "state of crowd" is comparable, e.g., to a state of coma or of depression. Cf. rapport.   T.D.E.

crowd, active. The crowd that has its behavior directed, usually deliberately by a leader, toward some object—person, thing, or situation—for the purpose of altering it, destroying it, or honoring it; it is the mobile crowd, or mob.   W.E.G.

crowd, expressive. The crowd that gets emotional through expressive behavior, such as dancing, shouting, weeping, etc.   W.E.G.

crowd, organized. An aggregation of human beings, not necessarily in proximity with each other, but welded into a unity, transitory or more or less permanent, characterized by rapport (q.v.) and having the attention of the members focussed on some common object.   W.E.G.

crowd, orgiastic. A crowd that has reached a peak of emotional expression of an ecstatic and inspired nature. It usually takes the form of ecstatic singing and dancing, although ritualistic behavior may also take place. It is found in religious revivals, armistice crowds, and other groups celebrating some occasion.   M.PT.

crowd, participant. "A "true" crowd, in which most of the people present feel themselves in rapport and taking a part in a common interest or experience; by contrast with a mere aggregation where persons' attention is not "polarized" and their behavior proceeds on an individualized basis—as at a market, fair or congested intersection, or with a movie audience.   T.D.E.

crowd, psychological. Cf. crowd, organized.

crowd intoxication. A figure of speech descriptive of a state of crowd in which its members are "carried away", "beside themselves" (ecstasy, standing outside), "possessed" by the "spirit of the crowd", behave under domination of the immediate stimuli without ordinary inhibition: an effect crudely compared to intoxication. Dionysus was god of wine, and his worshipers were doubtless possessed by spirits of wine. A worshiper dissociated in religious frenzy was said by the Greeks to be "drunk with the god", engodded.   T.D.E.

crowd opinion. Cf. opinion, crowd.

crowd suggestion. Stimuli from fellow members, from the locale, and from speakers, collective representations (q.v.), or platform-focus reinforce in each crowd-member the ascendency of the complex associated with the meeting and help to dissociate other, inhibiting phases of the personality, thus producing greater suggestibility and responsiveness.   T.D.E.

crowding. Occupancy of a dwelling unit in excess of a fixed number of persons per room. Usual standards are: one to one-and-one-half persons, crowded; over one-and-one-half but less than two persons, overcrowded; two or more persons, gross overcrowding. The critical significance of these ratios varies with size of unit and size of family.   S.S.

cult. A body of religious rites and practices associated with the worship or propitiation of a particular divinity or group of supernatural beings.   G.P.M.

cult, ancestor. An elaboration or extension of the ghost-cult (q.v.), consisting of practices and ritual observances associated with the worship or propitiation of the spirits of departed ancestors.   G.P.M.

cult, ghost. Cf. ghost cult.

cult, hero. The cult (q.v.) of the spirits of deceased heroes.   G.P.M.

cult of the dead. Ghost-cult (q.v.).

cultural. Pertaining to culture, having origin in culture, affected by culture. Cf. culture.   T.D.E.

cultural anthropoligy. Cf. anthropology, cultural.

cultural area. Cf. area, culture.

cultural change. Modifications in the civilization of a people, i.e., in the man-made environment, occurring either automatically or by design.   P.H.L.; N.L.S.

cultural competition. The more or less automatic claims of different cultural forms for adoption by different societies or social groups. The corresponding rivalry of specific minor type patterns within in the general cultural structure of society itself.

cultural convergence. Cf. convergence, cultural.

cultural determination. The operation and effect of factors geographic, biologic, psychologic, economic, social or cultural—influencing the origin, form, development and change of culture.   N.L.S.

cultural evolution. Cf. evolution, cultural.

cultural island. A local cultural area in which the prevailing cultural characteristics are unique as compared to those of surrounding areas. Such an area commonly occurs in rural territory where a group with a cultural background differing from that of the surrounding population works out an adjustment to its environment that is relatively uninfluenced by the culture of the surrounding people.   C.E.L.

cultural lag. Cf. lag, cultural.

cultural recreation. The type of leisure actively engaged in for pleasure that embodies a high standard of refinement and excellence, such as art, music, dramatics, and artistic or folk dancing. In a broad sense, all forms of established recreation are cultural traits or patterns.   M.H.N.

cultural variation. Tentative changes in society's folkways, mores, and institutions, subject to trial and comparison and then acceptance or rejection through societal processes. The individual—as inventor, borrower from other cultures, or adaptor—is the agent through which cultural variations are produced or offered for acceptance. The borrowing of elements from other cultures or from other subcultures (group, class) within a society is called acculturation.   A.M'C.L.

culture. A collective name for all behavior patterns socially acquired and socially transmitted by means of symbols; hence a name for all the distinctive achievements of human groups, including not only such items as language, tool-making, industry, art, science, law, government, morals, and religion, but also the material instruments or artifacts in which cultural achievements are embodied and by which intellectual cultural features are given practical effect, such as buildings, tools, machines, communication devices, art objects, etc. The scientific meaning of the term is therefore quite different from its popular connotation. It includes all that is learned through intercommunication. It covers all language, traditions, customs, and institutions. As no human groups have ever been known that did not have language, traditions, customs, and institutions, culture is the universal, distinctive characteristic of human societies. Hence, its importance as a sociological concept.

Foreshadowing of culture may be found in the animal world below man. But as no animal group possesses verbal language, the main vehicle for the diffusion and transmission of culture, their culture, if existent, is negligible. The origin of culture as a human trait must be sought in man's superior capacity to learn from experience and to communicate what he learns by means of symbols, the chief of which is language. Discovery and invention form the content of man's learning, and the accumulation and transmission of these by processes of teaching and learning results in the development of the distinctive culture of each human group.

As culture is transmitted by processes of teaching and learning, whether formal or informal, by what has been called "inter-learning", the essential part of culture is to be found in the patterns embodied in the social traditions of the group, that is , in knowledge, ideas, beliefs, values, standards and sentiments prevalent in the group. The overt part of culture is to be found in the actual behavior of the group, usually in its usages, customs, and institutions. But customs and institutions are nearly always the expressions of the ideas, beliefs, values, and sentiments of the group. The essential part of culture seems to be an appreciation of values with reference to life conditions. The purely behavioristic definition of culture is therefore inadequate. Complete definition must include both the subjective and objective aspects of culture. Practically the culture of the human group is summed up in its traditions and customs; but tradition, as the subjective side of culture, is its essential core. C.A.E.

culture, adaptive. The cultural adjustments, taken collectively, which a group has made to the material conditions of life; the totality of a group's ways of utilizing, exploiting, and controlling its material conditions; the folkways, mores, and institutions of a group in so far as they constitute an adjustment to such conditions.   H.E.J.

culture, collection. Cf. collection culture.

culture, continuity of. This term is used in two distinct, though related senses, which are often confused with each other: (1) The stability of the culture of a people or tribe, with the increments or changes in the process of adjustment to changing conditions, and the perpetuation of this culture whole, mainly through the family, by such instrumentalities as education and tradition. (2) The total cultural continuum, or the entire world accumulation of material and non-material culture in the course of history, the cultural achievements of various peoples being regarded

as steps or contributions in a never-ending series. There is agreement that some culture phases have a more definite continuity than others, but difference of opinion regarding whether the psychosocial aspects of a culture or the technological and related knowledges contribute more to the main or central stream of culture. Consensus seems to favor the latter. This allows for a history of development and progress to be put in terms of mechanical invention and science. S.J.

culture, criminal. Cf. criminal culture.

culture, fusion of. The process of uniting two or more cultures into one. This involves the retention of some traits, the modification of others, and the discarding of those that are supplanted. Cf. assimilation, social.   J.P.E.

culture, hoe. Cf. hoe culture.

culture, material. Those aspects of culture which consist of material objects, either artifacts or other objects to which the (non-material) culture attaches a meaning or value. The phrase is considered contradictory if culture is defined as exclusively psychic (non-material); in that case there is no other term for what is covered by this phrase. Cf. culture, non-material; artifact.   T.D.E.

culture, non-literate. (*anthropological*) a phrase preferred to "preliterate" or "primitive", since "preliterate" implies linear evolution, a preordained sequence, and a retarded or arrested situation; while "primitive" implies that this retardation or fixation preceded and prevented later social change along the lines of European culture, that the non-literate cultures are still "primitive" in the sense of having undergone no evolution of their own, and therefore are "living ancestors", i.e., that our prehistoric forebears lived as present-day non-literate tribes live. T.D.E.

culture, non-material. That part of the total culture which is intangible and without material substance. Synonymous with immaterial culture.   J.P.E.

culture, preliterate. A culture that has never acquired the use of writing. The exact point at which pictograms become "writing" is debatable. Cf. culture, non-literate. **R.E.B.**

culture area. Cf. area, culture.

culture base. The sum total of all the culture traits in use at any particular time and place. **J.P.E.**

culture borrowing. Diffusion (q.v.), especially from the point of view of the recipient group. **G.P.M.**

culture case study. The application of the method of constructive typology (q.v.) to problems in the social sciences which make necessary the analysis of social and cultural phenomena of more than limited scope. Weber's studies in the sociology of religion, utilizing a kind of constructive typology *idealtypische Methode,* are outstanding examples of successful culture case study. Although much less sophisticated, Toynbee's analysis of "the stimulus of penalizations" *re* the Ashkenazim, Sephardim, Dönme, and Marrarano Jews is another instance.

The necessity for culture case study in the social sciences, and especially in sociology, arises from the fact that generalizations backed by hand-picked illustrative fragments torn from their contexts (the old-fashioned "comparative method") is thoroughly unscientific and has long since been discredited. If the sociologist is really a scientist his ultimate goal will be prediction (q.v.), and prediction, retrospective or prospective, must always be couched in "if and when" terms. Now, "if and when" always refer to situations that either have already occurred or that can be envisaged in terms of what has already occurred.

The initial conclusions of a culture case study are limited to the area and period studied, but the basic method used—namely, constructive typology—may enable these conclusions to be transferred, after appropriate modification, to other areas and/or periods. Dated and localized types must be accumulated before there is any thoroughgoing attempt to build types of undated and non-localized form. Eventually, it may be possible to restate the constructed types in "if and when" terms, and then to search the record for other cases that will provide a checkup on the validity of the retrospective or prospective predictions made. This constitutes a genuinely comparative method. Only when validation of this pragmatic variety has been secured can there be any talk of far-reaching generalizations, and even with such validation it is altogether too much to assume that these generalizations will hold for all cases whatsoever. **H.B.**

culture centre. Cf. centre, culture.

culture complex. A name for a cluster of culture traits usually interwoven with a central trait and forming an interrelated whole; a chain of activities connected with some central culture trait. Culture traits are arranged in patterns which are known as "culture complexes". The complex embraces all the activities related to the central trait. For example, machine industry, monogamy, and monotheism are culture complexes in western civilization. The rice complex is very typical of the civilization of many Oriental peoples. Any culture or civilization of any group taken as a whole is composed of the sum total of culture complexes which it possesses; but taken together these constitute a definite culture configuration or gestalt (q.v.). The sum total of culture complexes possessed by a given people we call their culture. In a sense it is one large culture complex. The term, therefore, becomes very significant for the understanding of the civilization of any group and for the understanding of the social behavior and personalities of its members.

The interpretation of individual and group behavior in terms of culture complexes has, therefore, a realistic foundation of scientific social fact. No institution, and indeed no individual behavior or personality trait, is to be understood without reference to the culture complex in which it exists. Group ways, or folkways, follow the general pattern of some culture complex or of the whole culture of the folk. As they are habits of the group they become automatic and stereotyped through repetition. As they are often unreflectively performed they may be regarded as non-rational in the sense that they are not based upon any intelligent personal judgment. The usages and customs of people are hence intimately associated with the culture complexes which prevail in the group.   C.A.E.

culture(al) conflict. Cf. conflict, culture-(al).

culture(al) control. Cf. control, culture(al).

culture diffusion. The process by which a culture trait, culture complex, or culture pattern spreads from its point of origin to other points or areas. Cf. diffusion.   J.P.E.

culture evolution. The historic development of the systems of human experience, made up of the gradually changing objects, concepts, usages, associations, instruments, and skills, with which human beings satisfy their needs. Culture has a stable though changing framework of essential usages or institutions (such as home life, marriage, commercial exchange, governmental forms, religious worship, and public games). Each of these is developed as a customary expression and support of an essential class of social functions. These classes of elementary social functions, that give meaning to the institutions, may be indicated as the economic functions of sustenance and equipment, the reflective functions of information and education, the controlling functions of conduct and government and the appreciative functions of recreation and art, all being elaborations of the necessary modes of interested action of all people in the achievement of their projects. The historic stages in the evolution of their functions and institutions are indicated by shifts in emphasis of time and attention devoted to them, in the order above indicated: From the lower, more primitive and physical, economic activities, through the intermediate reflective and controlling activities, to the higher appreciative activities—the latter classes awaiting full development upon the adequate development of the former. This may be observed in the historic succession of types of human culture: (1) the savage or primitive culture, (2) the medieval or feudal culture, (3) the modern or industrial culture and (4) the contemporary, more worldwide and comprehensive, more democratic culture.   C.J.B.

culture lag. Cf. lag, cultural.

culture pattern. The arrangement or configuration of the culture traits and culture complexes that make up a particular culture at any given time.   J.P.E.

culture people. Cf. people, culture.

culture sub-area. A sub-division of a larger culture area, distinguished by the comparative completeness of the development of a particular culture trait, or the comparative readiness with which such a trait will be diffused.

culture trait. The simplest functional unit into which a culture is divided for purposes of analysis. This unit must be recognized as being either an abstract or a concrete entity in the total culture. J.P.E.

culture type. Total of characteristics and value-concepts societally valid within a given time or space.

cultures, cross-fertilization of. Cf. cross-fertilization of cultures.

cumulative evolution. Cf. evolution, cumulative.

current. A movement, trend or flow, as the current of the river. Otherwise, it is applied to the present status of a phenomenon; what is happening now, as current events. A file kept up to date may be described as current or active.   N.A.

curse. To invoke supernatural powers to wreak harm or injury upon a person or thing. Any act or word designed to produce supernatural harm.

curse, conditional. Cf. conditional curse.

curve of error. The normal or Gaussian curve, so called because it can be shown theoretically to represent the distribution of the sum of a large number of equal and independent errors, each of which is equally likely to be positive or negative. Practical experience has shown that the distribution of errors in a variety of types of measurement conforms approximately to this curve.   P.H.F.

custodial care. The care afforded in institutions to socially incompetent persons who need close supervision or require personal assistance in performing elemental human functions. J.W.M'C.

custody, close. Constant supervision of the prisoner on the assumption that he will not only run away if the opportunity is offered, but will make the opportunity. N.S.H.

custody, maximum. Care in that type of prison which provides the maximum security—high walls, tool-proof bars, numerous guards, rigid discipline, etc.—for the most hardened prisoners, e.g., Alcatraz among the United States' institutions. J.L.G.

custody, medium. Care in an institution for prisoners with a type of physical plant less strongly built and equipped and intended to house the less hardened and dangerous criminals, and to give them more freedom of movement and greater self-direction. J.L.G.

custody, minimum. Care of prisoners in an institution built, equipped and guarded with the least possible restraint required to keep them safely, and to allow the greatest possible freedom. Such an institution is exemplified by some of the camps and farms, by some reformatories, or by honor dormitories within an institution. J.L.G.

custody, protective. Detention by the police of persons essential to the prosecution of justice presumably in order to prevent reprisals against them by criminal elements for their part in furthering the investigation of crime. J.W.M'C.

custom. A socially prescribed mode of behavior, carried by tradition and enforced by social disapproval of its violation. Custom lacks the coercive backing of the state which characterizes the legal code or the extreme sanctions of the mores. Customs differ from institutions, among other ways, in their less definite recognition. Fashion is less permanent and both fashion and convention less intrinsically meaningful than is custom. M.K.

"custom, cake of". A phrase coined by Walter Bagehot to describe the total body of traditional ways and attitudes that cemented together the members of primitive societies in such a way that they are to the individuals involved much as the finished cake is to the included grains of flour. In current usage, the opposition to innovation or resistance to change which customary and habitual social conduct has built up. N.L.S.; F.E.L.

custom imitation. Cf. imitation, custom.

customary behavior. Cf. behavior, customary.

cut over area. A timbered area in which logging operations have left it depleted of its timber. P.H.L.

cycle, business. Cf. business cycle.

cycle, industrial life. Cf. industrial life cycle.

cycle, institutional. The typical life-cycle of an institution. The institution often has its origin in a reform movement in time of social crisis, or some other social situation demanding new adjustment techniques (in the latter case it may be established in a calculating manner); it develops leaders and the varied machinery typical of institutions and essential to their efficient functioning; it enjoys prestige and has authority in the lives of men and tends to become a cherished end in itself; it grows old and its administrators or other professional functionaries become complacent and even reactionary, its functioning becomes formal and mechanical, and its structures relatively inflexible; either it ceases to function altogether and eventually disappears, or, if it has a strategic place in the given society, it undergoes drastic reorganization during another crisis. It is possible to distinguish four periods of institutional organization and growth: (1) incipient organization; (2) efficiency; (3) formalism; and (4) disorganization. J.O.H.

cycle, life-. The span of the lifetime of an organism, or, by extension, of a group, nation, or culture, sometimes conceived as returning to repeat itself in another generation or epoch. A personal or family life cycle is marked by certain crises and episodes; conception, birth, identification, puberty, adolescence, courtship, marriage, menopause, senescence, death, bereavement. T.D.E.

cycle, plantation. Cf. plantation cycle.

cycle, secular. A variation of increase and decrease above or below a trend line

in which a century or more is required for the complete change to occur. H.A.P.

cyclical fluctuation. A form of recurrent change or cycle; a whole series of events within which there is no recurrence of separate parts, the chief features being a central condition, known as zero, the average or the normal, and positions of maximum variation above and below the central condition. M.S.

D

daimon. A higher supernatural being, i.e., one that cannot be identified with the soul (q.v.) or ghost (q.v.) of an individual human being; a spirit (q.v.) or god. G.P.M.

dance. Rhythmical motion, not motivated by work-use, as an original and symbolic expression of life. Its sociological importance lies in the creation of collective imagination, group-life and behavior pattern of we-feeling. J.H.B.

dance, jitney. Cf. jitney dance.

data, editing. Cf. editing data.

data, validity of. Cf. validity of data.

day dream. A thought process during waking life, which takes the form of trains of uncontrolled imagery, frequently of the character of imaginary adventures. M.S.

dead, cult of the. Cf. cult of the dead.

dead, door of the. A special opening made in the wall of a dwelling through which to remove a corpse, commonly because of a belief that, if the ordinary door were used, the ghost (q.v.) of the deceased would be able to find its way back and plague the survivors. After removal of the corpse the door of the dead is usually blanked out. G.P.M.

dead hand. A term commonly used to denote the control of certain affairs by a person after his death, through (a) the stipulations of his will, or (b) the terms of a legal agreement promulgated by him during his life, to be in force either for a stated time or in perpetuity. As a strictly legal term dead hand connotes a corporation, which by its very nature is perpetual. Also, by inference, the aggre-

gate weight of the influence of ancestors and predecessors, of the dead over the living. R.E.B.

Death, the Black. Cf. Black Death, the.

death rate. Cf. rate, death.

debauchery. Such excessive indulgence in eating, drinking or sexual gratification as to lead to temporary, or even permanent, incapacity for normal social activity. Distinguished from orgy (q.v.), in that it has no ceremonial or ritualistic social significance; in that it applies to individual rather than group behavior; and in that it is outside the mores. F.H.H.

debt-slavery. A customary or a mutually specified term of enslavement of debtor to creditor in liquidation of debt. E.E.M.

decadence. The process, or the result of the process, of social decay, by which institutions, social control, and culture traits generally lose their force, and a society dissolves into small units. The logical extreme of social decadence may be thought of as a thoroughly hedonistic and sensual individualism. Cf. disorganization, social; demoralization. F.N.H.

decadent. In a condition of decline, or state of being run-down. May apply to a family, a social set or people lacking in virility. The term may also be applied to the social or economic philosophy of a group; a sterility of imagination. N.A.

decentralization. Process (or condition) of division of some of the powers of a social unit among its parts. Often considered to involve a shift in the geographical location of power from a central area to a number of outlying districts, but geographical shifts are not synonymous with shifts of power.   M.S.

decentralization, urban. Cf. urban decentralization.

de-class. To degrade oneself by behavior considered suitable only for a person of lower social rank; to violate the manners and mores of one's own social group so as to lead to social ostracism.   F.H.H.

decorticate conditioning. Conditioning in the absence of the cerebral cortex.   M.S.

defect. Incapacity to conform to an established standard resulting from lack of, or a maladjustment of, essential parts of the whole. Sociologically the term defect refers to incapacity of an accepted social institution or agency to perform a designated or standardized function due to recognized deficiencies inherent in the structure or organization of the institution or agency. The term is applied to individuals, when referring to some physical or mental imperfection without specific reference to cause. Varying degrees of mental defectiveness have been distinguished for purposes of discussion as idiocy, imbecility, moronity.   J.M.R.

defect of personality. Cf. personality, defect of.

defective. Incomplete; lacking in some essential; faulty or imperfect. Sociologically it denotes failure of an institution, social agency or group to perform a recognized essential function due to a deficiency of structure or organization. As a noun and without a modifier it is nearly always used to denote a mentally deficient person. Used in this sense it usually refers to general inadequacy arising out of conditions present at time of birth, but not necessarily hereditary. Cf. mental deficiency.   J.M.R.

defective delinquent. Cf. delinquent, defective.

defectiveness. Cf. defective.

defectiveness, mental. Cf. mental defectiveness.

defender, public. An individual or organization rendering legal service to indigent persons charged with a criminal offense. The lawyer may be a representative of either a public or private organization. He may volunteer his services or receive a fee from public or private funds. The public defender is to be distinguished from counsel assigned by the court in a particular case, by the regularity of appearing as defense counsel. In the best developed public defender systems, such as exist in Los Angeles County and in the State of Connecticut, counsel devote full time to, and receive adequate salaries for, the preparation of cases and the defense of the accused.   N.F.C.

defense. That aspect of social conflict in which a personality or group seeks to prevent damage to itself or its allies.   H.H.

defense housing. War housing. Housing built primarily to meet the needs of civilian workers in war industries or in army or navy posts and of married army and navy enlisted personnel.   S.S.

defense mechanism. A psychological device employed by a child or a mentally immature person as a reaction against blame or criticism. Instead of admitting mistakes, accepting responsibility, and adjusting, the tendency is to fix blame on another or at least to make some excuse for oneself.   A.E.W.

deferred consumation. Cf. consummation, deferred.

deficit economy. Cf. economy, deficit.

definition. (1) A statement of identity of meaning between two expressions: the expression which is being defined (definiendum) and the defining expression (definiens); and (2) the process by which such a statement is arrived at. The expression to be defined always represents a concept, which refers to some class (or species) of individual objects, physical or mental. The defining expression usually consists of (a) naming a more inclusive class (called the genus) within which the species to be defined belongs; and (b) enumerating the differentiae, or specific characteristics which are necessary and sufficient to distinguish all members of this species from all other members of the genus.   H.H.

A complete definition must include such a verbal description of the concept as will make possible its identification at first contact, and will also provide an adequate understanding of it without any contact whatsoever.

definition, operational. A definition is operational to the extent that the definer includes among the differentiae (a) specification of the procedures, including materials used, for identifying or generating the definiendum and (b) the finding of a high index of reliability for the definition.   S.C.D.

defloration. The act or practice of depriving a woman of her virginity, especially when undertaken at or prior to her marriage for magical or ceremonial reasons either by mechanical means or by sexual connection with a man other than her husband. Cf. jus primae noctis; ritual union.   G.P.M.

deformation, cranial. Cf. cranial deformation.

degenerate. To sink to a lower organizational level, whether in genetic inheritance, personality organization, or social structure.   F.H.H.

degeneration. A decline in health, normalcy, efficiency, or viability due to pathological structural changes. During intoxication and disease various tissues suffer from disordered nutrition, function, and appearance. A certain degree of degeneration can be repaired in most kinds of tissue; in more severe cases the cells die. Organic philosophies of history like the Spenglerian or the cognate medically oriented type of Nordau, and organismic sociologies like those of Schaeffle and Ammon, interpret the increasing complexity, tensions, and multiplied conflicts of a complex expanding culture with its differential rates of evolution, as an irreversible, catabolic, quasi-biological process. Occasionally theories of this type actually suggest a palpable pejoration of the biological stock. This fatalistic pessimism obvi-

ously offers no fulcrum for any effective interference in the social process. Because degeneration connotes an organic conception of society and a definite pathology, the more neutral and functional term disorganization (q.v.) has supplanted it. In popular usage sex perverts and criminals are still referred to as degenerates with its implication of biological inadequacy and stigmatization though most perversion is socially conditioned.   E.F.

degradation. The demotion of a prisoner guilty of the violation of the prison rules from a higher to a lower grade with the loss of privileges belonging to the higher grade. Earlier the pillory, stocks, branding, the brank and similar methods were used as methods of social degradation.   J.L.G.

deliberation. The orderly communicational interaction of any number centered upon the examination and solution of problems; a careful weighing of evidence relative to a choice of action.   F.E.L.

delinquency. (1) Failure of an individual to perform a socially designated task; violation of a social obligation. (2) Used in juvenile court law to define juvenile offenses which come under the jurisdiction of the court. The juridically accepted distinction between a "criminal" act and a "delinquent" act is inherent in the theory that juveniles are not motivated by the same responsible considerations as are assumed to actuate adults. Legally and sociologically the distinction is justied by a recognition of the need for differential treatment of juvenile offenders. Cf. criminal responsibility; delinquency, juvenile.   J.M.R.

delinquency, juvenile. The anti-social acts of children or persons under age. Such acts are either specifically forbidden by law or may be lawfully interpreted as constituting delinquency. In most states, all offenses committed by children under sixteen are considered delinquency. A few states extend the term to include the offenses committed by those under eighteen. California extends the term to include offenders under twenty-one.   M.A.E.

delinquency area. Cf. area, delinquency.

delinquent. (1) A person guilty of anti-social conduct which generally speaking is considered less serious than the type of misconduct designated as "criminal." (2) In American penology the term "delinquent" usually refers to the juvenile offender whose misconduct is an infraction of the law. Such conduct is generally considered less offensive than an adult's misconduct because of the child's immaturity and the unfortunate environmental circumstances which so frequently occasion his behavior.   M.A.E.

delinquent, defective. A delinquent who has some defect in his physical or mental equipment. Generally speaking, the term refers to delinquents who are feeble-minded or otherwise mentally incompetent; hence incapable of assuming responsibility for their conduct.   M.A.E.

delit. A grade of crime. American criminal law has followed the English common law and dividing crimes into treason, felonies, and misdemeanors. The Continental European codes use a different although roughly comparable classification. In the French *Code Penal* crimes are classifified as *crimes* (felonies), *delits* (indictable misdemeanors), and *contraventions* (violations of police regulations). The Italian *Codice Penale* uses *delitti* for felonies and *contravvenzioni* for misdemeanors. The German *Strafgesetzbuch* employs *Verbrechen* (felonies), *Vergehen* (the French *delits* and American misdemeanor), and *Ubertretung* (violation of Police regulations).   N.F.C.

demagogy. A political epithet having reference to an opportunistic approach to issues with a conscious disregard for the social and economic implications. Demagogy waxes eloquent in platitudes and often in vilification. It promotes schemes of social or economic reform on the basis of half-truth analyses of the problems and takes advantage of popular unrest and misery, appealing to prejudice.   N.A.

demand, labor. Cf. labor demand.

democracy. A philosophy, or a social system, that stresses participation in, and proportional control of, the affairs of the community by the individual member, on the basis of his personal selfhood (q.v.) as a human being, regardless of his qualities, rank, status, or possessions. In the abstract, pure democracy takes no account of any individual characteristics whatsoever, race, sex, age, religion, occupation, wealth, intelligence, ancestry, etc. It is therefore a practical impossibility. No pure democracy ever existed, or ever could exist for more than a very brief period of disintegration. From the point of view of actual existence and administration, therefore, every democracy must be limited. The practical questions are; in what areas of social experience should the democratic principle be recognized and established, and what limitations or qualifications should be imposed in each area? Historically, the first major area in which societies have attempted to establish the principle of democracy is the political. Certain limitations were recognized as necessary almost intuitively. The first of these was age. No society, however democratic, has ever expected six-months old infants, or even ten-year old children, to take part in town meetings and vote in elections. Other limitations that were very common were sex, property, occupation, etc. The general trend of social evolution has been in the direction of removing or mollifying the restrictions and limitations on pure democracy in the political field, e.g., by extending the franchise to females. There has also been a strong movement to extend it into other great areas, particularly the familial and the economic. Recently, the area of race is also being emphasied. In the confusion and heat of controversy the necesscity of recognizing the principle of relativity is often lost sight of.

democracy, industrial. Cf. industrial democracy.

democracy, political. Rule by the people based on free and equal participation by all enfranchised adults: the election of public officers by a majority of the citizens voting, with (1) freedom to nominate alternative candidates; (2) the right of citizens to form political parties and present their candidates; (3) freedom to conduct campaigns; and (4) the right of defeated minorities to continue their propaganda. Cf. democracy.   R.N.B.

democracy, trade union. A condition within a trade union characteried by the application of the principles of political democracy (q.v.) and the additional safeguards against expulsion without a fair hearing, and against discrimination in admission to membership on the ground of race, religion, national origin or political belief. R.N.B.

democratic. Of, or pertaining to, a democracy (q.v.) in any particular usage of that term; of, or pertaining to, a person sympathetic with democracy in one or other of its phases. Contrasted with aristocratic and autocratic. T.D.E.

democratic mind. Cf. mind, democratic.

demography. The statistical analysis and description of population aggregates, with reference to distribution, vital statistics, age, sex, and civil status, either at a given time, or over time. G.M.F.

demonism. The belief in the existence of spirit beings, and the attendant practices of magic (q.v.), worship or other forms of ritual (q.v.) for the control or appeasement of such beings. The spirit beings may exist in a variety of imagined forms, such as goblins, ghosts, genii, witches, plant and animal spirits, and a host of the lesser deities, which are either benevolent or malevolent, as the case may be. Cf. animism. E.A.H.

demonology. The systematic study of demonism (q.v.) E.A.H.

demoralization. Loss of personal integrity or of group morale, as process or as condition; disintegration of an habituated scale of values, ideas, definitions of situations and conceptions of rôle. A demoralized family, for example, may retain its socio-legal pattern, or its members may be abandoned or deserted or divorced, or in custody, or non-wedlock relations may distort it; the essential thing in loss of group morale (social demoralization) is that solidarity has given way to individualism of ends. In societal demoralization the unity of an entire community, institution or nation is threatened. Personal demoralization, on the other hand, involves loss of integrity, dissociation, fantasy-thinking, self-deception, fear and furtivity, cumulative dishonesty, maladjustment, internal and external conflict, eventual loss of status and rôle, and personality breakdown. Distinguished from delinquency (q.v.), a situation-process which may or may not demoralize the person. Cf. morale; morals; mores. T.D.E.

demoralize. To break down seriously the habits, attitudes, or scheme of social values through which an individual maintains a normal adjustment to group life and expectations. F.H.H.

demos. A human group identified by its political unity, or regarded as a political unit. A people (q.v.) considered from the point of view of its political establishment.

demotic. Relating to or pertaining to the people, or to the population. F.H.H.

demotic composition. Cf. composition, demotic.

demotion. A reduction, by someone in authority, of the rights and privileges of another, amounting to a lowering of status. F.E.L.

denaturalization. The reversal, revoking, or annulment of naturalization (q.v.).

denomination. The accommodated religious group. The sect after its conflict stage is past. L.P.E.

density. The ratio of some index to units of space. The index may be number of persons or amount of any characteristic; the space may be linear, or areal, or cubic. An inverse density is the ratio of a space to an index as illustrated by street frontage per dwelling, area per person, gallons of water per capita, etc. S.C.D.

density (population). The number of units (persons, families, or dwellings) per acre or square mile.

density of population. Cf. population, density of.

dependability. A state or quality of trustworthiness that can be counted upon and accepted with considerable assurance, whether it be a social phenomenon or the behavior of an individual.   R.E.B.

dependency. A condition in which a person, not possessing the means of securing economic goods or services essential to the minimum standard of existence, is forced to seek and accept public or private assistance. Also, a legal state such as dependency of child upon parents, of wife upon husband for support.   E.E.M.

dependency, economic. The state of one who receives as relief from the community any of those goods and services which other members of that community receive in return for their labor or property, or by virtue of their favored position in the established order. When so used, the term connotes a condition of social pathology. The term may also be used to describe a normal relationship within the family group, when a child receives economic goods and services from its parents due to its age, or due to prolonged professional education. The term should not be confused with "financial dependence" which describes the normal position of any worker who produces for use and not for exchange; e.g., the housewife or any member of the family group who contributes services to the real income of the family group but receives no financial remuneration. Such a worker is a financial but not an economic dependent.   A.E.W.

dependency, emotional. The state of one who is not self-sustaining but constantly relies upon another for comfort, support and even for direction. A person who has never grown up emotionally but is always seeking for someone who can make his decisions for him and guide his course. A.E.W.

dependency, old age. A state of economic dependence upon public or private assistance resulting from the viscissitudes of old age—enfeeblement, unemployment, lack of savings, etc.   E.E.M.

dependent. Obliged by circumstances to receive support from another person or from a group or agency; or (noun) a person thus dependent. In our culture children and aged people have been normal dependents upon their own families' sup-

port. Statutes and moral codes require the support of normal dependents. Income tax laws recognize normal dependents. If family allowances and old age insurance provide state support regardless of poverty, such recipients will also be considered "normally" dependent. The word dependent is generally used, however (*social work*), to mean of abnormally dependent status, receiving part or all support from other than "normal" sources, whether personal, private or publicly supported, in cash or in kind, "indoor" or "outdoor" relief.   T.D.E.

dependent variable. Cf. independent variable.

depletion, social. Cf. social depletion.

depopulation. An extensive reduction of population by death through disease or war, by expulsion, or by voluntary migration.   E.E.M.

deportation. The forcible return by public authority of an alien to his country of origin, or rarely some other foreign jurisdiction. The process is particularly exemplified in connection with the administration of the United States immigration statutes. The grounds of deportation are of two main classes: (1) immoral, criminal, or politically prohibited behavior on the part of the alien, or (2) becoming an economic charge upon the public from causes existing prior to the arrival of the immigrant.

depreciation. (*housing*) Loss in value due to all causes, including functional and economic obsolescence and deterioration.

depression, business. A reduction in business activiy below an index of the normal. Cf. business cycle.   H.A.P.

derivations. Human efforts at justification of executed or contemplated actions; rationalizations. The term is used by Pareto and his followers to denote that large field of activity by which man tries to convince himself and his fellows of the logicality or "rightness" of his course of behavior. In this system four major categories of derivations are recognized: simple and repeated affirmation; appeal

to authority; appeals to values held dear by society; purely verbal manipulations. These may meet the needs for logical explanations, may substitute for logic, or may evade the logical issue. Cf. residues.
H.E.M.

descent. The rule governing affiliation with social groupings through kinship ties; called "linear", i.e., either "matrilineal" (q.v.) or "patrilineal" (q.v.) when affiliation is with the sib (q.v.) or other social group of either the mother or the father exclusively; "bilateral" when with both equally or with either indifferently; "double" when exclusively with a maternal group of one type and with a paternal group of another.
G.P.M.

descent, double. A rule of descent (q.v.) according to which a person is affiliated with one social group through his mother and with another through his father, belonging at the same time, for example, to the matrilineal sib (q.v.) of his mother and to the patrilineal sib of his father
G.P.M.

desertion. The unannounced cessation of cohabitation between husband and wife without formal divorce, separation or other mutually agreed to arrangement for support of family or care of children.
J.W.M'C.

desideratum. That which is desired (by specified people at a specified time as determined by a specified technic for maximal precision). It is any object of desire identified as that towards which people respond so as to increase it in amount, duration or proximity. A negative desideratum is that to which people respond so as to decrease it.
S.C.D.

despotism. Arbitrary political rule by a single head of government, unchecked by any controls whatever; usually applied to government headed by men who achieved power by violence and so maintain it. Cf. autocracy; dictatorship; tyranny.
R.N.B.

destination, country of. Cf. country of destination

detachment. A state of being emotionally removed from a problem or situation un-

er review. There is implied in the attitude of detachment an objective state of mind capable of fair analysis and thorough review.
N.A.

detention, house of. Cf. house of detention.

detention, juvenile. The function of providing custody and supervision of children whose cases are pending in the juvenile court to assure their appearance at the time of their hearing. Various types of place are now in use for such a purpose, including the children's own or boarding homes, jails, special detention homes maintained by the juvenile courts, or miscellaneous places, such as hospitals, almshouses, or police lock-ups, as the court may designate.
A.E.W.

detention, protective. Based on a policy of social defense or of protection, some countries and states have attempted to keep the defective, habitual, and unimprovable offenders in custody for an indefinite or life period after they would qualify for release if they had been ordinary offenders. Such an extended stay is in part accomplished by delaying the granting of parole or refusing parole. It is also accomplishable by use of third- and fourth-time offenders acts, under which a prisoner may be detained for periods up to life. But these laws have never been put into effective operation by judges. In some European countries, protective detention for habitual and abnormal offenders was written into laws of social defense. But even in these countries very few cases are handled under this measure for social defense.
W.C.R.

deter. To prevent a person from an act by threat or warning, or, as in penology, by example.
T.D.E.

deteriorate. To decline in quality, efficiency or value, whether the decline occur in goods, personal behavior, or social standards.
F.H.H.

deterioration. (*housing*). Impairment of condition of physical property.

deterioration, individual. Cf. individual deterioration.

92

deterioration, social. Cf. social deterioration.

deterioration, zone of. Cf. zone of deterioration.

determination, cultural. Cf. cultural determination.

determined, socially. A phenomenon is socially determined when it can be most adequately explained in terms of antecedent social conditions, i.e., by influences involved in the process of intercommunication rather than by biological, chemical, geographical or other physical or mechanical causes.   A.R.L.

determiner. A gene, or factor in inheritance. (Becoming obsolete.)   F.H.H.

determinism, economic. Cf. economic determinism.

deterrence. The penological theory that punishment, knowledge of which is widely disseminated, is the most important method of preventing crime. In the Classical School of penology (Beccaria, Bentham, etc.) this theory of punishment occupied first place in importance. The kind and severity of punishment was to be only sufficient to prevent the repetition of the crime.   J.L.G.

deterrence, social. Cf. social deterrence.

development, personality. Cf. personality development.

development, societal. Change or process involving social and non-social agencies or forces. Ex. secular, cyclical, evolutionary change. Cf. progress, social. H.A.P.

deviation, standard. Cf. standard deviation.

deviation from the mean. (*statistical*) The difference between a particular score or observation and the mean of the whole series of observations.   M.Pt.

devolution. A seldom used term to denote any process which is the reverse of evolution in the Spencerian sense: devolution moves from a more definite, more coherent, more heterogeneous and differentiated, more complex, organized and specialized condition toward a condition that is less definite and coherent, more homogeneous and undifferentiated, simpler and less highly organized and specialized.   T.D.E.

diagnosis, social. Cf. social diagnosis.

dialect. A specific variety of a language showing sufficient peculiarities of pronunciation, grammar, and vocabulary to be considered a distinct entity, yet not sufficiently disinct from other dialects to constitute a separate language; usually applied to local dialects with a geographic basis.   P.H.F.

dictatorship. A political system in which one person, or a small group of people, have complete authority over the lives and persons of all others in a given country. Civil rights, including freedom of speech, press, assembly, and petition, are nonexistent or very severely abridged; and the people have no means of turning out the person or persons in authority, short of revolution.   S.C.M.

dictatorship of the proletariat. The Marxist principle of the exercise of the State power exclusively by a minority, acting professedly in the interests of the working masses, in a period of transition from capitalism to socialism or communism.   R.N.B.

differences, racial. (*anthropological*) Differences in individuals considered to be common to, inherent in and characteristic of the race to which the individual's ancestors have belonged, being attributed to differences in heredity supposedly independent of environment, whether physiographic or cultural. Often confused with cultural or nationality differences, which may partake of true racial differences but are due also to differences in culture. In the empirical defining of racial differences historical accident and cultural selection play all important rôles. In the culture of the United States, known ancestry and pigmentation are most important, but hair, lips, eyes, head form, bone-composition and structure are also utilized as stigmata. Cf. race.   T.D.E.

differential association. Cf. association, differential.

differential fertility. Cf. fertility, differential.

differentiation. (1) Variation associated with interaction. With the individual, the acquisition of a rôle; with a group, the internal arrangement among the members. (2) The general result of the process of interaction, regarded by some as the main result. (3) In a classification, the noting of unlike characteristics between or among objects otherwise similar. (4) (*mathematical*) The operation of obtaining the differential or the differential coefficient. (5) (*biological*) Progressive changes in an organism.   B.M.

diffusion. The spread of culture traits, by borrowing or migration, from one area to another or from one group to another in the same area.   J.G.L.

diffusion, culture. Cf. culture diffusion.

diffusionism. The anthropological theory which explains culture growth largely in terms of the spread of culture traits from one culture to another. English diffusionism has emphasized the rôle of Egypt as the mother of culture from which lesser cultures have been nurtured. The German-Austrian school of diffusionism has attempted to establish the spread of large culture units (*Kulturkreisen*) over great areas of the primitive world from a limited number of diffusion centers.   E.A.H.

dimension, societal. A societal dimension is a measured amount of a societal phenomenon. It may be measured primitively, as existent or non-existent in any situation observed and recorded as an all-or-none dimension of two points, I or O, where the unit, I, is the nature of the phenomenon observed. Expressing the phenomenon in ordinal series (first, second, third, etc.), or in cardinal units (1, 2, 3, etc.), determines the dimension with greater precision. In geometric terms, a dimension is a vector, a line characterized by a length and a direction. The term is used in dimensional sociology to order societal phenomena to a n - dimensional societal space where n is the num-

ber of distinguished phenomena. In this space all dimensions have a common origin point at zero and radiate out from it to lengths determined by the amount of each phenomenon (as observed in a recorded situation) and at angles determined by the inter-correlation coefficients of the phenomena (when those coefficients are interpreted as cosines of angles).   S.C.D.

diminishing desirability (also known as diminishing gratification and as diminishing utility). The basis of an economic law that the intensity of desire, gratification, or utility of an article diminishes with each successive unit as consumption is satisfied.   E.E.M.

diminishing returns. Term used in relation to the economic principles of increasing and decreasing returns (or productivity): viz., as any factor in production is increased, other factors of production remaining fixed in quantity and efficiency, the output per variable factor may increase, but eventually becomes smaller. Also, in relation to population and natural resources—that condition wherein any net increase in population results in a lessened per capita yield from the resources.   E.E.M.

direct action. Cf. action, direct.

direct contact. Cf. contact, direct.

direct-contact group. Cf. group, direct-contact.

direction, social. Cf. social direction.

directive. A mandate or order prescribing a course of conduct. A decision by the people in an election may be a directive if the issue was made clear and the popular will indicated in the vote. The term has general rather than specific application. It would determine broad policies within the limits of which a program is executed.   N.A.

disapproval. Communicational interaction expressing highly critical or condemnatory judgments of another's point of view or behavior.   F.E.L.

disaster. A local event having dire consequences which may be blamable to persons or to an Act of God; an unusual condition which may call for unusual means in the treatment. The term is generally applied to sudden unexpected catastrophes, fires, floods, storms, explosions, rather than to such conditions as droughts, money panics, or depressions.   N.A.

disaster relief. Cf. relief, disaster.

discipline in prison. Cf. prison, discipline in.

discipline, self-. The ability of an individual to direct his own behavior in accordance with his own needs and with accepted standards of conduct. Through education, the individual has learned to regulate his own behavior from within in the main, rather than having it entirely controlled from without.   A.E.W.

discipline, social. Cf. social discipline.

discontinuity. With reference to temporal and causal sequences, the looseness between that which precedes and that which follows. This term, always employed in a relative sense (like its opposite—continuity) and implying many degrees, is very important for sociology. This comes to expression in several directions, regarding: (a) The discontinuity among different types of inclusive societies, as opposed to evolutionistic theories of uninterrupted (continuous) development; (b) The measure of discontinuity among depth layers of social reality (such as ecological basis, organized superstructures, patterns, symbols, valuations, group mentality, etc.) as opposed to more or less harmonistic and monistic theories of their continuity and unity; (c) The measure of discontinuity among social factors and social causes as well as between social causes and effects; (d) finally, the concept of "social time" and the measure of discontinuity which characterizes it. G.G.

discourse, universe of. The totality of concepts, ideas, meanings, and points of view which are shared in common by the members of a specific group   J.P.E.

discrimination, social. Cf. social discrimination.

disease. The absence of health; a failure of bodily function sufficient to cause discomfort, distress, or disability; a combination of symptoms, conditions, and observable bodily differences and changes such as to correspond to a "clinical entity" (as recognized by a diagnostician). A clinical entity is also by abstraction called a disease. Some portion of the body has failed to operate in coordination with other parts thereof; "organic" (i.e., gross structural) damage may or may not be present. By extension, failures of nervous and psychic and personal function or integration are also called disease (neuroses, psychoneuroses, q.v.) and have been classified and tested.   T.D.E.

disintegrate. To break up into integrant parts; sociologically, to lose the we-feeling and sense of common interests, and to separate into the district units which had previously constituted a group.

disintegration. Collapse of organizational unity; breakdown of integrity (unity of structure-function), organization, and solidarity, whether of person, group, institution, or nation; with disappearance of the entity as such. A stage immediately preceding dismemberment or dissolution. T.D.E.

disintegration, group. The process of interaction between members of a group in which conflict or lack of identification with the group results in a weakening or dissolution of the unity and structure of the group.   G.L.C.

disintegration, social. Cf. social disintegration.

dismemberment. Actual spatial separation, voluntary, involuntary or externally compelled, of one or more members of a group. It may or may not cause or be caused by demoralization (q.v.) or disintegration (q.v.)   T.D.E.

disorder, mental. Cf. mental disorder.

disorganization. The process of disintegration or breakdown of a scheme of orderly arrangement and functioning. Also the state or condition of confusion and malfunctioning which accompanies or follows the loss of, or absence of, coordinated and integrated behavior. The term is used in reference both to individual human personalities and to social groups.

disorganization, community. The disruption of established social relationships in a community.   P.F.C.

disorganization, economic. The disruption of an established system for the production, distribution, or consumption of wealth.   P.F.C.

disorganization, family. Interaction which runs counter to the social norms of the marriage and parental relationships. The norms of marriage, for example, include mutual love, sexual adjustment and exclusiveness, relative absence of conflict, a sense of unity and as much freedom for self-expression as is compatible with this unity, and so on. A lack of consensus in identifying family disorganization may exist because component norms are rated differently. Thus, a change in a patriarchal family which liberates the individual members with some loss of the sense of family interdependence may be variously described depending upon values. Another ground for disagreement as to the presence of family disorganization may exist because the indices of deviations from the norms are not reliable or valid. The fact remains, however, that much of the current family disorganization involves a departure from all norms, whether in terms of individual happiness or the quality of the relationship. The consensus in the diagnosis of family disorganization may be actually quite high.   M.K.

disorganization, personal. Any condition of inability or disinclination of an individual to conform to socially acceptable patterns of behavior which in turn leads to such a person's social maladjustment. In general, personal disorganization is the result of a conflict between the individual's attitudes and behavior and group (or social) values. The conflict may manifest itself in anti-social conduct such as crime or prostitution or the conflict may take place within the individual so that one set of attitudes censors another set of attitudes or behavior and thus may lead to an unstable personality, to mental and emotional disorders, or suicide. M.A.E.

disorganization, rural. The disruption of an established system of social, economic, or political relationships in an agricultural or open-country community. P.F.C.

disorganization, social. Cf. social disorganization.

disorganize. To disrupt an established system of relationships.   P.F.C.

disorganized. Characteristic of a condition in which a previously established system of relationships has been disrupted. The disruption may be either temporary or permanent, partial or complete
                    P.F.C.

disparity, social. Cf. social disparity.

dispensary. Originally, a place where medicines were distributed to ambulatory patients: modern, an institution which organizes the professional equipment and special skill of physicians for the diagnosis, treatment, and prevention of disease among ambulatory patients. E.E.M.

disperse. To participate in the process of dispersion (q.v.)

dispersed farmsteads. Cf. farmsteads, dispersed.

dispersion. The primitive form of population movement, whereby mankind carried out the initial stages of populating the habitable globe. Its motivation is essentially similar to the movements of subhuman species. It is regulated largely by the conditions of the physical environment and represents fundamentally an almost instinctive escape from population pressure. It is a movement of expulsion rather than of attraction, having no true destination. It is exceedingly gradual, so slow that those participating in it are not conscious that any true movement is taking place.

disposition. A term used to cover the various ways in which a court gets rid of an individual arraigned before it. The court may dispose of a case by a dismissal, fine, jail sentence, probation, suspended sentence, prison sentence, capital punishment, commital to an institution for the insane or for mental defectives. J.L.G.

dissociate. To withdraw from, or to refuse to enter into, association, whether from intense hate, mild dislike, or mere indifference. F.H.H.

dissociation. (*psychological*) The procescs or state of mind in which there is isolation of one idea, memory or complex from some other idea, memory or complex, so that they seem to be independent of one another in the subject's thought-process. A dissociated complex is inaccesible to the current conscious self. There may be a cleavage or split in the personality, sometimes amounting to amnesia or to multiple personality, by which in alternating conversions the same individual is two or more persons at different times, each dissociated from the other. T.D.E.

dissuasion. The marshalling of arguments, sound or unsound, for the purpose of detaching others from any belief, theory, or line of action. F.E.L.

distance, ecological. The separation in space of two points, measured in terms of costs (including time-costs) of transporting a given unit of men or materials along available routes. J.A.Q.

distance, social. Cf. social distance.

distribution, age. Cf. age distribution.

district, business. Cf. business district.

district, congested. Cf. congested district.

district jail. Cf. jail, district.

divided self. Cf. self, divided.

divination. Practices aimed at foretelling the future with supernatural aid or by magical means, embracing astrology (q.v.), augury (q.v.), necromancy (q.v.), scalpulimancy (q.v.), scrying (q.v.), sortilege (q.v.), etc. G.P.M.

division of labor. Cf. labor, division of.

divorce. The legal dissolution of an officially recognized marriage relationship. Its purpose is to give relief to those individual cases where the usual rigid marital controls are onerous. The breaking of marriage bonds with group approval is probably as old as marriage itself. Most primitive peoples have allowed dissolution of marriage under some circumstances, although the mores differ. Divorce patterns themselves are a clue to the status of women. In older patriarchal families divorce was relatively unknown and rights of women were proportionately limited. The present approach toward equalitarian families has witnessed a related growth in divorce. Reasons for modern divorce vary greatly. The most common legal causes are adultery, desertion, cruelty, failure to support, and drunkenness. All of the States except South Carolina permit divorce, but the grounds permitting it vary greatly. The divorce rate (q.v.) is not uniform throughout the United States, although its rapid rise in recent decades is well known. At the present time there is a rough equivalent of one divorce to less than six marriages. J.H.E.

divorce rate. Cf. rate, divorce.

dizygotic twins. Cf. twins, dizygotic.

Dr. Welfare. A designation for the Negro federal relief case worker. It is an expression of what such workers mean in the eroded lives of mass Negroes in large border state areas. They developed an all-inclusive social therapy beneficial to this peculiarly underprivileged social class. W.R.C.

doctrine. The tenets of a philosophy or way of life, or of a religion; the guiding principles by which a sect or other special group regulates the conduct of its members. N.A.

dogma. A rigidly formulated, and firmly supported, doctrine (q.v.), frequently applied with derogatory implications to describe the doctrine or the religious tenets of another group. Implied in the term is the assumption of an ideology learned and repeated by rote without question regarding its applicability. N.A.

dole. A donation given by a private or public relief agency to supplement the income of an individual or family, generally at regular intervals and in standardized amounts determined by some established law or policy. The term applies specifically to the British system of unemployment relief, but is loosely used to cover any systematic allotment made wtihout corresponding return in labor or otherwise.

dolichocephalic. Characterized by a relatively narrow head, with a cephalic index (q.v.) of less than 77.   G.P.M.

dolmen. A stone structure, or megalith, from the West European Neolithic and Bronze Ages. It consists of three or more boulders set vertically on their long axes to form a chamber. A flat boulder or slab of rock is laid horizontally as a cap, thus forming a ceiling to the chamber. Many dolmens were originally covered with an earth mound, known as the tumulus. Dolmens frequently (possibly always) served as sepulchres.   E.A.H.

domain, eminent. Cf. eminent domain.

domestic relations court. Cf. court, domestic relations.

domestic servant. A paid worker who is employed by the head of the household to perform certain tasks and render personal services in the household. The domestic servant has often worked long hours, without standards and without protection by social legislation. She has usually been forced to accept a status of social inferiority, both on the job and in the community.   A.E.W.

domestic service. The performance of tasks and the rendering of personal services within the home by paid workers rather than entirely by members of the family group. Historically, domestic service has often been performed by convicts, redemptioners, Negroes (both slave and free) and by others of inferior status. Therefore while the largest occupation for women in America, it is also the least standardized and the most stigmatized and shunned.   A.E.W.

domestic system. A system of manufacturing introduced just prior to the invention of power driven machinery, in which raw materials were furnished to workers in their homes by a merchant who re-

tained title to the material, paid for the service of manufacture, and assumed responsibility for the sale of the finished product. This system was fostered by the expanding markets at the close of the Middle Ages and acted as a transition between individual handicraft and the factory and wage-systems which followed the industrial revolution.   J.W.M'C.

dominance. Ascendancy, taking precedence. In Mendel's law dominance is contrasted with recessive; in personality types dominance is contrasted with submission; in ecology dominance designates some superiority of one community over another.   O.W.

dominant position. The place of greatest honor or authority in a social heirarchy.   P.H.L.

dominant trait. Cf. trait, dominant.

dominant wish. Cf. wish, dominant.

dominated. Under the control of; subject to.   M.S.

domination. That type of social interaction (q.v.) in which the structures, functioning, or purposes of the dominator determine those of the dominated.   H.H.

donatio. A kind of matrimonial property which became common in the Roman Empire and was called "the gift for the sake of marriage" (*donatio propter nuptias*). It consisted in a portion of the husband's estate set apart for the wife in case of his death or her divorce without just cause. The donatio remained, with the residue of his property, under the husband's control. However, if the husband became insolvent, the law of Rome forbade the use the wife's donatio to pay his creditors.   W.G.

door of the dead. Cf. dead, door of the.

dormitory town. A type of satellite community primarily devoted to residential use, in which most of the wage earners are employed in the central city or its environs. Community participation is usually incomplete and supplemented by cultural and other services of the central city.   S.S.

double descent. Cf. descent, double.

double sampling. Cf. sampling, double.

double standard. Cf. standard, double.

dower. A widow's share or interest in the property of her deceased husband. G.P.M.

dowry. A payment made to the groom, on the occasion of a marriage, by the father or kinsman of the bride, or the property brought by the latter into marriage. Cf. bride-price.

drawing and quartering. A mediaeval mode of punishing those guilty of lese-majesty. It was accomplished by fastening the victim to a platform by an iron band around the arms and chest and by another around the thighs, then fastening a rope to each arm and leg and attaching the other end of the rope to a whipple-tree to which was hitched a horse. At command the four horses started off in four different directions until the body was pulled apart. Often this final act was preceded by torturing by fire in order to produce the greatest possible suffering.
                                                        J.L.G.

drive. A form of motivation in which the organism is impelled by factors essentially beyond its control, to act without foresight of ends.   M.S.

drive, prepotent. A drive having dominant influence over another drive when the appropriate conditions of both are present. Sometimes applied to innate drives that are supposed to control the conditioning of motives and hence the motivation of the adult.   M.S.

drive, socialized. A drive which has been conditioned through social experience so that it contributes to the social adjustment of its possessor.   M.S.

drive, unsocialized. A drive unconditioned through social experience.   M.S.

drug addiction. Voluntary regular use of a drug accompanied by a psychological attachment to its use, usually evidenced by distress or uneasiness when the drug is not being taken. In the underworld the term is usually used to apply to the use of morphine, heroin, opium or other opiates, and sometimes to marijuana and cocaine.   A.R.L.

dual organization. The organization of a tribe into two primary subdivisions or moieties (q.v.).   G.P.M.

dualism, ethical. The prevalence of one code of ethics governing relations with members of the same social group, and of another, and more lenient, code governing relations with outsiders.   G.P.M.

ducking stool. A stool or chair in which common scolds were formerly tied and plunged into water. It is mentioned in the Doomsday Book, and was extensively used throughout Great Britain from the 15th to the beginning of the 18th century. The last recorded instance of it was in England in 1809.   A.E.W.

duel. A combat with weapons between two persons. The term may apply to any such combat but, more especially, to pre-arranged combats in which a ritual of performance controls the behavior of the participants and their accessories. E.A.H.

dugout. (1) A canoe hollowed from a single log. (2) In pioneer American life, a dwelling excavated in an earth bank.   G.P.M.

dumb barter. A common practice among primitive peoples of exchanging goods for other commodities without the physical meeting of the traders involved. Modus operandi; traders of one tribe deposit goods offered at a known place and retire, whereupon traders of the second tribe appear, place their exchange goods beside the offered commodities and withdraw. First traders reappear, take proffered goods instead of their own if satisfied, otherwise take back their own, and leave. Traders of second tribe reappear to collect their products, exchanged and original.   E.E.M.

dumbbell tenement. A type of "old law" tenement still common in New York, so called because narrow air shafts between buildings gave the plan of each floor a narrow-waisted dumbbell shape. Although the design won an early prize competition it is one of the worst residential building forms in the world.   S.S.

duress. A legal expression for coercion (q.v.) or threat of violence.   T.D.E.

duty. Behavior expected of one by virtue of his position, status, or occupation, or by virtue of membership in certain groups. The expectation of conformity to the mores.   A.R.L.

dwelling. A building designed or occupied as the living quarters for one or more families, or households, usually equipped with cooking, bathing, toilet, and, where necessary, heating facilities. Usually thought of as a detached single-family house.

dwelling, alley. Cf. alley dwelling.

dynamic. Energetic, forceful; introducing a new "force", a factor previously considered as outside and irrelevant to the situation, and now demanding re-equilibration. The terminology has been incorrectly carried over from physics to social sciences. Both static (latent) energy and kinetic energy are dynamic; but social philosophers have set off "dynamic" against "static", instead of kinetic vs. static (q.v.). The word is much abused colloquially as a favorable epithet for anything or anybody vigorous and energetic.   T.D.E.

dynamic civilization. Cf. civilization, dynamic.

dynamics. Change, force, motion, interaction, as opposed (in social references) to statics, meaning forces at rest or in equilibrium.   H.A.P.

dynamics, social. Cf. social dynamics.

dynastic incest. Cf. incest, dynastic.

dysgenic. Unfavorable to the perpetuation and intensification of desirable biological traits. The opposite of "eugenic" (q.v.). The term may be applied to qualities of the germ plasm, or to forms of marriage or mating.

dysgenic trend. Change involving deterioration of hereditary qualities of a population. Cf. eugenics.   M.K.

E

ecological competition. Cf. competition, ecological.

ecological concentration. Density of population as residentially distributed in an area. A high degree of concentration indicates great congestion of inhabited dwelling quarters. W.C.H.

ecological concepts. Cf. concepts, ecological.

ecological distance. Cf. distance, ecological.

ecological gradient. (1) Tne rate of increase or decrease of an ecological variable along a line of ecological distance. (2) The curve that represents this rate of increase or decrease. J.A.Q.

ecological interaction. That process of reciprocal modification, including both competitive and cooperative aspects, by which individual organisms or groups influence one another indirectly and impersonally by affecting some limited source of environmental supply upon which the others depend. J.A.Q.

ecological mobility. Cf. mobility, ecological.

ecological position. Cf. position, ecological.

ecological symbiosis. Cf. symbiosis, ecological.

ecology. The study of spatial-functional areal patterns that arise and change through processes of ecological interaction. J.A.Q.
   The study of the relations between organisms and their habitats; specifically, in anthropology, of the adaptation of human cultures to their geographical environments. Cf. anthropogeography. G.P.M.

ecology, human. That branch of science which treats of the reciprocal relations between man and environment: it includes human autecology, the study of reciprocal relations between the individual and his environment; and human synecology, the study of reciprocal relations between groups and their environments. Within the social sciences it includes human geography, the study of direct reciprocal relations between individuals (or groups) and their physical environment; and interactional ecology, the study of spatial-functional areal patterns that arise and change through processes of ecological interaction. J.A.Q.

ecology, social. Cf. social ecology.

ecology, urban. The study of the spatial distribution of people and institutions in cities from the developmental, non-moral, naturalistic point of view. Basic data include: "natural areas", individual and institutional competition for place in space, "expanding concentric" zones, spot maps, gradients, real estate values and trends, degrees of concentration, kinds of dominance and centralization, populational segregation, etc. This approach has permitted new interpretations of the growth and expansion of American cities, but ecology has up to date less to offer toward the understanding of urban decline, decentralization, and dispersion. W.C.H.

economic. Of or pertaining to the science of economics, or to the activities of producing and consuming. Also, frugal, saving in nature. E.E.M.

economic dependency. Cf. dependency, economic.

economic determinism. The theory that the dominant "forces" in social life and social change are economic interests, embracing land (natural resources), technology, property and other social relations involved in production and distribbution of wealth. The term is synonymous with "the economic interpretation of history." The theory was given its modern form and vogue by Karl Marx. As currently formulated, the theory emphasizes producer interests and producing classes, and could fairly be described as a producerist interpretation of history. Consumer interests are virtually ignored by economic determinists.   S.E.

economic disorganizaiton. Cf. disorganization, economic.

economic insecurity. Cf. insecurity, economic.

economic planning. The guidance and control of the economic life of people according to some prearranged pattern in order to achieve certain defined goals. Comprehensive economic planning began in 1928 in Russia with the instigation of the first Five Year Plan. The National Socialist regime in Germany adopted modified economic planning in order to achieve the re-armament necessary to pursue its policy of conquest. The demands of World War II forced economic planning upon all combatant nations. Economic planning requires four things: the definitions of the goals to be achieved, the estimation of the kind and quantity of goods necessary to achieve these goals, the marshalling of the necessary productive forces (capital, manpower and materials), and some system or organization to allocate and control materials for production and consumption. The basic dilemma of economic planning as visualized in the United States is to provide for economic planning without curtailing the economic or political freedom of the individual.   J.W.M'C.

economic status. Cf. status, economic.

economics. A study of the ways in which men organize natural resources, cultural achievements, and their own labor, to sustain and promote their material welfare.   E.E.M.

economy. The process of keeping a budget or balancing accounts or being thrifty; or, the actual structure of resources, intake, outgo, and distribution in nay given group situation. Social economy: The study of the structure of the actual and desirable means of organizing, conserving and utilizing social resources (inanimate and animate and superorganic), with organic community welfare and normal personal and family standards of living as criteria; or, the actual organization and utilization of social resources of materials and energy in any given economic habitat, area, nation or culture pattern.   T.D.E.

economy, collecting. Cf. collecting economy.

economy, deficit. A deficit economy or "pain economy" means an organization of social resources in relation to a population in which lack of natural resources such as land, raw materials, power, and climate, and/or lack of knowledges, techniques, talents, attitudes, or social organization, create a situation which will not support a "minimum of health and decency" for the entire population. "Population pressure" is felt: it is an economy of scarcity. Any who become wealthy must do so at the expense of others' destitution or extrusion from the group. If the situation is stabilized, the mores, morality, theology are affected in the direction of resignation, consolation, submission, by the poor. Sacrifice is glorified and pain and misery are taken for granted as God's will.   T.D.E.

economy, handicraft. Cf. handicraft economy.

economy, pain. Cf. economy, deficit.

economy, pleasure. Cf. economy, surplus.

economy, surplus. A surplus economy is one in which there are adequate natural resources accessible, and adequate cultural techniques for their development and distribution, so that everyone may live above the minimum of health and decency, and many may live in comfort without exploiting others. This sort of social economy may eventuate in an "economy of abundance." This ideal has hardly been realized anywhere on any large scale, but is potentially present. In many areas the resources are accessible and so are techniques of production; but failures of social organization and techniques of distribution still tend to produce deficit conditions. Even in an economy of only potential surplus, virtues of deprivation and restraint are less at a premium, and positive pleasures and luxuries are sought with less inhibition by all. A surplus economy is a "pleasure economy." T.D.E.

economy of abundance. Cf. economy, surplus.

economy of scarcity. Cf. economy, deficit.

editing data. Inspection of schedule entries to see that they are accurate, complete, consistent, and uniformly arranged. May include coding. M.PT.

education. The acculturation of the newer and/or younger members of society by the older. The institution-process whereby the accumulated ideas, standards, knowledge, and techniques of society are transferred to, or imposed upon, the rising generation. Ordinarily, education is conscious, purposeful, and deliberate. There is, however, such a thing as unconscious or incidental education, just as there is such a thing as the education of the old by the young. The essence of education is the inculcation of one individual with the mental accumulations of another.

education, adult. Education offered to those above the usual school-leaving age, outside of or in addition to the regular curricula of public and private educational institutions. Adult education in America was first offered in the form of vocational education for workers. Then followed Americanization classes in the public school system established to aid the foreigner to meet the educational requirements for citizenship. More recently classes for adults have been organized

under public and private auspices to teach hobbies, crafts, literature, art, and political and economic subjects. Generally speaking, any type of formal education which grants a degree, issues a certificate, or gives academic credit does not constitute adult education. Nevertheless, in Scandinavian countries adult education is so extensive that the *volkes schule* must be reckoned as part of the educational institution of the nation. J.W.M'C.

education, workers'. Education for adult workers after working hours in cultural, vocational and economic and political subjects. The development of workers' education began in the early decades of the 19th century, as an outgrowth of the interest in the wage-earning population shown by such groups as the Methodists and Quakers, and Cooperatives. and the trade unions. In America workers' education has been developed slowly, partly on account of the development of free public education. Radical political parties and some of the trade unions have established workers' schools, but their work has been sporadic and uncoordinated. The curriculum offered in workers' schools in both England and the United States has been the source of much debate, frequently of open conflict. Some have wanted the course of study to be strictly vocational, others have wanted it to be economic and political even to the point of training in techniques of strike and political conflict. A few have advocated purely cultural subjects. No general trend is apparent so far as America is concerned. In England economic and political instruction has been most important in recent years. J.W.M'C

educational sociology. Cf. sociology, educational.

effort, antagonistic. Directed activity which tends to eliminate or neutralize other activities. M.C.E.

effort, mutual. Cf. mutual effort.

egalitarianism. The doctrine that all so-called social classes contain approximately the same relative proportions of genius, talent, mediocrity and defectiveness. F.D.W.

ego. That part of the personality (q.v.)

which keeps the person in conscious recognition of the facts of reality.   H.H.

ego, super-. Those aspects of the personality (q.v.) which threaten or impose a sense of guilt or psychic suffering and which determine idealism; essentially the same as conscience.   H.H.

egocentricity. The tendency of the individual to make himself the center of the universe, expecting the world to revolve around his ego, and ignoring to a large degree the rights and needs of others.   A.E.W.

ego-centrism. Cf. centrism, ego-.

egoism. (1) One's persistence in centering his activities around what he considers to be his own advantage. It does not imply a complete disregard for others, for it implies a concern for the well-being of those whose happiness is considered necessary to one's own. What others claim as their right, however, is ignored. (2) Doctrine that all conduct is explicable in terms of self-concern. (3) Undue, i.e., exclusive esteem for one's own opinion. B.M.

egoism, collective. Cf. collective egoism.

egoism, national. Cf. national egoism.

egoistic. (1) Characterized by egoism (q.v), and usually restricted to describe the attitude of one using others for his own happiness. (2) Referring to the doctrine of egoism (q.v.), and thus opposed to altruistic.   B.M.

egotic. Having reference to the ego; selfish, but without any moralistic slur in the word. To be distinguished from "egotistic", which is more conceited than is "egotic"; also from egoistic, which while less adverse as epithet than "egotistic" or "selfish", suggests self-consciousness and self-reference. An egotic wish, impulse, etc., refers to personal pleasures of body or status.   T.D.E.

egotism, collective. Cf. collective egotism.

eidolism. Ghostism. The body of the belief about disembodied souls, or ghosts

(q.v.). It is convenient to distinguish this stage from animism. Cf. ghost cult.
A.G.K.

eidolon. A ghost (q.v.).

élan vital. The inner drive or impulse that leads to evolutionary development in definite directions and toward consistently changing forms. The central dynamic principle of "creative evolution" (q.v.).

electrocution. A method of capital punishment alternative to beheading, hanging, etc., based upon the theory that it is less painful, more certain, and less liable to accident than the older methods. It is administered by strapping the convict to a heavy chair wired to conduct an electric current of high voltage to electrodes applied one to the head and another to the lower leg of the prisoner.   J.L.G.

elements, social. Cf. social elements.

elimination. Physiologically, the term relates to the removal of wastes from the body, and in social relationships it has corresponding application; it also has application in various methods of research.
N.A.

élite. An aristocracy selected by birth in olden times, by ability to succeed at others' expense, regardless of means, under the competitive conditions of capitalism or the conflict conditions of war and fascism; conceivably chosen by planned tests for relevant intelligence, and aptitude and trained for responsible service. An established élite may prevent dangerous opposition by alert selection of rising talent and recruiting from its personnel those who are to share their power and succeed them. Class doctrines and racial ethnocentrism often assume that traits characteristic of the self-made élite are inherent in their offspring; even if true, such traits would not necessarily become overt in the absence of adequate conditioning.   T.D.E.

élites, circulation of. Movement of superior individuals from an inferior class to membership in an élite, one of a number of upper groups in a society who are distinguished by intelligence, aggressiveness, shrewdness, cruelty, or some other quality or combination of qualities. The ruling élite at a given time may dominate the upper class and its society through control of economic, military, religious, or ballot power. The term thus implies both the movement of individuals into élite groups and the movement of élite groups into and out of positions of societal dominance   A.M'C.L.

Elizabethan poor law. Cf. law, poor, Elizabethan.

Elmira System. The first system of reformatory management introduced in the United States. The system takes its name from America's first reformatory founded in 1876 at Elmira, New York. The system was designed for the reformation of young offenders by means of vocational training. Inspiration for the system came from the so-called Irish system which established a system of marking in which prisoners could earn points and privileges by exemplary behavior. Refinements of the Elmira system are due to the first administrator of Elmira, Z. R. Brockway. Under his direction daily schooling, occupational training, sanitation, military drill and moral training were added to the system.   J.W.M'C.

elopement. The practice according to which a man and a woman run away together informally, sometimes existing as a recognized mode of contracting marriage, sometimes occurring sporadically as a means of evading parental objections, requisite property payments, or other obstacles to an ordinary marriage.   G.P.M.

embezzlement. The illegal and fraudulent appropriation to one's own use of money or goods that have been intrusted to one's supervision or care by another. Embezzlement is distinguished from larceny in that the property in the case of embezzlement is intrusted to the embezzler; in the case of larceny the property was never legally in his possession.   J.M.R.

emergence. What happens when, out of the combination of known factors, a phenomenon arises which was unpredictable from the known attributes of the separate constituent elements. It can be noted on the chemical level; in astronomy (novæ); at critical points in physics; in the conception of an organism from two cells; in the mutations of species; in consummatory responses and conversions; in moments of insight into new configurations or discoveries and inventions; in creative poetry and arts; in creative discussion; in cultural cross fertilization (q.v.); and in crises and revolutions. The principle of emergence provides the only sense in which, assuming conservation of matter and energy, there can be anything new under the sun, at every point-instant in the total space-time manifold. Cf. critical moment.   T.D.E.

emergent evolution. Cf. evolution, emergent.

emigrant. One who participates in a movement of emigration (q.v.).

emigration. A population movement otherwise called immigration (q.v.), looked at from the point of view of the country of origin (q.v.).

eminent domain. The right of the State to take private property for public use upon payment of reasonable compensation.   F.W.K.

eminent man. Cf. man, eminent.

emotion. A complex state of an individual in which certain ideas, feelings, and usually motor expressions combine to produce a condition recognizable as such by the individual and frequently by others.   J.P.E.

emotional. Pertaining to or having a tendency to arouse an emotion in an individual. More than ordinarily inclined to experience, or be governed by, emotions.   J.P.E.

emotional dependency. Cf. dependency, emotional.

empathy. A variety of, or a contrast to, sympathetic behavior (q.v.).   H.B.

empire. A type of political organization involving a powerful central state and one or (usually) more dependences, held in subjection. Empire is the logical and characteristic product of conquest (q.v.). Typically the central state is on a higher cultural level than the provinces, particularly with respect to its economic, military, and political organization. The status of the provinces is definitely inferior to the central state, and their economic systems are regarded as tributary to that of the central power. The social and legal systems of the subsidiaries are frequently left as untouched as is consonant with their political and economic submission. Frequently the former ruling personnel is left in power, and simply integrated into the imperial system. Tribute is the primary objective. An empire differs from a colonial system (Cf. colonization) in several important particulars. In the first place, colonies are actually or prospectively settled by immigrants from the home state, as either the numerically preponderant or socially dominating element. Second, while the colonies are looked upon as politically subordinate to the home state, and their economy is often regulated with central prosperity in mind, yet the colonists themselves are not regarded as an inferior breed, being as they are an off-shoot of, and biologically related to, the home people. Third, colonies are ordinarily allowed a greater degree of self-government than provinces, and characteristically develop in the direction of practical political independence.

empiricism. The theory that knowledge arises solely out of experience. While generally accepted in this broad sense and contrasted with intuitionalism, it is sometimes opposed to rationalism conceived as the law of reason, and to the law of causation.   M.Pm.

employee, household. Cf. household employee.

employer-employee relation. The latest stage in the evolution of labor relations, to which modern industry is now endeavoring to adjust itself. Having passed through the slave-owner phase of relationship, then the lord-serf, followed by the master-man or mistress-maid relation, both employer and employee are now being educated to accept a more business-like, a more limited and a more democratic relation.   A.E.W.

employer's liability. A legal term denoting responsibility of an employer for an accident to an employee. This responsibility would become the subject of court action in which the burden of proof was upon the employee to give evidence in justifying claim for damages from the employer. The term became obsolescent when workmen's compensation abolished the necessity for demonstration of negligence and established the injured employee's claim to damages as a right in accordance with the legally established system of insurance. Cf. workmen's compensation.   M.VK.

employment, household. Cf. household employment.

emulation. Rivalry for socially acceptable goals; a combination of competition and imitation in which the more successful competitors are consciously used by others as models in order to achieve socially approved success and its satisfactions. But in emulation all may succeed, so the scarcity-characteristic of competition (that the objective cannot be achieved by all the competitors) is not present.   T.D.E.

encomienda. A grant of land to colonists in Spanish America, giving them the right to subject the aboriginal inhabitants to forced labor in return for the obligation of evangelizing and governing them. G.P.M.

endemic. (1) Of diseases: habitually or generally prevalent throughout a specified geographical area, continuously affecting a considerable proportion of the population; opposed to epidemic. (2) Of plants and animals; native to, or naturalized within, a specified country or region; opposed to exotic.   H.E.J.

endocannibalism. Cannibalism (q.v.) when practiced on members of the same social group.   G.P.M.

endogamy. The rule restricting marriage to members of the same tribe, village, caste, or other social group. Cf. exogamy.   G.P.M.

endogenic criminal. Cf. criminal, endogenic.

energy, social. Cf. social energy.

engineering, social. Cf. social engineering.

entity. The most inclusive of all genera; a class including all the actual and possible objects of perception or conception, regarded as being capable of definition and classification.   H.H.

entity, social. Cf. social entity.

entropy, social. Cf. social entropy.

enumeration district (*census*). The area canvassed by census enumerators for the decennial censuses. As a rule, one district is assigned to each enumerator.
                                                    M.Pt.

enumerator. One who enumerates or secures information from the population, e.g., census enumerator. Often used synonymously with interviewer, canvasser, field worker, field agent, or investigator for social surveys.   M.Pt.

environment. The field of effective stimulation and interaction for any unit of living matter. Within a cell, each molecule environs the others; within a tissue, each cell environs the other cells; within an organ each tissue environs the others; within an organism each organ environs and stimulates the others and is in turn stimulated thereby. Within the "mind" each unit of mentation operates in a field of stimulation (or inhibition, "negative" stimulation) from other areas of neural and glandular tension. The individual's environment has been classified as physiographic, bionomic, economic, cultural (material and non-material, institutional and symbolic) and personal-social. In a group, each person is part of each other person's personal-social environment. A group as a whole is environed as is an individual, and also by other groups. Environment is also definable as the field of adjustment of any responsive organism from molecule to United Nations. As such it merges with the ecological idea of habitat (q.v.). The conception of the planet, the solar system, and the universe as mankind's habitat-environment (forecast in religious poetry) may prove a revolutionary vision (Gestalt) when accepted as a working ideology.   T.D.E.

environment, geographic. Cf. geographic environment.

environment, social. Cf. social environment.

ephemeral group. Cf. group, ephemeral.

epidemic. (1) Of diseases: spreading rapidly through a population and affecting a large number at once, but for a limited period. (2) Of psychological and social phenomena: spreading rapidly through a population, as, an epidemic of fear, an epidemic of suicide.   H.E.J.

(3) A condition of contagion in which by contact a disease, an idea, or emotion spreads from person to person. The result may be an emergency as in the case of a plague. A social epidemic may involve the spread of an ism in a period of unrest in consequence of which the usual pattern of life may be disturbed or upset. If very widespread it is called ·pandemic or plague.   N.A.

epidemic, social. Cf. epidemic.

epidemiology. The science and art of mastering epidemics, including analyzing the possible routes of infection: viz., public (milk, water, markets), private (direct contagion), or by carrier (animal, insect, human); and of devising means for blocking the actual routes between the infected and the uninfected, by disinfection, injection, screening, filtering, quarantine, carrier control, public sanitation, inspection, condemnation, masking, embargo, segregation, etc.   T.D.E.

equality. Similarity of social status, rights, responsibilities, opportunities; an ideal principle realizable so far as social structure is concerned but conflicting with the results of the principles of liberty and competition, which lead to social selection, gradation, inequality. There is equal opportunity to become equal. Equality is a goal of social capillarity; the élite are not interested.   T.D.E.

equilibration. The state of being in balance or the process of maintaining equal poise among forces or factors.   N.L.S.

equilibrium. A state of proximate rest resulting from the equalization of forces; a poise or balance produced by the mutual counteraction of two or more forces. N.L.S.

equilibrium, social. Cf. social equilibrium.

equity. In connection with property: (1) broadly, any interest which will receive recognition in a court of equity, whether or not such interest rests on legal ownership; (2) specifically, the interest, usually expressed in money, of the equitable owner of a property over and above all liens against the property.

erogenous zone. A portion of the body having the potentiality of sexual stimulation. An endowment found more extensively in the female than the male body.   E.R.G.

erotic. Having to do with the stimulation or satisfaction of sexual passion or interest.   E.R.G.

error, compensating. Cf. compensating error.

error, constant (*statistical*). Cf. constant error.

error, curve of. Cf. curve of error.

escape mechanism, Cf. mechanism, escape.

escheat. A reversion or forfeiture of lands to the lord, the crown or the state occasioned by death of owner without heirs, or legal penalty for failure of some sort on part of owner.   E.E.M.

espionage. In law the act of covertly obtaining for a foreign government a military secret, in time of war or peace. Also used to cover practices in industrial strife by which one side obtains by covert methods information held secret by the other.   R.N.B.

esprit-de-corps. The "spirit of the body" or the group; morale or loyalty. The fidelity attitude of members of a group for one another and for the group interest.   N.A.

esthetics. The science and philosophy of beauty.   L.P.E.

estrangement. An increase of social distance, a cooling of affectional attitudes, usually referring to person-to-person or person-to-group relations. A step beyond isolation (q.v.) and misunderstanding; a step short of conflict (q.v.). One is hurt or grieved or bewildered, possibly resentful, but not hateful.   T.D.E.

étatism. Is the policy and process of integrating the governmental and economic functions of a nation under a unified but not necessarily autocratic direction. Its ideological base is the concept that the welfare of the state—be it autocrat, oligarch, or demos—depends as much upon economic as political integration and hence centralized control.   D.E.W.

eternalism. The concept of reality as unchangeable or eternal Being. In philosophy it is the ideology of Being in contrast to that of Becoming. In sociology and ehtics it is a term used in opposition to temporalism which considers incessant change as the true reality. From the idealistic point of view eternalism and temporalism are reconciled and constitute a synthesis. J.D.

ethical dualism. Cf. dualism, ethical.

ethics. The study of values and of their relations to action patterns and action programs. Those phases of sociology which deal with the mores, with social forces, with maladjustment, disorganization, social problems, reform movements, and social progress come properly within the scope of ethics. When used alone, without such modifiers as "social," the term "ethics" usually refers to the philosophy of right and wrong conduct. H.H.

ethics, Christian. That approach to social ethics which accepts as the fundamental criterion of value the teachings of Jesus and of the Christian Church.   H.H.

ethics, philosophical. That approach to ethics which seeks primarily for logically satisfactory concepts and propositions, with only subordinate reference to practical social problems. Cf. ethics, social.   H.H.

ethics, social. Cf. social ethics.

ethnic. Having to do with the ethnos (q.v.); characterized by unity of both race and nationality.

ethnic consciousness. Cf. consciousness, ethnic.

ethnocentrism. An emotional attitude which holds one's own group, race, or society to be superior to other racial or cultural entities, combined with contempt for the outsider and his ways; race-centeredness, but correctly used with broader connotations.   W.E.G.

ethnogenic. Having to do with the origin and development of ethnic groups.

ethnography. The branch of cultural anthropology (q.v.) concerned with the descriptive study of individual cultures, particularly those of primitive or preliterate peoples. Cf. ethnology.   G.P.M.

ethnology. The scientific study of ethnic groups. Cultural anthropology (q.v.), with special reference to the comparative study of the cultures (q.v.) of the various existing or only recently extinct peoples of the earth. Cf. archeology; ethnography.   G.P.M.

ethnos. A group bound together and identified by ties and traits of both race (q.v.) and nationality (q.v.). Numerous words beginning with this root are variously used, frequently in a sense almost synonymous with those beginning with the root "race" or "anthro-," or even "culture." Properly, terms built upon this root should apply exclusively to groups where the racial bonds and the cultural bonds are so interwoven that the members of the group itself are ordinarily unconscious of them, and unspecialized outsiders tend to make no distinction between them. Such groups are the logical product of human evolution under conditions of relative isolation and segregation. Cf. people.

ethos. The sum of the characteristic culture traits by which one group is differentiated and individualized from other groups.

etiology of crime. Cf. crime, etiology of.

etiquette. A trait of folklore, operating actually as a form of social control, regulating the outward relations of the individual and the group, and thus his external liberty. Closely connected with hierarchically organized society, etiquette is opposite ot convention (q.v.) which controls internal liberty; also distinguished from convention by its express rules, sometimes a written protocol.   J.H.B.

eugenic. Tending to improve the hereditary qualities of the members of society. May be applied to either physical elements or behavior patterns.

eugenics. The science based upon the principles of human heredity which has for its purpose the improving of the race.   E.R.G.

eunuch. A castrated human male.   G.P.M.

euphoria. A general feeling of well-being and sensuous satisfaction.

euphorimeter. Any paper-and-pencil instrument for obtaining approximate measurements of happiness (euphoria), using a scale in which zero represents the dividing line between happiness and unhappiness.   H.H.

euthanasia. The theory or practice of "mercy deaths"—permitting physicians or other socially authorized persons to give a lethal dose of medicine to persons painfully and incurably ill or hopelessly defective from birth. At present this theory is opposed to the law and the medical code of ethics; but a sample poll has shown that some 46 percent of the people giving opinions favored euthanasia under government supervision.   S.C.M.

ever-normal granary. The term used by Secretary of Agriculture Wallace and others to summarize a general agricultural program which would stabilize agricultural supplies through acreage control and government financed storage of surpluses in years when yields were good and release of these surpluses for use in years when yields were short.

evil eye. The alleged or assumed power to do harm to another by looking at him.

This belief (q.v.), is widespread among groups on a fairly high cultural level, as for instance some of the contemporary Mediterranean peoples. The quality of the individual that gives him this power is ill-defined, but among groups that are preponderantly dark-eyed, it may be simply the possession of blue eyes. In its broad application, the evil eye may be given through other means than a glance, such as a specified gesture. Charms against the evil eye are commonly worn by persons and even animals where this belief is prevalent. These may take the form of blue beads, a baby's shoe, a piece of garlic, etc., etc. The term may be also used to refer to the spell itself, as in the expression, "to give one the evil eye."

evolution. A process of change in which each succeeding stage has a connection with the preceding stage; a growth or development involving continuity.

evolution, creative. Cf. creative evolution.

evolution, cultural. The development of a culture (or of given culture traits) from simpler, less integrated forms to more complex and integrated forms, by a continuous process.   R.E.B.

evolution, cumulative. The resultant growth, modification and development of associated and related aspects of society, whose combined changes terminate in a general effect.   M.C.E.

evolution, emergent. Biological (or social) change by mutation, the emergence of something brand-new from new, unique combintaions of preexisting elements, at critical point-moments. Cf. emergence.   T.D.E.

evolution, personal. The growth and expansive unfolding of personality, along lines indicated in simple form during early childhood; the form taken being a comination of inherent characteristics and the influence of social and physical environmental forces.   M.C.E.

evolution, social. Cf. social evolution.

evolution, universal. The general comprehensive unfolding which is occurring in all the aspects of life, including all phenomena which may or may not affect social life.   M.C.E.

evolutionary. Displaying tendencies toward developmental changes growing out of previous conditions or situations. M.C.E.

evolutionary change. Continuous, orderly change in a definite direction, in a process of adaptation or adjustment to a given environment which itself may be varying, with an increasing differentiation, or complexity of structure, corresponding to a differentiation of function. Evolution implies the "unfolding" of forces potentially present from the beginning. What constitutes the specific dynamic factors of evolution depends upon the level of organization dealt with—inorganic, organic or super-organic (social).   S.J.

excess condemnation. The practice of condemning (q.v.) a larger area than is actually needed for the public improvement in question, with the purpose of taking advantage of the increased land values that result from the improvement itself.

excess development. Growth to such a great size as to bring about disharmony with the environment.   L.P.E.

exchange, medium of. Cf. medium of exchange.

exclude. To shut out, to eliminate by not permitting entry. Applied socially at the frontiers between in-groups of whatever size and out-group members. To be distinguished from extrude, to thrust out, to eliminate a former member or intruder by driving him forth—after which he is also excluded.   T.D.E.

exclusion. As related to population movement (q.v.), the definite prohibition of the immigration of specified foreign groups or individuals.

exclusion, policy of. Maintenance of homogeneity or integrity in a group by keeping out persons whose behavior or quality is thought to threaten its solidarity. By extension, a policy of exclusion includes extrusion of undesirables for the same reason.   T.D.E.

exclusive. As applied to groups, careful restriction of membership on the basis of criteria which are deemed honorific, such as: birth, money, status and so on. Snobbish.   A.R.L.

exhibitionism. An exaggerated tendency to display one's individual traits or features before a group, or the general public. In common usage, the term frequently refers to the unconventional display of sex features. In a general sense, it may be merely a form of extreme vanity.

exogamy. The convention, theory, or practice of marrying outside of certain locally defined and prescribed webs of relationship—the family, clan or race for example. For instance, among the Crow Indians exogamy is the inviolable rule, marriage within the clan being regarded as highly improper.   F.E.L.

exogenic criminal. Cf. criminal, exogenic.

exorcism. The driving out from the body of intrusive spirits or elements believed to be the cause of evil behavior or malaise.   E.A.H.

exotic. Brought in from a foreign country; not native to, or naturalized within, a specified country or region.   H.E.J.

expanded personality. Cf. personality, expanded.

expansion, group. The enlargement of a social unit either numerically or territorially.

expectation, social. Cf. social expectation.

expectation of life. A conventional function of the life table symbolized by $\overset{\circ}{e}_x$ and representing the "mean after-lifetime" or average number of years of life still remaining to persons attaining a specified age under given schedules of age-specific mortality rates. Cf. life table.   C.V.K.

experience, conscious. Attitudes, interests, or other qualitative data which are knowable through the senses even though they are not completely or directly measurable by scales or tests.   H.A.P.

experiential attitude. Cf. attitude, experiential.

experimental method. That branch of induction which attempts to confirm or disprove some tentative conclusion by repeated observations or demonstrations.   H.A.P.

experimentation. Cf. experimental method.

expert, the. A person having a special skill. One who is widely informed in a specific area of knowledge or who is especially qualified to perform special types of work.   N.A.

expiation. A theory of the purpose of punishment for crime based originally upon the belief that crime aroused the anger of the gods against the whole group, and that the only way to mollify that anger was to destroy the offender. Latterly the term has been widened in its meaning to include the turning away of the anger of the community at the offender. As thus used it is almost synonymous with retribution.   J.L.G.

explanation. Cf. principle; causation.

exploitation. The utilization of a subordinate group (as wage earners, female sex, Negro race), by a group in a superordinate position (as employers, male sex, white race), for its own economic or other advantage.   K.DP.L.

exploration. A preliminary and unrepresentative sampling study of any social unit, in order to ascertain the chief elements composing it, and as a rule, to prepare the way either for a systematic general survey, or for some intensive inquiry respecting one or more aspects of the unit.   G.M.F.

exposure. (1) Infanticide (q.v.), by abandoning newborn children in exposed or unfrequented places; (2) the practice of depositing the corpses of the dead in similar places to be destroyed by wild animals or the elements. Cf. burial.   G.P.M.
(3) Display of parts of the body in view of others.

expression, mimetic. A variety of sympathetic behavior (q.v.).   H.B.

extended family. Cf. family, extended.

extradition. The procedure by which a person who commits a crime in one jurisdiction and flees into another can be followed and arrested in the latter with its consent.

(1) Interstate extradition. The Constitution of the United States, several acts of Congress, and the statutes of the several states provide that a person charged with crime in one state who flees from that state into another may be extradited to the former. In order to be extradited the person (a) must be judicially "charged" with a crime in the demanding state; (b) must not be charged with a crime against the state to which he has fled; (c) must have been in the demanding state in order to have "fled from justice."

(2) International extradition. By treaties between the United States and most foreign countries provision is made for the extradition of fugitives from justice in specified cases. The several American states cannot act in this matter.   N.F.C.

extrapolation. The estimation, from two or more known values of a variable, of some unknown value which either precedes or follows all the known values. Thus, for example, one might estimate the population of the United States in 1960 from the known population in 1940, 1930, 1920, and so on.   P.H.F.

extra-social. Not involving human relationships.   P.F.C.

extroversion. The act of turning outward toward external things. The term at present most frequently relates to those individuals whose spontaneous interests and concerns are found in the world about them—in persons, events and physical nature. Such individuals aret called extroverts.   W.G.

extrovert personality. Cf. personality, extrovert.

exuvial magic. Cf. magic, exuvial.

F

Fabian socialism. Cf. socialism, Fabian.

face-to-face group. Cf. group, face-to-face.

facial index. Cf. index, facial.

fact. Any demonstrated, or demonstrable, item of reality.

fact, social. Cf. social fact.

fact-finding. Assuming that a fact is a phenomenon which has been defined by repeated and closely agreeing observations or measurements, fact-finding is the systematic and accurate assembling of social data with reference to certain social problems, policies, or trends. It is the first stage incident to a social survey or project in social research.   G.M.F.

faction. A type of conflict group, partisan in aim, of more or less fluid make-up and transitory nature, which frequently develops within communities and established organizations out of internal conflict situations.   K.DP.L.

factor. A cause, determinant, or necessary condition of an event or change. Less commonly the word is used to designate a component of a situation, whether with or without reference to its causal significance. Classifications of factors vary with the frame of reference. Thus, we may subsume causal factors under the three categories of culture, hereditary or original nature, and physiographic environment; or under the specialized group interests (in the sense of goal-centered activities) found in a situation; or again under the specified categories of behavior and experience, as thought, feeling, action, attitude, purpose. Factors as components are illustrated, in addition, by types of interaction in a social situation—competition, conflict, cooperation, etc.; or, in terms of personnel, by the rôles of the individual, the primary group, and special public or integrative organization sharing in a common undertaking.   S.E.

factorial analysis. The breakdown of a situation or phenomenon into its factors, as for example, into the underlying cultural, hereditary, and geographic determinants. A factorial analysis may follow a single approach or, instead, a combination of two or more approaches, such as are indicated under factor (q.v.). The latter would be a polydimensional analysis. Where interest centers on the elements rather than the determinants of a situation, componential analysis is a suitable designation.   S.E.

factory farm. Cf. farm, large scale.

factory system. The system of manufacturing characterized by the use of power driven machinery, housed under one roof and owned by the entrepreneur, or other owner, who hires men for wages to operate the machines. This system was the outgrowth of the discovery of new sources of power on the one hand and the invention of new types of machinery on the other. The origin of the factory system in England may be roughly placed at about 1750.   J.W.M C.

fad. A passing fancy or novelty interest. It may relate to slang phrases, types of jokes, modes of conduct, dress, or other phenomena. Fads originate generally and spread most rapdily in areas of high stimulation: Hollywood or Broadway. They are most likely to be associated with the interests of leisure or play. Cf. fashion.   N.A.

fakir. An oriental religious ascetic. One who renounces all property, lives on charity, devotes himself to religious contemplation and prayer, and sometimes performs thaumaturgical "miracles." Cf. thaumaturgy.   E.A.H.

familial. Connected with family life or pattern.   P.F.C.

familial behavior. Cf. behavior, familial.

familiar spirit. A guardian spirit (q.v.), or an evil or malicious spirit controlled by a sorcerer. Cf. witchcraft.   G.P.M.

family. The basic social institution. One or more men living with one or more women in a socially-sanctioned and more or less enduring sex relationship, with socially-recognized rights and obligations, together with their offspring. The four general forms (or types), in their order of known frequency, are: monogamy, polygyny, polyandry, group marriage.
                                          R.E.B.

family, composite. A social group comprising two or more related nuclear families (q.v.) who reside in a common household; an extended family (q.v.) or a polygynous family.   G.P.M.

family, extended. A social group consisting of several related individual families, especially those of a man and his sons or of a woman and her daughters, residing in a single large dwelling or a cluster of smaller ones.   G.P.M.

family, joint. Extended family (q.v.).

family, maternal. The type of family (q.v.) in which authority is formally vested in the mother, or female head, with some degree of subordination of the male to his wife's kinsmen. Cf. matriarchate.
                                          E.A.H.

family, nuclear. The social group consisting of a married man and woman with their children. Cf. composite family; extended family.   G.P.M.

family, paternal. The type of family (q.v.) in which authority is formally vested in the father, or male head, with the relative subordination of the female spouse and offspring.   E.A.H.

family, patriarchal. That type of family governed by the father, or, in ancient Rome, by the oldest male head—the patriarch. The patriarchal family, in rude form, is found among many primitive tribes. Ethnologists agree that the development of private property and the taking over of the chief functions of production by men have had powerful effects in the development and extension of father power and a paternal organization of peoples. The patriarchal family is found in Oriental countries and, in ancient times; it was firmly established in Palestine, Greece and Rome. Among the Romans this type of family attained its most complete expression. Consisting of wife, children, grandchildren and slaves, all under the power of the oldest male head, the patriarchal family in Rome was a religious, legal and economic unit, which has been called a state *in parvo*. It held firmly together through the centuries because in the patriarch were vested all religious rights, as priest of the family ancestor worship, all legal rights as the only independent person recognized by Roman law, and all economic rights, as the sole owner of all family property, real and movable. A modified form of the patriarchal family developed among mediaeval peoples in Western Europe which was handed on to modern times During the last century serious inroads on the power of the father have been made by law, until the family in the United States at least, has become a democratic organization, bound together by affection and with the rights of each member fully protected by law.   W.G.

family, plantation. The type of family that developed during the colonial and early national periods on the plantations of the South. These plantation homes were built in a virgin wilderness by men of English stock and strong ties of affection for England. A fortunate combination of fertile soil, relatively mild climtae, and valuable indigeneous products, such as cotton and tobacco, tended to make of these southern settlers with large holdings of land an aristocratic agricultural class, reproducing many of the customs and characteristics of their English forebears. Along the rivers of the Carolinas, Virginia and Maryland charming plantation homes were built in the midst of vast tracts of land cultivated in tobacco and cotton. The institution of slavery aided the settlers in establishing these "manor houses", rich in English furnishings, in which a gracious and leisurely mode of living often developed, quite unlike the sterner, more industrious home life of the northern colonies, especially New England. Not only did the southern planters seek to reproduce the manorial estates of England in their plantation homes, but they transplanted the English customs of primogeniture and entail, whereby the house and lands descended to the eldest son or his heir and ownership remained within the family.   W.G.

family, rural. A group of persons constituting a family which lives in an agricultural or open-country environment. This type of family is generally characterized by a relatively early age of marriage, high birth rate, and low divorce rate.   P.F.C.

family allowance. A modification of minimum wage provisions to permit variations in favor of families with children. Family allowances may be of two types. The first sets the standard minimum wage for a married man with no children; additional compensation is granted for each child. New South Wales was the first country to experiment with this procedure. The other type is designed to increase the birth rate and was adopted in France, Belgium and Italy after World War I. It is a payment in the form of bounty to every family to pay for the birth and maintenance of each additional child.   J.W.M'C.

family behavior. Cf. behavior, family.

family budgets. Regular financial statements of the recorded and projected revenues and expenditures of families, made to serve as guides for planning household and other activities. These statements are of important use today not only in assisting individuals and families to plan and regulate their own activities, but are also of use to social workers, econ-

omists, political leaders, and other authorities in carrying on their functions. As democratic concern for the changing prospects and plans of the common masses develops, these family budget statements, as useful examples, become increasingly important for orderly progress. They show the different status conditions of different classes, by the relative sizes of their incomes; and the proportions of expenditures for the different kinds of commodities, reflecting the habits, health, education, social privileges, and kinds of occupation and culture. The expenditures of the poorer and less privileged families go in larger proportions for the physical necessaries, and those of the wealthier and more privileged, in larger proportions for the education, controlling, recreational and aesthetic interests.   C.J.B.

family disorganization. Cf. disorganization, family.

family farm. Cf. farm, family.

family life of animals. Cf. animals, family life of.

family of nations. A metaphor which assumes that all the nations included within the framework of peaceful diplomatic, economic and cultural exchange thereby acquire sufficient similarity to the interdependence and mutuality characteristic of the normal human family to be termed a family. The absence in the political field of such central characteristics of the family as parenthood and infantile dependence, and the absence in the family of sovereignty in children disqualify the term for scientific use.   G.M.F.

family social work. Cf. social work, family.

famine. Extreme scarcity of something, especially food, existing on a group scale.   R.E.B.

farm. A tract or tracts of land operated under one management as a single working unit for the purpose of carrying on one or more agricultural enterprises such as the growing of crops or the raising of domesticated animals.   T.L.S.

farm, family. A farm of sufficient size to provide employment for its operator and the members of his family, who themselves perform the entrepreneurial and managerial functions and also do all, or at least the bulk, of the manual labor on the farm. In contrast with large-scale or factory farms such a unit is less rationally managed, more diversified, and more self sufficient. Operation of a family farm is to a considerable extent "a way of life." T.L.S.

farm, large scale or factory. Large and highly rationalized units in agriculture. Such a farm produces primarily for the market, hence tends to monoculture instead of diversification—a specialization by enterprises. It also involves great specialization by tasks, most important of all being the divorcement of the functions of the entrepreneur, the manager, and the laborer. Frequently the ownership of such a business is corporate, the capital is supplied by distant investors, the manager is a salaried employee, and the workers constitute a permanent rural proletariat. On large scale or factory farms profit is the dominating motive and farming is not "a way of life." T.L.S.

farm, part-time. A part-time farm is one whose operator divides his time between farming and non-agricultural enterprises, with the latter being nearly as important if not more important than the former. T.L.S.

farm, plantation. A term prinicpally used to designate a large-scale agricultural unit devoted to the production of cotton, sugar and rice such as exists in the southern portions of the United States. The name plantation is also given to the huge and highly rationalized units utilized in the production of tropical crops throughout the world. T.L.S.

farm, subsistence or self-sufficing. A farm in the operation of which the primary objective is the production of goods and services that will satisfy the wants of the operator and the members of his family. In the management of such a farm production for the market occupies a secondary position, the products sold consisting mainly of surpluses that cannot be util-

ized by the family. In colonial America most farms were of this type, but increasingly it has lost in relative importance. Those existing in the United States today are mostly small, highly diversified, and intensively tilled. On such a unit, farming continues to be more a "way of life" than a business. T.L.S.

Farm Bureau. An organization of farmers and those interested in agriculture for the improvement of agriculture and rural life. The county is the basic unit of organization. Counties are represented in state federations and the latter in the American Farm Bureau Federation. Farm Bureaus were originally fostered by the Extension Services of the U. S. Department of Agriculture and the State Colleges of Agriculture, but are now entirely separate from them in many states. D.S.

farm income. Income obtained from farm operations. The sum of receipts from sales, appreciation of inventory and value of living obtained from the farm (food and fuel, etc.) represent gross farm income. After expenses (such as cash paid out, decrease in inventory and depreciation) are deducted, the remainder is called net farm income. C.E.L.

farm laborer. A person who is gainfully employed by a farm operator to assist with the farm work. He may be a wage worker or a family member or other person working for perquisites. He may be regular or seasonal, local or migratory, full-time or part-time. Also a person who by experience or usual occupation may be classed as a farm laborer even though unemployed or temporarily employed in another occupation. C.E.L.

farm operator. A person who manages and directs the operation of a farm, or in other words an entrepreneur or hired manager who applies capital and labor to land for the purpose of carrying on one or more agricultural enterprises. A farm operator may exercise the functions of capitalist and laborer, but he must exercise those of manager. Farm operators may be divided into a number of categories in accordance with the manner in which they obtain the right to the use of the land utilized in the farming operations:

(1) the owner operator himself is proprietor of the land used in his agricutlural operations;

(2) the tenant operator or renter obtains the land he uses in farming operations through the payment of a rent to the owner. If the rent is paid in cash, so much per acre or for the farm, the operator is known as a cash tenant or cash renter; if it is paid as a fixed amount of the produce, he is classed as a standing tenant or renter; and if the rent is paid as a proportion or share of the produce, he is styled share tenant or share renter. Care must be taken to avoid confusing the farm operator who rents land on the share basis (the share tenant or share renter) with the agricultural laborer (see share cropper) who receives a share of the crop as his pay.   T.L.S.

farm population. All persons living on farms regardless of occupation. Farm population is usually subdivided according to the location of farms into rural-farm and urban-farm population.   C.E.L.

farmer, subsistence. Cf. subsistence farmer.

farmers association, cooperative. Cf. cooperative farmers association.

farmers' organizations. Organized groups of agricultural people. In rural sociological usage often confined to national organizations of farmers such as the Grange, Farm Bureau, and Farmers' Union.   P.H.L.

farming, part-time. Cf. part-time farming.

farming, subsistence. Operating a farm primarily for providing for the living needs of the operator and his family rather than for providing goods for the market.   P.H.L.

farms, prison. Cf. prison farms.

farmsteads, dispersed. Farms consisting of the homestead and its adjacent lands which are more or less isolated from others in contrast with village communities (q.v.).   D.S.

Fascism. The movement and principles which underlie the Fascist state in Italy. Fascism stands for an international ideology and policy following the "doctrines" and practices of Mussolini's Italy, in this respect closely related to German National Socialism (q.v.). The word is derived from the word fasces (a bundle of rods and an ax tied together), the badge of authority of the magistrates in ancient Rome. Fascism, in adopting this symbol, indicated its intention of restoring the glory of the Roman Empire. The movement had its beginnings in the 'interventionist group under the leadership of the former Socialist, Benito Mussolini, soon after the outbreak of World War I. It was officially created in March, 1919, as the *fasci di combattimento*. In an atmosphere of a disappointing peace settlement, economic depression and social unrest Fascism's promise of quick action appealed to dissatisfied army officers, an impoverished middle class, and industrialists afraid of Bolshevism. The movement seized power in the so-called "March on Rome" in 1922 and after an initial use of parliamentary machinery and established institutions (monarchy, army), it created a dictatorial one-party regime. Though not backed up by an elaborate and comprehensive theory of society, Fascism may be regarded as a reaction against the ideas of the French Revolution, against rationalism, liberalism, individualism. It has been influenced somewhat by modern syndicalism, and to a much greater extent by nationalistic ideas which found a fertile ground in this country of belated national unification. While Fascism's claims at being a social revolution have hardly materialized, its political dynamics have been evident in its militant structure and its international adventurers. It made good use of the slogan of a presumed "red peril" in post-war Italy. In differentiation from National Socialism, it may be regarded as a more conservative and less totalitarian system and as a primarily personal rule. Fascism is Mussolini-ism to a larger degree than National Socialism is Hitler-ism.   S.N.

fashion. (1) Relatively short-lived socially approved, continuous variations in dress, furniture, music, art, speech, and other areas of culture. These variations usually involve details of a more permanent form prescribed by custom or convention.

Fashion changes are not grounded in any utilitarian or artistic superiority of the new over the old. While the phenomenon of fashion as a whole fulfills certain functions, its particular contents are culturally indifferent. It is newness rather than tradition which recommends a fashion. Because of the functional irrelevance of a particular fashion, conformity to it is largely motivated by the prestige derived from the mere fact of conforming. "You have got to get used to it, madam; it is the new fashion." Habit and the prestige with which the current fashion is endowed affect the public taste so that fashion is followed also because it appears beautiful and right.

Customs and conventions are more lasting than fashion, and customs are also more meaningfully related to the mode of life and the general culture of the group. Fads are more superficial and ephemeral. Frequency of change makes conformity to fashion more conscious than conformity to custom.

(2) Any relatively short-lived cultural form, such as a school of thought, an artistic style which achieved prestige and, though intrinsically meaningful, is imitated by a given group superficially, for the sake of prestige derived from conformity.   M.K.

fashion imitation. Cf. imitation, fashion.

fatalism. A non-material culture trait in which the definition of situation involves a laissez-aller attitude with a frame of reference possibly but not necessarily sacred. Implicitly or explicitly ultimate controls are regarded as external to human effort, planning, and/or volition.   D.E.W.

father-right. Cf. right, father-.

favoritism. Manifestation of special interest, partiality, or bias toward a particular individual, group, idea, or practice when confronted with the necessity of making a choice between this one and others. J.P.E.
fay. A white person who seeks the company of Negroes.   W.R.C.

FBI (*The Federal Bureau of Investigation*). A federal government bureau in the Department of Justice charged with the investigation of all violations of federal laws (except those laws placed specifically under the jurisdiction of other government agencies) and other matters in which the federal government may have an interest. It was organized originally to give the Department of Justice a permanent investigating staff of its own. It remained a relatively obscure bureau until the reorganization of 1924 gave it better personnel and added functions. The increase in the number of federal crimes has increased the jurisdiction of the FBI. When racketeering became prevalent in the late 1920's the twofold job of supressing interstate crime and recapturing the lost prestige of the forces of law and order fell on the FBI. The Bureau also maintains one of the most extensive criminal identification divisions in the world, with extensive files on national and international criminals. During the emergency of World War II, the FBI was charged with the investigation of individuals and organizations believed to be engaging in un-American activity, and of applicants for important governmental posts.

J.W.M'C.

fear of ghosts. The fear of the supernatural, typified by the unlaid ghosts of the dead.   A.G.K.

fecund. Having fecundity.

fecundity. Physiological capacity to participate in reproduction.

federate. To form a federation.

federated financing. Cf. community chest.

federation. Cf. council of community agencies.

federation, group. Cf. group federation.

feeblemindedness. Mental deficiency (q. v.). In England the term feeblemindedness is usually applied specifically to the moron level of mental deficiency, whereas in the

United States feeblemindedness is used generically to include all degrees of mental deficiency.   C.F.S.

feeling. (1) Sense impressions or sensations from skin or underlying tissues.

(2) Elementary factor in affective experience.

(3) Affective experience, especially of pleasantness or unpleasantness.

(4) Any kind of process of experience.

(5) Opinion based on indefinite grounds.
                                                    M.S.

feeling, collective. Collective feeling is to be distinguished from identical or analagous feelings which, having the same or analagous content, are not necessarily collective. Collective feeling is participation of many subjects in the same feeling, the same joy, sadness, anger, etc. This participation may have several forms: (a) It can be founded on mutual sympathy (emotional understanding) among the participating subjects (for instance, in a "face-to-face group"); (b) It may occur without these assumptions, and even without any close relationship among the participating subjects (e.g. the feeling of a "public"); (c) It may be combined with a strong We-feeling, which is more than mutual sympathy and represents a peculiar kind of collective feeling (to be defined separately). Collective feelings play a very important rôle in social life, manifesting themselves in emotionally colored social symbols and valuations, as well as in direct aspirations and reactions of groups and entire societies.   G.G.

feeling, group. Cf. group feeling.

feeling, nationality. Any feeling that exists because of the affiliation of an individual with a nationality (q.v.). They include sentiments of loyalty, approbation, and devotion to specified cultural traits or patterns, particularly those of language, religion, dress, decoration, recreation, and the patterns of family, state, and economic organization.

feeling, race. Any feeling that has its origin in race character. It may be sympathetic or antipathetic. In its significant practical use it applies to the distinctive feelings which, in theory, may be associated with the characteristic physiological and hereditary traits of any race (q.v.). Narrowing the concept still further, it is most commonly used to indicate antipathetic attitudes on the part of the members of one race toward those of another. The actual existence of true race feeling is exceedingly difficult to demonstrate as the expressed attitudes of human beings are always more or less qualified by experience and cultural environmental factors. This difficulty of demonstration, however, does not disprove the validity of the concept, which is theoretically quite conceivable. Actually, much of what passes for race feeling is really nationality feeling (q.v.).

feeling, we-. A distinctive type of collective feeling, in which many subjects participate not only in the same feeling, but in the feeling of the same We as the center of the act of feeling. We-feeling presupposes a collective emotional intuition of the We, e.g., an interpenetration of the emotional consciousnesses of many persons and groups. Its most intense forms may be observed in the collective love of the same group as a We, and in religious group ecstasies. The we-feeling plays an important role in group life and in the opposition and struggle among groups. On the other hand, such a sociological category as Nation, as distinguished from functional unions (political society, economic society, etc.), and from superimposed organizations, is impossible without the implication of a we-feeling.   G.G.

fellow-traveler. A political phrase originating after the Russian revolution to characterize a person who sympathizes with the objectives of the Soviet Union and international Communism, but who from considerations of self-interest or public influence declines to become officially identified with the movement. R.N.B.

felon. A term derived from the legal classification of crimes as felonies and misdemeanors. The former category includes those crimes regarded as the more heinous which usually involve confinement in a State or Federal prison or death as punishment. A felon is therefore one who commits a felony or who habitually commits felonies.   A.R.L.

felony. A high or major crime punishable by a sentence of more than one year in a state or federal prison. This is a rule of thumb definition, but no more substantial description can be given until the basis of criminal prosecution and punishment is made more consistent and more logical. The present system of penalties depends largely upon the state of public disapproval at the time the law is passed prohibiting it. The seriousness of a crime in relation to other crimes or the social consequences of a crime have little bearing upon which crimes are considered as felonies and which are not.   E.H.S.

feminism. A social movement to obtain for women an equal status with that of men in political, economic, and other spheres.   M.K.

fence. Cf. criminal fence.

fence, criminal. Cf. criminal fence.

feral man. Cf. man, feral.

fermentation, social. Cf. social fermentation.

fertile. Expressing fertility.

fertility. Fecundity expressed in performance and therefore measurable; virtually synonymous with natality.

fertility, differential. Variations in the fertility of different elements of the population, such as those by rural-urban residence, nativity, color, religion, occupation, education, and income.   C.V.K.

fertility rate. Cf. rate, fertility.

fetish. An object—natural or artificial, inanimate or animate—which is believed to possess supernatural power of efficacy of any sort, particularly if its special virtue is attributed to its occupation or "possession" by a spiritual being, and which is consequently either propitiated or employed for magical purposes. Cf. amulet; idol.   G.P.M.

fetishism. Belief in the occupation or "possession" of things, inanimate or animate, by indwelling spirits other than their own souls or a type of religion especially characterized by the use or worship of fetishes (q.v.) as in the case of many West African religions. Cf. animism.
                                              G.P.M.

feudalism. That social system which was firmly established in Western Europe in the centuries between the tenth and the seventeenth. Under this system the land was divided into fiefs, large or small, which were held on condition of pledging allegiance and rendering military service to an overlord. The largest fiefs were held by powerful nobles who owed military service directly to the king. In return for the armed services rendered the overlord, he, in turn, was responsible to his vassals for the protection of their lands and persons. The effects of feudalism upon the property rights, the inheritance of estates, the legal status and the guardianship rights of English women were profound, tending in every instance to a lowering of the status and a curtailment of the rights which they had enjoyed in Anglo-Saxon times prior to the Norman invasion. W.G.

fictions. Assumptions upon which people act as if they were actual. Under certain conditions such action actually validates the fiction, in the sense that social structure is actually built about such assumptions and develops in actuality the conditions previously assumed. Personal fictions serve to rationalize one's behavior into some more or less integrated or at least intelligible life organization pattern which may thus corroborate the fiction. Group myths and legal fictions may serve an analogous function. Fictions as social causes are very real. Cf. belief.   T.D.E.

fief. The land held by a vassal under the feudal system on condition of pledging allegiance and rendering military and other stipulated services to an overlord. During the Middle Ages all of Western Europe was divided into fiefs, large and small.   W.G.

field. An area of influence or of interest. In public or private administration the term is used to distinguish those phases or aspects of the program not identified with the central office. In research the term describes the area embraced within a study, and in trade it may be the area of sales contract. N.A.

field work (*social survey*). Process of collecting primary data from a population distributed geographically. M.Pt.

filiate. To establish in the relationship of a child to a parent or as a branch or derivative of another group or organization. J.P.E.

filiation. The view of the philosophic evolutionist that all natural phenomena are genetically interdependent, the more simple and general giving rise to the more complex and highly differentiated by processes of natural evolution. Thus astronomical phenomena preceded and generated the physical, and there followed in order the chemical, the biological, the psychological and the sociological. Thus the sciences are filiated, or related as parent and child, and dependent upon each other in an order representing the order of nature. Cf. affiliation, (2). F.H.H.

financing, federated. Cf. federated financing.

fine arts. Cf. arts, fine.

finger printing. A means of identifying persons which has many applications, but is principally used in the identification of criminals. It is based upon the hypothesis, never disproved, that the patterns or ridges on the finger tips remain unchanged for every person from birth to death, and are never alike for any two persons. Finger prints, left upon objects that are handled, can be revealed by sprinkling appropriate powders over such objects. They then can be photographed, recorded and classified for the purpose of comparison with other recorded prints. A.E.W.

fission. Splitting; mitosis. Group fission is the splitting of one group into two separate groups. T.D.E.

fittest, survival of the. Cf. survival of the fittest.

fix. A method of securing partial or complete immunity from punishment for crimes by the application of financial, political or other social pressures to witnesses, victims, or the agents of the system of criminal justice. Organized fixing involves a person who has an established business as a fixer, and the pressures become thoroughly commercialized. E.H.S.

fixation. (1) An arrest of a component impulse of the libido, or its attachment to an early (usually pregenital stage) of the psychosexual development of the individual; an arrest of some phase of the emotional life on a childhood level. (2) Fixation hysteria refers to a form of hysteria the symptons of which have a casual relation to an organic disturbance. J.M.R.

fixation, parental. An abnormally strong and persisting emotional attachment of an offspring to a parent. M.Pt.

flagellation. (1) The act of scourging with a whip or rod. (2) The practice of religious cults, e.g., the Penitentes, whereby devotees whip each other in ascetic zeal. An exorcising rite of whipping as used in initiation rites of Pueblo Indians. E.A.H.

flattery. Gracious commendation, overly favorable complimentation, even exaggerated and lying tribute, used as a means of attracting attention and winning good will. As a rule it is a method of social climbing used by inferiors. F.E.L.

floater. (1) An irresponsible person without community attachments; a person who moves from place to place without the motivation of specific goal or purpose. (2) One who shifts about to avoid arrest or to keep out of jail. (3) Police or court order directing one to leave the community on pain of arrest. J.M.R.

fluidity. An ecological term denoting movement without change of residence, such as the daily ebb of population to and from the business centers of a large city. C.F.S.

focus of attention. Cf. attention, focus of.

focus of consciousness. Cf. consciousness, focus of.

folk. The societal composite product of the associational processes integrated in the cultural and areal setting. The heart of society. The universal societal constant in a world of historical variables. Many variations of this concept. (1) The folk as bearers of culture. While the folk connotes the people, the two terms are in no wise synonymous. The people constitute the population in terms of measurable units. The folk, on the other hand, represent the composite essence of the mental and cultural interactions nearest the primary associational level. The folk, at any time and in any place, approximate the product and process of the people in their associational interactions among each other and their interactions between their regional, physical environment and their cultural development. Thus, as bearers of culture, the folk represent a general term, applying to the mode of the people in any given area and time which conditions and determines the culture of the people at that time. Illustrations are abundant in the history of culture and civilization, reflecting situations in which, within a single great civilization, it was possible to observe different folk societies within the major society. This is clearly the case in such great aggregate societies as those of India, Russia, and the peoples of Central Europe. It was true in the Old South of the United States, where there was a fourfold pattern of the folk society: the upper levels of the plantation aristocracy; the upper levels of the middle white South; the slave level of black folk; and the lower level of disadvantaged whites. (2) Folk as a substitute for race. This meaning of the folk as being the societal composite product of the associational processes in balance with regional, phsyical, and cultural environment makes it the correct designation of an entity frequently miscalled "race" (q.v.). Illustrative of this would be the use of the term "folk conflict" in contradistinction to *der Rassenkampf*, or race conflict, which Gumplowicz made the elemental force in societal development. This definition of the folk is comprehensive enough to explain the power and dynamics of Hitler's Germany, in which the ideology of race purity and super-race really refers to the folk. The conflict between Japan or China is one of folk-society, not of race. (3) The folk uni-versal, not primitive only. A chief value of this general concept of the folk is to divorce it from the pure ethnological concept and the popular interpretation which made the folk synonymous with the primitive or only early society. This larger meaning is still accurate as applied to earlier cultures. The specialized meaning can still be applied to literary and technical use with reference to folklore, folk songs, and the like as distinguishing the unwritten and written culture. (4) The folk in contrast to the state. This meaning of the folk and folk society is of importance furthermore in the definition of the state society and of the corresponding terms, stateways (q.v.) and technicways (q.v.), which are in contradistinction to the earlier accepted organic folkways and mores. Thus, the state society and the stateways reflect primarily organizational and coercive processes as opposed to voluntaristic and informal primary group processes. The state society as organizational, while referring primarily to political sovereignty and the development of social control through government, is also reflected in such other organizational control as the Catholic encyclical, other church formal processes of control, and various other institutional organizations whose mode of procedure is primarily organizational. A maximum development of the stateways is reflected in current trends towards totalitarian institutions as almost completely coercive of the individual and voluntaristic institutions, aided and implemented by the sweep and power of modern science and technology. This becomes the state society de luxe in contradistinction to the folk society. (5) Folk culture in contrast to civilization. This concept of the folk also provides bases for the measurable distinction between the folk society as culture and civilization as the specialized culture of state-urban-technological society. That is, culture represents the total processes, products and achievements of the folk in all aspects of their life and development, whereas civilization represents a special advanced cross section of culture in the higher brackets of technological and organizational achievement. Cf. folkways; mores.

H.W.O.

folk-regional society. The elemental unit

of the folk society consolidated in areal patterns susceptible of laboratory study through folk sociology and regionalism. The folk-regional society is the smallest unit of society in which all aspects, including spacial and historical evolutionary factors, can be studied. The folk-regional society is universal and organic in contradistinction to mere levels of the regional-folk society as descriptive of cross sections of early or primitive society. H.W.O.

folk society. The basic, elemental, definitive level of all spontaneous society. Cf. folk sociology.   H.W.O.

folk sociology. Cf. sociology, folk.

folklore. The surviving beliefs, myths, stories, traditions, in short, the so-called wisdom of a folk—a folk being (1) any primitive kindred or tribe, (2) the simpler, less-educated members, or (3) the masses, of any population.   F.E.L.

folkways. The popular habits and traditions. E.g., taking off hat to a lady. Good manners. Breach punished informally, by exclusion, avoidance, ostracism.   A.G.K.

force, appetitive. Force primarily dependent on internal organic conditions, although capable of being influenced by environmental stimuli.   M.S.

force, psychic. Force primarily dependent on the conscious experiences.   M.S.

force, social. Cf. social force.

forced labor. Cf. labor, forced.

forces, societal. Cf. societal forces.

forecasting. Cf. prediction, sociological.

forecasts. Predictions of future events by extrapolation or extending statistical trends according to their probable direction and within the limits of probable error. Cf. prediction; trend.   H.A.P.

forked merging. The bifurcation (q.v.) of relatives combined with the classification of geneologically unlike relatives into like relationship categories. Cf. classificatory system; merging.   E.A.H.

form of settlement. Cf. settlement, form of.

formal. Pertaining to the form, structure, rules, or relationships that are found in society without regard to the meanings which are attached to them.   J.P.E.

formalism. The practice or the doctrine of strict adherence to the form, structure, rules, or relationships of society without regard to the meanings which are attached to them.   J.P.E.

formula. A rule, law, or principle expressed in algebraic or other symbolic form.   H.A.P.

fornication. Illicit sexual cohabitation of unmarried persons. An unmarried person who engages in illicit sexual intercourse is guilty of fornication whether or not the others be married. In this respect fornication differs from adultery (q.v.). For instance, if an unmarried woman has intercourse with a married man, the offense would be fornication in the case of the woman and adultery on the part of the man.   J.M.R.

foster home. Cf. home, foster.

fostering. The nursing or rearing of a child by a person or persons other than its parents.   G.P.M.

foundation sacrifice. Cf. sacrifice, foundation.

fragmentation of holdings. This expression denotes the condition prevailing when the land owned and operated by a farmer consists of many non-contiguous tracts. Fragmentation of holdings is most prevalent where the village form or pattern of settlement is used in arranging the farm population on the land.   T.L.S.

frame of reference. A universe of discourse (q.v.); a connected set of "facts" and "axioms" in reference to which members of a group do their thinking, their defining of situations, their conceiving of personal and group rôles in such situations, and their communicating of such thoughts and attitudes.   T.D.E.

franchise. A special privilege or liberty conferred by government and vested in particular individuals or corporations; in the United States, franchises are generally exercised by corporations created for the purpose and deriving their powers under general or special laws most commonly conferring railroad or transit rights and privileges.   F.W.K.

franking. The privilege given to certain persons to receive the benefits of free postage.   F.W.K.

fraternal polyandry. Cf. polyandry, fraternal.

fraternity. The type of association characterized in general by relatively close acquaintance, easy understanding, familiar cooperation, and friendly good willl of persons associated—promoting the welfare of each other as is common between brothers. Historically fraternal associations have been and are influential social forces, often securing larger rights and privileges for the weaker members of the community; beside developing more or less privilege and political power for themselves. They frequently are organized with secret rituals, uniforms, ceremonies, symbols, with somewhat democratic forms of government and insurance protection against accidents, sickness, poverty and death for their members.   C.J.B.

fraud. That method of exploitation (q.v.) or domination (q.v.) in which the purposes of the exploiter or dominator are imposed on the exploited or dominated by deceiving them, or by concealing from them the real purposes of the exploiter or dominator. Cf. coercion.   H.H.

free love. Unregulated sex relations, without the ordinary obligations and responsibilities of marriage. A vague term, running all the way from complete promiscuity to "outside affairs" on the part of a married individual. The term has no scientific precision unless its exact meaning is made clear in the context.

free speech. A political principle in democracies, claimed as a natural right or a constitutional guarantee, by which citizens may discuss public questions without governmental interference or restraint; limited, however, by laws against slander, obscenity, profanity and direct incitements to special unlawful acts. R.N.B.

free will theory. (1) The theory that course of thought or action may be directed by the individual himself, regardless of external influences. (2) The theory that course of thought or action may be directed by the individual, regardless of all other influences.   M.S.

freedom. Ability to act in accordance with one's own inner motivation. "Freedom" in the sense of whim or choice independent of the situation-process in which a person is operating is no longer accepted. Freedom is often loosely identified with liberty. It is the positive internal aspect of independent action. Liberty is negative in that it is merely absence of external restraint. One may have liberty but not have freedom if one has no will to express, or has limitations and inhibitions which he feels are part of him. One may retain moral freedom even when denied liberty.   T.D.E.

freedom, academic. A phrase used to assert the right of teachers to expound their subjects without interference, in the classroom or outside; and by extension, to claim protection from disciplinary action by academic authorities for any activities as citizens outside their institutions. The use of the phrase is confined to higher educational institutions, since courses of study and the selection of texts in high and elementary schools are regulated by administrative authorities.   R.N.B.

freedom of assembly. The right of the people peaceably to assemble, freely to discuss public policies, and to petition the government for a redress of grievances or other modification of law or administrative policy. In the United States, this right is assured by the 1st Amendment to the Federal Constitution and made binding upon the States by judicial interpretations of the 14th Amendment. Problems created by urban congestion, societal tensions, and war have brought the implications of this freedom into conflict with governmental policing policies. The judgment of the U. S. Supreme Court in Hague v. C.I.O. (307 U. S. 496) seems to indicate that speakers may talk in peacetime without previous permission from anybody but that they remain fully responsible for what they say. In wartime, the right is strictly limited.   A.M'C.L.

freedom of the press. The right assured citizens of certain democratic countries to express and circulate opinions in printed form. In the United States, this right is assured by the 1st Amendment to the Federal Constitution and made binding upon the States by judicial interpretations of the 14th Amendment. Freedom of the press in the daily and weekly newspaper fields has been limited more and more by technological advances and other changes that have increased costs and have restricted access to adequate supplies of news and features. Individual citizens and small groups who cannot obtain space in established printed media must thus satisfy themselves with circulars, pamphlets, and books. The U. S. Supreme Court's Jehovah's Witnesses and Handbill Cases of 1938-39 broadened the free press doctrine to give protection against local legislation impeding or prohibiting the circulation of certain types of literature. Because of their vested interest in freedom of the press, the publishers of large newspapers through their trade associations have also fought through cases that strengthen the aspects of the doctrine protective of their interests   A.M'C.L.

freedom of speech. The right assured citizens of certain democratic countries to voice their opinions on political, economic, religious, and other social matters. In the United States, this right is assured by the 1st Amendment to the Federal Constitution and made binding upon the States by judicial interpretations of the 14th Amendment. Freedom of speech is interpreted as including not only the related Constitutional guarantees of freedom of assembly, the press, and religion but also such means of expression as "peaceful picketing (Thornhill v. Alabama, 310 U. S. 88), recognized by the Supreme Court as "the working man's means of communication." In free speech actions and discussions, the maintenance of the principles of free discussion in the case of unpopular sentiments or persons is essential to their preservation; in no other case will any effort be made to test and maintain those principles.   A.M'C.L.

frequency. The number of observations or measures in a class of a frequency distribution. The size of the class. Cell frequency is the number of cases in a cell.   M.Pt.

frequency distribution. A tabulation of frequencies in classes when the classes are arranged in order of magnitude. Frequencies may be indicated by tally marks or by numbers as in a frequency table. To be distinguished from historical distribution.   M.Pt.

friendship, guest. Cf. guest friendship.

friendship, Platonic. Cf. Platonic love.

frustration. Emotional tension produced by failure to attain a desired goal or to terminate an act successfully. Inner conflict arising as a result of opposing wishes or by external thwarts to the fulfillment of one's desires.   J.M.R.

function. (1) The type or types of action of which a structure (q.v.) is distinctively capable. (2) To engage in the specific type, or types, of action of which the type of structure involved is distinctly capable.   H.H.

function, correlate. A procedure related to other procedures, but differentiated by its particular characteristic action. It may represent a class within a larger society as teachers, carpenters, farms or merchants. Their particular activity and its relationship to the larger social process determine the correlate function of their class in society.   M.C.E.

function, social. Cf. social function.

functional. Special form of responsibility, which is the normal or characteristic action of a particular part of the entire structure. The performance of this particular activity is what distinguishes the part from the whole or from other parts. The functional value of a class or group may be determined by its specific contribution to the general social process.   M.C.E.

functional group. Cf. group, functional.

functional relation. Cf. relation, functional.

functional society. Cf. society, functional.

functionalism. Social organization based upon rigid groupings and classifications determined by activity, use, or specific contribution.   M.C.E.

functionary, social. Cf. social functionary.

funeral. The rites preceding and attending the disposition of the corpse of a deceased person. Cf. burial; mourning; rites of passage; second funeral.   G.P.M.

funeral, second. A ceremony, held some time after the original disposal of the body, at which the bones of the deceased are exhumed or otherwise retrieved and then disposed of in a different fashion, e.g., in an ossuary (q.v.). Cf. burial. G.P.M.

fusion. The joining of groups or factions having relatively uniform purposes, but differences regarding methods or leaders. Perhaps the joining may be a temporary one in the face of some emergency on issues concerning which the factions can take common ground.   N.A.

fusion of culture. Cf. culture, fusion of.

G

galleys. Ships, usually war-ships, propelled partly or wholly by oars before the days of sail. In ancient maritime nations the rowers were either mercenaries, or, with the growth of slavery, slaves and criminals. In the Middle Ages the galleys were manned by criminals. The use of the galleys, however, continued in France until 1748.   J.L.G.

Galton-Henry Method. A system of classification of fingerprints designed by Francis Galton in 1891 and elaborated by Edward R. Henry in 1897. It is the most widely employed of all systems and is in general use in English-speaking nations.
                                              T.S.

gamete. A matured germ, sex, or reproductive cell; a sperm or egg.   F.H.H.

gang. A primary group which develops spontaneously in face-to-face association and achieves some degree of solidarity as a result of conflict or antagonism in its social environment. It may originate as a play-group, from which it is to be distinguished because of its solidarity due to conflict. It may act as a mob, but it differs from a mob in that it has a tradition and a higher degree of morale. The mob is dispersed and does not re-form; the group that behaves like a mob and re-forms again under the same leadership is a gang. A gang may be made up of people of any age grouping beginning at 7 or 8 and continuing through adolescence and adulthood. While most gangs are composed of boys or young men, some gangs include girls and in rare instances gangs may be composed entirely of girls. The gang is an interstitial group forming at those periods in life when other types of group have least influence and forming in those areas where more stable types

of social organizations are absent. Thus, ganging is primarily a phenomenon of adolescence, although gangs may exist throughout adult life under special conditions. The gang is particularly characteristic of the intramural frontier, that is, those urban or rural areas where social organization is at a low ebb and the gang fills in the social interstices. Gangs have also flourished on frontiers between civilization and the wilderness or between nations where social control is relaxed. As the members of adolescent gangs become older, the gang tends to break up, particularly when its members marry. The natural history of the gang includes an amorphous stage when such groups are very unstable and constantly forming and re-forming. The gang may next enter a stage of high integration which is characterized by strong solidarity and definite leadership. And in a third stage it may become conventionalized and form an athletic or social club, a phase which usually precedes its decay and disintegration. The gang is to be distinguished from the merely orgiastic crowd (q.v.) whose behavior is characterized by dissipation or emotional expression. While the gang is quite capable of this type of behavior, it possesses a degree of morale and solidarity unknown in the orgiastic crowd as such. The orgiastic crowd disappears in the face of opposition while the gang remains to fight, as long as the odds are not too great, for its morale is less than that of a disciplined conflict group and its methods of conflict usually follow no rules but its own.   F.M.T.

gang, chain. The term used to designate groups of county jail prisoners working on projects outside the jail. Sometimes used formerly also for inmates of state prisons working outside the walls. Formerly the chain attached to one leg was connected with a heavy ball. Usually now there is a short chain joining two iron cuffs rivetted one upon each leg above the ankle. In either case the object is to prevent escape.   J.L.G.

Also, according to a practice formerly prevalent in a number of Southern states, groups of convicts chained together to prevent escape while employed in outside public works, such as road construction.   M.A.E.

gang, criminal. Any group of criminals which operates as a cooperative unit in the commission of crime or in realted matters.   A.R.L.

gang age. A period of childhood characterized, especially in the case of boys, by a striking development of social activities carried on with others of the same age and sex; the age shows a great growth of interest in the standard team games and a negative attitude (shyness) toward members of the other sex.   P.H.F.

gangster. A member of a gang or racketeering organization.   A.R.L.

garden city. A more or less self-contained urban unit surrounded by an agricultural belt, planned to provide ideal residential conditions in a garden environment, restricted as to maximum size and population, and possessing all the utilities of an ordinary city of its size and industries to provide employment for its inhabitants.   E.E.M.

gemeinschaft. A German word, commonly contrasted with *gesellschaft,* variously translatable as fellowship, community, or traditionalistic society. A close equivalent is sacred society (q.v.).   H.B.

gene. The elementary unit in inheritance carried by the chromosomes (q.v.), or small bodies in the germ cell, usually definite in number and shape. The gene is invisible under the strongest microscope and therefore, unlike the chromosome, is a hypothetical unit of heredity. Nevertheless, its existence is almost universally accepted by biologists. The functional significance of genes in the development of the diverse characters of the individual is at present a subject of much discussion, and divergent views have been expressed regarding the relationship of the genes to the characters which they determine. Biologists and geneticists have recently uncovered abundant evidence that each gene may affect many characters at the same time. Indeed there is reason to believe that every gene contributes to every part of the body, even while it affects some parts more than others. It is these parts that are selected for convenience in the study of heredity. A further inference, based on considerable evidence, is that the character of the individual is the result of a definite balance (or interaction) between the activities of the genes. If the balance is changed the end result is affected, as in the case of sex determination. The theory of balance in gene activities leads to the assumption that a normal environment is necessary to the maintenance of this balance and to the end result.   W.G.

genealogical method. A method in anthropological field work, consisting in the collection of pedigrees, their compilation into genealogical tables, and the relating of information thereto, for the purpose of working out inductively the kinship system (q.v.), marriage regulations, forms of social organization, mode of reckoning descent and inheritance, etc.   G.P.M.

genesis. Origin, generation; special usage by Lester F. Ward to denote aspects of evolution prior to planned or controlled change, which he called by contrast telesis (q.v.); emergence of the new through unplanned combination, coalescence, or creative synthesis of preexisting elements or factors.   T.D.E.

genesis, social. Cf. social genesis.

genetic. (1) Having reference to earliest traceable appearance, and, by extension, to the development. (2) Referring to a common origin.   B.M.

genetic aggregate. Cf. aggregate, genetic.

genetic change. A concept used, chiefly on the part of the evolutionary sociologists and anthropologists, to explain the variety of social systems by their manner of origin, or genesis. How technical processes and objects evolved was an early problem of archaeologists and students of primitive material culture, and the origin of most social institutions was eagerly investigated, in the belief that a true causal explanation of their progressive differentiation in time could be obtained, and a total picture of social evolutionary change and progress could be built up, for the complete history of man and his development.   S.J.

genetic group. An aggregate which has been recruited chiefly or wholly by its own birth rate, as the natural family of parents and children, clan or larger kinship group.   N.L.S.

genetics. The study of origins. In biology, the study of the transmission of characteristics of organisms by heredity.   B.M.

genius. A man possessing qualities which, under circumstances, lead to the attainment of superlative success in a field of specialization; one who demonstrates by achievement the possession of a brilliant intellect or extraordinary inventive ability. Also, great talent as such. Genius, since it is closely related to fame and circumstances, is no longer considered in social science to be exclusively hereditary. W.C.H.

genotype. The category which accounts for the underlying nature and causes of things. Cf. phenotype.   M.S.

gens. A sib (q.v.) or unilinear exogamous kin-group, especially when characterized by patrilineal descent.   G.P.M.

gentleman. A man of good family whose dress, education, speech, work, recreational habits, manners, and dwelling place set him apart from the mass, the commonalty. Originally, a man above the yeoman class, not a nobleman but entitled to wear a coat-of-arms; frequently one of the non-titled "extra" sons of the nobility.   W.C.H.

geographic environment. Those natural phenomena that affect the origin or development of physical or social life, such as climate, temperature, seasons, sunshine, rainfall, floods, droughts, soil, minerals, topography, land or water formations, altitude, latitude, longitude. Dicta, discussions and debates from the time of Aristotle to the present have attempted to establish the importance of the geographic environment, especially the relative importance of heredity and the geographic environment. Recent knowledge concerning the mechanisms of heredity shows that some factors in the geographic environment assist and that others harm or prevent the development of some hereditary traits. Many writers have tried to show the importance of the geographic environment in influencing or determining social activity.   O.W.

geography, human. Cf. human geography.

geophagy. The practice of eating earth. Clay is eaten by numerous poverty-stricken people in the tenant farm areas of Alabama and Georgia as a food substitute, primarily to make up for dietary deficiencies.   W.R.C.

geopolitics. Governmental policies derived from the sciences of the earth and its resources in relation to a nation's population. First developed in Germany after 1920, it was taken over as part of the ideology of National Socialism.

The word is just emerging (1942) into use. Closely associated is geo-economy, which determines geopolitics and in turn has its scientific base in geography and population studies, economics, political science, and technology. A new word, geotechnology, has been coined to include all the mineral arts and sciences, from metallurgy to ceramics.   M.VK.

George Junior Republic. A private institution founded in 1891 at Freeville, New York, for facilitating the adjustment problems of young persons. Only five per cent of the "citizens of the republic" have been sent by the courts, but most of the cases are delinquents or problem children referred by families or social agencies. Each boy or girl achieves the right to vote and to help determine the policies of the institution at sixteen; he or she must be self-supporting in the token money of the institution; must obey the laws or suffer punishment. The whole plan aims to promote a sense of social responsibility and training in good citizenship. Critics differ as to the value of such a plan for all delinquents.   M.A.E.

germ plasm. The special type of cells which have the capacity, and the biological function, of transmitting hereditary traits from one generation to the next. These cells have an independent existence and life cycle of their own, and in one respect the body may be thought of as simply their host or carrier. However, they have the remarkable capacity, upon reaching the appropriate stage in the biological sequence, to divide themselves into two portions, one of which remains germ plasm and the other becomes body plasm or somatoplasm (q.v.) with the type characters which they themselves determine. Cf. heredity, biological; chromosome; gene.

gerontocracy. Rule of the elders; an early stage in the development of government wherein the old men—heads of families, natural repositories of the extant wisdom, those with magical powers and therefore with prestige—rule all others. For example, "the elders of Israel" as a distinct body are often referred to in the Bible. There are many survivals of this usage to our own day.   F.E.L.

gerrymander. To alter unfairly the political map for the purpose of advancing partisan interests; an unnatural and arbitrary redistricting of a state or of a political division for purposes of electoral manipulation.   F.W.K.

gesellschaft. A German word, commonly contrasted with gemeinschaft, variously translatable as company ("in bad company" or as "Jones and Co."), association, society, or "worldly connections." A close equivalent is secular society (q.v.).   H.B.

gestalt. An undivided, articulated whole consisting of interdependent parts. The whole is formed by integration (q.v.), rather than addition of parts. Each part is a member of the whole and the nature of the part depends on its membership in the whole. The basic conception of the gestalt school of psychology. Cf. configuration.   M.S.

gestalt movement. An approach to the study of phenomena in the social science field, the particular aim of which is to find in mass phenomena coherent, functional and meaningful wholes and to understand the behavior of wholes as well as of the parts constituting the wholes and the relations between parts and wholes, and to find what points of nature stand in cause-effect relations from whole-laws rather than from part-laws. The proponents of the movement do not claim that it is a completely original approach but acknowledge that students of former times and operating in other specialized scientific fields have recognized the importance of wholes and that wholes possess attributes not possessed by the parts of which they are composed. As a social science movement, the gestalt approach was first advanced in the field of psychology about 1895 by Charles von Ehrenfels in Germany and, after a lapse, was given new direction by Max Wertheimer and Wolfgang Köhler about 1912. Since that time, and particularly after the coming into power of the Nazi regime, the movement has produced considerable technical literature in the United States in the field of animal and human behavior. Its proponents have discarded the strict factual sequence method and the assumptions of faculty psychology. It has produced a considerable technical and mathematical terminology and its own system of special and interaction constructs. The movement embodies a frame of reference system which is most fruitful for purposes of observing relationships.   F.W.K.

gestalt psychology. Cf. psychology, gestalt.

gesture, social. Cf. social gesture.

ghetto. (1) Place outside the walls of a town where Jews: (a) voluntarily live; (b) are compelled or legally required to dwell. (2) A natural area of the city, where a minority, not necessarily Jewish, settles. Life under these conditions has resulted, for the Jews at least, in a fixed pattern of folkways and mores, of intrinsically urban character, eventually forming neuroses.   J.H.B.

ghost. The disembodied soul (q.v.) or surviving spiritual counterpart of a deceased person, whether inhabiting the spirit world or appearing among the living as an apparition. Cf. spirit.   G.P.M.

ghost cult. The cult (q.v.), i.e., the practices and ritual observances, associated with the propitiation or avoidance of the ghosts (q.v.) of the dead. Cf. ancestor cult.   G.P.M.

ghost fear. Cf. fear of ghosts.

ghost town. Originally coined to describe abandoned mining and lumbering towns, the term is now being used in connection with war housing which may be left stranded after the liquidation of war industries.   S.S.

ghosts, fear of. Cf. fear of ghosts.

gifta. During the early Middle Ages in Western Europe gifta was the act of handing over (or "tradition") of a girl to her suitor, after she had been contracted to him by the crude ceremony of beweddung. By this act the woman was transferred from the power of her father to that of her husband. Originally it is probable that gifta immediately followed beweddung, or the fulfilment of the contract to pay to the father cattle, arms or money for the woman. But much later, under the influence of the Roman Empire and the Christian Church, gifta was slowly transformed, step by step, into the marriage ceremony.   W.G.

gigolo. A professional male escort; one who is paid to accompany women as a partner in dancing or other social activities.

gild (guild). (*medieval.*) An organization of producer-traders (merchant gild), or of craftsmen associating with others skilled in the same occupation (craft gild) for mutual protection and monopolistic control in their respective fields. (*modern.*) An association of persons with like interests, generally social or religious rather than economic, viz.: parish gild, sewing gild.   E.E.M.

glabella. The smooth prominence of the forehead just between the eyebrows.

glandular theory. The belief that the endocrines or glands which are related to the emotions and behavior will, when functioning abnormally, account for antisocial and criminal acts. Endocrinologists are not in agreement regarding the importance of the glands in determining behavior.   N.F.C.

goal. An objective or purpose to be attained and toward the achievement of which the policies and procedures of a program are fashioned.   N.A.

goal, social. Cf. social goal.

goods, consumption. Material objects used to satisfy immediately and/or directly some human want, need, or desire. The end product of economic activities. The distinction between consumption goods and production goods (q.v.) lies not in the form of the object, but in its use. A diamond worn in a ring or necklace is a consumption good; a diamond set in the point of a glass cutter and used by a glazier is a production good. Consumption goods are not necessarily destroyed in the using. A diamond ring or a stone residence may outlast generations of users.

goods, production. Material objects used in the production of wealth or economic services. Capital (q.v.). Production goods are distinguished from consumption goods (q.v.) not inherently by their form, but by their use.

goods, stolen, receiver of. Cf. receiver of stolen goods.

gossip. A face-to-face spreader of copious, superficial, often vulgar and untrustworthy news or tales; an idle tattler. Also the content spread. Also the act of spreading such content.   F.E.L.

government. The personal embodiment of the state. The state in action. As a process, the term refers to the functioning of the state in all its aspects. As an objective entity, it refers to the individuals and agencies who are charged with the responsibility of carrying out state action. Confusion often exists between "government" and "form of government." Correctly interpreted, the government may change without any change in the form of government, as is in general the case with the administration of democratic or republican societies at the time of each periodic election. Similarly, a government may in theory be overthrown "by force or violence" without changing the form of government or the organization of the state. In the case of revolution, such an overthrow may be designed to bring the actual government into closer conformity with the form of government and the type of state established and approved within a given society.

government, invisible. Government is the sovereign general system of social controls in a community, by which the parts are compelled to cooperate in rendering required social services. In earlier times the services rendered by different classes or groups having different privileged status, were less equal in essential values for human welfare than are the public services usually today, as democracy increases. Generally the regular, legally established modern government is publicly visible in the sense of being easily recognized and observed in the community, and, as such, it tends to progress with the advance of democracy in enforcing just claims for equal values in exchange. The invisible government, on the other hand, tends to be a survivor of the old general form of government by privileged or irregular groups. Generally today these groups are unknown, such as criminal gangs, lobbies, political cliques and corporate combines operating unobserved by the masses of the people, and inclined to exact from them undue and unjust incomes.   C.J.B.

gradations, social. Cf. social scale.

gradient. Any series of magnitudes which varies between high and low values,

by progressive steps or degrees. In sociology gradations of magnitude are usually related to spatial distances between points or areas.   M.S.

gradient, ecological. Cf. ecological gradient.

gradualism. The tactic of promoting social change by specific reforms, all aimed at the ultimate goal of creating a socialist society, and opposed to revolutionary tactics of change.   R.N.B.

graft. The process whereby an officeholder accepts money for dispensing privileges and contracts by favoritism rather than by merit; or the money accepted for such services.   J.W.M'C.

graft, honest. A term coined by the famous Tammany Hall chieftain, George Washington Plunkitt, to identify the profit secured by a politician in making use of his foreknowledge of public building and improvement, for example, the buying up of a piece of swamp land that the city was subsequently to use for a public park, and the profiting greatly from the resale of the land to the city. Dishonest graft is payment for non-existent jobs and services to persons who return a portion of the payment to the politician who made it.
                                          J.W.M'C.

grant-in-aid. A grant of money made by a central government to a unit of local government in order to encourage or to bring up to standard a necessary social service. The first grants-in-aid were made by states to local government for education and highways. Now the federal government is using this method extensively to secure general acceptance by the states of social legislation. The basic problem in the grant-in-aid is the formula used to determine the amount granted to each recipient. Matching, need, per capita tax and many other criteria have been used for this purpose but none has been completely satisfactory. By inference the term is also applied to allotments made by private organizations such as foundations.   J.W.M'C.

grave escort. Widows, slaves, or other persons sacrificed at a funeral to provide the deceased with an escort to accompany him to the other world and serve him there. Cf. human sacrifice.   G.P.M.

grave-goods. Weapons, ornaments, or other objects deposited with a corpse, e.g., in a grave. Cf. sacrifice.   G.P.M.

greenbelt. A strip of vacant, recreational or farm land encircling a community intended to protect the community against intrusion of objectionable real property uses from adjacent communities or to provide for the community's orderly future expansion. The land is owned and controlled by a public agency or the community. The term is occasionally used in city planning to denote a temporary open use area around a commercial or industrial district to permit future expansion without invasion of residential districts.   S.S.

greenbelt town. A planned town, with a protective strip of land in agricultural or recreational use around it. The town provides shelter, services, stores, schools, and other community facilities, is permanently held in one public or corporate ownership, and is administered together with its greenbelt with full representation of the inhabitants. Such a town may or may not include industry. Existing American examples are largely dormitory satellites of metropolitan centers.   S.S.

gregariousness. The social tendency to seek interaction with others of one's kind.   E.A.H.

group. Two or more people between whom there is an established pattern of psychological interaction; it is recognized as an entity, by its own members and usually by others, because of its particular type of collective behavior.   D.S.

group, component. Any aggregate within a natural society that in most respects, though not in all, is complete and independent and capable by itself of maintaining existence and perfecting a complete social life.   N.L.S.

group, compound. An association of persons in which the structure of the group includes relations not only of individuals to the group as a whole but of subgroups

of individuals recognized as entities and related to the whole as subgroups.   G.L.C.

group, consanguine. A social group which is defined on the basis of blood relationship, putative or fictitious. In the latter case, arbitrary rules of kin relationships may exclude certain actual blood relatives from the consanguine group, and certain persons who are not actual blood relatives (e.g., adopted persons) may possibly be included. Cf. lineage; clan; moiety; kinship.   E.A.H.

group, direct-contact. A social group in which the members are able to respond immediately to sensory stimuli emitted by each other.   J.P.E.

group, dyadic. A pair, or couple, of human beings in sociation (q.v.), usually but not necessarily of associative character.   H.B.

group, ephemeral. An aggregation, or even a functional group, which forms for a brief period only, because of some momentary common stimulus or purpose.   T.D.E.

group, face-to-face. Equivalent of group with presence (q.v.).   T.D.E.

group, functional. A social group whose membership is chosen from persons who perform the same function or service in the social order.   J.P.E.

group, genetic. Cf. genetic group.

group, horizontal. A social group whose membership is chosen from the same social stratum.   J.P.E.

group, in-. Any group regarded from the point of view of one of its members, in contrast to outside groups. Virtually equivalent to we-group (q.v.).

group, intermittent. A functional group which meets face-to-face periodically or sporadically, but continues to operate in absence in the intervals. Cf. group with presence; group without presence.   T.D.E.

group, intimate. A (functional, human) group within which person-to-person affective contacts and relations are extremely close, whether of love or of conflict. T.D.E.

group, kindred. A group identified by the biological unity of common ancestry. The members of such a group are more closely related to each other by ancestry than they are to the members of other comparable groups. Strictly considered, the kin group may run all the way from a single family to a race, or even to humanity itself.

group, kinship. Cf. kinship group.

group, local. A social group consisting of persons who normally reside in the same locality and maintain face-to-face association, e.g., a band (q.v.), village, or neighborhood. Cf. clan. G.P.M.

group, locality. Any group which is defined chiefly by its geographical or spatial boundaries, as a neighborhood, rural community, village, city, or region. D.S.

group, marginal. An incompletely assimilated group; one which has partially relinquished its former culture and which has not yet won full acceptance in the new culture within which it is living. A term used in connection with immigrant groups in which there has been considerable mixture of different cultures, so that attitudes and values and resultant behavior patterns are characteristic of neither; the group occupying a sort of social no-man's land. Where overt characteristics make identification easy, this stage in the assimilation process may be occupied for decades, as in the case of Orientals and Latin-speaking peoples in the U. S., and such groups may evolve a fairly well integrated culture of their own containing elements drawn from both the social orders concerned. Cf. conditioned participation. H.E.M.

group, minority. A sub-group within a larger group (ordinarily a society), bound together by some special ties of its own, usually race or nationality, but sometimes religion or other cultural affiliations. Even in the common types of democracy, minority groups are precluded from expressing themselves in proportion to their numerical strength through the operation of the principle of majority rule. Cf. proportional representation.

group, natural. A rather inaccurate term used in recent years in social work terminology to define an association of persons united by close ties of congeniality or friendship who have formed themselves into a group by their own spontaneous efforts. It is contrasted in this sense with groups formed by organizations or individuals outside the group itself and with those in which interests other than those of personal friendship create the dominant bond between the members. This use of the term natural group is used to define especially groups of adolescents without the implication of anti-social purpose associated with the term "gang" (q.v.) or the implication of social exclusiveness associated with the word "clique." G.L.C.

group, neighborhood. An association, frequently informal, of persons living near one another. W.P.

group, organized. A social group (q.v.) so organized that functions through which group purposes are to be achieved are divided among its members, who may carry out these functions as separate persons and/or as subgroups. H.B.

group, others.- All people outside of a group considered as the we-group or in-group; or, a specific group considered by members of the we-group as "others", alien. Difference and separateness are implied, and a degree of isolation (q.v.) may produce estrangement (q.v.); but estrangement is not a necessary element in attitudes toward others-groups as thus defined. Cf. we-group; in-group; they-group. T.D.E.

group, pressure. An actual or alleged group utilized by its leaders to force modifications in the policies of other groups or of a larger organization with which it is affiliated. This pressure usually takes the form of representations by group spokesmen that their proposals are merely expressions of the conscious needs and demands of their constituency. Examples range in the United States from the National Association of Manufacturers, the Congress of Industrial Organizations, and the American Federation of Labor, to the Roman Catholic Church and the Federal Council of the Churches of Christ in America, and include the Farm Bloc, American Legion, Chambers of Commerce, and many more localized groups. A pressure group usually concerns itself with the promotion of some aspect of the "general public interest," i.e., with obtaining special privileges for its leaders and members.   A.M'C.L.

group, primary. A (functional, human) group characterized by affectional (as vs. utilitarian) motives, direct face-to-face or intimate contact, and (because of the limitations on these) small size; called "primary" by Cooley because the family neighborhood and play groups are the first groups in which (in our culture) a child is socialized, and such groups have the aforementioned characteristics. Secondary groups are "second" in sequence in a child's life. Difficulty is experienced, however, in that (a) the phrase has come to be used chiefly to denote any sympathetic or intimate groups, even those joined late in life, and (b) many indirect-contact groups-in-absence retain affectional bonds. The word primary in this connection, though rather heavily entrenched in sociological usage, is confusing and might well give way to a terminology more descriptive of the essential traits meant: viz.: affectional or intimate groups, based upon affectional motives and attitudes and sympathetic bonds (vs. utilitarian); direct contact groups in or with presence (q.v.) vs. groups in absence or without presence (q.v.); original groups vs. derived groups (for chronological sequence).   T.D.E.

group, secondary. A group-form distinguished from a primary or face-to-face group by its type of social contact and degree of formal organization. The secondary group is larger and more formal, is specialized and indirect in its contacts and relies more for unity and continuance upon the stability of its social organization than does the primary group. An army with its formal orders, hierarchy of ranks, and rigid discipline is an illustration of a secondary group.   F.D.W.

group, shifting. A play group characterized by changing membership; characteristic of pre-school children not yet sufficiently socialized to form a stable group.   P.H.F.

group, social. Cf. social group.

group, they-. A group external to the one to which the individual in question belongs, and toward which he feels such a sense of separation that he would ordinarily use the third personal pronoun instead of the first personal pronoun in referring to its members. The term is just one of several forms of expressing the emotional distinction between the insider and the outsider, the sympathetic and the antipathetic, the emotional near and far. Cf. we-group.

group, vertical. A social group whose membership is chosen from two or more social strata.   J.P.E.

group, we-. Any association with which one feels identified; to which one belongs —in the sense of longing for when away from it; the members of which are governed by attitudes of loyalty, devotion, sympathy, respect, and cooperation to it, as well as a certain sense of exclusiveness and pride. When members are made aware of outsiders, the latter are regarded with indifference, repulsion, and even enmity. Cf. they-group.   F.E.L.

group acceptance. The response to any one member of a group by the other members indicating their preference or lack of preference for him and so establishing his status within the group.   G.L.C.

group accommodation. Cf. accommodation, group.

group behavior. A concept which covers the subject matter of most of the social sciences, if looked at from the standpoint of mass phenomena. Group behavior is a matter of ordinary human experience, and there is no reason to believe that it is a fallacy or an illusion. The behavior of a football team, for example, is definitely something very different from the behavior of its individual members. Such mass behavior is brought about by the mutual adaptation or adjustment of the behavior of the individual members of the group, so that the group becomes a functioning unity, virtually a human machine. Most sociologists consider that social groups and their behavior constitute the chief subject matter of sociological theory. As the group is constituted, however, by the interactions of its individual members, social interaction may, with perhaps equal validity, be regarded as the subject matter of sociological theory. In any case, most recent sociology considers that the origin and development, structure and functioning of human groups present the chief problems of the science of sociology. This conception, however, varies but little from the older conception that sociology concerns itself with the process of association of human beings. The rise of the group, of group egoism and group interests, probably has had some influence upon making group behavior a central conception in sociological theory. Over a hundred different kinds of groups have been listed by sociologists. Among the more important of these for the understanding of group behavior in our human world are primary (q.v.), or face to face, intimate groups, and secondary (q.v.), or non-face to face groups; also we-groups and others-groups; also voluntary groups or associations and non-voluntary, or genetic groups. Communities come under this last heading.

Sociological theory of the present regards group behavior as largely a product of culture or civilization. Very definite group behavior is found among many animals below man, probably upon a purely instinctive basis. All human group behavior seems to be dominated by the customs (q.v.) and traditions (q.v.) of the group, and these customs and traditions are always learned. In historic times the behavior of many communities and other larger groups has been dominated by some obedience-compelling authority, such as the state. Democratic groups aim to secure unity and harmony in their group behavior by voluntary means involving communication, education, and many other forms of control which appeal to the intelligence and will of the individuals in the group.   C.A.E.

group centrism. Cf. centrism, group.

group contact. Cf. contact, group.

group disintegration. Cf. disintegration, group.

group expansion. Cf. expansion, group.

group fallacy. The practice of "social animism", i.e., of ignoring the fact that plurels (q.v.) exist only in the sense that social actions of appropriately constitutive kinds have a high probability of recurrence. For some purposes, of course, it is quite permissible to speak of various plurels, such as church or state, in a substantive sense, i.e., as nouns, in spite of their basically verbal character. Otherwise, intolerable circumlocution and pedantry would result.   H.B.

group federation. Cf. community organization. An organization of groups of people (usually organized clubs) cooperating for some common objective.   W.P.

group feeling. The feeling of persons in association, as opposed to that of persons in isolation, usually expressing itself in either attitudes or overt behavior. It involves a consciousness or partial consciousness of the feelings of others in the group.   R.E.B.

group fusion. The process of anastomosis, blending or merging of two previously separate groups (functional or merely aggregate) into one group, whether organized or unorganized. Opposite of group fission, (q.v.).   T.D.E.

group integration. Cf. integration, group.

group interest. Cf. interest group.

group marriage. A hypothetical form of marital union between a group of men and a group of women. Cf. sexual communism.   G.P.M.

group mind. Unified, and perhaps organized, attitude toward any subject prevailing among, and practically dominating, a group. Cf. social mind.

group momentum. Cf. momentum, group.

group morality. Cf. morality, group.

group opinion. Cf. opinion, group.

group perpetuation. Cf. perpetuation, group.

group play. Play characterized by social cooperation; sometimes thought of as an intermediate stage between the parallel play of young preschool children and the more fully socialized play of older preadolescents.   P.H.F.

group process. Continuous actions or series of actions constituting and developing from the psychic interactions of persons associated in a group. The group process includes not only the physical and psychological interactions of the persons in the group with each other but also the resulting patterns of interaction between individuals and the group as a whole as aspects of the group process, such as the process of group control or the process of group thinking.   G.L.C.

group settlement. When in the settlement or colonization of new lands a new colony or community is established as an offshoot from an older one, similar to the swarming of a hive of bees, the process is known as group settlement.   T.L.S.

group situation. Cf. situation, group.

group slavery. Enslavement of an entire societal group without reference to individuals therein.   E.E.M.

group stimulation. Cf. stimulation, group.

group thought. Cf. thought, group.

group tradition. Cf. tradition, group.

group unity. The unity of interacting personalities which characterizes any functional group, and is recognized as a larger unity by each of its functioning members. It is dependent on both common purpose and structure.   T.D.E.

group will. Cf. will, group.

group with presence (or in presence). A group that functions only when face-to-face; an aggregation or functional group when it is meeting face-to-face. Equivalent of face-to-face group, opposite of group in absence.   T.D.E.

group without presence. A human group which functions and may be organized, but the members of which do not meet: they transact business by like response to the stimuli from central headquarters, or through indirect, symbolic contact. Most such groups depend, however, upon occasional face-to-face contacts with representative members, and a nuclear (executive) committee and/or staff among whom there are constant face-to-face contacts or intermittent face-to-face meetings. Equivalent to group in absence.   T.D.E.

group work. The function of professional social workers in assisting groups or communities to enlarged opportunities of living.   R.N.B.

group work, social. Cf. social group work.

groups, blood. Cf. blood groups.

growth. The process of development. P.F.C.

growth, adaptive. Development which involves adjustment of the organism to its physical or social environment.   P.F.C.

growth, social. Cf. social growth.

growth, urban. Cf. urban growth.

growth process. The way in which development takes place.   P.F.C.

guardian spirit. An individual protective spirit, often acquired, especially in North America, through a dream or vision. Cf. familiar spirit.   G.P.M.

guardianship. The protection, care and management of the person or property, or both, of an individual, as of a minor or a person incapable of managing his own affairs. For many centuries the guardianship of minor children was the prerogative of the father, no rights being granted to the mother save after the decease of her husband. In the popular view the father was held to be the natural guardian of his children down to modern times. In England and in several states of America the guardianship rights of mothers, even at present, are unequal to those of fathers. Where the parent fails to appoint a guardian by will, the court may appoint such guardian to care for the person and property of orphaned children until their legal maturity. Also the court may appoint a guardian on request in the case of a person mentally incapable of managing his affairs.   w.g.

guest friendship. A formalized rule of hospitality, characteristic of the Arabs and other peoples according to which a guest, whether friend or stranger, is guaranteed entertainment and inviolability during his visit.   g.p.m.

guidance. A very general term, having reference to all efforts put forth by an individual or group to shape the understanding and activities of another individual or group towards the attainment of certain goals. Cf. vocational guidance.
     f.e.l.

guild socialism. Cf. socialism, guild.

guillotine. A machine invented by Dr. Guillotine, a Frenchman, for beheading those sentenced to capital punishment. It obviated the uncertainty of the headsman's ax, since the blade was fixed in grooves in two uprights and fell with exactitude upon the block below.   j.l.g.

gynecocracy. Matriarchate (q.v.).

H

habeas corpus. A writ which must be granted on application to any court of general jurisdiction to review the legality of the confinement of any person by a public authority. The right to such a writ may be suspended, according to the U. S. Constitution, only in cases of invasion or rebellion where the civil courts cannot function. R.N.B.

habit. An acquired attitude or tendency to act in a specific way, which has become, in a measure, largely unconscious and automatic; custom is sometimes referred to as group habit. W.E.G.

habitat. Area suited to the occupancy of a species, group or person. The term is more specific in application than environment, having a spatial implication. Habitat may have somewhat of an associational meaning in so far as it relates to an area of living in which the essential activities of life are carried on. Contrasted with range (q.v.). N.A.

habitation area. A section of the earth's surface considered as the place of residence of a relatively stable and organized human group—society, tribe, or race.

habitual. Characteristic of gradually acquired forms of response to repeated situations; according to habit. Habitual reactions are easily elicited, relatively invariable, nearly automatic, and typically require a minimum of conscious direction or attention. M.Pt.

habitual criminal. Cf. criminal, habitual.

habitual criminal laws. Many American states and other countries have passed laws which provide increased penalties for offenders with previous criminal records. The provision for the increased

penalty is either permissive or mandatory. The habitual criminal law is invoked after conviction of a second, third or fourth felony. The advocates of such laws believe the increased severity of penalty will eliminate or considerably reduce serious crime. Cf. Baumes Law. N.F.C.

habitual offender. Cf. criminal, habitual.

hamlet. A small cluster of homesteads in rural territory. A small village. D.S.

handicapped. Possessing a physical defect which reduces one's efficiency in performing one's personal and social obligations according to a socially determined standard. Since the degree of defect and the test of social adequacy vary with the individual and the community no hard and fast definition of handicapped is possible. A person with such a defect. J.W.M'C.

handicraft economy. A society which derives its chief support from the products of manual labor unaided by power machinery. G.M.F.

hanging. A method of capital punishment devised in ancient times and in use at present in many countries. As originally used death came about by strangling, but as now used there is either a drop of about seven feet, or a sudden jerk upward which usually breaks the neck and causes supposedly instantaneous death. Originally hanging was public on the theory that the horrible sight would deter others from crime. At present in most countries of the Western world the execution is private with only witnesses and newspaper reporters present. J.L.G.

hard labor. An additional punishment added in England to simple imprisonment

intended to make the sentence more deterrent. In practice the sentence to hard
labor in prisons is obsolete, since under
the restrictions placed now upon the sale
of prison made goods it is impossible to
make the inmates work as hard as free
workmen. J.L.G.

harmonism. The theory that the concept
of singularism (that the individual is the
only social reality) and of universalism
(that society is the only reality) are inseparable and that the two concepts are
merely two aspects of the same reality.
Syn.: integralism. J.D.

haruspicy. Divination (q.v.) from por-
tents, especially by observing the entrails
of sacrificed animals. G.P.M.

hashish. A narcotic derived from the Indian hemp plant. It may be inhaled,
chewed or smoked in order to produce a
type of exhilaration accompanied by the
disorganization of the central nervous
system. The use of hashish is particularly prevalent in the Near East. J.W.M'C.

Hawes-Cooper Act. A law enacted by
the Congress of the United States and
approved by the President January 19,
1929, which became operative after five
years. It provided that all prison-made
goods entering into interstate commerce
are subject to the laws of any State or
Territory of the United States to the same
extent and in the same manner as prison-
made goods manufactured in that State
or Territory. It was aimed at the contract, piece-price and public account systems of prison labor. J.L.G.

head-hunting. The practice, widespread
in Indonesia and adjacent regions, of
making raids on hostile tribes to secure
enemy heads either as trophies or to
satisfy ceremonial requirements. G.P.M.

headman. The leader or head of a band,
village, or other social group, especially
when his position and authority are but
slightly institutionalized, being founded
primarily on personal influence. Cf. chief.
G.P.M.

headship. A position of power as distinct
from the individual who holds the position.

Headship may be inherited, acquired
through the exercise of force or fraud,
by election, or by promotion. W.E.G.

health cooperative. Cf. cooperative,
health.

health insurance. Cf. insurance, health.

heckling. A form of political debate, between a speaker and his audience, characterized by interruptions of an address
by a member of the audience, and designed either to embarrass a speaker or
to bring out points avoided or neglected.
Regarded in England as normal and useful practice in political life, where the
term carries no connotation of rude interruption, as in the United States. R.N.B.

hedonism. The doctrine that moral duty
is fulfilled by making pleasure the chief
good. L.P.E.

hepatoscopy. Divination (q.v.) by observation of the livers of slaughtered animals. G.P.M.

herd. In the animal world a group of
animals (specifically, certain larger mam-
mals) given to moving about as a unit.
In the social world of man a group of
persons motivated by common desires and
marked by the absence or relative weakness of patterns of rational control. E.A.H.

heredity, biological. The transmission of
the physical (including the innate psychical) characters of parents to their offspring. The physical basis of heredity
lies in the development of the offspring
from one or more living cells derived
from the parent organisms. In human
sexual reproduction these germ cells (the
egg and the sperm) unite, after each has
lost half of its chromosomes (q.v.). The
true bearers of the hereditary characters
are held to be the invisible genes (q.v.)
within the chromosomes. Heredity is never
shown completely in the offspring but is
always modified by more or less variation,
which results in differences between individuals. If the variation is marked
enough it may eventually result in a new
species. In addition to new characters appearing spontaneously in an organism,
other characters may be acquired by the

individual in contact with its environment, e.g., the abnormal growth of a part due to continuous use, or its atrophy due to disuse. The theory of the inheritance of such acquired characters by offspring is no longer held by most biologists. At present the relative importance of heredity and environmental influences in shaping the individual is a question warmly debated by biologists, geneticists, and sociologists.   w.g.

heredity, social. Cf. social heredity.

heresy. An opinion not accepted by the established authority. A deviation, usually somewhat formalized, from accepted dogma.   L.P.E.

heritage, social. Cf. social heritage.

hermaphrodite. In human beings, an abnormal and rare individual having both male and female reproductive organs, one set of organs usually being rudimentary or imperfect.   R.E.B.

hero cult. Cf. cult, hero.

heroin. One of the opium family isolated in the search for non-habit forming anesthetics to take the place of morphine. Heroin is a trade mark name which has become identified with a white crystalline form of morphine derivative. It is definitely habit-forming and has become one of the most widely used of the narcotics. It produces a quiet, pleasant, dreamlike slumber.   J.W.M′C.

hetaerism. A system of prostitution in ancient Greece, involving both slaves and free women. Many of the latter were well educated—a few being famed for their learning and culture and much sought by prominent men.   R.E.B.

heterogeneity. The quality characteristic of a population when the individuals within it show markedly traits which are biologically or culturally dissimilar. Cf. homogeneity. Racial heterogeneity exists when the members of a group are derived from different races, and are dissimilar in their physical traits because of different ancestry. Cf. race. Ethnic heterogeneity exists when the members of a group are

derived from several different ethnic groups, and when they maintain their ethnic traits within the larger community. Cf. ethnic. Cultural heterogeneity occurs when the members of a group are diverse as to cultural traits. Cf. culture.   B.B.W.

heterogeneous. Characterized by heterogeneity (q.v.). Communities are heterogeneous when composed of two or more diverse groups. The specific groups within the community may of themselves be racially or culturally homogeneous as for example—Negro, Chinese, Jewish, etc. When an increasing number of individuals are of mixed descent as a result of the crossing of diverse strains, the community tends to become homogeneous both racially and culturally—racially because the individuals are alike as a result of admixture, culturally because of the assimilation of cultural traits into a new cultural pattern.   B.B.W.

hierarchy of the sciences. The sciences arranged in an orderly series based usually on comparative complexity of data and/or precision of methodology and on the dependence of one on others; since Comte and Spencer the range has been ordinarily from the inorganic through the organic to the social sciences.   A.J.T.

hinterland. The outlying areas, of an area central or dominant to them. The term carries the implication of remoteness, of less congestion and less responsiveness to influences of change. The town or the village is associated with the hinterland. It is the area of raw materials, supply of essentials and is the area which gives the city its sphere of influence and its market.   N.A.

historical materialism. Cf. materialism, historical.

historical sociology. Cf. sociology, historical.

history. The chronicle of the past and the discipline which investigates and narrates it in accordance with certain accredited methods. History stands in close connection with sociology both in content and through historical development. It is one of the major sources of raw materials for sociology, together with anthropology (pre-history) and the statistical and interpretative study of contemporary events. In the evolution of sociology the connection with history has been very close, the earliest systems being summarizations and cross-sectional studies of history from the viewpoint of distinctive philosophies of history. As to method, history has been differentiated from sociology by its addiction to the ideographic as contrasted with the nomothetic method characteristic of the latter. Moreover the recession of sociology from the tendency toward over-ambitious generalizations of history and its greater concentration on empirical studies have also resulted in a diminution of the antithesis and indeed have made the historical approach one of the techniques of sociological research. Furthermore both sociology and history have points of contact in that they both deal with human beings and must take motives, intentions, meanings, and values into consideration, as opposed to the method of a reductive positivism which tends to deny their reality or significance by reducing them to allegedly more fundamental physical or bio-chemical components. Also both disciplines must put under contribution schemata of the explanation of conduct oriented to depth psychology. Finally both are value-centered in the choice of their subjects, the aspects of society past or present which they undertake to study because they interpret them as somehow significant in terms of their own culture. Hence both are open disciplines, continually to be written as viewpoints and needs change. While both are scientific disciplines with specific methodologies of control a certain political trend may be discerned: generally concentration upon history has been associated with a conservative political tendency as was generally true of the historical school of romanticism (although primitivism has sometimes been employed to validate a progressive movement); whereas the comparative tendency of sociology tends to be associated with an oppositional point of view.   E.F.

history, life. Cf. life history.

hobby. A leisure activity to which considerable time is devoted but irregularly.

It is pursued with enthusiasm and vigor at times, followed by periodic lags of interest. A wide range of activities can become hobbies, depending upon the interest and enjoyment which they afford. Cf. avocation.   M.H.N.

hoe-culture. A primitive type of agriculture in which the hoe is the principal implement.   G.P.M.

holdings, fragmentation of. Cf. fragmentation of holdings.

holocaust. A burnt offering, especially when wholly consumed by fire; hence, by extension, a wholesale or extensive sacrifice (q.v.).   G.P.M.

holy war. Cf. Jihad.

home. The most essential, relatively stable central institution of face-to-face human relations, generally in an accustomed place, with dwelling house, equipment and surroundings presumably adapted to the needs of the family living in it. It is naturally and usually the place with the refreshing and encouraging social atmosphere, cooperative management and daily cultivation of the more intimate human interests and values:—those of conjugal love, sex relations, birth and rearing of children, mutual human recognition and appreciation, economic sustenance, refuge from social perplexities and dangers, sleep, rest, health care, recreation, morale building, and general training in the social courtesies and amenities approved by the community.   C.J.B.

home, broken. A family in which one or both the parents are removed.   W.P.

home, foster. The home of a private family in which orphaned, neglected, or potentially delinquent children are placed on the theory that institutional care is too artificial an environment for the social development of a growing child. The foster parents are paid an established fee for their services. Roughly 250,000 children are cared for in foster homes in the United States. While the the theoretical superiority of the foster home over the institutional care is admitted, the foster home has problems of its own. Exploitation and mistreatment by persons of questionable qualification for the work of parenthood constitute one of the most serious difficulties.   J.W.M'C.

home bureau. An organization of farm and rural women for the improvement of homemaking and rural life, originating as a department of the Farm Bureau (q.v.) and associated with it in its work.   D.S.

home relief. Cf. relief, home.

homestead. (1) A property which is the subject of a "declaration of homestead" whereby the property is exempt from attachment or seizure to satisfy a judgment rendered in favor of a creditor. (2) A property occupied by its owner as his home.

homework. Manufacturing done in the home using materials furnished by an entrepreneur who pays for the work of manufacture by the piece. Homework was once an important source of exploitation of women workers but social crusades since 1890 have brought it under control.
                                            J.W.M'C.

homicide. The killing of one person by another. Homicide in the legal sense may be either justifiable or unjustifiable. In the former there is no occasion for court action; in the latter case the person may be charged with and tried for either manslaughter (q.v.) or murder (q.v.). J.W.M'C.

hominine. Characteristic of all members of genus homo, their behavior, quality, etc., whether or not of species sapiens, and whether or not possessed of culture and therefore human (q.v.).   T.D.E.

homogeneity. The quality characteristic of a population when the individuals within it show marked likeness of biologic or cultural traits. Racial homogeneity exists: (1) When the members of a group are derived from the same race, or physical type; when they are relatively of pure stock; i.e., they show similar physical traits due to common ancestry and continued in-breeding, or (2) when the members are derived from two or more dissimilar groups between whom there has been continued cross breeding. A popu-

lation may be heterogeneous in origin and through inter-marriage achieve homogeneity; i.e., all members of the group are of mixed ancestry — carrying diverse strains in similar fashion. Ethnic homogeneity exists when the members of a group have the same ethnic and cultural origin, and/or when they display likemindedness and cohesion due to group membership, tradition and cultural patterning common to the group. Cf. ethnic. Cultural homogeneity occurs when the members of the group are characterized by similarity of culture. Cf. culture.
                                            B.B.W.

homogeneous. Characterized by homogeneity (q.v.). A population is homogeneous: (1) When it is relatively of pure stock; i.e., the individuals within it are derived from the same race or physical type and have physical or cultural traits in common due to common ancestry, the result of inbreeding; (2) when originally heterogeneous—the population has become admixed through continued crossing of diverse strains, i.e., when the members have similar physical traits due to common ancestry arising from cross breeding. Cf. heterogeneous.   B.B.W.

homosexuality. The perversion of sexual desire that makes persons of the same rather than the opposite sex attractive.
                                            E.R.G.

honest graft. Cf. graft, honest.

honeymoon. Originally the term is said to have referred to the moon which, at the full, is nevertheless about to wane. At present the word signifies a short holiday period after marriage, which is spent by a newly wedded pair in traveling or otherwise, before settling down to their new life together.   W.G.

honor system. A method of prison discipline intended to relieve the prisoner from constant oversight and direction and place upon him, with a limited degree of liberty, the responsibility for his conduct. It is applied not only to "trusties" within the institution, but to prisoners who drive trucks, and go outside the walls for other work connected with the prison, and to those who work on farms and in camps connected with the institution. These are often called "honor" camps and farms. J.L.G.

horde. A loosely organized social group. The term is of very dubious scientific value inasmuch as it is applied to groups ranging in size from a small band, as in Australia, to a great agglomeration of tribes, as in Central Asia. G.P.M.

horizontal group. Cf. group, horizontal.

horizontal mobility. Cf. mobility, horizontal.

hospital social service. A system utilizing the functions of specialized social service workers in connection with hospital patients or recently discharged patients as a supplement to medical care. E.E.M.

hospitalization. A system of insurance offered by hospitals and private insurance companies whereby a person can be assured of necessary hospital care in return for the payment of a small premium. The care offered is limited in amount and applies only for certain types of ailments; incidental hospital fees may also be paid. Participation in the plans is usually limited to members of bona fide groups such as employees of a firm. Beginning in the early 1930's the growth of hospitalization plans has been rapid. Also the commitment of a patient to a hospital. J.W.M'C.

hostage. A person given by one power or group to another as security against the breaking of a contract or a promise. One held by another individual or group to insure compliance, by others, with a demand. The term hostage usually refers to a person held by a warring power to secure advantages over the enemy. J.M.R.

house, apartment. Cf. apartment house.

house of correction. English institution established in the sixteenth century for vagabonds, prostitutes, rogues, and the unemployed. In the United States, place of confinement for offenders whose violations of the law are of a minor nature. Usually for short-term offenders. J.P.S.

house of detention. A building maintained by local government to detain young persons pending juvenile court action or other disposition of their cases. In some states by law, and in others by common consent, children below a certain age are not housed in local jails. Consequently the house of detention becomes a catch-all for children who cannot be set at liberty immediately. Juveniles charged with serious crimes are thrown together with children held as witnesses, deserted children and runaways. J.W.M'C.

house of refuge. Early American institution for the confinement of juvenile delinquents. A forerunner of contemporary juvenile institutions. J.P.S.

household. That economic and social unit which is composed of all those persons who live together in a single dwelling-place, be it a house, apartment, tenement, tent, or igloo. As contrasted with the family which is a biological and social unit including only those related by ties of marriage and blood, the household includes servants, boarders and temporary or permanent guests. A.E.W.

household, census. A family or any other group of persons living together, with common housekeeping arrangements, in the same living quarters. Includes servants, other employees, and lodgers who sleep in the house if such is their usual place of residence. M.Pt.

household administration. The determination of the objectives of, and policies for, the management of the household. Household administration is one of the functions of the husband and wife relationship, and includes plans for the delegation of responsibility for the management and detailed work of the home. A.E.W.

household employee. The paid worker who is employed by the head of the household to perform certain tasks and render personal services in the household, on the same basis as are workers engaged in other industries which accept standards of hours, wages, living conditions, and protection by social legislation. A.E.W.

household employment. The performance of the tasks and the rendering of personal services within the home by paid workers rather than entirely by members of the family group. Cf. domestic service.   A.E.W.

household management. The detailed direction and supervision of all the processes which take place daily in every normal household. As contrasted with household administration, household management is the carrying out of the policies determined upon jointly by the administrators of the household.   A.E.W.

housing. (1) The development of living facilities for human beings. (2) Living facilities for human beings.

housing, company. Cf. company housing.

housing congestion. The overcrowding of land areas with houses of multiple or one or two-family types. Cf. overhousing.   E.E.M.

housing cooperative. Cf. cooperative, housing.

hulks. Unseaworthy vessels anchored in rivers or still waters which were used as places of confinement for offenders. J.P.S.

human. Ordinarily used to include all representatives of the species homo sapiens, or any qualities supposed to be common to the entire species. Sociologists tend to restrict the word to culture man, i.e., men with at least the essential elements of a culture (speech, ideas, ability to transmit, ability to make and use artifacts). Anthropic (q.v.) man and feral (q.v.) man would be excluded from this definition, as well as idiots. Cf. human nature; hominine.   T.D.E.

human, infra.—Literally, "below the human"; hence, belonging to a species of organisms inferior to the human, or possessing the traits, characteristics, or qualities of such a species.   H.E.J.

human behavior. Cf. behavior, human.

human being. Cf. being, human.

human ecology. Cf. ecology, human.

human geography. That branch of science which treats of the direct reciprocal influences that take place between individual men or groups of men and their physical environment.   J.A.Q.

human intelligence. Cf. intelligence, human.

human nature. The general character of mankind at any particular epoch, especially with respect to the motivation of behavior. It is the product of cumulative cultural modifications of basic biological instincts, capacities, and drives.

human nature, laws of. The observed, regular sequences and coordinations of the behavior of people organized in the development of interesting projects, for the growth and enrichment of human personality. These observed uniformities follow a necessary sequence of need, effort, and satisfaction, developed in social institutions as follows: (1) The stage and functions of physical maintenance; (2) the stage and functions of reflective investigation; (3) the stage and functions of collective control; (4) the stage and functions of aesthetic appreciation. In this order the classes of social functions appear to have developed historically in regard to the time devoted to them, exact efficiency, public concern, and social attention. Elaboration of these more fundamental of human folkways, mores and civil and criminal laws.   C.J.B.

human phenomena. Cf. phenomena, human.

human sacrifice. Cf. sacrifice, human.

humanistic. Characterized by an attitude centering upon human interests, especially the academic humanities.   L.P.E.

humanitarian. (1) An adherent of the doctrine that moral duty is dependent only on human relations. (2) A philanthropist.   L.P.E.

husband. The term is derived from the Middle English word husbonde, meaning master of the house or family. At present the term is used to mean a man with a wife, or as the correlative of wife.   W.G.

hybrid. The first generation offspring of parents belonging to different species, varieties or strains, and thus differing in one or more hereditary traits. Human hybrids include not merely half-breeds, such as true mulattoes or mestizos, but children of any couple having different gene constitutions. If the parents differ by one gene only, the children nevertheless would be hybrid for that one trait.   F.H.H.

I

iconoclasm. Image breaking; attacking cherished beliefs as shams.   L.P.E.

id. That portion of the personality (q.v.) reposing in the unconscious and containing the repressed primitive and anti-social wishes and impulses, constituting the reservoir of libido.   H.H.

ideal. An imaginary or non-existent, culturally defined situation, characteristic, or behavior pattern which serves as an aim or goal for the activity of a person or a group.   J.P.E.

ideal, primary. Any ideal which has been defined by the culture as being essential to the welfare of the individual or group adhering to this culture. Usually believed to be derived from the intimate relationships existing in the family. J.P.E.

ideal civilization. Cf. civilization, ideal.

ideal of society. A form of society sincerely approved as desirable to achieve. E.g., in the opinion of many, democracy, understood as a more perfect union, in which the social services or essential functions are so organized and promoted by the members as to render efficient and equally helpful assistance to all .   C.J.B.

ideal personality. Cf. personality, ideal.

ideal type. A configuration or gestalt of characteristics constructed by bringing together those most often observed in specimens of the category under consideration. Not all such characteristics need to be present in any one example, but all must be present in a high proportion of such examples and none must be incongruous with the other characteristics listed. It is assumed that an absolutely "pure" example of the category would display all such elements: hence the ideal type may be used to identify members of a class and also to measure the extent of typicality. It must be observed that "ideal" as here used carries no connotation of "better" or "poorer", i.e., is entirely non-normative. Cf. typology, constructive.   H.E.M.

ideal-typical method. Cf. typology, constructive.

idealism. The theory or practice of judging social institutions and practices by their degree of conformity to some ideal of perfect type; the tendency to be dissatisfied with achievements that fall short of perfection.

idealism, social. Cf. social idealism.

idealistic. (1) An expression of a thought or any behavior suggestive of perspective or of approximation to an ideal. Striving for or imagining a state of perfection. (2) A type of culture which recognizes both spiritual and material values but considers the material values only as a means of realizing an ideal. It is interested in the transformation of the external world as well as of the individual man, and is like the ideational type in interest in the things that are distant in perspective, durable and fundamental.   J.D.

idealization. The process of creating imaginary forms different from, and preferable to, those that actually exist, usually with the expectation of striving for them and the hope of eventually achieving them or at least approximating them. The setting up of new norms (q.v.). Idealization is an indispensable pre-requisite for a conscious, voluntary, planned improvement.

ideals, moral. Tested and desired patterns of human cooperation, facilitating or producing peace, order, union and general prosperity through voluntary, intelligent team work for the common good. These patterns imply recognition by the authorities of the equal rights of all citizens to legal protection and liberty of communication, worship and exchange within the limits set by the common welfare; as honestly, intelligently and freely determined by the majority of the people, through their chosen representatives. While moral ideals may transcend or contradict the existing civil law, they operate to defend and improve the laws in the interests of the common welfare.   C.J.B.

ideals, social. Cf. social ideals.

ideational. (1) Any expression of a thought or any behavior suggestive of perfection. (2) A type of culture which exalts the spiritual above material values and imposes restraint in the use of material values as a means of realizing a spiritual good. This type is further characterized by attention to the things that are distant in perspective, durable and fundamental, and by interest in the transformation of the individual with little or no interest in the transformation of the external world. Reality is perceived as nonsensate and nonmaterial, everlasting Being (*Sein*). The needs and ends are mainly spiritual. The extent of their satisfaction is the largest, and the level, highest. The method of their fulfillment or realization is self-imposed minimization or elimination of most of the physical needs, and to the greatest possible extent. These major premises are common to all branches of the ideational culture mentality.

ideationalism, active. Identical with general ideationalism in its major premises, it seeks the realization of the needs and ends, not only through minimization of the carnal needs of individuals, but also through the transformation of the sensate world, and especially of the socio-cultural world, in such a way as to reform it along the lines of the spiritual reality and of the ends chosen as the main value. Its bearers do not "flee from the world of illusion" and do not entirely dissolve it and their own souls in the ultimate reality, but strive to bring it nearer to God, to save not only their own souls but the souls of all other human beings.   J.D.

ideationalism, ascetic. This seeks the consummation of the needs and ends through an excessive elimination and minimization of the carnal needs, supplemented by a complete detachment from the sensate world and even from oneself, viewing both as mere illusion, nonreal, nonexisting. The whole sensate milieu, and even the individual "self", are dissolved in the supersensate, ultimate reality.

identical twins. Cf. twins, identical.

identification. (1) The process by which a person defines himself, the self's identity, from the not-self. That which is accepted and integrated in his will, that is, subject to immediate control and consonant with the integrity of the rest of the self at the time, is introjected. Introjection includes a new experience, or a reappraisal experience, in the self by identifying it with the self. That which is intolerable to or beyond the control of the self is rejected, or projected: the self refuses to identify with it, even though it be an actual deed of the individual, or a dream or fantasy from within his own subconscious. Riddance may take the form of excretion, encystment, dissociation, repression, or projection of a "devil." Special phases of projection (psychiatric) include hallucinations (attribution of actuality to a fantasy) and illusions of persecution (attribution of motives to outsiders which have arisen from within the person). Putting oneself emotionally in the place of another.   T.D.E.

(2) The process of establishing the identity of a person accused or suspected of a crime.   F.W.K.

ideograph, ideogram. (1) The graphic representation of an object or idea by a single symbol, as distinguished from representation by the use of letters, syllabic signs or words. (2) A tracing giving a direct record of muscular movements due to changes of thought.   M.S.

ideology. The aggregate of the ideas, beliefs, and modes of thinking characteristic of a group, such as a nation, class, caste, profession or occupation, religious sect, political party, etc. These ideologies are conditioned and determined by the geographical and climatic situation, habitual activities, and cultural environment of their respective groups. They are not necessarily mutually exclusive and may overlap. Thus two individuals of the same nationality but of different occupations may share their national ideology but differ in their respective occupational ideologies.   M.Pm.

idiot. A feeble-minded person with a mental development not exceeding that of a three-year-old normal child, i.e., with an intelligence quotient of less than 25. The lowest level of mentality. The few at the extreme left of the bell-shaped curve. Cf. mental deficiency.   P.H.L.

idle rich. Those persons who have amassed wealth either by inheritance or through their own efforts, and who live off their accumulated possessions without regular occupation or without making further efforts in the interest of the common welfare.   A.E.W.

idol. An image or representation of a supernatural being in which the latter is believed to have his seat or abode and before which sacrifices or other acts of worship are performed. Cf. fetish. G.P.M.

igloo. A dome-shaped Eskimo dwelling built of blocks of snow laid in spiral courses.

illegitimacy. The state of being illegitimate; not according to law or established custom, usually applied to one whose parents were not married in some legal manner.   O.W.

illiteracy. The state of being illiterate, uneducated. As it is used in the United States census, illiteracy refers to anyone ten years of age or over who is unable to read and write in any language.   O.W.

imagination, scientific. Resourcefulness in research as shown in each step in the

scientific method; it appears most inclusively in "imaginative synthesis."   H,A.P.

imbecile. A mentally deficient person with an intelligence quotient of from 25 to 49, or a mental age for an adult equivalent to that of a child of from 3 to 7 years.
                                                 J.W.M′C.

imbecile, moral. According to nineteenth century Italian psychiatrists certain persons were supposed to be tainted with a form of insanity known under various names such as "moral insanity" or "moral imbecility." Such individuals lacked any moral or social sense or had had it atrophied. Moral imbecility could be accompanied by apparent soundness of mind.
                                                 N.F.C.

imitate. To copy or reproduce action of another.   M.S.

imitation. Any behavior, conscious or unconscious, which is patterned after observably similar behavior or traits of another being considered as sentient, responding to the model whether the latter be conscious or unconscious, deliberate or accidental in that rôle. As an "instinct", imitation is no longer so considered. As a capacity, it is roused either on an ideomotor basis without central motivation, or on a basis of wishful identification: the person wants to be like the model either because of admiration or in order to get results or status that the other has got (rational imitation, learning imitation).
                                                 T.D.E.

imitation, conventional. The more or less intentional copying of the attitudes and behavior patterns of one's age group or contemporaries.   N.L.S.

imitation, custom. The form of imitation whereby the individual develops conformity to the folkways of his group, usually unconsciously through the operation of persuasive control.

imitation, fashion. Imitation of models for the sake of status, based upon identification with the class which has status, notably through honorific expenditures on clothes, accessories, furnishing, and personal adornment. The imitators compose the mode, which, however, is always skewing toward the pace-setters, some of whom are employed to serve as models, others of whom serve as such because of prestige of notoriety or position. Variants at the other extreme ignore the mode but follow in its wake more or less willy-nilly as the market is glutted with bargains of passing fashion. Yesterday's pace-maker provides today's mode and tomorrow's lag.   T.D.E.

imitation, suggestion. Imitation, conscious or unconscious, that is the result of suggestion (q.v.).

imitative magic. Cf. magic, imitative.

immigrant. One who participates in an immigration movement.

immigration. A population movement between two countries on approximately the same culture area, the former being relatively older, more densely populated and less attractive politically, economically, or socially; the latter being relatively sparsely populated with definite attractions in the way of economic opportunity or political, religious, and social liberty. True immigration is voluntary on the part of the migrants, and in the majority of cases is on private resources, although there is frequently state support or subsidy of some sort. True immigration always crosses a political boundary. The country of destination (q.v.) may be an independent state or may be a colony. Immigration differs from emigration only in the point of view—the individuals involved are identical.

immobility, social. Cf. social immobility.

impairment. A fault, break or condition of flaw marking a deviation from normal in a process or structure. The recognition of an impairment may or may not involve the possibility of repair. N.A.

impaling. A form of capital punishment at least as old as the ancient kingdom of Assyria. It was used also in ancient Persia and Rome. It took various forms, sometimes a stake or spear was driven through the body just below the breast bone, and at other times and places the culprit was thrown from a height upon spears or stakes set in the ground. There was an element of brutality in it, because it usually involved slow death.   J.A.G.

imperative, social. Cf. social imperative.

imperialism. The national policy and practice of expansion either by the forcible annexation of adjoining territory or by gaining possession of alien colonies, dependencies and protectorates. The recent opening up of vast unexplored and unexploited regions stimulated greatly the international rivalry for colonies and spheres of influence as outlets for the export of surplus capital and commodities of the more highly industrialized nations. The modern form of imperialism is therefore predominantly economic rather than political. It includes the struggle for concessions, for the control of colonial markets, for monopolies of raw materials, and sometimes of cheap native labor. Protective and preferential tariffs, subsidies to national industries, and other forms of economic discrimination, play their part in this economic warfare, which often leads to military and naval warfare. Cf. empire.
                                                  M.Pm.

impulse. (1) Tendency to act without voluntary direction or reflection. Action tendency appearing not to be traceable to stimulation.   M.S.

impulsive action. Cf. action, impulsive.

inbreeding. The process by which a group or institution tends to become static or retrogressive for lack of the introduction of new biological or psychological elements, or new personalities.   G.M.F.

incantation. A verbal formula, the recitation or chanting of which is believed to have magical efficacy. Cf. spell.   G.P.M.

incentive. (1) An extraorganic stimulus which combines with one or more intraorganic factors to produce activity. (2) An extraorganic stimulus which serves to direct or maintain motivated conduct. M.S.

incest. Sexual intercourse between relatives to whom marriage is prohibited.
                                                  G.P.M.

incest, dynastic. The practice, prevalent in certain royal families, of contracting marriages between brother and sister, or other near relatives, in contradiction to the incest taboos observed by the general population.   **G.P.M.**

income, farm. Cf. farm income.

income level. The plane of living which any individual or family is able to enjoy, based on their earnings or other sources of income. The term includes the following: (a) the subsistence level (the emergency or relief standard); (b) the minimum standard of health and decency; (c) the comfort standard; (d) the luxury standard.   **A.E.W.**

incorporated village. Cf. village.

incorrigibility. The unmanageable or uncontrollable behavior of a child or minor which is generally classified as an act constituting juvenile delinquency, and hence warrants the authorities making the child behaving thus a ward of the juvenile court.   **M.A.E.**

increase, natural. The numerical excess of births over deaths in a given population during a specified period of time. The reverse situation (excess of deaths over births) is a natural decrease, but is frequently entered in tabular material as a minus quantity (—) under the general heading, natural increase. Natural increase differs from total growth or actual increase in that its computation takes no account of gains or losses through migration. Through age-selections, however, natural increase is often indirectly influenced by migration.   **C.V.K.**

increment, unearned. Cf. unearned increment.

independent variable. Cf. variable, independent.

indeterminate sentence. Cf. sentence, indeterminate.

index. (1) A catalog or list, an orderly array of classified information through the use of which added information may be obtained. (2) A numerical symbol of a proportion.   **N.A.**

index, census tract street. An index of streets usually for a large city (and sometimes for its adjacent area) with house number entries for each street classified according to census tracts. The census tract street index is used to facilitate the rapid allocation of data according to census tracts.   **C.F.S.**

index, central. Cf. social service exchange.

index, cephalic. The ratio of the maximum breadth of the head to its maximum length as measured from the glabella (q.v.) to the most distant point on the occiput, determined by multiplying the breadth by 100 and dividing by the length. Cf. cranial index; brachycephalic; dolichocephalic; mesocephalic.   **G.P.M.**

index, cranial. The ratio of the maximum breadth of the skull to its maximum length as measured from the glabella (q.v.) to the most distant point on the occiput, determined by multiplying the breadth by 100 and dividing by the length.   **G.P.M.**

index, crime. A crime rate employed as an indirect measure of criminality. The total criminality is an unknown quantity; the recorded criminality includes only that part of the total which is known to the law enforcement, judicial, and penal agencies. It is assumed that in the case of certain types of offenses, certain rates of recorded criminality may be used to measure not only law enforcement activity, but indirectly the trends, etc., of total criminality. Statisticians have paid little attention to the theoretical aspects of this problem and the concept of an index is therefore still crude.   **T.S.**

index, facial. A proportional measure of the breadth to the length of the face, technically defined in anthropology.

index, nasal. The ratio of the breadth of the nose or nasal aperture to its length, determined by multiplying the breadth by 100 and dividing by the length. Cf. leptorrhine; mesorrhine; platyrrhine. **G.P.M.**

index, replacement. A measure of the reproductive trend of a population with reference to population replacement. Specifically, a measure derived from census data on number of children (e.g. P_{0-5}) and number of females (e.g. P^F_{20-44}) relative to the age distribution of the corresponding life table population (L):

$$P_{0-4}/P^F_{20-44}//LO\text{-}5/L^F_{20-45} \qquad \text{F.L.}$$

index, vital. A birth-death ratio designed to afford an index of the "biologic vigor" of a population under consideration. In the crude but common form

$$\frac{\text{Total Births During Year x 100}}{\text{Total Deaths During Year}}$$

the index is subject to the limitations of the crude birth and death rates in so far as influences of age composition, sex-ratios, etc., are concerned. To avoid limitations of this character the indices are sometimes restricted to women of child-bearing age and are presented in age-specific form

$$\frac{\text{Births During Year to Women 20-24x100}}{\text{Deaths During Year Among Women 20-24}}$$
C.V.K.

index number. One of a series of numbers expressing the relative changes in a variable or in a group of variables from time to time or from place to place. A simple index which shows the fluctuations in a single variable (e.g., price of pig iron) is more correctly called a relative or percentage relative. The term index number usually refers to a composite index number used to express fluctuations in the magnitude of groups of phenomena (e.g., retail prices as a whole, business activity, cost of living, employment, etc.). The items entering into the composite may be unweighted (called simple index) or weighted in accordance with such numbers as quantities produced or consumed. The value of the index number at the reference point chosen as the base (usually a given year or group of years) is taken as 100. Index numbers are usually expressed as percentages of the values in the base period, but they may be mere aggregates.   M.Pt.

indictment. The list of crimes with which a person is charged and for which in the opinion of the grand jury there is sufficient evidence of guilt to hold the accused for formal trial. The formal indictment should be clearly distinguished from the bill of indictment which the prosecuting attorney reads to the grand jury and upon which they deliberate.   J.W.M'C.

indirect contact. Cf. contact, indirect.

individual action. Action not influenced by the presence or activity of others.   M.S.

individual adjustment. The process by which an individual consciously modifies a socially acquired characteristic in order to make it conform to a desired standard or norm.   J.P.E.

individual ascendancy. Ascendancy of one individual over another.   M.S.

individual authority. Consciousness of the effective and ample superiority of one value-system over another, represented by a person or group. Such authority can be: (1) original or (2) derivative. The recognition of the original can be through experience or perception, the latter through achievement or intuition. The recognition of derivative authority lies in the superiority of the value system to which the person or group which acts or speaks authoritatively belongs.   J.H.B.

individual aversion. Personal dislike or antagonism which is not the result of group experience or tradition.   P.F.C.

individual behavior. The manner of acting of a specific individual in a given situation.   J.P.E.

individual contact. Relatively temporary interaction between two or more persons.
P.F.C.

individual demoralization. Cf. demoralization.

individual deterioration. The process of growing worse or declining from some previous condition regarded as a norm, such as a given degree of physical or mental health, conformity with the mores, social adjustment; the state of having so declined.

individual progress. Change, movement, or development of an individual toward a predetermined goal or objective. This goal may be determined by the individual, by others, or jointly.   J.P.E.

individual reorganization. The establishment of a new set of values in the life of an individual.   P.F.C.

individual representation. Any privately meaningful, but uncommunicated, item of the individual person's experience. Cf. representation, collective.   M.S.

individual satisfaction. Acceptance of and agreement with the hierarchy of values of his society by an individual.   J.H.B.

individual survival. A concept of indefinite survival attempted, even if indirectly; physically and bodily through procreation; and/or spiritually and symbolically through creation, in order to enter history which man recognizes as the objectivized residuum of survival.   J.H.B.

individual telics. An intellectual system of ideas and purposes organized around the goal of personal betterment.

individual type. Conception structure of instrumental forms through embodiment in a sociologically definable object. J.H.B.

individual will. The will of an individual.   M.S.

individual wish. Wish possessed by an individual for the satisfaction of individual desires.   M.S.

individualism. An attitude, doctrine, or policy of control which stresses the supremacy or importance of the individual person or personality,—either as means or as end, and either selfishly ("each man for himself") or altruistically ("the greatest good for the greatest number"). Classic economics offered a specious synthesis: "The self-interest of each will produce the best interest of all." Individualism as an ideology is linked with doctrines of hedonism, utilitarianism, self-interest, free contract, free enterprise, free competition, individual initiative, laissez faire (q.v.), liberty of exploitation ("rugged individualism"); the historical results of these doctrines in action have led to much

common illfare for which collectivistic or class conscious policies have attempted to compensate. Not to be confused with individuality (q.v.). Cf. collectivism. As an attitude it stands for personal independence, not in relation to tradition or authority as such, but from collective motivations, which are often but not always supported by tradition and authority. But individualism may also be reinforced by its own tradition and authoritarianism.
                T.D.E.

individualism, rugged. Cf. rugged individualism.

individualistic. Possessing or pertaining to the characteristics of the individual or individualism.   J.P.E

individuality. The configuration of characteristics which makes a personality (q.v.) unique to the outside observer. Cf. selfhood.   H.H.

individualization. The process by which one human being acquires characteristics which differentiate him from others. J.P.E.

individualization of punishment. Cf. punishment, individualization of.

individuals. Those human beings comprising any social aggregate when they are considered from the point of view of the characteristics which make each one different from the others.   J.P.E.

indoctrinated attitude. Cf. attitude, indoctrinated.

indoor relief. Cf. relief, indoor.

industrial arbitration. Cf. arbitration, industrial.

industrial area. Cf. area, industrial.

industrial city. Cf. city, industrial.

industrial democracy A phrase used variously to characterize either; formal participation by employees in determining the conditions of their labor, as by trade union contracts and employee representation systems; and the set-up of industry as a whole where relations between owners and workers are determined by collective bargaining and governmental protection of workers' freedom to organize, and of minimum standards of hours and wages. Cf. democracy. R.N.B.

industrial life cycle. A term derived from the theory of cyclical fluctuations of social phenomena. In this view industry is seen to manifest a more or less definite pattern of social change, with an initial period of rapid development, then a long period of stabilization marked by varying degrees of exploitation of men and resources, the development of conflict situations and other factors affecting the health of the industry, with, in the long run, a tendency toward diminishing returns; and finally, a period of decline. Population changes, technological innovations, the changing state of domestic and world markets, and numerous other social and economic factors apparently are fully recognized as influencing the course the cycle takes. While some industries and industrial communities may cease to exist, presumably the stage of decline does not necessarily imply this. It may mark a transition from one cycle to another. A decadent industry or industrial community which takes on new life (as under the impetus of wartime expansion) would simply be beginning a new life cycle, or so it would seem. The theory is vague at many points. K.DP.L.

industrial organization. A culture pattern characterized by the extensive use of machinery, large-scale operation, mass production, and non-human power. The self-maintenance type characteristic of capitalism.

industrial policy. Group aims relating to the conduct of industry. The term is commonly applied to pronouncements by business organizations, firms and leaders, with reference to moot issues; also to stated aims and rules of procedure laid down by laws, government officials and departments; also to pronouncements in the platforms of political parties. It is sometimes used in a more inclusive sociological sense to refer to any stated long-time aims and programs concerning industrial organization and control, whether formulated by business, labor or other groups. K.DP.L.

industrial prison. Cf. prison, industrial.

industrial relations. The organization and practice of relations between workers and management in an industrial enterprise or an industry, or in all the industries of a community or a nation. M.VK.

Industrial Revolution. An inclusive term used to cover the complex of changes that ushered in modern industrialism. It is especially applied to the classic period of change of the late eighteenth and early nineteenth centuries in England at which time technological innovations completely altered the productive process and brought about the shift of industry from the home and small workshop mode of production to the factory system. Changes most frequently cited are those that occurred in the textile industry where a succession of inventions, in particular the spinning-jenny, water-frame, mule and power-loom transformed production. Also important were new developments in the production of iron and steel. Emphasis is given to changes in motive power, first in the application of water-power, and later, in the early nineteenth century, in the application of steam, the development of the steam engine in turn revolutionizing land and water transportation with consequent expansion of commerce and trade. Simultaneous division of labor and acceleration of mechanization in production everywhere typified the industrial changes in this period, with multiplication of productive efficacy the result. The many economic and social changes which are associated with the early stages of industrialism may be considered features of the Industrial Revolution. Cf. industrialism. Some economists speak of the "second industrial revolution", to refer to late nineteenth and early twentieth century changes, marked by the development of electrical power and the use of the lighter metals, together with advanced developments in the mechanization of industry. K.DP.L.

industrial society. Cf. society, industrial.

industrial spy. A person engaged by an employer to operate among employees as an informer concerning trade union activities, discontent and agitation. Cf. stool pigeon; rat. R.N.B.

industrial symbiosis. Cf. symbiosis, industrial.

industrial union. Cf. union, industrial.

industrialism. The stage of advanced technological development by means of applied science, the typical characteristics of which are large-scale production with the use of power machinery, a wide market, a specialized working force with intricate division of labor, and accelerated urbanization. The term is sometimes used in the case of a society in process of becoming industrialized, but it is not strictly applicable unless and until a decisive portion of the total production is carried on under such conditions. Where the process has gone far, mechanization may extend not only throughout most of industry but in some degree to agriculture; large-scale production, specialization and the division of labor are seen on a wide scale; the means of communication and transportation reach maximum development; electrical energy, through the development of large power projects, more and more displaces older forms of motive power. Accompanying the economic changes goes a complex pattern of change in social groups and the social process.

Typical of the early stages, along with urbanization, were rapid increases in population and in the mobility of populations. Also there were significant alterations in social customs and mores affecting all types of primary and secondary groups, and secondary groups were seen to play an even larger rôle. Especially characteristic were the effects upon the occupational status and skills of the working population, upon family life and the status of women, and upon traditions and habits in the consumption of goods. Conflict between classes, races and other groups, has been observed as a typical concomitant, as has also the increasingly complex nature of the process of accommodation.

Historically, industrialism has been limited in its application to the capitalist form of economic organization, with certain additional economic features commonly mentioned, such as economic expansion into undeveloped parts of the world, business cycles, with booms, crises, underemployment and unemployment, and new patterns of ownership and control by industrial and, latterly, financial interests. In contemporary usage the term is not thus confined. It is often used as likewise applicable to the industrialization process under socialist economic organization. However, due to many characteristic differences in the development of various traits and problems, the term as defined here refers to industrialism only under its capitalist form. Cf. capitalism.   K.DP.L.

industrialization. The process of technological development by the use of applied science, characterized by the expansion of large-scale production with the use of power machinery, for a wide market for both producer's and consumer's goods, by means of a specialized working force with division of labor, the whole accompanied by accelerated urbanization.   K.DP.L.

industry, large-scale. The organization of production under conditions of modern industrial society in enterprises of considerable size. The term large-scale has been applied to enterprises antedating the factory system, such as shipbuilding. Also it is often loosely used today with reference to vast integrated concerns under a single control, such as banking, insurance, construction and similar undertakings. Usually, however, it refers to manufacturing or mining operations, carried on by power machinery, with the use of advanced production techniques, requiring the employment of a considerable labor force working simultaneously in proximity, under a common management and control.   K.DP.L.

inequality. A condition of disparity arising from individual differences of sex, age, and mentality influence, and social economic stratifications of class, caste and rank.   K.DP.L.

inequality, social. Cf. social inequality.

inertia, social. Cf. social inertia.

infamous punishment. Cf. punishment, infamous.

infant mortality. Deaths of children under one year of age. Infant mortality rate: The number of deaths of children under one year of age during one year per 1,000 live births during the year. c.v.k.

infanticide. The act or practice of killing unwanted children at birth. Cf. abortion.

infecund. Cf. sterile.

infecundity. Cf. sterility.

inferiority, constitutional. Cf. constitutional inferiority.

infertile. Manifesting infertility; synonymous with childless.

infertility. Absence of fertility; synonymous with childlessness.

infibulation. The attachment of a ring or other contrivance to the female genitals for the purpose of preventing copulation.
G.P.M.

influence. Inclusive term for controls, subhuman, subsocial, social, super-social; but reserved ordinarily for informal person-to-person or person-to-group controls.
T.D.E.

information. A bill of particulars concerning the part the accused played in the commission of a crime, made up by the prosecuting attorney and submitted to a trial judge who determines on the basis of the facts presented whether there is sufficient evidence to hold the accused for trial. The information is gradually supplanting the indictment by grand jury as a swifter and fairer method of determining whether a person should be held for trial. Grand juries have already been abolished in favor of the information in England.
J.W.M′C.

infra-human. Cf. human, infra-.

in-group. Cf. group, in-.

inheritance. The rule governing the transmission of property, being "patrilineal" (q.v.) if it follows the male line, e.g., from father to child, and "matrilineal" (q.v.) if it follows the female line, e.g., from mother to child or from maternal uncle to sister's child. Cf. avunculate; descent; succession.
G.P.M.

inheritance, social. Cf. social inheritance.

inheritance of criminality. Cf. criminality, inheritance of.

inhibition. (*physiological, psychological*) A positive nerve impulse conflicting with another nerve impulse sufficiently to offset and block its path or its effect; a negative control restraining some particular attitude or behavior, but felt to be internal to the subject, even if due to mores, taboo, morals, religion, or law: if these be accepted (introjected) by the subject, the restraining effect is inhibition rather than prohibition (q.v.).
T.D.E.

inhibition, social. Cf. social inhibition.

inhibitive (or inhibitory). Tending to inhibit, hold back, restrain, or hinder a function which is already active.
M.Pt.

inhumation. The practice of earth burial, i.e., of interring the corpses of the dead in graves or beneath mounds. Cf. burial.
G.P.M.

initial cause. Cf. cause, initial.

initiation rites. Cf. rites, initiation.

initiative. A political device for getting a proposal before the people for vote, submitted by petition of qualified voters, with a provision commonly for opportunity for action first by the legislative body. R.N.B.

innovation. Something new, a departure from prevailing practice. An adaptation to a changing situation.
N.A.

inpatient. One who is received into a hospital or similar institution, generally for temporary medical treatment and care.
E.E.M.

insane, criminal. Cf. criminal insane.

insane criminal. In its legal sense, any person who commits a crime, but who, because of a permanent defect or disease of the mind, is considered incapable of entertaining a criminal intent. A criminal intent is, generally, an essential element of every crime, hence no insane person is criminally responsible for his acts. Cf. criminal insane.
N.F.C.

insanitary dwelling. A dwelling in which infestation, dampness, lack of ventilation, natural light, or heating or sanitary facilities exist to a degree prejudicial to the health of its occupants.   s.s.

insanity. An antiquated term used to designate mental defect or unbalance. In legal procedure where the term is most generally used insanity indicates a person who cannot judge right from wrong, consequently one who is likely to menace the health and safety of society. In sociology insanity has given place entirely to such terms as mental disease or mental defect and others more descriptive of the character of the ailment. Insanity (mental disease) may be classified roughly into neuroses (q.v.) and psychoses (q.v.), which may be either organic or psychological in origin.   J.W.M'C.

insecurity, economic. The uncertainties surrounding the means of livelihood attendant on modern industrial social organization, relating in particular to limited occupational opportunity, low income, unemployment, sickness and old age.
                    K.DP.L.

insight. The direct, immediate, or sudden apprehension of the meaning of a situation without recourse to involved mental processes.   J.P.E.

insight, sympathetic. The direct apprehension of the meaning of a situation as it affects others combined with an understanding and appreciation of the emotional factors involved.   J.P.E.

insignia. Emblems of office, authority, or rank. Cf. regalia.   G.P.M.

inspiration. (1) The supposed communication of ideas or actions to human beings by supernatural, or divine, beings. (2) The formulation of ideas or actions without conscious recourse to established methods of reasoning.   E.A.H.

installment buying. A plan of consumer credit enabling the person to have possession (though in some cases not legal title) of an article by making a small initial payment and a contract for future periodic payments until the sale price is entirely paid. There are endless varieties of installment plans each attempting to present a less painless schedule of money payments than the other. The practice of installment buying is so widespread as to have a profound effect upon the operation of the economic system.
                    J.W.M'C.

instinct. (1) The innate propensity to satisfy basic needs, especially the biological, believed present in all organisms. This propensity is presumed to be automatic in becoming activated, so that the stimulus merely releases it; here the emphasis is on the purposeful motivation, the implication being that instincts are directive. (2) An inherent tendency of an organism to respond to a stimulus according to a regular pattern. Though this reaction may be serviceable, neither it nor the services attained need to be consciously appreciated. Here the emphasis is on the response activity, and the implication is that the instincts are driving forces. *Note*: The term is not fixed in meaning, and usage involves adaptations or combinations of these definitions.   B.M.

instinctive. Referring to activity presumably associated with instincts, and sometimes regarded as motivated by them. B.M.

institution. (1) An enduring, complex, integrated, organized behavior pattern through which social control is exerted and by means of which the fundamental social desires or needs are met.   H.E.M.
(2) An organization of a public, or semi-public, character involving a directive body, and usually a building or physical establishment of some sort, designated to serve some socially recognized and authorized end. In this category fall such units as colleges and universities, orphan asylums, hospitals, almshouses, etc.

institution, operative. An institution which carries on, in a systematic manner, specific activities or services for a given group at a given time, as, for example, a social settlement, the Y.M.C.A., the Boy Scouts, a library, a charitable organization. Operative institutions should be distinguished from the more universal regulative institutions which emphasize compulsory norms and serve as social molds or channels for the behavior of human beings generally in the common social relationships, as the family, the state, or property.   J.O.H.

institution, remedial. A culture complex (q.v.) in which the major purpose is to correct maladjustments or to achieve more adequate adjustments, and in which a building or a system of buildings plays a major and central rôle. Examples are hospitals, jails, old people's homes, orphanages, and the like.   H.H.

institution, social. Cf. social institutions.

institutional. Pertaining to or partaking of the nature of an institution in structure and/or function, or other identifiable characteristic. For example, the term may be applied to a person or persons, as institutional administrator, institutional personnel, or to a culture trait or complex, as institutional rule, institutional code, institutional building.   J.O.H.

institutional adjustment. Cf. adjustment, institutional.

institutional church. Cf. church, institutional.

institutional competition. Cf. competition, institutional.

institutional control. Cf. control, institutional.

institutional cycle. Cf. cycle, institutional.

institutional process. Any operation or occurrence caused by or relating to an institution. The term has at least two specific connotations: (1) The procedures or operations in effect, the change undergone, as a social function or social relationship emerges or develops as an institution. (2) The operation of an institution as it carries on its appropriate or established social function; and two more general or all-inclusive means: (3) The total career of institutions Cf. institutional cycles. (4) The semi-total of the special processes characterizing the life of most institutions (emergence, development, conflict,

competition, persistence, disorganization, reorganization).   J.O.H.

institutional relief. Cf. relief, institutional.

institutional stereotype. Prejudiced and oversimplified estimate of the manner in which a social institution operates and of the ways in which it functions and is utilized in social control. Such an estimate reflects chiefly these factors in the mental orientation of an individual holding a given stereotype: (1) His social statuses; (2) the sub-cultures of the groups to which he belongs; (3) his functional relationship to the institution in question; (4) the history of his relationship with that institution. Personnel managers spend considerable time and effort ascertaining employees' stereotyped views of the employing institution and correcting such institutional stereotypes in terms of management's interests. Public relations counselors are concerned with the popular stereotypes of the institutions they represent. Labor leaders make conscious efforts to correct workers' institutional stereotypes to terms consistent with the aspirations of the labor movement. A.M'C.L.

institutional systems. The groupings of institutions according to the major or pivotal fields of social life in which the institutions perform their basic social functions, such as the economic system (institutions of production, exchange, consumption, transportation, etc.), the marriage system (kinship, marriage, inheritance, family), the political system (administrative, legislative, judicial, military, public health, etc., institutions). In arranging the institutions of any given society by systems the division and allocation, of necessity, is more or less arbitrary, since the specific institutions overlap, intertwine and support each other; few institutions perform a single function. Thus while the family is primarily a domestic institution it also has and does perform educational, religious, recreational, health, and economic functions.   J.O.H.

institutions, correctional. Jails, reformatories, and prisons. Modern society has recognized that institutions for offenders not only have a punitive function but also have a custodial and rehabilitative function. As the institutions for juvenile and adult offenders enrich their programs and develop their facilities for effective handling of inmates, the punitive function gives way to the custodial and rehabilitative function. Hence, these institutions become more correctional than penal.

W.C.R.

institutions, primary. The great, universal institutions, found in some form and degree of development in all cultures, which regulate and standardize the behavior of the members of the society with respect to the basic and omnipresent social needs, such as physical maintenance (economic institutions), sex regulation and the production, maintenance and social induction of the young (domestic institutions), adjustment to the unknown and the hereafter (religious institutions).   J.O.H.

institutions, secondary. The institutions serving less important social functions, or those derived from or functionally amplifying the primary institutions. Such institutions as morals, education and aesthetics may be considered secondary because they are less essential to group maintenance and security. Cf. institutions, primary.   J.O.H.

institutions, social. Cf. social institutions.

insurance, accident. Indemnification for physical injury suffered as a result of unknown or unavoidable circumstances. Workmen's compensation providing payment for industrial injury resulting in disability is compulsory throughout the United States and most foreign countries, but insurance for non-industrial accident is voluntary although a few states insist upon automobile owners carrying liability insurance.   J.W.M'C.

insurance, health. A general term covering all plans for offering medical care, hospitalization and cash disability benefits or any one of these separately on a pre-payment basis. The most extensive and controversial of these plans are the government sponsored plans prevalent throughout Europe. While not typical of all such plans English health insurance comes closest to American thought on the

subject. The government, the employer and the employee contribute to a pooled fund. In order to receive cash benefits for disability the insured joins a club through which the benefit is paid. Medical care is offered by any one of a panel of doctors in the local community that the patient selects. Doctors are paid by the government a per capita fee for all persons selecting them as attending doctor regardless of the amount of medical service rendered. In the United States similar plans are proposed or in operation but they are sponsored through private rather than public agencies.   J.W.M'C.

insurance, old age and survivors. Cf. old age and survivors insurance.

insurance, social. Cf. social insurance.

integralism. Cf. harmonism.

integrate. To unite separate entities into a cohesive whole which is something different from the sum of the parts, as in the merging of different tribes, or states into one nation, or the complete assimilation of different cultural elements so as to produce a homogeneous culture of mutually adapted traits. Cf. assimilation, social.

integration. That social process which tends to harmonize and unify diverse and conflicting units, whether those units be elements of personality, individuals, groups or larger social aggregations.   A.E.W.

integration, group. The process of interaction between members of a group which results in reciprocal accommodation and an increased sense of identification with the group. More recently the term has acquired a specialized meaning applied to a process of accommodation within small groups. In this sense integration is a type of group thinking in which out of the differing contributions of each a consensus is created which welds the group into unanimity involving both intellectual and emotional responses. Such integration is to be contrasted with compromise or subjugation of a minority to majority control.

G.L.C.

integration, social. Cf. social integration.

intelligence. The quality of a living organism that enables it to meet and solve problems, particularly new and unfamiliar ones, in ways adapted to its own needs and with a minimum expenditure of effort, time, and energy. As ordinarily interpreted, this quality is a generalized one, and is presumed to be established in the hereditary constitution of the individual. It is presumed not to be affected by environment, experience, or education. It develops normally with the chronological age of the individual, and attains increasing scope and effectiveness up to a certain age, perhaps fourteen or sixteen years in human beings. This is what practising psychologists have sought to isolate and grade in the process of intelligence testing. The validity and precision of the concept have not yet been completely demonstrated, though there is little doubt that intelligence tests do furnish a practical working measure of the ability of the individual to function normally in his own social environment.

intelligence, human. Combination of those aspects, peculiar to human beings, of the ability to profit by both present and past experience in adjusting to existing conditions and in preparing for successful adjustment to future conditions.   M.S.

intelligence quotient. The numerical ratio between the chronological age of a person and his mental age times 100 in order to give a whole number. For example, if a child of ten takes an intelligence test and makes a score equivalent to that of a ten-year-old his IQ is 100. If on the other hand his score equals that of a 12-year-old, his IQ is 120; or if only equal to that of an 8-year old his IQ is 80. The intelligence quotient of any person is only a relative rating as judged according to a test which gauges an undefined set of mental abilities called intelligence (q.v.). Efforts have been made to eliminate the influence of culture and training but these inevitably influence both the character of the test and the degree of mental competence shown by the individual. The usefulness of the IQ as a measure of ability can be determined only on the basis of the achievements of those persons who have previously taken such tests. Such experience tables increase the probability

of accurate prediction concerning persons taking the tests in the future.   J.W.M´C.

intelligentsia. Social group of a population concerned with science, art and cultural life. Sometimes used almost in the sense of a caste with a somewhat derogatory connotation for its liberal attitudes toward social problems and its only theoretical efforts toward their solution; outstanding in Russian writings; played an important rôle in discussions of the early New Deal era.

intent, criminal. Cf. criminal intent.

interact. To influence reciprocally; to mutually modify behavior by the exchange of stimuli within a group.

interaction. Any process in which the action of one entity causes an action by, or a change in, another entity.   H.H.

interaction, ecological. Cf. ecological interaction.

interaction, multiple. The operation of numerous agencies or forces in the social relations of groups. Cf. collective action.
H.A.P.

interaction, non-social. The operation of sub-human and non-human agencies and forces. E.g., any physical, geographical, biological, or physiological action or cause of action.   H.A.P.

interaction, reciprocal. Relationships between members of a group which modify the behavior of all participants in different degrees or amounts. Cf. factorial analysis.   H.A.P.

interaction, social. Cf. social interaction.

intercommunication. Reciprocity of communication. We have, for example, communication with the ancients and even with primitive times. But intercommunication is possible only between the contemporary members of a group.   C.A.E.

intercourse. An interpersonal relationship involving some degree of give and take, usually with the assumption of a gain in values on both sides. It may be mental, verbal, or emotional, and in common usage frequently applies to sex relations. Cf. coitus.

interdependence. Relationships between social units in time, space, and quality.   H.A.P.

interest. (1) The relation between a person and anything which he believes will satisfy one of his desires. An objectified desire. The object of an interest may be a material thing, another person, an act, an experience, or a physical or mental state. The purposeful and voluntary acts of human beings are always in pursuit of interests. (2) A group which is bound together by the identity or similarity of the interests of its individual components. For example, the banking interests, the racing interests, the metal trade interests.

interest, class. The common concern of a social group growing out of like economic status and problems.   K.DP.L.

interest, group. An alert condition of consciousness in individuals, working in organized social groups to attain ends or values, achieved in performing the social functions, thought essential for carrying on human life. Interests are involved in originating, promoting and concluding human projects, through the universal successive stages of need, effort and satisfaction.   C.J.B.

interest, public. General social welfare. Proposals are said to be in the public interest when they are, or can be made to appear to be, contributions to this general welfare rather than to the special privileges of a class, group, or individual. In practice, the term is frequently used to obscure the selfish nature of special-interest proposals.   A.M'C.L.

interest, vested. An economic interest of a privileged group in maintaining the status quo. The term was first used by Henry George.   S.C.M.

interest group. A group organized about some special concern, desire, or want. In contrast with local groups, interest groups are more specialized and more dependent upon promotion or deliberate action. J.H.K.

interhuman. An inclusive term covering human relationships of every sort.   C.A.E.

intermittent group. Cf. group, intermittent.

internal. Relating to phenomena within a body or group; or to relationships within a group or class, or within a political or geographical area.   N.A.

internal migration. Cf. migration, internal.

international. Relating to conditions of widely extended social relations appearing where persons or groups have interests, investments, acquaintanceships, fraternal societies, and other connections between two or more nations. The term becomes increasingly significant today as national sovereignties merge into wider systems of social control before the advance of world-wide communication, commerce, travel, missions, education, and war.   C.J.B.

international law. Cf. law, international.

international prison congresses. Meetings of persons from many nations interested in the discussions of problems of criminology and penology. They grew out of the London Congress of 1872, which was the result of American initiation. It was contemplated that they would be held every five years. The first was held at Stockholm, 1878; the succeeding ones met at Rome, 1885, at St. Petersburg, 1890, at Paris, 1895, at Brussels, 1900, at Budapest, 1905, at Washington, 1910. That planned for 1915 at London was not held because of the outbreak of World War I. The last met at Berlin, 1935.   J.L.G.

international trade. Cf. trade, international.

interpolation. The estimation from two or more known values of a variable, of some intermediate unknown value. Thus, for example, one might estimate the population of the United States in 1933 from the known population in 1930 and 1940.   P.H.F.

interstate compacts. Arrangements between states providing for the supervision of probationers and parolees from the state in which convicted by the supervising authorities of the state to which they are sent to serve their probation or parole. In 1937 twenty-two states in the United States had such compacts concerning probationers, and in 1939 thirty states had such arrangements affecting parolees.   J.L.G.

interstitial area. Cf. area, interstitial.

interview. The securing of information through a professional conversation with an individual for a research study or to aid in social diagnosis or treatment. w.p.

interview, application. Cf. application interview.

interviewer or investigator. One who secures information from people, or who collects schedule data.   M.PT.

intimate group. Cf. group, intimate.

introjection. Cf. identification.

introspection, sympathetic. Behavior in which a person, through a combination of observations of himself and others with imagination, is able to understand and appreciate the experiences of others. M.S.

introvert. A self-centered person or group, given to dwelling upon its own feelings and limitations, and comparatively indifferent to its social relations and responsibilities.   G.M.F.

introvert personality. Cf. personality, introvert.

invasion. (1) A population movement involving two political units, one relatively rude, low in culture, but vigorous and aggressive; the other relatively high, settled, and enjoying material wealth and prosperity. Invasion is a hostile movement initiated by the people of lower culture. The movement, while not as gradual as that of dispersion (q.v.), is still at such a slow rate that the invading people must be able to live and conduct their daily affairs on the march. Historically speaking, the invading people has usually been a tribe; the whole group, or a large section of it, moves as a unit, men, women,

children, and livestock. Frequently a period of hundreds of years elapses between the actual start of the movement and the arrival at its destination. . . .

(2) By analogy, an ecological term describing the entrance into an area of a new class or type and the resultant displacement of certain other classes or types. The process may, however, involve an amalgamation (q.v.) of the invasion types with resident types.   N.A.

inversion. (1) Departure from the expected or the normal. (2) Assumption of the rôle of the opposite sex; homosexuality.   J.M.R.

investigation, social. Cf. social investigation.

Irish system. A system of punishment developed by Sir William Crofton, which provided for progressive stages in the prison term and for release under supervision before final termination of sentence.   M.A.E.

irredentism. A national movement to recover formerly owned territory (*Italia irredenta*). It is based upon the principle of nationality and implies the identification of a nation with the state.   M.Pm.

isolate. To separate from social relations; to reduce or eliminate social contacts.

isolation. From the sociological point of view, a triply relative concept: (1) It is impossible to have an organized self, and in this sense to be a human being, it complete separation from other human beings from birth onward, or during certain crucial phases of development, has prevailed; (2) persons may nevertheless be prevented from initiating or maintaining social relations which they think desirable, and therefore may be in some degree isolated; (3) what is believed to constitute isolation varies from person to person and from society to society. Because of this relativity, therefore, a truly general definition of isolation can be negative only: it is a condition in which certain relations with other human beings are lacking.

For less general purposes, however, we may distinguish (a) strictly physical isolation, of Alexander Selkirk, solitary confinement, or Pitcairn Islander type; (b) social isolation, of sacred society (q.v.), Gypsy, Jewish, Untouchable, or "marginal man" variety; and (c) mental isolation (using "mental" as one aspect of the functioning of a total organism rather than dualistically). This latter kind of isolation may range all the way from the self-contained thought patterns of a dog-matist to the autistic reveries of a schizophrene, or from the naive ethnocentrism of a nonliterate people to the racial arrogance of highly educated "Aryans". Physical isolation may of course foster or further the other sorts and, under some circumstances, vice versa.   H.B.

isolation, social. Cf. (b) under isolation.

J

jail (English spelling gaol). A local city or county prison for detention of criminals pending trial and for incarcerating short-term convicts. Originally all prisons resembled modern jails in that they were essentially places for holding the accused pending trial or disposition of his case. Today jails serve two major purposes: places of detention for those for whom bail is denied or in case bail cannot be furnished, and places for incarcerating prisoners guilty of minor offenses. Occasionally, however, sentences for six months or a year are served in jail. M.A.E.

jail, district. A proposal to obviate the difficulties due to small numbers incarcerated in the county jail in counties of small population by combining several counties into a single jail unit. Such an arrangement, it is suggested, would enable such a jail to provide more adequate hospital and work facilities, hire more and better equipped officials, permit of better classification within the institution, and lessen the cost per inmate. J.L.G.

jihad (transliteration of Arabic). The holy war of Islam. To wage it is one of the secondary responsibilities of the devout Muslim. Its purpose is the expansion of the realm of Islam: the forceful conversion of new adherents to the Faith. The call to arms is a function of the Kalif. Partly because only pseudo-Kalifs have held office for centuries, and partly because recent attempts to mobilize it have been in compromising political alliances with infidels, no jihad has occurred in recent decades. The increasing social accessibility of Muslim populations and secularization of their political structure render unlikely any future occurrence of jihad. D.E.W.

jitney dance. A dance for a nickel. While the term may refer to a cheap dance at which the admission is five cents, it is more commonly used to designate a dance with a hostess in an entertainment establishment, not usually a dance hall. Girls are employed by cheap eating or drinking places to dance with customers who drop five cent pieces (jitneys) into automatic music machines known as "juke boxes". These girls also solicit customers to buy food and drink. F.M.T.

jive. Loose talk; vernacular expression common to Harlem. W.R.C.

joint family. Cf. family, extended.

joking relationship. A special relationship of privileged familiarity or license between particular relatives. Cf. avoidance relationship. G.P.M.

Judaism. The religious system of the Jews; the term is generally reserved for the Jewish religion since the fall of the Kingdom of Judah (586 B.C.).

judgment. The final order of a court in an action. F.W.K.

judicial torture. Cf. torture, judicial.

juge d' instruction. A French magistrate whose duty it is to investigate crime, gather evidence concerning the accused, and determine whether or not prosecution should follow. Without a counterpart in Anglo-American court organization, the office of the *juge d'instruction* is found in many of the continental administrative systems, such as in Italy (*giudice d'istruzione*) and in Germany (*Untersuchungsrichter*). T.S.

164

Junior Republic. A privately operated, minimum security reform school which emphasizes self-government, training in adjustment to the economic and social aspects of community life, the association of boys and girls, and of delinquents and non-delinquents on a basis of equality. The Junior Republic originated with the George Junior Republic (q.v.) in New York State and has been copied in several other states. The record of this type of school is not as yet conclusive.   J.W.M'C.

junior right. Cf. ultimogeniture.

jural pluralism. Cf. pluralism, jural.

jurisdiction. The power to act legally; the territory within which a government or its agencies has power to act legally; the power, or one of several recognized types of power, possessed by or conferred upon courts.   F.W.K.

jurisprudence. In the strict sense of the term, an art or a technique which comprises the systematized prediction of what the tribunals will do, with the practical aim of facilitating the work of counselors, judges, and other practitioners. In the light of the fact that there can and must be as many different jural techniques as concrete systems of law and corresponding types of inclusive societies, jurisprudence has rightly been characterized as "social engineering" (q.v.) according to particular social conjunctures and needs. Different trends in jurisprudenec, viz.: historical, philosophical, analytical, normative, sociological, and realistic jurisprudence, are just different techniques of this engineering, which can be justified only by analysis of concrete situations in the life of law and society.

Unfortunately, every interpretation of jural technique has manifested, more or less, a tendency to affirm itself also as separated theoretical knowledge of law, and in this way has contributed to the confusion of jurisprudence as a sum of varying techniques with such purely theoretical disciplines, as history of law, philosophy of law, and sociology of law. So arose a misleading enlargement of the term jurisprudence, which came to be conceived not only as an art, but also as science; the confusing of both led to dogmatism.   G.G.

jury. The body of men (and/or women) usually eleven or twelve in number who are officially entrusted with weighing the evidence and deciding whether or not the defendant in either a criminal or civil trial is guilty. These persons are usually selected by lot from voters in the local community. Theoretically jurors are the peers of the defendant and are presumed to prevent any miscarriage of justice.   M.A.E.

jus primae noctis. The right of a chief, lord, or priest to cohabit with a bride on the first night of her marriage. Cf. defloration.   G.P.M.

justice. The ideal in law by which judges are expected to be guided. That abstract objective which is at best only approximated in the administration of the law.
                                        N.A.

justice, criminal. Cf. criminal justice.

justice, social. Cf. social justice.

justice, sporting theory of. The term applied to the contentious method of judicial procedure in criminal trials. In this form of procedure, characteristic of criminal procedure derived from Anglo-Saxon precedents, the prosecution presents all the evidence against the accused, the defense all favorable, while the function of the judge is to act as umpire to see that the game is played fairly according to the rules of procedure laid down in the law and in court decisions.   J.L.G.

juvenile court. Cf. court, juvenile.

juvenile delinquency. Cf. delinquency, juvenile.

juvenile detention. Cf. detention, juvenile.

K

kakistocracy. Rule by the worst; a degenerate state of human relationships wherein the governmental machinery is in control of and managed by rulers, all the way from ignorant, vote-buying bullies to astute but unscrupulous gangs and rings. F.E.L.

kalifate. The accessible sacred structure of Islam identical with the secular structure of the dominant Muslim state—the international political organization of Islam, under the Kalif, or "successor" of the Prophet, Muhammad. Although the legitimate succession ended in 661 A.D., series of secular rulers of Muslim countries were able to maintain the definition of situation by which they were regarded as the sacred rulers of all Islam. The Ottoman Sultans from 1517 to 1922 held this office. Since 1922 the kalifate has been vacant with little prospect of reinstitution despite the candidacy of several minor kings. This amorphous organization has passed through the stage of a sacred social institution which in turn became non-existent through secularization. D.E.W.

kangaroo court. The social pattern in many American jails which allows previously committed prisoners to regulate the treatment of the newly admitted prisoners, forcing them to submit to indignities, furnish "treats", etc. M.A.E.

katabolism, social. Cf. social katabolism.

kidnap. To seize, carry off, or entice an adult or child from his home or country or to detain him or hold him in service against his will. F.W.K.

kin. Persons related by blood. The recognition of blood relationship, however, is often determined by cultural prescription, so that persons in certain categories of relationship are counted as kin, while other relatives are dogmatically not recognized as such. Cf. classificatory system, relationship systems; kinship system. E.A.H.

kindred. A group of near relatives based on bilateral (q.v.) descent. G.P.M.

kindred group. Cf. group, kindred.

kinship. A relationship between two or more persons on the basis of recognized common ancestry. Cf. kin. E.A.H.

kinship, totemic. The real or supposed blood-relationship existing between the various members of a sib who share a common totem. J.G.L.

kinship group. A form of societal organization based on blood relationships. P.H.L.

kinship system. The terms of relationship current in a particular society, together with the statuses and patterns of behavior associated with them. Cf. classificatory system. G.P.M.

kismet. The fatalism of Muslims. It is a non-material culture trait in which the definition of the situation involves a laissez-aller attitude with a religious frame of reference. According to the credo implied and/or expressed, the major controls are divine—not subject to human effort, planning and/or volition. It is a trait consistent with both the doctrines of Islam (islam means "surrender"—submission to the will of Allah), and the mode of life—pastoral and agricultural, without the application of scientific controls—characteristic of most Muslims. D.E.W.

kitchen midden. A heap of shells and accumulated refuse marking the former habitation of a primitive people who used shellfish extensively as food.   G.P.M.

kiva. A subterranean or semi-subterranean ceremonial chamber in a Pueblo Indian village, used for certain secular purposes but especially for religious rites.   G.P.M.

kultur. In German sociological writings, a synonym for civilization, i.e., a specific system of values for all phases of life, which is passed on by tradition. Some German writers, however, use *Kultur* as opposed to civilization, *Kultur* being the internal, inherited spiritual structure of national or supernational life, intangible and basically unchanging, mostly derived from the original agricultural state, rooted in the totality of the people, transmitted by tradition; civilization then being understood as the outward systematization of life, mostly of urban origin, tangible, progressive, transmitted by technicways.   J.H.B.

kulturkreis. Area or space where a specifically determined *Kultur* is valid and from which it radiates.   J.H.B.

L

labor. (1) Human energy expended toward some consciously recognized goal. Specifically, one of the basic factors in a wealth producing unit or business, of which the other indispensable factor is land. As culture develops, there are added capital, organization, and ownership.

(2) That element in the population which contributes to the self-maintenance of society (q.v.), by providing a combination of physical energy and human intelligence to the productive process. In practice it is differentiated from other participants by the relative prominence of physical energy as contrasted with intellectual ability or specialized education and training; ordinarily, also, the term is practically synonymous with wage labor, that is, productive activity paid for by someone else. In common practice, labor is divided into unskilled, semi-skilled, and skilled.

labor, child. Regular full-time employment in factory or farm of children under a socially or legally determined age. At present the legal minimum age for employment in the United States (as defined by the Fair Labor Standards Act of 1938) is sixteen years; in hazardous occupations, eighteen. Since this law does not apply to intra-state industries the standard is not consistently observed throughout the nation. Like all standards the specific requirement varies from time to time. For child labor the minimum age has been rising ever since the first employment of young children in cotton mills during the 18th century.   J.W.M´C.

labor, contract. The system of prison labor in which a private contractor provides the machinery and other equipment necessary for the production of goods, while the prison furnishes the building, light and heat, and the guards. The contractor pays the prison so much per man per day for his labor for a certain stint of product, often paying the prisoner so much per piece over his daily stint.   J.L.G.

Also, any wage labor, particularly that of immigrants, in connection with which the employer assumes a specific obligation in advance of the beginning of work.

labor, division of. The distribution and differentiation of the tasks and services to be performed in any society among those who actually accomplish the work. The economic and other social needs of an individual in modern society are multitudinous. Only through specialization with its generally attendant increase in efficiency and reduction of costs may most of these needs be met. The term "geographical division of labor" is frequently used to indicate international adjustments whereby different areas supply the products for which they are peculiarly fitted.   J.H.E.

labor, forced. Services obtained through compulsion, usually by or with sanction of governmental authority and for wages in money or goods.   E.E.M.

labor, hard. Cf. hard labor.

labor, prison, Cf. prison labor.

labor demand. The recognized and expressed need of employers at any given time for wage workers Cf. labor market; labor force; labor supply.

labor dispute. Conflict situation arising between employers and labor groups in pursuit of their separate interests. K.DP.L.

labor force. The total number of people actually in the labor market (q.v.) at any

168

given time. The census definition includes those working, those with jobs but temporarily not working, those on public emergency work, and those actively seeking work. It excludes those able and willing to work, but not working and making no effort to find employment. The labor force of the U. S. was estimated at 54,-000,000 in 1942. Cf. labor reserve; labor supply.   s.c.m.

labor legislation. A body of laws and their administration, establishing standards of working conditions, safety, and health; regulating terms of employment, such as wages and hours; or dealing by law with any phase of the terms or conditions affecting employees in a given industry, occupation, or area of governmental jurisdiction.   M.VK.

labor market. A general expression to describe that area of economic intercourse within which employers seek workers and workers seek jobs. In some respects the labor market, like the market for goods, is regulated by the laws of demand and supply. There are in this market, as in the market for goods, various interfering influences, social, economic or political, which may condition the availability of workers regardless of the demand for labor. Collective bargaining arrangements between unions and employers may close out classes of workers. The labor market breaks down into many lesser markets because of the classifications of workers, types of jobs, and the disposal of workers as well as the jobs. For classes of work involving little skill the market may be more limited in area than for skills only occasionally and intermittently in demand, or for which the demand may be national in scope.   N.A.

As ordinarily used, only persons in the labor force are said to be participants in the labor market. Students or other persons who have not been part of the labor force are said to have "entered the labor market" when they start working or looking for jobs.   s.c.m.

labor mobility. Positional changes within the laboring population, the most common types of such movement being geographical change or migration, and employment change or horizontal mobility.

A change in class position of laboring people, or vertical mobility, may also occur. Migration and horizontal mobility are regarded as highly typical of modern industrial society; vertical mobility is evident in some degree wherever open-class systems are found.   K.DP.L.

labor movement. An inclusive term to describe all forms of organized group action, political as well as economic, on the part of wage earners to improve their status and/or conditions.   K.DP.L.

labor problems. The relationships and conditions affecting the laboring class in modern industrial society. Broadly used, the term touches nearly all aspects of the labor field, including such questions as labor and employer organizations past and present, collective bargaining, strikes and lock-outs, the closed and open shop, the legal status of labor, protective and social security legislation, problems of special groups such as women, children and racial minorities, standards of living, compulsory and voluntary arbitration, labor and government, and many others. Strict usage may differentiate between problems, policies and practice in the labor field, and between problems, history and theory of labor, but ordinarily the term is more loosely used.   K.DP.L.

labor relations. The process of conflict and accommodation continuously manifest in the interaction of employer and labor groups.   K.DP.L.

labor reserve. The total of all persons who are potential but not present members of the labor force. Includes persons 14 years of age or older who are neither working nor seeking work, but who would be willing to take a job for wages if one were available within a short space of time, such as thirty days. By this definition, the WPA Division of Research estimated the U. S. labor reserve at 7.6 million full-time workers and 5.7 million half-time workers in 1942. Over four-fifths of the full-time labor reserve consisted of housewives, with students next in importance. Those with physical handicaps or those who considered themselves "too old" to seek work under ordinary conditions made up the remainder of the group. s.c.m.

labor standards. The changing norms relating to wage rates, hours of work, social security, working conditions of women and children, and the like, arrived at by agreement between labor and management, or by government action. As manifestations of social control in economic relations, they signify accommodation of conflicts between employer and labor groups by self-action, or by intervention of the state. K.DP.L.

labor supply. The sum total of available workers in the labor market at any one time. In viewing the labor supply attention is directed to the heterogenous character of the workers. They must be regarded in terms of age, sex, race, skill and other differentials. Each demand for labor calls for workers of a type needed by the job. There may be an ample overall supply but a shortage in critical skills, or the workers may be inaccessibly distributed. The labor supply may increase as demand and inducements attract marginal workers (self-employed, staying at home, etc.) into the market. Reverse conditions may diminish labor supply. Cf. labor demand; labor force; labor market. N.A.

labor turnover. The change in personnel in a given labor force (establishment, industry), commonly measured by calculation of separations and replacements. While a certain amount of change is considered normal, an exceptional amount is regarded as symptomatic of maladjustments in the economic and social situation affecting labor mobility (q.v.). K.DP.L.

labor union. A secondary conflict group, comprised of wage and salary workers, organized along economic lines, for the purpose of improving and protecting their immediate status and conditions. K.DP.L.

laborer. One who engages in labor, i.e., applies his personal energy to the production of some desired good. One who supplies the factor of labor to a business. In ordinary usage, the term is restricted to the type of worker whose manual or physical capacities and exertions, rather than his mental, distinguish his activities. In a capitalistic economy a laborer is ordinarily thought of as one who is employed by some one else and works for wages Cf. labor.

laborer, farm. Cf. farm laborer.

labret. A wooden plug or other ornament worn in a hole pierced through the lip. G.P.M.

la colonie agricole. A French term designating the agricultural workhouses which began to be established widely on the continent a hundred years ago as means of penal treatment of vagrants, beggars, and drunkards. T.S.

lag, cultural. Retardation in the rate of change of some one part of an interrelated cultural complex, the lack of synchronization producing maladjustment. M.K.

lag, culture. Cf. lag, cultural.

lag, moral. The situation that exists when a general public ethical evaluation is not made promptly to apply to significant new forms of behavior, e.g., in the field of high finance. The unspoken implication in the term is that an ethical evaluation ought to be applied to the behavior in question. A.R.L.

lag, social. Cf. social lag.

laissez-faire. The doctrine which emphasizes giving to the individual maximum freedom to follow his own interests, particularly in his economic relationships, with a minimum of social interference or regulation, particularly of an official or governmental character. The logical analysis that has been used to justify this theory may be briefly summed up as follows: "Every individual will do his best work where he receives the highest reward. Society will give an individual the highest reward for the thing he does best. Therefore, if an individual is given the maximum freedom to discover in what way he can demand the highest reward for himself, he will thereby be rendering the greatest service both to himself and to society." The doctrine is obviously predicated on the assumption of free competition, and is central in the classical system of economics and in the societal patterns that are associated with it.

land. The sum total of the material components and configuration of the globe, solid, liquid, and gaseous. The basic source of all material wealth, and the spatial setting for human beings. From the point of view of human utility, land presents two main aspects—area and productivity. Productivity, in turn, may be divided into agricultural fertility and mining resources Cf. agriculture; mining.

land bank. A bank which uses land as its financial basis instead of the customary stocks, bonds, and other securities.

land grant. A transfer of title of a part of the public domain to an individual or legal person in return for some service or valuable consideration. In the United States land grants have been used as a means of developing the unsettled areas of the country, particularly by promoting railroads, educational institutions, public buildings, etc.

land grant college. In the United States, an educational institution established on the basis of an endowment derived from the sale of lands granted to the states or territories by the federal government in accordance with the Morrill or Land Grant Act of July 2, 1862, and subsequent related legislation.

larceny. The unlawful carrying away of property with intent to deprive the owner of its possession. Grand and petite (or petty) larceny are the major classifications. They are differentiated by the amount or value of the property stolen. The amount varies from state to state in the United States.   J.W.M'C.

large-scale farm. Cf. farm, large-scale.

large-scale industry. Cf. industry, large-scale.

larger parish. A grouping of two or more Protestant churches and their ministers to serve all the people of an area rather than separate parishes.   E.des.B.

larithmic. Having to do with larithmics. Relating to the quantitative or numerical aspects of population.

larithmics. The scientific study of population in its numerical and quantitative aspects, as eugenics (q.v.) is in its qualitative aspects.

latifundia. Large landed estates exploited by absentee landlords for profit to the neglect of all other interests.   N.S.

law. (1) A statement of an orderly and dependable sequence, presumably of a causative character Cf. causation. All the true laws of nature are of this character. Natural laws are man's statements of the way things have been observed uniformly to happen in nature. They presuppose an antecedent and a consequence They are statements that if a given set of factors is present under given conditions, a specified result may be expected to follow. They contain no commands or prohibitions. They are beyond human alteration, and have no moral or ethical implications, and no intrinsic concern with human welfare. Men can use them for their own good by learning their operations, and playing one natural law off against another. But human beings can neither amend nor break natural laws.

(2) The expressed will of the state (q.v.). A command or a prohibition emanating from the authorized agencies of the state (Cf. government), and backed up by the authority and the capacity to exercise force which is characteristic of the state. Law is one of the most explicit and concrete forms of social control, though by no means the only or the most influential form. The evolutionary development of law is correlated with the development of the state. In modern societies the law is always written, and ordinarily includes specifications for penalties, imposed for violations, which are themselves a part of the law. Human law may be broken (as is implied in the provision of penalties), and is broken to such an extent that practically every mature member of a fairly complex society is a law breaker. Cf. social laws.

law, canon. The body of ecclesiastical laws adopted by the early Christian Church and chiefly set forth in the Corpus Juris Canonici (body of canon law). These laws were originally brought together and interpreted in the Decretum, a compilation of Church law made probably before 1150. Included in this important work were the decretals, or decrees of the popes, determining disputed questions of ecclesiastical law. The original Decretum comprised the papal decretals up to and including those of Innocent II (1130-1143). Later there were added to the work the decretals of succeeding popes through the period of Clement V (1305-1314). An official edition of the Corpus Juris Canonici was published in 1582, which is even now the authoritative source of the canon law of the Roman Catholic Church.   W.G.

law, common. The body of law built up from English local custom in the 9th and 10th centuries and elaborated subsequently by judicial interpretation. The most significant characteristic of common law is that its origin lies in custom rather than in statute. However, for all practical purposes little difference exists between common law and statutory law since codification of common law by Coke, Blackstone and other famous jurists provides as definite a starting point for legal interpretation as any statute. Provisions of common law in most states of the United States have usually been defined and modified by legislative enactment.   J.W.M'C.

law, criminal, positivist school of. This is a term applied to legal scholars who in the latter half of the nineteenth century urged the reform of the criminal law in the light of scientific discoveries concerning the causation of criminal conduct. The impetus was derived from the Comtian positivistic philosophy on the one hand and the researches of the criminal anthropologists on the other. Its leading exponent was the Italian scholar Enrico Ferri and it greatly influenced criminal law reform, particularly on the continent.   T.S.

law, international. The system of rules that govern the relations between states, based on custom and treaty. It differs from municipal (domestic) law in the method of its creation, and in its sanctions. Courts have been instituted by agreement between parties, including the Permanent Court of International Justice, which has a limited obligatory jurisdiction in legal matters over those states which have been willing to grant it. Since 1939, much of this has been withdrawn.

The international legal system, having to deal with sovereign states, is necessarily both limited and primitive. So long as states insist, as they do, on maintaining their own armies, their tariffs and other indicia of sovereignty, it is impossible to proscribe the use of force by single nations and impossible to substitute a so-called community or group force. The effort to make international law more coercive than its subject-matter, states, permit, has done international relations great harm. International law rests on custom, not consent, and dissent from custom is not permissible. International law must prevail over contrary municipal law, otherwise it would hardly be a legal system. But the attempt to "enforce" it—except as self-help—or "enforce peace", acts as a blight and has a withering effect on the system. It destroys that confidence and trust which is essential to any effective cooperation. The political aspects of the League of Nations Covenant, thought by many to constitute the new international law, have been detrimental to respect for international law and have driven the nations apart. The primitive nature of the system is revealed by the fact that the only way to create new law, by treaty, requires the consent of the nations that are to be bound by it.   E.M.B.

law, natural. The sum total of the orderly and dependable sequences implicit in the constitution of the universe. All that is known by human beings about natural law is the product of accurate and scientific observations and recordings. Whatever exists above and beyond this, is a matter of belief (q.v.). This includes all convictions regarding the consistency of unknown data with known data, and regarding the continuance into the future of established sequences and relationships. Scientific knowledge stops at the threshold of the future. We can know only that which has transpired. The projection of this knowledge into the realm of things to come is a matter of belief and faith. Natural laws, in the plural, or the laws of nature are human statements of the items of natural law. They are records of the way things have been observed uniformly to happen. Cf. law.

Historical note. In earlier usage, the phrase "natural law" meant binding uniformities in nature laid down (as in edict or statute) by Nature (more or less deified); or (as in Roman Catholic usage) laid down by God for the governance of nature, and therefore having divine sanction. The suspension of "natural law" is in this sense a supernatural act, the exclusive prerogative of divine will, and constitutes a miracle.　　　　　　　　T.D.E.

law, poor. An antiquated name still frequently applied to the body of laws governing the administration of public assistance. The name dates from 16th century England and is best known in relation to the Elizabethan Poor Law of 1603, which consolidated the numerous poor laws passed by Parliament in the century preceding. The name was borrowed by the colonies and continued in use to designate various state laws dealing with relief of poor and dependent persons. Public welfare and public assistance are terms which are gradually replacing the term poor law. In a wider sense poor law is synonymous with a degrading and shortsighted system of poor relief based upon severe laws of settlement, pauper oaths, standards of relief below that of the poorest paid common laborer, and relief in kind.　　　　　　　　　　　J.W.MᵃC.

law, poor, Elizabethan. A law enacted by the English Parliament in 1603 summarizing and consolidating a variety of laws concerning poor relief passed during the preceding century. The law required the local community to assume responsibility for the care of its own poor, established the principle of settlement and destitution as tests of eligibility for assistance, and decreed that relief could be granted only in return for work in places provided for housing the poor. The principles of public assistance established by the Elizabethan Poor Law governed the administration of relief in England and the United States for over three-hundred years.　　　　　　　　　　　J.W.M'C.

law, sociological. Cf. sociological law.

laws. The individual items within the broad field of law (q.v.), natural or manmade. Scientific laws are particular statements of generalized truths, especially those having to do with causative sequence. Juristic laws are the items on the statute books of states, in ordinary usage the current statutes of any particular state. These fall into three main categories: (1) general laws, which apply to all citizens or persons, or to all persons within legally recognized groups or classes, and (2) special laws, enacted for particular purposes, and (3) private laws, passed for the benefit of particular individuals. Scientific laws are divisible into (1) quantitative laws, which are principles or generalizations explaining the aspects of quantity or of metricization within a field of operations, and (2) qualitative laws, which are principles or generalizations explaining the aspects of quality or non-metricization within a field of operations.　　　　　　　F.W.K.

laws, habitual criminal. Cf. habitual criminal laws.

laws, social. Cf. social laws.

laws, sumptuary. Laws designed to regulate the expenditure of persons for food, clothing, and other consumption goods, especially luxuries; to restrict or forbid the use of certain goods. A common method of control is through taxation.　　　E.E.M.

laws of human nature. Cf. human nature, laws of.

laws of settlement. Cf. settlement, laws of.

laws of social defense. Cf. social defense, laws of.

layman. A person without technical training or competency in a specified calling, such as a science, medicine, or the ministry. Common usage of the term carries the connotation of superficiality and passivity; but lay participation in a specialized field of interest does not necessarily have these characteristics. In some types of social analysis, a comprehensive term is needed for the non-vocational participants in all fields embraced in the prevailing system of specialization. Layman is the most available term for this purpose. By this definition, the terms layman and specialist (as broadly defined) are correlatives.　　　　　　　　　　S.E.

leader. (1) In the broadest sense, one who leads by initiating social behavior; by directing, organizing or controlling the efforts of others; or by prestige, power or position. The effective stimulus-giver in social behavior.

(2) In a restricted sense, one who leads by means of persuasive qualities and voluntary acceptance on the part of followers. M.S.

leadership. (1) A situation-process in which a person (or persons) because of his actual or supposed ability to solve problems in the field of current group interest, is followed by others in the group and influences their behavior. (In a leadership situation the character of "followership" is equally important.) Leadership may be based upon spontaneous personal ascendency (physical, courageous, congenial), or upon prestige of skill, knowledge, age, alleged supernatural endowment, or position, or upon a combination. Leadership does not include all direction of many by one. It should be distinguished from domineering, in which the group perforce accepts a dictator or through fear or strategic disadvantage submits reluctantly; and the underlying motives of the domineerer are egotic rather than altruistic or collective. Many situations, of course, partake of mixed motivation. A dictator may call himself "leader", seize a problem situation or crisis, and successfully feign collective interest, though it be his wishes for new experience, manipulation, power, recognition or even sadism in which he finds satisfaction. Cf. domination. T.D.E.

(2) The act of organizing and directing the interests and activities of a group of persons, as associated in some project or enterprise, by a person who develops their cooperation, through securing and maintaining their more or less voluntary approval of the ends and methods proposed and adopted in their association. The two socially most significant types of leadership, present in all communities, are the conservative and the progressive. The conservative leader develops interest in maintaining the social order or situation in status quo, generally, so far as this concerns the distribution of its values and rewards, to its main beneficiaries,—with some maintenance or increase of techni-

cal efficiency. The progressive leader, on the other hand, develops interest in changing the social order or situation so as to distribute more widely its benefits, to those who have been stinted or excluded, also with some interest in increasing technical efficiency. C.J.B.

leadership, indirect. Leadership in which the influences of leader over follower are transmitted by other people or by artificial means. M.S.

leadership, recreation. Cf. recreation leadership.

learning process. Cf. process, learning.

lease. An agreement which, for a consideration, conveys the right of use and occupancy of a property for a specified term, and under specified conditions. Cf. rent.

lease system. Cf. convict lease system.

lease system, convict. Cf. convict lease system.

left wing. A term describing the extreme radical parties in democratic states, derived from their location on the floor of European legislative bodies, and commonly covering Socialists, Communists and others with a revolutionary program based on the abolition of capitalism. By extension the term is used to describe the elements in any organization advocating the most extreme program within it. The term right wing (q.v.) is used to describe the opposing conservative parties or sections. R.N.B.

legal aid. A social service through which those who need legal assistance are helped to overcome the obstacles met in the effort to obtain justice. W.P.

legal aid bureau. An organization established in cooperation with public-spirited lawyers to give legal counsel to worthy poor persons. Applications may be made to the bureau by the individual directly or a case may be referred to the bureau by magistrate. In some cases the bureau is entirely supported by private funds, in others the municipal government may also assume some responsibility. Three stages have marked the growth of legal aid bureaus. In the first the work was confined to assisting immigrant persons; in the second, the work was expanded to care for all poor persons in need of legal aid but only civil cases (usually unpaid wage claims) were handled; the third stage has been marked by an extension into the criminal case field and by the growth of legal aid bureaus in small as well as large cities.   J.W.M'C.

legalization. The process of making that which was unlawful, lawful; applying the characteristics of the law to other professions or fields; dwelling upon or emphasizing technicalities.   F.W.K.

legalize. To make that which was unlawful, lawful; such as to make an illegal relationship between a man and woman legal; mostly applied to status, conditions, and relationships.   F.W.K.

legislation, social. Cf. social legislation.

legitimize. To remove by law the status of illegitimacy or bastardy.   F.W.K.

leisure. Free time after the practical necessities of life have been attended to. The adjective leisure means being unoccupied by the practical necessities, as, leisure hours; the adverb leisurely applies to slow, deliberate, unhurried undertakings. Conceptions of leisure vary from the arithmetical one of time devoted to work, sleep, and other necessities, subtracted from 24 hours—which gives the surplus time—to the general notion of leisure as the time which one uses as he pleases.   M.H.N.

leisure class. That element in society which by social custom can maintain a plane of living, usually considerably above the average, without engaging directly in self-maintenance activities. The basis of its privileged position may be hereditary status, unearned income from land or capital, or special privileges.

leptorrhine. Characterized by a narrow nose, i.e., with a nasal index (q.v.) of less than 47, as measured on the skull, or of less than 70 as measured on the living head. Cf. mesorrhine; platyrrhine. G.P.M.

lesbianism. Sapphism. Homosexual relations between women (by various methods, including oral stimulation of the genitals and the wearing of an artificial phallus by one partner). The term is derived from the extreme sensuality of the women of Lesbos, circa, 600 B.C., where Sappho, a famous poetess of aristocratic birth, wrote passionate love lyrics and reputedly indulged in erotic relations with her female pupils.   R.E.B.

lethal chamber. A room or place within or adjacent to a prison or jail where prisoners convicted of capital crimes are put to death.   A.E.W.

level, income. Cf. income level.

level, occupational. A class of occupations defined in terms of the skill required or in some cases of the function performed. For example, skilled, semi-skilled or unskilled levels, or in census classification proprietary, professional or skilled labor levels.   G.L.C.

level, poverty. Cf. poverty level.

level, social. Cf. social level.

level, subsistence. A plane of living which includes only the minimum of food, clothing and shelter necessary to maintain life.   E.E.M.

level of living. Sometimes used to describe the average plane of living of a group. Cf. plane of living.   T.D.E.

levirate. The rule according to which a man may, or must, marry the widow of his elder brother or other near kinsman. Cf. sororate.   G.P.M.

lex talionis. (1) Law of retaliation; example "an eye for an eye and a tooth for a tooth." (2) In modern times, also the acts of one nation in retaliation for the acts of another. These may include amicable retaliatory acts.   J.M.R.

liability, employer's. Cf. employer's liability.

liability to arrest. A differential risk for various categories of offenders to become acted on by police. In American society, negroes have a greater liability to arrest than the whites. In societies with a marked class system, offenders of the lower class are more liable to be arrested than offenders of influential circumstances. Likewise, police act differentially on men. Hence, women are less liable to be arrested for offenses.   W.C.R.

liaison. (1) (*adm.*) Functional connection and coordination. (2) (*crim.*) Illicit sexual intimacy. Connections maintained for mutual illegal operations.   J.M.R.

libation. A sacrifice (q.v.) of wine or other beverage or liquid; a drink offering. G.P.M.

libel. Any misrepresentation of another person whether spoken, written or printed, calculated to injure his reputation, or to expose him to ridicule, contempt, or derision.   J.M.R.

liberal. Characterized by liberalism (q.v.). Interested in the general welfare of mankind, and the wide spread of social benefits. Concerned with the remedy of social maladjustments rather than with the idealistic reorganization of the social structure.

liberalism. A social attitude characterized by interest in the increase and wide dissemination of welfare, without drastic changes in the structure of society. Broadminded principles and theories unrestricted by traditional prejudices and other *a priori* positions. A doctrine of intellectual tolerance that rules out selfish considerations and other evidences of unfairness and bias in the formulation of economic, political, and other social policies. More specifically, the doctrine of orthodox intellectual liberals at a given time and in a given country. This somewhat crystallized body of principles and theories takes shape as a moderate alternative to the pragmatic positions of radicals, conservatives, and reactionaries. It develops in the minds of humanitarian intellectuals as a means of moral and ethical orientation in a shifting and otherwise confusing world. Such persons attempting to enforce their orthodoxy upon peripheral individuals, groups, and journals of fact and opinion. Liberalism, in this area, thus becomes identified as a catchword with such others as "scien-

tific" and "scholarly." A catchword of respectability attached to any humanitarian, humane, democratic, or socialistic doctrine in order to give it wider acceptance. Trades unionism, consumer cooperation, communism, republicanism, and many other doctrines have thus been labeled.   A.M'C.L.

libertarianism. (1) Originally the theological and philosophical doctrine of freedom of the will. In modern times the theory and advocacy of individual liberty as an end in itself, most fully exemplified in the movement for civil liberties in the Occidental world.   M.Pm.
(2) The modern philosophy of liberty, especially as conceived by those to whom the goal of society is the establishment of institutions which will make unnecessary the forms of compulsion associated with the State and the private ownership of industry. A term adopted by many groups of anarchists to avoid misinterpretation of their beliefs. Used also to describe the advocates of civil liberty, and those in larger fields committed to principles of expanding liberty without regard to any ultimate goal.   R.N.B.

liberties, civil. The freedom claimed by or accorded to persons to speak, write, publish, assemble and organize without interference or penalty. The phrase is associated chiefly with the practices of political democracy stemming from English institutions in which the civil power is dominant over the military, and in which judicial review of all confinements is guaranteed by habeas corpus. The equivalent phrase in continental countries is the "rights of man", which also includes what under English and American law are known rather as civil rights (q.v.) than as civil liberties. While all ten of the original amendments to the U. S. Constitution (the Bill of Rights) are often characterized as civil liberties, the phrase applies correctly only to the political guarantees, not to the guarantees to defendants in the criminal courts.   R.N.B.

liberty. Absence of restraint, general or specific. Civil liberties include certain specific legal guarantees, or restrictions on governmental powers and agents, which purport to protect so-called natural liberty or natural rights (q.v.). Legal personal liberty in general is never absolute, being limited in the interest of the equal liberties of others, and by the general welfare and public safety. Liberty needs often to be distinguished from freedom (q.v.); and occasionally from "license", the "abuse" of liberty (usually a matter of subjective judgment). Policies of liberty are patterns of social control in which various techniques are employed to permit or even encourage variation from the mode, free expression, individuality, experimentation, etc.   T.D.E.

liberty, religious. Freedom to worship God according to the dictates of conscience, and to organize associations for that purpose free of governmental supervision or control; and to express the principles of religious belief in conduct which does not violate the equal rights of differing believers, nor transgress the accepted limits of social morality and public order; with complete separation of religious bodies from governmental functions, and with no governmental support of any religious body nor preference among them. As a corollary, the right to deny Deity, to oppose religious concepts, and to be free from compulsion by government over individual or group conscience based on authority asserted to be superior to man-made law.   R.N.B.

libido. Instinctive sexual energy or desire which finds dynamic expression in attachment to the ego or to external objects or persons.   J.M.R.

license, ceremonial. Cf. ceremonial license.

lie detector. Accurately speaking, the "lie-detector" consists of a number of instruments combined into one, commonly referred to as a polygraph. It is made up of a cardiograph which records the pulse wave, the sphygmograph which records the blood pressure, the galvanograph which records the galvanic reflex, and the pneumograph which records the respiratory movements. Such involuntary changes in bodily processes as one undergoes when one is questioned concerning a crime are recorded and compared with the record of the same subject made during an initial test period when no questions concerning

the crime are asked. Deviations in the readings provide the basis for interpreting whether deception has occurred.   N.F.C.

life. A structure-function in protoplasm such as can maintain its energy-balance by response to environing fields.   T.D.E.

life, change of. Cf. change of life.

life, expectation of. Cf. expectation of life.

life cycle. Cf. cycle, life.

life history. The method of tracing the environmental and internal factors entering into the development of a person or a group by describing accurately and in detail, either its entire career, or a considerable period of time in it.   G.M.F.

life-organization pattern. Cf. pattern, life-organization.

life span. The length of life characteristic of a given species when life is terminated by normal processes of old age.
  C.V.K.

life table. A conventional set of computations built up from age-specific probabilities of dying within one year, which, in turn, are based upon age-specific mortality rates of a population under consideration. The life table expresses the meaning of observed age-specific mortality rates in terms of expectation of life and other functions at successive ages for an hypothetical cohort of persons starting life together (conventionally 100,000 started at birth) and assumed to be subjected throughout the course of their entire lives to the age-specific mortality rates in the population under study. The functions include, among others: 1_x, the number of the original cohort surviving to exact age x; q_x, the probability of a person age x dying within another year; p_x, the probability of a person age x living another year; T_x, the total number of years of life remaining for combined survivors of the original cohort at age x; $\dot{e}_x$, expectation of life (the "mean after lifetime" or average number of years of life still remaining to survivors at age x).
  C.V.K.

like-mindedness. Similarity of mental content and/or mental process on the part of two or more people.   M.S.

line sample. Cf. sample, line.

line village. Cf. village, line.

lineage. A group of relatives, commonly a subdivision of a sib (q.v.), who trace actual descent unilinearly from a common ancestor. Cf. descent; extended family.   G.P.M.

linguistics. The branch of cultural anthropology (q.v.) concerned with the study of languages, their elements, forms, structure, inter-relations, historical development, and principles of growth.   G.P.M.

literate. Able to read and write or to communicate by means of writing. Such capabilities evidence the capacity of a person or people to become articulate in symbols.   N.A.

livelihood. The living earned by work. The term involves many elements having to do with the state of the industrial arts, the status of workers, whether independent or employed, the purchasing power of the money used in payment, the occupational skill or ability of the worker, and the interrelationships of the home, the community, and the occupation. In its complex significance, the term has historical recognition in its Chinese equivalent because the first President of China, Sun Yat-sen, outlining the basis of a program for the nation, declared the "principle of livelihood" to be one of the "three principles of the people." In western industrialized nations increasing labor productivity and the problems of marketing a surplus have created the paradox of insecure livelihood due to lack of opportunity to work, i.e., to be hired under prevailing conditions of employment.   M.VK.

living, plane of. Cf. plane of living.

living, standard of. An ideal or normative level of consumption which represents the goal of living which a group of people are striving to reach or maintain. When a group has achieved its goal, the standard of living coincides with actual consumption performance. But, owing to the fact that standards are fundamentally psychological, the standard of living usually represents something above or beyond actual performance. The actual consumption level of a large group or class, expressed as an average, is sometimes treated as a measure of the standard of living of the group. This is done on the assumption that, on the average, such a group or class will be able to express its standards in actual consumption performance. Cf. level of living; plane of living.
                                              C.E.L.

living wage. Cf. wage, living.

lobola. The bride-price (q.v.) among the southeastern Bantu tribes of Africa. G.P.M.

local group. Cf. group, local.

local option. A plan of liquor control in which each state decides for itself whether to abolish or restrict the manufacture and sale of intoxicating liquors.   J.W.M'C.

localism. A phenomenon which is confined to a relatively limited geographical area or small social group.   P.F.C.

locality. A limited geographical area.
                                              P.F.C.

locality group. Cf. group, locality.

localize. To confine a phenomenon to a relatively limited geographical area or specific social group.   P.F.C.

locate. To determine the position which a specific fact has in relation to other related facts; as to determine the position of an item on a map, or to indicate the place of residence of an individual. P.F.C.

location. The place which an object or fact has in reference to other related objects or facts.   P.F.C.

lock-out. An employer-employee relationship in which the employer during a labor dispute closes the place of business and refuses to admit any workman pending the settlement of the dispute.   J.W.M'C.

lodging house. A building in which persons are accommodated either over night or for extended periods for compensation. It differs from a hotel in that accommodation is by agreement rather than to whomever may apply and that the proprietor's duties and liabilities are not those of an inn-keeper to a "guest" but of a lessor to a lessee. A rooming house.   s.s.

logistic curve: A curve used to describe the normal progress of growth. First used by P. F. Verhulst in 1838 to represent the growth of human populations. Later rediscovered and developed by Raymond Pearl and Lowell Reed—after whom the curve is frequently called. It is the curve of the equation $y = \dfrac{K}{(1+e^{a+bx})}$ in which y is the growing mass or population, x is time, and a, b, and K are constants. Also called logarithmic curve. In chemistry called the curve of autocatalytic growth.   M.P.

looking-glass self. self, looking-glass.

love. Deep and sincere affection for any object, usually accompanied by loyal devotion and solicitude. The object may be a person, a group, or even an abstract entity like "country." The term has many recognized sub-divisions, such as sexual, filial, parental, consanguinial, romantic, platonic, etc. For scientific exactitude the context should always make clear which precise variant is involved.

love, free. Cf. free love.

low-rent housing. Decent, safe, and sanitary housing provided specifically for low-income families. Except in rare instances such housing is not low-cost and the difference between economic rent and the rent paying capacity of low income families is met by subsidy.   s.s.

luck. That which happens without any apparent influence on the part of any human agent, particularly the person immediately concerned. The crossing of two seemingly unrelated causative sequences. Cf. aleatory element.

lust. The possession of abnormally strong sexual cravings.   E.R.G.

lynch. To practice the custom of enforcing certain mores by death or of punishing violations of certain fundamental regional mores, without due process of law. The avenging group is composed of at least two persons. This practice is commonly referred to as lynch law.   W.R.C.

lynching. Execution of a person by mob action under circumstances in which the machinery of law is circumvented and sometimes in open defiance of established authority.   N.A.

M

machine. A combination of mechanical devices used ordinarily for the production of material wealth. Every machine includes three essential parts, a tool and a device for holding the tool, a device for holding the material to be operated on, and a device for the transmission and purposeful application of power. The nature and purpose of machinery are primarily to supplant human labor, accomplishing production with greater speed, scope and economy than are possible by the use of human labor aided only by tools.

McNaghten Case. English decision by the House of Lords setting forth the legal definition of insanity. J.P.S.

Mafia. A form of organized and generally violent crime, supposed to have originated in Sicily as an unofficial police system on the large estates to protect the owners during the period of disorganization following the Napoleonic invasion, and to have become a distinctly criminal organization when it turned against the owners and became an independent secret group. Its behavior includes tests for admission, and an oath not to refer any controversy to the legal authorities. The Mafia was introduced into the United States in the last part of the nineteenth century. E.H.S.

magic. Beliefs and practices concerned with producing effects by the coercion of supernatural forces or agents, as through the manipulation of fetishes or rituals, or by following out some mystical principle or association of ideas, e.g., that like affects like; differentiated from religion by the absence or minimization of the element of propitiation, and from science, which has evolved from it by a process of refinement and correction, by its largely fallacious character; called "black magic" when pursued for private or sinister ends; hence, by extension, sorcery (q.v.) or witchcraft (q.v.) in general. Cf. contagious magic; imitative magic. G.P.M.

magic, contagious. Magic (q.v.) based upon the assumption that things which have once been in contact continue to exert an influence upon each other after they have been separated, so that, for example, a person can be injured by performing rites of black magic over his nail parings, food leavings, discarded property, etc. Cf. imitative magic. G.P.M.

magic, exuvial. A form of contagious magic (q.v.) in which parts of the body cast off by the chosen victim of the magic are worked upon by the magician. Through fixation of the charm upon the cast off part, the effectiveness of the charm then operates upon the victim. E.A.H.

magic, imitative. Magic (q.v.) based upon the assumption that things which resemble one another can influence each other, so that, for example, a person can be injured by damaging an effigy made to represent him. Cf. contagious magic. G.P.M.

magistrate's court. Cf. court, magistrate's.

magnitude (*statistics*). A quantitative datum resulting from the use of a measuring scale; an aggregate arrived at by counting or totaling individual elements which are independent. M.Pt.

maiming. A former method of punishment consisting of cutting off some portion of the body. Sometimes the part excised was the organ connected with the commission of the crime, as the tongue in the case of perjury or slander, the hand of the thief, the sexual organs of the rapist. But sometimes the part maimed was not thus connected with the crime, as the eye or the ear.   J.L.G.

majority. More than half of a group. This concept is widely accepted as a basis for democratic, political, and other administration. In practice it may result in subordination of, and injustice to, one or another minority group (q.v.).

mala prohibita. Offenses that are made so solely by reason of statutory prohibition. Such acts may be in themselves morally indifferent. They become right or wrong, just or unjust, as the legislative body deems necessary for the protection of the welfare of society. Municipal ordinances are a case in point. Most indictable crimes are mala in se, and derive no additional moral turpitude from being declared unlawful by legislation; whereas in the case of mala prohibita their wrongful character is established solely by ordinance or statute. Cf. malum in se.   A.E.W.

maladaptation. (1) In biology, a state of disharmony between an organism and its environment due to its possession of traits, characteristics, or structures which are disadvantageous to it under the prevailing conditions of life; the failure of an organism to develop by variation and natural selection the structural traits suitable to its changing environment. (2) In the social sciences, sometimes erroneously used as a synonym for maladjustment, malaccommodation, malassimilation and other terms connoting social and cultural, as distinguished from purely biological, processes.   H.E.J.

maladjustment. A situation-process in which a personality or a group is continuing to fail to "compensate", i.e., to solve its problems, in such a way as to resolve its internal and external conflict-tensions; inadequacy of adaptation or accommodation as judged by some standards of values. Normally problems are solved within the ordinary resources (habitual, mental, economic, social) of the person or group, after a period of "unadjustment" (q.v.). If "normal" resources prove inadequate, a

crisis situation supervenes, and if the crisis is inadequately met, maladjustment follows, leading to further abnormality, further crisis, and disintegration (q.v.), or to intervention by successive remedial, curative, ameliorative (q.v.), agencies from outside the circle of normal dependency (q.v.).   T.D.E.

maladjustment, personal. A condition or state in which the individual is not in harmonious relationship with a given social situation; only in extreme form may it be called pathological; since all persons are both adjusted and maladjusted in certain respects and to some extent to particular situations, it is simply faulty adjustment.   W.E.G.

maladjustment, social. Cf. social maladjustment.

maladjustment of personality. Those types of relationship between the parts of a personality (q.v.) and between the personality and its environments, material and social, which tend to thwart or damage the long-run interests of the personality, and which tend to violate the requirements of the social groups on which the interests of the personality depend.   H.H.

malfeasance. Commitment of an act forbidden by the moral code or by contract. The doing of an act which one has no right to do and against which a court action may be instituted. Malfeasance is distinguished from misfeasance in that the latter term denotes an improper act which one may lawfully perform. Malfeasance has come to be commonly used in referring to the misconduct of public officials.   J.M.R.

malinger. To feign illness or physical injury for the purpose of avoiding a duty or the performance of a task, or to secure damages or compensation.   J.M.R.

malnutrition. Originally, a general term used chiefly to designate cases of acute starvation or effects of disease, but later developed into a clinical entity much broader in scope, including not only low weight for height and age (the latter largely repudiated by later experience), but specific symptoms of listlessness, slouched posture, flabby ligatures, sallowness, hollow eyesockets, protruding scapulae. Not confined to the poorer classes, it is traceable to a multitude of emotional and habit factors, family factors, social factors, ecological factors. More broadly, the word covers not only general malnutrition but over-nutrition, glandular imbalance cases, and other specific malnutritions such as vitamin deficiencies and mineral deficiencies, including the diseases therefrom resulting.   **T.D.E.**

Malthusian theory. A scientific explanation of the growth of population, its factors, its limitations, and its consequences developed by Thomas R. Malthus, an English clergyman and economist. Malthus based his system on two fundamental postulates, viz., that food is necessary and that the passion between the sexes is permanent. If granted these two postulates, he claimed to be able to disprove the possibility of the perfection of human society. The essence of the Malthusian theory is that population tends to increase at a geometrical ratio, while it is not humanly possible to increase food at more than an arithmetical ratio. Population, therefore, will always be pressing on the food supply to such an extent as inevitably to induce serious social ills.

The two ways through which the inescapable restraint upon population growth may be exercised are through the increase of the death rate or the decrease of the birth rate. Factors operating in the former field are called positive checks, those in the latter field preventive checks. Malthus recognized that both types of checks involved misery, but maintained that the misery of the preventive checks was much less than the misery of the positive checks. He believed that an intelligent society could take its choice between these two alternatives but denied that by this choice it could escape social evils. As far as Malthus ventured to give advice to individuals it was to the effect that they should refrain from marriage until they felt sure that they could provide reasonably for whatever children might come. He made no place in his system for the voluntary restriction of children within marriage, although there is no doubt that he was familiar with some of the contraceptive

knowledge of his day. Malthus recognized clearly the influence of the standard of living and economic culture upon the actual size of a given population and the core of his theory may be summed up in the statement, "Population tends to increase up to the supporting power of the land on a given stage of the arts and a given standard of living."

malum in se. A crime which is so by reason of its inherent nature, or one that is intrinsically evil, such as murder or rape. It is one that deeply offends our sensibilities, or our notions of probity, justice, decency, humaneness, and so on. Offences at common law are generally mala in se.   **A.E.W.**

man. (1) The human species in general as distinguished from sub-human organisms. Homo sapiens. (2) An adult male member of the human species.

man, criminal. Cf. criminal man.

man, eminent. A man who has received widespread social recognition for power, achievement or position.   **M.S.**

man, feral. Any human being who has been nurtured in complete social isolation from other human beings, either by animals, or through indirect contact with human caretakers.   **E.A.H.**

man, marginal. In the broadest sense, a person who is not a fully participating member of a social group. Most marginal persons are marginal to two or more groups, as is true of partially assimilated immigrants.   **M.S.**

man, medicine. Cf. medicine man.

mana. Impersonal supernatural power, i.e., the mysterious force, not associated with individual supernatural beings, to which some peoples, especially in Oceania, attribute good fortune, exceptional qualities in things and persons, and the efficacy of magic. Cf. animatism; orenda; soulstuff; wakanda.   **G.P.M.**

management, household. Cf. household management.

management, scientific. Cf. scientific management.

mandate. In politics, a directive from the people, as when an issue has been decided at the polls. The term also has use in relationships between nations. For example, by agreement between first-class powers, the jurisdiction over lesser or backward peoples may be assumed. Thus a mandated area is placed in a position of tutelage or protective supervision to major power.   N.A.

manes. Ghosts (q.v.) or spirits of the dead; also, in classical mythology, the chthonian divinities.   G.P.M.

manic-depressive. Having reference to manic-depressive psychosis, a type of mental disorder characterized by excitement or depression.   B.M.

man-land ratio. The ratio or relationship between numbers of human beings and land (supporting power) which may exist at any given time for a given geographical area. The ratio is alterable (1) by natural forces, drought, famine, pestilence, change of climate and the like and (2) by the application of human forces in the form of productive techniques and processes on the land or nature side, and by the control of numbers through such practices as infanticide, abortion, celibacy, volitional restraint and birth control induced by pressure of population on resources or by standards of living.   E.E.M.

manorial system. The social organization and relationships including the customs, rules and regulations pertaining to the holding of large landed estates and the exploitation of serf labor and free tenants by feudal lords; the form of feudal land holding and social organization.   N.S.

manslaughter. The killing of one human being by another without malice or forethought. Involuntary manslaughter is killing in the performance of some unlawful act (not a felony) or in the performance of some lawful act by unlawful means, for example, killing someone through negligence. Voluntary manslaughter is killing in the heat of passion with sufficient provocation.   J.W.M'C.

manufacturing. Sometimes used very loosely to mean the production for sale of any article by any method, whether hand or machine. By some of the earlier economists it was used with reference to handicraft production involving simultaneous division of labor. In the usually accepted meaning, under conditions of modern industrial society, it refers to the system of factory production with the use of power machinery and complex division of labor.   K.DP.L.

manumission. The act of freeing a slave.   G.P.M.

marginal. Lying on the borderland of any recognized and relatively stable area, either territorial or cultural. The term carries implications of dissociation, unadjustment, and some degree or form of abnormality.

marginal area. Cf. area, marginal.

marginal group. Cf. group, marginal.

marginal man. Cf. man, marginal.

marginal uniqueness. A perceptible difference between persons who have points of similarity, particularly one that attracts others, contributing to leadership.   M.S.

marginal utility. The importance or value attaching to the marginal or last unit acquired in a stock of like goods; actually, to any single unit in a stock of like goods.   E.E.M.

marijuana. A native wild plant of Mexico and the southwest United States. When dried and smoked in a cigarette, popularly referred to as a "reefer", it induces advanced hallucination somewhat in the manner of opium.   E.A.H.

marital abstinence. Cf. abstinence, marital.

marital continence. Cf. continence, marital.

market, labor. Cf. labor market.

markets, conjuncture of the. Cf. conjuncture of the markets.

maron. A French term derived from the Spanish word *Simaran* meaning monkey. The use of the term Maroons by American Negroes as applied to West Indian Negroes is probably a mispronunciation of Maron. This deduction is based upon the custom of referring to West Indian Negroes as "monkeys" and "monkey chasers."

W.R.C.

maroon. Hog hunter. An appellation applied to fugitive Spanish Negro slaves.

W.R.C.

marriage. The social institution that provides the recognized form for entering into matrimony or setting up a family unit. The state of being married. Two principal forms of marriage have been the monogamous in which there is one male united to one female, and the polygamous in which there is a plurality of either husbands (polyandry) (q.v.) or wives (polygyny) (q.v.). Among many primitive peoples and in some of our ancient civilizations marriages have peen arranged by the parents, usually the male. The marriage may indicate a customary, legal or religious sanction of the provisions for forming a new family. It has frequently been accompanied by an exchange of economic goods or a provision for such an exchange at a later time. In countries in which the Christian religion is prominent marriage is usually formalized by a religious officiant after the parties have received a legal sanction in the form of a marriage license. The legal qualifications for marriage are established by a great variety of state laws regulating age, physical and mental fitness, parental consent, kinship, securing a license and other factors.

O.W.

marriage, clandestine. A private, lay and often secret union entered into by a man and woman without the services of church or civil officials. This type of marriage originated in Europe as early as the ninth century and grew out of the conflict between the Christian Church, which held that marriage is a religious rite, and the rooted idea of Teutonic and Anglo-Saxon peoples that marriage is a civil contract. While the Church steadily sought to extend its control over marriage, some laymen, both on the continent and in England, insisted on a private and sometimes secret or clandestine ceremony without witnesses. The difficulty encountered by the Church in stamping out these irregular unions was due in large measure to its own advocacy of the view that if a man and woman were contracted in words of the present tense ("I take thee to be my wedded wife—.") they were in very truth man and wife. In the twelfth century the canonical laws on marriage made a clear distinction between legal and valid marriages. Unions contracted in church and blest by the priest were legal; those in which the man and woman took each other for man and wife in words of the present tense (*per verba de praesenti*), either before witnesses or secretly, were valid but not legal. Because the Church was unwilling to declare clandestine marriages null and void and the offspring of such marriages illegitimate these secret, lay unions became common from the thirteenth to the sixteenth century, on the continent as in England. Since it was easy for dishonorable men to repudiate these informal unions, public scandals frequently grew out of them. At the Council of Trent in the middle of the sixteenth century, the Roman Catholic Church solved this perplexing problem by one clear stroke. The Council decreed that henceforward all marriages not celebrated in the presence of a priest and two or three witnesses should be null and void. In England, where individualism has always been strong, clandestine marriages became a public scandal during the seventeenth and eighteenth centuries, against which the Anglican Church struggled in vain. It was not until the Hardwicke Act was passed by Parliament in 1753 that England freed itself of this social evil. But in America clandestine marriage, lay but not always secret, lives on in many states in so-called "common law marriage." W.G.

marriage, common law. Marriage by reason of cohabitation for an uninterrupted period of seven years. In the absence of any statute to the contrary common law marriage has the same standing before the law as formal marriage. However, the number of states with laws removing legal recognition from common law marriage is increasing; by such laws the wife and children cannot legally claim the husband's name, support, nor inheritance. Cf. clandestine marriage.   J.W.M'C.

marriage, companionate. A proposed form of trial or provisional marriage, designed particularly for young people who are not yet ready to assume the full burdens of the family, but who wish nevertheless to enjoy the benefits of marital life. According to the assumption, the couple would be instructed in birth control, and upon the birth (or possibly conception) of their first child the marriage would become regular.

marriage, continence in. Cf. continence in marriage.

marriage, group. Cf. group marriage.

marriage, matrilocal. The type of marriage among primitive peoples where the husband takes up his residence with or among the wife's relatives.

marriage, morganatic. A marriage between a man of rank and a woman of inferior position whereby the wife and offspring are debarred the husband's rank and inheritance.   F.W.K.

marriage, pair. A form of marriage in which both parties have equivalent rights and obligations. It is the type of marriage which would be consistent with the full emancipation of woman, and her establishment upon a social plane equal to that of man.

marriage, patrilocal. That type of marriage among primitive peoples where the wife goes to live in her husband's clan or tribe. Patrilocal marriage is found where the patronymic, or paternal, kinship system has developed. As civilization advanced and the power and prestige of the father, as fighter and producer, increased patrilocal marriage became general. In ancient society the custom was universal and was handed on through medieval to modern times.   W.G.

marriage, tree. A ceremony, prevalent in parts of India, symbolically uniting a man or a woman in marriage to a tree, performed sometimes as a part of the wedding ritual, sometimes to enable a younger sibling (q.v.) to marry before an elder.   G.P.M.

marriage, trial. Any actual or proposed matrimonial system designed to permit a man and woman to live together in full intimacy while attempting to discover whether they are sufficiently compatible to cause them to wish to perpetuate the relationship, and allowing them to either stabilize or terminate the relationship without social condemnation or loss of status.

marriage at the church door. As early as the tenth century in Western Europe it became customary for gifta (q.v.), or handing over by her father of a contracted girl to her suitor, to take place at the church door in the presence of a priest. Marriage was still regarded as a lay and private matter, based on the consent of the parties and the "tradition" or giving of the bride to the man. But the growing influence of the Church over marriage is clearly seen in the fact that gifta now took place at the door of the church, with a priest present at the lay ceremony in England. Even as late as the end of the twelfth century, the York ritual of marriage showed that the essential part of the wedding ceremony took place at the church door. Here the bride's dower was assigned; here the priest asked, "Who giveth this woman to this man?" After these essential acts in marriage, the priest blessed the married pair. Only then did the bridal party enter the church and attend the "bride mass", which was followed by another priestly blessing. W.G.

marriage broker. An intermediary who arranges marriages in certain cultures where the patriarchal institutional type of family is still dominant and the companionship type is only imperfectly developed. Marriage in various primitive tribes and civilized peoples has often been a commercial transaction redounding to the advantage of the parents of one or the other mate. In many European countries the bride brings her husband a dowry, and there are legal arrangements for the settlement of a portion of the groom's property on the bride. Royal marriages are usually contracted for considerations of state, which leads to the institution of morganatic marriage. In all these cases the services of an intermediary are frequently invoked to make the necessary arrangements. The practice of resorting to a marriage broker remains operative even in the midst of metropolitan individualized cultures, particularly among immigrant groups. Thus among Jewish immigrants the shadchan arranges meetings between clients of the opposite sex, after they have paid him a stipulated registration fee. Then if the couple finally decides to marry, they are contractually obligated to pay him a definite sum as remuneration for his brokerage service. Not to be confused with marriage brokers are various introduction bureaus and dating agencies.   E.F.

marriage by capture. A mode of marriage according to which a man obtains a wife by forceful abduction, sometimes genuine but more frequently merely a ritual pretense after a previous agreement with her kinsmen. Cf. elopement.   G.P.M.

marriage by exchange. A mode of marriage according to which two men exchange sisters or daughters, each thus securing a wife either for himself or for a son or brother.   G.P.M.

marriage by purchase. A mode of marriage according to which a man obtains a wife by paying a bride-price (q.v.) to her father or kinsmen, or sometimes, conversely, whereby a woman obtains a husband through the payment of a dowry (q.v.).   G.P.M.

marriage class. An exogamous group in an aboriginal Australian society, superficially resembling a sib (q.v.) but differentiated therefrom by the prevalence of double descent (q.v.). Though prominent in the theoretical literature, the term is now obsolescent, having been replaced by "moiety" (q.v.) where there are two such classes, by "section" where there are four, and by "subsection" where there are eight.   G.P.M.

marriage contract. The formal agreement arranged between the parents of a young man and woman prior to betrothal, regarding the amount of the dowry the girl should bring in marriage and the property settlement the suitor should make on his widow in case of his death. In ancient Rome these contracts were regarded as of the utmost importance and the docu-

ments recording them were carefully preserved. Under the influence of Rome the verbal marriage contracts of peoples in the early Middle Ages slowly gave place to formal written agreements. Until late in the eighteenth century marriage contracts were customary among families of property in Europe and the American colonies. These contracts were not uncommon during the nineteenth century and are sometimes drawn up between people of wealth at the present time. w.G.

marriage counselling. A counter movement to increasing disorganization of the family, designed to provide therapy and education. Among the activities sponsored by the general movement in public and private agencies, including universities, family welfare agencies, domestic relations courts, etc., are courses and discussion groups on the problems of marriage in colleges, secondary schools, community and adult education centers, and counsel and treatment of particular cases of family disintegration that come to the attention of physicians, psychiatrists, social workers, and sociologists. It operates with theories of the probability of predicting happiness in marriage and emphasizes the importance of rôles, personal behavior patterns, parent-child relationships, similar cultural backgrounds, and an adequate philosophy of life.   E.F.

marriage ritual. The more or less formal ceremonies by which a man and woman enter into the marriage relationship. Even in barbarian societies certain crude rites were observed in handing over a woman to a man as his wife. Among the ancient Hebrews, Greeks, and Romans it was customary for the father to give the girl in marriage before an assemblage of family friends. After the father had handed over his daughter to the groom a gay procession escorted the bride to her husband's home. This marriage procession was an important feature of the ritual of marriage in all ancient societies. During the Middle Ages, the Christian Church gained a large measure of control over marriage and the marriage ritual. One of the earliest of these written rituals in English is that of York cathedral in use at the end of the twelfth century.   w.G.

Marxism. The body of revolutionary doctrines originated by Karl Marx and Friedrich Engels, based primarily on what they conceived to be the historic rôle of the working classes to abolish capitalism and class privileges, and to create a classless society, ultimately without a State apparatus; but preceded by a dictatorship of the proletariat (q.v) as set forth most succinctly in the Communist Manifesto of 1848. Cf. socialism; communism. R.N.B.

masochism. An abnormal inclination which makes pain, or some expression of cruelty, in mild or greater degree, sexually stimulating. E.R.B.

mass, masses. Mass is a particular kind of social connection (sociability, sociality, sociation) characterized by the lowest degree of intensity and depth in the partial fusion of minds and behavior into a "We." The more intense and deep degrees are expressed in "community" and "communion". The mass may be characterized as the lowest degree of fusion and the highest degree of pressure. Often confused with "crowd" or with "gathering" and even with "herd", which moves by simple contagion. Sometimes, the term "mass" is conceived in the sense of a statistical frame of reference, e.g., the numbers of suicides, consumers, voters, newspaper subscribers or readers, etc. Sometimes under the term "mass", or in this case rather "masses", there is understood a "union penetrated with the spirit of negation and construction", a "union of pariahs", which appears only in the periods of decadence of a society, and prepares the way for a radical overthrow of the established order. This conception appears arbitrary and expresses certain negative value-implications, derogatory to the "mass" and "masses", e.g., as something located very low on value scale. Sociologically significant is the distinction between the unassembled masses (e.g., malcontents, poor, unemployed, aliens, scholars, readers of certain newspapers, etc.), and assembled masses. Normally, the masses are unassembled, and become transformed into an assembled mass in rather exceptional circumstances. Between the two, there are obviously many intermediary forms. G.G.

mass movement. An uprising of large numbers of the common people under the influence of dissatisfaction with some social institution or doctrine, in which the logical and critical faculties are submerged by the emotions, and there is a contagious tendency among the people to follow dogmatic leaders blindly. In the Occident, the most extensive mass movements have been either religious, as in the Crusades, the Lollard and the Wesleyan revivals; or political, as in the French and Bolshevist revolutions; or social, as in the anti-slavery and anti-liquor agitations in the United States. In India, the term is applied to the breaking away of untouchables and low caste Hindus, as village units, from the traditional prescriptions of caste and their adhesion to the Christian movement. G.M.F.

mass phenomena. Any observable facts or events associated with a large aggregate of persons. J.P.E.

master-servant relation. A special type of human relationship well known in Roman and feudal society but distinctly absent from employer-employee relationships in modern transportation, mass production industries, and the present-day civil service. The typical master knows his servant, his servant's family and its problems. The master's demands upon the servant are regulated in great part by custom; his responsibilities to his servant are real and recurringly demonstrable. The servant, in turn, is devoted to his master, makes no categorical or imperative demands, exercises exceeding patience, and is habitually respectful. House servants typically enjoy special prestige, security, and personal privileges. In the northern part of the United States householders have forgotten, largely, the rôle of the master; servants reject the rôle of the servant. The result is the "servant problem." W.C.H.

material culture. Cf. culture, material.

materialism, historical. A complex theory of history and social causation involving a definite metaphysics (and, less explicitly, a theory of knowledge). Sometimes known as economic determination (q.v.), this theory, which came into prominence through the Marxist movement of which it was the prepotent ideology, abjures all idealistic explanations of history, culture, and social change. Committed to an outright anthropocentric philosophy it interprets history as the career of man's adjustment to the world and society, which proceeds through a series of class struggles growing out of fundamental economic differences. It inclines to a theory of monistic causation, attributing primacy to economic and technological factors, and regarding the other major social organizations and structures as being somehow derivative. Thus political and legal institutions, art and letters, philosophy and religion are regarded as secondary effects of the fundamental economic processes and changes. All absolutes are denied and knowledge becomes an instrumental and adjustive reaction to the world, with inescapable activistic imperatives. This instrumentalization of knowledge provides leverage for the manipulation of society in the direction of a collectivized social order, conceived as the only equitable ordering of human affairs. The specifically political consequences of this social philosophy, viz., the inevitability of the classless society through an inherent dialectical process, the ultimate disappearance of the state, the dwindling of the middle class, and the election of the proletariat, with all the organizational consequences drawn from these theorems by the socialist and communist parties are not necessarily connected with the theory of historical materialism, and in some cases represent deviations. Whatever may be said regarding the validity of historical materialism as a metaphysics or a philosophy of history or of society, there is no denying its great value as a heuristic instrument in discovering the functional relationship of the inextricably inter-woven ramifications of a culture. Of course the awareness of the latter and also of the indubitable importance of economic factors have always been present in anthropology and to some extent inherent in the whole approach of the historical school.

E.F.

maternal and child health. Services aimed to protect, promote and conserve the mental and physical health of children from the prenatal period through adolescence, and of their mothers throughout the reproductive cycle.   W.P.

maternal family. Cf. family, maternal.

mating, assortive (assortative). Cf. assortive (assortative) mating.

matriarchate. A purely hypothetical form of early social organization in which women are alleged to have wielded both political and domestic authority. Cf. motherright; patriarchate.   G.P.M.

matrilineal. Reckoning descent, inheritance, or succession (q.v.) exclusively or preferentially through females. Cf. patrilineal.   G.P.M.

matrilinear. Cf. matrilineal.

matrilocal. Pertaining to customary or preferential residence on the part of a married couple, at the home of the wife or her kinsmen. Cf. patrilocal.   G.P.M.

matrilocal marriage. Cf. marriage, matrilocal.

matrilocal residence. Living with the wife's people, a custom found in several islands between Asia and Australia and among the Pueblo and Iroquois Indians of North America. The custom is frequently found among people who have the maternal system of kinship. Among some peoples matrilocal residence alternates at specified times with patrilocal residence. o.w.

matrimony. A joining in wedlock, a union formed by marriage; the state of being married.

matripotestal. Characterized by the exercise of authority, especially in the family or household, by the mother or maternal grandmother. Cf. patripotestal.
                                             G.P.M.

matrix, algebraic. A rectangular arrangement or tabulation of entities in rows and columns. The degree of the matrix is the number of series which are cross-classified. A series of rows only constitutes a first degree matrix, a series of rows cross-classified with a series of columns constitutes a second degree matrix, while a third series expanding each cell of a second degree matrix into a sagittal array would constitute a third degree matrix, etc. S.C.D.

matronymic. Cf. metronymic.

maturation. The process of development of a characteristic by normal growth or ripening, in the absence of learning. M.S.

maturation, criminal. Cf. criminal maturation.

maturation process. The process by which an individual achieves social adjustment through outgrowing his tendency to delinquent or criminal conduct. M.A.E.

maturity, social. Cf. social maturity.

mayhem. Intentional maiming or disfiguring the body of another. At common law the term referred generally to an act depriving another of a limb essential for fighting, as an arm or leg, but not an ear since it was assumed to have no value for defensive purposes. Modern statutes make no distinctions on this ground. J.M.R.

maximum custody. Cf. custody, maximum.

mean (*statistical*). The sum of any series of numerical items such as scores or observations, divided by the number of items in the series. This is the arithmetic mean, and is the most-used type of average. Cf. mode; median. M.Pt.

mean, deviation from the, (*statistical*). Cf. deviation from the mean, (*statistical*).

meaning. The definition of anything as the result of a reflective process. This process is as follows: When the empirical or automatic interaction between the human organism and its environment is interrupted, consciousness develops universally as the focusing of attention on the interrupting conditions and becomes an emerging or growing thought, purpose or active project indicated in the question: This is What? In this live form of the actively developing judgment, meaning appears as the identification of the unfamiliar percept or subject, This, through the placing or locating of it as to its function in the more familiar system of experience, indicated by the predicate, is What? The predicate is made up of a tentative, experimental series of familiar, emotionally valued concepts of similar situations drawn from memory of the past. As unreflective, overt action is checked and thinking thus develops about the subject of attention, the effort of consciousness is to observe experimentally what kind of a situation the subject functions in. Determination of this functional relationship of the subject to the experience of the thinker is the process of identification; and this ends in the invention or memory of a name, which gives the meaning or functional relation of the object, in the experience of the speaker. This determination of meaning reinstates the interrupted functioning of the human organism in its environment. C.J.B.

mechanism. A structure or a well-established pattern of behavior by which the individual or the group is prepared and equipped for action. Examples include the reflexes or the individual organism, the attitudes of persons, and the language, folkways, rituals, myths, and institutions of the group. W.E.G.

mechanism, compensation or compensatory. A system or pattern of psycho-physical structure-function by which an organism or person or group as a whole so responds or behaves as to resist or offset conflicts, difficulties, shortcomings, defects, in an effort to maintain or adjust its balance, equanimity, integrity. In a sense all life is a compensatory process-condition, equilibrating inner and outer forces. Cf. defense mechanism; escape mechanism. T.D.E.

mechanism, defense. A system or pattern of psycho-physical structure-function by which an organism, person or group, as a whole, so responds or behaves as to resist or offset dangers, threats, attacks, injuries, accusations, actual or imagined, in an effort to maintain or adjust its balance, equanimity, integrity. Cf. escape mechanism. T.D.E.

mechanism, escape. (*psychiatric*) A pattern of attitude and behavior by which a person avoids, evades, postpones, or attempts to escape from disagreeable situ-

ations or problems, by distraction, repression, rationalization, dissociation or amnesia, drink, drugs, actual running away.
    T.D.E.

mechanistic theory. The operation upon man, as a biological organism, of forces external to man, the individual being passive in the process. One form of the theory consists of attempts to subject social phenomena to categories developed in conjunction with the biological and physical sciences. This is known as "mechanistic analogy." Examples are such analogical notions as mass, energy, attraction and repulsion, law of least resistance, equilibrium, and the like when applied to social life.   W.E.G.

mechanization. The substitution of machinery for tool-using human labor in any productive process.

median. That average which is the point on a distribution scale below and above which half of the cases fall; the midpoint of a frequency distribution.   M.PT.

mediation. The act or process of intercession or intervention, usually applied to the settlement of a dispute; the interposition of a person or agency between two persons to harmonize or reconcile them without the use of sanctions directly or indirectly.   F.W.K.

medical social work. Social case work practiced in a clinic or hospital or other medical setting, or in regular association with a physician. It is especially concerned with the social problems related to illness.   W.P.

medicine, socialized. Cf. socialized medicine.

medicine man. A primitive practitioner of the curing arts, and commonly also of magic, witchcraft, and thaumaturgy often with the aid of personal supernatural helpers or familiar spirits; a shaman (q.v.).   G.P.M.

medium custody. Cf. custody, medium.

medium of exchange. An article or commodity freely accepted in exchange for other goods and constituting a conventional standard by which the relative value of other things is measured; money (q.v.) (in its most inclusive sense). G.P.M.

meliorism. A philosophy of action and a program which avoids the extremes of pessimism or optimism. It recognizes realistic facts in the situation and proceeds with a program planned to meet challenge for partial betterment.   B.B.W.

melioristic. Remedial and realistic; based on a theory of meliorism. Cf. meliorism.
    B.B.W.

Mendelian. Characteristic of, or relating to, Mendel or his laws of inheritance; specifically relating to the processes of hereditary transmission carried out by the chromosomes.   F.H.H.

Mendelian ratio. The ratio of chance combinations of the genes, or hereditary factors, in the offspring of crossbred plants and animals. Such ratios may be either genotypic, i.e., carried in the germ plasm, or phenotypic, i.e., manifest in the somatoplasm. In popular usage this term often refers to the genotypic ratio of 1:2:1 and the phenotypic ratio of 3:1 among offspring of monohybrids. In other words, in the typical case, the statistical probability is that three-fourths of the offspring of such hybrids will manifest in their bodies the dominant form of the trait and one-fourth will manifest the recessive form; however, in their germ plasms, one-fourth will carry genes only for the dominant form of the trait and one-fourth for the recessive form only, while the remaining half will, like their parents, carry genes for both forms of the trait. Cf. genotype; phenotype. F.H.H.

mens rea. Every crime consists of two elements, the criminal act or omission, and the mental element or "criminal intent", the mens rea. The mens rea is the particular state of mind which accompanies the particular act defined as criminal. Hence, the mens rea, or mental element of each crime will be different. Thus, in the crime of receiving stolen goods, the mens rea is the knowledge that the goods were stolen; in the case of murder, the mens rea means malice aforethought; in

the case of theft, an intention to steal.
N.F.C.

Menshevik. Derived from menshinstvo
(meaning minority) referring to the Second Congress of the Russian Social Democratic Party held in Brussels and London,
1903, where the group in question secured
only a minority of the vote for the Central Committee. In fact, numerically the
Mensheviks comprised a majority of the
Socialist followers in pre-revolutionary
Russia. They represented the moderate
wing of the Workers' Party adhering to
the concepts of an evolutionary socialism,
democratic techniques and cooperation
with middle-class parties. The eventual
victory of Bolshevism led to the elimination of the Mensheviks in Russia. Cf.
Bolshevik.
S.N.

mental defectiveness. Mental deficiency.
Frequently the term mental defectiveness
is specifically limited to borderline conditions in which the person is legally competent but slightly subnormal in intelligence. The intelligence-quotient range
for the mentally defective is generally
considered to be 70 to 79.
C.F.S.

mental deficiency. Feeblemindedness;
amentia; mental subnormality; mental
defectiveness. A state of mental retardation or incomplete development, existing
from birth or early infancy, by reason of
which one is unable to meet the social expectation of his own society. Mentally deficient persons of the higher grades can
be enabled to be self-supporting, but only
with exceptional guidance, care, and direction. The mentally deficient as a whole
are conventionally differentiated into
three grades as follows: (a) the moron,
who has an intelligence quotient (I.Q.)
of from 50 to 69 or a mental age (M.A.)
of from 84 to 143 months. It is this type
which is capable of self-support under
the terms mentioned above, and the higher
grades, or borderline cases, are frequently
difficult to distinguish by the layman from
normally minded individuals. (b) The imbecile, who has an I.Q. of 25 to 49 or a
M.A. ranging from 36 to 83 months. Such
a person is capable of protecting himself
from elemental dangers, but not of playing an even approximately mature rôle in
society. (3) The idiot, who has an I.Q.

of less than 25 or a M.A. of not more than
35 months. Idiots are so lacking in intelligence that they cannot live without
constant care and attention.
C.F.S.

mental disease. A term of relatively recent origin designating a state of mental
disorder, unbalance, or derangement which
prevents the individual from assuming responsibility for his own support or makes
him a positive menace to the health and
safety of the community. Mental diseases
are classified as neruoses (q.v) and psychoses (q.v.) of organic or psychological
origin. Further classification is a subject of controversy. The term insanity is
gradually giving place to mental disease,
the latter term being more accurate and
less socially derogatory and humiliating.
J.W.M'C.

mental disorder. A situation in which the
personality is maladjusted and under
strain physically and/or socially-emotion-
ally, and becomes disorganized, distorted,
disordered, or even disintegrated in a
variety of ways classified by psychiatrists.
Whether or not certain mental phenomena
are to be considered "normal" and are
therefore not further complicated by social stigma and maladjustment, is largely
a matter of definition of situation in terms
of the current culture. The current culture also provides or affects the content
of any "illusion" or imagery, and the
subjective interpretation thereof by the
person affected. Certain cultures set up
frustrations and conflicts, and therefore
mental disorders, which are not found in
other cultures. Cf. disease; mental disease; maladjustment.
T.D.E.

mental hygiene. The science and practice
of maintaining mental health.
W.P.

mental interstimulation and response. A
psychological phrase which has practically
the same content as "social interaction".
As we ascend in the social scale of life,
the various forms of interstimulation and
response become more or less conscious;
hence they might be said to become more
and more "mental interactions", though
strictly there is no direct connection between the minds of individuals. Each individual mind responds to the stimuli in
its physical medium, and among these

stimuli are the symbols of thought and feeling created in the physical medium by the voice, the features, and the bodily movements of other individuals. These are reacted to and mentally interpreted; thus communication between individuals becomes possible through mental interstimulation and response.   C.A.E.

mental mobility. Cf. mobility, mental.

merging. The use of the same kinship term for both lineal and collateral relatives, e.g., for both father and paternal uncle. Cf. classificatory system.   G.P.M.

mesaticephalic. Cf. mesocephalic.

mesocephalic. Characterized by a head of medium breadth, with a cephalic index (q.v.), of between 77 and 82.   G.P.M.

mesognathous. Characterized by an intermediate facial profile, i.e., by a facial profile angle of between 80° and 85°. Cf. orthognathous; prognathous   G.P.M.

mesorrhine. Characterized by a nose of medium breadth, i.e., with a nasal index (q.v.) between 47 and 51, as measured on the skull, or between 70 and 85 as measured on the living head. Cf. leptorrhine; platyrrhine.   G.P.M.

messiah. In Christianity, the Annointed One, i.e., Christ.   Any religious leader who is the founder of a revolutionary cult promising a new and improved way of life, in the present, or hereafter, for its followers.   E.A.H.

mestizo. A person of mixed blood, especially, in Spanish America, the offspring of a European and an American Indian.   G.P.M.

metabolism, social. Cf. social metabolism.

metempsychosis. Reincarnation (q.v.).

method, experimental. Cf. experimental method.

method of the artist. For the artist, his work is mainly the expression of a conflict of his inner with the outer world. Working according to certain traditions of production, he will, usually uncon-

sciously, create in a general style.   In his artwork he can bear witness to his understanding of life and his ethical convictions.   Such understanding, however, will not become science, nor will the expression of his conviction become religion. Both science and religion are valid only within their own systems and the artwork, while sometimes instrumental, is not indispensable to the fulfillment of their missions.   The artist is independent of any particular system of values.   J.H.B.

metronymic. Deriving the personal or family name from the mother or other matrilineal relative.   Cf. patronymic.

metronymic or mother name system. That form of social organization among primitive tribes in which kinship is traced through mothers only.   In some tribes, as the Malayans, the father's relationship to his children was totally ignored.   Under the matrilocal system, whereby the husband goes to live with his wife's kin, not only kinship but property descend through women. Perhaps the extreme development of the system was attained among the Pueblo Indians of Southwest America. In this tribe kinship and property descend through women who own the home and all the household goods.   If any difficulty arises between the husband and his wife's relatives they may expel him from the house and compel him to return to his mother's home, which is in reality his own.

metropolis. A large principal city commonly surrounded by contiguous or nearby urban communities more or less dependent, economically and socially, upon the metropolis.   E.E.M.

metropolitan area. Cf. area, metropolitan.

metropolitan district. For the 1940 Census a metropolitan district was defined as an area including one or more cities of 50,000 people or over, plus all adjacent and contiguous minor civil divisions (e.g., townships, precincts) with an average density of 150 or more persons per square mile with occasional modifications according to local circumstances.   The 1930 definition was similar but only areas with an aggregate population of 100,000 or more were considered metropolitan districts.   S.S.

middle class. A social stratum recognized in the Roman republic by the equestrian rank, in the empire by the title of decurio, in medieval Europe by various forms of the word burgher. A social class resting between the aristocracy and the proletariat on the social scale, characterized by its cult of respectability, interest in secular education, care of its own children, indefatigable business and professional enterprise, and usually by its moral inhibitions. In the middle class cleanliness is next to godliness, and idle time is lost forever. The greatest goal in life is to be independent, the next is to work, but usually not with the hands in direct production. The middle class is usually associated with town life, although prosperous American farmers, German *Landgutsbesitzer,* and English gentry are in the middle class. In Holland and Switzerland cultural diffusion of middle class habits has been so complete that proletarian culture has been all but obliterated. w.c.h.

The modern middle class emerged midway between the landed aristocracy and the free peasants and serfs in Europe during the period of the breakdown of the feudal system. It was composed first of the traders who acquired wealth as a result of the increased use of coined money, and later also included those who put a part of mercantile wealth into industrial enterprises. These merchants and industrialists were town dwellers and hence were known as burghers or bourgeoisie (q.v.), which latter term came to be synonymous with the capitalist class.

In the later development of capitalism (q.v.) a distinction was drawn between the more powerful and wealthier capitalists (gross bourgeoisie) and smaller capitalists (petite bourgeoisie). This latter division of the population known in the United States as "small business and industry" became the core of the new middle class. But with the increase of professional services and other intellectual pursuits the term middle class was made to include those providing these services also, particularly those with moderate incomes. Well-paid skilled workers and prosperous farm-owning farmers also were covered under the term. Thus, in the United States, down to approximately the middle of the nineteenth century, "middle class" designated small property owners, intellectual workers with modest incomes, skilled artisans and prosperous farmers. From about the middle of the nineteenth century there began an extensive increase in the number of salaried workers, office workers, managers and superintendents of branch stores or shops or departments of larger enterprises. This group of "white collar" and salaried workers, most of whom are technically wage earners, are, because of their education and character of work, more nearly allied with the property-owning and intellectual workers than with industrial wage-earners. Hence, usually they are regarded, and regard themselves, as middle class.

Middle class therefore today is a term designating a heterogeneous section of the population made up chiefly of small businessmen and small industrialists, professional and other intellectual workers with moderate incomes, skilled artisans, prosperous farmers, white collar workers and salaried employees of larger mercantile, industrial and financial establishments. They have few common economic interests. Whatever unity they possess lies in their educational standards, their standard of living and ideals of family life, their mores and recreational interests. They constitute the overwhelming bulk of the Protestant Church membership and a considerable element of the Catholic Church and Reformed branch of the Jewish community.

midwife. A woman who practices the art of assisting women in childbirth. Many midwives are untrained but modern states are now requiring a more or less thorough period of training for this exacting work. w.g.

migrant. One who participates in a movement of migration (q.v.).

migration. The form of population movement which in the course of cultural evolution follows dispersion (q.v.). The participants are sufficiently advanced in economic culture, intelligence, and geographical knowledge so that they are conscious of a true destination. The movement is planned, purposeful, and deliberate. The movement is as rapid as the available means of transportation make possible. Migration as a whole falls within the historical period and manifests four chief distinct forms—invasion (q.v.), conquest (q.v.), colonization (q.v.), and immigration (q.v.).

migration, internal. Population movement within the central territory of a political unit. It should be distinguished from movement to dependencies of the home state. Cf. colonization; conquest.

migratory worker. Cf. worker, migratory.

milieu. A word synonymous with environment (q.v.). Although in French the word means "middle", in English-American sociology this literal translation is altogether misleading. "In the midst of" is as close in meaning to the French "middle" as can be found.   W.C.H.

millet. A vicinally accessible, socially isolated sacred (non-local) community enjoying, in most phases of its life, autonomy in quasi-theocratic organization and control, yet within the territory of a dominant state. Most prominent examples have been the several Christian communities in the Ottoman Empire (1299-1922), each being an ecclesia with sectarian tendencies, in which the patriarch was also temporal ruler and the members of the hierarchy frequently performed secular functions. The arrangement was congenial to the Sultans because the law they administered, with the aid of Muslim ecclesiastics, was sacred to Islam and its adherents.   D.E.W.

milling. The pointless moving about of people in a crowd, denoting a state of leaderless confusion.   N.A.

mimetic expression. Cf. expression, mimetic.

mimetic response. Cf. response, mimetic.

mind, class. Cf. class mind.

mind, democratic. The aggregate of the attitudes, ideas and beliefs in matters of social concern shared by members of a society in which equality of opportunity and of rights exists and no privileged class dominates. Hence it can develop only in a classless society.   M.Pm.

mind, group. Cf. group mind.

mind, mob. The mental state of the members of a crowd which has reached a high degree of emotional excitement and is bent upon some unreasoned or impulsive action.

mind, social. Cf. social mind.

mindedness, like-. Cf. like-mindedness.

mindedness, mob. Cf. mob mindedness.

mindedness, social. Cf. social mindedness.

minimum custody. Cf. custody, minimum.

minimum wage. Cf. wage, minimum.

mining. The extraction of non-replaceable materials from the land. It includes not only the extraction of solids, such as coal, copper, granite, etc., but also liquids such as oil, and gas. The process of mining really depletes the land, and ordinarily results in the diminution of natural resources, since these materials are seldom recoverable after final consumption.

minority. Less than half of any group. In practice, the term is usually applied to subdivisions of a society, the numbers of which are so small as to give them a limited social potential (q.v.). Cf. minority group.

minority group. Cf. group, minority.

mir. The village assembly or "council" of the ancient Russian community. Sometimes, though strictly speaking incorrectly, used to designate the ancient Russian village itself as a community.   N.L.S.

miscarriage. A lay, non-medical term for detachment or expulsion of the fetus before viability; a spontaneous abortion. In lay language miscarriage is distinguished from abortion or premature birth. In clear medical discourse the term miscarriage is rarely used, but is represented by one type of abortion (q.v.).   N.E.H.

miscegenation. The mixture of different racial stocks through physical interbreeding. It is the primary process in amalgamation (q.v.). In customary usage, the term has somewhat derogatory implications. This is due probably to two factors, first the confusion of the syllable mis (from a Latin root meaning "to mix") with a similar form implying error or evil; and second, from a widespread, undemonstrated belief that all race mixture, beyond certain narrow limits of variation, is unfavorable. The scientific truth as to the socially significant effects of miscegenation has not yet been established.

misdemeanor. One of the two major classifications of crime. It designates minor violations, as contrasted with felony (q.v.) which is the name for high crimes. The basis of differentiation between felonies and misdemeanors is vague, the rule of thumb guide being the length of sentence as established by statute. Misdemeanors carry a sentence of less than one year, or small fine. Traffic violations, originally classified as misdemeanors are now frequently placed in a separate category.
                                              J.W.M'C.

missionary. A sacred stranger whose vocation is the conversion (q.v.) of outgroup individuals to profession of his sacred dogma and membership in his ecclesia.   D.E.W.

missions. The organizations charged with missionary (q.v.) activity; the institutions of denominational religious organizations which undertake programs of activity for the sake of making converts.
                                              D.E.W.

mistress. (1) A woman having power and ownership who exercises authority as chief; a female head of a family or school. (2) A woman with whom a man habitually consorts outside of marriage; a woman living with and supported by a man as his paramour, or illicit love.   w.G.

mistress-maid relation. That stage in the evolution of labor relations where the mistress no longer owns the person of the worker (as in slavery) but considers that she owns most of the maid's time, energy and devotion. The maid has often accepted subservience and inferiority as her rôle and status.   A.E.W.

mitigation of punishment. Cf. punishment, mitigation of.

mob. A crowd in active motion in relation to a common objective; usually violent, usually having previously "milled about" or undergone a barrage of suggestion and some "galvanizing" or "polarizing" emotional stimuli of symbol, slogan, or demagoguery. Cf. crowd.   T.D.E.

mob mind. Cf. mind, mob.

mob mindedness. A high degree of emotional tension which actuates the individuals of a crowd in irresponsible, aggressive collective behavior. (*crim.*) Motivated by and loyal to a criminal group called the mob.   J.M.R.

mobility, ecological. The (a) capability, (b) amount, or (c) speed of change in ecological position.   J.A.Q.

mobility, horizontal. (1) movement of individuals and groups from one social position to another within the same social stratum, as, for example, a change in occupation from masonry to house painting. (2) Diffusion of culture traits:—material objects, customs, values—from region to region, group to group within the same social stratum, as, for example, spread of a Hollywood fashion among the middle classes from California to other regions.
                                              M.K.

mobility, labor. Cf. labor mobility.

mobility, mental. A term used to designate the social-psychological aspects of social change. The members of a rapidly changing society are mentally mobile in various ways and degrees, in contrast to the mentally immobile members of a society changing slowly or not at all. It should be noted, however, that it is entirely possible for a personality to be mobile in one segment and immobile in another.   H.B.

mobility, occupational. (1) Change from one occupation to another. (2) Change from one occupation to another, as a result of which the number and variety of social interactions is altered.   M.S.

mobility, social. Cf. social mobility.

mobility, vertical. (1) The movement of individuals or entire groups from one social stratum to another, either ascending or descending. The hierarchy involved may be the social class hierarchy as a whole or its components, such as the economic, occupational, or educational hierarchies. The impoverishment of a well-to-do family, the promotion of an employee to a managerial rank, the elevation or lowering of entire classes in revolutions are examples of vertical mobility. (2) The diffusion of any culture trait, such as invention, knowledge, custom, value up or down the social strata. The pyramid involved may be economic, occupational, educational, or any other associated with the social status hierarchy. M.K.

modal. Pertaining to a mode or the mode. T.D.E.

modality. The tendency in a given statistical population, type-group, or category of phenomena for degrees of a trait to be distributed in such a way as to vary from the mode (q.v.). T.D.E.

mode (*statistical*). That average which is defined as the value of a score or measure that occurs the greatest number of times in a frequency distribution. M.Pt.

modification, reciprocal. The change that takes place when two organisms processes or things impinge upon each other and each of them is altered in the process. Symbolic intercommunication involves reciprocal modification of the parties involved. A.R.L.

modify. To alter or change; the term finds its most general use in relation to change in the direction of a lesser emphasis or compromise. N.A.

modus operandi. A method of identifying one who has committed a crime by examination of the method used in its commission. It is based upon the theory that each professional criminal has a method of committing a crime peculiar to himself. It was devised by Major Atcherley of Yorkshire, England. It is used to supplement the finger print method. J.L.G.

Mohammedanism (called Islam by its adherents). A religious system founded by Mohammed (c571-632 A.D.). P.H.F.

moiety. A phratry (q.v.) or large sib (q.v.), where the tribe is primarily divided into two such groups. Cf. dual organization. G.P.M.

momentum, group. The force exerted upon individual members of a group. The cumulative force of the entire body, which tends to keep all moving in a general direction, and tends to overcome temporary retardation of parts or efforts to change the direction of emphasis. M.C.E.

monandry. A form of marriage in which one man is ordinarily united to only one wife at a time, although not necessarily permanently or to the exclusion of polygyny (q.v.) in individual cases. Cf. monogamy. G.P.M.

money. A medium of exchange and a common denominator of value (unit of account) the function of which is to facilitate the exchange of goods and services in any given economy. Money functions also as a store of value and as a standard for deferred payments. The medium chosen is determined by cultural conditions, by the stage of development of the economy, and by the materials available. A good modern medium should be generally acceptable, easily recognizable, easily divisible, homogeneous, portable and durable. In modern societies many forms of credit substitute for money, e.g., bank credit, retail credit, consumer credit, installment sales, etc. Like money, all these influence the equation of exchange, hence the price level, inflation and deflation. Currency is a type of money subject to public regulation. While we think of money as bills, coins, etc., in primitive societies many different objects (e.g., cattle, shells, furs, salt, various instruments), many of them not meeting the ideal characteristics of money, served as such. Money may thus have originated in some commonly prized object of barter. Such objects were generally acceptable and recognizable in the particular culture though they were not always divisible, homogeneous, etc.

These circumstances show that cultural

and even geographic factors as well as purely economic factors, influence the choice of the medium of exchange. At the other end of the time scale, in modern western civilization, we see the influence of changing cultural conditions on the monetary system in the widespread abandonment, at least temporarily, of the gold standard and the adoption of controlled foreign exchange by the governmental manipulation of funds. The development of total war has caused the monetary system to be used not simply to facilitate exchange internally and externally; the monetary system has become an instrument of economic warfare to serve political and nationalistic purposes quite independent of economic welfare as that term was understood in the nineteenth century.   N.E.H.

money, blood. Cf. blood money.

mongrel. A plant or animal of mixed breed. This is a popular, not a scientific, term and hence has no precise meaning. It is often used, sometimes disparagingly, to designate persons or groups of mixed racial descent.   F.H.H.

monocracy. Literally, rule by a single individual; a state or condition of human affairs wherein the governmental machinery is in control of a single individual; undivided authority, such as is said to be characteristic of Hitler. Cf. autocracy.
                                         F.E.L.

monoculture. Cultivation of a single money crop or other exportable product to the virtual exclusion of others.   G.P.M.

monogamy. A form of marriage, socially sanctioned and institutionalized, in which one man is united with one woman to the exclusion, on principle, of any plurality of spouses. Cf. monandry; polyandry; polygyny.   G.P.M.

monopoly. (1) Non-competitive possession of, or access to, any object. Monopoly may be partial or complete, temporary or permanent. The degree of monopoly varies in inverse relation to competition (q.v.). Factual monopoly is always socially tolerated and may be socially sanctioned or socially guaranteed. The commonest usage of the term is with reference to natural resources or other economic materials or functions.

(2) An enterprise in which the element of competition is wholly or partially eliminated. This exclusive control has been especially developed in the field of economics (exclusive control or possession of a commodity or service, involving command over its price or the extent of its use). Though elements of monopoly control were also common in the medieval society (craft guilds, etc.), it was fully developed in theory and practice not before the end of the nineteenth century; in fact, it has often been identified with the most recent stage of economic development, i.e., capitalism of a monopoly state. Totalitarianism as practiced by modern dictatorships represents, in its complete suppression of independent competitive action and its exclusive control of the power and privileges, machinery and masses of the state, an "ideal type" of political monopoly.   S.N.

monozygotic. Resulting from a single zygote (q.v.).

monozygotic twins. Cf. twins, monozygotic.

moral. Pertaining to morality, rightness and wrongness, good and evil. In conformity with the prevailing moral code (q.v.).

moral code. Cf. code, moral.

moral community. Cf. community, moral.

moral conduct. A form of behavior that involves a consideration or choice of right and wrong, appraised in terms of a standard of values or a code of morals, toward which a person recognizes a duty or feels a sense of responsibility. Broadly speaking it includes both acceptable and unacceptable or immoral forms of behavior, according to the mores of the group, as contrasted with unmoral acts. The phrase "immoral conduct" is commonly interpreted as a violation of sex mores. M.H.N.

moral holiday. An occasion during which crimes are committed by individuals who are otherwise habitually orderly. Thus, New Year's Eve, election night, football celebrations, national conventions of fraternal organizations are occasions leading to tensions which are sometimes expressed in brawls, assaults, and destruction of property. Such minor offenses are expected to occur upon these occasions and most often the prosecutor's office, as well as the police, is indulgent. Only few of these crimes are prosecuted.   N.F.C.

moral ideals. Cf. ideals, moral.

moral imbecile. Cf. imbecile, moral.

moral lag. Cf. lag, moral.

moral order. The element of order in a society that is produced by common orientation of the members toward shared ultimate needs or values. This may be contrasted with legal order, economic order and the like.   R.C.A.

moral phenomena. Phenomena associated with the mores or the moral code, i.e., with those ways of behaving which are associated with ideas of right and wrong in a conventional sense.   A.R.L.

moral restraint. Cf. restraint, moral.

moral standard. Cf. standard, moral.

morale. Esprit de corps. Fidelity, zeal, confidence, and hope for current dominant ideals with which a group works, thinks, and/or fights under leadership. Morale gains from a close apparent similarity between the group's moral principles and its leader's and members' moretic practices, by a willing acceptance of the tenets of the group's morality as they bear upon the group's current objectives. Morale also gains as group faith and consciousness of kind are strengthened by common sacrifices and other experiences. Such experiences have to contain enough examples of what the group regards as successes to maintain hope and idealism.   A.M'C.L.

morality. The essence of the moral code (q.v.), and conformity thereto. Specifically, morality as regards the members of a particular society can be defined only in terms of the moral code of that society. There is no universal morality except in so far as certain items of behavior are similarly covered in the moral codes of all societies. Morality is to be sharply dis-

tinguished from ethics (q.v.) which is the philosophical study of the foundations of right and wrong behavior, and is in essence supra-societal. Ethical standards are a matter of individual conviction, although influenced by, and largely derived from, the cultural environment. Ethical mandates may frequently require given individuals to violate the moral code, that is to practice immorality. Cf. mores.

morality, class. (1) Moral ideas or morals of a social class. Ethical principles members of the class seek to instill in themselves and to impose on each other and their children. Contrasted with the moretic behavior patterns or mores adhered to by members of the class as a matter of societal necessity and expediency. (2) Degree of adherence by members of a class, or by the class aggregate, to the general moral code of the society of which it is a segment. Class virtue. Usually defined for the several classes of society from the standpoint of an individual in one class, as for example in class-oriented theories of criminology.   A.M'C.L.

morality, group. (1) Special moral ideals of a neighborhood, professional, religious, political, or other social group. Sometimes formalized into codes of ethics, suitably short for printing and framing. Group morality, in this sense, contains a strong element of the rationalization of the necessary and expedient moretic practices of the group, its ways of pursuing its objectives, its social status. Cf. morality, class, (1). (2) Degree of adherence by members of a group to the general moral code of the society of which it is a part. Cf. morality, class, (2).   A.M'C.L.

morals. Mores insofar as they have acquired sufficient importance to have suprarational sanction such as that of theology, of a political economic ideology, or to be embodied in the moral code.   T.D.E.

morbidity. An unhealthful or diseased condition; a sickness or disorder; the prevalence or amount of illness in a population at a specific time; the rate or incidence of illness as indicated by frequency of attacks or by number of new cases of a particular illness per unit of time and population.   C.V.K.

mores. Folkways which are held by common consent to be conducive to the welfare of society. E.g., having only one wife at a time. Elementary morals. Breach punished more formally and severely than in case of folkways, eventually by law.   A.G.K.

mores, organizational. Traditional definitions of the basic social structures and relationships of society that a given society regards as essential to its stability at a given time and place. These mores —and accompanying folkways—are so inclusive that an adult member of society finds himself equipped to handle most problems involving social relationships in their terms rather than through reference to more objective procedures. Only in times of critical maladjustment in society do the organizational mores fail to furnish mores-controlled individuals with "instinctive" guidance in their social relationships. At such times, the resulting bewilderment emphasizes the all-embracing character of such traditional guidance and the trauma occasioned by being forced to face trying social problems without a preconceived formula.   A.M'C.L.

moretic. Adjectival form of mos (plural, mores). Used to avoid confusion occasioned by employing moral as the adjectival form of both the ethical term, moral (noun), and the behavioristic sociological term, mos.   A.M'C.L.

morganatic marriage. Cf. marriage, morganatic.

morgue. (1) A public depository or building for temporarily holding bodies for identification and from whence the unknown or unclaimed dead are taken to the Potter's Field. (2) The files of a newspaper office for storing news clippings and pictures.   N.A.

moron. A person of deficient mentality whose intelligence quotient ranges from 50 to 69 and who has a mental age of from 7 to 12 years. The moron is in the highest classification of mental deficiency. For this reason morons are the most difficult of all persons of sub-normal intelligence to deal with, for they are frequently able to adjust well enough to society to

escape detection, but under stress or unfavorable environmental conditions they prove unable to assume responsibility for their actions, thus causing unexpected difficulties and serious problems.   J.W.M'C.

mortality. The condition or event of death; the number of deaths or the death rate in a given population. Cf. death rate.   C.V.K.

mortality, infant. Cf. infant mortality.

mortality of criminal justice. Cf. criminal justice, mortality of.

mos. Singular of mores (q.v.).

mother right. Cf. right, mother.

motivate. To supply an incentive adequate to induce deliberate and purposeful action. Cf. motive.

motivation. The process of initiating conscious and purposeful action. Cf. motive.

motive. An urge, or a combination of urges, adequate to induce conscious and purposeful action. A motive is ordinarily a compound of feelings, appetites, inclinations, and perhaps instinctive impulses. It becomes objectified as an interest, and unless impeded by internal or external obstacles leads to action in pursuit of that interest.

mourning. The observance of customary forms of behavior expressive of bereavement on the part of relatives of a person recently deceased, e.g., seclusion, self-mutilation, the assumption of a distinctive garb, the observance of special taboos.   G.P.M.

movement, social. Cf. social movement.

moving average. Cf. average, moving.

mulatto. The offspring of parents, one of whom is white and the other Negro. Technically and legally, all non-full blooded Negroes whose physical appearance indicates intermixture with white persons, thus including quadroons and octoroons. In the vernacular, they are designated as dark, light and very light mulattoes.   W.R.C.

multiple causation, theory of. Cf. causation, multiple, theory of.

multiple causes of crime. Cf. crime, multiple causes of.

multiple choice. Cf. choice, multiple.

multiple correlation. Cf. correlation, multiple.

multiple interaction. Cf. interaction, multiple.

mummification. The practice of preserving the bodies of the dead, especially by embalming, desiccation, and swathing with bandages. Cf. burial.   G.P.M.

municipality. The urban community, as a political unit created by state authority, provided with a specific type of local government and administration, generally varying in scope and function with the size of population.   E.E.M.

murder. The killing of another human being with malice aforethought. In recent years murder has been classified in some states of the United States as first and second degree murder. First degree murder includes cases in which the killing is deliberate, premeditated, especially cruel, or in the performance of a felony.   J.W.M'C.

mutation, biological. As used at present, a sudden variation by the offspring from its parents in a certain important character or characters. This meaning, first employed by DeVries, should be distinguished from an earlier usage of the term as a gradual variation, in which the new characters of the offspring become fully developed only in the course of many generations. The occurrence of mutations and the hereditary transmission of the new characters thus appearing, under certain conditions, are well established facts of biology and genetics. Perhaps not so firmly established is the theory that mutation has been an important factor in the evolution of existing species and of those now extinct.   W.G.

mutation, social. Cf. social mutation.

mutilation. As a punishment, the same as maiming. (q.v.).   J.L.G.

mutual. Being offered, undertaken, or shared alike and reciprocally by each member of a group.   J.P.E.

mutual aid. Spontaneous and informal reciprocal help or direct cooperative effort for the benefit of the participants; contrasted in evolutionary science with survival of the fittest. The cooperative factors as against the competitive in social development.

mutual bond. A tie, covenant, or force which holds two or more persons or groups in reciprocal relations to each other.   J.P.E.

mutual effort. A joint or combined attempt, trial, or endeavor on the part of two or more persons to accomplish a desired end.   J.P.E.

mutualism. In its narrow economic sense the cooperative movement to form mutual aid societies in industry, agriculture, insurance, banking, etc. In its broader meaning the recognition of mutual interdependence and tendency to mutual aid as expressed in any form of collectivism, more particularly as used by the philosophical anarchists who regard it as an innate trait of the organic world.   M.Pm.

myth. A traditional story of religious import, especially an account of the activities of supernatural beings or a fictive explanation in narrative form of the origin of religious rites, social usages, or natural phenomena.   G.P.M.

mythical. Relating to a belief, person, or object of unproven existence. Derived from myth or legend.   E.A.H.

mythology. The body of myths (q.v.) in a particular culture, or the scientific study of myths in general. Cf. folklore.   G.P.M.

N

nasal index. Cf. index, nasal.

natality. The birth performance of a group, correlative to mortality; natality rate is synonymous with birth rate.

nation. A nationality that has achieved the final stage of unification represented by its own political structure and territorial establishment. A nationality (q.v.) may exist without political identity or self-control, and on the other hand, a state (q.v.) may exist without harmony of nationality. The true nation is probably the most stable and coherent large-scale human group yet produced by social evolution.

national egoism. A belief in the superiority of national customs, usually carrying with it a determination for national aggrandizement even at the expense of other nations, a sensitive pride in national history, and an attitude of dominance toward other nations.   B.M.

national socialism. Cf. socialism, national.

nationalism. Emphasis upon the realities and bonds of nationality. Any principle or doctrine which recognizes the nationality—or in practice the nation—as the basis for group action.

nationality. A human group bound together by specific ties of cultural homogeneity. A true nationality is animated by consciousness of kind (q.v.) and has a fundamental similarity in its mores (q.v.). There need not be, and seldom is, complete uniformity in all cultural traits; but there must be conformity, or at least sympathy and cooperation, with reference to a number of the basic institutions such as language, religion, dress and ornamentation, recreation, moral code, political system, family pattern and ethical ideas. The essence of nationality is we-feeling (q.v.). The members of a nationality feel a bond of sympathy to each other different from that they experience toward the members of another nationality. They desire to share a common life. This desire may not be realized but as long as it exists it serves to give reality to the nationality. The component units of a particular nationality may be scattered among various political units. The best contemporary example of this situation is furnished by the Jewish people. On the other hand, a well-knit political unit may include several nationalities (i.e., Switzerland), and what is practically a single nationality may be divided into two or more political units (i.e., Canada and the United States). In other words, political unification is not an essential component of nationality. Cf. nation. The term nationality may be used to refer to the group itself or to the culture complex that unites the group. Cf. ethnos; demos.

nationality feeling. Cf. feeling, nationality.

nationalization. The process of substituting the traits of one nationality for those of another nationality. It is the process undergone by an immigrant who is molded by the influences of his new social environment. It may be partial or complete. When complete, the responses of the foreigner to social stimuli cease to manifest any trace of his national origin, and his individual behavior becomes what it would have been if he had always been a member of his adopted nationality. Obviously, complete nationalization is seldom, if ever, achieved on the part of an immigrant who changes residence after infancy or very early age. Cf. assimilation; Americanization.

native behavior. Cf. behavior, native.

native endowment. The physical equipment—more particularly the innate mental capacity—one receives through his biological inheritance.   R.E.B.

natural. Pertaining to nature. Characteristic of objects that have not been modified or affected by the application of human intelligence. The antonym of natural is artificial. All the features and functions of the human organism that are not under the control of the intellect, or have not been modified by the application of human intelligence in the past, are natural. There is obviously, therefore, no value judgment involved in the concept of natural. The qualitative connotations that custom has associated with the word unnatural are unfortunate. The word nonnatural, though awkward, is less subject to misinterpretation.

natural area. Cf. area, natural.

natural group. Cf. group, natural.

natural increase. Cf. increase, natural.

natural increase, crude rate of. Cf. rate, crude, of natural increase.

natural increase, true rate of. Cf. rate, true, of natural increase.

natural law. Cf. law (1).

natural resources. Undeveloped raw materials and unutilized energies or aspects of nature in their original state. Cf. conservation.   T.D.E.

natural rights. Personal liberties and freedoms justified as established "by Nature" (occasionally identified with "'Reason" conceived as a reflection of nature). Being in the "nature" of mankind, natural rights were considered inborn, inherent, and unalienable. A modern reinterpretation finds a justification of similar "natural rights" in the "nature" (actual structure-function) of society and culture. Cf. liberty; rights; natural law.   T.D.E.

natural science. Accurate, systematic, generalized knowledge concerning phenomena, forces, and causative sequences that are not affected by the human intelligence. Cf. law; natural law.

naturalization. The process of substituting one legal citizenship for another. It is strictly a formal process, having nothing necessarily to do with any change in the attitudes or loyalties of the individual, however much such changes may be assumed. It has reference to a particular political state, with respect to which the alien, through this process, becomes a citizen.

nature. That which exists, or would exist, without the intervention of the human intelligence. The simple antithesis of man and nature is unsound. Much of man belongs to nature, and much that is external to man has been modified by the application of his intelligence, and is therefore no longer strictly a part of nature. The emphasis upon *human* intelligence is obviously arbitrary and artificial, but it is in accordance with customary usage, common sense, and sociological utility. No other animal uses its intelligence to modify the face of the globe to any significant degree, but rather its intelligence is a part of the whole structure and balance of nature.

nature, conquest of. Cf. conquest of nature.

nature, human. Cf. human nature.

nature, original. Man's hereditary endowment as distinct from his nurture or environment. It is the new organism with its unique set of potentialities, created when a human ovum and sperm meet at fertilization.   F.D.W.

nature people. Cf. people, nature.

Nazism. Cf. socialism, national.

necromancy. Divination (q.v.) by communion with the ghosts of the dead; hence witchcraft (q.v.) in general.   G.P.M.

negative conditioning. Cf. conditioning, negative.

negativism. A habit of reacting in a contrary manner to command or suggestion; usually associated with attitude of emotional resistance to persons exercising authority, or disliked.   T.D.E.

neglected child. Cf. child, neglected.

negligence. A loose designation for the law applied to cases arising out of accidents, usually with reference to automobiles and public conveyances.   F.W.K.

neighborhood. A small community, characterized by limited area and highly developed personal, face-to-face relations.

neighborhood group. Cf. group, neighborhood.

neighborliness. The social characteristics of people living in direct contact and practicing mutual aid; the reciprocal assistance and exchange of sympathies and favors normally prevalent among peoples in close proximity.   N.L.S.

neo-Lombrosians. Criminologists who emphasize psycho-pathological states as causes of crime.   J.P.S.

neo-Malthusianism. Literally new Malthusianism, i.e., the social doctrine that limitation of population is desirable to prevent poverty and depressed levels of living. It differs from Malthusianism on the best means to achieve population control: birth control rather than "moral restraint" (i.e., postponed marriage accompanied by premarital chastity). The term was first coined in Dutch (*nieuw-Malthusiaanisms*) by Dr. S. Van Houten about 1870 and began to be used in England in English about 1885. Between 1860 and 1880 the term Malthusianism was sometimes used to mean neo-Malthusianism. It was not so commonly used in the U.S.A. as in England (where it became an organized social reform movement). In England in the 1920's the birth control (q.v.) movement began to differentiate itself from the social movement for neo-Malthusianism, first by emphasizing the health aspects rather than the prevention of poverty.   N.E.H.

neonatal. Characteristic of, or related to, new born infants.

nephew-right. Cf. right, nephew-

nepotism. Favoritism granted to relatives without due regard for merit; family favoritism. Used especially to indicate favoritism in placing near relatives into positions whether they are qualified or not.   O.W.

neurosis. A functional disorder of the nervous system; psychogenic disease of nervous system where no actual lesion is demonstrable.   J.M.R.

neurotic. Characterized by a relatively minor disorder of the nervous system having its origin in psychic causes, or by aberrant behavior as judged by the norms of a particular social group.   J.M.R.

neutrality. The status assigned by international law to states that remain out of war. It embodies a complex of rights and duties, the result of a compromise between the conflicting claims of belligerent and neutral, the product of 300·years of evolution. In 1911 Sir Thomas Barclay regarded the creation of the status of neutrality as the highest achievement yet attained by international law. In recent years there has been a tendency to belittle, ridicule, and attack the status of neutrality, in the interests of a so-called "collective security" by which all states theoretically shall join in the hue and cry against an "aggressor" and thus in theory preserve the peace. Objections to this doctrine are based on the claim that nations never agree on such a subject as "aggression", since the disfavored is always an "aggressor", because the decision is or would be reached not on evidence but on prejudice or political interests, and because the posse commitatus would give rise to a counter-alliance and thus necessarily lead to war. That has happened. But the idea of "collective security" still persists. More lately the term "non-belligerency" has come into use on the part of neutrals, though not a legal term and having no authority in law. It seems designed either (a) to justify a neutral country in departing from the obligations of neutrality without incurring the penaities of war, or (b) to enable certain neutrals to call certain belligerents non-belligerents, and thus to afford unneutral facilities in their ports to these belligerents. This interpretation takes the matter out of the field of law into that of politics. The consequence of these innovations cannot yet be estimated.   E.M.B.

new poor. A term descriptive of the large numbers in the population who are precipitated into dependency for the first time by widespread unemployment occurring during prolonged economic depressions.   K.DP.L.

news. Report of an event regarded by reporters and editors as having sufficient potential mass interest to justify its publication in a medium of mass-communication. Since readers and listeners cannot make their criticisms felt in detail, reportorial and editorial traditions play an appreciable rôle in defining news policies. News values include (1) timeliness, (2) proximity, (3) prominence, (4) human interest, (5) unusualness, (6) conflict, (7) suspense, (8) mystical elements. The rules of news selection depend upon the character of news media in their rôles as advertising media, as business institutions, as public utilities protected from special governmental controls in democratic countries by provisions of the organic law, as employers of adult and child labor, as instruments of economic, political, and even religious control.   A.M'C.L.

nexus, social. Cf. social nexus.

nigh-dweller. A term used by urban sociologists in place of the older word neighbor. One who lives in the apartment across, above, or below—with whom one has only the most formal dealings and about whom one hopes never to have to know anything.   W.C.H.

nihilism. A term first applied by Turgenev in his novel "Fathers and Sons" (1862) to a theory of revolutionary action commonly held at that time and indeed until the overthrow of the Czarist regime, in which there was more agreement as to the negative aspects than the positive. The former entailed the immediate need to destroy, by assassination and arson, all existing social and economic institutions and their leading representatives, in advance of any reconstruction, about which there was no unanimity except for the necessity to establish a parliamentary government. The movement was individualistic and not centralized, with small groups and individuals encouraged to perpetuate independent acts of terrorism. Many nihilists were intellectuals who shared the ideas of socialist and anarchist writers; and their positive programs were generally moderate in comparison with the revolutionary demands of 1917. It is the more general and positive aspects of the theory, not the practical directives to terrorism, that have been retained in the other meanings of the term. More generally nihilism denotes a radical rejection and devaluation of the ideals and values of a culture or a class, e.g., the totalitarian denigration of democracy or the communist rejection of bourgeois civilization. The most comprehensive usage refers to the complete relativization of all values and their consequent assessment as ideologies or rationalizations.   E.F.

nirvana. In Buddhism, the attainment of complete divorce of the spirit from the body by so observing the highest religious precepts that all personal consciousness is absorbed into the divine force of the universe. It represents the ultimate in escape from the mundane while still alive.   E.A.H.

niyoga. A custom, occurring in India, according to which a childless man may choose a substitute to get a son and heir by his wife.   G.P.M.

nobility. That part of a population which receives—altogether as a result of inheritance—special distinction, rank, and privilege. Recently historians and sociologists have ceased to emphasize the aspect of kingly prerogative in the recruitment of a nobility. The latter aspect is extraneous to the nature of a true nobility, which desires no royal hand to appoint newcomers to its ranks. It is now emphasized that kings usually arose from among noblemen, themselves products of social situations long antedating the kingship. The nobility of Europe was not, as is so commonly asserted, created by the whimsy of kings to whom commoners had rendered "personal service." In general its oldest members were noble in Roman and Germanic life, its later additions were entitled to entrance by their high standing, already largely hereditary, in office and bourgeois enterprise.   W.C.H.

nomadism. The habitual or traditional movement of peoples in response to their needs for subsistence. In pastoral cultures there had to be the seasonal wanderings to follow the grass supply, but there were also cyclical wanderings as when there was a long period of drought. It is a moot point whether latent traces of nomadism exist in some types of modern wandering; the families that migrate north or south to work in the seasonal jobs' of agriculture. Not to be confused with true migration (q.v.).   N.A.

nomadism, primitive. A mode of life in which the primitive band habitually changes its location of dwelling. Such nomadism is ordinarily a movement from one traditional camping site to another within a recognized band territory. Movements are seasonal and synchronized with variations in food-getting opportunities.   E.A.H.

nomadism, seasonal. A semi-nomadic mode of life in which a people shifts its abode with the seasons from place to place within its own restricted territory, e.g., to take advantage of different food-gathering, hunting, fishing, or grazing grounds as they become successively available or productive. Cf. nomadism.   G.P.M.

nominal wages. Cf. wages, nominal.

non-conformist. A person who is unable or unwilling to adjust himself to the ordinary conventions and even to the more important customs of social living. Specifically, the term may apply to certain religious bodies, other than those of the Established Church.   A.E.W.

non-cooperative. A person who is unable or unwilling to do team work and to unite with others in various types of group action. Specifically, the term may apply to a technique developed by Gandhi to register disapproval, particularly of British governmental policies.   A.E.W.

non-cooperative response. Cf. response, non-cooperative.

non-literate. Pertaining to a people or culture without letters, i.e., without a written language. Preferred to "primitive" (q.v.) and "preliterate" (q.v.) in that it does not imply any fixation at a prehistoric level nor any preordained sequence of development or "progress" in cultures. Not to be confused with illiterate, which refers to unlettered persons in a literate culture.   T.D.E.

non-literate culture. Cf. culture, non-literate.

non-material culture. Cf. culture, non-material.

non-social. Cf. social, non-.

non-social being. Cf. being, non-social.

non-social interaction. Cf. interaction, non-social.

non-social stimulation. Cf. stimulation, non-social.

non-support. Failure to provide maintenance for one's legally recognized dependents.   J.M.R.

non-violent coercion. Cf. coercion, non-violent.

non-wedlock. Pertaining to or deriving from an unmarried mating; *unehelich* (German); "illegitimate"; as, non-wedlock relationship, non-wedlock father, mother, child, inheritance, parentage, case. The term is gaining favor as it avoids the now objectionable words "bastard" and "illegitimate" (as applied to children), the long, awkward phrase "children born out of wedlock" and the occasionally ambiguous phrases "unmarried father" and "unmarried mother". A married man (or woman) may be a non-wedlock parent.   T.D.E.

norm. A standard or criterion for judging the character or conduct of an individual, or any societal form or function. Any single aspect of a smoothly functioning social system. Cf. normality.

norm, social. Cf. social norm.

norms, sociological. Cf. sociological norms.

normal. (1) Consistent with the total structure and functioning of any system. Any unit of a social system is normal when its characteristics or condition are such as to promote the efficient functioning of the system as a whole. There is no such thing as a normal society, except in the sense that a single society is considered as a part of some multi-social system. (2) Average, customary, usual. Used in this sense, the term has no qualitative implications. Thus reference may be made to a normal typhoid rate, normal unemployment, normal infant mortality.

normality. (1) Conformity to a norm. The characteristic of any part of a system which conduces to the smooth and efficient functioning of the system as a whole. As applied to any particular case, normality is a strictly relative concept. A particular social feature, such as wife purchase, patria potestas, or an individual wage bargain may have normality in one society and not in another. Normality is accordingly entirely free from any abstract or intrinsic ethical or moral implications. It is a question of consistency of a part with the whole. (2) Conformity to the average, or customary, situation.

normalize. To bring into harmony with an accepted norm. To achieve smooth functioning with respect to any given social system.

normlessness. The absence of any applicable norm.

nouveau riche. A "newly rich" person who uses his wealth ostentatiously for the purpose of gaining recognition among persons who honor the possessors of riches as such. He may also expend it to attract the attention of aristocrats of waning fortunes who are sometimes persuaded to compromise high principles of exclusiveness for immediate material advantage. Excessive wealth is offered as a substitute for other qualifications usually required in the attainment and maintenance of a high social position.   w.c.h.

nuclear family. Cf. family, nuclear.

nucleated settlement. Cf. settlement, nucleated.

nucleus, social. Cf. social nucleus.

nudism. A type of cult interest shared by persons who for health, esthetic or other reasons meet in groups to associate in nakedness, and who sometimes make nakedness the object of their association. Nudism not only has its literature, but its code, its leaders and its gathering places.   n.a.

number, pattern. Cf. pattern number.

nuptials. The wedding ceremony; the rites used in marriage.   w.g.

nurture. All those elements of the social environment to which individuals are subject, or to which they subject themselves, from conception onwards, and which affect their physical, mental or personality development, in contradistinction to nature, or heredity.   f.h.h.

nymphomania. A condition of very strong sexual desire in females.   b.m.

O

oath. A solemn affirmation supported by appeal to some high authority, usually divine. By analogy, the careless or profane use of the name or attributes of divinity.

oath, pauper. Cf. pauper oath.

objectification. Act or process of making an idea or concept objective, especially of giving objective existence to illusions and delusions of the mind. F.H.H.

objectify. To give external existence to ideas or concepts, especially when these are illusory or delusional. F.H.H.

objective approach. Cf. approach, objective.

objective value. Cf. value, objective.

objectivity. The ability to detach oneself from situations in which one is personally involved, and to view facts on the basis of evidence and reason rather than prejudice and emotion, without bias or preconceptions, in their true setting. A.E.W.

obscenity. Whatever is considered by opinion, law or the public authorities offensive to purity of mind, morals or public taste. Applied to personal behavior, dress, language, works of art, literature and the stage to cover whatever is considered obscene, lewd, lascivious, filthy, indecent or disgusting. F.H.H.

obscurantism. An attitude or policy adverse to the sharing and diffusion of knowledge, especially among the masses. T.D.E.

observer, participant. A researcher who looks at social phenomena from the inside as well as from the outside, e.g., a labor problems' student who works in mines, factories, and fields; a criminologist who sleeps in jails and prisons; a military strategist who leaves his maps and charts and goes into the front lines for close-up observation of weapons, morale, and operations. W.C.H.

obsolescence. A condition of being old and because of age, outmoded. The aging process may be measurable as in the use of equipment, and provision may be made for replacement when efficiency is impaired to the point of diminishing returns. The term may be applied variously to social phenomena. N.A.

occultism. Belief in the supernatural; mystic doctrines and practices based on belief in the supernatural. Cf. magic; religion. E.A.H.

occupation. A form of activity in which an individual regularly engages for remuneration. J.H.E.

occupational hierarchy. The order in which vocations are typically rated by a society. Blacksmiths, e.g., are ranked high in some cultures, low in others. In the United States agricultural labor for wages is rated low; white collar work is usually more honored than manual labor. Garbage men and grave diggers exercise lowly occupations. Living from landed estates has always been especially honored in England, as it was in ancient Rome. Law and teaching have slipped considerably in rank in the United States because of the influx of increased members into their ranks, diluting the dignity of the professions by too much competition and by introducing elements from non-professional and lower class family backgrounds. W.C.H.

occupational level. Cf. level, occupational.

ochlocracy. Government by the populace or multitude; a state of human affairs wherein the ultimate authority rests with, and the governmental machinery is in the control of, the mass of the people—populace being defined as the common people and excluding all distinguished by rank, office, education or profession. Theoretically, this might be regarded as an approach to democracy; in practice, however, it is mobocracy.   F.E.L.

octoroon. A legally determined concept. A person, supposedly, of one-eighth Negro and seven-eighths white blood. Rarely used by Negroes in conversational reference to light-skinned Negroes.   W.R.C.

odalisque. A member of a harem with servile, or inferior marital, status.

ofay. A white person who seeks the company of negroes. The word has several variants, such as "fay", "old-fay" or "ole-fay", the latter two of an especially colloquial character.   W.R.C.

offender, psychopathic. Cf. pathological criminal.

offenders, sex. Sex offenders may be divided into two classes, persons committing illegal acts such as rape, sodomy, and indecent exposure, which indicate physical or mental abnormality, and individuals who commit such acts which in themselves do not indicate abnormalities but which have been declared unlawful, such as solicitation, maintaining disorderly houses (commercial vice), and seduction.   N.F.C.

offering, votive. Cf. votive offering.

old age and survivor's insurance. Federal benefits under the Social Security Act given persons of a certain prescribed age, who have contributed, and whose employers have contributed, to a pension fund.   W.P.

old age assistance. Relief given old people who have reached a certain age and are destitute or partially so.   W.P.

old age dependency. Cf. dependency, old age.

oligarchy. Government by a few; a form of government in which the supreme power is vested in or has been seized by a very few members of the society, say, the elders, a military clique, revolutionists.   F.E.L.

omen. Any phenomenon believed to have supernaturally inspired portent and, hence, interpreted as a reliable indication of future happenings of a good or bad nature.   E.A.H.

ontogenetic. Having to do with the origin and preservation of the individual. Cf. self-maintenance.

open shop. Cf. shop, open.

operational definition. Cf. definition, operational.

operationism (or operationalism). That philosophy of science which seeks to reduce all statement of truth to verifiable predictions of either form (a) or form (b), as follows: (a) If a specifically defined observer makes a specifically defined observation under specifically defined conditions, the probability is P that that same observer, or another specifically defined, can make a second specifically defined observation under specifically defined conditions; or (b) if a specifically defined operator performs a specifically defined operation, the probability is P^1 that either he or another specifically defined observer can make a specifically defined observation. Operationism is often mistakenly confused with positivism (q.v.) or with behaviorism (q.v.).   H.H.

operative institution. Cf. institution, operative.

opinion. (1) A judgment held as true, arrived at to some extent by intellectual processes, though not necessarily based on evidence sufficient for proof. (2) A view or estimate on a particular subject or point, e.g., regarding the appropriateness of a policy. (3) A statement of one regarded as an expert, when consulted, on a problem.   B.M.

opinion, collective, (rare). A type of public opinion in which, in a given group, organization or public, a consensus has been recognized and formulated as the opinion of the group as a whole.

opinion, crowd. Verbal reactions by members of a crowd to a stimulus-event. Such reactions achieve in a crowd a higher degree of unanimity than in groups that have not established such a high degree of mental isolation and rapport. Crowd members only express such crowd opinions on stimulus-events within the interest area that focused its members into the crowd situation. Crowd opinions are typically on a somewhat more emotional and hysterical plane than ordinary public opinions.   A.M'C.L.

opinion, group. Verbal reactions by members of a group to a given stimulus-event. Such reactions are products of the group's societal culture and its own sub-culture, of pertinent remembered events, of current social tensions apparent to the group's members, and of relevant societal structure. Cf. opinion, public; opinion, crowd.   A.M'C.L.

opinion, public. The attitude of a significant portion of a population toward any given proposition, based upon a measurable amount of factual evidence, and involving some degree of reflection, analysis, and reasoning. It is a partially intellectual product, in contradistinction to public sentiment (q.v.), which is essentially a matter of emotion, and may and does exist without any adequate factual basis whatever. Propagandists characteristically give the impression that they are seeking to modify public opinion, while in actuality they are appealing to, and seeking to utilize, public sentiment. Cf. prejudice.

opium. A narcotic drug produced from the gummy juice of one species of poppy. In commercial use opium usually appears in the form of one of its derivatives, the most important of which are morphine, heroin, and codein. The invention of the hypodermic syringe in the 19th century greatly stimulated the use of opium derivatives as narcotics. The effect of this drug in whatever form taken is the depression of the higher nerve centers and the crea-tion of a mental feeling of blissful calm known as euphoria (q.v.).   J.W.M'C.

opposition. Expenditure of energy against an object considered to be moving in a contrary direction; resistance to, or efforts to prevent or offset, the efforts or ideas of another person or group, not necessarily accompanied by attitudes of anger or purpose to destroy or injure the opponent. It is frequently argued by those who glorify struggle that conflict is universal in all nature and even serves to bind systems together and to make locomotion possible, and that conflict is therefore either inevitable or a blessing, or even an indispensable means of progress. Such doctrine fails to distinguish between mere opposition, of which the argument would be true, and conflict (q.v.), in which there is hate, or wish to injure an enemy. T.D.E.

opposition, social. Cf. social opposition.

optimum population. Cf. population, optimum.

oracle. (1) In classical religions, the place of worship of some divinity where questions could be put to the god, and answers were returned by the priest, or priests, who served the god. (2) A god or priest endowed with mystic and supernatural capacity to reveal hidden answers to questions.   E.A.H.

ordeal. A test of endurance, courage, and fortitude used in societies of limited scientific development to establish the innocence or guilt of an accused person. The ordeal persisted as a common feature of judicial procedure in Europe as late as the thirteenth century. Common forms of the ordeal are by fire, by battle, and by water. Escape from death or injury is taken as proof of innocence.

order, social. Cf. social order.

orenda. The Iroquois concept of impersonal supernatural power or magic force. Cf. mana.   G.P.M.

organ, social. Cf. social organ.

organic analogy (organismic analogy). The comparison of the structure and functioning of society to those of biological organisms, involving detailed parallelism between the systems of nutrition, communication, transportation, etc., with the structure-function systems of animals. This concept was so highly developed by Herbert Spencer as to give the impression that he was trying to convince his followers that society actually is an organism.

organic concept of society. Cf. society, organic concept of.

organic society. Cf. society, organic.

organic welfare. Cf. welfare, organic.

organism. A living being composed of parts capable of maintaining existence as a unitary system and of acting in a coordinated manner toward the environment.
M.S.

organism, social. Cf. social organism.

organismic. Pertaining to an organism.
M.S.

organismic behavior. Cf. behavior, organismic.

organization. That process which differentiates one part from another in a functional sense and which at the same time creates an integrated complex of functional relationships within the whole.
J.P.E.

organization, business. Cf. business organization.

organization, community. Cf. community organization.

organization, criminal. Cf. criminal organization.

organization, dual. Cf. dual organization.

organization, industrial. Cf. industrial organization.

organization, rural social. Cf. rural social organization.

organization, social. Cf. social organization.

organizational mores. Cf. mores, organizational.

organized crime. Cf. crime, organized.

organized group. Cf. group, organized.

orgiastic crowd. Cf. crowd, orgiastic.

orgy. A festival or ceremonial celebration characterized by a temporary relaxation of customary taboos and restraints, and hence by an excess of singing, dancing, and indulgence of appetite. It is often a magico-religious celebration in honor of a deity, as in the Dionysian and Bacchanalian orgies; not infrequently, especially among primitive peoples, it is an occasion for the relaxation of sex taboos.
F.H.H.

orientation. Placement, especially of a dwelling, a temple, or a body in a grave, with definite reference to the cardinal directions.
G.P.M.

orientation, social. Cf. social orientation.

origin, country of. Cf. country of origin.

origin, social. Cf. social origin.

origins, social. Cf. social origins.

original nature. Cf. nature, original.

ortho-cousin. A parallel cousin (q.v.) in the same line of descent, i.e., a father's brother's child under patrilineal descent or a mother's sister's child under matrilineal descent.
G.P.M.

orthognathous. Characterized by a relatively receding jaw and perpendicular face, i.e., by a facial profile angle of 85° or higher. Cf. mesognathous; prognathous.
G.P.M.

ossification, social. Cf. social ossification.

ossuary. A place where bones of the dead are deposited.
G.P.M.

ostracism. A form of punishment administered within the group, in contrast with banishment. Neighborly help is forbidden, and even aid by the members of one's family is denied. Often it is accompanied by sneers and contemptuous attitudes, or by complete indifference. Today the attitude of the public towards the ex-convict or the parolee is one of ostracism. J.L.G.

other world. Spirit world (q.v.).

others-group. Cf. group, others-.

outbreeding. (1) Mating outside of a given group. (2) The introduction into a group or an institution of new personalities or ideas which stimulate fresh patterns of thought and behavior, much as cross-fertilization in animal and vegetable reproduction develops new characters. The introduction may be either intentional or accidental. G.M.F.

outdoor relief. Cf. relief, outdoor.

out-group. Cf. group, others-.

outpatient. An ambulatory patient receiving medical care from a hospital or clinic. Also called a "walking patient." N.A.

overcrowding. A number of occupants per room or apartment unit, commonly measured by cubic air content, light and ventilation standards, in excess of that deemed permissible for minimum health requirements. E.E.M.

overcrowding in prisons. Cf. prisons, overcrowding in.

overhousing. An excessive covering of land areas with dwellings; in particular, building upon an unduly large proportion of lot. E.E.M.

overorganization. The condition of organization in which the purposes or ends become subordinated to the means, and in which the details of management, the importance of rules and the trappings of authority take precedence over the work to be done. N.A.

overpopulation. A condition of society in which the numerical population is too large to achieve or maintain some recognized and socially accepted objective. The term has no precise meaning unless the particular objective is specified. The actual measures of overpopulation in a given society at a given time may vary widely according to the particular social values used as criteria. For example, the measure of overpopulation, considered from the point of view of military efficiency, may be very different from that based upon standard of living.

overt behavior. Cf. behavior, overt.

ownership. Socially established, recognized, and enforceable command over any object, involving the right to use, destroy, or transfer. Such rights may be complete or partial, exclusive or shared, but are always socially conferred and socially limited. The relationship of ownership is closely connected with the institution of property (q.v.).

P

padrone. A boss or employer who operates within the padrone system (q.v.).

padrone system. A type of self-maintenance mores wherein an individual maintains control of a small group of workers, usually young and frequently children, by use of whom he operates a small-scale business unit. Historically, the system has developed among certain Mediterranean peoples, notably the Greeks and Italians, and by immigrant representatives has been introduced into the United States, where at one time it flourished extensively. The characteristics of the system are the almost complete control over the lives of the workers by the boss, including communal housing and eating arrangements and strictly controlled occupational activities. The system lends itself particularly to such activities as bootblacking. There are many similarities to the early apprenticeship system.

pain economy. Cf. economy, pain.

pair marriage. Cf. marriage, pair.

palliative. Temporary, superficial, not reaching causes, relieving suffering but not curative. A palliative measure stops, or at least slows, the downward course of the client, the situation does not deteriorate as rapidly as if no treatment had been undertaken, or as if self-defeating methods of "aid" had been tried; but the treatment does not rise to the ameliorative or remedial level.　　T.D.E.

panel technique. Repeated survey of the same groups over a period of time to study changes in situations or opinions. The panel may be one of individuals, of families, of addresses, or of other sampled units of the population.　　M.Pt.

panhandler. A street beggar, moocher, mendicant who solicits money from pedestrians. The origin of the term is obscure. The term "panhandle" has attained an approved derived meaning among various private charities that send out persons to beg for clothing, furniture and other salvage material which is repaired and given or sold to the needy.　　N.A.

panic. A disaster in the money market when credit falls. It may involve runs on banks, hoarding, migration. The term has valid use also in describing a state of alarm and confusion as when a crowd caught in danger gets out of control. N.A.

panopticon. Circular form of prison architecture.　　J.P.S.

papoose. An American Indian child or infant.　　G.P.M.

parallel cousin. A child of a parent's sibling (q.v.) of the same sex, i.e., a father's brother's child or a mother's sister's child. Cf. cross-cousin.　　G.P.M.,

parallel play. Cf. play, parallel.

parallelism. The independent development of similar culture traits in different regions.　　J.G.L.

paranoia. A form of psychosis characterized by persistent and systematic delusions, usually of grandeur or persecution, and sometimes hallucinations. J.M.R.; B.M.

parasite. One who lives, in whole or in part, at the expense of others, or of the community at large, through the use of fraud, favoritism, sex appeal, simulation or pretense.　　F.H.H.

212

parasite, social. Cf. social parasite.

parasitism, social. Cf. social parasitism.

pardon. Use of the power exercised by the head of a state, i.e., in the United States either the governor of a state or the President of the United States, to release a convicted man and prevent the infliction of all or part of the penalty. The power to pardon extends to all crimes save those of treason and impeachment. In the several states where the power to pardon is exercised more frequently there is associated wtih the governor a board whose duty it is to investigate and recommend cases for pardoning. Cf. pardoning power.
                                    J.W.M'C.

pardoning power. The authority residing usually in the chief executive of a state to forgive the convict his crime and release him from the sentence imposed upon him by the court. Under this power lie all sorts of executive clemency — conditional and absolute pardon, commutation of sentence, and restoration of civil rights. This power is usually given to the executive by the constitution, but grants to the legislature the right to prescribe methods of application, and rules of procedure. J.L.G.

partial correlation. Cf. correlation, **par-**

parental relations. The relation between either a mother and child, or father and child. It is part of the constellation of family relationships, which include also the relation between husband and wife, and the relation between the siblings. Child training, education of the child in the home and discipline are among the problems of this relationship. There is also the need for understanding, affection and emotional security on the part of both parents and children.   F.D.W.

parenthood. The state of one who has begotten or brought forth offspring. R.E.B.

parenthood, voluntary. A term used increasingly for birth-control as emphasizing the positive rather than the negative aspects of the movement, i.e., the conscious planning of parenthood in the light of the health conditions and the economic status of the parents, and the desired spacing of the children, if there is to be more than one. Synonymous with planned parenthood.   F.D.W.

pariah. A member of a low or despised caste or class; an outcast.   G.P.M.

parity, social. Cf. social parity.

parole. Release from a correctional or penal institution, under the supervision of the parole authorities, in the attempt to adjust the prisoner to life in free society. Usually parole supervision is limited to the unserved balance of the maximum sentence for which the prisoner was committed to the institution.   J.L.G.

parole board. An administrative board which by law has charge of granting paroles, and of supervising the parolees. Usually the board is governed by law as to who may be granted parole, and the length of time parolees remain under its control. Originated by Maconochie for transportees to Norfolk Island as a method of improving discipline, and called ticket-of-leave.   J.L.G.

parole contract: A statement of the conditions which the parolee is to observe while on parole. Violation of these conditions is ground for the revocation of the parole and for the return of the parolee to the institution.   J.L.G.

partial correlation. Cr. correlation, partial.

participant. Taking part, partaking in, playing a rôle in, being an active member in a functional (usually face-to-face) group; (of a group) showing active participation by members; (of behavior) pertaining to an active rôle in a functional group situation. As a noun, a sentient creature taking part in or playing a rôle in a functional group situation.   T.D.E.

participant crowd. Cf. crowd, participant.

participant observer. Cf. observer, participant.

participation. Entry into, identification with, as through communication or common activity, some defined social situation.   J.H.K.

participation, conditioned. Cf. conditioned participation.

participation, social. Cf. social participation.

partile. A class name for percentiles, deciles, quintiles, quartiles, tertiles, etc. A partile is the amount of a distributing characteristic (i.e., abscissa or X score) which corresponds to some fraction of the distributed population (i.e., area or frequency cumulated from the lower limit of the distribution). Thus the first quartile, Q, is that amount of the characteristic below which occur 25% of the population, and the second quartile Q_2, which is also the medium, is that amount of the characteristic which divides the population into two equal halves.   S.C.D.

part-time farm. Cf. farm, part-time.

part-time farmer. A farmer who engages in part-time farming (q.v.).   C.E.L.

part-time farming. A type of family farming in which only part of the family labor is devoted to farm work, a major portion being devoted to some non-farm occupation. The farm provides a living site, home produced products and usually some cash from the sale of products. However, much of the cash income is derived from the non-farm occupation. C.E.L.

party. (1) A person who takes part in a legal transaction or in a legal action or proceeding. (2) A group of people organized for political purposes.   F.W.K.

passive resistance. A calm refusal to be influenced by commands or physical force. Non-violent non-cooperation has a similar but somewhat narrower meaning.   M.S.

pastime. A short time diversion for the pleasure which it affords. That which amuses, diverts, and serves to make free time pass agreeably.   M.H.N.

pastoral. Pertaining to herding peoples or their typically nomadic mode of life. Cf. nomadism.   G.P.M.

paterfamilias. The paternal head of the ancient Roman family, who exercised almost unlimited power over his wife, children and grandchildren as well as his slaves. The strong unity of the Roman family was preserved through centuries because in the paterfamilias was vested all religious rights, as priest of the family ancestor worship, all legal rights, as the only "person" of the family recognized by Roman law, and all economic rights as the sole owner of the family property, real and movable. It was not until the first century of the Empire that the power of the paterfamilias began to be limited by Roman law.   W.G.

paternal family. Cf. family, paternal.

paternal rights. Cf. rights, paternal.

paternalism. Protection and control, like that of a minor child by a parent, exercised by the government over the governed, employer over employee, or in similar relationships.   R.E.B.

pathological. Diseased. (*medical*) Pathological diatheses—disease tendency believed to be usually inherited. (*criminal psychological*) Pathological lying; falsification out of proportion to desired ends. (*psychological*) Persistently morbid or unnatural behavior not otherwise defined. (*social*) Undesirable social manifestations or conditions, which threaten social well-being. It usually refers to those socially undesirable conditions and trends that by analogy can be conceptualized as social diseases, such as abnormal dependency, crime and delinquency, vice, increasing defectiveness.
                    J.M.R.

pathological criminal. Cf. criminal, pathological.

pathology. (a) The science dealing with causes, development and effects of disease. (b) The diseased or abnormal condition itself. Cf. social pathology.   O.W.

pathology, social. Cf. social pathology.

pathos. The aura of intellectual untouchableness with which we surround a cherished notion, mos, idea, symbol, institution, functionary. It is the glamor of sentiment that grows up around such elements and protects them from objective examination and criticism.   A.M'C.L.

214

patria potestas. The Roman term for the power of the father over the members of his family (*familia*), including the slaves. This power was expressly recognized in the Laws of the Twelve Tables (c. 450 B.C.) and was almost absolute, extending to life and death. In only one respect was the power of the pater familias over his children limited: he must summon a family council of adult members of his gens (or "great family") before condemning a son to slavery or death. A son remained under the patria potestas as long as his father lived. Even after his marriage the son was under his father's power and so likewise were his offspring. No male under power, even if he held high public office, could control his property or earnings, nor could he make a will so long as his father lived. It was not until the Empire was well established that Roman law took the first steps to limit the patria potestas.   w.g.

patriarchal family. Cf. family, patriarchal.

patriarchal society. Cf. society, patriarchal.

patriarchate. (1) A type of social organization characterized by patrilineal descent, inheritance, and succession, patrilocal residence, patripotestal authority and the legal subordination of women and children. Cf. father right; matriarchate. (2) The dominance, authority, province, office or residence of a patriarch.

patrilineal. Reckoning descent, inheritance, or succession exclusively or preferentially through males. Cf. matrilineal.
                                                        g.p.m.

patrilinear. Cf. patrilineal.

patrilocal. Cf. patrilocal residence.

patrilocal marriage. Cf. marriage, patrilocal.

patrilocal residence. Cf. residence, patrilocal.

patriotism. Love of one's fatherland, devotion to its soil and its traditions, defence of its integrity. The etymological origin shows that patriotism is based upon the experiences of the formative years of childhood and youth and upon the primary attachment to soil and immediate environ-

ment. It arouses deep-seated emotions though they may be less rational and even less conscious to the patriot than the reactions of a nationalist. A phenomenon of all historical periods, patriotism has often been used in the age of nationalism and imperialism as an inspirational force and justification for political dynamics and national expansion. While essentially pre-supposing due respect for another people's homeland and traditions, patriotism may easily be connected with a myth of the mission of one's country, thus justifying in the name of patriotism the subjugation of another people and the hatred of the stranger and his way of life. Cf. collective egotism.   s.n.

patripotestal. Characterized by the exercise of authority, especially in the family or household, by the father or paternal grandfather. Cf. matripotestal.

patrolman. A policeman whose regular duty is to cover some specified section.

patronymic. Deriving the personal or family name from the father or other patrilineal relative. Cf. metronymic.
                                                        g.p.m.

pattern, acquired. A learned way of behaving as opposed to an instinctive response to stimulus; a pattern acquired through social transmission instead of biological heredity.   r.e.b.

pattern, action. Cf. action pattern.

pattern, behavior. (1) A relatively uniform series of overt activities; observable regularity of conduct. Though there may be variations within the series so that the behavior pattern differs from the stereotype, such a pattern is found when acts, otherwise distinct, are organized in relation to each other. (2) A type of conduct serving as a model.   b.m.

pattern, conceptual. The arrangement, form, or organization of the concepts which have been abstracted from a specific field of learning.   j.p.e.

pattern, culture. Cf. culture pattern.

pattern, life-organization. A conception of a career, or rôle, viewed longitudinally (through time), by a person appraising his own life or by an outside observer, in which some consistent plan, orderly sequence, or type of character development is seen as a dominating "entelechy."

T.D.E.

pattern, plurality. Plurality pattern.

pattern, social. Cf. social pattern.

pattern, societal. Cf. societal pattern.

pattern, type. Cf. type pattern.

pattern, typical. Cf. typology, constructive.

pattern, universal, of culture. Common-human elements in culture patterns; similarity of array of culture complexes observable in all known cultures; a classification of cultural activities and complexes applicable to the analysis of all known human cultures. Sometimes erroneously called "universal culture pattern." T.D.E.

pattern number. A number for which the people of a society show a preference, so that it recurs frequently in various contexts, e.g., in the grouping of figures in mythology and in the repetition of elements in folk tales and ceremonials. G.P.M.

patterning, behavior. Cf. behavior patterning.

patterns, quasi-legal. Patterns found in fields related to the law based upon or resembling legal patterns; particularly applied to procedural patterns of administrative agencies in the United States.

F.W.K.

patterns, symbolic. Those patterns which are linked with cultural values and ideas which they symbolize through sense expressions. Symbolic-cultural patterns play a decisive rôle in Religion, Morality, Law, Education, and other forms of social control. Cultural-symbolic patterns presuppose the intervention in social life of spiritual meanings and ideals, of which the symbols are the intermediaries adapted to concrete social situations. G.G.

patterns, technical. Technical patterns are standardized images of collective behavior, the ascendency of which is founded only on repetition and habitual routine. The main examples are the patterns of production in economic life. In some types of society (for instance, the primitive), the symbolic-cultural patterns exercise a strong influence on the technical patterns; also some intermediary forms are built up by interpenetration of both. G.G.

pauper oath. (pauper's oath.) An oath taken by an applicant for public assistance swearing that he is utterly destitute and without means of support for himself and family. The oath is used in most states as a means of retaining legal power over those obtaining relief under false pretenses. However, progressive social workers look upon the oath as unduly and unjustly humiliating to persons who through no fault of their own are forced to apply for assistance. The general trend is toward the removal of the pauper oath from state welfare laws. J.W.M'C.

pauperism. A state of economic dependency on other sources than those recognized as normal in the mores of any particular society. In ordinary usage, the sources of support are public authorities of some sort.

pauperization. The process of undermining an individual's or community's interest and ability to self-support. W.P.

peaceful access. The right to enter the territory of a tribe unmolested, sometimes granted to aliens to enable them to avail themselves of some monopoly of natural resources located therein without embroiling the two groups in perpetual warfare. Cf. safe-conduct. G.P.M.

peaceful picketing. Cf. freedom of speech.

penal colony. Cf. colony, penal.

penitentiary. The name first given to those prisons the purpose of which was conceived to be not punishment, but reformation. Later when imprisonment came to be looked upon as primarily for correction the term "penitentiary" came to be synonymous with "prison." J.L.G.

Pennsylvania system. The system of imprisonment originating in the Eastern

Pennsylvania Prison when it was opened in 1829. It was characterized by having each prisoner confined in a separate cell without contact with any human beings except the warden and chaplain, and by work in the cell to occupy the prisoner primarily to prevent brooding and ultimate insanity. It was believed that by this system the prisoner would be kept from contamination or from being a contaminating influence and also that he would not be recognized by other inmates after release. This system was borrowed by most European countries, but has entirely disappeared from the prison system in the United States.   J.L.G.

penology. That field of applied sociology which deals with the theory and methods of punishment for crime. Penology is gradually losing itself as a special branch of knowledge, being absorbed by the general field of criminology.   J.W.M'C.

penology, school of, classical. Cf. classical school of penology.

peonage. A status or condition of compulsory service based upon indebtedness.   J.W.M'C.

people. Though not infrequently used as a synonym for two or more persons viewed distributively, as "enough for three people," this term usually designates a category, an aggregation, or a collectivity of persons, distinguished from the rest of the community or of mankind by one or more traits common to them all. The distinguishing trait may be any socially significant characteristic, location, physiological, racial, regional, occupational, political, etc., as the Pine Grove people, red-headed people, old people, Nordic peoples, upper-class people, city people, the American people, professional people, etc. As a collectivity, as in the American people, the Jewish people, colored peoples, it may include a variety of races or nations. Cf. nationality; demos; ethnos.   F.H.H.

people, culture. Civilized men. Used in contrast to the unscientific term "nature people" (q.v.). A literal translation of the German *Kulturvolk*. Its implication in English translation that civilized man

has culture (q.v.) and primitive man does not gives rise to a spurious distinction that makes the term invalid for proper usage.   E.A.H.

people, nature. Primitive, non-literate, uncivilized tribes. Used in contrast to "culture people" (q.v.). A literal translation of the German *Naturvolk*. The distinction between nature people and culture people is spurious, however. The term has no place in modern social anthropology.   E.A.H.

perception, social. Cf. social perception.

perpetuate. To cause to continue without such changes as are implicitly assumed or explicitly stated as specific conditions.   F.L.

perpetuation. (1) Continuance without specific changes (cf. perpetuate), e.g., the continuance of a population without decrease in number. (2) Creation of conditions tending to effect such continuance.   F.L.

perpetuation, group. The continuance of a population considered as part of a larger aggregate.   F.L.

perpetuation, self-. Cf. self-perpetuation.

person. An individual human being who plays a social rôle in group life according to the culture or cultures in which he has been conditioned. Human nature as embodied in one individual.   W.C.H.

personal. Of or pertaining to the person (q.v.). Personal relationships, for example, are intimate and informal contacts between human beings. Impersonal relationships are formal and hierarchical or stand-offish.   W.C.H.

personal adjustment. Cf. adjustment, personal.

personal ascendency. A class of social situations in which one member of a face-to-face group (q.v.) is in control by virtue of spontaneous leadership and submission; based upon personal qualities and differences rather than upon differences of known status or rank, or upon known previous achievements, power or skill. Personal ascendency may be based on physical dominance, voice, fearlessness, tact, problem-solving in crisis, charm, humor, skills.   **T.D.E.**

personal disorganization. Cf. disorganization, personal.

personal evolution. Cf. evolution, personal.

personal maladjustment. Cf. maladjustment, personal.

personality. That dynamic organization of ideas, attitudes, and habits which is built upon the foundation of the biologically inherited psycho-physical mechanisms of a single organism and of socially transmitted culture patterns, and which embodies all the adjustments of this individual's motives, desires and purposes to the requirements and potentialities of his social and sub-social environments. The personality includes: (a) the focus of consciousness; (b) the pre-conscious area of sensori-motor experience and of unrepressed memories, ideas, wishes, attitudes and purposes; (c) the unconscious, including repressed memories, ideas, wishes, and attitudes; and (d) the patterns of behavior which can be overtly observed and operated upon by others. Cf. consciousness, focus of; ego; expanded personality; id; individuality; self.   **H.H.**

personality, defect of. A trait or combination of traits of personality which constantly injure oneself and others, but which one has not the insight or character to correct.   **A.E.W.**

personality, expanded. The physical organism of an individual, plus the belongings, loved ones, social organizations, ideas, habits, skills, memories, and purposes toward which the individual gives reactions similar to those which he gives to his own body. The antipathies of an individual consist in the objects, people, ideas, habits, memories, and possible future events, toward which he gives reactions, similar to those which he gives to physical pain. These antipathies are the opposite, or negative, of the expanded personality.   **H.H.**

personality, extrovert (extravert). Personality in which one's attention and interests are directed mainly toward external, socially perceptible phenomena. Because few personalities are completely extroverted there is no factual justification for speaking of an extrovert personality type. Cf. personality, introvert.   **M.S.**

personality, ideal. Personality corresponding to a standard of desirable superiority or perfection.   **M.S.**

personality, introvert. Personality in which one's attention and interests are directed toward his own mental behavior or self. Although morbid introvert personality is more common than completely extroverted personality, there is little justification for speaking of an introvert personality type. Cf. personality, extrovert.   **M.S.**

personality, symbolic. (1) A stock character. (2) A personality stereotype that has become the symbol for a government, movement, tribe, association, type of thought or music or art.   **A.M'C.L.**

personality development. A gradual and balanced growth of all the many aspects of a human personality including the physical, mental, emotional and social. Cf. self-realization.   **A.E.W.**

personality stereotype. Cf. stereotype, personality.

personality type. (1) Simplified example of personality chosen to characterize a group of similar personalities found with some frequency in society. (2) An example of personality chosen to indicate one of a number of possible kinds of personality to be found in more or less mixed form in society. A wide range of terminology has been developed for personality types, e.g., pyknic, asthenic, athletic, and dyplastic; extrovert and introvert; anal, oral optimist, oral pessimist; ascendent and submissive; etc. Current psychological and sociological usage discards categorical concepts of personality type for characterizations based upon (1) physiological equipment and (2) type-situations in the life-histories of individuals in given cultures and in given statuses within cultures.   **A.M'C.L.**

personnel work. A term used in applied sociology, economics and psychology, more or less synonymous with labor relations or employment management, and frequently including welfare work; concerned with the personnel rather than the materiel of production, emphasizing human relations; includes hiring, classifying, training, promotion, transfer, wage rates, bonus systems, discharge, health, recreation, sometimes also public relations and arbitration. The word itself has come into general use only since about 1930; but its content derives from early English progressive employers like Robert Owen, was stimulated by Taylor and other protagonists of "scientific management," and during World War I by use in the United States Army and in civilian production.   A.J.T.

persuasion. The use of arguments, true or false, designed to secure the adoption by others of certain beliefs, theories, or lines of action.   F.E.L.

perverted. Turned against its proper function; (*moral*) "against nature" (q.v.) bestial, etc.; (*psychiatric*) pathological or abnormal; (*social work*) so incompetent or neglectful as to defeat any ameliorative (q.v.) objective and make a situation worse than it would have been had not the agency attempted the treatment; e.g., most jails, prisons, reformatories, some asylums, orphanages and baby-farms, occasional hospitals and relief agencies. Cf. palliative; remedial.   T.D.E.

peyote. A species of small cactus, or the powerful drug decocted therefrom by the Indians of Mexico and the western United States and widely used for medicinal, ceremonial, and religious purposes.   G.P.M.

Pharisees. The Jewish religious school, prominent at the time of the four Gospels and later, who laid stress on ritual correctness and who have become the symbol in modern social thought of persons and groups who cling to special economic and social privilege and substitute liberal phrases and alms-giving for social justice.   G.M.F.

phase, social. Cf. social phase.

phenomena. Basic units, elements, or constants which are used in sociological systems as relatively stable, observable, and objective starting points in the scientific study of society. E.g., culture, family, group, process, a strike, robbery, gift.   H.A.P.

phenomena, human. Sociological data, distinguished from non-social and physical data. E.g., attitudes, values, wishes, opinions.   H.A.P.

phenomena, repetitive. Products of reciprocal interaction; social relationships and processes, such as conflict, competition, and assimilation.   H.A.P.

phenomena, social. Cf. social phenomena.

phenomena, societal. Cf. societal phenomena.

phenomena, sociological. Cf. sociological phenomena.

phenotype. A descriptive category which accounts for external appearance. Cf. genotype.   M.S.

philanthropy. The spirit of active good will towards one's fellow man as shown in efforts to promote his welfare. Cf. charity.   W.P.

philosophical ethics. Cf. ethics, philosophical.

philosophical pluralism. Cf. pluralism, philosophical.

philosophy, social. Cf. social philosophy.

phobia. An exaggerated, persistent and usually pathological fear of a particular stimulus or situation or class of stimuli or situations. The term phobia is frequently used as a suffix in a popular or quasi-technical sense, for example, Russophobia and is contrasted with -philia or -mania.   C.F.S.

phratry. A primary tribal subdivision, commonly characterized by exogamy (q.v.) and unilinear descent (q.v.), especially when further divided into sibs (q.v.) Cf. moiety.   G.P.M.

phrenology. Theory and practice based on Gall's hypothesis that mental traits and therefore human character conform to the shape of the human skull and are localized in certain specific brain and skull areas; of significance to sociologists because it was used for vocational and marital guidance before the present vogue of tests and statistical correlations for predictive purposes.   A.J.T.

phylogenetic. Having to do with the origin and preservation of the group. Cf. self-perpetuation.

physical anomalies. Cf. anomalies, physical.

physical anthropology. Somatic anthropology (q.v.).

physics, social. Cf. social physics.

Physiocrats. A school of French social thought in the XVIII century, affirming "a fundamental and essential order of society" which the State is incapable of modifying and to which it is always forced to give way. The Physiocrats considered the "spontaneous social order" as a real whole and fought against contractual theories of society; they became simultaneously promoters of sociology ("social physics") and founders of political economy. But in the last domain, they did not maintain their sociological views and merely formulated the demand of their time for "laissez faire", as well as insisting on the necessary predominance of agriculture over industry. Principal representatives are: Quesnay, LeTrosne, Dupont de Nemours, Mercier de la Rivière, and to some extent, Turgot.   G.G.

physique, asthenic. A human physical type characterized by relatively small trunk, long angular body and limbs, and low constitutional vitality. Believed to be associated with schizophrenic mental traits. Cf. athletic physique, pyknic physique.   J.M.R.

physique, athletic. Medium proportioned human body type with well developed musculature suggesting the athlete. Athletic physique is one of the three human body types (the other two being asthenic (q.v.) and pyknic (q.v.) distinguished in an attempt to establish a relationship between personality traits and type of body structure.   J.M.R.

physique, pyknic. Round, heavy-set human body type with short limbs. One of three types identified as significant in establishing a consistent relationship between physical and psychological human types. Cf. asthenic physique; athletic physique.   J.M.R.

picket. A person or group involved in a labor dispute trying to obstruct passage in or out of the premises of the erstwhile employer. The picket may resort to various active tactics as permitted under the law, but his object is to injure the offending employer in pocket and social standing.   N.A.

picketing, peaceful. Cf. freedom of speech.

pictogram. An integrated series of pictographs (q.v.) which relates a whole story or records a more or less complex event.   E.A.H.

pictograph. A representation of an object, action, or idea by a picture or symbol suggestive or imitative thereof. G.P.M.

picture-bride. Bride selected by correspondence methods, a practice once popular among Japanese in this country who sought wives from women in Japan. Upon the basis of such negotiations the arrangements were made to migrate the pledged brides.   N.A.

pile dwelling. A dwelling raised on posts or piles, often but not always over a lake or marsh.   G.P.M.

pillory. A wooden framework upon a raised platform to which a culprit was fastened either with head and hands through holes in a board or by a chain about the neck in order that he might be the object of public scorn. Often it was set up in the market place where the occupant could be pelted with over-ripe fruit and eggs by the people.   J.L.G.

pilot study. Preliminary survey preceding a social survey for purposes of testing and perfecting technique. Used synonymously with pre-survey, test-tube survey.   M.Pt.

pimp. A person who serves as procurer or agent for prostitutes.   J.P.S.

pirrauru. A relative of opposite sex, among certain Australian tribes, belonging to the marriage class (q.v.) from which a spouse may be taken, with whom sexual relations are permitted under the prevailing form of sexual communism (q.v.). G.P.M.

plane of living. The actual consumption performance of a group of persons, expressed in terms of the average quantities and qualities of goods and services consumed per unit of time, conveniently a year, and per typical unit of the group, ordinarily a family. Precision of interpretation requires a sharp distinction between this concept and standard of living (q.v.). The latter term applies correctly to an ideal or objective goal, the existence of which is primarily mental, and which therefore does not lend itself readily to precise measurement.

planning. The projection of ends and arrangement of means for their fulfillment, involving a systematic pattern of activities permitted by the background of the general social order. All planning is the arranging of a cooperation of parts or members in a functional union, in an effort to secure the full service the parts can render in a desired project for human welfare. Planning is thus always the second step in the project form of human experience, which has four general stages, viz.: (1) felt need; (2) reflective interpretation; (3) social control; and (4) aesthetic appreciation. C.J.B.

planning, agricultural. A system of organization for the analysis and adjustment of state and local agricultural problems, sponsored by Bureau of Agricultural Economics and Agricultural Extension Service with the expectation that it become autonomous in state ànd counties. Composed of county committees and state committees made up of representatives of county committees. Generally problems of land use are the first attacked; others, such as farm labor, taxation, credit, health, housing and education, follow in whatever order each committee decides is desirable. It began about 1938, and was originally called land use planning. More recently it has been called county agricultural planning or **agricultural planning.**

Committees are referred to· as County, or State, Agricultural Planning Committees. C.E.L.

planning, city. The guidance and control by government of the form and use of public and private real property according to a comprehensive plan for the physical development of the community. City planning includes the demolition of old buildings, zoning, and the pre-arranged construction of trunk or through highways, parks, recreation centers, and public buildings. For the larger cities, city planning to be effective must be articulated with county or regional planning. The first attempts at city planning appeared in Europe in the 18th century. Sweden had a building law for towns early in that century and Paris was placed under planned growth in 1790. The most comprehensive legislation on the subject appeared in the Housing and Town Planning Act passed by the English Parliament in 1909. J.W.M'C.

planning, economic. Cf. economic planning.

planning, regional. Cf. regional planning.

planning, social. Cf. social planning.

plantation cycle. A term derived from the theory of cyclical fluctuations of social phenomena. In this view the plantation, like other social institutions, follows a more or less definite pattern of change, its early stage showing exploitation of land and labor at a rising rate, followed by a long, relatively stable period, after which the plantation form gives way to some other form of agricultural economy. However, during the so-called stable period there may be seen many evidences of an unstable equilibrium, such as conflict between planters and laborers, uneconomic exploitation of the soil, changing labor forms (such as wage labor vs. sharecropping), all affected by larger social and economic forces such as the state of the domestic and world market for products of the plantation economy and technological changes affecting the culture and harvesting of crops. Wide disparities found in an industrial society between wages and living standards of plantation and industrial labor constitute a dynamic factor, as does so-called "land hunger" of the farming population. Apparently a transition from the plantation form to smaller land holdings is implied. But the theory is vague on many points.   K.DP.L.

plantation family. Cf. family, plantation.

plantation farm. Cf. farm, plantation.

plantation system. In American usage, the agricultural complex of the South, characterized in the main by large-scale landholding, concentration on a single cash crop, and cheap labor forms—Negro chattel slavery in antebellum times, and sharecropping in postbellum,—the whole developing characteristic class and caste relations. Cf. colonization.   K.DP.L.

plasm, germ. Cf. germ plasm.

plasticity. That quality of human nature which permits behavior patterns to be modified by early conditioning and the cultural factors of environment into many diverse forms.   F.D.W.

Platonic love. Comradeship of a non-sexual, non-carnal, spiritual nature. Modern usage confines this state of affection to persons of the opposite sex, but there is nothing in Plato's writings to justify this strict limitation.   W.C.H.

platyrrhine. Broad nosed. When the nasal index is determined on a skull it expresses the relation between the breadth of the nasal aperture at its widest point and its length as given in the distance from the juncture of the middle point of the nasal bones and the frontal bone above (nasion), to the inferior border of nasal aperture. If the breadth is over 51 per cent of the length, the nose is platyrrhine. On living subjects, nose breadth is the distance between the two widest points of the fleshy wings, or alae. Length is measured from the nasion to the juncture of the septum with the upper lip. If the breadth, so measured, is more than 84 per cent of the length, the nose is platyrrhine.   E.A.H.

play. A form of recreation; the relatively free, happy, spontaneous activity,

chiefly of children, engaged in for pleasure and amusement, as contrasted with work, toil, chores, compulsory school attendance, and other required tasks. As a general term, it has been regarded as practically synonymous with recreation (q.v.).   M.H.N.

play, group. Cf. group play.

play, parallel. A form of play in which each individual engages in the same type of activity as the others but without overt cooperation with them.   P.H.F.

playground. An area or place with facilities for supervised play activities, and the organization and promotion of recreation programs.   M.H.N.

pleasure economy. Cf. economy, pleasure.

plebiscite. The method often adopted in peace treaties by which the inhabitants of a particular territory are allowed by vote to determine their political allegiance, whether to their old state or to a neighboring or annexing state. Numerous instances are provided in the Treaty of Versailles, when the Saar, Silesia and other areas surrounding Germany were afforded this opportunity. There is objection to the system by some writers, maintaining that it covers a disguised annexation; but if properly conducted, there is no reason why it cannot be honest. Functioning usually in times of political tension, there is an especial need for careful planning and supervision by independent and impartial authorities.   E.M.B.

pluralism. A conception affirming a multitude of irreducible and equivalent ultimate principles, realms, forms of reality. Pluralism presupposes discontinuity. Its opposite term is monism.   G.G.

pluralism, jural. A conception affirming the existence of many conflicting and equivalent jural orders in the same system of law. Jural pluralism insists on the capacity of particular groups and social connections to engender autonomous jural regulations, and on the impossibility of establishing a priori a primacy of the legal order of the state over other competing jural orders. The relationship among different jural orders is considered as depending upon varying social and jural conjunctures.   G.G.

pluralism, philosophical. A conception affirming a multitude of irreducible and equivalent ultimate wholes, ideas, values and value scales, as well as experiences in which they are tested. Consistent philosophical pluralism is opposed not only to monism, but also to rationalism, and is linked with radical empiricism. Philosophical pluralism may be affirmed without necessarily implying a sociological, jural, or political pluralism (q.v.). On the other hand, jural and political pluralism presuppose philosophical pluralism.   G.G.

pluralism, political. A conception proposing a reorganization of the state through a set of institutions guaranteeing its effective limitation, e.g., by some other independent organizations (cf. Guild-Socialism and Syndicalism) which serve as checks. Political pluralism is teleological and practical. It does not necessarily follow either from jural or sociological pluralisms, which are purely theoretical and descriptive, and admit different practical applications, according to circumstances.   G.G.

pluralism, sociological. A trend in present day sociology affirming: (a) an irreducible multiplicity of the forms of sociality within each particular group; (b) an irreducible multitude of particular groups in each type of inclusive society; and (c) an irreducible diversity of types of inclusive societies themselves. Sociological pluralism sees in social reality a "microcosm" of irreducible social connections, groups and social types. It is opposed to all oversimplifications in sociology, insisting on the impossibility of unilinear evolution, as well as of a universally valid hierarchy of social forms, which varies with every social conjuncture. Jural pluralism is directly an aspect of sociological pluralism; on the contrary, political pluralism is only a possible, but not necessary, consequence of it as applied to the present day situation.   G.G.

pluralistic behavior. Cf. behavior, pluralistic.

plurality pattern. A plurality of existing sociative relationships so interwoven that a pattern is formed. This pattern is manifested in vocal or other mutually understood gestures corresponding to certain relatively permanent states of social distance, private and/or public. Churches, states, classes, families, etc., are plurality patterns. Closely related terms are plurel, social structure, group (in the broad sense), etc.   H.B.

plurel. A category of persons. It is any number greater than one of human beings who are characterized in common by at least one attribute.   S.C.D.

plutocracy. Government by the wealthy; a form of government in which the supreme power resides with very wealthy men or the wealthy classes; rule by the rich primarily because they are rich. It refers also to a controlling group of wealthy people.   F.E.L.

poetic punishment. Cf. punishment, poetic.

pogrom. A massacre or wholesale slaughter spontaneously generated or incited and organized by a government or ruling class against a group of unarmed persons because of popular hatred or some sort of prejudice. It refers especially to the large scale killing of Jews in Czaristic Russia which from time to time was incited and organized by the governing class.   N.L.S.

polarity, social. Cf. social polarity.

polarization (*of a crowd*). A situation-process observed in crowds (q.v.) when the attention of all or most members is focussed upon one person, symbol, sound, or idea. The word is used sociologically by a figure of speech derived from the physics of magnetism. (*of public opinion or an estrangement situation*): a situation-process in which opposing and competing ideas, interests, and antagonisms in a total group situation are becoming clearly contrasted, and two conflicting modes, or subgroups, or rallying-points are observable.   T.D.E.

police. Agents of the law charged with the responsibility of maintaining law and order among the citizens.   J.M.R.

police, state. A police force organized and directed by a state government. Until late in the 19th century police forces in the United States were under the jurisdiction of local governments. Then in order to abolish extensive private police forces maintained by large industrial companies, the state of Pennsylvania established the first state constabulary. Since then twenty-seven states have set up state police forces. Not all state police have the same powers. In some states the state police are merely highway patrolmen who can make arrests for traffic violations only. In others they can make arrests for any offense committed on the highway. And in eight states the power of the state police extends to any crime committed in territory not directly under the jurisdiction of a competent local police force.   J.W.M'C.

police clearances. The number of offenses "cleared by arrest" indicates the number of crimes for each of which at least one of the offenders has been apprehended and made available for prosecution. Police clearances considered by themselves can be misleading without the additional information regarding the subsequent procedural outcome.   N.F.C.

policeman. Cf. police.

policewoman. Female members of the police force of the larger cities in the United States. They are usually women of good education, superior intelligence and social casework experience. They were first appointed as a special detail at the Lewis and Clark Exposition in Portland in 1905. Their work consists mainly of supervising dancehalls, tracking down wayward girls, and controlling prostitution. About 200 cities now have female members in the police force.   J.W.M'C.

policy, industrial. Cf. industrial policy.

policy, social. Cf. social policy.

political action. Cf. action, political.

political democracy. Cf. democracy, political.

political pluralism. Cf. pluralism, political.

political refugee. A person seeking or securing asylum in a foreign land after fleeing from political persecution in his native country.   R.N.B.

politics. The theory, art, and practice of government.

poll, public opinion. Survey of the opinion or attitude of the public. Pre-election counts of voting intention of a sample of the electorate used for forecasting election outcome.   M.Pt.

poll tax. Cf. tax, poll.

pollyanna. A person with happy, unrealistic, optimistic type of mind reminiscent of a character by that name in a novel of the same name by Eleanor Hodgman Porter. Pollyanna had a faculty for cancelling the ills of life by counting her blessings and reasoning that the bad could have been worse.   N.A.

polyandry. A form of marriage in which one woman may be united with two or more recognized husbands at one time. Cf. cicisbeism; monogamy; polygamy; polygyny.   G.P.M.

polyandry, adelphic. Fraternal polyandry (q.v.).

polyandry, fraternal. A type of polyandry (q.v.) in which the husbands of a woman are, by preference, brothers of one another.   G.P.M.

polygamy. A form of marriage in which a person of either sex is united to more than one spouse; includes polyandry (q.v.) as well as polygyny (q.v.), with which it is often incorrectly confused.   G.P.M.

polygyny. A form of marriage in which one man may be united with two or more recognized wives at one time. Cf. concubinage; monandry; monogamy; polyandry; polygamy.   G.P.M.

polygyny, sororal. A type of polygyny (q.v.) in which the wives of a man are, by preference, sisters of one another. Cf. sororate.   G.P.M.

poor, new Cf. new poor.

poor law. Cf. law, poor.

poor relief. Cf. relief, poor

population An aggregate of individuals defined with reference to spatial location, political status, ancestry, or other specific conditions, either (a) at a specific time, or (b) in a temporal continuum.   F.L.

population, balanced. A population which is, for the time being, stationary in size, with an equal birth rate and death rate, and equal immigration and emigration. The condition may be temporary or even momentary; wherefore, the concept is not to be confused with stabilized population (q.v.).

population, density of. Number of individuals in a population relative to space (crude density) or specific factors affecting economic development (economic density).   F.L.

population, farm. Cf. farm population.

population, optimum. A population of the right size to achieve and maintain some recognized and accepted social goal. Various criteria have been suggested as the basis for computing optimum population. The most generally accepted and widely used is the standard of living (q.v.). The optimum population of any given society is a moving quantity, changing with all the factors which combine to determine the total social pattern.

population, rural. Cf. rural population.

population, stable. (1) (*hypothetical*) A population so distributed by age and sex that, with continuance of given age-specific rates of fertility, sex ratio at birth, and age- and sex-specific rates of mortality, its crude rates of natural increase, death and birth and its age and sex distribution will remain constant. Note. A hypothetical stable population may be an increasing, decreasing or stationary population.   (2) (*actual*) A population with conditions approximating those of a hypothetical stable population. Note. The term, when applied to actual population is re-

stricted (unless otherwise stated) to populations with intrinsic rate of natural increase in the vicinity of zero.   F.L.

population, stabilized. A population which quantitatively has been brought into conformity with some significant social value. A stabilized population may grow or diminish, provided its relation to the value is not altered. For example, a population which was stabilized at the optimum would grow or diminish according to changes in the factors affecting the optimum, but would not be excessive in either direction. Not to be confused with balanced population (q.v.).

population, stationary. (1) (*hypothetical*) A population with zero intrinsic rate of natural increase, i.e., a life table population. (2) (*actual*) Same as stable population, definition (2).   (3) (*transitional*) A population which is not increasing or decreasing at a particular time, without regard to structure and intrinsic trend. Cf. population, balanced.   F.L.

population change. (1) Increase or decrease of number of individuals in a population through a specified temporal continuum (total) including effects of migration or (natural) apart from such effects. (2) Change in the distribution of characteristics of the individuals comprising a continuous population, especially change resulting from population change as defined above (1).   F.L.

population mobility. The act of changing position in space; also the capacity to do so. Two general types may be distinguished: physical mobility and social mobility. Physical mobility (sometimes called territorial mobility) refers to movement of population units in physical space. Although vertical movements, such as the number of persons who leave the ground by aeroplane, may be significant for some purposes, sociological significance attaches chiefly to the movements of the population upon the land and water surface.

Social mobility refers to change of position in social space, i.e., change in the system of relationships with respect to men and institutions. Theoretically, social mobility may occur in any direction, but typologically, the directions of greatest sociological significance are vertical and horizontal. Social movements are said to be vertical when the unit moved changes position in the social strata or levels, either up or down. Social movements are said to be horizontal when the unit moved changes from one position to another at the same social level, or in the same social stratum. Cf. social mobility.   C.E.L.

population movement. A transfer of human groups from one geographic setting to another. The number of persons involved, necessary to bring any particular shift within this category, is indeterminate, but it must always be sufficient to constitute a genuine group phenomenon. It may be inter-societal, or intra-societal, and may be temporary or permanent. The two basic types of population movement are dispersion (q.v.) and migration (q.v.).

population pressure. The force originating in the numerical increase of a population to the point where it passes beyond the optimum and creates overpopulation (q.v.).

population trend. Cf. trend, population.

position, ecological. (1) The spatial relation of an object within a given areal frame of reference, involving both (a) ecological distance and (b) direction from the point of reference along available routes of transportation. (2) The dominance-subordination relation of an ecological unit to a given point of reference within a functionally-integrated ecological unit. (3) The niche occupied by an ecological unit or class of units within a functional ecological chain.   J.A.Q.

position, spatial. An ecological term indicating location, or location in relation to other objects, perhaps in a pattern.   N.A.

positive checks. Cf. Malthusian theory.

positivism. A system of philosophy originated by Auguste Comte, who used the name to indicate the last and highest stage of knowledge, which was described as having risen from the primitive theological or fictitious through the metaphysical or abstract to the positive or scientific. A theory which definitely abandons all search for ultimate causes and limits knowledge to the laws of phenomena as being the only knowledge that is both attainable and useful. Positivism reduces all knowledge to natural science and all scientific methods to objective methods of observation and classification of phenomena as they are actually experienced in their invariable relations of co-existence, succession, and resemblance, which observed relations give the laws of phenomena.   N.L.S.

possibilism (possibilisme). Theory stated by Vidal de la Blache and Febvre which holds that geographic conditions make possible but do not determine the culture of a region; hence opposed to geographic determinism. Man, it follows, is a vital geographic factor, introducing and maintaining plants and animals in regions where they could not occur under natural conditions; and often failing to make use of apparently favorable environmental factors. Non-material culture traits, in such a theory, are as important as geographic conditions in producing the current pattern or configuration, so that historical factors are essential to an understanding of the exploitation of the region. From this it follows that the "natural resources" of a region will depend as much upon the non-material culture of the time and place as upon the nature of the geographic endowment.   H.E.M.

post-parole period. The period or time starting immediately after the parolee has been officially released from the control or supervision of the parole authorities and is again a member of free society.   N.F.C.

potential, social. Cf. social potential.

potential, social, difference of. Variation among individuals as to capacity to affect social change or direct social action.

potentiality, social. Cf. social potentiality.

potlatch. A ceremony, characteristic of the Indians of the northern Pacific coast of North America, in which property is lavishly given away or destroyed in order to acquire or maintain social status. G.P.M.

poverty. The state of being (relatively) poor; more specifically, a situation in which a given person's or family's plane of living, or a given group's level of living, seems to be below the standard of normal living of whatever community is used as basis of reference; lack of goods or services serious enough to cause misery if not provided from sources outside the channels of income considered normal for the given culture. Distinguished from dependency (q.v.) and pauperism (q.v.).

Primary poverty is poverty due to lack of money income serious enough to preclude purchase at the given price level of goods and services needed to maintain a plane of health and decency accepted in the community as a minimum standard of living. Secondary poverty is poverty due to ignorance, incompetence, neglect or other circumstance preventing such use of money income as will produce a real income adequate for maintenance of the given person or group at or above the community's minimum standard of health and decency. Cf. real wages.   T.D.E.

poverty level. A state where the individual or family is unable to provide the amounts of food, clothing and shelter necessary for independent existence.   E.E.M.

power. The ability or authority to dominate men, to coerce and control them, obtain their obedience, interfere with their freedom, and compel their action in particular ways. It may be the outcome of personal charisma, which induces obedience to the genius of an individual leader, or of tradition, the sacrosanct character of an institution, or rational acceptance; or the result of a monopoly of wealth or military force. Every social order is a system of power relations with hierarchical super- and sub-ordination and regulated competition and cooperation. The power of the state is greater than that of all other associations and individuals within the given territorial area, by its control of the system of law, and its possession of the most powerful and efficient organization. The state has a monopoly of legal power and aims to find moral authority and sanction for its principles. Military power is an indispensable component of political power. In democracy political power is the resultant of the struggle of constitutional political parties and machines. Actually power resides chiefly in a controlling minority of parliamentary and other leaders, who dominate the machines and direct political responses to the major economic pressures.   E.F.

power, social. Cf. social power.

power age. An economy characterized by the extended and diversified use of material-physical power in the characteristic productive processes. The term is frequently used to designate the economic era following World War I, during which industrial power rose to a dominating position in a way comparable to the rise of capital at the beginning of the capitalistic era. One important feature of the power age, directly dependent upon technological developments in the field of electricity, is the use of multiple, mobile, small scale power units.

practical sociology. Cf. sociology, practical.

praetorianism. The condition in any society when a minority, like the Praetorian Guard in ancient Rome, by force, fraud, venality or illicit pressure, acquires and exercises actual control of the policies and activities of the society, but functions through the titular officials.   G.M.F.

praise. The expression, in any manner, of the approval of others in sincere and appropriate terms—as contrasted with flattery which is insincere and uses extravagant terms. Praise flows downward from superordinates to subordinates, whereas flattery flows upward.   F.E.L.

prayer. A formal petition to a supernatural being, often accompanying a sacrifice (q.v.).   G.P.M.

preanimism. The theory that animatism (q.v.) rather than animism (q.v.) is the original and basic element in religion.   G.P.M.

precipitating crisis. Cf. crisis, precipitating.

pre-coded schedule or questionnaire. Collection form with code symbols printed on form to enable interviewer or informant to record information in terms used for tabulation. Schedule data are coded in the field rather than in the office. M.PT.

predictability. The degree of probability to which a phenomenon is capable of prediction. This quality rests on regularity or uniformity of occurrence or of causal connection; but it also holds for those scientific or statistical estimates of future events or social trends, where certain variable conditions are held constant or assumed to operate in designated manner. F.H.H.

prediction. The act or process of forecasting, with greater or less probability, the outcome of an event or series of events, by inference from a scientific, especially a statistical, analysis of known events. In view of the multiplicity of causal conditions affecting social events, prediction in the sociological field is less precise than in the physical sciences. Moreover, in view of the wide variation in the intensity of known causal factors and the presence of unknown causal factors, prediction is usually made on the assumption that certain major and known factors continue to operate in a given manner. Cf. natural law. F.H.H.

prediction, sociological. There is much confusion over what is meant by sociological prediction; the most common misconception is that it is equivalent to prophecy, forecasting, foretelling. Strictly, however, it refers only to the "before-saying" (prediction) of certain kinds of recurrence.

To predict the recurrence of phenomena is, in a certain sense, to control that recurrence if it is possible to reinstate or reconstruct the conditions under which previous recurrences have taken place. The scientist may not have any interest whatever in bringing about actual recurrence; he may be quite content to say that "if and when" certain factors are combined in certain ways, the results are predictable. This is *conditional prediction*. The supreme test is experimental, but when a number of experiments sufficient to diminish chance to insignificance have been performed—and a very small number, under some circumstances, may suffice—the scientist has achieved all the control he seeks: "When this is done, these—within a small range of variation—must be the consequences."

Further, the scientist may get the prediction he is after even when he is not able to reinstate the conditions of previous recurrence, i.e., when actual, manipulative experiment is impracticable or impossible. He may, in other words, attain hypothetical prediction through mental recognition and/or extension of such reconstruction. Instance: Astronomers are able to say, because of the study of certain aspects of the heavens over a long period, that time, mass, and motion are in certain definite relations with each other. They can therefore say that if the mass of the moon were altered in a determinate amount, its orbit and its cycle would also be changed in determinate amounts. Now, this "if the mass of the moon were altered" is hypothetical prediction, on the basis of previously observed recurrences of related phenomena, of phenomena never yet specifically observed.

The varieties of prediction thus far discussed, whether hypothetical or actual, have all had an orientation toward the future, both with regard to the predictive act itself and with regard to the phenomena predicted. Putting it differently: there has been an effort to make clear the implications of *actual prospective prediction* and *hypothetical prospective prediction*. There need be a prospective reference, however, only in the predictive act itself; it is not necessary that the recurrence of the phenomena under examination take place in the future.

Appropriate example: Paleontologists, on the basis of fragmentary evidence, frequently reconstruct animals long extinct, and then venture assertions like this: "If and when a complete skeleton is discovered, our reconstruction will be found to be substantially correct." This is *retrospective prediction*, for the skeleton which will eventually provide the full validation lies under strata deposited millenia ago. The only essential reference toward the future is in the "will", which is the inseparable component of the predictive act. There is no actual prospective prediction; the biology supply houses which stock our laboratories do not yet breed dinosaurs for the market. There is no hypothetical prospective prediction, for no living animal species known at present is evolving in the dinosaur direction. The prediction is hypothetical in the same way as "altering the mass of the moon" is hypothetical. Finally, to repeat, the prediction is retrospective because the occurrence which will provide the validation presumably has already occurred; it is only the validation which lies in the future, and it is only to this that the future-ward orientation implied in "before-saying" or "pre-diction" refers. All else is past.

Astronomy, geology, paleontology, archeology, zoölogy, botany, philology, ethnology, sociology, and several other sciences make much use of retrospective prediction. More use would unquestionably be made of it were it not for the prevailing confusion between the logic and the psychology of prediction.

Logically, there is not a particle of difference between prospective and retrospective prediction. Psychologically, retrospective prediction may open the door to tampering with the evidence, self-deception, rationalization, and other difficulties. When the event to which predictive techniques are applied has already occurred, there is the besetting temptation to reconstruct the earlier recurrences and functional interrelations in such a way that the solution appears inevitable. What can be learned about the interdependence of social personalities, processes, and structures by applying the appropriate procedures (especially constructive typology [q.v.]) to the task of retrospective prediction may eventually be of much use when prospective prediction of the actual variety is the goal.   H.B.

preferential mating. Marriage regulations favoring or prescribing unions between persons related to one another in a particular manner, e.g., between cross-cousins (q.v.) of opposite sex. Cf. also levirate; sororate.   G.P.M.

preferential shop. Cf. shop, preferential.

prejudice. An attitude, usually emotional, acquired in advance of adequate evidence and experience. It is based upon varying combinations of suggestion, imitation, belief, and limited experience and may be either favorable or unfavorable. No specific prejudice is innate, although all individuals have genetic capacities of prejudice. Specific prejudices are forms of sympathy or antipathy, and may have as their objects individuals, groups, races, nationalities (or the particular traits of any one of these), or ideas, social patterns, and institutions. In brief, the range of prejudice is virtually as wide as that of attitude.

prejudice, class. Discriminatory attitudes directed in blanket fashion against persons of another class (q.v.), especially with regard to their ideas and behavior. Also—in regard to the social classes—scorn of the upper classes for the lower, and surly, vengeful attitudes by the lower toward those above them. Any conscious condemnation of one class by another. Prejudicial attitudes make for one form of social distance (q.v.). Religious intolerance and discrimination are of a similar order but should not be identified as class prejudice.   W.C.H.

prejudice, race. Cf. race prejudice.

preliminary hearing. The fifth amendment in the Bill of Rights of the United States Constitution provides that no one may be prosecuted for an "infamous crime", i.e., a felony, without a presentment or an indictment. Therefore, one charged with a felony is detained until arrangements are made for a preliminary hearing before a magistrate. The sole purpose of this hearing is to determine (a) whether or not the alleged felony has actually been committed and (b) whether the defendant in question is in some way connected with its commission. If the magistrate conducting the preliminary hearing believes both (a) and (b) have been established he commits the defendant to jail (or grants him bail) to await the action of the grand jury. The preliminary hearing is not a trial. It is a hearing to determine whether the defendant is to be held for the action of the grand jury. The latter body decides whether the defendant is to be indicted and then tried, or whether he is to be released. The defendant is entitled to have witnesses in his behalf as well as counsel present during the hearing. He is entitled to be confronted by the witnesses against him. He must be told by the magistrate that he need not make any statement, that if he does speak anything he says may be used against him at the subsequent trial. The defendant, at the outset, may waive his rights to the preliminary hearing and simply await the action of the grand jury.   N.F.C.

preliterate. Characteristic of a tribe which has not yet acquired a written language. Preferred to primitive (q.v.) except when referring to prehistoric peoples; but less correct than non-literate (q.v.) which does not imply either inferiority or a fixed linear sequence of cultural evolution. T.D.E.

preliterate culture, Cf. culture, preliterate.

premarital license. The relatively unrestricted liberty in sexual matters allowed to the unmarried in many primitive societies.   G.P.M.

premature birth. Cf. birth, premature.

prepotent. Having tendency to take precedence over.   M.S.

prepotent drive. Cf. drive, prepotent.

prepotent reflex. Cf. reflex, prepotent.

prepotent response. Cf. response, prepotent.

prepotent stimulus. Cf. stimulus, prepotent.

pre-sentence investigation. To help the courts decide on the nature of the sentence to be imposed upon a convicted offender some states require that an investigation of the character and backgrounds of the offender be made and the data submitted to the judge. This report aids the judge, when and if he uses it, to decide whether the offender should be placed on probation, and under what conditions. The investigations are made by the probation officers attached to the court.   N.F.C.

press agent. Specialist in placing or inspiring news, feature, pictorial, and edi-

torial matter in newspapers, magazines, radio programs, etc., in behalf of a client. His work may take the form of creating and stage-managing events in such a manner that the media of mass-communication are likely to carry reports and other notices of them; he thus is able to have some characteristic, policy, or service of his client dramatized to a large audience. The client may be a church, trade association, trade union, college, privately-owned public utility, debutante, Congressman, political party, or bank president. The term apparently derives from the commercial entertainment field, especially from the "press agent" sent in advance of a traveling circus, theatrical company, or museum. While this prototype frequently handles paid advertising as well as the so-called "free publicity," the modern press agent in non-entertainment fields usually has no more than advisory contact with paid notices.   A.M'C.L.

pressure, group. Cf. group pressure.

pressure, social. Cf. social pressure.

prestige. Social position or status in public esteem, attained by the social recognition one receives in his associations, or perhaps in the press.   N.A.

prevailing wage. Cf. wage, prevailing.

preventive. (*social economy and social work*). Descriptive of measures and agencies which, coming before social maladjustment sets in, stand in the way of the development of serious social situations. By extension the word may be too loosely used to describe ameliorative (q.v.), remedial (q.v.) or even palliative (q.v.) measures, in as much as these prevent situations from being as bad as they might have been; but strictly the word should be reserved for measures and agencies that keep normal people normal, or that correct community conditions which are considered evil because they threaten the normality of persons or families or community standards. Cf. palliative; remedial; normality.   T.D.E.

preventive checks. Cf. Malthusian theory.

prevision. A seeing in imagination of a possible future. The vividness of such imagination may operate as a threat or as a promise, thus exerting personal or social control. To be distinguished from prediction (q.v.), which strictly is telling rather than seeing the future, and refers, on the one hand, to alleged "prophecy"; and, on the other, to statistical forecasts based upon projected trends, or to scientific forecasts based upon formulations of uniform behavior of phenomena under controlled observation (both of which assume many constants under given conditions).   T.D.E.

price. The amount of money for which a good or service is exchanged; a measure of value in terms of money.   E.E.M.

primary conflict. Distinguished from secondary conflict on the basis of whether the conflict is occurring within (or between) "primary groups" (q.v.) or members thereof, on the one hand, so that the battle is "personal" in its motivation, or on the other hand, within (or between) "secondary groups" (q.v.) or members thereof.   T.D.E.

primary contact. Cf. contact, primary.

primary group. Cf. group, primary.

primary ideal. Cf. ideal, primary.

primitive. Related to the beginnings of human culture; in a condition supposed to be similar to that of the original prehistoric ancestors of European man; undeveloped, arrested in cultural development. The use of the word to describe peoples and cultures of small cultural base is thought to suggest misleading ideas; viz.: that our own ancestors had a similar culture, that the cultures of such tribes have always been in their present state, are arrested, or would or should eventually develop in some predetermined sequence similar to our own.   T.D.E.

primitive man. (1) A term used to refer to ancient and prehistoric men collectively. Any man or group of men who lived before the dawn of history, i.e., before the invention and development of writing. In Europe, Africa, and Asia men who lived during the Eolithic, Paleolithic, Neolithic and Bronze Ages. (2) Any man who belongs to a society possessing a non-literate culture. Temporally, the society and culture may have occurred in antiquity, or they may be contemporary. In this sense the term is used to describe a cultural condition of man which is uncivilized. Primitive man in addition to being non-literate (or pre-literate) possesses an economic culture which may be agricultural or non-agricultural (food gathering, hunting and fishing, or pastoral) but is non-industrial and usually non-urban.   E.A.H.

primitive nomadism. Cf. nomadism, primitive.

primitive society. Cf. society, primitive.

primogeniture. The exclusive or preferential right in inheritance (q.v.) of the eldest son, child, or other heir. Cf. ultimogeniture.   G.P.M.

principle, compensatory. Cf. compensatory principle.

principles. Generalized and abbreviated statements of policy or fact; in social references to value or policy, they mean the agreement or consensus of a number of competent authorities; in sociological references, they are the inductive explanations of sociological laws. Ex. the principle of population in the Malthusian theory is natural selection. Cf. law. H.A.P.

principles, descriptive. Generalizations concerning human interaction which are not sufficiently complete to make them acceptable as scientific explanations but which are useful as guides to further study. Ex. the four wishes, cultural lag, (the principle of) limited possibilities.
                              H.A.P.

principles, explanatory. A principle is an adequately tested explanation. The use of the redundant objective "explanatory" is necessary to include competing or complementary explanations from geographical, biological, psychological, and cultural studies whose principles presumably explain the same types of human interaction but which are not acceptable as scientific because they have not been proved. Ex.

"a culture into which a man is born makes him into a being after its own image."

H.A.P.

principles, Rochdale. Cf. Rochdale principles.

principles, sociological. Cf. sociological principles.

principles, universal. Basic and fundamental generalizations which are used to explain human interaction and culture; general theories. Ex. (the principles of) continuity, evolution, the stage theory of social development, the materialistic interpretation of history; diffusion; behaviorism; organic and social cycles. H.A.P.

priority. The order of preference in which persons or interests stand in relation to one another. In the administration of public relief it indicates the order in which persons or families stand to receive public benefits. In the rationing of materials essential to war it relates to the order in which requests for such materials are recognized. N.A.

prison. A penal institution operated (in the United States) by either the state or the federal government and used only for adult offenders whose sentences exceed one year. The prison should be differentiated from the jail which is operated by local governments and houses petty criminals whose sentence is less than one year and also miscellaneous persons whose detention is required, such as witnesses, accused persons awaiting trial, and suspects. J.W.M'C.

prison, discipline in. All those measures used by the prison administration—the grade system, degradation and advancement in grade, privileges and denial thereof, isolation in cell or in solitary cells; "good time," etc.—designed to promote good behavior in the institution. J.L.G.

prison, industrial. A term more common in Europe than in the United States to designate a prison in which the inmates carry on production of useful articles and with a minimum emphasis upon vocational or other training intended to prepare the discharged prisoner for life in society.

The inmates are those who are looked upon as relatively hopeless for reformatory methods. Originally it meant a prison for those sentenced to hard labor as distinguished from those sentenced to simple imprisonment. J.L.G.

prison community. Social structure, social relationships, and social processes in prison. The quality of staff-staff, inmate-inmate, and inmate-staff relationships; class stratification, informal group life, leadership, and folkways in prisoner society, the rôle of gossip and public opinion as means of social control; the processes whereby the guards become institutionalized and the inmates "prisonized"—all these aspects are included. Cf. Bolshevo.

N.S.H.

prison congresses, international. Cf. international prison congresses.

prison farms. Farms for convicts, of four general varieties: (1) First, the farms which are owned by counties or municipalities where misdemeanants are committed who would otherwise serve short terms in a county or city jail. (2) Second, farms run as an auxiliary to state prisons, partially as a means of segregating a special group of offenders, as for example, first offenders, or habitual offenders, and partially for providing meat and vegetables for the prison kitchens. (3) Third, privately owned farms or plantations in the South to which the states leased convicts at considerable profit. Such private farms assumed responsibility for guarding and disciplining the men, and providing their food and shelter in return for their labor. Most of such privately operated farms have been abolished because of abuses. (4) Fourth, the prison farms now owned and operated by a number of Southern states, including Louisiana, Texas, and Mississippi, as a basic part of their prison system. Prisoners are first sent to a receiving center from which they are allocated to the different farms. Usually an attempt is made to place the prisoners on the different farms according to their types. M.A.E.

prison labor. This is the name given to that phase of prison organization concerned with the employment of prisoners.

232

It has always been the theory that prisoners should work, both for the economies to be gained and for the mental and physical discipline of prisoners. There have been so many humanitarian and economic arguments against the various plans of prison labor that the present program is quite inadequate. The manufacture of articles for state use (the state use system) which now prevails concentrates the work in a narrow range of objects with special emphasis upon household tasks in the maintenance of prisons such as laundry, bakery, and clothing manufacture. Economy in state appropriations restricts prison industry to antiquated equipment. In jails, where the sentence of prisoners is much shorter than in the prisons, the problem of finding adequate employment for prisoners is much more acute.   J.W.M'C.

prison psychosis. Characteristic attitudes on the part of some of the inmates due to the rigid system of discipline in many prisons. They become more or less apathetic and dull, or rebellious and violent. Extreme deviations of these sorts have been observed in prisons throughout the world. The longer the period of confinement the more marked are the reactions. There is little opportunity for initiative, the prison atmosphere is repressive, and the daily program monotonous. Inmates are robbed of will. They compensate by daydreaming and phantasizing, or by marked aggressive behavior which sometimes takes the form of destroying everything in the cell. This kind of prison stupor or aggression has been labelled "prison psychosis." The term is not used in a critical sense.   N.F.C.

prisoner. A person under arrest, in custody, or in prison, as punishment or held captive by the enemy. Treatment of prisoners varies according to the legal status of the prisoner. A person charged with crime and held for trial is innocent and is entitled to considerate treatment. Persons tried and convicted of crime are isolated by the state from the rest of society as punishment. Treatment of prisoners of war is defined by international conventions.   J.W.M'C.

prisoners, classification of. Cf. classification of prisoners.

prisoners' aid association. Private organization designed to aid discharged prisoners with advice about jobs, often providing a place to live while seeking work, giving counsel and sometimes money or credit.   J.L.G.

prisons, overcrowding in. The optimum-maximum number of inmates in a prison is generally considered to be five hundred. However, most countries throughout the world build much larger prisons. Even with the larger prisons overcrowding is generally found. In only five or six American states are prisons not overcrowded. The per cent of overcrowding in the American prison varies from about 5 per cent (Minnesota) to over 115 per cent (West Virginia). Overcrowding makes the classification and segregation of prisoners difficult, and complicates the problems of discipline, employment, education, and health.   N.F.C.

prisons, receiving. Induction centers for prisoners to which they are sent for assignment to the particular prison or prison facilities which best fit them. Some prison systems have reception prisons; others have reception facilities at larger prisons. A reception center is supposed to enable classification committees to assign each admitted prisoner to the proper custody, work, and education. During his period of reception, often called the period of quarantine, the prisoner is given the preventive and corrective medical attention necessary for induction, is interviewed for his social and criminal background, is examined psychologically, and is processed for identification.   W.C.R.

prisons, sex perversions in. Abnormal pathologic sex conduct, such as homo-sexualism or Lesbianism, arising out of the abnormal situation when hundreds of men or women are crowded together in prisons for long periods of time without contact with members of the opposite sex. N.F.C.

privacy. A desired degree of seclusion, not involving isolation from society, the group or the family. It may relate to the opportunity of an individual or a family to be alone at times when being alone is essential.   N.A.

privilege. Advantage based upon special edict or discriminatory legislation and not available to others on equal terms; unfair advantage sanctioned by law or based upon power, exploitation, or fraud. Usually used as an adverse epithet, applied when privileges are used for further exploitation or domination for their own defense, or to grasp further power and privilege. Bases of privilege include sex, age, skill, prowess, birth, race, status, position, property, wealth.   T.D.E.

probability. The likelihood of the occurrence of an event. Sometimes expressed as the ratio of the number of equally likely ways in which a particular event can occur to the total number of occurrences possible.   M.Pt.

probation. The special treatment of a convicted delinquent or criminal whereby his sentence to any penal or correctional institution is suspended during his good behavior. Ideally, such treatment requires that the probationer be placed under the supervision of a well-trained probation officer. In practice, except in the larger urban centers, American communities seldom have professionally trained officers competent to give such supervision. In many communities no supervision is given although the probationer may be required to report regularly to the presiding judge.   M.A.E.

The word is also used in educational and other institutions to denote a form of discipline or supervision over students or others who fall below prescribed standards, or who offend regulations.   R.N.B.

probation, adult. A modern system of placing adults who have been convicted of penal or criminal offenses under the supervision of trained workers for the purpose of social rehabilitation after suspension of sentence by the court.

probation officer. A court official responsible for supervising the conduct of persons placed on probation after conviction, and for investigating prior to sentence the life records of convicted offenders.   R.N.B.

problem. A situation defined as a difficulty to be solved, mastered, or adjusted to; an unadjusted situation. There are both normal and abnormal problems, personal and social problems. A problem is purely personal and normal so long as it is being dealt with within the person's usual resources of means, intelligence and contacts.   T.D.E.

problem, behavior. Cf. behavior problem.

problem, social. Cf. social problem.

problems, labor. Cf. labor problems.

problems, sociological. Cf. sociological problems.

process. Any change in which an observer could see a consistent quality or direction, to which a name is given (e.g., gravitation, refraction, osmosis, capillarity, mitosis, metamorphosis, tropism, commensalism, succession, evolution, institutionalization).   T.D.E.

process, behavior. The sequence of activity which takes place when an individual reacts to stimuli in a particular situation.   J.P.E.

process, group. Cf. group process.

process, growth. Cf. growth process.

process, institutional. Cf. institutional process.

process, learning, (inter-learning). The process by which cultural changes and cultural development take place in human groups; also a psychological name for the processes called the transmission and diffusion of culture. Animals learn by the sensory and muscular exploration of objects. Man's main method of learning seems to be acquisition from other members of his group through some form of inter-communication, especially verbal langage. All customs and traditions of human groups are learned in this way, and they constitute the bulk of all that is learned by human beings. Human beings learn, in other words, not so much by doing, or even by private experience, as by intercommunication and social imagination. As learning necessarily accumulates in human groups and is stored in language in its various forms, it becomes the basis of tradition and custom, and so of the whole social life of mankind. It also becomes a basis for social progress and explains why progress is possible in human groups. Inter-learning, which is found to only a negligible degree among the animals below man, becomes in mankind the main factor in his cultural and social life. Through inter-learning it is possible for great groups of men to profit from the experience, the inventions and discoveries of a single individual.   C.A.E.

Psychologically, it includes conditioning, the building up of new series of complexly coordinated motor responses, the formation of character, the fixation of items in memory, and the acquisition of ability to respond adequately to a situation. It is generally implied that the behavior of the organism takes place more promptly, easily and accurately with successive repetitions.

According to the gestalt school of psychology, it is confined to the process of acquiring insight into a situation, which is not contributed to by repetition and may occur without previous experience of the situation.   M.S.

process, maturation. Cf. maturation process.

process, situation-. Cf. situation-process.

process, social. Cf. social process.

process, societal. Cf. societal process.

process, telic. The regular sequence of purposive acts or the steps whereby some desired objective, ideal, program, project or goal is sought or attained.   N.L.S.

procreation. Participation in the biological process of reproduction.

producers' goods. Cf. production goods.

production. The sum total of the processes involved in the creative phase of the self-maintenance (q.v.) of society. The extraction of raw materials from the land, and the conversion of them by the application of labor, capital, and organization into forms useful to man, either as production goods (q.v.) or consumption goods (q.v.), with the latter as the final objec-

tive, and the transportation of such goods to the places where they are to be used. Commercial activities are a part of production. The term may also be considered to include the provision of economic services.

production goods. Cf. goods, production.

profession. An occupation, or calling. More specifically a particular type of calling characterized by considerable social power and high social status, e.g., medicine, law, divinity, university teaching, engineering, etc., and a marked degree of institutionalization. It is characterized by a high degree of technical skill, entailing specialized preparation generally at recognized institutions of learning, official regulation and licensure, a strong feeling of class honor and solidarity, manifested in vocational associations to secure a monopoly of the service, and in codes of ethics enjoining the responsibility of the profession to the collective it serves. With the passage of time and the change of folkways the differential status of the various professions changes; moreover new ones emerge either de novo or as the changed status of what were formerly merely occupational groups, to meet the needs of a rapidly expanding complex civilization for experts and trained specialists.   E.F.

professional. A member or practitioner of a profession (q.v.) or of a professional group.   E.F.

professional criminal. Cf. criminal, professional.

profit. The social reward permitted in any economic system to the owners of businesses as such. Historically speaking, true profit is a distinctive characteristic of what is called the capitalistic system. In this system the four universal and indispensable factors in a productive unit are land, labor, capital, and organization or management. Each of these factors is in some way privately owned and each owner respectively is socially entitled to his particular reward—rent, wages, interest, and salaries. The productive unit as a whole is also privately owned, and this ownership may be, and in theory is, entirely detached from any of the other particular forms of ownership. In the full development of the capitalistic system, the characteristic form of ownership is the joint stock corporation. The actual owners of the business are the common stockholders, and true profits are common stock dividends without any element of rent or interest. In an individually owned business, the owner in theory is compensated for his business ownership separately from any return for land or capital that he may own, or labor and management that he may supply.

profit sharing. One of a number of practices introduced by employers to stabilize employer-employee relationships. It is a plan to share the earnings of business with employees on the theory that they will work harder and more efficiently and be less likely to change jobs if they are rewarded for such services. Public opinion has been widely divided on the plan. Employers said it allowed workers to share in profits without sharing in losses. Employees claimed it was meaningless since the workers' "profit" probably came out of wages anyway. With the depression of 1929 the plan was generally abandoned in the United States.   J.W.M'C.

prognathous. Characterized by a relatively projecting jaw and sloping face, i.e., by a facial profile angle of less than 80 degrees. Cf. mesognathous; orthognathous.
                                                        G.P.M.

progress. Movement in the direction of a recognized and desired goal or objective.

progress, individual. Cf. individual progress.

progress, social. Cf. social progress.

progressive. Related to any deliberate act or any occurrence which from some point of view promotes or indicates progress. Cf. progress.   J.O.H.

progressive system. In penology, a prison program patterned after the so-called Irish system (q.v.). According to the Irish system, instituted by Crofton, a prisoner advanced progressively from initial cell isolation and lack of privileges

to congregate life with increasing privileges. Such advancement into a new grade or class was earned by acquiring credits for good behavior, industry, and interest in education. The later phases of progressive advancement were supposed to include minimum custody in an intermediate prison, where self-control could be fostered and the prisoner prepared for discharge by parole. The system is sometimes called the graded system. It has never been completely followed but many modern prison systems have incorporated phases and general principles of the progressive system, especially the earning of privileges, promotions to jobs of trust, and classification for degree of custody, such as close, medium, and minimum. In general the prison systems which have used the principles embodied in the Irish system do not have the inmate pass through all the stages of custody but classify him at admission as to what degree of custody he requires. But he can be reclassified as time and circumstances warrant both upward and downward in custodial level.
                                                        W.C.R.

progressive taxation. Cf. taxation, progressive.

progressivism. A force in the field of politics reflecting the attitude of liberalism (q.v.) but commonly identified with programs of immediate action.   R.N.B.

prohibition. The attempt to prohibit by law the manufacture, sale or use of alcoholic beverages. In the United States such prohibition was the goal of the temperance movement during the 19th and early 20th centuries, which was reached by gradual stages that culminated in the adoption of the 18th amendment to the Constitution of the United States in 1920. After thirteen years of ineffectual enforcement this amendment was repealed in 1933. Sociologically, prohibition may be defined in terms of a cultural conflict, or series of such conflicts, between urban and rural areas, foreign and native born, workers and their employers, and certain evangelical Protestant sects in contrast with other groups who are either not religious, or who do not subscribe to the mores of these sects.   A.E.W.

project. A social undertaking of an experimental character, intended to throw light on specific problems.   G.M.F.

project-problem method. (*education*) A plan of learning in which pupils are given (or select and set up for themselves) a project or goal for achievement, each such project being analyzed into a series of problem-situations which must be solved in the course of completing the project-goal. In the process of problem-solution the learning processes are implied. (*penology*) If correctional treatment be considered and operated as a re-educational process, principles of the project-problem method are applicable in connection with delinquency situation-processes: probation, indeterminate-sentence, prison training, parole.   T.D.E.

projection. Thrusting forth, or locating in the external (objective, actual) world, an experience which is subjective in origin; (*psychiatric*) imputing to an object or to another person, as actual, qualities, feelings or attitudes imagined by the subject. Events may corroborate projections of the latter sort; they are "pathological" only when so appraised by an observer who notes discrepancies between a "psychosis" and the consensus of others' judgments in the "same" situation. A fear may lead to a projection of hate, i.e., an imputation of hate motives to another person or group. Personification, animatism and animism are examples of projection. In a broader sense, projection is the reverse of introjection, both being aspects of the process of identification; any new experience, or remembered experience, is either incorporated in the self (introjected, identified with) or ejected by the self as not a part of it (projected, identified from), and imputed to "outside" sources, natural or supernatural, real or unreal. A compensatory resistance at the frontier of integrity is thus maintained by the self against the uncontrollable or intolerable.   T.D.E.

Ascribing to others one's own repressed mental processes.   M.K.

projective. Relating to the tendency to ascribe to others one's own unconscious drives and attitudes.   P.H.F.

projectivism. The conception of the next life in terms of this one.   A.G.K.

proletarian. Cf. proletariat.

proletariat. A distinct social stratum characterized by (a) consciousness of its existence as a social body; (b) ability to agitate for concessions on threat of creating social unrest; (c) social status as free but insecure propertyless people who form the "mass" base above which the "class" hierarchy towers. That social layer without social esteem or social honor but not lacking in political influence, real or potential, through mass action, formalized or spontaneous. The IWW of 1918 was a proletarian movement. White collar workers and the aristocrats of labor (except sand-hogs and truck drivers) are usually lower middle class affiliants, not proletarians. People on relief, on WPA, unskilled and mass production workers, and residents of slums such as those of Harlem are modern equivalents of the Roman proletariat.   W.C.H.

proletariat, dictatorship of the. Cf. dictatorship of the proletariat.

promiscuity. The acceptance indiscriminately of sexual intercourse.   E.R.G.

proof. A demonstration of any proposition that is of such a character that any person who is mentally competent to understand the demonstration must accept the conclusion. A test to determine the accuracy of conclusions reached in sociological research.

propaganda. The presentation to the public of facts, actual or alleged, arguments and opinions so organized as to induce conclusions favorable to the interests or viewpoint of those advancing them. R.N.B.

In order that such efforts may have the maximum effect, it is quite generally important that the sources of the pronouncements should not be obvious. Since propaganda is in essence biased, if its originators were known there would be a possibility and tendency to discount the statements because of the known attitudes and interests of the sponsors. Skilful propagandists make their material appear like genuine news, or "uninspired" editorial comments, recreational programs, or entertainment features. Propaganda need not necessarily be untrue, nor need its sponsors be either dishonest or animated by selfish or anti-social motives. The hallmark of propaganda is the effort to make biased, prejudiced, interested statements appear completely factual and objective.

propagation. (1) Multiplying by generation. (2) Spreading or disseminating something, such as an idea. R.E.B.

propagation, social. Cf. social propagation.

property. Any valuable right or interest, considered primarily as a source or element of wealth. A thing to which a person has legal title, especially land or buildings, but also goods, money, and intangible rights. The right to exclusive possession of an object which carries with it the right to enjoy or to dispose of the object possessed. Cf. ownership. J.W.M'C.

property, community. Cf. community property.

prophecy. The activity of religious prophets (q.v.) found in various religious traditions, particularly in Israel, and exerting various degrees of social influence. In its early manifestations it resembles closely the practice of seers, ecstatics, soothsayers, and diviners, and relies upon divers magical manipulations for the solution of particular problems and predictions of the future. E.F.

prophet. One who speaks by inspiration for another, especially for a God. A seer. One who foretells future events. L.P.E.

prophylaxis social. Cf. social prophylaxis.

propitiate. To use gift offerings, including even human sacrifice, prayers or ceremonials, thought to be pleasing to the deities which man believed inhabited the abode of the gods, as a technique of dealing successfully with them. In order to get the help of ghosts, spirits and deities, and to avoid the harm they might do him, man invented ways of pleasing them. The avoidance of certain other acts thought to be displeasing to them constituted a large part of taboo (q.v.). F.D.W.

proportional representation. A system of voting in which electors specify more than one choice among candidates for each office, and minority groups (q.v.) are guaranteed representation if they fulfill certain minimum requirements as to size of vote. S.C.M.

proportional sampling. Cf. sampling, proportional.

proportional taxation. Cf. taxation, proportional.

prosecutor. A public official, representative of the national, state, county or municipal government in criminal cases in courts of record, having broad powers, as determined in the United States by the statutes of the Federal Government or of the several states, including the issuing of warrants, making investigations, securing and assembling evidence, examining witnesses, participation in preliminary hearings, summoning of grand jury, drawing indictments, disposing of cases before trial, presenting the State's case to the trial jury, advising with judge on disposition of cases after verdict of guilt, and so on for other related duties. Besides these functions in relation to criminal procedure, in some states prosecutors have many responsibilities in civil cases. The term is also sometimes applied to a prosecuting witness. A.E.W.

proslavery. A term prevalent in the antebellum period of American history to designate those groups and individuals throughout the United States who actively favored the perpetuation of the institution of chattel slavery. K.DP.L.

prospective prediction. Cf. prediction, sociological.

prostitution. The sale of sexual services usually engaged in by women. However, there are male prostitutes, although rare. The services rendered by prostitutes are many, ranging from the normal coitus to very special perversions. Ordinarily prostitution is a transaction of strangers and in this sense is bartered promiscuity or bartered vice. The prostitute may operate as an independent solicitor, may be available on call, or accessible in a house of prostitution or brothel along with other prostitutes. In some eastern countries, prostitution is institutionalized. In western lands, it is either tolerated as a part of police policy or has illegal status, surviving because of lack of law enforcement.   W.C.R.

protective custody. Cf. custody, protective.

protective detention. Cf. detention, protective.

protectorate. A tribe, nation, or other political unit in which internal authority is exercised by hereditary or other internally determined authorities, while foreign relations and external military protection are controlled by a more powerful protecting power.   G.M.F.

Protestantism. The religious movement within Christianity which originated in the early sixteenth century under the leadership of Luther, Calvin, Zwingli and Knox and gave rise to the many denominations and churches known as reformed, evangelical and state churches. Primarily it was an effort to substitute the authority of the Bible for that of the Roman Church, and the autonomy of the individual believer without the mediation of a priest. Secondarily, it was a phase of the political struggle accompanying the dissolution of the Roman Empire, and of the assertion of the rights of non-military, non-aristocratic classes against the feudal system.   G.M.F.

protocracy. A theoretical social and political system in which authority and power are exercised by the most competent citizens, regardless of their social status, as contrasted with a society dominated by a hereditary aristocracy or monarchy, on the one hand, or with a democracy ruled by a mixture of competent and incompetent officials, on the other.   G.M.F.

protoplasm, social. Cf. social protoplasm.

province. The characteristic dependency of an empire (q.v.), distinguished from a colony (q.v.) by the degree and character of political subordination, and the preponderance of the native population both numerically and in the localized societal pattern.

provincialism. A backward, rural or hinterland state of mind. The opposite of cosmopolitanism. A provincialism is an expression of opinion or behavior reflecting a background of isolated experience. It may be characteristic of city dwellers as well as rural people.   N.A.

provision, social. Cf. social provision.

psychiatric social work. Cf. social work, psychiatric.

psychiatry. The branch of medicine dealing with the study and treatment of mental disorders.   S.C.M.

psychic force. Cf. force, psychic.

psychoanalysis. A school of psychology specializing in the clinical treatment of individuals with neurotic tendencies. It is based on the theory that many of our desires, especially those involving sex, are subconsciously repressed early in our lives, and can be dealt with only by bringing them out into the open through such methods as free association and dream-analysis.   S.C.M.

psychological crowd. Cf. crowd, psychological.

psychological repression. Cf. repression, psychological.

psychological sociology. Cf. sociology pschological.

psychology. Systematic knowledge of psychic phenomena, including what is called, sensation, perception, imagination, memory, thought, judgment, voluntary behavior, the self, beliefs, attitudes, desires and the like. Psychology also deals with relationships between psychic and non-psychic phenomena.   M.S.

psychology, collective. The part of social psychology dealing with collective behavior (q.v.).   M.S.

psychology, gestalt. The school of psychology whose most important concept is the gestalt. The gestalt is considered to be the unit of observation or study and to be incapable of subdivision. Every conscious process is considered to be a gestalt. Each important concept of traditional psychology is said to be capable of restatement so as to be articulated into the resulting psychological system. Field Theory is an offshoot of gestalt, as in Topological Psychology.   M.S.

psychology, social. Cf. social psychology.

psychoneurosis. A mental disorder in which functional factors, those without known organic basis, seem to predominate. Thus defined the term is approximately synonymous with neurosis. Neither psychoneurosis nor neurosis, as usually defined, is entirely distinct from psychosis.   M.S.

psychopathic offender. Cf. pathological criminal.

psychopathy. (1) Any specific mental disorder of a minor character. Sometimes synonymous with mild psychosis. Thus defined the term is of little value. (2) Serious emotional instability without clear mental derangement. Mental functions remain intact, but capacity for social adjustment is generally impaired by the emotional instability. This is the preferred definition.   M.S.

psychosis. (1) A relatively severe mental disease, involving a loss or disorder in mental processes. So defined, the term remains vague and indefinite, and has little value. (2) Any specific mental state, conscious experience or mental condition at any given moment.   M.S.

psychosis, prison. Cf. prison psychosis.

psycho-social. That which is constituted partly of psychic and partly of social phenomena.   M.S.

psycho-social control. Regulation of behavior of individuals or groups by devices of a psychological or sociological nature as contrasted with regulation by physical force or violence.   P.H.L.

puberty. The period of life at which a person attains the biological maturity necessary for reproduction.   E.A.H.

puberty rites. Rites, puberty.

public. (1) Subject to examination by relative strangers, people other than intimates; opposed to private. (2) A public: A group that includes individuals outside the intimate family circle. A social area of communication that may be defined by any common non-familial group-making interest or interests; on matters outside of such common interests, it need not achieve unanimity of sentiment or opinion. Thus, in many respects, a public is a social area of interaction. (3) The public: A protean conception that refers to people generally or to the people living in some geographical area. A common catchword in political and economic struggle and competition. Cf. group; class.
   A.M′C.L.

public assistance. The process of providing public relief or the organization responsible for this activity.   W.P.

public consciousness. Cf. consciousness, public.

public defender. Cf. defender, public.

public enemy. A term used by some officers of law enforcement to describe a dangerous criminal.   N.S.H.

public health. A term used to describe (1) the condition of health of the masses of a population; or (2) a type of social organization; or (3) a social reform movement within the medical profession. Thus we speak of our improving level of public health as measured by a declining death rate from certain specific diseases. The state or condition of public health is often measured by death rates, morbidity rates, by the extent and quality of sanitary and preventive measures for guarding the health of the masses. Trends in rates are often indicative of alterations in the state or condition of public health and suggest needed control measures or new emphases in control measures. Public health as a form of social organization is somewhat distinct from private medicine of the traditional, historic sort. Initially concerned with the public control of infectious diseases (for which work private physicians were inadequately organized), its domain has gradually widened to include a broad program of prevention. Although private medicine naturally influences the health of the general public, public health as a social organization is mainly centered in governmental agencies, federal, state, local—to some extent there is international organization—supplemented also by the research, community demonstrations, and financial aid of private charitable foundations. As a social movement, the public health movement aims, like socialized medicine (q.v.), to fill in some of the gaps left by the inadequacies of private medicine as it functions within the framework of modern capitalism. For example, contemporary private physicians spend a very small proportion of their time in group activities calculated to prevent disease and morbidity. Most of their work is limited to direct and personal relations with private patients; and perhaps healing rather than prevention receives the emphasis; whereas in public health medicine the stress is exactly reversed. It works mainly through and for groups, is governmental rather than private, and emphasizes preventive, long-run measures. It is not essentially, therefore, in conflict with private medicine but should be considered as supplementary—as filling a gap that socially needs filling. Only where areas of function overlap is conflict reasonably to be expected.   N.E.H.

public health nurse. A graduate nurse with special postgraduate education employed by an organized community agency, either public or private, to render service to the individual, family and community. Her service includes the interpretation and application of medical, sanitary and social procedures for the promotion of health, the prevention of disease, and the correction of defects; the participation in community education for the promotion of an adequate health program; and may include the skilled care of the sick in their homes.

public interest. Cf. interest, public.

public opinion. Cf. opinion, public.

public recreation. Cf. recreation, public.

public relations. Cf. relations, public.

public relations counselor. Specialist in public relations. Specifically, an expert in (a) analyzing public relations malad-

justments, (b) locating probable causes of such maladjustments in the social behavior of the client and in the sentiments and opinions of publics, and (c) advising the client on suitable corrective measures. The latter requires "bedside" techniques as delicate and complex as those utilized by the psychiatrist in many cases. The public relations counselor has a field of competence that overlaps somewhat those of press agents, public opinion analysts, lobbyists, organizational experts, etc., and requires him to be in a broad sense a societal technician, proficient in the application of scientific social theories and tested publicity techniques.   A.M'C.L.

public sentiment. Cf. sentiment, public.

public service. Cf. service, public.

public spirit. Interest in community welfare, joined with a willingness to serve it, to work for the public interest. Cf. public interest.   A.M'C.L.

public utility. An economic service which is so closely related to the basic needs of all members of society as to demand special governmental interest and perhaps regulation or control. Conspicuous examples have to do with transportation, such as trolley lines, bus lines, and railroads; with communication, such as telephones, telegraphs, and radio; or with vital human needs, such as water, light, and heat. Public utilities may be privately or publicly owned, but are by nature subject to special community control. In their commonest development in the United States they are municipal in scope, but the general tendency of social change is to extend both the scope and the variety of services included in this category.

public utility society. Cf. society, public utility.

public welfare. Cf. welfare, public.

public works. As distinct from public service, which is another type of public work by agencies of government, public works include construction projects of one type or another; roads, buildings, water and sewer systems, airports and airway facilities, docks, canals. Within the embrace of public works is included those activities incidental to the construction of such facilities or their repair and improvement. Their maintenance and operation is public service.   N.A.

publicist. (1) A writer or other expert on public affairs, with special reference to domestic and international political situations and theories. (2) A press agent. (3) A specialist in public relations. A.M'C.L.

publicity. Data made available to common knowledge, given public circulation. The dissemination of information through any of the channels of mass-communication. In simpler societies and in neighborhoods, the media are gossip, public announcements, etc. In larger and more complex societies, the media include also newspapers, radio broadcasting stations, billboards, etc. These channels are available through advertising and "free publicity," i.e., paid and free announcements.
    A.M'C.L.

publicity and interpretation in social work. The process of informing the public—contributors and clients—about the objectives and programs of social work agencies. w.p.

pueblo. A large, flat-roofed, communal dwelling of the sedentary Indians of Arizona and New Mexico, constructed of stone or adobe in several stories or terraces, and entered by ascending a ladder and descending through a trapdoor in the roof; also a village composed of such dwellings.   G.P.M.

punishment, capital. The use of the death penalty as punishment for crime. From an estimated 240 crimes punishable by death in the 18th century in England the number has been reduced to three: murder, treason, and interstate kidnapping. At present there are six states in the United States which have abolished the death penalty as punishment for crime, although nine other states have abolished it and since reinstated it. The effectiveness of capital punishment as a deterrent to crime has long been a subject of controversy and in addition humanitarian arguments against the use of the death penalty have carried great weight. Never-

theless, the trend toward the abolition of the death penalty seems to have been reversed in recent years.   J.W.M'C.

In the United States the general methods of execution are by electrocution or hanging. Nevada executes through lethal gas. The chief offense in the United States punishable by execution is premeditated murder. In a few jurisdictions rape, robbery or burglary are still treated as capital offenses. Treason is also a capital offense. Cf. crime, capital.   N.F.C.

punishment, corporal. Bodily pain or suffering inflicted as punishment for crime. Cf. poetic punishment.   M.A.E.

punishment, individualization of. Corrective treatment of the offender based upon an analysis of the interrelated factors in the background and personality which have led to his conflict with the law. Such treatment is "making the punishment fit the offender," rather than "making the punishment fit the crime."
    M.A.E.

punishment, infamous. Punishment for what is held by society at a given time to be an infamous crime. The United States Supreme Court has decided that death, or imprisonment in a state prison for a term of years at hard labor, especially for treason or felony are infamous punishments (114 U. S., 417, 426, 429), and later that disqualification for office as a punishment for crime is infamous (112 U. S. 76).   J.L.G.

punishment, mitigation of. The reduction in severity of a sentence regularly imposed for an offense, because of some special personal aspects of, or surrounding circumstances in, the case.   N.F.C.

punishment, poetic. A punishment adapted to the particular crime committed, e.g., cutting off the hand of a thief, tearing out or piercing the tongue of a false witness, emasculating the rapist, parading a fishmonger who had sold spoiled fish with a string of rotten smelts around his neck.
    J.L.G.

purification rites. Cf. rites, purification.

Puritanism. The doctrines, ideas or practices of the Puritans. Adherence to, or advocacy of, a stricter code of behavior than the one usually prevailing; especially along pleasure, moral or religious lines.

       o.w.

purpose. Cf. value.

purposive sampling. Cf. sampling, purposive.

pyknic physique. Cf. physique, pyknic.

Q

quasi-legal patterns. Cf. patterns, quasi-legal.

questionnaire. A form or schedule used for collecting data from the population. It usually refers to forms submitted by mail or filled out by the informant without the assistance of an interviewer. M.Pt.

R

race. A biological subdivision, based upon similarity of ancestry and consequent physical kinship. A variety of a species. The ideal race is a group of organisms all descended from a single ancestor, or pair of ancestors, without the introduction of any external germ plasm during the entire series of generations. Carried to its extreme, according to this definition any particular family is a race. This concept, while a reductio ad absurdum, is nevertheless useful in formulating an accurate and workable notion of race as applied to human beings. Accepting the general evolutionary theory, the whole mass of mankind is a race—the human race—descended, not probably from any single pair of individuals, but from a small group of creatures whose evolution had proceeded far enough along certain lines to justify calling them men. This original race of men, by a long process of dispersion, became localized in separate broad areas of the earth's surface. Thus were constituted the basic races of mankind, ordinarily subdivided into three or five categories.

The question whether this primary subdivision into localized groups took place after a particular branch of the animal kingdom had evolved far enough to be called man, or before, underlies the controversy concerning the monogenetic or polygenetic origin of the human species. If the early pre-human stock broke up into two, three, or more subdivisions while it was still so unspecialized that it could not be called human, then the human species may be said to have had a corresponding number of separate origins. If, on the contrary, biological evolution had proceeded to the point where humanity definitely existed before this primary separation took place, then the monogenetic theory holds good. The problem, while of

much theoretical interest, has no particular bearing on modern affairs.

If, after this original separation, each of these basic groups had remained completely isolated and segregated from all of the others, so that there had been no interchange of germ plasm, then all the contemporary descendants of each of these groups would constitute a pure race, on this primary level. But actually, each of these basic groups proceeded to undergo a similar subdivision and relocation. Once more, if each of these subdivided groups had reproduced solely from within itself there would have been created other pure races on a lower level.

The abstract concept of race, as a biological entity, is therefore perfectly simple. The essence of race is closeness of kinship and unity of ancestry through strictly biological continuity. The development of any particular race in its area of characterization (q.v.), involving factors of adaptation to the physical environment, inbreeding, and possible sexual selection, has occasioned the development on the part of each such group of distinctive hereditary physical traits. These traits have come to be regarded as race criteria, and as the identifying marks of race. Since it is always impossible to trace the actual ancestry of any human individual back more than a few generations the genuine racial affiliation of such an individual cannot be determined genealogically. The practice has therefore arisen of determining racial affiliation by examination of the traits of the individual, and assigning him to a particular racial group on the basis of these traits. As a result of this procedure there has arisen the common notion that an individual belongs to a particular race because he has certain traits. The truth is that he has certain traits because he belongs to a particular race. An illustration of this principle, and of the corresponding fallacy, is found in the case of the so-called Mongolian idiot. On the basis of the traits alone such an individual might easily be assigned to the Mongolian race. The facts of his ancestry show him clearly to be an aberrant specimen of whatever race his parents belong to.

Further confusions in the concept of race have arisen from the fact that human groups in isolation develop distinctive cultural traits along with their characteristic biological traits. In the eyes of early explorers and inexpert travelers these two types of traits are not easily distinguishable. As a consequence, a large variety of cultural features come to be spoken of in racial terms. The outstanding example, probably, is language. The developed form of this tendency is manifest in the common usage of the term race to apply to any group of people which has had a somewhat extended historical continuity, accompanied by geographical localization and social, political, and economic integration. This misinterpretation lies at the bottom of innumerable racial fallacies and practical confusions. Probably the outstanding single example is the exaltation of the Aryan race. There is no such thing as an Aryan race —Aryan is a strictly cultural designation. Cf. ethnos; nationality.

race antipathy. A feeling of alienation, ranging all the way from indifference to antagonism, arising out of the racial constitution of two or more different individuals or groups. A manifestation of consciousness of kind (q.v.), when the we-group and the they-group are differentiated on racial grounds. In actual experience, race antipathy is so intertwined with various other feelings and attitudes that it is exceedingly difficult to isolate and observe in detachment, and consequently the scientific understanding of it is extremely meager. Not to be confused with race prejudice (q.v.).

race conflict. Conflict between two groups of different race, motivated primarily by race consciousness (q.v.). Probably a rare phenomenon and difficult to identify, because true racial motives are almost invariably associated with, and to some extent obscured by, other group feelings.

race consciousness. Awareness of affiliation with a particular racial group and of differentiation from other racial groups, ordinarily combined with sentiments of race superiority and race interests.

race contact. Political, economic and social interrelations between members of different racial groups.   E.E.M.

race feeling. Cf. feeling, race.

race mixture. The fusing or blending of races through offspring resulting from sex relations between persons of different race groups. Cf. amalgamation.   E.E.M.

race prejudice. An antipathetical attitude toward an individual or a group predicated upon traits or characteristics which are, or are erroneously believed to be, racial in origin, but without any adequate foundation in fact or experiential acquaintance. A common form of stereotype response (q.v.). To be carefully distinguished from race antipathy (q.v.).

race relations. Cultural contacts between people of different races, involving different degrees of prejudice and conflict and often a condition of subordination-superordination, as well as the processes of toleration, accommodation, and possible assimilation.   R.E.B.

race suicide. Cf. suicide, race.

racial differences. Cf. differences, racial.

racialism. Cf. racism.

racism. The philosophy or doctrine which tends to stress the real, or alleged, features of race, and supports the use of them as grounds for group and inter-group action. This term can have no more exactness or scientific validity than the term race (q.v.) itself as used in any particular context. As a designation of a standardized philosophy or program it has no precision whatever.

racketeer. One who is able to extort money from a large number of individuals over periods of time by threats of physical violence, destruction of property, and threats to withhold or prevent delivery of essential services. Usually a racketeer is surrounded by an effective criminal organization ready to do his will although he may maintain a front of strict respectability. Beginning with bootlegging, racketeering has reached out to dominate many legitimate as well as illicit trades and occupations. It may be primarily a local activity or it may encompass the state or nation.   J.W.M'C.

radical. By derivation, concerned with the roots of things. In its sociological application, the term applies in general to those who believe in drastic measures for the improvement of social conditions, and in particular to those who believe in and/or advocate sweeping changes in the political and/or economic structure of society. The word has no precise connotation, and is commonly used, often opprobriously, to designate any individual or group whose views are measurably further to the "left" than those of the speaker.

radicalism. A viewpoint favoring drastic social change in the fundamental aspects of society. Derived from radix, root: hence, going to the root of a problem. In the political field, it is properly used to refer to such schools of thought as socialism and communism, which advocate a change in the class basis of society. It is often misused to refer also to extremist political groups of the right, whose aim is rather to preserve the basic relationships already existing in our society.   S.C.M.

radio. A technical medium of communication; the transmission and reception of signals and programs by electric ground or sky waves without connecting wires. More specifically, it is an instrument for the reception of programs broadcast over the air, commonly known as a receiver. Radio emerged as a significant culture trait when sound—music, human voice, and other sound effects—was added to telegraphic signals.   M.H.N.

ragged and industrial schools. A term first used in 1842 to apply to missionary schools established in Clerkenwell, England. The name attracted attention and became popular. A Ragged School Union was formed in 1844 with the seventh Earl of Shaftsbury as president. The aim

of the schools at first was to provide a broad religious and character building program for underprivileged and destitute children. As the movement expanded the schools also provided food, clothing and lodging to those who needed it. Industrial education was also added and the Ragged School movement thus constituted the origin of the Industrial Schools of Great Britain. When education was made free and compulsory by the First Education Act in 1870 these schools became less important though many were retained as supplementary social agencies. The ragged schools were regarded in their time as important instruments in the prevention of juvenile delinquency.   A.R.L.

"railroad" apartment. A type of apartment common in the older sections of some large cities consisting of five or even six rooms arranged in a straight line, one behind the other, from street to alley. Most of the rooms are windowless (except for air shafts). The term arose because of the similarity to a string of box cars. s.s.

ramage. A lineage (q.v.).

ranch. An establishment, with its estate, for the grazing and rearing of horses, cattle or sheep; especially the buildings occupied by owners and employees, with the adjacent barns, corrals, etc.; also, the persons on the estate collectively.   C.E.L.

random sampling. Cf. sampling, random.

range. That portion of a habitat (q.v.) which is actually occupied by a specified group. The emphasis here is upon geographical space, rather than upon environmental features.

rank. That form of status or position in a group which has reference to the degree of prestige or honor, power, or rights and privileges enjoyed, in comparison with the prestige, power, or rights and privileges of others in the same group.

rape. The carnal knowledge of a woman forcibly and against her will. At common law rape means the having of unlawful carnal knowledge of a female over the age of ten years, forcibly and against her will, or such knowledge of a female child under the age of ten years either

247

with or without her consent. In statutory rape the "age of consent" has been raised from ten years to an advanced period up to 18 years, the precise age when consent becomes legally possible varying among the states. Above the age of consent force and resistance are essential elements of the crime, while under the age of consent they are not.   A.E.W.

rapport. (1) A condition of mutual responsiveness between two or more people such that each is capable of responding immediately, sympathetically, and with apparent spontaneity to every other. (2) Relation between hypnotist and hypnotized person during hypnosis, characterized by apparent insensibility of the hypnotized person to all stimuli from sources other than the hypnotist.   M.S.

rat. An informer. A member of the underworld who gives damaging information concerning another underworld character to the authorities. Also known as "fink," "snitch," or "stool pigeon."   A.R.L.

rate. A proportion, with a time element added. Ordinarily, the relationship between a significant variable and some arbitrarily fixed base within a defined spatial area and some conventional time period.

rate, birth. The number of births in a given population per unit of time and population. Although sometimes used in connection with various indices of human fertility, the term, unless otherwise specified, is generally synonymous with "crude birth rate," which expresses for a given population the number of live births during one year per 1,000 persons alive at the middle of the year (or per 1,000 living persons in the average population for the year).

Live Births During Year x 1,000
———————————————————
Mid-Year (or Average) Population

Cf. fertility rate; reproduction, gross and net rate of.   C.V.K.

rate, crime. A measure of the recorded criminality of given geographical areas or population groups expressed in numbers proportionate to a population unit. Such rates may be crude (per 100,000 population), refined (per 100,000 persons

capable of committing a crime), or specific (e.g., per 100,000 native-born males, 21-30 years of age). No generally accepted terminology to distinguish different types of rates exists. The unit of "crime" or "criminality" employed in computing these rates varies. Cf. crime index; criminal statistics.   T.S.

rate, crude, of natural increase. The excess of the crude birth rate over the crude death rate of a given population. The term thus conventionally expresses for a given population the excess of births over deaths during one year, per 1,000 persons alive at the middle of the year. The reverse condition resulting from a higher crude death rate than crude birth rate is a crude rate of natural decrease, but is frequently entered in tabular material as a negative (-) rate of natural increase.
                                   C.V.K.

rate, death. The number of deaths in a given area or population per unit of time and population. Examples: crude death rate, the number of deaths from all causes during one year per 1,000 persons alive at the middle of the year (or per 1,000 living persons in the average population for the year),

All Deaths During Year x 1,000
———————————————————
Mid-Year (or Average) Population

Age-specific death rate; death rate among individuals of specific age or ages,

Deaths During Year at Specific Age x 1,000
———————————————————————
Mid-Year (or Average) Population at
Specific Age

death rate from specific causes, death rate (all ages or age-specific) for individual causes or groups of causes of death,

Deaths From Specific Causes During Year
(All Ages or Specific Age) x 100,000
————————————————————————
Mid-Year (or Average) Population
(All Ages or Specific Age)

standardized death rate, the average of age-specific death rates weighted according to the proportionate importance of successive age groups in a population taken as a standard. Note: The word "mortality" (q.v.) is interchangeable with the word "death" in all above types of rates.   C.V.K.

rate, divorce. The ratio between the number of divorces, within a given area and a time period, and some specified base. The problem of determining the correct, or most useful, base is difficult, and has never been adequately solved. Logically, the most significant and useful base would be the total number of marriages. The proportion of all marriages that end in divorce in a given country is what most people are really interested in. But the difficulty of establishing a time factor, and even a spatial factor, in the use of this base is practically insuperable, particularly because the accumulation of comprehensive data would extend over a long period of years. Most logarithmic rates are computed on the basis of the calendar year. In keeping with this procedure, other bases for the divorce rate which have been suggested are (1) the total population estimated as of the midyear, (2) the estimated number of married couples, (3) population fifteen years old and over, (4) the number of marriages performed in a year. Until more standard procedure has been attained by specialists in this field, the term can be considered as precise only when its specific application is made clear in the context.

rate, fertility. A measure or index of birth performance or reproduction of a species. In a generic sense, all indices of fertility are "fertility rates." In technical usage, however, students of population apply this term, with proper adjective or description, to indices in which fertility is expressed in relation to a given number of women, or married women of childbearing age. Examples: general fertility rate, the number of live births during one year per 1,000 females of childbearing age (often 15-44); marital fertility rate, the number of legitimate live births during one year per 1,000 wives of childbearing age; age-specific fertility rate (general or marital), the number of live births during one year per 1,000 females (or wives) of specific age; standardized fertility rate (general or marital), the average of age-specific fertility rates weighted according to the proportionate importance of successive age groups in a population taken as a standard; ratio of children under 5 to women (or married

women) of childbearing age, as usually expressed, the number of enumerated living children 0-4 years of age per 1,000 enumerated females (or married women) 15-44 years of age; cumulative fertility rate, total number of past live births per 100 wives among a group of married women under consideration. (For a time-control this rate should be expressed in age-specific form, or standardized for age if a summary figure for wives of childbearing age is desired.) Data on total number of children ever born to wives of completed fertility (45-49, 45+, etc.) are also frequently used for computation of proportions childless and proportions with given fertilities in completed families. For other indices of human fertility, Cf. birth rate; reproduction, gross rate of; reproduction, net rate of.   C.V.K.

rate, gross, of reproduction. The average number of daughters that would be borne per woman among a cohort of females starting life together and surviving the childbearing period, if, as they pass through successive ages of the childbearing span, they are subjected to a given schedule of age-specific fertility rates. Thus, if 1,000 newly-born females all live throughout the childbearing period and give birth to 860 daughters, the gross reproduction rate is 0.86 (per woman). The assumption of universal survival of all in the cohort throughout the childbearing period differentiates the gross reproduction rate from the net reproduction rate and affords a device for measuring the implicit ratio of fertility in two successive generations, apart from the influence of mortality. Although not generally computed in such detail, the gross reproduction rate for a given population and year is equivalent to the sum of the average number of daughters born during the year per female of each successive age within the childbearing span. In practice, if the basic data are in the form of five-year age groups, and relate to births rather than to daughters during the year considered, the sum of the observed age-specific fertilities is multiplied by 5 and then reduced on the basis of a reasonable sex-ratio at birth. Various indirect methods have also been devised for computing reproduction rates from census data concerning numbers of children under 5 and females of childbearing age. Cf. reproduction, net rate of. C.V.K.

rate, net, of reproduction. The average number of daughters that would be borne per female among a cohort of females starting life together and subjected to given schedules of age-specific fertility and mortality rates. Thus, if the survivors of 1,000 newly-born females give birth to 750 daughters, the net reproduction rate is 0.75 (the average number of daughters per female in the original cohort). The net reproduction rate is differentiated from the gross in that it makes allowance for age-specific mortalities of females from birth to the end of the childbearing period. With the exception of this additional step, the gross and net rates of reproduction are similar in concept and in method of computation. Cf. reproduction, **gross rate of. The net** reproduction rate may also be described as an index of the "self-replacement" potentiality of a population with given age-specific rates of fertility and mortality. Thus, a net reproduction rate of 0.75 is 25 per cent below the requirements for "self-replacement" of the population on a permanent basis. With a net reproduction rate of 1.0 a population is said to be exactly reproducing itself on a permanent basis. C.V.K.

rate, true (intrinsic), of natural increase. The rate of natural increase that would ultimately obtain within a population if a given schedule of age-specific fertility and mortality rates continued in operation and if the population remained a closed one in so far as the influences of migration are concerned. The true or intrinsic rate of natural increase is, therefore, one implicit in the age-specific fertility and mortality rates and one that would be yielded in a "closed" population with an age-specific fertility and mortality. The true rate of natural increase computed for a current population thus serves to remove the influence of abnormalities in the age structure arising from migration and from fertility and mortality trends of the past. C.V.K.

rating scale. A device permitting individuals called raters or judges to give quantitative expression to their judgments of the magnitude of a variable. P.H.F.

ratio. The relation between two similar magnitudes expressed as the quotient of one divided by the other; often a convenient method of expressing facts in the social sciences, as, the ratio between males and females in the population. P.H.F.

ratio, man-land. Cf. man-land ratio.

ratio, Mendelian. Cf. Mendelian ratio.

rational selection. Cf. selection, rational.

rationalization. Assignment of socially acceptable reasons for one's conduct where giving the real reasons would result in less social approval or in social disapproval. This is an often subconscious process, indulged in to keep oneself from recognizing one's own shortcomings. S.C.M.

reaction. (1) A typical, standardized, essentially spontaneous or automatic response to a (usually external) stimulus. (2) Action of one body designed to offset or neutralize action on the part of another body. In social relations, specifically the attitude and/or activity which seeks to oppose change and restore or maintain the status quo. Cf. reactionary.

reaction, circular. (1) In psychology, a process in which the last action of a series functions as a stimulus to the repetition of the entire process. (2) In sociology, a form of social action in which the overt actions of one or more organisms stimulate others whose responses become, in turn, additional stimuli to further actions by the original agents. The actions may be of any sort. M.S.

reactionary. A person, movement, sentiment or epoch which seeks to counteract or undo the progressive forces and trends of a period, thus favoring the return to a bygone order. In this sense, reactionary expresses a negative attitude as measured by the progressive tendencies—an evaluation which may or may not conform to its objective qualifications. Specific periods in modern history, such as the decades following the age of the French Revolution and the Prussian development between 1850 and 1858, have been generally called periods of reaction. Cf. liberal; radical. **S.N.**

realism. The philosophical theory that objects of human cognition actually exist as opposed to nominalism and subjective idealism. In science, literature and social movements it is opposed to idealism, subjectivism, and romanticism, and is assumed to be a depiction of the facts or of phenomena as they really are. **M.PM.**

reality. Degree of permanence of meaningfulness discovered in any given experience, or attributed to any object, person, memory, idea, value, symbol, or even "illusion". Contrasted with actuality (q.v.), which is objective existence verifiable by other observers using similar and other instruments and getting consistent results. **T.D.E.**

reality, social. Cf. social reality.

realization self-. The balanced development of the human personality. This term should be contrasted on the one hand with self-expression which connotes various degrees of unconventionality, including libertinism; and on the other hand, with self-repression, which signifies varying degrees of self-denial, including asceticism. Self-realization implies an acceptance of the various parts of the personality which are blended into a balanced whole in which no part dominates. **F.D.W.**

rear building. A separate structure on the same lot with a front building but not attached to it; a rear building may share a wall or walls with other rear buildings. Access to it is either from a narrow alley or, in some cases, through the front building from the main street. **S.S.**

recapitulation. A summary conclusion, a review in brief of the essential items of a presentation. It may also describe a gathering of forces for a final showing or final effort. **N.A.**

receiver of stolen goods. One who buys or handles goods known by him to be stolen. When the receiver makes a business of handling such goods he may be spoken of as a "fence". **A.R.L.**

receiving prisons. Cf. prisons, receiving.

recessive. Tending to recede or go back; failing to come to expression. In biology, said of an inheritable trait which does not appear in the offspring because it has been inhibited by a dominant contrasting trait inherited from the other parent. **H.E.J.**

recidivism. The repetition or recurrence of delinquent or criminal conduct. **M.A.E.**

reciprocal action. Cf. action, reciprocal.

reciprocal behavior. Cf. behavior, reciprocal.

reciprocal interaction. Cf. interaction, reciprocal.

reciprocal modification. Cf. modification, reciprocal.

reciprocity. (1) In sociology, the mutual action and reaction between persons participating in social relations; a state of social interaction in which the act or movement of one person evokes a corresponding act or movement in some other person or persons. (2) In law, equality of privileges between citizens of different governments or states to the extent established by treaty or other legal agreement. **H.E.J.**
(3) The use of the same kinship term for another by two relatives of different categories, especially if they belong to different generations. **G.P.M.**

reclamation, slum. Cf. slum reclamation.

reconstruction, social. Cf. social reconstruction.

recreation. Any activity pursued during leisure, either individual or collective, that is free and pleasureful, having its own immediate appeal, not impelled by a delayed reward beyond itself or by any immediate necessity. Recreation includes play, games, sports, athletics, relaxation, pastimes, certain amusements, art forms, hobbies, and avocations. A recreational activity may be engaged in during any age period of the individual, the particular action being determined by the time element, the condition and attitude of the person, and the environmental situation. A person pursues a recreational activity because he chooses to do so without compulsion other than inner drives—interest, enthusiasm, absorbing attention, enjoyment, and the satisfaction of wishes. Originally recreation meant a more deliberate form of re-creative activity, engaged in chiefly by adults, following exhaustive effort. Cf. play.   M.H.N.

recreation, commercial. A pleasurable activity, or amusement provided for spectators, organized for profit. A commercial recreational enterprise is an organization for profit to provide pleasurable activities or amusements, or to deal in commodities required in leisure. A commercial amusement has reference to a relatively passive entertainment provided for spectators, as contrasted with active recreation.   M.H.N.

recreation, community. Cf. community recreation.

recreation, cultural. Cf. cultural recreation.

recreation, public. Governmental provision of facilities, leadership, and programs of recreative leisure activities. Tax supported playgrounds, parks, beaches, resorts, etc.   M.H.N.

recreation, social. Cf. social recreation.

recreation center. A place where play, entertainment, and other leisure activities are provided.   M.H.N.

recreation leadership. The direction, supervision, organization, and promotion of play and other activities pursued during leisure. Instruction and guidance in spending free time.   M.H.N.

recreation movement. A series of collective efforts intended to provide for a large number of people wholesome and enjoyable activities pursued during leisure, usually occasioned by an unsatisfactory social situation, involving stages and transitions in its development, and moving toward more or less clearly defined objectives or common goals.   M.H.N.

redintegration. Literally, reintegration: the act of reproducing a pattern of behavior acquired unconsciously in the interactional process; often mistaken for imitation. Examples: the acquisition of a peculiar accent, some mannerism, or idea; much so-called plagiarism may be nothing more than redintegration. Cf. imitation.
                                              W.E.G.

reference, frame of. Cf. frame of reference.

referendum. A vote of the people on a law or constitutional amendment enacted by a state legislature; in cities, on an ordinance or charter amendment. Similarly in private organizations, a vote of the membership on a proposal submitted by the elected governing committee or officers.   R.N.B.

reflex. A native, involuntary, and relatively invariable form of response of a specific muscle group, e.g., eyelid reflex, knee-jerk or patellar reflex.   M.Pt.

reflex, conditioned. Cf. conditioned reflex.

reflex, prepotent. Certain coordination of reflexes, such as starting and withdrawing, rejecting, struggling, hunger, sensitive zone, and sex reactions, either present at birth or involving later maturation of receptors and effectors. They are of the highest importance for the survival and welfare of both the individual and the species. They provide the innate sources of human behavior, and determine the subsequent acquisition of knowledge and skill through the process of conditioning. The concept has been developed by some psychologists as an alternative to the older term instinct which, they felt, laid too great stress upon the determination of human behavior by inherited biological factors, and failed to give adequate recognition to the rôle of learning and social experience in the explanation of both individual and social activities.   H.E.J.

reform. Improvement in a particular social pattern with especial emphasis upon function rather than upon structure. Reform movements, strictly so called, aim to alleviate distress and to correct maladjustments without attempting to alter the basic plan of society itself.

reform, social. Cf. social reform.

reformatory. (1) An institution originally designed to rehabilitate the younger adult and post-juvenile offenders. In general, such institutions receive those convicted of first offenses who range between the ages of 16 and 30 (some institutions place the maximum age much lower). Ideally the reformatory purports to offer educational and vocational training while serving an indeterminate sentence. All persons sentenced to reformatories are eligible for parole. Today, most features of the reformatory have been adopted by our prisons, hence most reformatories differ little from prisons except in the age and experience of the inmates. In fact, reformatories today are often characterized as "junior prisons." (2) The institutions to which women are sentenced are frequently termed reformatories irrespective of any age or offense classification.
M.A.E.

reformism. The advocacy of social change by gradual, piecemeal improvements, of a nature to preserve and fortify the status quo. (Not synonymous with reform.)
K.DP.L.

refuge, city of. Cf. city of refuge.

refuge, house of. Cf. house of refuge.

regalia. Emblems or symbols of kingship; hence insignia (q.v.) in general.   G.P.M.

regeneration. (*theological*) Spiritual rebirth, conversion, shift to a new focus within the personality; (*social control*) a policy (or a technique) of regeneration" in social telesis (q.v.) is contrasted with a "policy of structural reform": the former is based upon an assumption that a given system will work if the participants' (especially the leaders') "hearts" or characters are right, while the latter assumes that people will respond rightly or wrongly according to the structural stimuli and channels provided by constitutions, laws, organizations, systems, etc.   T.D.E.

regimentation. The organization of people through doctrinaire teaching and discipline, perhaps for the conscious purpose of developing uniformity in behavior and stereotyped sterility in thought. While this may not be the conscious objective of all training regimentation may result from much of it, especially in large standardized school systems.   N.A.

region, the. A measure of areal and cultural differentiation of human society, delineated in scientific units of observation of likenesses and differences. The region is essentially a measure of homogeneity as a delineated composite unit in some total society. It provides an areal laboratory adequate to comprehend all factors involved, historical, evolutionary, and spatial, and small enough for exhaustive inquiry. The specific nature and traits of a region are determined by the nature of the indices of homogeneity utilized. The region may be characterized by major attributes somewhat as follows: Beginning with the elemental factor of space, the region is, of course, first of all an area, a geographic unit with limits and bounds. Yet, in the second place, the region differs from the mere locality or pure geographic area in that it is characterized not so much by boundary lines and actual limits as it is by flexibility of limits, by extension from a center, and by fringe or border margins which separate one area from another. The third attribute of the region is some degree of homogeneity in a number of selected characteristics. The definitive nature of the region and the aspects of its homogeneity will be determined by the fourth attribute of the region, namely, some structural or functional aspect or aspects through which the region is to be dominated. Yet there must be a limit to the multiplicity of regions, so that in general a fifth attribute must be found in the relative, composite homogeneity of the largest number of factors for the largest number of purposes in view, to the end that the region may be a practical, workable unit susceptible of both definition and utilization. A sixth attribute of the region is, therefore, that it must be a constituent unit in an aggregate whole or totality. Inherent in the region as opposed to the mere locality or the isolated section is the essence of unity of which it can exist only as a part. A seventh attribute is found in the organic nature of the region. A region has organic unity not only in its natural landscape, but in that cultural evolution in which the age-long quartette of elements are at work—namely, the land and the people, culturally conditioned through time and special relationships. The sociologist's region is differentiated from what is ordinarily described as a natural region, determined by geological factors climatic factors, and geographic factors.   H.W.O.

regional planning. Social planning based particularly upon the concept of the region. A localized type of planning which recognizes the region as a significant and identifiable social unit, and attempts to integrate the life of a particular region with respect to certain accepted values, without any implication of isolation or antagonism between it and the larger society.   H.W.O.

regionalism. The study of the regional societies as component and constituent units of total society and in the consequent programs of regional balance and interaction processes. This application of regionalism may be made with equal scientific accuracy to a total national or continental society with its delineated regions and the synthesis of their culture into the total integrated society or to world society, with its regional delineations and programs for regional world planning. Regionalism, therefore, is essentially the opposite of localism, separatism, provincialism, and sectionalism. More specifically, regionalism is a tool for both research and planning and provides the folk-regional laboratory for the study of society in its historical and spatial setting. As a science of the region, it provides not only for exhaustive empirical studies, but for the analyses of regional, interregional, and intra-regional processes and their syntheses in sound theory. Regionalism as methodology takes concrete shape through its cultural, statistical approach in a comprehensive scientifically controlled principle capable of wide adaptation and utilization in the cooperation and coordination of the social sciences and of the physical sciences and social sciences working together. Regionalism has sometimes been defined as world ecology, in which

the total factors of time, spatial relations, and cultural gestalt are all comprehended in the total principle and methodology. Cf. folk regional-society; folk sociology; the region.   H.W.O.

registration area. Cf. area, registration.

regress. To move backwards in respect to some direction, norm, or value considered by the interested appraiser to be "progress"; (*psychiatric*) to revert to patterns of behavior characteristic of earlier life.
                                                 T.D.E

regression. A situation-process which is considered the opposite of "progress" (q.v.); (*psychiatric*) a mental-emotional process in which a person reverts to patterns of behavior analogous to those of some earlier period of life.   T.D.E.

regressive. Tending to regress, exerting effort against values or trends considered progressive; (*psychiatric*) symptomatic of or tending to facilitate reversion to behavior patterns of earlier periods of life.
                                                 T.D.E.

regressive taxation. Cf. taxation, regressive.

regular interval sampling. Cf. sampling, regular interval.

regulation, administrative. Cf. administrative regulation.

rehabilitate. To restore a person or thing to its original state or capacity, e.g., a slum area to a good residential area; a cripple to economic or social usefulness.
                                                 E.E.M.

rehabilitation. The process or technique of reeducating and redirecting the attitudes and motivations of the delinquent or criminal so as to bring his behavior into full harmony with the law and his own willing acceptance of social regulations and legal restrictions.   M.A.E.

rehabilitation, vocational. Cf. vocational rehabilitation.

reincarnation. The translation of the soul of a deceased person into another body, human or animal.   G.P.M.

rejected companion. Cf. companion, rejected.

relapse. A reversion to old habits of delinquent or criminal conduct following a seemingly satisfactory social adjustment.   M.A.E.

relation. Any connection between two or more individuals, two collectivities, or an individual and a collectivity. Such connection may be associative or dissociative, direct or indirect, immediate or remote, real or imaginary.   F.H.H.

relation, employer-employee. Cf. employer-employee relation.

relation, functional. A partially or completely dependent relation between two variables such that alteration of one will be accompanied by a corresponding alteration of the other. The dependent or altered variable is known as a function of the so-called independent or altering variable.   M.Pt.

relation, master-servant. Cf. master-servant relation.

relation, mistress-maid. Cf. mistress-maid relation.

relation, social. Cf. social relation.

relations, industrial. Cf. industrial relations.

relations, labor. Cf. labor relations.

relations, parental. Cf. parental relations.

relations, public. (1) Relations of an individual, association, government, or corporation with the publics which it must take into consideration in carrying on its social functions. These publics can include voters, customers, employees, potential employees, past employees, stockholders, members of antagonistic pressure groups, neighbors, etc. (2) The body of theory and technique utilized in adjusting the relationships of a subject with its publics. These theories and techniques represent applications of sociology, social psychology, economics, and political science as well as of the special skills of journalists,

artists, organizational experts, advertising men, etc., to the specific problems involved in this field of activity.   A.M'C.L.

relations, race. Cf. race relations.

relationship, avoidance. Cf. avoidance relationship.

relationship, joking. Cf. joking relationship.

relationship, social. Cf. social relationship.

relationship system. Cf. kinship system.

relativity. The state or condition of interdependence or reciprocal dependence; the probable accuracy of a trend or law which is stated within limits of truth.   H.A.P.

reliability, sampling. Cf. sampling reliability.

reliability of data. The consistency or constancy obtaining between data secured by repetition of the same measurements on the same individuals or phenomenon under identical or highly similar conditions. Not to be confused with validity of data.   M.Pt.

relief. Money or necessaries given people who are in need.   W.P.

relief, disaster. The assistance given to individuals, families and communities who have suffered from some form of group catastrophe.   W.P.

relief, home. Shelter, fuel, food, clothing, light, necessary household supplies, medical, dental and nursing care, etc., furnished by a municipal corporation, to persons or their dependents in their abode.   W.P.

relief, indoor. Public or private charity, generally of the kind made available to persons lodged in camps, poor houses or institutions rather than in their homes. Cf. outdoor relief.   N.A.

relief, institutional. Assistance given an individual through providing for him in some form of institution, i.e., home for the aged, hospital.   W.P.

relief, outdoor. Relief given individuals or families in their own homes. Cf. home relief.   W.P.

relief, poor. Relief provided for those whose chief problem is economic need. Home relief is the term used at present.
W.P.

relief, work. Various types of employment activity of community value provided for those who are unemployed and in need.
W.P.

relief-in-cash. A method of providing public assistance to needy families in cash in their own homes. The relief authorities estimate the needs of the family according to a general budget, and a check is sent covering these needs, but the family is free to spend the money anywhere and for whatever articles it sees fit. Only for gross mismanagement is the privilege of receiving cash replaced by relief-in-kind (q.v.). This plan of relief is supported by progressive social workers because of the greater independence it gives the relief client.   J.W.M'C.

relief-in-kind. A method of public assistance whereby the necessary food and clothing are provided for needy families either in their own homes or through a commissary. In the latter case orders for the necessary amount of goods are issued to the family to be surrendered when the goods are obtained. In this way no money is used. This plan of relief is based upon the theory that it is cheaper for the community and safer for the recipient since the relief authorities may determine the amount and kind of articles to be given and arrange for mass purchase and distribution.   J.W.M'C.

religion. The social institution built up around the idea of a supernatural being or beings, and the relation of human beings to them. In any particular culture this idea becomes formalized into a social pattern, or patterns. Such a pattern comes to be known as "the religion" of a particular group. Every true religion involves three major aspects. (1) A conception of the nature and character of divinity. (2) A set of doctrines concerning the reciprocal duties and obligations between divinity and humanity. (3) A

set of behavior patterns designed to conform to the will of God and to assure to the individual believer the approval of his conscience and whatever rewards or freedom from penalties in this world or the next are included in the doctrines of his particular faith. Since the higher beings in the religious nexus are in essence supernatural, the whole of religion necessarily lies outside the scope of science and is a matter of belief (q.v.). Because of this fact there has been, and still persists, a widespread notion that religion and science are inherently incompatible, or that the relation between them must be one of conflict. This notion tends to fade away as the truth becomes clear that science, as well as religion, has its limitations, and that the fields of the two are distinct, and not superposable. Cf. magic; superstition.

religion, comparative. The branch of cultural anthropology (q.v.) concerned with the study and comparison of the various religious systems of mankind.   G.P.M.

religious liberty. Cf. liberty, religious.

remedial. Curative, ameliorative (q.v.); describes a level of social case work, group work or custodial care which is above the merely palliative (q.v.) in that the situation of the client becomes better than it was when the treatment was initiated, and may even be brought up within the range of normality (q.v.).   T.D.E.

remedial institution. Cf. institution, remedial.

rent. (1) Payment for the use of any object, ownership remaining fixed. (2) More specifically, payment for the use and occupancy of real estate, including land and buildings or improvements. (3) In economic analysis, the money paid periodically for the use of land as a factor in a productive unit or business (q.v.).

rent strike. The collective refusal of a group of tenants to pay rents until alleged abuses are corrected or excessive rents reduced.   S.S.

reorganize. To establish a new system of relationships or values, particularly after a period of disorganization or rapid change.   P.F.C.

reorganization, individual. Cf. individual reorganization.

reorganization, social. Cf. social reorganization.

reparation. The provision that a convicted offender make restitution to the victim in accordance with the damage the latter suffered. Thus, one of the conditions of probation in some jurisdictions is that the offender make weekly or periodic payments to the victim of his criminal offense for the injury done to persons or property.   N.F.C.

repetitive phenomena. Cf. phenomena, repetitive.

replacement, population. A tendency toward continuance of equal number of individuals in successive generations, defined with reference to births or to adults in the reproductive age classes.   F.L.

replacement index. Cf. index, replacement.

representation, collective. Literal translation of Durkheim's *représentation collective.* The French is much better rendered, however, as "publicly intelligible symbol." This stands in contrast to "privately understood happening", *représentation individuelle.* "The communicable as opposed to the ineffable" is another way of putting it. The communicable is "social" or "collective" for it acquires its communicability in and through an interactional process involving two or more persons. Above all, a collective representation is not merely something like a flag, which presumably "represents" a "collectivity."   H.B.

representation, individual. Cf. individual representation.

representation, proportional. Cf. proportional representation.

representation, symbolic. Collective representation (q.v.). Cf. catchword; ritual; symbol.

representative. In sociological statistics, a sample of any social aggregate which is sufficiently large and diversified to include all the major characteristics of the individuals composing the aggregate, in approximately the proportions found in the aggregate.   G.M.F.

representative control. Cf. control, representative.

repression, psychological. The inability or refusal to respond in a way ordinarily evoked by stimuli. Also the suppression of recollections of unpleasant events, the memory of which is painful or shame-provoking. Fear of social disapproval frequently causes the inhibition (repression) of recall or action and this sometimes results in phobias, anxieties, and illusions. Repression is a poor, although common, attempt at adjustment—it is itself tension-producing. Much repression concerns excretive and sexual functions of the human body.   W.C.H.

repression, social. Cf. social repression.

reprieve. An order, usually by the executive of the state, temporarily postponing the execution of a sentence in order to provide the time for further investigation into the guilt of the convicted offender. A respite or reprieve is sometimes granted in order to investigate the offenses of others upon which the convicted may throw light. Reprieves are granted in connection with death sentences. A "stay of execution" is the newspaper phrase for a reprieve.   N.F.C.

reproduction, gross rate of. Cf. rate, gross, of reproduction.

reproduction, net rate of. Cf. rate, net, of reproduction.

research, social. Cf. social research.

residence. The rule governing the location of the household of a married couple, being "matrilocal" (q.v.) if the husband normally goes to live with his wife or her kinsmen and "patrilocal" (q.v.) if the wife customarily joins her husband's household. Cf. descent.   G.P.M.

residence, matrilocal. The practice among primitive peoples where the couple establishes residence with or nearby the wife's parents. Such location of residence may be for the full duration of the marriage, or may be limited for a specific period immediately following marriage. It may alternate with patrilocal residence in accordance with established annual cycles or other periods. Matrilocal residence tends to predominate in cultures characterized by a horticultural economy.   E.A.H.

residence, patrilocal. Pertaining to customary or preferential residence on the part of a married couple, at the home of the husband or his kinsman.   G.P.M.

residues. A term popularized by Pareto and his followers to connote manifestations of the basic sentiments out of which human motivation arises. In the Paretan system there are six basic categories of such motivating factors: the instinct for forming combinations; the persistence of aggregates or conservatism; the desire to externalize sentiments; the urge to sociality; the need to preserve the integrity of the individual against the demands of society; and the desire for sexual expression. This concept partakes of the nature of the Freudian libido, or racial memory as expounded by Jung and others, of instincts, of basic and universal wishes. In each case the effort is to postulate some fundamental drive or set of drives in terms of which all other activity may be explained. Cf. derivations.   H.E.M.

resistance, passive. Cf. passive resistance.

resources, natural. Cf. natural resources.

resources, social. Cf. social resources.

response, collective. (1) Response of a plurality of persons in which each shares and to which each contributes. (2) Response of a plurality of persons under the influence of an emotionalized state of mind, in which each person shares and to which he contributes. Such responses are usually dependent on face-to-face proximity of large numbers of people, and occur most frequently in periods of social change and unrest.   M.S.

response, conditioned. Cf. conditioned reflex.

response, cooperative. Cf. cooperative response.

response, emotional. Response accompanied by sensations and perceptions and/or motor expressions of excitement. The excitement, which is accompanied by increased physiological activity, appears to interfere with discriminatory mental processes and complex motor habits.   M.S.

response, mimetic. (1) Response by means of which one organism assumes some characteristic of another in order to escape danger or to reach a positive goal. (2) Response through which one organism reproduces the action of another which serves as a stimulus. Cf. imitation.   M.S.

response- non-cooperative. Response not contributing to the attainment of an objective jointly desired by two or more social agents.   M.S.

response, prepotent. A response which has the ascendency over all competing responses when the stimuli appropriate to all such responses are present simultaneously. Thus in Sherrington's experiment on a decerebrated dog, the postural reflexes maintaining the extended position of the limb, the scratching response to the stimulus of tickling the shoulder, and the withdrawal response to the stimulus of pricking the foot, remained intact. But when all these stimuli were applied at once, the withdrawal response inhibited the others and controlled the movement of the limb. In this case the withdrawal is the prepotent response and the prick is the prepotent stimulus. H.E.J.

response, social. Cf. social response.

response, stereotype. A response in the form of words or actions that is provided for a given stimulus by the folk-beliefs of a group or society. It contrasts with responses defined by non-cultural factors, situational and psychological.   A.M'C.L.

response, stereotyped. Response patterned by a definition of the situation or conception of rôle previously habituated in the responding person's mind.   T.D.E.

response, struggle. Unlearned response to stimuli which interfere with freedom of movement, usually characterized by strong, general excitement and absence of skilled muscular coordination.   M.S.

responsibility. Accountability for actions and their consequences. The term implies some degree of comprehension of the nature and consequences of an act and the deliberate or voluntary carrying out of the act. Responsibility is thus not attributable to the insane or the very young, nor would it be ascribed to an individual who was coerced into doing something against his will.   A.R.L.

responsibility, criminal. Cf. criminal responsibility.

restraint, moral. A Malthusian term to indicate late (postponed) marriage accompanied by premarital chastity. It specifically does not mean abstention from intercourse within the marital relationship.   N.E.H.

restraint, social. Cf. social restraint.

retainer. A person attached to a chief, lord, or household by the obligation to render certain services, but enjoying a status superior to that of a slave, serf, or servant.   G.P.M.

retaliation. The term applied to private vengeance for wrongs. The avenger was supposed to make the offender suffer as much as the victim had suffered. Because the avenger in his anger might cause more suffering than the victim had suffered, the law of retaliation (lex talionis) placed a limit upon the extent and kind of reprisal, "An eye ·for an eye, a tooth for a tooth, wound for wound, burning for burning." In other words, the term carries the idea that punishment for an injury is of like kind with the injury.   J.L.G.

retention. Capacity of the nervous system to accept impressions and to hold what is learned.   N.A.

retribution. Punishment which balances the injury done both to the injured and to society of which he is member. This theory is based upon the supposition that crime disturbs the balance of the social universe, which must be restored by inflicting upon the offender a punishment appropriate to restore this balance. Aristotle first formulated the law of what he called "corrective justice." Cf. retaliation.   J.L.G.

retrogression, social. Cf. social retrogression.

retrospective prediction. Cf. prediction, sociological.

revenge. The infliction of suffering upon the offender by a private individual who has been injured. A broader term than retaliation (q.v.) in that revenge has no limits as to kind or degree of suffering returned upon the offender.   J.L.G.

revenge, blood. Cf. blood revenge.

revolution. A sweeping, sudden change in the societal structure, or in some important feature of it. A form of social change distinguished by its scope and speed. It may, or may not, be accompanied by violence and temporary disorganization. When changes of equal magnitude are accomplished gradually and without exceptional conflict or violence, it is ordinarily an expression of social evolution. The essence of revolution is the sudden change, not the violent upheaval which frequently accompanies it. Indeed, there is excellent support for the theory that the genuine revolution, as a social phenomenon, starts well in advance of the violent manifestation and has been practically accomplished before that manifestation takes place. The violence is merely the overt evidence that the change has occurred.

revolution, commercial. The sudden and extensive expansion of trade relations that accompanied, and was intimately associated with, the Industrial Revolution (q.v.). Significant features were the creation of a world market, increase in the speed and facility of transportation, the development of international finance, increased importance and complexity of international political trade relations, etc.

Revolution, Industrial. Cf. Industrial Revolution.

revolution, social. Cf. social revolution.

revolution, vital. The marked change, historically viewed, in human reproduction by which a given population, whether increasing, stationary or decreasing, is achieved by a low birth rate and a low death rate instead of by the historically prevalent vital conditions of a high birth rate and a high death rate. The essential feature of the change is the increased economy of human reproduction under recent developments in sanitation and preventive medicine.   N.E.H.

revolutionary change. A major social change, affecting or altering the relations of social classes to one another, as well as the ideas, traditions and loyalties (ideology) which sustain the social structure. More careful analysis has been made of political revolution, because of widespread interest and the dramatic quality of the action, than of other forms of revolutionary change. Briefly, its two characteristic features are: first, its apparent suddenness; second, the shifting of power from one socio-economic class to another. The end-process has usually been preceded by a long period of intellectual fermentation and agitation which paves the way for the revolutionary moment, crisis or struggle resulting from the seizure of power and the displacement of the governing bureaucracy, class or group by technically illegal and violent means. Long-term, fundamental changes in the technological, economic, religious or social structure, and any other deep-seated change in systems of thought and habit, if transpiring gradually and without violence, are evolutionary rather than revolutionary.
                                              S.J.

revolutionary conflict. Cf. conflict, revolutionary.

revolutionary syndicalism. Cf. syndicalism, revolutionary.

reward. As a general sociological concept, the amount of valuable goods and services that a society permits any of its constituent units to receive in return for its participation in the total social proc-

ess. For example, wages are the reward of labor, rent the reward of the landlord, interest the reward of the capitalist, salaries the reward of managers, and profits the reward of business owners. More specifically, a special payment or gift in recognition of some unusual service.

rhythm. Foreseeable regularity of recurrence of any kind of phenomenon in life and thought.   J.H.B.

rhythm, social. Cf. social rhythm.

rhythm method. Cf. safe period.

rich, idle. Cf. idle rich.

ridicule. A critically, even caustically, humorous exaggeration of certain characteristics of others, by way of revenge or for the purpose of encouraging their disappearance. It is not easy to distinguish from derision, banter, raillery, burlesque, mockery, irony, satire, etc.   F.E.L.

right. (1) That which any social unit, individual or group, is entitled to expect from its social environment in accordance with the norms of that society. Philosophically or ethically the term is often used to apply to benefits or privileges which the individual or group feels that it ought to receive from society or from the world at large. Sociologically, rights have reality only as they are guaranteed and will be enforced by some social agency. All practical rights are socially conferred and socially guaranteed and have no existence beyond the extent to which they will be socially supported. (2) In keeping with any socially accepted standards or codes. Conformable with the mores (q.v.).

right, father-. A type of social organization characterized by patrilocal residence, patripotestal authority (q.v.), and patrilineal descent, inheritance and succession. Cf. mother-right; patriarchate.   G.P.M.

right, junior. Ultimogeniture (q.v.)

right, mother-. A type of social organization characterized, in its most extreme or consistent form, by matrilocal residence matripotestal or avuncular authority, and matrilineal descent, inheritance and succession. Cf. father-right; matriarchate.
                                              G.P.M.

right, nephew-. The avunculate (q.v.), with special reference to the right of a nephew to inherit from or succeed his maternal uncle.   G.P.M.

right, riparian. Any right appurtenant to a parcel of land which appertains to water bordering on, or within, or under such parcel; e.g., the rights to natural flow unobstructed by artificial checks or barriers, to freedom from unreasonable pollution, of access to the water, or accretion.

right of asylum. Cf. asylum, right of.

right of sanctuary. Cf. sanctuary, right of.

right of way. (1) A right of passage. (2) The area over which the right of passage exists.

right wing. That section of any ideological group that tends toward relative conservatism or reactionism; or within a group, that element which supports the least extreme form of the characteristic ideas or principles of the group.

rights, bill of. The first ten amendments to the U. S. Constitution, prohibiting the federal government, or in certain amendments the states, from interfering with political liberties, and guaranteeing to persons charged with crime the protections of fair procedure. The Civil War amendments (13th, 14th and 15th) are also commonly classed as part of the Bill of Rights. Most state constitutions also include the equivalent of the federal guarantees, and when codified together these are referred to as Bills of Rights. The phrase was used earlier in England in the course of the struggle between King and Commons, and there characterizes the similar guarantees won by the people.   R.N.B.

rights, civil. The right to vote, seek office, serve on juries, etc. Also the legal guarantees protecting all persons in a democracy from attack on personal liberties (freedom to live, travel, possess property, etc.) either by governmental agents or mobs. Civil rights comprise the guarantees to defendants in courts of law for fair trials, and against discrimination on account of race, religion or national origin.   R.N.B.

rights, natural. Cf. natural rights.

rights, paternal. The rights of the father over the persons and property of the members of his family. Until the second half of the nineteenth century these rights were almost unchallenged. At present, however, in England and the United States wives have won control over their persons, property and wages. Children, also, are protected by the State from cruel punishments and from the denial by a father of educational privileges.   W.G.

riparian right. Cf. right, riparian.

rite. A formal or conventional act or series of acts, especially of a magical or religious character. Cf. ceremonial. G.P.M.

rite, social. Cf. social rite.

rites, birth. The ceremonies practiced by savage tribes and ancient peoples at the birth of a child. They were designed to cleanse both mother and child from the impurities of child-birth, to protect the infant from evil spirits and to give him strength and energy. The purification rite has persisted into modern times, as shown in the Anglican prayer book in the ritual for the "Churching of Women."
                                                 W.G.

rites, initiation. Ceremonies, usually of supernatural import, attending admission either to the status of adulthood (Cf. puberty rites) or to a secret society, age-grade, sect, or other association.   G.P.M.

rites, puberty. Ceremonies at adolescence, for boys and girls, or both sexes, marking their transition to adult status or marriageability, and frequently involving seclusion, food taboos, physical ordeals, moral instruction, and investiture with some outward evidence of the new status. Cf. initiation rites; rites of passage. G.P.M.

rites, purification. The rites performed in many primitive tribes which are designed to purify both mother and child from the "uncleanness" of childbirth. Among rude peoples there exists very generally an awe and fear of pregnancy and childbirth, phenomena that they do not understand. A pregnant woman is often regarded as abnormal and a potential source of evil to her community. Therefore she is subjected to certain taboos and is not rarely compelled to live in a hut separate from her family. After the birth of the infant both mother and child are sometimes quarantined while purification ceremonies take place. The umbilical cord is very generally disposed of in customary rites designed to ward off harm. Cf. rites, birth.   w.g.

rites of passage. The ceremonies which cluster about the great crises of life, or periods of transition from one status to another, notably birth, puberty, marriage, and death.   g.p.m.

ritual. A form of behavior prescribed by custom, law, rule or regulation. Among many primitive peoples ritual is thought to be particularly pleasing to the gods and deviations from the established ritual are punished. Ritual is considered especially important in church, fraternal, governmental and formal social activities; in admitting new members, in baptism, in initiation, in induction into office, in introducing members to each other or to the group. It is found in ceremonial dances, feasts, sacrifices, burials and many other established forms of activities. Ritual may refer to the list of ceremonies governing such activities. It may include prayers, testimonies, standing, bowing, kneeling, clasping the hands, marching, singing, carrying a cross, staff or other insignia.
                                                o.w.

ritual, marriage. Cf. marriage ritual.

ritual continence. Cf. continence, ritual.

ritual union. Cf. union, ritual.

ritualism. A system or procedure putting into practice a ritual, the use or observance of a ritual. Churches, lodges, military organizations and many other formally organized groups adhere to a prescribed form of behavior known as ritualism.   o.w.

rivalry. Personalized competition, but subject to rules (mores, code, etc.) to prevent or at least mitigate conflict.   t.d.e.

Rochdale principles. A set of eight principles, or rules of procedure, for developing a consumers' cooperative association, based upon the rules and aims as devised by the twenty-eight founders of the Rochdale Society of Equitable Pioneers in Rochdale, England, in 1844. These principles have been stated with some variations but in the main are: (1) open, voluntary membership; (2) only one vote to one member; (3) limited rate of interest on capital with no speculative profits; (4) business done on a cash basis only; (5) market prices; (6) patronage refunds; (7) political and religious neutrality; and (8) continuous education and expansion.

rôle. The function or expected behavior of an individual in a group, usually defined by the group or the culture.   j.p.e.

romanticism. A preponderance of spontaneity, sensitivity, passion, or fancifulness in mood or temper; an attitude or doctrine which glorifies feeling and élan rather than form in the fields of aesthetics and ethics, and considers impulse as self-justifying in its expression. Its tendencies are therefore individualistic, pluralistic, even anarchic, rather than toward solidarity, order, or stability. Distinguished from romance, the situation-process of aesthetic excitement in the reciprocal exploration of one another's feelings and personality in the process of courtship (q.v.); and from the romantic complex, a cultural or personal complex concentrated upon stereotypes of romance, courtship and marriage.   t.d.e.

roomer. One who occupies a rented room, on a basis at least as permanent as weekly or monthly.

rugged individualism. A popular phrase connoting a high degree of self-reliance and self-sufficiency such as characterized the American pioneers; also the state of a social order in which there exists a minimum of social control and group concern for the individual, leaving the individual largely free to achieve such satisfaction as he can secure through his own unaided and unhindered efforts. Cf. laissez-faire.

rural. Defined by the United States Census as inhabitants of incorporated places

of less than 2,500 and residents in the open country or unincorporated territory.
J.H.K.

rural community. An area of face-to-face association larger than a neighborhood in which a majority of the people use a majority of the social, economic, educational, religious and other services required by their collective life and in 'which there is general agreement on basic attitudes and behaviors, usually village or town centered.
E.des.B.

rural community organization. Rural community organization may be considered: (1) As the process of developing relationships between groups and individuals in rural communities that will enable them to act together in creating and maintaining facilities and agencies through which they may realize their highest values in the common welfare of all members of the community. (2) As the existing state of such relationships.
D.S.

rural disorganization. Cf. disorganization, rural.

rural family. Cf. family, rural.

rural-farm population. All persons living on farms located in rural territory without regard to occupation. Persons living on farms located within the incorporated limits of a city are classed as urban-farm population. Farm laborers not living on farms are excluded from the farm population.
C.E.L.

rural industrial community. A community, rural in size, dominated by a single industry, such as a textile village, lumbering village, etc.
E.des.B.

rural non-farm population. All persons living in rural territory except those living on farms. Includes all persons living in incorporated villages of less than 2500 inhabitants, all persons living in unincorporated villages and persons living in the open country on tracts of land not definable as farms. Includes most farm laborers.
C.E.L.

rural population. The population living in rural areas as contrasted to the urban population living in urban areas. Rural and urban areas may be variously distinguished, but, in statistical practice, the factor most frequently used to distinguish rural and urban population is size of place. The term includes the population living in unincorporated territory and also the population of those incorporated places which are smaller than the minimum size assigned to cities. Since 1910, 2500 has been in the United States the generally accepted lower limit of cities, all the population of smaller places being classified as rural.
C.E.L.

rural problem area. An area in which the combination of population, natural resources and cultural development peculiar to the area has failed to produce a level of living and a degree of economic security consistent with the minimum standards of society as a whole. Such an area finds it necessary, and may be encouraged by the larger society of which it is a part, periodically or continually to request public assistance to support its population. Because of maladjustment between resources and population, the area is chronically at or near the economic margin, though the vicissitudes of the business cycle alternately tend to relieve and accentuate the difficulties of adjustment.
C.E.L.

rural social organization. The art of planning social relationships in the rural environment by the use of the methods of science; a technology using various sciences and disciplines for the practical improvement of rural welfare, but based chiefly upon the application of sociology and social psychology.
D.S.

rural sociology. Cf. sociology, rural.

rurality. The degree to which a given community or area approximates a wholly rural status or condition.
E.des.B.

ruralization. The process by which rural attitudes and practices are carried over into urban behavior.
E.des.B.

rurban. A contraction of rural and urban designed to describe the community relations of country and village or small city.
J.H.K.

rurbanization. Interaction of rural and urban, an intermediary process of rapprochement.
J.H.K.

S

sabotage. Any act of obstruction of industrial processes, usually secret or covert, committed by individuals or groups of employees to further a private interest; either to force recognition of workers' grievances and claims (industrial sabotage) or in war time to serve the purposes of a foreign country (political sabotage). The word is also properly, but not commonly, applied to employers' limitation of production, or destruction of products, to maintain prices or to force governmental concessions. The term originated in France, traced variously to the slow clumsiness of workers' wooden shoes (sabots) or to their reported use to obstruct machinery to call attention to grievances. Sabotage takes on varied forms of obstruction, not only by damage to property, but by soldiering on the job (known in Scotland, and widely elsewhere, as "ca' canny") by spreading false rumors or by publicly revealing unfavorable truths about goods (open-mouthed sabotage), and by increasing costs through using expensive materials.   R.N.B.

sachem. The supreme chief of a tribe or federation of New England Indians; hence any tribal chief of the Indians of northeastern North America.   G.P.M.

sacra privata. The rites and sacrifices of family worship in ancient Rome. In these ceremonies performed in worship of Vesta, goddess of the hearth, the Lares, spirits of ancestors, and the Penates, who blessed the family store, the father acted as Priest, assisted by his wife and children, the latter of whom acted in the capacity of *camilli* and *camillae* or acolytes. Some writers have suggested that the reason why young Roman boys were permitted to wear the purple stripe on the *toga praetexta* (toga of boyhood), a privilege restricted to priests and magistrates, was because of their active participation in domestic worship.   W.G.

sacra publica. The ceremonies held in early Rome on the day called *Liberalia*—the sixteenth of March—after the Roman boy had exchanged the toga of boyhood for the *toga virilis,* symbolizing his attainment of manhood. The day began with worship of the domestic gods at the family altar, on which the boy laid his favorite toys and the *bulla,* or amulet against evil charms, that he had worn around his neck since his naming day. There followed a solemn ceremony held in the public forum. Surrounded by his relatives and friends the patrician boy was led to the forum and then to the Capitol, where sacrifices were offered to the national gods of Rome.   W.G.

sacred society. Cf. society, sacred.

sacrifice. An act of offering or dedication to a supernatural being or to sacred use, ordinarily involving the destruction of the object offered. E.g., blood sacrifice, foundation sacrifice, grave-goods, holocaust, human sacrifice, libation, prayer, scapegoat, vicarious sacrifice, votive offering.   G.P.M.

sacrifice, blood. A sacrifice (q.v.) of blood, especially by blood-letting.   G.P.M.

sacrifice, foundation. A sacrifice (q.v.) made in laying the foundation of a building or other structure, especially of a human victim to provide the structure with a protective or guardian spirit.   G.P.M.

sacrifice, human. The sacrifice (q.v.) of a human being. Cf. foundation sacrifice; grave-escort; suttee.   G.P.M.

sacrifice, vicarious. A sacrifice offered for another, e.g., of an animal in place of a human victim. G.P.M.

sadism. An abnormal and wanton exercise of power on the part of a person or group, in order to torture, abuse or fiercely oppress other persons, commonly associated with some perversion of sexual passion. G.M.F.

safe-conduct. A guarantee of security or protection granted to a messenger or other person enabling him to pass safely through a hostile territory or war zone. Cf. peaceful access. G.P.M.

safe period. One or more groups of days in the menstrual cycle of the human female within which she is incapable, or thought to be incapable, of conceiving. A sterile period relied upon by some as a birth-control measure. Exact determination of the days is still somewhat subject to medical controversy. In the case of any given woman it is impossible, by any simple and certain method, to determine the date of ovulation, and hence to calculate the sterile days. For most women with a normal 28-day cycle, the safe period approximates days 1 - 8 and 21 - 28 counting from the onset of bleeding. Possibly the 7 days preceding the projected onset of the next menstruation are safer than the first 8 days. N.E.H.

salpingectomy. A surgical operation in which the Fallopian tube is severed or tied off to prevent the passage of the ovum into the uterus. Used in the treatment or prevention of disease and especially as a form of sterilization. O.W.

salutation. A form of greeting or farewell. G.P.M.

sample, adequate. A sample containing enough cases to yield the accuracy required for the purpose at hand; a sample large enough to have a sampling error within specified limits. Not necessarily an unbiased or representative sample. M.Pt.

sample, biased. A sample that is unrepresentative of the universe of which it is supposed to be a true cross-section. M.Pt.

sample, line. A sample obtained by selecting cases falling on specified lines in a listing arranged on lined paper. Sampling procedure used in U. S. Decennial Census of 1940. M.Pt.

sampling (*statistical*). The process or method of drawing a finite number of individuals, cases, or observations from a particular universe. Selecting part of a total group for investigation. Survey procedures having to do with the selection of the sample, collection of information from sample cases, and statistical treatment of findings so as to yield a representative group. M.Pt.

sampling, block. Selecting a sample of the population by first grouping the units of investigation into contiguous blocks, then numbering the blocks and drawing a sample of blocks. Within the blocks chosen, the entire population may be included in the sample. If only a portion of each block is selected, the term "block-segment sampling" applies. M.Pt.

sampling, controlled. Method of sampling in which some control is exercised over the choice of sample cases in order to insure the desired representation of the various groups or categories of elements in the population. The sample may be controlled so that a fixed number of cases will be secured from each stratum, regardless of the number of units in the stratum, or it may be controlled to insure proportional representation. M.Pt.

sampling, disproportional. Process of sample selection in which the number of cases drawn from each of the various strata in the universe is not in proportion to the number of units in the strata. M.Pt.

sampling, double. Use of two or more methods of sample selection at different levels of an investigation. For example, random selection may be used in a short survey of the population, and from the random sample, a smaller stratified sample might be selected for a more time-consuming investigation. Also called mixed sampling. M.Pt.

sampling, proportional. Selecting a sample in which all significant elements are represented in the same proportion as they occur in the universe.   M.Pt.

sampling, purposive. Selection of a portion of the population which has the same average or other measures as the universe in regard to one or more characteristics which are already a matter of statistical knowledge. E.g., to sample the population of a state for a study of earnings, several counties might be selected which have the same average age as the state population. It is then assumed that the average earnings, or any other investigated variable which is correlated with age, will be the same for the counties as for the state.   M.Pt.

sampling, random. Process of sample selection in which each individual or element in the universe is assured an equal and independent chance of being included. Also called simple sampling and random selection. Should be distinguished from careless, unsystematic, accidental, or opportunistic sampling because careful planning and systematic procedure is required to assure random choice.   M.Pt.

sampling, regular interval. Selecting of sample cases at evenly spaced points of a list or other catalogue of the universe. E.g., every 10th item on a list.   M.Pt.

sampling, stratified. Selection of a sample by first dividing the population into classes or strata, and then sampling each stratum. The selection may be proportional or disproportional from each stratum. Disproportional samples are usually weighted to achieve the effect of a representative sample of the universe.   M.Pt.

sampling reliability. The extent to which a given sample accurately characterizes the universe from which it is selected. The stability of a measure from sample to sample. Reliability of a statistic is usually measured in terms of the standard error which tends to be inversely related to the square root of the number of cases included in the sample.   M.Pt.

sanction. (1) A permission or social approval of any act or form of behavior. (2) The legal, or other regulatory, provisions for the enforcement of a legal or social imperative, and accordingly the penalty for the violation of such an imperative. (3) By a peculiar process of inversion, not uncommon in the history of language, a prohibition or proscription. It is in this latter sense that the term has acquired wide vogue in recent years, particularly in connection with international agreements, and the system of enforcement included in the organizational establishment of the League of Nations. In contemporary usage, the phrase, "to apply sanctions," ordinarily means to apply restraints, prohibitions, or penalties.

sanction, social. Cf. social sanction.

sanctioned. (1) Socially permitted or approved. (2) Subject to social, particularly legal or conventional, restraints, prohibitions, or penalties.

sanctuary. A place or object, access to which is recognized as giving an accused person protection against a pursuer, particularly an avenger under the mores of retaliation. One who takes sanctuary commits himself to the orderly legal processes of society. Cf. city of refuge.

sanctuary, right of. Ancient and medieval law permitting certain offenders to escape punishment by civil authorities if they reached certain areas or buildings designated as under the protection of God. Cf. city of refuge.   J.P.S.

San Michele. The first modern penal institution. It was built in Rome in the 16th century to house delinquent boys pending their reformation. In architecture it foreshadows many of the modern prisons and reformatories emphasizing cellular subdivisions.   J.W.M'C.

sapphism. Cf. lesbianism.

satellite community. Cf. community, satellite.

satire. An unanalyzable mixture of humor and criticism applied, for correctional purposes, to human foibles and faults. It is not designed for the correction of major social diseases such as crimes, depressions, and war.   F.E.L.

satisfaction. The quenching of the desires, wants and needs of the constituent parts of a given society.   J.H.B.

satisfaction, individual. Cf. individual satisfaction.

satisfaction, social. Cf. social satisfaction.

satyagraha. A campaign of civil disobedience or nonviolent resistance (*ahimsa*) as practised by Gandhi and his followers in India. Literally, it means "insistence on truth." It entails disobedience to laws that are felt to be unjust. It includes refusal to pay taxes or to patronize stores operated by those considered to be oppressors. It may include refusal to supply food or other necessaries to aggressors, general strikes, etc. It excludes, theoretically, physically aggressive action against the enemy.   S.C.M.

scab. An epithet applied to a worker who refuses to join a union or who takes the job of a worker on strike. Any activities of non-union workers if they are injurious to the collective of union members may be called scabbing.   N.A.

scale, attitude. Cf. attitude scale.

scalping. The practice, especially prevalent among the North American Indians, of removing a portion of the skin of an enemy's head, with the hair attached, as a trophy.   G.P.M.

scapulimancy. Divination (q.v.) by the observation of animal bones, especially by heating a shoulder blade and reading meanings from the resulting cracks.   G.P.M.

scarcity, economy of. Cf. economy of scarcity.

scarification. The practice of cutting the skin, sometimes for purposes of bloodletting or self-torture, but more especially in order to raise scars for personal adornment. Cf. tattoo.   G.P.M.

schedule, or schedule form. Collection form, sheet, card, or booklet designed for recording research data. Sometimes used synonymously with questionnaire, although technically, the questionnaire is a form of schedule.   M.Pt.

schizophrenia. Literally "splitting of the mind." A form of psychosis characterized by negativism and hypochondrial, dissociative tendencies. The term is tending to replace dementia praecox in scientific usage since it emphasizes the character of the disease rather than age at which the manifestations began.   J.M.R.

school. (1) A social unit devoted specifically to the process of education. It ordinarily includes some physical setting, particularly a building or buildings, and personal participants divided into the two categories of teacher and pupil. (2) The followers of a scholar who in their teaching and writing seek to emulate him and to promote his doctrines. Any group of thinkers whose theories are in accord, and who join forces to further their doctrines.

school, consolidated or centralized. A school which combines two or more district schools, frequently serving all the children of a community from first grade through high school.   E.des.B.

school nurse. A public health nurse whose services are employed for the benefit of the school children of a community or rural area. Her services include the promotion of health, the prevention of disease, the securing of healthful environment and teaching of proper habits of living for school children, based upon individual needs as seen in periodic medical examinations. She works in the school, and in the home with both school personnel and parents, as well as with the children themselves.

schools, ragged and industrial. Cf. ragged and industrial schools.

science. A kind of human activity directed toward the systematic statement of the probability of the hypothetical or actual recurrence of phenomena which for the purposes in hand are regarded as identical. Under this definition geology, comparative philology, biology, sociology, etc., are sciences even though they often times lack the precision of physics and chemistry; history, mathematics, logic, and similar studies are activities directed toward ends of differing sorts and hence are not sciences. Science is not an honorific but a descriptive term; therefore activities which are not scientific are not necessarily of lower value; they are simply different from science.   H.B.

science, natural. Cf. natural science.

science, social. Cf. social science.

science of society. The body of knowledge derived from the systematic observation and conceptualization of those social relationships and social processes which exist as a result of human association.   J.P.E.

sciences, hierarchy of the. Cf. hierarchy of the sciences.

scientific management. The name given to new techniques of plant organization and employee-employer relationship first introduced by Frederick Winslow Taylor, hence often called "Taylorism." The plan calls for the hiring of the most efficient workmen available, the payment of wages high enough to hold these men, the standardization of work practices, and the detailed planning of all operations. Modern large scale production methods are an outgrowth of Taylor's ideas. Taylor interpreted his plan as the application of engineering techniques to management.   J.W.M'C.

scrying. Divination (q.v.) by gazing fixedly, as into water or a crystal.   G.P.M.

seance. A group sitting, usually in darkness and with other conditions favoring illusions and hallucinations, for the alleged purpose of observing psychical or extra-sensory phenomena.   M.Pt.

seasonal crowding. Overcrowding which periodically occurs when one or more rooms in a dwelling are unusable in winter because of lack of heat, or in summer because of high temperatures, poor ventilation, infestation, etc.   S.S.

seasonal nomadism. Cf. nomadism, seasonal.

second funeral. Cf. funeral, second.

secondary contact. Contact, secondary.

secondary group. Cf. group, secondary.

second-settlement area. Cf. area., second-settlement.

secret society. Cf. society, secret.

sect. A religious we-group characterized by exclusiveness (as contrasted with evangelistic zeal and programs), relative mental immobility, and stubborn adherence to creedal formulae. It usually is a minority group, and frequently is organized for conflict or at least for highly self-conscious accommodation to the majority. That accommodation is a defense against assimilation into the patterns of the outgroup. Even though the organization of a sect be political in form, it is theocratic in its conception and definition.   D.E.W.

sectarian. A member of a sect (q.v.). Relating to a sect.

sectarianism. Conduct characteristic of sect (q.v.) members.   H.B.

secular cycle. Cf. cycle, secular.

secular society. Cf. society, secular.

secularization. A process by which an isolated, sacred social structure is transformed into an accessible, non-sacred pattern of controls and interactions. Generally it is a highly self-conscious process depending upon the leadership of liberated (but not disintegrated) individuals. The process involves mental mobility on the part of all active participants together with emphasis on rationality, analysis and planning, and frequently it is accompanied by programs which are definitely opposed to stereotypes and institutions of religion and the supernatural. Secularization may be segmental, e.g., the political life of a nation may be secularized without direct effects to individual faith and/or ecclesiastical or sectarian activity therein. D.E.W.

security. Safety, a condition of refuge, insurance against hazard. The concept is normally used in relation to economic considerations. Social security conveys the assurance of freedom from the dangers of penniless old age, unemployment without compensation, etc.   N.A.

security, collective. Cf. collective security.

sedition. The advocacy of unlawful means of changing the form of government, such as the "overthrow of government by force and violence," or encouragement of the violation of law with the purpose of promoting disloyalty or disaffection to the government.   R.N.B.

seditious conspiracy. The agreement of two or more persons to act together in promoting unlawful means of changing the government or of encouraging the violation of law for the purpose of promoting disloyalty or disaffection to the government.   R.N.B.

seduction. The legal offense whereby a man induces a woman to have unlawful sexual intercourse with him.   F.W.K.

segregate. To separate or set apart one or more categories of the population, either through conscious social purpose or through the unconscious selective action of personal and cultural influences. F.H.H.

segregated district. Used in connection with surveys of prostitution in American cities, a more or less tolerated concentration of vice resorts or houses of prostitution in a local area of a city, usually in the slums of large cities. There was at one time a disposition to believe that the police actually corralled the houses of prostitution within set boundaries and in this sense segregated them. But observation showed that many houses of prostitution existed outside the segregated district and that most of the business of independent solicitors took place outside the district. The segregated district was probably more of a product of a natural segregation of brothels whose invasion of, and survival in, a blighted area, was not threatened by protests of the residents or by the law enforcement policies. The so-called anti-vice crusades, often accompanied by preliminary vice surveys which exposed the evil, have succeeded in closing the segregated districts in most American cities.   W.C.R.

segregation. The act, process or state of being segregated. It may be the result of law, as in authorized red-light districts or separate schools for Negroes; of social custom, as in the usual class lines of a democratic society or the castes of a stratified society; of temporary social attitudes, as in some cases of social ostracism; or of the emergency use of force, as in concentration camps and restricted zones during war time. Lines of segregation in a democratic society are based on economic status, birth, education, and other marks of respectability.   F.H.H.

selection, automatic. The survival and unpremeditated selection through the concurrence of numbers of persons, of a particular way or mode of action (folkway or mos) which seems to have satisfied a human need or interest better than other tentatives.   E.E.M.

selection, rational. The deliberate selection in the light of verifiable knowledge and with the concurrence of numbers of persons, of a particular way or mode of action (folkway or mos) believed to satisfy a human need or interest.   E.E.M.

selection, social. Cf. social selection.

self. A personality's conception of its own personality. Cf. consciousness, focus of; ego; personality.   H.H.

self, divided. Pathologic disunity of personality, ranging all the way from sense of inner conflict (e.g. St. Paul) to alternating more or less complete and separated personalities (e.g., in fiction, Dr. Jekyll and Mr. Hyde).   A.J.T.

self, looking-glass. The social self, i.e., the judgment one makes about oneself as seen reflected in the attitudes of others toward oneself.   F.D.W.

self, social. Cf. social self.

self-consciousness. (1) Awareness of one's own existence and characteristics, usually in relationship to other people or objects.
(2) Popularly, an emotional state of awareness of the evaluations of others towards oneself, usually involving embarrassment.   M.S.

self-control. Cf. control, self-.

self-direction, societal. Cf. societal self-direction.

self-discipline. Cf. discipline, self-.

self-gratification. The satisfaction of the intellectual and emotional needs of the individual. The achievement of status and recognition from the group. Activities arising in this connection grow into the mores revolving around the Sumnerian concept of "vanity."

selfhood. The subjective uniqueness which gives to each personality (q.v.) its own focus of consciousness and its viewpoint from which to observe and to operate; the privateness of the inner experience of each personality. Cf. individuality.   H.H.

self-maintenance. Mores which promote, or are believed to promote, societal survival within given life-conditions. Institutional forms: industrial, military, governmental, religious organizations as adjustments to the physical, social, and supernatural environments.   A.G.K.

self-perpetuation. Mores which promote, or are believed to promote, societal survival beyond the living generations. Institutional forms: marriage and the family, adjustment to environment, with the distinctive adjustment to the intrinsic condition of bisexuality.   A.G.K.

self-realization. Cf. realization, self-.

self-regard. 1. Consideration for one's own interest. When of moderate strength it may be termed "enlightened self-interest"; in extreme form it becomes wholly selfish and unsocial—anti-social if necessary.
2. Self-respect.   R.E.B.

self situation. Cf. situation, self.

self-sufficing farm. Cf. farm, subsistence.

sentence, indeterminate. A prison sentence imposed upon a person convicted of a crime without specific time limits, usually dependent upon the behavior of the con-

vict while incarcerated. However, such indeterminate sentences have always provided some maximum and often some minimum limit. There are no completely indeterminate sentences in American penal law.   M.A.E.

sentence, short. A sentence that runs from a few days to a few months, imposed on petty offenders, who often cannot afford to pay the alternative of a fine, if such is given. Short sentences are usually served in municipal or county jails, except in those few places where special institutions for misdemeanants are maintained.   A.E.W.

sentence, suspended. An interval existing between conviction and the imposition of the penalty. It resembles reprieve, except that the latter term means the postponement of the execution of sentence to a certain day; whereas a suspension of sentence is for an indefinite period of time. Perhaps the most important area within which suspension of sentence functions in modern times is in relation to probation (q.v.), a procedure which permits certain convicted offenders to live in the community under a suspended sentence and under the supervision of a probation officer. In such cases it should be noted that the suspension of sentence is conditioned upon the good behavior of the offender during the period of his supervision.   A.E.W.

sentiment. Generalized patternings of emotion, thought, and action; the culturally and physiologically determined major premises underlying folkways, mores, and institutions in a group, class, or society. Psychologically complex emotional biases and canalizations of emotional drive. Frequently ambivalent. Sometimes, as in the case of mother love, it includes such a range of factors as fear, joy, sorrow, and anger, all related to the pattern of the sentiment. Like the Freudian id or subconscious, individuals are rarely able to define their own sentiments with any accuracy and candor. Not only are their sentiments not always understood on a verbal plane by individuals but the description of many actual sentiments in such terms is taboo. Cf. public sentiment; public opinion.   A.M'C.L.

sentiment, public. A fairly standardized attitude on the part of a considerable proportion of the members of a society toward a given object, based on emotion, prejudice, intuition, and personal predilection, rather than on the deliberate and rational interpretation of experience and factual evidence.

sentiment analysis. A method of reporting, analyzing, and interpreting public sentiments relevant to the formation of opinion concerning a current or forthcoming event. As a means of estimating and predicting public opinions, the technique is based upon a recognition that events, conflicts, and sentiments are the dominant factors in opinion-formation. In gathering facts for such an analysis, much more detailed and mature interviews are required than for opinion polling purposes; the interviewers also follow lines of social organization rather than rules for mathematical sampling in selecting interview subjects. Cf. poll; public opinion.
                                                    A.M′C.L.

separation. (1) A cessation of cohabitation between husband and wife by mutual agreement in pursuance of a contract between them providing for the wife's support, and custody of the children. Such contracts are legalized in England and in some states of the United States being granted by the courts where the charges are not sufficient to warrant a divorce.
                                                    J.W.M′C.

(2) The termination of an employer-employee relationship.

sept. A localized social group or tribal subdivision based on common descent, especially where the latter is reckoned bilaterally, i.e., through both the male and the female lines; sometimes used for, but preferably to be distinguished from, a unilinear kin-group or sib (q.v.).   G.P.M.

sequence. Succession of events, when one event follows another either causally or accidentally.   H.A.P.

serf. A person who, in a feudal system, is bound to a tract of land and owes duties and services to whoever holds title to the latter, but who is not, like a slave, the immediate personal property of his lord.
                                                    G.P.M.

serial action. Cf. action, serial.

servant, domestic. Cf. domestic servant.

service, civil. Cf. civil service

service, domestic. Cf. domestic service.

service, public. That type of public work of an agency of government which ministers to the needs of the public. Examples are the postal service, the regulation of public utilities, regulation of labor relations, regulation of financial securities and such direct services to individual citizens as relief, pensions, education, recreation and services relating to health and safety.
                                                    N.A.

service, social. Cf. social service.

service agencies. A term used by rural sociologists to designate the institutions, organizations, businesses or professions serving a given area.   D.S.

set. A temporary readiness of the organism to respond in a particular manner. The set itself is unconscious, but may sometimes be accompanied by a vague background of awareness.   M.Pt.

settlement. (1) An institution serving a neighborhood by means of various forms of recreational, educational, social and civic programs. The trend in recent years has been toward greater neighborhood participation in administration of the program, and selection and direction of settlement activities. This has resulted in varied activities and a less standardized program.

(2) The period of residence required before an individual or family is eligible for benefits under the public welfare laws of a state.   W.P.

settlement, form of. Form of settlement, type of settlement, and pattern of settlement are terms used to denote the manner in which the agricultural population is arranged on the land. The various settlement forms or patterns may be classified into three principal types:

(1) Village or nucleated settlements are those in which the farm homes are not situated on the land amid the fields

but are found clustered together in a more or less compact village or hamlet. In such a pattern the cultivated areas, pastures, and woodlands lie in the area about the residential center and it is necessary for the cultivators to commute between their homes and their fields.

(2) Scattered or isolated farmsteads is a form of settlement in which the homes of the farm population are located on the land, each amid the fields cultivated by the family and with little or no tendency for homes to be grouped in close proximity to one another.

(3) The line village is a semi-nucleated type of settlement in which residence on the land is achieved without a widespread dispersion of farm homes. Such a settlement pattern arises when farm lands fronting on a water front, road, ridge, etc., are divided into strips and the various farm families locate their homes at the same end of the holding. Such an arrangement of the population on the land gives rise to a long row of houses stretching across the landscape, or, if fronted on the other side of the road or stream, to a long one-streeted village extending through the countryside.   T.L.S.

settlement, group. Cf. group settlement.

settlement, laws of. Laws found in every state and most counties of the United States defining the length of residence within the community required before a person is eligible for public assistance. Settlement laws are an inheritance from old English poor laws, particularly the Elizabethan poor law of 1603 from which most state laws on the subject of poor relief were originally derived. In making the locality responsible for the maintenance of its own poor it was necessary to define who was a resident of the locality. Requiring a minimum period of residence was designed to suppress an increasingly large group of itinerant beggars which was fostered by the liberal almsgiving of churches and monasteries during the Middle Ages. In the United States at present laws of settlement vary greatly. Some states require a minimum residence of one year while others require as many as seven years. Many of the laws are worked out in elaborate detail, indicating how the laws of settlement apply to widows, divorcees, orphans, minors, convicts, aliens, and illegitimate children.
                                              J.W.M'C.

settlement, nucleated. A type of rural settlement. Cf. form of settlement.

settlement, social. Cf. social settlement.

sex. Physical characteristics that distinguish male and female.   E.R.G.

sex distribution. The composition of a population by sex. The sex distribution may be stated by expressing the number of each sex as a percentage of the total population. More frequently it is stated in terms of the "sex ratio" which usually expresses the number of males per 100 females.   C.V.K.

sex experience. A vague term, the use of which varies between such wide extremes as to afford no basis for a precise definition. It has no place in scientific discussions, unless the particular meaning is made clear in the context.

sex intercourse. Sexual union. Coitus.

sex offenders. Cf. offenders, sex.

sex perversions in prisons. Cf. prisons, sex perversions in.

sex ratio. The ratio of the number of males in a given population per one hundred females, at any specified time. Cf. sex distribution.   M.K.

sex totemism. Cf. totemism, sex.

sexual. Relating to sex.

sexual communism. Cf. communism, sexual.

shadchan. Cf. marriage broker.

shaman. A mediumistic healer, magician or exorcist of the Siberian tribes, who, by means of his special relationship with personal spirit helpers, is able to act as a mediator between his fellow men and the unseen world of spirits; hence a primitive medicine man (q.v.) in general, especially one versed in spirit possession.
                                              G.P.M.

sharecropper. A name commonly applied to the agricultural laborer in the Southern part of the United States who performs the manual labor on a given tract of land in the production of cotton and is paid a share, usually one half, of the crop. Such a laborer furnishes none of the workstock and agricultural equipment, but his account is debited for one-half of the fertilizer bill and the ginning fees. As a rule he is permitted to live in a cabin located amid the field on which he and the members of his family do the work. Usually he receives a stipulated advance per month, either in cash or in credit at the plantation commissary, which is repaid with interest when the crop is sold.   T.L.S.

share tenant. Cf. farm operator.

shibboleth. A criterion, test, or watchword employed without regard to its intrinsic validity.   L.P.E.

shifting group. Cf. group, shifting.

shop, closed. An employer-employee relationship in which only members of the union with which the employer has a contract may be hired to work in his plant or factory.   J.W.M′C.

shop, open. A employer-employee relationship marked by the fact that any person whether union or non-union may hold a job in the plant or shop. In general, an open shop tends to become a non-union shop, although in theory union men have equal rights with non-union men.
    J.W.M′C.

shop, preferential. A type of employer-employee relationship created by Louis Brandeis when he served as arbiter in the New York dressworkers strike in 1913. Under a preferential shop agreement an employer must hire union workers as long as capable union men are available; if such is not the case he may hire whom he pleases. When lay-offs are necessary the employer must dismiss non-union men first. Hence union men get preferential treatment in both hiring and firing.
    J.W.M′C.

shop, union. An employer-employee relationship in which the employer may hire whom he likes on the condition that the person or persons hired must within a stated period join the union. This is a variation of the closed shop allowing the employer a larger amount of discretion in hiring workmen.   J.W.M′C.

short sentence. Cf. sentence, short.

shrine. A place where sacred objects are kept and prayers or offerings made. G.P.M.

sib. A unilinear and usually exogamous kin-group based upon traditional common descent, either matrilineal (q.v.) or patrilineal (q.v.), and frequently characterized by a common totem (q.v.). Often used synonymously with clan (q.v.), but preferably reserved for a non-localized group, i.e., one comprising brothers and sisters in one line of descent irrespective of their place of residence. Cf. descent; exogamy; gens; lineage; phratry; sept.   G.P.M.

sibling. A brother or sister; a child of the same parents irrespective of sex. G.P.M.

sign language. A system of gestures, either imitative or conventional, used for intercommunication by tribes speaking different languages, e.g., by the Plains Indians of North America.   G.P.M.

silent trade. Cf. trade, silent.

single cause. Cf cause, single.

singularism. A sociological theory that society is a mere sum of its members and that there is no ontological entity called society.

There are three variations of the theory.

1. Extreme or consistent singularism which holds that the individual is the only social reality and is therefore the supreme ethical value, and that society has value only as it serves to enhance the life of the individual. This variety of singularism is hedonistic and utilitarian.

2. Moderate singularism, which concedes that society as well as the individual is of supreme value and that individual freedom or happiness is limited by the equal interest of society.

3. Collectivistic singularism which, while considering society as merely the sum of the individuals, claims the superior-

ity of the collectivity over the individual. For example, Fascism or Hitlerism.

Historically singularism has alternated with universalism and mystic unity or integralism.   J.D.

situation. The totality of all the factors, inner and outer, organic and environmental, significant for the behavior under investigation, as they appear to an observer on objective scientific analysis.   H.E.J.

situation, conflict. A set of circumstances involving mutually antipathetic and overtly coercive or destructive relationships of individuals or groups.   M.S.

situation, group. A set of circumstances involving one or more collections of persons considered as preserving social relationships with one another. The circumstances may be those within one group or those between or among groups.   M.S.

situation, self. The organized whole of an individual's nature which refers to a specific set of social relationships or general class of social relationships.   M.S.

situation, social. Cf. social situation.

situation-process. A phrase which, by hyphenation, draws attention to the inseparability, in actuality, of the relatively-stable, or momentarily-observed aspects of experience (structure, form, situation, gestalt, event, product) and the changes (function, process) which are occurring even as observation is made. Practically every "social process" may be reconsidered as situation-process.   T.D.E.

situational approach. A way of viewing and analyzing problems (personal or social), not in terms of single causes or of individual traits and blame, but as situation-processes: any given situation, as discovered, being considered as emerging from the preceding situation-sequence and as still evolving subsequent situations, into which the observer (in a participant rôle) may or may not be introducing new elements. Many conditions or events, considered in an individualistic culture as individual traits or acts, are seen, under such analysis, as situations: e.g., leadership, goodness, criminality, insanity, pauperism, poverty, common sense, competence, genius, success, sainthood, witchcraft.

In social case work, the situational approach considers the unit of diagnosis and treatment to be the problem situation rather than the person who happens to be the focus of attention in the records of the case. The problem "situation" is itself an abstraction or cross section from the total space-time manifold, and is to be compared with the situation after treatment. It is limited for practical purposes to those elements of personality and environment considered sufficiently and significantly related in etiology or therapy so as to be dealt with as a unit. The workers and agencies become part of the situation.   T.D.E.

skill. Manual dexterity. The capacity to perform specific types of work. Skill is an art learned by practice, acquired or retained well or not depending on the capability of the learner.   N.A.

slavery. The ownership and control of the person and his services by another. E.E.M.

slavery, debt. Cf. debt slavery.

slavery, group. Cf. group slavery.

slogan. Derived from the Gaelic, *sluagh-ghairm*, meaning army-call. Hence, a battle cry and, more broadly, a rallying cry for a political party, a catch phrase for a commercial organization, a terse and catchy phrase or statement associated with a product, movement, organization, institution, or country. Although no longer thought to be indispensable to an advertising campaign, advertisers of the latter part of the nineteenth century did much to make the European and American publics "slogan-conscious," and they and other publicity men still utilize them. Examples: "Remember Pearl Harbor," "Keep That School Girl Complexion," and "For God, for Country, and for Yale." Sociologically, slogans have the same characteristics as catchwords (q.v.).   A.M'C.L.

slum. An area of physical and social decadence. On the physical side, the slum is identified by the presence of run-down, over-aged neglected houses and facilities.

On the social side it is identified by poverty, vice and the various forms of social disorganization. The existence or absence of a slum in any city is determined on the basis of relative considerations. It may be said that the slum in any community is where the poor people and social outcasts live. In a large city there may be various types of slums, each of which may be occupied by a different population or social class.   N.A.

slum clearance. The removal of a slum condition by demolition of all existing structures. This should not be confused with the construction of new housing upon the same site.

slum reclamation. The improvement of a slum area or of a cleared slum site in order to provide for a more suitable use.

sociability. A way of being bound to a whole and by a whole. Different forms of interdependence among self, alter ego, he, they (relations with others) and different forms of partial fusions into the we (mass, community, communion) are examples of forms of sociability. Sometimes, the term sociability (or sociality) is understood in a looser sense, that of the capacity of individuals to be integrated in group life, even in the sense of the measure of their cooperative spirit.   G.G.

social. Having to do with the reciprocal relations of interacting human beings, either as individuals or groups. A comprehensive term, including all the phenomena which are the subject matter of sociology.

social, anti-. Any behavior, attitude, or value which is believed by the members of a group to be detrimental to the welfare of that group. It usually pertains to the dominant group in a particular society.   J.P.E.

social, non-. Characteristic of the relation between an individual and his group where the former has no conscious identification with the latter, makes no deliberate effort to contribute to its welfare, and is indifferent to it. The term non-social is to be contrasted with anti-social (criminal); pseudo-social (parasitic); and social. The last term describes a situation in which

the individual actively identifies himself with his group and is concerned with its welfare. The non-social person, in contrast, remains largely an individual, living and letting live, but having no purposeful interaction with his group.   F.D.W.

social abnormality. Abnormality (q.v.) manifesting itself in either the relations of an individual or a group to its social environment, or the structure or functions of society itself.

social achievement. The process (or the result) of bringing a project to a successful conclusion by a number of individuals acting together.   M.S.

social acquisitiveness. The quality of having a strong desire to receive or possess social status, group affiliation, or some other social value defined by the group of which the individual is a member.
                                             J.P.E.

social action. (1) Any expenditure of effort by a group as such; all conscious or unconscious concerted or collective endeavor.
                                             N.L.S.
(2) Organized effort to change social and economic institutions, as distinguished from social work (q.v.) or social service (q.v.), the fields of which do not characteristically cover essential changes in established institutions. Social action covers movements of political reform, industrial democracy, social legislation, racial and social justice, religious freedom and civil liberty; its techniques include propaganda, research, lobbying. Cf. social reform.
                                             R.N.B.

social adaptation. That relation of a group or institution to the physical environment which favors existence and survival or the process, passive or active of attaining, the same. Sometimes improperly used in place of adjustment or accommodation to mean a favorable or advantageous relation of the individual to the group or the process of attaining the same.   N.L.S.

social adjustment. (1) (a) Those types of relationship between personalities, groups, culture elements, and culture complexes which are harmonious and mutually satisfactory to the personalities and groups involved. (b) Those processes which tend to produce such relationships.   H.H.

(2) This is one of the most widely used terms in contemporary biology, education, psychology, social psychology, and sociology. It is also one of the vaguest and most ambiguous, ranging from Spencer's "Life is the adjustment of internal relations to external relations" to Dale Carnegie's "Success means adjustment to others." In most cases, therefore, it is well to specify exactly what, in the context, adjustment is to mean—i.e., whether passive conformity, active self-reformation, mutation, infinitesimal variation, habituation, subservience, unobtrusive manners, ethical laxity, and the like.

A survey of current usage yields several principal sociological meanings of adjustment. Among the most important of these are: (a) *Interactive,* in which man adjusts to others as he functions in economic, religious, and other ways. The existing interaction may be characterized as competitive, cooperative, etc. (b) *Striving,* in which there is deliberate effort toward a better or improved adaptation. (c) *Accommodative,* described as some relatively stable and mutually accepted relationship among the participants. (d) *Associative,* in which adjustment is treated as a step or stage in a general associative process. Less social distance is present than in advance, but more than in accordance. The participants have reached a *modus vivendi* in some respects, as it were, and for the rest "agree to disagree." (e) *Normative,* wherein "good" or "efficient" or "adequate" adjustments, adaptations, "fits", or "integrations" are worked out between persons or technologies or organizations or institutions. Antonyms are unadjustment, maladjustment, disintegration, or disorganization.

social agencies, administration of. Directing the operation and planning the development of an agency; primarily the executive or managerial function; supporting or facilitating activities of the executive function.   W.P.

social aggregate. The totality of the people inhabiting a given territory, considered as a collectivity merely from the standpoint of relative propinquity to one another, but not from the standpoint of organization or interaction.

social anabolism. The constructive development taking place in society through the absorption and adaptation of new ideas, attitudes and practices.   M.C.E.

social analysis. Comprehensive examination of complex social facts to distinguish a) the constituent parts b) the relation of such parts to each other, c) the relation of the single part to the whole; resulting in systematic description of social interrelationships according to formal and material classification; to be distinguished from the research techniques known as analysis of social data and/or factor analysis.   J.H.B.

social anatomy. The structure and organization of society. The function, relative position, and interdependence of the different social groups and their relation to society as a complete working unit. M.C.E.

social and economic areas. The rural areas defined by common use of certain service agencies (q.v.) located at designated centers.   D.S.

social anthropology. Cultural anthropology (q.v.).

social anthropometry. The comparative, quantitative, and statistical treatment of social phenomena. Cf. statistics, social.
                    E.A.H.

social arts. Arts not produceable by an individual but created through pooling cooperative artistic efforts.   J.H.B.

social ascendancy. The movement of individuals, families, or groups upward on the scale of social rank, power, prestige, and honor. This concept is not to be confused with domination.   W.C.H.

social assimilation. The process by which different cultures, or individuals or groups representing different cultures, are merged into a homogeneous unit. The analogy is with the biological process whereby a living body ingests external matter of various different kinds, and transforms it into body cells of harmonious types. It is important to note that this physiological assimilation does not result in identical body cells, but in various types of cells that are adapted to, and normal in, the entire organism no matter how complex it may be. Likewise, social assimilation does not require the complete identification of all the units, but such modifications as eliminate the characteristics of foreign origin, and enable them all to fit smoothly into the typical structure and functioning of the new cultural unit.

The most frequent and important instances of assimilation are afforded when more powerful groups overmaster and absorb weaker groups, or when, by the process of immigration, representatives of external cultures are admitted within the territory of another country. In essence, assimilation is the substitution of one nationality pattern for another. Ordinarily, the modifications must be made by the weaker or numerically inferior group. Cf. nationality.

social attitude. An attitude which (1) is communicable—shareable, or (2) is favorable to societal as contrasted with individual interests. For example, if the militarist or the conscientious objector is able to spread his ideas, or if he values social welfare above individual welfare, his attitude is said to be social.   F.E.L.

social authority. Consciousness and recognition, enforced by means of institutional social control, of the superiority of one value-system established for common group-ideals.   J.H.B.

social aversion. Antagonism which is derived from the culture of a society. P.F.C.

social balance. A condition of society in which the various elements, demographic and cultural, exist in proximate equilibrium or are freely functioning with none exercising a dominant or disproportionate influence.   N.L.S.

social being. (1) Man in his interrelationships to other human beings.
(2) The totality of processes basic for human interrelationships and especially those crystallizing into definite forms, thereby acquiring the character of reality, as opposed to the appearance of doing so.   J.H.B.

social capillarity. A situation-process in which members of a 'lower' class are attracted upward and seek to raise their status, creeping up into higher status through interstices in the stratified class structure. In an open class system competition makes capillarity accepted and relatively widespread. In a caste system there are few leakages upward, though a person may lose caste in many ways.
                T.D.E.

social case work. A method of helping people through social services and personal counselling in order to release their capacities and to bring about personal and family adjustments. Cf. case work; case study method.   W.P.

social causation. Causation (q.v.) manifesting itself in the sequences of social phenomena. The principle in social relations which justifies the conclusion that a given set of factors or conditions may be expected to be followed by a specified event or condition.

social cause. The productive force of a social conjuncture having as sequence a change in a social situation. Social cause must be distinguished from physical, biological, and psychological causes and can be found only in the social realm itself. Furthermore, social cause is not the same as social factors, which are only abstractions from the total social conjuncture, whose relative importance varies according to changing frames of reference; e.g., the types of society and groups. G.G.

social change. Variations or modifications in any aspect of social process, pattern, or form. A comprehensive term designating the result of every variety of social movement. Social change may be progressive or regressive, permanent or temporary, planned or unplanned, uni-directional or multi-directional, beneficial or harmful, etc., etc.

social circulation. That form of social mobility (q.v.) which pertains exclusively to vertical social class movement, both to the upward flow of individuals and families on the social scale and to the descent of others in social rank. Social circulation is a refined term, a distinct form of social mobility. Cf. circulation of élites. W.C.H.

social class. A stratum in society composed of groups of families of equal standing. Cf. social clique. All persons of the same social level of prestige and esteem, who consider themselves to be social equals, form a relatively distinct social class. Cf. class.

Family backgrounds and connections, friendships, moral attitudes, amount and kinds of education, success in occupation, taste in consumption, possession of usable wealth, type of vocation, degree of prestige of one's political, religious, and racial affiliation all contribute to fixing or identifying one's social class status.

In the United States the social classes have been recently delineated in the following general terms: upper, upper middle, middle, lower middle, upper lower, and lower lower.   W.C.H.

social climber. Any person who seeks to loosen ties with older acquaintances and cultivate the favor of persons on higher levels. A person whose contacts with others are planned consciously to improve his own social standing.   W.C.H.

social clique. A local unit of a social class. A group of families which accept each other as social equals and associate intimately with each other, largely to the exclusion of the rest of the local community. A social clique is the next larger unit above the family in social class formation.   W.C.H.

social code. A system of regulations backed by social sanctions.   M.K.

social cohesion. Stability of social organization. Syn. social solidarity. Ant. social disorganization.   H.A.P.

social competency. The state of being competent; able to compete in maintaining status and playing one's social rôle (aside from mere occupational competency). Cf. competent.   T.D.E.

social competition. The activity of the person or group in seeking status or social position without conscious reference to the strivings of others and subject to limitations imposed by the social order. W.E.G.

social composition. (*demography*) the make-up of a population in respect to national or cultural origins, religious affiliation, language, occupation, income, citizenship, length of residence, and other important social-economic and cultural factors.   T.D.E.

social configuration. Cf. configuration.

social conflict. That species of social opposition (q.v.) in which (a) the immediate objective consists of the capture of or damage to part or all of one or more of the opposed personalities or groups, or of their property or culture complexes, or of something for which they have developed an attachment, so that the struggle takes the form of attack and defense; or in which (b) the activities of one personality or group unintentionally block the functioning or damage the structure of another personality or group.   H.H.

social consciousness. (1) Awareness of social relationships between individuals. This elementary definition is the counterpart of the scientific definition of self-consciousness.

(2) Awareness that experiences are common to or shared between persons. This definition, widely used by sociologists, implies greater insight than does the elementary definition.   M.S.

social constitution. That system of related social services, or social functions essential to maintain the normal life of society. The form or pattern of this self-sustaining system is naturally that of the elementary types of activity that people always find themselves engaging in for the achievement of any project. Briefly stated, these essential steps or stages of experience are those of need, effort, and satisfaction; as illustrated, for example, in the building of a home. Inadequate functioning calls for new experience—new understanding and enlargement of the activities of the social constitution.

(1) The first stage of the project is always that of making sure of the physical factors basic to any life, which are sustenance and equipment. Out of them develops the maintenance functions or vocations.

(2) The second stage of the project is always that of planning, experiment, and trial, activities that give rise to the reflec-

tion functions of information and education.

(3) In the third stage, with identification or plan of the subject clear, moral and political adjustments appear, involving the control functions of morals and government.

(4) And in the fourth stage of any project, the activities become those of recreative and aesthetic appreciation according to the values achieved.   C.J.B.

social constraint. A type of negative social control exercised by authority in the name of the group, subjecting offenders to custody or limitation of freedom supposedly of sufficient rigor to prevent their repetition of offenses.   T.D.E.

social contact. Such a relation of one human being to another as will initiate some form of interaction or response. The primary requirement for all social processes. Contact and isolation may be considered as the poles of social distance (q.v.), though each may vary in degree of intensity, and seldom if ever exists as an absolute.

social contagion. Social interaction by which impulses are passed from person to person with the result that a uniformity of response is elicited. It has application to situations involving fads, perhaps panic or exhiliration.   N.A.

social content. A body of sentiments, values, beliefs, traditions, attitudes and forms of interaction out of social experience that influence behavior and give it significance with respect to a specific situation, place, time or group.   J.M.R.

social continuation. The extension of procedures, organization and forms by means of expansion or reaching into areas or groups not previously included within a particular culture or institutional designation.   M.C.E.

social continuity. Essentially an alternative term for culture (q.v.), but one of more restricted and specialized emphasis. The persistence of social groups, forms of social interaction, customs, traditions, beliefs, and the like, to a degree which causes many of these features of social life to preserve a recognizable identity, even though they are continuously undergoing change.   F.N.H.

social contract. A (reciprocally) binding agreement or covenant entered into by members of a group, setting up reciprocal grants and privileges, rights and responsibilities, powers and duties, as a basis of government. It may be set up between a sovereign and subjects, or between persons and their sovereign collectivity considered as reciprocally responsible in a democracy (q.v.). The special theories positing a state of nature or absolute individual liberty preceding all government, which arose through a social contract, are now discarded.   T.D.E.

social control. The sum total of the processes whereby society, or any sub-group within society, secures conformity to expectation on the part of its constituent units, individuals or groups. It exhibits two main forms: (1) coercive control and (2) persuasive control. Coercive control emanates from the agencies of law and government, and is accomplished by force or the threat of force. The types of behavior specifically designated for coercive control fall under the general category of crime. Persuasive control operates through all the various agencies and instrumentalities that induce the individual to respond to the standards, wishes, and imperatives of the larger social group. The means of social control are numerous and varied, and rest upon the dynamic characteristics of the units to be controlled. The law is the most concrete, explicit, and obvious instrument of social control but by no means the most powerful or comprehensive. Much the greater bulk of social control falls in the persuasive category, and is achieved by such agencies as suggestion, imitation, praise, blame, reward, recognition, and response. When the controlling group is society, social control takes the specific form of societal control.

social correlation. The precise comparison by statistical methods of two or more characteristics of social units, such as the relation between income and fertility.
    G.M.F.

social crisis. A serious condition of social affairs in which the course of events reaches a point where change, either for better or for worse, in respect to the welfare of the group or the community, is imminent; and the influences of social control are uncertain as to their power of direction. Generally the ultimate criterion of social welfare involved in the crisis is whether the union is to be promoted and enriched or the reverse.   C.J.B.

social cultural lag. Cf. lag, cultural.

social defense, laws of. A continental European term made popular by the positive school of criminal law and designating laws that primarily aim to provide special treatment or internment for habitual or defective criminals.   T.S.

social demoralization. Cf. demoralization.

social depletion. The occurrence of the drawing off, or gradual removal, of strong social elements, leaving a socially ineffectual residue. Ex. The reduction of population in a community by the removal of certain age or sex groups, or mentally and technically equipped persons, so that the effectiveness of social institutions is impaired.   M.C.E.

social deterioration. The process within a group, as a community, a nation, an international organization, of growing worse or declining from a previous condition regarded as a norm, in such matters as the welfare of the members, the degree of social unity and cooperation, adherence to the codes and standards of the group; the state of having so declined.

social deterrence. Inhibitions upon behavior through the agency of group pressures.   A.R.L.

social diagnosis. The determination of the essential facts bearing upon any individual's social difficulties in order to understand the individual's behavior in the light of his social relationships, and to formulate a plan for social treatment.
                                        A.E.W.

social differentiation. The process whereby social differences of persons and groups

occur, due to biological heredity and physical characteristics—age, sex, race, consanguineous and individual; variations in vocations, social status, cultural background, and acquired personality traits and accomplishments; and differences in group composition and social relationships. Social differences are both phases and products of the process of differentiation.
                                        M.H.N.

social direction. The line or course of change in which modifications in human activities are tending. The trends of social change.   M.C.E.

social discipline. The direction and control of individual behavior from without the individual, by the famly, the community or the nation. Cf. social control.
                                        A.E.W.

social discrimination. Unequal treatment of groups of basically equal status. Discrimination carries with it the element of unfair, unreasonable and arbitrary distinction in the imposition of burdens and the distribution of favors. The crucial question of social discrimination is not differentiation as such but the general validity of the yard-sticks for admission to the in-group as defined by the predominant element. Whether differentiations are regarded as discriminatory or not depends on the denial or recognition of such gradations in a given society. Social discrimination is obviously existent in a society which confesses basic principles of equality yet does not practice them in their daily application. Such a discrepancy may be due to conscious deceit or ignorance, to uncontrolled emotional reactions or traditional residues of prejudice.   S.N.

social disintegration. The break-up of a group into separate units following upon the loss of social organization and the feeling of common interests; the state of being so broken-up.

social disorganization. Any disturbance, disruption, conflict or lack of consensus within a social group or given society which affects established social habits of behavior, social institutions, or social controls so as to make relatively harmonious functioning impossible without some significant intermediate adjustments. By virtue of the dynamic character of social life and social change, social disorganization must always be a relative term. A certain amount of social disorganization is present at all times, but in general sociological practice, the concept (social disorganization) is applied whenever these disrupting forces exceed or threaten those making for social stability. The term is also applicable to ideational conflicts. These in turn may be considered as the counterpart of other cultural disturbances. Since old habits and institutions become vested with sanctity, any social change is certain to divide society into conflicting groups, those which believe in the validity of the status quo and those which insist upon altering old institutions to meet present needs. This division of opinion or lack of consensus is in itself a disruptive force as well as an evidence of lack of harmony cr of social disorganization.

M.A.E.

social disparity. Differences in social behavior or in status.   A.R.L.

social distance. (1) Reserve or constraint in social interaction between individuals belonging to groups rated as inferior and superior in status. The differences giving rise to social distance may be those of race and nationality, of class, of institutional rôle, as between officer and soldier or teacher and student. Social distance so defined need not preclude a certain kind of intimacy, circumscribed by rules governing the relation of the superior and the inferior.

Social distance must be distinguished from the emotional tone of the relationship; it need not imply aversion. Master and servant may be devoted to each other. Nevertheless, especially in ·race and nationality relations, social distance is often accompanied by fear and hostility.

Reserve in interaction involving superiority-inferiority attitudes is sometimes referred to as vertical social distance.

(2) Reserve in social interactions resulting from cultural differences without involving superiority-inferiority attitudes. This is sometimes called horizontal social distance. The cultural differences giving

rise to it may be those of nationality, religion, mores, and the like.

Social interaction may be conceived as extending from a superficial contact to the most intimate and intense interaction. Horizontal social distance refers to the lesser or greater obstacles to free interaction. In contrast to vertical, horizontal social distance does imply lack of intimacy. It is not to be identified with antagonistic attitudes but is, in fact, often accompanied by some suspicion or hostility.

(3) Some writers use "social distance" to denote also reserve in interpersonal relation due to personal and not only social factors, as in the case of two persons who are not congenial to each other. In the opinion of other writers, this identification of social distance with any bar to mutual understanding makes the concept too general to be useful.   M.K.

social drive. A general term descriptive of a wide range of springs of human action (including impulses, urges, wants, wishes or desires, emotions, sentiments, interests, attitudes, and habits) that develop in the course of social interaction. The motivating forces (drives) have a complexity of sources ranging from inherited conditions and biological needs to those growing out of the reflective thinking, experience, and cultural background of a person. Cf. social forces.   M.H.N.

social dynamics. The science or study of the vital urges or powers of human beings organized in the collective activities of functioning groups. These urges are essentially the system of human interests involved in carrying on the social functions.

The human interests, appearing as a logical series in the stages of any project, form the natural, basic frame of reference for any classification of human functions, vocations and institutions, which are the dynamic units of social organization; and this basic system of natural forces in human nature constitutes the subject matter of social dynamics. c.j.b.

social ecology. That branch of science which treats of (a) the spatial-functional structure of areas of human habitation, and (b) the spatial distributions of social and cultural traits or complexes, which phenomena arise and change as the result of processes of both social and ecological interaction.   J.A.Q.

social elements. The simplest units of human behavior which may be communicated to others, e.g. attitudes, culture traits, or the general attributes within a given frame of reference.   M.C.E.

social energy. The vital power of a group together with all its other available resources in goods and accumulated culture.   N.L.S.

social engineering. The application of established sociological laws and principles to the accomplishment of specific and recognized social objectives. Social engineering differs from social reform (q.v.), in that it deals primarily with structure instead of function, and is concerned more with the creation of new forms and patterns than with bringing behavior into conformity with existing norms. As in the case of all forms of engineering, every social engineering project starts with a problem. The engineer, as such, is not concerned with setting the problem nor with passing upon its merits. His task is to work out a scientific solution and carry it to a successful completion. Social engineering differs from other branches of engineering in that the materials with which it deals are human rather than inanimate, and the forces which it utilizes are social forces. Cf. sociology, applied.

social entity. The most inclusive of all social genera; a class including all beings and groups of beings who are to be regarded as having conscious states which need to be taken account of when attempting to predict or to control their behavior.   H.H.

social entropy. The doctrine of inevitable social decline and degeneration derived from the field of physics and particularly from the Second Law of Thermodynamics, which conceived that the energy of the universe, fixed and limited, was being given off to futile heating of empty space, and was not being replaced.   A.J.T.

social environment. Society looked upon as the setting for the life activities of the individual. The human analogue to the physical habitat (q.v.). The sum total of social institutions, forms, patterns, and processes that impinge directly upon the socius (q.v.).

social epidemic. Cf. epidemic.

social equilibrium. A state of socio-cultural integration in which all parts are functioning harmoniously. Cf. normality.   N.L.S.

social ethics. That approach to ethics which seeks primarily for practical guidance in relation to specific social problems, including the broad issues of political and economic policy and also such questions as sexual morality.   H.H.

social evolution. The development, planned and unplanned, of culture and forms of social relationship or social interaction. The processes of social evolution are conceived to be more or less analogous to those of biological evolution, i.e., variation, struggle for existence, selection, and adaptation; but they are not identical with these processes. The term evolution differs from progress (q.v.) in that the former does not necessarily imply change for the better, or even increase in complexity. It is usually understood to refer especially, but not exclusively, to the long-run aspects and consequences of social change, and to those which may be regarded as cumulative or irreversible, rather than repetitive. Cf. revolution.   F.N.H.

social expectation. The attitude of society with respect to the sum total of individual behavior, required by the mores (q.v.) and subject to control by any form of social pressure.

social exploitation. Cf. exploitation.

social fact. Any identifiable item which pertains to the nature of a social relationship, process, or value.   J.P.E.

social fermentation. The process by which a society or social group is brought to a state of unrest or dissatisfaction with regard to existing situations in order to bring about some desired change in them. This process is usually instigated and controlled by some specific group which is interested in the desired change.   J.P.E.

social force. Any effective urge or impulse that leads to social action. Specifically, a social force is a consensus on the part of a sufficient number of the members of society to bring about social action or social change of some sort. In the plural, the social forces are the typical basic drives, or motives, which lead to the fundamental types of association and group relationship. These have been variously identified, but are practically always understood to include hunger, sex love, and certain other desires such as the desire for recognition and response, preferably favorable, the desire to know, and the desire for the good will and assistance of supernatural beings.

social function. A series of service activities carried on by an organized group of persons in a society for the benefit of its members. The functions performed as organized services by social groups tend to become more specialized, interdependent and efficient as society grows more complicated, extended and organically united today. The general classes of functions growing out of the elementary individual needs, are those of physical maintenance, intellectual enlightenment, moral control, and aesthetic appreciation.   C.J.B.

social functionary. A person occupying a social status in which he is an instrument of group or societal action, policy, ritual, or leadership. Examples: king, president, judge, soldier, citizen, priest, physician, teacher, student, etc.   A.M'C.L.

social genesis. Growth and changes in social relationships, institutions, or values.   H.A.P.

social gesture. An abbreviated act, or a symbolic representation of an act, used by an actor who understands its referent and who anticipates that others will understand it or respond to it as he does.   A.R.L.

social goal. An end, objective, project, or program proposed, desired or sought by collective effort.   N.L.S.

social gradation. Cf. social scale.

social group. A number of persons between whom exists a psychic interaction and who are set apart by that interaction in their own minds and in those of others as a recognized entity. The social group requires for its existence a durable contact between persons out of which continuous interaction may arise, a consciousness of sufficient likeness or common interest to establish some degree of identification of each with the group and some structure recognized by the members as essential to achieve its continued existence as an entity.   G.L.C.
A somewhat redundant term, since every group must have social features.

social group work. The process of helping people in groups to further their individual and common interests and needs.   W.P.

social growth. The development of individual traits in conformity with established social patterns.   P.F.C.

social guidance. The skillful direction of each individual by those in authority including the family, the school and other social institutions to the end that each member of society may develop his potentialities, learn self-direction and make his utmost contribution to society.   A.E.W.

social heredity. The transmission of established culture traits. The contribution made to present-day society by the accumulated experience and achievements of past generations. The term is loose and inappropriate, and should be abandoned in favor of social transmission (q.v.).   M.C.E.

social heritage. The body of social customs, folkways, mores, thoughtways and cultural achievements which has been received from predecessors. An inaccurate term. Cf. social heredity.   N.L.S.

social hygiene. A part of social work dealing with the control of prostitution and elimination of venereal diseases.   W.P.

social idealism. An attitude centering upon the unattained welfare of humanity.   L.P.E.

social ideals. Standards of social wellbeing set up in accordance with certain ethical concepts: specifically, in the United

States, the socio-ethical formulations agreed upon by representative religious bodies, such as "The Social Ideals of the Churches," first adopted by the Federal Council of the Churches in Christ in America in 1912; and the pronouncements of the National Catholic Welfare Conference, and of the Conference of American Rabbis. G.M.F.

social immobility. A condition wherein social class rigidities prevent all significant rising and falling in social esteem on the part of families within a society, also wherein occupations and organizational affiliations tend to be hereditarily fixed. Feudalism, if studied strictly from the short term view, presents a noteworthy example. The tendency of many scholars, however, to find in some periods of human history a great deal of social mobility and in others practically none at all is extremistic dichotomous thinking. There is always some and never very much social mobility. W.C.H.

social imperative. An extraordinarily binding custom. A.R.L.

social inequality. Differences in social prestige, based chiefly on differences in family backgrounds, social conventions, wealth, income, political influence, education, manners, and morals, in a homogeneous society. Possession of differing degrees of social power, privilege, and influence by the diverse social groupings in society indicate the extent and kinds of social inequality. These differences in degrees of social prestige are largely transmissible from parents to children through family institutions, contacts with other persons in the same social class, and institutions of property ownership and inheritance. Racial and religious differences are of another order and typically do not correlate with social inequality. W.C.H.

social inertia. Resistance to social change. The continuance of outmoded, impractical, or actually harmful practices which have become established but do not meet present needs. Their persistence results in social stagnation due to lack of enough social energy to make the necessary effort to bring about an effective change. M.C.E.

social inheritance. A loose and inaccurate designation of the process of transmission or tradition. Cf. social heritage.

social inhibition. A restraint of conduct imposed by group standards. P.H.L.

social instability. A condition of disequilibrium as between the various units of a society. An absence of accepted adjustment or accommodation between such units, which results in tension and, possibly, conflict in the accompanying struggle for status and power.

Instability may result from the destruction of the functions or the traditional rôles of certain groups so that they are forced to take a new position in the social structure. Or, it may be the consequence of groups aspiring for the acquisition of functions or status held by other groups. Or again, it may result from the invention or introduction of entirely new functions into the culture of the society concerned. Mass disturbances and upheavals are frequently connected with it. W.C.H.

social institutions. The sum total of the patterns, relations, processes, and material instruments built up around any major social interest. Any particular institution may include traditions, mores, laws, functionaries, conventions, along with such physical instruments as buildings, machines, communication devices, etc. The more generally recognized social institutions are the family, the church or religion, the school or education, the state, business, and such minor items as recreation, art, etc. Institutions are the major components of culture.

social insurance. Provision by government for payments to all individuals affected by an experience to which the total group is liable, such as unemployment, accident, sickness, occupational disease, old age, maternity, and widowhood, based on predetermined contributions by employers, insured individuals, or government, or a combination of these, and given to the individual as a right and not as relief. M.VK.

social integration. The process of coordinating the various classes, ethnic groups or other diverse elements of a society into a unified whole. N.L.S.

social interaction. Social processes (q.v.), when analyzed from the standpoint of the interstimulations and responses of personalities and groups. The chief forms of social interaction are opposition (including competition and conflict) and cooperation. Accommodation and assimilation are often mentioned as co-operative forms of interaction, but they may be regarded even better as social processes related to social change and social adjustment. Isolation may be regarded as the zero degree of social interaction. Cf. isolate. H.H.

social investigation. A term used to describe all forms of inquiry into social situations, from the most intensive and original research, through surveys which combine the compilation of existing data with some original studies, to the most uncritical and extensive descriptive surveys. G.M.F.

social isolation. Cf. (b) under isolation.

social justice. The intelligent cooperation of people in producing an organically united community, so that every member has an equal and real opportunity to grow and learn to live to the best of his native abilities. These ideal conditions of justice through social union are essentially those of democracy. They may be briefly and simply stated as follows in the practical terms in which they are being more widely recognized and achieved: (1) For every child a normal birth, a healthy environment, abundant, good food and a liberal, appropriate education. (2) For every mature person a secure job adapted to his abilities. (3) For every person an income adequate to maintain him efficient in the position of his highest social service. (4) For every person such influence with the authorities that his needs and ideas receive due consideration by them. With the possibility of economic abundance for all, now in some countries becoming a reality for the first time in history, the above fundamentals of social justice would appear to be no longer impossible. C.J.B.

social katabolism. The destructive phase of social metabolism (q.v.). The normal wearing down of component parts of the social structure normally replaced by social anabolism (q.v).

social lag. The failure of social institutions and attitudes to keep abreast of technology with which they are interrelated, the lack of synchronization producing maladjustment. M.K.

social laws. Formulations of uniformities of social behavior under similar conditions, the validity of which has been tested by repeated observations and by various logical and heuristic methods. Sociologists of recent years have been less confident in announcing "social laws," most of which have turned out to be unverified social theories, or at most social principles. Distinguished from axioms, which are supposedly universal self-evident truths; from hypotheses, which, like theories and principles, are plausible guesses in respect to causes, origins, and trends, pending demonstration and proof. T.D.E.

social legislation. Laws designed to improve and protect the economic and social position of those groups in society which because of age, sex, race, physical or mental defect, or lack of economic power cannot achieve healthful and decent living standards for themselves. The term social legislation was coined by William I of Germany in 1881 in a famous speech before the Reichstag urging the adoption of public accident and health insurance. J.W.M'C.

social level. A stratum in the hierarchy of social classes. The social level of a family is indicated by the stratigraphic position of its class. Conversely, if a family should move from one locality to another, it will find its place within the new community at approximately the same level as before. W.C.H.

social maladjustment. Any type of relationship between personalities (q.v.), groups (q.v.), culture elements, and culture complexes (q.v.), which is unsatisfactory to the personalities and groups involved. H.H.

social maturity. The degree to which an individual's attitudes, socialization, and emotional stability reflect a characteristically adult adjustment to his environment. P.F.H.

social metabolism. The balance of intake of raw materials, energy conservation and outgo (production, efficiency) in the social economy. The "katabolic" phase, however, is not destructive except by itself and therefore should not be considered homologous with social disorganization; and similarly, organization, while it is "built up", is not exclusively "anabolic": an organization may spend as well as build up energy and materials, on a normal, balanced basis. Cf. social anabolism; social katabolism.   T.D.E.

social mind. A concept used by many sociologists to express the mental unity of social groups, or the collective mental life of a human social group. The term is a very old one, but was given definite connotation by Professor Emile Durkheim and his school. Professor Durkheim held that just as the sensations and perceptions of the individual mind are compounded into concepts and individual representations, so the ideas and sentiments of individuals in a social group get compounded into what he called "collective representations" (q.v.). These may be ideas, opinions, beliefs, sentiments current in the social group. Durkheim held that these are still psychic, though objective to the individual. Instead of being made by the individual mind they are made by the minds of the members of a group in interaction. Thus there is a social mind, though there is no social brain. Most sociologists would reject the term "social mind" as unfortunate and misleading. They would say that Durkheim was simply describing culture on its subjective or mental side. While they recognize the reality of ideas and values in circulation in a group and dominating its behavior, they would prefer some other term to designate this process. There are such recognized terms as public opinion, popular sentiment, and popular will.   C.A.E.

social mindedness. A personal attitude of shared responsibility for solutions of social problems or improvement of social conditions, based upon awareness of such conditions and their multiple social-economic causation and upon faith in their modifiability or solubility. Distinguished from public spirit, which has to do with willingness to participate in civic or military enterprises, but is not necessarily aware of basic evils or remedies.   T.D.E.

social mobility. The movement of persons from social group to social group. Changes in religious or political affiliations are usually considered as horizontal social mobility. Changes in social status are identified as vertical. Inter-racial marriages frequently draw the contracting parties and their offspring in an oblique direction, to a half-caste position. The term social mobility is not related, conceptually, to the physical mobility of a population.
                    W.C.H.

social movement. A concerted action or agitation, with some degree of continuity, of a group which, fully or loosely organized, is united by more or less definite aims, follows a designed program, and is directed at a change (or to a countermovement at the preservation) of patterns and institutions of the existing society.
                    S.N.

social mutation. (By extension from biological mutation) a sudden metamorphosis or realignment of societal structure-fashion, usually occurring as a phase of crisis-behavior, either resolving the critical conflicts or precipitating further conflict and crisis and mutation. If social disorganization (q.v.) and societal disintegration (q.v.) have created conditions for reorganization of old elements, the emerging new structure is a social mutation.   T.D.E.

social nexus. The inter-connection linking individuals and groups through social dependence, mutual understanding or common origin.   M.C.E.

social norm. Any socially sanctioned mode or condition of behavior.   M.K.

social nucleus. The central or focal unit within society which contains the germs of a new idea, a social procedure or new social order. The term is applied sometimes to a particular organization or institution, as "the Sunday school" is the nucleus of tomorrow's church, or "the family" is the nucleus of society. M.C.E.

social opposition. That species of social interaction in which personalities or groups seek to attain any objective under such conditions that the greater the immediate or direct success of one personality or group the less the immediate or direct success of the others. Social opposition includes competition (q.v.) and conflict (q.v.). It is the opposite of cooperation.　　　　　　　　　　　　　　　　H.H.

social order. In general, the term refers to the totality of human relationships and culture of any given area or time; the constellation of social institutions. Critically the reference is to a certain quality, namely, the smooth, efficient, logical, aesthetic and ethical interactional functioning of individuals and groups within any such totality; it is a condition comparable to health in the individual. It is not the same as peace, for conflict may be orderly; it is not the same as organization, for organization always implies an amount of complexity not necessarily found with order.　　　　　　　　F.E.L.

social organ. A specialized group in society serving a distinct and necessary function demanded by a complicated social system.　　　　　　　　　　　　M.C.E.

social organism. A social organization or society considered to be analagous to a biological organism.　　　　　　　　M.S.

social organization. The organization of a society into sub-groups, including, in particular, those based on differences in age, sex, kinship, occupation, residence, property, privilege, authority, and status.　　　　　　　　　　　　　　　G.P.M.

social orientation. The general direction of the thought and effort of a social group, as determined by its dominant social values, or its philosophy of group welfare. Thus the social orientation of a society devoted to the ideals of democratic individualism differs from that of one devoted to socialistic, communistic or fascistic ideals; that of a religious order differs from that of a chamber of commerce.　　　　　　　　　　　　　　F.H.H.

social origin. The beginning, in human society, of a culture trait or pattern of mental or overt behavior, such as a belief in the supernatural being or the establishment of the "right" of private ownership of property.　　　　　　　　　R.E.B.

social origins. The first or earliest observed forms of societal and social phenomena, to which all current societal agencies and factors may be traced. H.A.P.

social ossification. The hardening of tradition, custom, or other prevalent social behavior patterns so that they resist change even though they may no longer fit the social needs for which they were designed.　　　　　　　　　　　R.E.B.

social parasite. A person who lives off of society. The term may include "the idle rich" at one extreme, and the beggar at the other. It always implies being a social debtor in that one does not make a fair return to society for the goods and services which one consumes.　　　F.D.W.

social parasitism. A type of human symbiosis (q.v.) in which, as in vegetable or animal parasitism, one person or group lives at the expense of another person or group, without corresponding contribution to his "host" or to the community. This includes criminals, defectives, exploiters, privileged income receivers, racketeers, idle women and the idle rich, but not normal dependency (q.v.). Cf. leisure class.　　　　　　　　　　　　　　　T.D.E.

social parity. Equality of status.　A.R.L.

social participation. Sharing by sentient beings in social interaction. The term ordinarily refers to conscious human participation. It may refer to utilitarian groups, or to sympathetic and affectional groups. In the latter there is more thorough identification of the personality with the group, through shared feelings of affection and loyalty, joint responsibility, sentiment, tradition, and personal friendship.　　　　　　　　　　　　　T.D.E.

social pathology. (1) A study of social disorganization or maladjustment in which there is a discussion of the meaning, extent, causes, results and treatment of the factors that prevent or reduce social adjustment; such as: poverty, unemployment, old age, ill health, feeblemindedness, insanity, crime, divorce, prostitution, family tensions.　　　　　　　　　O.W.
(2) The diseased or abnormal condition itself.

social pattern. Any oft-repeated bit of interactional behavior—three meals each day or family prayers each morning; or a coherent web of such behaviors. It involves the coordination and synchronization of the activities of two or more individual participants; the coordination and synchronization may develop unconsciously or be planned.   F.E.L.

social perception. Perception of social objects, qualities, relations or events.   M.S.

social phase. A stage through which a social activity may pass in its change from a simple to a compound activity.   M.C.E.

social phenomena. Events, facts, or occurrences of social interest susceptible of scientific description and explanation. They may be either conditioning, or of problem, phenomena: determining a social activity or the activity itself. The basic material of social science.   M.C.E.

social philosophy. The interpretation and estimation of social phenomena in terms of ethics and intimate values. Whether philosophy be understood as a criticism of concepts and of the presuppositions of knowledge, or as a synthesis of all scientific knowledge through logical inferences, it is closely related to sociology. Philosophy in the first sense bears directly on questions of sociological methodology. In the second sense it relates to the synthesis of the scientific knowledge afforded by the social sciences. Many of the problems in the social sciences cannot be solved by strictly scientific methods. For example, the problem whether planned social improvement is possible on a wide scale, can be dealt with only by the method of rational inference. Most of the burning problems of the day partake of this character. For example, should social planning be toward a free democratic type of society, or in the direction of Fascism or Communism? These questions, because they involve values, necessarily involve social philosophy. While the boundary between strictly scientific conclusions and philosophical conclusions should always be observed, the social scientist can have no objection to a social philosophy which reasons from the facts of human experi-

ence. Among the best philosophical methods of the present is critical realism, and critical realism should be of much aid to the social sciences.   C.A.E.

social physics. The description of and analysis of social phenomena as natural phenomena or data similar to physical data in their capacity to be observed.   H.A.P.

social planning. The interactional process —investigation, discussion, agreement—of projecting order upon human relationships; it involves a number of people reaching agreement as to what may be in human relations; to prepare a program for any body or organization.   F.E.L.
The apparently socialistic implications of this concept, as it has developed in recent years in the United States, have created the assumption of incompatibility between social planning and the capitalistic system, and have accordingly aroused opposition on the part of extreme champions of individualistic capitalism. Cf. idealization; social engineering.

social polarity. Forces in any social aggregate which are sharply contrasted and which tend by their opposition to keep the aggregate in equilibrium; as in the tension between major political parties, between agricultural and industrial interests, and between youth and age.   G.M.F.

social policy. A consistent attitude toward the direction of social control, whether in respect to its goals or its methods. This attitude may be verbalized, and even announced, by those who pursue the policy. It may be announced but not consistently maintained, in which case it may be called merely an ostensible policy. Or, it may be maintained without formulation, even unconsciously, by those in control, the pattern being noted and named by an outside observer. Among social policies the following (and their opposites) may be noted as important examples: centralization (q.v.), collectivism (q.v.), regeneration (q.v.), exclusion (q.v.) obscurantism (q.v.), diversification, reward, reaction.   T.D.E.

social potential. Capacity to influence social action or social change. This differs greatly among different individuals but is not entirely lacking in any individual no matter how humble or insignificant.

social potentiality. Cf. social potential.

social power. Any of a number of types of energy, force, or strength derived from social relationships and from the functional characteristic of social structure. It is "fluid" in the sense that it can be activated, canalized, and projected towards goals in the social-pressure operations of individuals and groups. It is most readily available for use in the form of pressure groups, armies, money, prestige and status, and social sanctions. Leaders can activate and gain control of social power through the manipulation of symbols, verbal and event propaganda, and existing political, economic, and religious organizational structures. Certain statuses are focal points of social power, e.g., the physician, priest, chieftain, precinct leader, congressman, banker, general, professor, football hero, actress, orator, journalist, scientist. The achievement of such statuses is a significant aspect of the struggle for power. As conditions change in society, aggressive individuals seize and strengthen the power-focusing characteristics and even create new ones to meet new needs, such as labor leadership. Dictators systematically integrate into their power structures statuses and contributing social structures that can be useful to them and attempt to undermine and destroy such elements as cannot be so assimilated. Cf. power; social potential.

A.M'C.L.

social pressure. Efforts directed toward individuals and groups with the purpose of modifying their behavior to attain certain clearly defined goals. Specifically, social pressure in the form of public opinion is often brought to bear on individual public officials or legislative bodies to bring about certain action in connection with specific social problems. A.E.W.

social problem. A situation inherently requiring ameliorative treatment, which either (1) arises out of the conditions of society or the social environment, or (2) calls for the application of social forces and social means for its improvement. The two classes frequently merge, and show common characteristics. In Category (1) fall such defects, maladjustments or inadequacies of individuals, families or small groups as are directly traceable in some part to the human environment and would not exist in an ideal society even though the individual units concerned were precisely as they are. Illustrative of this category are many types of unemployment, disease, destitution, vice, etc. In Category (2) belong defects and maladjustments of the societal structure and functioning itself, which lie beyond the power of any single individual or small group to correct, such as war, cyclical unemployment, political corruption, etc. Remedial measures in Category (1) tend to be of the type of social reform; those in Category (2) correspond chiefly to social engineering (q.v.). The tendency of modern sociological theory and practice is to regard an increasingly large proportion of the problems of individual life as social, that is to recognize the influence of the human environment upon the development and experience of all individuals, regardless of their genetic constitution and equipment. This trend also recognizes the increasing complexity and interdependence of modern social life with a correlated impossibility of the individual, no matter how great his social potential (q.v.), to provide independently for his own needs and welfare.

social process. Any social change or interaction in which an observer sees a consistent quality or direction to which a class name is given; a class of social changes or interactions in which by abstraction a common pattern can be observed and named (e.g., imitation, acculturation, conflict, social control, stratification). No social process is good or evil in se, but in relation to the situation in which it occurs, as appraised in relation to some set of subjective values or norms. It should be noted that social processes, like all other processes, are changes in structure (q.v.) and that social structure like other structure is only relatively permanent. It should also be noted that most social process words are also used to describe the situations in which the process has been and is operating, as abstracted from the total space-time manifold and at a given time: like a snapshot or a single still in a motion-film. Every social process has four or five possible forms. 1. Intra-personal, when the interaction is between selves or complexes of a personality; 2. Person-to-person; 3a. Person-to-group; 3b. Group-to-person; 4. Group-to-group. Cf. situation-process; structure-function. T.D.E.

social product. Collective product; the state of being in any social situation-process at any given moment; or, the material results of a given unit of social or economic interaction, whether deliberate or unplanned. T.D.E.

social progress. Social change or movement in the direction of some recognized and approved goal. The telic activities of society when wisely conceived and efficiently administered. Sheer change, even though of an evolutionary character, is not necessarily progress. Nor can progress be determined merely by discovering whether society appears to be moving forward or backward. If an ancient automobile with a low level of gas in its tank encounters a hill so steep that it can be negotiated only by turning around and driving up backward the car is still making progress. Since society itself is a complex structure, different parts of which may move at different speeds (Cf. lag, cultural) or even in different directions, social progress does not necessarily affect the whole of society at any given time. Progress may be appraised with reference to almost any one of the major societal interests. When reference is made to social progress in general, there is, or should be, ordinarily some assumption of general values that are either ultimate in character, or have been demonstrably accepted by the society in question.

To philosophy belongs the problem of what is the ultimate good, and so the ultimate question as to what constitutes specific progress or improvement. In a relative sense social progress is verifiable if we accept the ordinary tests and values of common sense. For example, the lengthening of human life has usually not been questioned as an evidence of progress. Even in such cases, however, one has to admit that the subjective values of human beings play a part in determining what is accepted as betterment.

Nearly all sociologists hold that social progress must be defined in terms of control—control over physical nature, on the one hand, and control over human nature and human relations, on the other. Such control is almost the whole content of culture. The only improvement in human relations which man knows evidently must come through the improvement of culture. Whether anything like general progress is possible depends upon our answer to the question whether a general high level of culture is possible for the whole of mankind. The concept of social progress, and the possibility of achieving it, are bound up with social philosophy (q.v.). Cf. idealization.

social propagation. The dissemination, or spreading from person to person of ideas, ideals, attitudes, and practices. M.C.E.

social prophylaxis. The prevention and guarding against negative social forces and social deterioration. M.C.E.

social protoplasm. The unformulated elements in society which contain the germ of ideas, social growth and organization. M.C.E.

social provision. (*social economy*) A social economic situation-process in which some element in the plane of living is provided to all persons and families through public or cooperative channels; e.g., street cleaning, fire protection, water, schooling, libraries, playgrounds, parks. The cost of goods and services socially provided may be prorated by meter or otherwise, or may be covered by taxes. T.D.E.

social psychology. The scientific study of the mental processes of man, regarded as a socius or social being. The distinction between social psychology and any other psychology is essentially abstract and academic, since it is impossible to study any human being entirely detached from social relationships.

social reality. The basic content of sociology. Ant. nominalism. H.A.P.

social reconstruction. Reorganization of society as a whole or in some specific part. H.A.P.

social recreation. A leisure activity that affords opportunities for social contact and sociability, such as parties, social dances, dining, and social games.   M.H.N.

social reform. The general movement, or any specific result of that movement, which attempts to eliminate or mitigate the evils that result from the malfunctioning of the social system, or any part of it. In its concept and scope, social reform lies somewhere between social work (q.v.) and social engineering (q.v.). It rises above and beyond the mere alleviation of individual and family hardships, but it does not aim at the sweeping changes in social structure that are involved in social engineering. Social reform is closely affiliated with the ideas of social progress that characterized 19th century thought in Western culture. It accepted the existing framework of society, and sought to correct the ills that were associated with it. There have been numerous reform movements such as the extension of the electorate, the protection of the less powerful elements in society, and the control of vice.

social relation. An inclusive term designating both social processes (q.v.) and social relationships (q.v.).   H.B.

social relationship. A form pattern of social conduct, i.e., interaction between persons and/or plurels in which space positions are more conspicuous than time sequences, and quiescence is more conspicuous than motion. The social relationship is one aspect of the graphic, the structural, the morphological patterning, wedlock, kinship, citizenship, etc. Note the suffix -ship, denoting state or condition. This is not an essential feature of terms of social relationship, however; it is merely an occasional indication.   H.B.

social reorganization. The establishment of a new system of relationships or values in a social group or society, particularly after a period of disorganization or rapid social change.   P.F.C.

social repression. Elimination or prevention of deviant behavior through collective effort.   A.R.L.

social research. The application to any social situation of exact procedures for the purpose of solving a problem, or testing an hypothesis, or discovering new phenomena or new relations among phenomena. These procedures must conform as closely as possible to the accepted scientific requirement that each process shall be susceptible of being repeated approximately by subsequent investigators. Social research differs from social survey in being more intensive and precise, and more concerned with the discovery of general principles.   G.M.F.

social resources. All persons or organizations which can be of help to an individual or a social work agency in solving problems.   W.P.

social response. Response of one social agent to the stimulation of another social agent or to the stimulation of some inanimate object having social significance.   M.S.

social responsibility. Cf. responsibility.

social restraint. Negative control exerted within a group; a condition in which some form of restraint is imposed by a group upon its members; or, a form of internal control in which a person is inhibited by cultural requirements or appreciation of the group situation or demands of membership. Distinguished from social constraint (q.v.), in which there is physical control imposed by law, and (usually) custodial care.   T.D.E.

social retrogression. Regression in respect to achieved levels in any given scale of social values, or in respect to some goal, standard, or criterion accepted by a group; 'the opposite of social progress (q.v.).   T.D.E.

social revolution. The sudden passing of a social order, especially its social class hierarchy. A social revolution is a thoroughgoing revamping of the constellations of power, prestige, and privilege in a society, wherein the upper orders are almost completely dislodged from dominance and control.   W.C.H.

social rhythm. Any succession of identical or closely similar thoughts, feelings and actions of groups that is punctuated periodically. The waltz with its triple measure, the three-meal-a-day pattern, the repetitious behavior in church and lodge rituals, and business cycles—in so far as they are true cycles—are examples.   F.E.L.

social rite. Standard of behavior designated by law, custom or religion as the correct form. Cf. ritual.   O.W.

social sanction. Any threat of penalty or promise of reward set by or for a group upon the conduct of its members, to induce conformity to its rules or laws. Legal sanction is a form of social sanction; but the phrase may also be used, by contrast, to indicate those group sanctions other than legal. Cf. sanction.   T.D.E.

social satisfaction. (1) The capacity of the social organization of a given society to bring the large majority of its members, or groups of members, to acceptance of and agreement with its concepts of values. (2) The state of mind induced by the quenching of desires, wants, needs and ambitions of groups and masses through effective social division of labor, thereby reducing and softening revolutionary activities and ideas.   J.H.B.

social scale. A hypothetical measuring standard whereon the social classes distribute themselves by giving and receiving deference, rank, and precedence. The "Four Hundred" enjoy prestige at the top of the scale; the "Bowery bums" live in the social morass at its base. The social scale is never identical with the economic; it includes values far in excess of the possession, acquisition, and expenditure of wealth.   W.C.H.

social science. A general term for all the sciences which are concerned with human affairs; such sciences are economics, government, law, education, psychology, sociology, anthropology.   H.A.P.

social selection. A situation-process in which certain persons or groups, in conscious or unconscious competition with others for status in a given culture (or between cultures), succeed and win recognition, prestige, power, or social survival

because of adaptability to the changing situation. Often such selection occurs at crises (q.v.).   T.D.E.

social self. (1) The individual viewed by others solely from his social experiences, or that aspect of the individual's personality which others treat as significant in their dealings with him. (2) An individual's consciousness of his abilities to adopt demanded rôles, or a sense of esteem for what is believed to command recognition in others.   B.M.

social service. Organized efforts to improve the conditions of disadvantaged classes; synonymous with social work, a more professional term. Also extended to cover the wider field of agencies for health, recreation, etc., public and private, known as the social service agencies of a community, or the social services. Cf. service agencies.   R.N.B.

social service exchange; confidential exchange; central index; social service index. A central clearing bureau of all the case records of a given geographic area. Names, addresses and other information of help in identifying individuals and families using the private and public social work agencies which register with it are filed.   W.P.

social settlement. A neighborhood center in the poorer districts of cities, supported largely by private contributions, staffed by persons of education and training, with the objects of enlarging the neighborhood opportunities for living, and of interpreting to the whole community the problems of disadvantaged sections and classes. Cf. settlement.   R.N.B.

social situation. The environmental circumstances of a unit containing one or more other units with which social relationships may exist or social behavior may occur.   M.S.

social solidarity. Cf. social cohesion.

social standard. A minimum or maximum, modal degree, or model to which a given group expects its members to conform their behavior, costume, food, housing, etc., in particular respects, considered conducive to maintenance of social values (q.v.). Traditional standards are part of the mores. Other standards may be set up in the light of current scientific knowledges. Cf. expectation.   T.D.E.

social statistics. Quantitative data relating to human society and social relations, collected, analyzed, and organized in mathematical form. Cf. statistics.

social status. A position in a social group or in society. Relative position, rank, or standing. Locus in the social scale of an individual or group. Within the limits prescribed by an individual's status in society generally, he may occupy different statuses in different groups and institutions. The assignment of statuses and the definition of their duties and rewards are crystallized in and sanctioned by the folkways and mores. Individuals in a preferred social status thus have a vested interest in maintaining the cultural patterns that assure the persistence of their status. Persons occupying social statuses in which they are instruments of group action, policy, ritual, or leadership are called social functionaries. Some of the criteria by which status is judged are leadership, dominance, ability, accomplishment, occupation or other means of recognition designated by title, degree, membership, dress, behavior, or other devices for securing attention.   A.M′C.L.; O.W.

social stimulation. Stimulation by the presence or action of one or more other persons.   M.S.

social stimulus. A stimulus that brings a response from people as group members rather than as individuals. Such stimuli —in the form of rumors, news reports, parades, catastrophes, etc.—elicit such social responses as public opinions, group-formation, folkway - making, cultural change, crowd and mob phenomena, etc.
                                        A.M′C.L.

social stratification. The arrangement of societal elements into groups on different horizontal levels. The establishment of status on terms of varying superiority and inferiority.

social structure. (1) The established pattern of internal organization of any social group. It involves the character of the sum total of the relationships which exist between the members of the group with each other and with the group itself.

(2) A general term for all those attributes of social groups and types of culture which make them susceptible of being viewed as composite or complex wholes, made up of interdependent parts. Two kinds of social structure may be distinguished from each other in the abstract: (a) the division of social groups into part-groups and ultimately into individual members or persons, often differing from each other in rôle and status; and (b) the division of a type of culture, i.e., the total body of culture of a society or group, into constituent elements such as folkways, mores, culture complexes, institutions, and beliefs.   F.N.H.

social suggestion. Suggestion employed on one person by another.   M.S.

social surplus. That margin of energy (vital power or cultural accumulation) existing in or available to a social group over and above what is necessary for survival at its cultural level; the residue of social energy possessed by any group after its existence and survival demands have been provided for and satisfied. N.L.S.

social survey. A cooperative undertaking which applies scientific method to the study and treatment of current related social problems and conditions having definite geographical limits and bearings, plus such a spreading of its facts, conclusions, and recommendations as will make them, as far as possible, the common knowledge of the community and a force for intelligent coordinated action. It draws upon and utilizes in a single endeavor the knowledge, experience and skills of: 1. The civic and social workers in discovering in their everyday service to the community clues to current social situations needing better understanding; 2. The engineer in seeing the structural relations of different types of community conditions to each other; 3. The surveyor in relating his work and study to a definite geographical area; 4. The social research worker, in formulating specific questions for study, investigating and analyzing the pertinent facts, and drawing warranted generalizations; 5. The physician, city planner, and social worker, in bringing problems down to human terms and in prescribing or planning treatment; and 6. The journalist and publicity worker in interpreting facts and new knowledge in terms of human experience and presenting them in ways which will engage the attention and stimulate democratic action.

social survival. Factual remembrance of social aggregates by means of tradition. Cf. symbol; tradition.   J.H.B.

social symbol. A symbol which is not merely personal, but, having a shared meaning, may communicate this meaning; e.g., gestures, words, signs, devices, heroes. Distinguished from collective symbols in that the latter are symbols or collective representations which stand for the collectivity, and more especially for the history and values of the group, as a whole. T.D.E.

Any person, word, mark, sound, or other object or expression that is used to direct attention to a social program, idea, movement, object, or service. Social symbols include, to be more specific, such as the following: a church, school, capitol, or other building; Jesus Christ, Charles Darwin, Abraham Lincoln, or other personality; priest or minister, teacher or professor, governor or judge, or other functionary; cross, school book, scales of justice, swastika, fasces, or other objects; music, intonation, medal, uniform, etc. In fact, the term's connotations are so broad that it refers to a way of looking at practically all socially-recognized and even many socially-ignored objects, ideas, institutions, and other phenomena. The socially-ignored phenomena become symbols of the vulgar and criminal. Cf. stereotype.   A.M'C.L.

social synthesis. A drawing together or combination of social elements and persons or groups into a more organized system of relations, giving meaning, recognition and support to one another, usually involving an increase of mutual understanding and reciprocal service.   C.J.B.

social technique. The development of principles, methods and means for the practical study and improvement of society.
                                           M.C.E.

social technology. The applied social sciences, arts, and skills underlying social work as a profession and social planning (q.v.) and social engineering (q.v.) as social controls.   T.D.E.

social telesis. The conscious choice by society of desired goals, and the intelligent direction of natural and social forces to achieve such chosen objectives. Cf. social planning; social progress.   A.E.W.

social telics. A system of conscious idealization and effort based upon the consensus of an influential section of society, and aimed at the goal of societal betterment.

social tension. An emotional state, resulting from the repressed friction and opposition existing among social groups, developed, generally, over a considerable period of time, and caused partly by the pressure of interest groups, partly by mutual ignorance and differing traditions, partly by designing or incompetent leaders, and partly by forces in the environment beyond human control, such as adverse climate or terrain, or meagre resources.
                                           G.M.F.

social theory. Any generalization concerning social phenomena that is sufficiently established scientifically to serve as a reliable basis for sociological interpretation.

social thought. The totality of man's thought about his relationships and obligations to his fellow men. The earliest social thought was such in the literal sense of the term; that is, it was the product of folk thinking, the cumulative experience of men in association embodied in myths, legends, proverbs, folklore. Since the days of the Greek social philosophers, social thought has become increasingly the conscious product of critical reflection on the part of individual thinkers. Social thought has matured into social science to the degree that it has achieved objectivity through the development of methods of verification.   H.E.J.

social tradition. The product of the transmission from generation to generation, usually by oral or written language, though also by means of ceremonies, of the ideas, sentiments, and values connected with the life of a social group. Briefly, social tradition is the subjective side of culture passed along by various forms of inter-communication, while custom is the objective, behavioristic side. Tradition is dominantly a way of thinking and feeling handed down from generation to generation, while custom is a way of doing which is handed down. The chief vehicle of social tradition is oral and written language. Custom and tradition make up the culture of the group. Sociologists are divided as to which is the main element. The behaviorists hold that custom, or patterned actions, is the main element. Non-behaviorists hold that in human groups, especially in the more culturally advanced groups, nearly all customs are sustained by the social tradition. The patterns of action, in other words, are lodged in the minds of individuals through language and other forms of communication, and in this way, even more than through imitative action, customs are transmitted from generation to generation and persist.

Man must have started without a definite social tradition, as tradition requires verbal language as a vehicle. As soon as articulate speech developed, however, human groups began to accumulate traditions. As they accumulated knowledge, ideas, sentiments, and values, they passed these along, and human groups came to live more and more through and by means of their traditions. The compulsive power of the social tradition is due wholly to its acceptance and the opinion of the living members of the group. Nevertheless, it is true that as tradition represents group experience, accumulated often through many generations, it seems to have a weight which is not possessed by the opinion of the moment.   C.A.E.

social transmission. The process whereby culture traits are passed on from generation to generation, thereby achieving continuity. Its instrumentalities are imitation, education, indoctrination, taboo, and various forms of social control.

social trends. The predominant tendencies and the particular course which social developments show as manifested in the sum of reactions and prevailing institutions of a given period. These trends may well differ from specific occurrences and individual presentations, important though the latter may be.   S.N.

social type. Rational superstructure over social life, or part of it, modeled according to a specific form (gestalt) determined by qualities of a sociologically defined object. Cf. gestalt; social entity.   J.H.B.

social units. Elements or basic object-matter in social study, so called because they are observed within given limits and are comparatively constant and measurable. E.g. person, family, standard of living, attitude, propaganda, crime. Units, thus, may be either elementary and studied as actual parts of a whole complex, or they may be combinations of constants whose stability, uniformity, and interaction have been analyzed operationally.   H.A.P.

social unity (group unity). Unity of action in a social group is brought about by the mutual adjustments made in the behavior of the individual members of the group, so that the action of the group as a whole has a single aim. For example, the members of a football team so adjust or coordinate the activities of individual members of the team that the whole team works as a human machine to put the ball over the goal. While the football team is a very artificial group, yet all human social groups are characterized by some mutual adjustment of the behavior of their members, so that they function to achieve some objective goal. Their action is the result of the integration or coordination of the individual actions, feelings, and purposes of the members of the group. Thus the behavior of a social group becomes often so highly unified that we speak of the solidarity of the group. The process is called "group integration." Social or group unity does not imply that all members of the group act in the same way or have the same thoughts and feelings. On the contrary, differences of behavior and of thought and feeling, when they favor coordination or adjustment, are necessary for the integration of a group. The unity of the group results from integration of the adaptive feelings and purposes of the members of the group. They unite in order to achieve some collective purpose which is usually desired by all the members of the group. Human group unity is not simply due to the pressure of environment, but even more to adaptive ideas, feelings, and purposes.

C.A.E.

social unrest. Friction or frustration in the relationships of social groups. If the unrest is undefined it may be manifest in confusion and incoherent expression. If it is defined it may find expression in any of a variety of actions, depending on the leadership that emerges. A labor union may be formed, a political pressure group or even a mob.

N.A.

social values. Objects, inanimate or animate, human, artificial, or non-material, to which some value for the group (collectively or distributively) has been imputed by group consensus. The value may be positive or negative. The attitudes of persons often reflect group consensus toward social values, and may also affect and thus modify the group consensus.

T.D.E.

social welfare. Private or public services to ameliorate conditions of need or social pathology in a community. In the general application of the term there is implied an organization of purpose and possibly a systematic method of rendering social welfare service. Cf. public welfare.

N.A.

social wholes. Systems of social relationships, such as the social institutions, in which the sub-parts have been identified, and in which the parts and relationships have meanings only as they are observed in their interaction to each other.

H.A.P.

social will. Combined will of two or more interacting participants. A much disputed concept. Cf. group will.

M.S.

social wish. Wish in which only the image of its satisfaction is social, or both the impulse and the image of its satisfaction are social. Two forms may be distinguished: (a) wish of an individual for satisfaction obtainable only in social situations; (b) a joint wish of two or more agents for satisfaction obtainable only in social situations.

M.S.

social work. The processes involved in adjusting an individual's relationships with other persons and with his wider social and economic environment, including case work and group work. Also organizing and administering agencies for this purpose. Cf. social technology; societal technician.

W.P.

social work, family. Social case work with families. The problem presented is usually one involving the whole family rather than any one individual.

W.P.

social work, psychiatric. Social case work practised in a psychiatric hospital or clinic or child guidance setting, or in regular association with a psychiatrist. It is especially concerned with behavior problems.

W.P.

social work, publicity and interpretation in. Cf. publicity and interpretation in social work.

social worker. A person engaged in social work.

W.P.

socialism. A social philosophy, or a system of social organization, based on the principle of the public ownership of the material instruments of production and economic service. It is essentially an economic concept, rather than a political one. The extensive confusion on this point arises mainly from two sources; first, the recognition that political action will ordinarily be required to establish socialism in a society that does not possess it; and second, the realization that socialism can hardly be expected to function with smoothness and stability in anything but a democratic society. Theoretically, socialism could be established in almost any type of state, and it is significant that some of the most dictatorial forms of state characterize themselves as socialistic. However, the public ownership of the instruments of production can hardly function efficiently under government despotism, and on the other hand, a society in which socialism is well established will necessarily, and almost automatically, demand and achieve a democratic form of state.

Like democracy, liberty, and freedom, to which it is closely related, socialism is a matter of relativity. It can exist in widely varying degrees of comprehensiveness. To take the United States as an example, there already exist within its economic system innumerable and widely diverse socialistic enterprises, such as publicly-owned waterworks, electric light and power systems, public schools, roads, post office, transportation facilities, Army and Navy, flood control establishments and so on through an almost interminable list. There are, however, many significant differences between partial socialism and complete socialism. Under partial socialism, workers, at least in theory, have the choice between public and private employment. Under socialism every worker, (and it is assumed that every able bodied adult will be a worker) must be in the employ of society.

The distinction between socialism and capitalism is not in the character of the productive mechanism, but in the location of the ownership of Capital, Land and Business. The effect of complete socialism would be to wipe out entirely what has been called "property" or "ownership" income, and leave only "service" or "doership" income. There need necessarily be no limitations to the accumulation of consumer goods under private ownership but there would be no possibility of deriving income from the ownership of production goods, or from what in socialistic terminology is called "the exploitation of labor."

In its fundamental principle, socialism is practically identical with communism. It differs from communism primarily in the matter of the tempo and method of transition, and in the basis of compensation of the worker. Communism is characteristically committed to rapid, and if necessary forcible, change, while socialism is content to make its gains by gradual, piecemeal methods. Communism, in theory, holds either that all workers should be compensated alike, no matter what their economic function or contribution, or that income should be adjusted to need.

The classless state, which looms so large in socialistic discussions, is not an integral component of socialism itself, but a goal toward which the socialistic community strives, and which it hopes eventually to attain. The assumption, quite prevalent in the United States, that socialism involves the centralized ownership and administration of all economic func-

tions has no foundation in socialistic theory. The public units which, under socialism, would conduct the economic activities are ordinarily identified in the public mind with existing political units, but they need not necessarily be so, and certainly there could be as many, and diversified, types of economic divisions as the efficiency and economy of the entire system called for. There would, naturally, be a tendency towards nation-wide integration and coordination.

Historically there have been many branches of socialistic theory, such as Marxian Socialism, Fabian Socialism, Guild Socialism, National Socialism, and others. The only historical example of the establishment of virtually comprehensive socialism on a large scale is furnished by the Union of Soviet Socialist Republics.

socialism, Fabian. Fabian socialism presents a constitutional and gradual transition to state ownership of the means of production. No place is given to revolutionary techniques. Rather its methods are educational. It seeks in an opportunistic and practical way to utilize all legislative means of regulating hours of work, health, wages, and other labor conditions. This form of socialism has as its sponsoring organization the Fabian Society, founded in 1884. Leadership in this English social movement has come from a small group of intellectuals, among whom are George Bernard Shaw, Lord Passfield, Beatrice Webb, Graham Wallas, and G. D. H. Cole. One of their members J. Ramsay MacDonald, twice became Prime Minister of Great Britain.   J.H.E.

socialism, guild-. A trend in the British labor movement which enjoyed great ideological success in the period between 1916 to 1926, and of which the main idea, parent to the foundation of French syndicalism, was the autonomous organization of a planned economy through the effective control of it by workers and consumers, limiting and balancing the political state. A special league for guild-socialism was founded which produced some practical achievements in the building industry. Guild-socialism was strongly opposed not only to communism, but also to all forms of centralist and collectivistic socialism. Its difference from French syndicalism lies in a more consistent pluralistic view and a closer connection with the liberal tradition (e.g. "group liberalism" favorable also to individual liberty). Sociological interest in guild socialism is linked with its practical application of some theoretical principles of the "social and jural pluralism" and its contribution to the typology of particular groups. G.G.

socialism, national. The theory and practice of present-day German dictatorship. The very name indicates an adroit combination of the two powerful dynamic tendencies in modern society: nationalism and socialism. It also suggests the purposeful ambiguity of the movement and its successful appeal to the most divergent social groups and ideological forces —a fact which makes it difficult, if not impossible, to give national socialism a certain, conclusive meaning. National socialism has been in turn called the personal instrument of Hitler's one-man rule; a subservient tool of doomed capitalism; an efficient weapon against Bolshevism; a revolt of the strata in society most seriously affected by the crisis, uprooted by war, inflation and economic depression; a militant movement of a proud people who want to avenge their defeat and to renew a drive toward world conquest which they failed to achieve a generation earlier. Each of these interpretations and many more may signify an important aspect of this dictatorship and in specific stages of its development such formulae possibly characterize the most essential driving forces of the movement. Probably the analysis which comes closest to an inclusive definition is one which recognizes in national socialism an unrestrained lust for power, ready to make use of any element of unrest, internal and international, that will feed the continuous dynamics of a permanent revolution.

Four features of national socialism stand out: First, it is totalitarian, embracing all social groups and all fields of activity. Secondly, its quasi-democratic character is expressed in its demagogical leadership, its "legal" seizure of power, its use of democratic machinery, its constant craving for popular acclaim (propaganda). Thirdly, its institutional framework guarantees the daily functioning of the complex political body, and its well-established party machine may even bring about the survival of the dictatorship system beyond the life span of its creator, momentous though the personality of Hitler has been in the making of the movement. Finally national socialism is government for war. This militancy permeates all agencies, policies, and attitudes of the Third Reich and exclusively dictates its foreign relations. Belligerence and expansion are of its essence. The strategy of international affairs has been successfully tried out within the nation and is now merely applied to wider fields of activities (E.g. treatment of minorities, fifth column, psychological warfare). Hitler's Reich can never be appeased, and even the peace of its "New Order" is a perpetuation of the rule of a warrior caste (based upon the myth of the supremacy of the master race). The rise, development and survival of national socialism are inextricably tied up with continuous dynamics. S.N.

socialist. One who adheres to the doctrines of socialism, and who advocates the establishment of a socialistic order.

sociality. The quality of being socialized. Ant. individuality. H.A.P.

socialization, rural. Processes in the growth of a society, identified essentially by the primary group, agriculture, relatively simple form of industry, the small locality group, a relatively small, homogeneous, and immobile society. H.A.P.

socialization process. A socio-psychological process, whereby the personality is created under the influence of the educational institutions; a process intertwined with (a) the institutions wherein the general conditioning process relates itself to the school process, the family, play groups, racial groups, community, church, motion-pictures, and the like—and with (b) some problems of the sociology of groups formed in the educational process, and of the groups engaged in education—teachers, professors, administrators, school boards, state legislatures, preachers, pressure groups. It is a process centered fundamentally around the school, the base of all organized educational efforts and aims, which gives the whole educational process a definite direction. Cf. school. J.S.R.

socialize. The process of teaching the individual, through various relationships, educational agencies and social controls, to adjust himself to living in his society. It does not imply moral values but rather sufficient adjustment to the folkways and mores of his time and place to be a functioning member of his community. F.D.W.

socialized drive. Cf. drive, socialized.

socialized medicine. A broad term to indicate a new emphasis in modern medical practice; emphasis on new forms of medical practice designed to get modern scientific treatment to all the people regardless of income or ability to pay for it—and to do this systematically and beyond the charity of private physicians and local governments (e.g., city hospitals). Socialized medicine, therefore, to some extent overlaps the organization and work of the public health (q.v.) movement. In the broad sense socialized medicine includes state medicine; in a narrower and more accurate sense it excludes it. Since socialized medicine may well prove to be a transition type of social organization, its form is somewhat amorphous. Some of its more "radical" features are various forms of group organization rendering free service outside that rendered by private physicians, and outside state medicine; more frequently it is associated with partial prepayment often on an insurance basis with subsidies by the government to cover aid to the lowest income groups. Some of its more conservative (i.e., more nearly traditional) features are group practice, plans for total prepayment (i.e., without subsidy) of unusual and sudden medical expenses, "blue cross" hospital plans, etc. N.E.H.

sociation. A term including all interhuman relations, or social interaction, whether of associative, dissociative, or mixed associative-dissociative character. Approximate synonyms are social behavior, conduct, "the social process," human relations, etc. H.B.

societal. Having to do with society. Relating to, or characteristic of, any large group or groups that are included within the concept of society. As compared with social (q.v.), the emphasis of the term societal is upon group structure and functioning, rather than upon associational relationships.

societal control. A category of social control (q.v.) comprising control exercised by a society as a whole upon its members, or over its own structure-function. T.D.E.

societal development. Cf. development, societal.

societal forces. Assuming "forces" as entities, societal forces are such constellations or resultants of personal social forces as are organized or seen as patterned wholes, representing the impact of collectivities upon other major compositions of social energies. As examples: The Catholic Church, Masonry, The Comintern, The United States Steel Corporation, "Sofina," The International Postal Union. "Historical forces" are societal forces in time dimension, such as The Renaissance, The Industrial Revolution. Cf. social forces. T.D.E.

societal pattern. A composite arrangement of social and non-social phenomena, such as a universal culture, a civilization, or the divisions thereof. H.A.P.

societal phenomena. Phenomena connected with the structure or functioning of society, as contrasted with "social phenomena," which may involve only individuals or small groups.

societal process. Any social process (q.v.) in which the changes under observation involve the structure-function of a society as a whole. T.D.E.

societal self-direction. Societal control (q.v.) under deliberate planning and responsible leadership; social telesis (q.v.). It does not necessarily premise a societal "self", in a personified sense. T.D.E.

societal technician. A specialist in analyzing institutional structure, function, and change, in diagnosing maladjustments, in facilitating adjustments, in estimating the wise rôle for a client in a prevailing situation, and in predicting future possibilities. His facilitation of societal adjustments necessitates as adequate as possible a knowledge of the techniques of social cultural manipulation as well as of the trend and range of permissible experimentation in the pertinent social situation.

As public relations counselor, management specialist, labor relations consultant, personnel director, political manager, sentiment analyst, or whatever, the societal technician avails himself—to the extent of his time, curiosity, and ability—of what has been learned about society by social scientists as this knowledge has a bearing on the solution of practical problems. Cf. public relations counsel; clinical sociology; social work.   A.M′C.L.

societal variables. Social and non-social changes of different magnitudes and degrees which modify human interaction.   H.A.P.

societal wholes. Systems of societal patterns in which each pattern is a combination of social and non-social forms, relationships, and changes, and each pattern may be considered as a whole. Ex. population; social organization; social change.   H.A.P.

societary. Cf. societal.

society. A group of human beings co-operating in the pursuit of several of their major interests, invariably including self-maintenance and self-perpetuation. The concept of society includes continuity, complex associational relationships, and a composition including representatives of fundamental human types, specifically men, women, and children. Ordinarily, also, there is the element of territorial establishment. Society is a functioning group, so much so as to be frequently defined in terms of relationships or processes. It is the basic, large-scale human group. It is to be sharply differentiated from fortuitous temporary or non-representative groups or aggregations such as a mob, the passengers on a steamship, the spectators at a ball game, or the inhabitants of an army camp.

society, component. A society viewed from the point of view of its demotic and social composition. Cf. constituent society.   T.D.E.

society, conspirital. A society in which exploitation by the dominant group has roused opposition in the aggrieved groups, which, however, must be organized secretly because of suppression; a society in which conspiracies and conspirital groups are to be found.   T.D.E.

society, constituent. Society viewed from the point of view of its constitution, i.e., its organic structure-function; or, a society considered as a constituent (functional) element in the structure-function of a larger society. Cf. component society.   T.D.E.

society, folk. Cf. folk-regional society.

society, folk-regional. Cf. folk-regional society.

society, functional. A group of people associated together, within, and partly supported by, a more extensive society, for the purpose of carrying on, facilitating or enjoying a particular social function. Examples of such functional groups: literary, fraternal, religious, research, athletic, economic, or political societies. C.J.B.

society, ideal of. Cf. ideal of society.

society, industrial. Group life organized with reference to the pattern of industrialism, the indispensable condition for which is widespread transformation in industry itself, as seen in advanced technological development by means of applied science, large-scale production with power machinery, and specialization and the division of labor. Accompanying the changes in industry are other striking changes, chief among them being transformations in the means of communication and transportation, a widening market, migration and accelerated urbanization of the population, and alterations in consumption habits. Likewise there is the ever larger rôle played by secondary groups and alterations in customs and mores affecting primary group relationships. Conflicts between classes, races and other groups reflect the typical features of the new situation, as does the more complex nature of the accommodation process.   K.DP.L.

society, organic. An association of people whose system of social functions is so highly organized that their mutual services are thoroughly reliable in maintaining its existence, or in discharging the services required of it by the larger community of which it may be a member.   C.J.B.

society, organic concept of. A concept that may include the organismic analogy (q.v.); but more broadly or by contrast may indicate a recognition that a community or a society is organized, i.e., that parts and units are working together in a larger unity. An organization, as well as an organism, is organic.   T.D.E.

society, patriarchal. A society whose culture places notable dominance and power over others in the hands of the male head of the household or kinship group (q.v.), as the case may be. It may, but not necessarily, include such features as patrilocal residence (q.v.), patrilineal descent (q.v.), and patronymy.   E.A.H.

society, primitive. In the strict sense, any society which has not acquired written language. A society which is uncivilized.   E.A.H.

society, public utility. A private corporation organized under British law for the construction and operation of working men's dwellings, and limited as to profits or dividends. To be compared with American limited-dividend housing corporation.   E.E.M.

society, sacred. A society in which many binding, generally accepted norms, united in a functional whole, prevail; there is a maximum of social control, internalized and/or externalized. In such a society resistance to change is usually quite high in comparison with the resistance of secular societies (q.v.). Indeed, for some purposes a strongly sacred society may be characterized as one in which there is marked inability and/or unwillingness to respond to the new. Approximate equivalents are: ideational society, folk society, community, culture (in a special sense), *gemeinschaft*, status society, etc.   H.B.

society, science of. Cf. science of society.

society, secret. A closed association, the membership of which, usually male, is secret and unknown to the members of the community at large. Some of its activities may be performed in public, in which case, the functioning members are usually masked or otherwise disguised. However, most of the secret societies' activities and ritualistic performances are carried out with none but the society members present. Regalia and ritual are regular features. Secret societies, primitive and modern, usually stress mutual benevolence, and nourish primary social intercourse between the members. They may take on secondary functions of social control through attempted imposition of their will upon non-members by means of threat or force.   E.A.H.

society, secular. A society in which few binding, generally accepted norms prevail; there is a minimum of social control, externalized and/or internalized. In such a society resistance to change is usually quite low in comparison with the resistance of sacred societies (q.v.). Indeed, for some purposes a strongly secular society may be characterized as one in which there is marked inability and/or unwillingness to refrain from responding to the new. Approximate equivalents are: sensate society, urban society, civilization, *gesellschaft*, contractual society, etc.   H.B.

society, static. A society without change; one in which no agencies other than those connected with the "static-dynamic" processes are in operation.   N.L.S.

sociogenetic. Having to do with the origin and preservation of society in its distinctly human aspects, particularly aesthetic, spiritual, and intellectual.

sociological. Relating to sociology. (q.v.). Having to do with the scientific study of the phenomena of human association. Not to be confused with social (q.v.) or societal (q.v.).

sociological concepts. Cf. concepts, sociological.

sociological interpretations. The analysis and explanation of social events by sociological methods in terms of sociological units of investigation and sociological concepts (social forces, social relations, social forms, social situation-processes).   T.D.E.

sociological investigation. Research within the limits of accepted scientific methods. Cf. operationalism.   H.A.P.

sociological law. A statement of scientifically established causal relations and of causal sequences and continuity; a social law that has been proved. Cf. law. H.A.P.

sociological methods. In general, in respect to methods of research, sociological methods are substantially the same as those of any other branch of science, viz.: (1) giving attention to a subject arising as an unidentified and somewhat challenging or disturbing feature of the social situation; (2) construction of a working hypothesis as to its nature: that is, trying to identify it by trying to place it in its functional position in the more familiar background of experience as represented by a series of tentative predicates applied to it; (3) the validity of this placement aimed to give meaning to the subject is determined by a comprehensive search and experimentation:—the assembly of data describing the phenomena known to be associated in objective relations with the subject, so as to throw light on its character, or meaning, as a functioning part of the community; (4) the result is an enlargement and better definition both of the particular subject and of the community life of which it is found to be a part.   C.J.B.

sociological norms. Logically reliable criteria or indexes of social relations, such as rates, cycles, trends.   H.P.F.

sociological phenomena. The basic subject matter of sociology. Social and societal data which can be defined in a logical frame of reference or pattern. H.A.P.

sociological pluralism. Cf. pluralism, sociological.

sociological principles. Scientifically demonstrated explanations of social relations.
                    H.A.P.

sociological problems. Unsolved areas in the realm of sociological science. Unsupported hypotheses and unverified theories. Any body of incompletely observed, analyzed, and interpreted sociological phenomena presents problems for scientific treatment. Any unfilled gap in the total range of scientific sociological generalizations presents a problem in the way of a challenge. To be sharply differentiated from "social problems" (q.v.).

sociological trends. Statements of recurrence in the association of events; the sequence or continuity that is demonstrated in a sociological law. Ex. rural depopulation; urbanization.   H.A.P.

sociological units. Elements which are logically substantiated as observable and relevant data and which are uniformly interpreted. Such units may be expressed in words, numbers, formulae or other symbols.   H.A.P.

sociology. The scientific study of the phenomena arising out of the group relations of human beings. The study of man and his human environment in their relations to each other. Different schools of sociology lay varying emphasis upon the related factors, some stressing the relationships themselves, such as interaction, association, etc., others emphasizing the human beings in their social relationships, focusing their attention upon the socius in his varying rôles and functions. Whether sociology, as developed hitherto, is entitled to the rank of a science is still a matter of some disagreement, but it is uniformly recognized that the methods of sociology may be strictly scientific, and that the verified generalizations which are the earmark of true science are being progressively built up out of extensive and painstaking observation and analysis of the repetitious uniformities in group behavior.

sociology, applied. The deductive phase of scientific sociology. The accurate and precise use of sociological generalizations to assist in the solution of social problems (q.v.). The application of sociological laws and principles to particular cases. Applied sociology may be an instrument of either social reform (q.v.) or social engineering (q.v.).

sociology, biological. A somewhat ill-defined area of sociological inquiry centering in the study of the social correlatives and consequences of the biological processes of heredity, variation, selection and reproduction in human populations. In its broadest historical connotation this term includes the bio-organismic theories of society; the anthropo-sociological, or social selectionist, theories of racial and individual differences and their social effects; the "struggle for existence" theories with their emphasis on the rôle of war; and even the demographic theories emphasizing the social effects of size and density of population.   F.H.H.

sociology, clinical. That division of practical or applied sociology that reports and synthesizes the experiences of (a) social psychiatrists with functional problems of individual adaptation and (b) societal technicians with functional problems of institutional adjustment. Chiefly in the first group, at least in emphasis, is the experience of social workers, personnel managers, psychiatrists, career guidance experts, etc., and chiefly in the second group is that of public relations counselors, professional politicians, sentiment and opinion analysist propagandists, advertisers, etc. Clinical sociology thus stresses the development of effective manipulative and therapeutic techniques and of accurate functional information concerning society and social relationships.   A.M'C.L.

sociology, educational. Sociology applied to the solution of fundamental educational problems. One—sociology—examines the field, knows its structure, and describes its functioning; the other—education—attempts to enlighten and improve this same order.   J.S.R.

sociology, folk. A branch of sociology based specifically upon the recognition of the "folk" as a significant basis of social relationships. It is closely identified with the concept of "region," and stresses the localized relations of geographically and culturally unified sub-groups. Cf. folk; region; folkways.

sociology, historical. An aspect of sociology in which data from the past, ordinarily defined as "history", are utilized for predictive generalization rather than for the presentation of unique, particularized wholes; the latter kind of utilization is strictly historical rather than sociological. The sociological prediction referred to may be of retrospective or prospective,

hypothetical or actual character; all that is necessary is the formulation: "If and when these typologized factors recur, these are the typologized consequences." Above all, historical sociology should not be confused with the history of sociology.
                                                          H.B.

sociology, practical. Cf. sociology, applied.

sociology, psychological. A division of sociology which stresses the prior importance of mental factors as explanations of social phenomena.   H.A.P.

sociology, rural. Sociology as especially applied to the phenomena of rural society.

sociology, rural and urban. Specializations in sociology addressed to the study of rural communities or urban communities. Actually, rural sociology, while being descriptive of rural society and social problems, must approach the subject with the urban community in the background. On the other hand, urban sociology approaches the social phenomena of the city by viewing such phenomena against the background of rural society. In the case of either rural or urban sociology there are points at which both must rest on common ground where city meets hinterland.
                                                          N.A.

sociology, systematic. General sociology which excludes non-scientific value-judgments and stresses the systematic interrelation of its component concepts and constructs with the object of extending the scope and accuracy of scientific prediction of sociative recurrence.   H.B.

sociology, urban. The scientific study of the socio-economic adaptations and adjustments induced by the concentration of population within limited geographical areas.   E.E.M.

sociology of art. Science concerned with the definition, classification, and interpretation of artworks and artists in their effect on society and society's effect on them.   J.H.B.

sociometry. An approach to the study of sociology which emphasizes the operational definition of sociological concepts and the description of human relationships and other social phenomena in quantitative or mensurative terms.   J.W.M'C.

socius. The individual human organism regarded as a participant in social relationships or social behavior. The ultimate particle of sociological science. M.S.

sodomy. Unnatural sexual relations between persons of the same sex, or between persons of either sex and beasts, or between persons of different sex in an unnatural manner. Consent does not affect its criminality, but makes the consenting party an accomplice in the crime. The statutes prohibiting sodomy as a crime against nature are broadly interpreted so as to include all acts of unnatural carnal copulation with mankind or beast. The crime is punished with great severity, and in some states with imprisonment for life. A.E.W.

solidarity. Internal cohesiveness of a group. The integrity of a group to the unifying elements that hold it together. N.A.

solidarity, social. Cf. social solidarity.

solitary confinement. Cf. confinement, solitary.

somatic. Pertaining to the body. Variously contrasted with the environment, the germ cells or germ plasm, and a part of the body. Most prevalent contrast is with the mind, as in psycho-somatic. Since this usage suggests that mental phenomena are disembodied, it must be used with caution. M.S.

somatic anthropology. Cf. anthropology, somatic.

somatoplasm. All of the body except the germ plasm; the protoplasm of the soma or body, as distinct from that of the germ cells. Also called the somaplasm. F.H.H.

sorcery. The exercise, as in divination, of supernatural power acquired with the aid of spiritual beings or by magical means; hence black magic or witchcraft (q.v.) in general. G.P.M.

sororal polygyny. Cf. polygyny, sororal.

sororate. The rule permitting or requiring a man to marry the younger sisters of his first wife, or one of them, whether as additional wives during her lifetime or as a substitute after her death. Cf. levirate. G.P.M.

sortilege. Divination (q.v.) by the casting of lots. G.P.M.

soul. The separable spiritual double and animating principle of an individual human being or other organism or object. Cf. animism; ghost; spirit. G.P.M.

soul loss. A primitive theory of disease which attributes illness to the departure of the soul (q.v.) from the body, e.g., as a result of magical or supernatural enticement. G.P.M.

soul-stuff. Impersonal supernatural power in general, or the diffuse spiritual essence associated with a particular human being or object. Cf. mana; soul. G.P.M.

souteneur. Cf. pimp.

sovereignty. The qualification of supremacy attributed to a power, group or jural order. There are three different applications of the term sovereignty which often are confused: (a) jural sovereignty is the primacy of a jural order over other jural orders, for instance of international jural order over the national jural order, or of the national jural order over particular jural frameworks (such as of the state and of economic society); (b) political sovereignty is the monopoly of the state to dispose of unconditional constraint within the limit of its jural competency. It is obvious that the state can possess political sovereignty without possessing jural sovereignty; actually, it can be asserted that even in the epochs of de facto jural predominance of the state, it never possesses jural sovereignty; (c) sovereignty of the people is the inalienable prerogative of the people for self rule. According to different interpretations sovereignty of the people may mean sovereignty of its will (power) or sovereignty of the spontaneous law engendered by the national community. The second interpretation of the term brings it in close relation to "jural sovereignty" of which it becomes, in this case, a special form. Theories of the "absolute sovereignty of the state" (first elaborated in the 17th and 18th centuries) confused jural and political sovereignty, by assuming the impossibility of both, without their combination by attributing them to the same organization. Cf. state; law.   G.G.

soviet (from the Russian). A council or counsel: to hold council, to deliberate. The Soviets are bodies of elected delegates or representatives of the people who form governing legislative bodies. In the USSR there are Soviets (councils) for villages, cities, regions, autonomous republics and for each one of the sixteen (as of June, 1941) Soviet constituent republics forming the USSR. During the rule of the Tsar there was a High Council of State, responsible of course only to the Tsar, which was also called a Soviet. The Soviets representing the people first arose during the unsuccessful Revolution of 1905. In many cities the working class population elected a Soviet of workers' delegates. Soviets reappeared again in the Spring Revolution of 1917. The Soviets as a form of State was ushered in with the successful November Revolution. Accordingly the November Revolution is often referred to as the Soviet Revolution.

specialist. An individual or group characterized by intensive interest in, and fitness for, a particular activity or function, especially in the field of self-maintenance. By common usage, the term is restricted to individual persons and is now applied almost exclusively to members of professions, such as the medical, legal, and engineering. The rank of specialist is almost always dependent upon some concentrated education and experience. The development of specialists is in keeping with the characteristic trends of societal evolution, involving such forms as the division of labor.

specialization. Division of labor, whether on a biological, geographic, institutional, industrial, vocational, or other basis. The term connotes some complexity of structure, two or more parts of the given system which may assume different functions, and also the coordination of these functions into a viable whole. It presupposes the interdependence of the specializing parts. Specialization and integration of specialized functions thus defined characterize the interrelations of familial, economic, educational, religious, and political institutions; of different communities, regions, and countries, so far as they are in communication; of the various industries embraced by an economy; and of the vocations also included in an economy. Specialization is found in other realms as well; and in the smallest as well as the largest groups or organizations. Thus, it is exemplified in the field of sport and recreation generally, of which there are countless varieties; and also in almost any game shared by several players. Currently, the term is most commonly applied to the division of labor among occupations and industries.   S.E.

specialized court. Cf. court, specialized.

spell. A verbal formula the utterance of which is believed capable of bringing about a certain desired result by magical means. Cf. incantation.   G.P.M.

sphere of influence. A loose concept used in the field of international relations and diplomacy, not having legal significance, meaning a geographical area claimed by a sovereign state to be under its protection or subject to its influence for one or more purposes and implying the impairment, to that extent, of the sovereignty of the area so subjected.   F.W.K.

spinster. The name given in England and America, especially in the seventeenth and eighteenth centuries, to an unmarried woman who had passed the age (fifteen to twenty) at which it was customary for girls to marry. The term referred to the custom whereby these unmarried women, regarded as social failures, spent most of their time in spinning.   W.G.

spirit. An animating soul or a disembodied ghost, or an independent supernatural being; preferably restricted in scientific discourse, for the sake of precision, to the last of the three senses, i.e., to that of a spiritual being inferior in power and status to a god but not identifiable with a particular human being, and living a relatively independent existence as a demon, tutelary genius, petty divinity, or the like. Cf. daimon.　　　　　G.P.M.

spirit, familiar. Cf. familiar spirit.

spirit, guardian. Cf. guardian spirit.

spirit, public. Cf. public spirit.

spirit helper. A guardian spirit (q.v.) or familiar spirit (q.v.).　　　　　G.P.M.

spirit world. A region believed to be the abode of ghosts or departed souls of the dead. Cf. projectivism.　　　　　G.P.M.

split-ballot technique. Research device according to which two alternative questionnaire forms with different wording on each form are submitted to comparable cross sections of the population in order to test the effect of differences in phrasing of questions in surveys and public opinion polls.　　　　　M.Pt.

sponsalia. The Latin term for espousals, or the plighting of troths in the betrothal ceremony. In the Middle Ages the Church made a sharp distinction between the formal promise to become man and wife at some future time (*per verba de futuro*) and the promise to become man and wife in words of the immediate present (*per verba de praesenti*). A troth in words of the present tense, e.g., "I take thee to be my wedded wife," was held by the Church to be a valid marriage until the sixteenth century.　　　　　W.G.

sporting theory of justice. Cf. justice, sporting theory of.

spouse. A person espoused or married to another.　　　　　W.G.

squad leader (in social surveys). A person who supervises a group of interviewers in the field. Usually he does some interviewing also.　　　　　M.Pt.

squatter's right. The right to occupancy of land created, in the absence of legal title or arrangement, by virtue of long and undisturbed use.　　　　　S.S.

squaw. An American Indian woman. G.P.M.

stabilize. To establish and to maintain a state of dynamic equilibrium among the social forces of a community, a social group, or an institution.　　　　　F.H.H.

stabilized population. Cf. population, stabilized.

standard. (1) That which is customary, usual, and expected, within a given field, as a standard typewriter, a standard gear shift, a standard gauge, standard deviation. (2) A measure or criterion by which actuality is judged. Such a standard may have no factual existence. It is striven for, but may never be attained. Its existence may be a matter of idealization (q.v.).

standard, double. The moral standard, tacitly recognized by Christian nations for many centuries, whereby lapses from the current ideal of chastity were condoned in the man and severely punished in the woman.　　　　　W.G.

standard, moral. That which is established by mores, authority, tradition, or general consent, as a mode or example of living; a definite level, degree, criterion, or ideal of conduct by which attitudes, habits, and social acts are judged. An elevated mode of life regarded as essential to human welfare and desirable for personal purity.　　　　　M.H.N.

standard, social. Cf. social standard.

standard deviation. A certain measure of dispersion; it equals the square root of the mean of the squares of the deviations from their mean of the individual measures in a series.　　　　　P.H.F.

standard of living. Cf. living, standard of.

standardization. A social situation-process in which differentiation is checked in the interest of uniformity; a type of social control in which a social standard (q.v.) is set up and behavior of group members is brought (by whatever techniques) toward conformity therewith; a policy of social control in which uniformity with a standard type of behavior, opinion, personality, or product is the goal; opposite of diversification.   T.D.E.

standardize. To bring into conformity with a standard.

standards, labor. Cf. labor standards.

state. That agency, aspect, or institution of society authorized and equipped to use force, i.e., to exercise coercive control. This force may be exerted in the way of control of the members of the society or against other societies. The voice of the state is the law, and its agents are those who make and enforce the laws. These agents constitute the government. State and government should be carefully differentiated; the former includes traditions, political instruments, such as constitutions and charters, and the whole set of institutions and conventions that have to do with the application of force. The latter is a group of individuals entrusted with the responsibility and equipped with the authority to carry out the purposes of the state.

state police. Cf. police, state.

state-use system. That system of prison labor in which all prison-made goods are sold only to public agencies and institutions. The system favored primarily by the labor unions, manufacturers, and merchants on the theory that this system best prevents competition with free labor and private industry. Aimed chiefly at the contract system of prison labor and the piece-price system, which gave the contractor, it was claimed, an unfair advantage in the market.   J.L.G.

stateways. The formal, organizational, coercive ways of society for meeting needs, especially for social control. They follow the folkways and mores in the order of evolutionary development of slow-moving society, the order generally being folkways, mores, morals, institutions, stateways, the stateways ultimately working to conserve and integrate the folkways, mores, and institutions. The stateways assume balance and equilibrium between the folkways and stateways as the ideal society. The stateways, developed to their extreme in a modern, urban, in-

dustrial, intellectual, and technological world, tend to develop into technicways and totalitarianism. Cf. technicways; folkways; mores.   H.W.Q.

static. A term borrowed from mechanics, and having reference to a relatively stabilized, imperceptibly changing, and predictable state of human relationships; opposed to dynamic—a rapidly changing and relatively unforeseeable condition. Statics is the branch of mechanics which deals with the equilibrium of forces and bodies at rest.   F.E.L.

static civilization. Cf. civilization, static.

static society. Cf. society, static.

statics, social. Cf. social statics.

stationary population. Cf. population, stationary.

statistic. A summarizing value of a particular series of quantitative observations. A value calculated from a sample in order to characterize the universe. E.g. mean. Used in contradistinction to parameter, which is the expected or true value in the universe.   M.Pt.

statistical universe. Cf. universe, statistical.

statistics. Body of methods dealing with the collection, classification, analysis, and interpretation of masses of numerical data; statistical methods. Statistical data; groups of numerical facts, observations, or measures.   M.Pt.

statistics, criminal. Cf. criminal statistics.

statistics, vital. Collection, presentation, analysis and interpretation of numerical data concerned with human beings, especially births and deaths. The term includes also methods, principles and systematization.   J.H.B.

status. Social standing or prestige of a person in his group or of the group in the community. The position that a person or group holds in public esteem. Status may be vague in some respects, but fairly defined in others, depending on the social or other rules. Economic status may be determined by the size or the source of one's income. Economic status alone may not insure social prestige. This may rest partly on wealth but may also be determined by race, nationality, religion, family lineage, or other factors.   N.A.

status, economic. Position or standing judged by a standard of wealth or lack of wealth.   O.W.

status, social. Cf. social status.

statute. A formally enacted law, e.g., one established by an act of a legislative body.   A.R.L.

statute of limitations. A statute in Anglo-American jurisdictions specifying precise time limits within which different types of actions and proceedings may be instituted in the courts or before governmental agencies, and in connection therewith, the conditions under which they may be brought. It was passed to eliminate the uncertainty under common law resulting from the presumption or fiction that if a cause of action were not prosecuted within a reasonable time, it would be presumed to have been satisfied.   F.W.K.

steatopygia. An excessive fatty development of the buttocks, especially characteristic of Bushman and Hottentot women.   G.P.M.

stereotype. A folk-belief. Group-accepted image or idea, usually verbalized and charged with emotion. Simplified, even caricaturized conception of a character, personality, aspect of social structure, or social program which stands in the place of accurate images in our minds. A.M'C.L.

stereotype, institutional. Cf. institutional stereotype.

stereotype, personality. Prejudiced and oversimplified estimate of the way in which a person is organized. Usually based upon (a) traditional interpretations of personal appearance (weight, build, features, etc.); (b) gossip; and (c) in the case of public figures, reports in newspapers and other mass-communication media. Characterizations based largely on the latter are sometimes referred to

as an individual's "newspaper personality."   A.M'C.L.

stereotype response. Cf. response, stereotype.

stereotyped. Made into a stereotype. Simplified into a type pattern.   A.M'C.L.

stereotyped response. Cf. response, stereotyped.

sterile. Lacking fecundity.

sterile period. Cf. safe period.

sterility. The lack of physiological capacity to participate in reproduction.

sterilization. The policy or act of preventing propagation, especially of the congenitally feebleminded, insane, epileptic, and others revealing grave hereditary defects, by means of a surgical operation rendering the subject sterile. The operation is slight in the case of men but more serious in the case of women. During the last thirty years the educated public has gradually awakened to a realization of the enormous costs involved in permitting the congenitally unfit to propagate. Movements for the sterilization of these unfortunates, under proper safeguards, have sprung up not only in America but in Great Britain and Germany. Since 1907 sterilization laws have been passed in at least thirty states of America, although many have been allowed to lapse. Cf. salpingectomy; vasectomy.   w.G.

stigmata. Physical defects or characteristics believed influential in producing criminal conduct. Cf. anomalies.   J.P.S.

stillbirth. A viable fetus that shows no sign of life after delivery. Stillbirths are differentiated from abortions and miscarriages in that the latter represent losses of fetal life before the fetus has reached the stage of viability (capable of living outside the uterus). Although there is no universal agreement regarding length of period of uterogestation required for viability, it is usually considered to be about 26 weeks.   C.V.K.

stimulation. Excitation of a sensory receptor or of the nervous system as a whole by some object or situation external to the receptor or system. Of particular importance to any theory dealing with action or function.   M.S.

stimulation, group. Stimulation of a group or the act of stimulation carried out by a group.   M.S.

stimulation, non-social. Stimulation by an object or situation not involving social relationships or social behavior.   M.S.

stimulation, social. Cf. social stimulation.

stimuli, stored. Material culture-objects and symbols, stored by accident (in habitat-sites or in ruins) or in tombs, libraries, and museums, so that, to later inhabitants or explorers, they may serve as stimuli, having meanwhile lain idle.   T.D.E.

stimulus, prepotent. A stimulus which has the ascendency over all simultaneously competing stimuli in controlling the response of the organism. Cf. prepotent response.   H.E.J.

stimulus, social. Cf. social stimulus.

stocks. A device formerly used to punish offenders by placing them in a very uncomfortable position in a public place subject to the scorn of passersby. The stocks consisted of two upright posts with usually three strong planks set from one post to the other with holes cut in the planks into which were fitted the ankles and wrists of the offender. The planks were high enough from the ground so that when the offender sat on the ground his body was in a very uncomfortable position. Usually employed for minor offenders.   J.L.G.

stone boiling. The method of boiling liquids in a basket or other vessel, by dropping in heated stones.   G.P.M.

stool pigeon. A term used chiefly in labor and radical circles to describe an informer in their ranks secretly serving the interests of opponents. Also used to describe secret informers among inmates of prisons.   R.N.B.

stored stimuli. Cf. stimuli, stored.

St. Paul Project. A project sponsored by the Children's Bureau of the United States Department of Labor for coordinating the various social agencies in St. Paul for the purpose of demonstrating possibilities for community organization in preventing delinquency, discovering delinquency in its initial stages and developing effective plans for treatment for different types of individuals and cases. A child welfare unit staffed and financed by the Children's Bureau has directed the project.   M.A.E.

stranger. A person living within a community and, therefore, affecting to some degree the life of the place, but not given status as one of the in-group by the natives; one who accepts such lack of identification with the group within which he lives and feels a lack of compulsion to submit to the more subtle forms of social control prevailing. Such a person is characterized by a relative mental and physical mobility, objectivity of attitudes, freedom to accept or reject native values or conventions. He is, to a greater or lesser degree, a man without a country, though he will accept some elements of the cultures of both his former and present places of abode. Such a person at once attains freedom denied natives or members of the in-group, and is denied the freedom of participation which is the unquestioned right of such members.   H.E.M.

stratification. (1) The horizontal division of society into fairly definite and identifiable layers, such as class, caste, and status. (2) The occurrence, in an archeological site, of successively deposited layers indicative of human occupation.

stratification, social. Cf. social stratification.

stratified sampling. Cf. sampling, stratified.

strike. An employer-employee relationship in which the employees as a group refuse to work until certain conditions of employment are granted by the employer. The act of going on strike is not synonymous with quitting work, and under present law the employee has numerous guarantees against arbitrary dismissal for engaging in strike or organizing activities.   J.W.M′C.

structural. Of the nature of, or pertaining to, structure. But in actual spacetime what is structural is also functional: the two words represent abstracted aspects of a total operating organization or organized operation.   T.D.E.

structural condition. Real Property Surveys classified residential structures on a four-fold basis: "unfit for use" indicates an unsafe or insanitary dwelling, usually with the implication that rehabilitation is economically unfeasible; "major repair" indicates structural defects so serious that immediate repair is necessary to prevent the building from becoming unfit for use; "minor repair" indicates less serious defects; "good condition" indicates that no repairs of consequence are needed. The complicated field-judgments i n v o l v e d proved difficult and considerable lack of uniformity resulted. The 1940 Housing Census uses only two classifications: "no major repair" and "major repair needed."
                                                                            S.S.

structure. A relatively permanent or persistent organization of parts which, as an organization, can go into action in specified ways, and whose type is defined by the kinds of action into which it can go.
                                                                            H.H.

structure, class. Cf. class structure.

structure, social. Cf. social structure.

structure-function. A compound phrase to denote the inseparability or integrity of "structure" and "function" in any actual space-time situation-process.   T.D.E.

struggle. One of the basic forms of social interaction, synonymous with opposition, and including competition, contravention, conflict. The effort to secure advantage for one's self by matching one's strength with another's.

struggle, class. The efforts of a class of people to secure a position or conditions of better welfare in the community, with respect to the rights, privileges and opportunities of its members. Specifically, conflict between organized capitalists, especially industrial entrepreneurs and managers, and organized labor. The sum total of actions centering around strikes, boycotts, lockouts, wage-hour negotiations and agreements, pressure lobbies and party groups representing laborers or capitalists. Politico-economic warfare arising out of the almost wholly unregulated hire-and-fire power of the owners of business enterprise and the attempt by free articulate labor groups to circumscribe and limit that power; in detail not comparable to other forms of social unrest such as slave rebellions, serf uprisings, and political revolutions; although it may logically be argued that both Bacon's and Shay's Rebellions were agricultural counterparts of the nineteenth century class struggle.   C.J.B.; W.C.H.

struggle for existence. The biological competition of organisms to live and reproduce. This involves efforts of the organism to win sustenance and shelter from nature, to dominate or utilize other species, and to compete with other members of the same species for sustenance, shelter and opportunity to reproduce. Strictly speaking, the human struggle for existence has been chiefly confined to early man's struggle with nature and with other species, war, and the unconscious competition involved in differential birth rates. Most human struggle is and has been for better living, economic security, power, prestige, rather than for existence.

struggle response. Cf. response, struggle.

stub. The title of a horizontal row in a statistical table; phrasing placed at the left of a row. To be distinguished from caption or column heading.   M.Pt.

sub-area, culture. Cf. culture sub-area.

subhuman controls. Cf. controls, subhuman.

subincision. A genital mutilation, widespread in Australia, involving the making of an incision in the under side of the penis to the urethra. Cf. circumcision.
                                                                            G.P.M.

subjectify. To make subjective, or to bring an observation of the external world into harmony with the internal mental state;

especially, to interpret an experience in terms of previous mental bias or prepossession. F.H.H.

subjective. Relating to internal mental states, such as emotions, feelings, attitudes or concepts; especially, interpreting experience in terms of such states, with insufficient regard for reality as determined by scientific attitudes, experiment, or investigation. F.H.H.

subjective approach. Cf. approach, subjective.

subjective value. Cf. value, subjective.

sublimate. To change energy from one form to another; in psychological literature usually meaning to utilize sexual impulse for some other than its natural expression. E.R.G.

sublimation. The act of directing sexual or other energy to some other than its characteristic expression. E.R.G.

submission. The process of yielding, resigning, or surrendering to the power or will of another party. J.P.E.

subordinate. Lower in rank, class, or authority. Applied to persons, races, and classes engaged in integrated activity.

subregion. A minor division of a larger region. Subregions are usually delineated on such bases as geographical homogeneity, population distribution, agricultural and industrial similarities or differences, and cultural traits such as languages, standard of living, fertility, etc. Thus, the Pacific Northwest as a major region might be divided into the Puget Sound, Inland Empire, lower Columbia and Willamette River Valley, Oregon Coastal, and Desert subregions, chiefly on the basis of geography, economic activities and population distribution. S.C.M.

subsistence farm. Cf. farm, subsistence.

subsistence farmer. One whose farm operations aim primarily at providing for the living needs of the operator and his family rather than for goods for the market. P.H.L.

subsistence farming. Cf. farming, subsistence.

subsistence level. Cf. level, subsistence.

sub-social. Between or among human beings but involving no psychic response. Mere aggregation and mere coercion are sub-social. T.D.E.

sub-social control. Cf. control, sub-social.

substitution. A physio-psychological situation-process in which an alternate satisfaction-object is sought and found, or provided and accepted, either with or without competition from the former satisfaction-object. The desire, wish, appetite or interest involved remains similar. Distinguished from sublimation (q.v.) in which not only the love-object but the quality of the want and satisfaction is supposed to be changed into something more acceptable in the culture, libido being (according to the theory) convertible like mechanical energy to other forms or channels. To provide a foster-child to a bereaved mother is substitution; to replace pugnacity with pageantry, or sex.with salvation would be "sublimation." T.D.E.

suburban. Areas often rural in size but wholly urban in outlook and habits, the economic base of which is employment in nearby metropolitan centers, rather than in agriculture or local industry. E.des.B.

suburban trend. Cf. trend, suburban.

suburbs. The peripheral portions of a city or town. The outlying regions adjacent to a city, usually economically dependent upon the city but composed of independent political units. E.E.M.

subversive activity. Organized political movements, less often individual political actions, regarded by officials and defenders of the status quo as hostile to existing institutions and designed to overthrow them by illegal means. When used by governmental agencies the phrase covers a wide variety of actions construed to interfere with the operations of public authority, most of which can be brought under specific categories of offences, such as spying, sabotage, conspiracies to thwart the enforcement of law, etc. When used in relation to other than governmental authority, the phrase commonly covers activities aimed at capitalism and the institutions of private property. The most common use of the term in recent years has been in relation to Communist activity, and to a less degree Fascist. R.N.B.

succession. (1) An ecological term descriptive of the order in a series of occupations as one species in a habitat is forced out or replaced by another. N.A.

(2) The rule governing the transmission of authority as by seniority, election, or kinship affiliation; in the last case, it is "patrilineal" (q.v.) if it follows the male line e.g., from father to son, and "matrilineal" (q.v.) if it follows the female line, e.g., from mother to daughter or especially from maternal uncle to sister's son. Cf. descent; inheritance. G.P.M.

suffragette. A term coined in the 19th century to describe an ardent female advocate of equal voting rights for women. Suffragettes secured much adverse publicity by their unwomanly demonstrations, their peculiar dresses, and their vicious attacks upon public officials who would not support their cause. J.W.M'C.

suggestibility. Susceptibility to suggestion. M.S.

suggestion. (1) A stimulus which controls consciousness and behavior in an immediate manner, relatively uninfluenced by thought, by means of building up or releasing elementary action tendencies or by augmenting responses that are being carried out. (2) A stimulus resulting in an uncritical release of action patterns already learned. This view fails to recognize the possibility of reeducation and similar results of suggestion. (3) Popularly, presentation of an idea or intimation to the mind. (4) That, which is suggested. M.S.

suggestion, auto-. Suggestion emanating from the individual himself. Contrasted with heterosuggestion which emanates from another. M.S.

suggestion, contra-. suggestion, contrary;

suggestion, counter. (1) A response opposite to one suggested. This usage, now rather rare, confuses response with stimulus. (2) A suggestion opposed to a previous suggestion. M.S.

suggestion, crowd. Cf. crowd suggestion.

suggestion, social. Cf. social suggestion.

suggestion imitation. Cf. imitation, suggestion.

suicide. The taking of his own life by a human being, a legal offense in some jurisdictions but in others abolished as such. A person who kills himself.

suicide, race. A tendency for a group or class to fail to have a sufficient number of children to maintain its own numbers. A term applied specifically by President Theodore Roosevelt to members of the so-called upper classes, or ethnic groups, who voluntarily limited the size of their families to one or two, or none at all. F.D.W.

sumptuary laws. Cf. laws, sumptuary.

sun-language theory. The thesis that awe of the sun stimulated the first vocalization of man associated with wonder and thought, and hence that human speech is associated with reactions to observation of solar phenomena. This monogenetic theory was about the final phase of Turkish chauvinism. Called the *gunes-dil teoresi* (sun-tongue theory), its proponents found the first sound uttered by man to have been ag (agh), a prominent syllable in Turkish. Following this line of reasoning it was easy to demonstrate the primacy, or at least the universal affiliations, of the Turkish language. Interest in this propaganda line has diminished as the new republic reaches maturity and a sense of security in relation to European intellectual life. D.E.W.

supercision. A genital mutilation involving the making of a longitudinal incision in the prepuce or foreskin, as contrasted with the excision of the latter as in circumcision (q.v.). G.P.M.

super-ego. Cf. ego, super-.

superordinate. Higher in rank, social class or authority. Indicating the relative position of persons, races or classes in the social order, or in any aspect thereof, when their relations are viewed as an integrated activity.   F.H.H.

superordination. The process (or result) of acquiring superiority of influence or position of one over another. Cf. subordination.   M.S.

super-social control. Cf. control, super-social.

superstition. A religious belief or practice surviving from out of the past and lacking an adequate basis in either the prevailing religious system or the existing body of scientific knowledge; a religious survival (q.v.).   G.P.M.

suppression. (*psychiatric*) Conscious but vigorous inhibition of an act or complex. Distinguished from repression, in which not only the complex but the resistance or block upon it has become unconscious. (*social-economic-political*) Forcible restraint or constraint of a given activity, group, or mode of expression by a group in power.   T.D.E.

supremacy. The ascendancy of a person, a social set, or a people in relation to others. The hallmark of success in an area of social or economic competition.   N.A.

surplus, social. Cf. social surplus.

surplus economy. Cf. economy, surplus.

survey. A term common in applied sociology especially since publication of the Pittsburgh Survey in 1912; used rather loosely to indicate a more or less orderly and comprehensive gathering and analysis of facts about the total life of a community or some special phase of it, e.g., health, education, recreation; techniques derived from pioneers like Le Play and Charles Booth, more recently from statisticians, experts of The Russell Sage Foundation, and specialists in universities; little used in continental Europe, but extensively in the United States and England.   A.J.T.

survey, social. Cf. social survey.

surveys, crime. Cf. crime surveys.

survival. (1) Continuation of existence, with possible limitations relative to time and place, of individuals and groups, objects and ideas.   J.H.B.
(2) An element of culture which has endured, with altered or diminished function, after the social circumstances which gave rise to it, and to which it was originally adapted, have disappeared.   G.P.M.

survival, individual. Cf. individual survival.

survival, social. Cf. social survival.

survival of the fittest. In the theory of evolution, the preservation and reproduction of those varieties or organisms best adapted to cope with the prevailing conditions of life. The phrase was coined by Herbert Spencer to express the result of natural selection. It has popularly been misinterpreted by the so-called "social Darwinists" to mean the survival of the most brutal, selfish, aggressive, and cunning. But this view finds no scientific support in evolutionary theory, which recognizes man's social, cooperative, and altruistic qualities as among the most important conditions of his survival. Cf. survival value.   H.E.J.

survival value. Cf. value, survival.

suspended sentence. Cf. sentence, suspended.

suttee. The Hindu practice of cremating a widow on the funeral pyre of her husband, or the woman thus sacrificed. G.P.M.

swaraj. East Indian term for independence. Literally, self-rule.   S.C.M.

sweat-box. A form of disciplinary punishment occasionally found in some southern road camps or chain gangs and consisting of a small box so constructed that the prisoner shut up therein could not stand upright, lie down, or sit in any comfortable manner.   T.S.

sweat lodge. A small, air-tight, hemispherical hut, widespread in aboriginal North America, within which steam baths are taken by sprinkling water over heated stones.   G.P.M.

symbiosis. A mutual relationship between animal species involving an exchange of services; a division of labor as that between certain species of ants and lice in which each serves the subsistence needs of the other. Similar relations exist between certain plants and insects. The term has been employed to describe ecological relationships in human society; for example, the mutual-support relations between theatres and hotels in the Broadway area of New York City. Cf. antagonistic cooperation.   N.A.

symbiosis, ecological. The co-existence aspect of ecological interaction, i.e., that impersonal relation which exists between the co-existing inhabitants of an area by virtue of (a) their common dependence upon a limited source of environmental supply, or (b) their positions in niches of a functional chain.   J.A.Q.

symbiosis, industrial. The grouping within a community of independent manufacturers, who are able to benefit by using each other's products. In Kingsport, Tennessee, which was planned on this basis, the containers and packaging of several firms are supplied by a local box factory and certain concerns finish and distribute the raw products of others. The economic justification of such systems rests on the elimination of unnecessary cross hauling and transport costs.   S.S.

symbiotic. Pertaining to mutual subsistence relationships between species. Cf. symbiosis.   N.A.

symbol. That which stands for something else. Particularly, a relatively concrete, explicit representation of a more generalized, diffuse, intangible object or group of objects. A very large part of the social processes is carried on by the use of symbols, such as words, money, certificates, and pictures. A true symbol excites reactions similar to, though perhaps not quite as intense as, those created by the original object.

symbol, social. Cf. social symbol.

symbolic behavior. That overt activity the performance of which regularly refers to a meaning other than that involved in the action taken by itself.   B.M.

symbolic contact. Cf. contact, symbolic.

symbolic patterns. Cf. patterns, symbolic.

symbolic personality. Cf. personality, symbolic.

symbolic representation. Cf. representation, symbolic.

symbolism. The practice of using acts, sounds, objects or other means which are not of importance in themselves for directing attention to something that is considered important; the substitution of a symbol for the thing symbolized.   O.W.

symbolism, mathematical. The use of mathematical terms to express relationships which are subject to logical classification.

sympathetic behavior. Cf. behavior, sympathetic.

sympathetic contact. Cf. contact, sympathetic.

sympathetic insight. Cf. insight, sympathetic.

sympathetic introspection. Cf. introspection, sympathetic.

sympathy. Literally, feeling with another. Reacting to the experiences and stimuli of another as if they were one's own. The sharing of emotions and interests. Cf. sympathetic behavior.

sympodial. A term introduced into sociology from botany by Lester F. Ward to describe the zigzag or meandering course of evolutionary development. To Ward belongs the distinction of pointing out that the theory of organic evolution of his time was radically incorrect in presenting the course of evolution as arborescent or monopodial. In this type of growth, the stem or axis of growth continues to extend in the direction of previous growth by the continuous development of a terminal bud, all the branches originating as lateral appendages. In sympodial growth, however, the main stem gives off a branch which becomes a new axis of growth. The original stem is reduced to a branch or twig, or may disappear entirely through atrophy. The new axis of growth continues until it gives rise to a new branch along which the main processes of development now take place as before, and this is repeated indefinitely throughout the life of the plant. If the true course of evolutionary development is sympodial, then the genera and species of each succeeding geological epoch are not the off-spring of the specialized forms of preceding epochs, but of more primitive generalized forms. Ward was thus able to answer those critics of evolution like Dr. William Buckland and others who pointed out that the great species which formed the Carboniferous forests are now represented only by insignificant club-mosses and horsetails, and insisted that there had not been evolution. but degeneration. This sympodial theory Ward verified by his researches in paleobotany, and extended to the evolution of animals, races, peoples, and societies. Ward's theory is now generally accepted in its main outlines. H.E.J.

syncretism. The process of amalgamation of conflicting, or at least different, parties or principles or cultures. More specifically, the assimilation of foreign groups. The foreign elements disappear as physiological and cultural entities into the majority, and the majority adopts both the individuals and a selection and adaptation of their culture traits. Cf. assimilation; acculturation; amalgamation. A.M'C.L.

syndicalism. A trend in the French labor movement which considers labor unions and their federations as cells of the future socialist order, and insists on the complete independence of labor unions from political parties. Syndicalism enjoyed a great ideological success in France in the period between 1899 and 1937. The powerful French Confederation of Labor (*Confédération Générale du Travail*) applied syndicalist ideas in practice. Whereas, at the start of the movement, syndicalism preached the exclusive right of workers to control industry, after the first World War, it admitted the equal right of the consumers. All forms of French syndicalism were anti-statist (their device was:

to socialize, but without reinforcing the state—*"socialiser sans étasier"*). Some interpretations denied the right of the state at all, and others wanted only to limit and to counterbalance the state by an independent economic organization (this interpretation of syndicalism is very close to British guild socialism). On the other hand, there were a reformistic-moderate and a revolutionary trend, in the French Syndicalism. G.G.

syndicalism, criminal. Cf. criminal syndicalism.

syndicalism, revolutionary. A radical trend in French syndicalism, particularly influential in the period between 1905 and 1914. Revolutionary syndicalism preached "direct action," the "general strike," and a radical antimilitarism. It attached importance to the initiative of "revolutionary élites," and was, throughout, hostile to the state in all its forms. G.G.

synergy. Unconscious "cooperation" among people who, following their own interests and seeking their own goals, produce unplanned societal structure-function, community patterning, and cultural products. Distinguished f r o m true cooperation (q.v.), telesis (q.v.), societal self-direction. T.D.E.

synthesis. A combination of elements or traits in a pattern or compound. Ant. analysis. H.A.P.

synthesis, social. Cf. social synthesis.

system. An aggregate of related interests or activities. There is the assumption of an organization of parts or phases in orderly arrangement. A philosophy in all its related phases may be so regarded; also a communication or transportation system; or an economic system. Whatever the system, its related character is identified by harmony in operation and the integration of its structure. N.A.

systematic sociology. Cf. sociology, systematic.

T

taboo (tabu). A prohibition whose infringement results in an automatic penalty; a prohibition resting on some magico-religious sanction; social control by abstention, taking into account the dangerous aspects of supernatural power and surrounding these with strict observances; more loosely, any sacred interdiction. J.G.L.

talisman. An object believed to furnish protection against evil or to bring good luck, especially if it owes its efficacy to astrological arts. Cf. amulet; fetish. G.P.M.

tattoo. An indelible mark or pattern on the skin, usually decorative in intent, made by introducing pigment under the surface by pricking with a needle or similar implement. Cf. scarification. G.P.M.

tax, poll. A tax levied upon each individual as a prerequisite to voting. The poll tax was first introduced by liberal states as a substitute for a property qualification. It gradually disappeared during the 19th century only to be revived by the southern states to combat the heavy Negro vote and the rising power of the Populist movement among the poor whites. By various manipulations the poll tax is used to exclude undesired voters from elections. The constitutionality of the poll tax has been upheld by the Supreme Court, and on several occasions the United States Senate has rejected legislation outlawing it. J.W.M'C.

taxation. The act of levying or imposing taxes upon the subject or particular classes of subjects by governmental authority. A system of raising public revenue. E.E.M.

taxation, progressive. Imposition of taxes at ascending rates whereby a larger proportion of large incomes or properties is taken than of smaller ones. E.E.M.

taxation, proportional. Imposition of taxes at a fixed rate, irrespective of size of income or property. E.E.M.

taxation, regressive. Imposition of taxes at descending rates, whereby a larger proportion of small incomes or properties is taken than of larger ones. E.E.M.

taxes. Compulsory charges levied by public authority for public purposes upon specific bases, such as persons (head or poll tax), incomes, inheritances, lands, houses, imports, chattels, etc. E.E.M.

taxi dance hall. A public dance hall in which hostesses are provided by the management to dance with male patrons at a standard fee of ten cents a dance. Each dance lasts approximately a minute, less at night, the termination of each dance being indicated by the ringing of a bell. Although advertising states that couples are invited, only unaccompanied men attend. The analogy between the hostess and the taxi which picks up new fares every few minutes is obviously the basis of the name taxi dance hall. However, the aim of the taxi dancer is to get a gentleman partner to "sit-out" dances for which pleasure the partner pays at the rate of six dollars per hour. Tables are provided for this purpose and the hostess encourages her partner to purchase drinks and cigarettes from the sale of which she gets a commission. J.W.M'C.

technical patterns. Cf. patterns, technical.

technicways. The developed habits of the individual and customs of the group for meeting needs and survival in a technological world. The technicways transcend the old folkways (q.v.) and supplant the mores (q.v.), thus accelerating the rate of societal evolution and negating the slow processive development of morals, institutions, and mores. The technicways in contrast to the folkways and mores have their origin in definite, specific, technological situations and arise quickly and are measurable in terms of statistical objectivity. The technicways are measures of social change and process and reflect not only what happens in the impact of technology upon culture, but how it happens.   H.W.O.

technique, social. Cf. social technique.

technocracy. A school of thought which stresses the importance of the technician in modern society, the restrictive influences of the "price system" in preventing the full use of technological developments, and the need for giving engineers control of our economy. It originated during the depression from the research and writings of a small group of engineers, economists, and publicists led by Howard Scott. Interest in technocracy reached the proportions of a major fad in 1932, and subsequently declined sharply.   S.C.M.

technological change. Technology is the combination or totality of techniques employed by a people or at a given period for the purpose of adaptation to their biophysical environment. More broadly, it includes elements of social organization such as cooperation, division of labor, management, etc. An equilibrium or adjustment is attained between a given environment, with its potential resources, and a people inhabiting this environment, with their technical skills and knowledges. Technological change is shown to be an enduring force of history, through the increasing differentiation in the form of tools and implements used by man, the constant additions to the range of inventions, the gradual increase in empirical knowledge and the resulting greater ability in utilizing and exploiting the natural environment for his needs. Factors making for technological change may be migrations, or change of locality, and changes in techniques and knowledge, through inventions within the group, or the introduction of new techniques from without. In modern times, the broader cultural base

made possible by the widening of contacts and communication between peoples has led to an ever-increasing rate of technological change.   S.J.

technology. The branch of cultural anthropology (q.v.) concerned with the study of material culture (q.v.) and the industrial arts.   G.P.M.

technology, social. Cf. social technology.

teknonymy. The practice of naming a parent after his child, e.g., of calling a man, after the birth of his first child, merely "father of so-and-so."   G.P.M.

teleology. The study of the purpose, ends, goals, final causes or ultimate values which are immanent in natural phenomena.   J.P.E.

telesis. A mode of thinking or a program of action that assumes certain values as ends to be attained by deliberate, consciously planned conduct towards that end. *Individual telesis.* Telesis as applied to individual planning and personal action. *Social telesis.* Telesis as applied to group planning, social control. *Collective telesis.* (a) Telic conduct on the part of a collectivity or group, such as a consumer cooperative. (b) According to Ward, the collective action of society in directing, controlling, restraining, and otherwise utilizing the natural forces of society for recognized ends. All forces are to Ward an expression of cosmic or universal energy and are included under "natural force"; psychological and social forces are natural forces, the intellect being the final cause and the directive agent.   B.B.W.

Conscious direction of social change toward recognized goals by human intelligence; antithesis of "natural" or "spontaneous" evolution, of the idea that social change is directed by supernatural or divine forces, and of such theories as geographic determinism and laissez faire. The idea that mind and reasoning ability make it possible and imperative that man direct his own fate. As a corrollary of this proposition it follows that the artificial, man-made, is superior to the natural.   H.E.M.

telesis, social. Cf. social telesis.

televising. The physical process by which images, motion pictures, and other objects are picked up by a tube within a camera and transmitted to distant places for reproduction on screens by electricity. M.H.N.

television. The device of communication which projects images or motion pictures to a distant point by electricity where a reception device reconstructs the identical picture elements on a screen. The process includes the flooding of the televised area with light, breaking the secluded or grouped object pictures into a number of elements, transmitting these elements through screened sets, and reconstructing them into identical images on a screen some distance away from the point of origin. Facsimile transmission differs from television in that graphic material is transmitted and recorded on paper at a distance, reproducing a carbon copy of the original. M.H.N.

telic. Purposive; with reference to a given end. B.B.W.

telic change. Cf. change, telic.

telic process. Cf. process, telic.

telics, individual. Cf. individual telics.

telics, social. Cf. social telics.

temperament. The emotional aspects of character (q.v.); the prevailing or characteristic mood of a personality (q.v.); the characteristic and hence predictable modes in which a personality utilizes and displays neuromuscular energy. H.H.

temporalism. The concept of reality as an incessant change. In philosophy it is the ideology of Becoming and in sociology and ethics it is a term used as the opposite of eternalism which considers eternal Being as the true reality. From the idealistic point of view, temporalism and eternalism are reconciled and constitute a synthesis. J.D.

temporary housing. In war housing terminology: housing, usually of light construction utilizing substitutes for critical material, built on leased land, or not in conformity with building codes or restrictive covenants normally governing in the area, or under pledge of post-war removal, or of short life expectancy at reasonable maintenance costs. S.S.

tenancy. Use and occupancy of land or dwelling of another on a rental basis. The sociological use of the term is primarily in the field of rural sociology where farm tenancy is considered a problem. P.H.L.

tenant. One who uses and/or occupies land on the basis of tenancy (q.v.).

tenant, cash. A farm operator (q.v.) who pays rent in cash as distinguished from a sharetenant who pays rent in a share of the crop. K.DP.L.

tenant, share. Cf. sharecropper.

tenant, sharecropper. Cf. sharecropper.

tendencies, criminal. Cf. criminal tendencies.

tendency. An inherent impulse in a given direction. That which would happen to an object if there were nothing to prevent it. For example, all material objects on this globe have a tendency to fall toward the center of the earth, but in the great majority of cases, at any given time, this tendency is neutralized by a greater force. Not to be confused with trend (q.v.).

tension, social. Cf. social tension.

tension, societal. Societal tension in operational terms is the ratio of the total intensity of desire of a plurel to the total amount of the available desideratum. S.C.D.

tensions. Chemical, mechanical, and neutral differentials in the organism felt as pressures and stresses and objectively observable and even measurable in the operations of the body and the behavior of the personality. The whole organism, in unstable equilibrium with and in its environment, represents an infinitely complex configuration of tensions, the more persistent of which are referred to as structure (q.v.), attitude (q.v.), character (q.v.). The more rapidly changing tensions are called interests, wishes, emotions, dispositions, instincts, motor sets, reflex arcs, etc., depending upon the scientist and upon the locus in the organism. **T.D.E.**

tenure. As used in rural sociology and agricultural economics, the nature of the property rights under which land is held and utilized. In the United States almost all property rights in land are lodged in the land owner through the system of ownership in fee simple, the state merely retaining the right of eminent domain. In descending order according to the completeness of their rights to the use and control of the land, the agricultural population may be classified as follows: owner, tenant or renter, and laborer. **T.L.S.**

terrorism. A technique of minorities seeking power or defending their autocracy, in which violence and threat of violence, suppression, secrecy and kidnapping are used to crush active opponents, stifle discontent and intimidate the general population. A device of super-social control (q.v.). **T.D.E.**

tertiary contact. Cf. contact, tertiary.

test, aptitude. Cf. aptitude test.

thaumaturgy. The art of working marvels, as by legerdemain, jugglery, etc. **G.P.M.**

theatre. The art through which a living spectacle is communicated to an audience. It originated from magic and ritual dances, which led to self-transfiguration of the dancer. It represents dramatically a mostly social conflict. The main forms of the theatre are: tragedy, comedy, opera, ballet, pantomime, shadow, and marionette-theatre, etc. Semi-theatrical forms: circus, processions, movies, audio-scripts, etc. Cf. magic; social conflict. **J.H.B.**

theocracy. Government of a state by ecclesiastics as representatives of God. **L.P.E.**

theory, social. Cf. social theory.

theory of responsibility. The theory underlying the greatest part of our criminal and penal law which assumes any individual to be responsible for his conduct so long as he is able "to tell the difference between right and wrong." This concept is generally rejected by psychiatrists and psychologists as an unsatisfactory basis for differentiating types of human conduct or understanding delinquent behavior. **M.A.E.**

they-group. Cf. group, they-

third degree. The popular term given to the practice of beating and intimidating suspect persons prior to arraignment in order to obtain information or a confession. Between the time a suspect is arrested and the time he first appears before the lowest court (magistrates court in the cities) the police alone are in charge; no court authority exercises jurisdiction. This is the opportunity used by the police to administer the third degree. Although completely unlawful, it is almost impossible to secure sufficient evidence to bring the police to trial for such actions. **J.W.M'C.**

thought, class. That aggregation of ideas, values, attitudes, and concepts peculiar to the members of a given social stratum. **J.P.E.**

thought, group. The combined thought of two or more minds possessing the implication that group thought is different from the thought of each participating mind and from the sum of the thoughts of the inter-related minds. A much disputed concept. Cf. social mind. **M.S.**

thought, social. Cf. social thought.

threat. The communication of a disagreeable alternative to an individual or group, by one in authority or who pretends to be; the confrontation of an opponent by an "either-or" situation. **F.E.L.**

throwback. The alleged biological phenomenon of atavism; the cropping out, in an apparently "pure" stock, several generations after a single miscegenation, of an individual markedly like the opposite race of the original miscegenation. Anthropologists are not able to verify such claims. **T.D.E.**

thwart. To block or frustrate an activity. To interrupt or prevent the activity of a person or group, especially by means not readily circumvented, perhaps eliciting disagreeable responses.   N.A.

ticket of leave. Printed card bearing formal conditions under which a person in penal servitude was permitted to leave penal colony.   J.P.S.

tip. A gratuity given by a customer to a worker in a service industry, which becomes significant in social practice when regarded as a customary part of workers' remuneration, to be considered in all decisions related to determination of a fair wage or entering into computation of rights in social insurance.   M.VK.

tipi. A conical tent of dressed skins stretched over a circular framework of poles meeting near the apex, characteristic of the North American Indians of the Plains and adjacent areas.   G.P.M.

tolerant. A quality characteristic of one who manifests restraint or forebearance toward ways or customs differing from his own.   .E.E.M.

tolerate. To exercise toleration, or consciously to permit the continuing of social practices or the expression of opinions and beliefs which one does not approve, or which one even believes harmful to social welfare, under the moral principle that freedom of expression in such matters is, in the long run, less injurious to the social order than forceful suppression.   F.H.H.

tolerated companion. Cf. companion, tolerated.

toleration. An attitude or social situation-process in which the rights of others to differences of behavior and opinion are conceded without, however, approving such out-group traits. Associated with policies of liberty in the field of social control; distinguished from active encouragement of variation.   T.D.E.

tong war. Cf. war, tong.

torture. Suffering caused by various devices employed in ancient times and during the Middle Ages to induce the accused to confess. It was based on the theory

that if the guilty suffered sufficiently he would confess his guilt. The trouble with this method of determining guilt or innocence is that it gave advantage to the most insensitive human beings, and often led to confessions by innocent persons. Beccaria and the Classical School of penology protested it, and led to its final abandonment.   J.L.G.

torture, judicial. The application of physical or mental pain and suffering to prisoners accused of crime and having as its purpose the extraction of confessions of guilt or of the names of accomplices. An integral part of the criminal procedure of the Middle Ages, it was not abolished by law in some European nations until the 19th century and still survives in the illegal police practice known as the "third degree" (q.v.). Cf. torture.   T.S.

tory. A reactionary devoted to the maintenance of a system of political, social and economic privileges, derived from the popular name of the British Conservative Party.   R.N.B.

totalitarianism. The exclusive control of the body politic embracing all spheres of activity and all social groups. As such a political monopoly, a totalitarian regime does not allow any opposition and criticism, or recognition and representation of a divergent group, and aims at a complete subservience of the individual. Modern dictatorships as differentiated from the autocratic regimes of earlier absolutism do not suffice in a control of the merely political institutions and forces but subordinate practically every social agency and social act to their will. They do not recognize any sphere of privacy outside of the totalitarian state.   S.N.

totem. An animal, plant, or natural object from which a sib name is derived, and toward which the sib members feel a special relationship and display special attitudes.   J.G.L.

totem pole. A carved pole, with figures of animals or birds, from which the totemic myths and ceremonies take their character. The totemic carving represents a kind of crest or coat-of-arms connected with totemic experience.   J.G.L.

totemic. Having to do with a totem.
J.G.L.

totemic kinship. Cf. kinship, totemic.

totemism. A form of social organization and religious practice typically involving an intimate association between sibs and their totems, which are regarded as ancestors or as supernaturally connected with an ancestor, which are tabooed as food, and which give the sibs their names. J.G.L.

totemism, sex. The association of totems with each sex, as in southeastern Australia. G.P.M.

totemistic. Pertaining to totemism. J.G.L.

town. The word is used in two senses: (1) In New England, Michigan, New York, and Wisconsin the town is a subdivision of the county for local government and is the same as the township of other states; (2) town is also used colloquially to designate any large village or small city, but in some states this term is the legal name for small incorporated places. Some rural sociologists have distinguished urban places of 500 to 2500 inhabitants as towns. J.H.K.

town, company. Cf. company town.

town, dormitory. Cf. dormitory town.

township. A geographic area for land description and local government, usually, in regions other than New England, six miles square, 36 square miles in area. In New England it is known as the town and does not follow the checker-board pattern but is irregular in both size and area.
J.H.K.

trade. The exchanging of goods for goods or for money equivalents; economic transactions or commerce within a country (domestic trade) or with other countries (foreign trade). Also, an occupation or employment usually of a manual or mechanical nature as distinguished from the professions or entrepreneurship. E.E.M.

trade, international. The interchange of wealth across major political boundaries.

It had its beginning largely in commodity exchange. In most cases the natural expansion of domestic trade led to the purchase and sale of goods beyond national lines. Exchange of products from tropical countries for goods from the temperate zones has long existed. But it was not until the development of industrialism, together with improvements in transportation facilities, that traffic in commodities assumed tremendous size. An early consequence of industrialism was the growth of trade between agrarian and raw material countries on one hand and industrial countries on the other. But as industrialism spread, the total of trade among manufacturing nations was even greater than between them and agrarian nations.

Trade is no longer limited to commodities. Maturing industrialism was accompanied by a flow of capital and services to relatively under-developed areas. These so-called "invisible" exports and imports now must be counted as important both in size and in their social implications. The theory of international trade emphasizes that regional specialization either in skills, abundance of raw materials or capital, together with unrestricted flow of these goods and services, promotes the efficient utilization of productive factors. The blighting effect of ignorance and the willful application of trade barriers by vested and selfish interests tend to reduce standards of living in the total economy. Cf. commercial revolution. J.H.E.

trade, silent. Dumb barter (q.v.).

trade area. Cf. area, trade.

trade center. An expression used in rural sociology to designate any hamlet, village, town, or city to which farmers resort for the purposes of selling their produce and making purchases. Where scattered farmsteads are the prevailing mode of settlement, as in the United States, the village is primarily a trading center. The modern American rural community consists of two parts, the village or town trade center and the surrounding trade area or trade basin. T.L.S.

trade union. A voluntary association of working people organized to maintain or further their rights and interests, with particular respect to wages, hours, and conditions of health, efficiency, security, education, insurance, etc. Originally, in the middle of the nineteenth century, trade unions were exclusively composed of male wage earners, excluding women, industrial executives and professional workers. Recently women's locals have been admitted into the larger federations; though, as a rule, in the local unions, women are not members with the men, but cooperate through women's auxiliaries, mainly on social recreations. Salaried professional workers, such as teachers, are beginning to organize for similar purposes in local federations, admitted to the larger organizations of the wage workers; and occasionally unions with both employer and employee members are found, though this is contrary to trade union principles. Unions emphasize the need of wage workers' solidarity in the struggle of organized labor for public recognition of their democratic rights of consent and advice in the management of industry, as well as in the general governmental control. Failure of some management, and of some leadership in the trade unions, clearly to recognize this point, has resulted in two important developments: (1) the formation of industrial unions including many more of the unskilled workers with the skilled, sometimes in locals with thousands of members; and (2) the invention and use by them of the "sit-down strike" in which the strikers remain in the factories continuously day and night, during the stoppage of work, thus preventing more easily the other employees from taking their places. This method, although still in most localities technically illegal, is beginning to be recognized by the general public as morally warranted as a last resort to maintain the workers in their positions, when wide unemployment makes is impossible to find work elsewhere. In the United States recently, there has taken place the formation of two separate national federations of trade unions: the older American Federation of Labor, and the newer Congress of Industrial Organizations. The latter promoted the newer form of the industrial union. Under the pressure of war conditions and public sentiment for wider union, these two general associations have been trying to arrange the wider federation necessary for better democratic efficiency in industry and in the life of society. C.J.B.

trade union democracy. Cf. democracy, trade union.

tradition. A social situation-process in which elements of the cultural heritage are transmitted from generation to generation by contacts of continuity; or, the non-material cultural content so transmitted, having the prestige sanction of antiquity. By extension, in an institution where personnel turns over more frequently than once a generation, practices, ideas and lore transmitted over a series of such "turn overs" are called traditions. Cf. social tradition. T.D.E.

tradition, group. The subjective aspect of the culture of a group which is transmitted from generation to generation through language in the form of meanings, values, beliefs, sentiments, attitudes, and other ways of thinking, feeling, and acting in so far as they are capable of verbal symbolization. H.E.J.

tradition, social. Cf. social tradition.

traditional. Following or conforming to an established way, such as a long-accepted code of morals, or a well known order of procedure handed down from the past (such as a traditional way of opening a court session or of celebrating Easter or Christmas). R.E.B.

traditionalism. That attitude or philosophy which accepts, reveres, and upholds social institutions and beliefs as being right and best solely because they have been handed down from the past; a system of faith founded on tradition or competent authority in disregard of critical or rational processes. N.L.S.

trait. An independent item in a general pattern, either that of an individual personality, a society, a culture, or a process. (*biological*) A physical characteristic heritable as a unit, determined by a "gene" in the chromosomes, according to the "Mendelian" pattern of inheritance (*psychological*) A persistent behavior pattern or attitude in the personality or character, to which a name has been assigned in our culture (such as cheerfulness, secretiveness, reliability, cowardice). (*anthropological*) A unit of culture, material or nonmaterial, capable of independent diffusion and accumulation (such as a method of making fire, a decorative pattern, a god's name, a specific gesture, a domesticated animal, a rare metal). A culture complex transmitted as a unit would by this definition be also a culture trait; but a culture complex is a configuration of traits, and a complex so transmitted (e.g., the Peyote Cult, or Chess) is seldom called a trait on that account. The diffusion of the nuclear trait of a complex usually carries the complex with it. Cf. complex.   T.D.E.

trait, cultural. Cf. culture trait.

trait, culture. Cf. culture trait.

trait, dominant. Gene characters of the germ plasm which appear in the somatic structure of the offspring as compared to recessive characters which do not appear in the somatic structure. For example, if in the cross of a pure white and a pure black line black is dominant, all offspring in the first generation will be black in color.   P.H.L.

trait complex. Cf. complex, trait.

transition, area of. Cf. area of transition.

transition, zone of. Cf. zone of transition.

transitional area. Cf. area of transition.

transmigration. Reincarnation (q.v.), especially through a succession of forms or incarnations.   G.P.M.

transmission, social. Cf. social transmission.

transportation. (1) The carriage or removal of persons or things by a conveyance on land, water, or in the air, e.g., by beast, human or animal drawn sledge or vehicle, boat, railroad, automotive vehicle, or aircraft. Also, the material instruments involved.   E.E.M.
(2) A method of punishment originally devised by England for the most hardened criminals. It had a precedent in that country in the practice of outlawry where-

by certain persons could escape hanging by abjuring the realm. It first received legislative sanction during the reign of Charles II. Felons were first transported to the colonies of North America. When the American Revolution put an end to the practice, transportation to Australasia was put into operation in 1787.   J.L.G.

transvestite. A person who adopts the dress of the opposite sex. Cf. berdache.   G.P.M.

travois. A rude vehicle of the Plains Indians of North America, consisting of two poles attached like shafts to a single dog or horse, trailing on the ground behind, and supporting a burden.   G.P.M.

treason. The offense of the attempted overthrow of a government by one or more of its citizens, or the betrayal of its interests to a foreign power. More narrowly defined in the U. S. Constitution to cover levying war against the United States or adhering to its enemies in time of war.   R.N.B.

treatment. The process by which the individual is helped to a greater use of his own capacities or social resources. Used also more rarely in relation to group or community.   W.P.

treaty and convention. These terms are used interchangeably. Treaty is the name assigned to a formal agreement between nations, usually approved or ratified by some branch of the national legislature or Executive. Treaties may be bilateral or multilateral. Many rules have accumulated around the institution of treaties. They cannot be unilaterally denounced; but since times change, political treaties often cease to be convenient to both parties. Politics then dictates either negotiation for change or unilateral breach. The fact that change is a law of nature is recognized by Article 19 of the Covenant of the League of Nations, which provided for the recommendation of change whenever conditions warranted; but the procedure was so loosely drawn as to make the article impossible of application. The fact of change has brought a demand for short-term treaties with a definite date of termination, unless the parties both or all wish to continue it. International law recognizes the doctrine of *rebus sic stantibus*, i.e., that a change of factual conditions on which treaties were premised justifies release from or change in the treaty. But like Article 19, this has not been implemented, so that it has merely served to excuse unilateral breaches of treaty without proof of or impartial judgment on the justifying facts. Novel political treaties, like a Kellogg Pact—even if they meant what optimists assumed—have no chance for survival in the face of uncongenial political conditions; to go beyond the hard facts makes such treaties worse than useless; it arouses unfulfillable hopes and then recriminations and hostility. Treaties, especially multilateral treaties, are often signed with reservations, which, when accepted by the co-signatories expressly or by implication, exempt the reserving state from the particular obligation excepted.   E.M.B.

tree marriage. Cf. marriage, tree.

trend. A general movement in a specified direction. The term may be applied to an abstraction or to concrete objects. Thus it may be said that there is an upward trend in the price level, and that there is a trend of population from the country to the city. An expressed tendency (q.v.).

trend, dysgenic. Cf. dysgenic trend.

trend, population. A continuous function expressing changing or constant rates of population change, or a conceptual generalization of such rates and their effects on the number and composition of a population.   F.L.

trend, suburban. The persistent movement of the urban population away from the congested areas in the heart of the city, out to the smaller towns and communities near or adjacent to the city. The trend, made possible by the development of easy and rapid transportation, has given rise to numerous residential communities in the periphery of nearly every great cit'   R.E.B.

trends, social. Cf. social trends.

trends, sociological. Cf. sociological trends.

trends, urban. Social or economic trends or movements evolving in urban communities, such as apartment house life, deferred marriages, commercialized recreation. Also, the trend or flow of population toward urban centers.   E.E.M.

trial by newspaper. The practice among newspapers of "taking sides" or editorializing in news stories relating to crimes so as to give a general impression of the guilt of the accused and thus inevitably to influence the verdict of the jury.   M.A.E.

trial marriage. Cf. marriage, trial.

tribadism. Homosexual relations between women by rubbing their genitals together.   R.E.B.

tribe. A social group, usually comprising a number of sibs, bands, villages, or other sub-groups, which is normally characterized by the possession of a definite territory, a distinct dialect, a homogeneous and distinctive culture, and either a unified political organization or at least some sense of common solidarity as against outsiders.   G.P.M.

tribes, criminal. Cf. criminal tribes.

tropism. A tendency, inherent in the biological constitution of an organism, to react in a particular way to a given external stimulus.

truancy. The offense of a child absenting himself from school without acceptable excuse; habitual absence from school without leave; one of the types of child behavior constituting a strong factor leading to juvenile delinquency, and in most states of the United States specified by law as actually belonging in that category.   F.W.K.; M.A.E.

trusties. The term applied to some of the more trustworthy prisoners, who serve as messengers or other helpers within a penal institution, or are sent on errands of various sorts outside the prison. They are put on their honor not to escape and are given various privileges and threatened with loss of good time, and other privileges if they violate their trust.   J.L.G.

twins, dizygotic. Two individuals born at the same time and derived from two distinct ova. Also called diovular, binovular, fraternal, or ordinary twins. They may be of like or of unlike sex. There are a few cases where such twins are known to have had different fathers. F.H.H.

twins, identical. Popular name for monozygotic twins (q.v.). Somewhat inaccurate since such twins are never precisely alike in all respects. F.H.H.

twins, monozygotic. Two individuals, always of the same sex, born at the same time but derived from one ovum through division of the zygote or the embryo. Also called monovular or uniovular, and, popularly, identical or duplicate twins. They are also described as monochorionic, but this term is now known to be sometimes inapplicable since these twins may have separate chorions when their separation occurs at a very early stage of development. Where such separation starts at a late stage and is incomplete, Siamese or conjoint twins (double monsters) are produced. F.H.H.

type (also called **ideal type**). Rational construction derived from the integration of one or more characteristics of a social entity; a conceptual instrument for systematic description of social life and formal or material classification-schemata. The so-called average type is not a sociological but an empirical, mathematical, statistical instrument and concept. J.H.B.

type, culture. Cf. culture type.

type, ideal. Cf. ideal type.

type, individual. Cf. individual type.

type, personality. Cf. personality type.

type, social. Cf. social type.

type pattern. Rational model-structure for and of standard characteristics of a social entity. J.H.B.

typical. Corresponding to a type.

typical attitude. Cf. attitude, typical.

typical pattern. Cf. typology constructive.

typology, constructive. A kind of scientific method in the social sciences which lays stress on the construction of types made up of criteria (so-called "elements," "traits," "aspects," etc.) which have discoverable referents in the empirical world. (Cf. culture case study for examples.) This construction should always take place in relation to a definite problem and should be oriented toward a clear-cut hypothesis; the type of highest usefulness is not merely classificatory. The conception of science (q.v.) underlying constructive typology is that scientific activity is essentially predictive; even though predictions must often be cast in retrospective rather than prospective terms, and even though they are frequently hypothetical rather than actual, the logic of scientific prediction (q.v.), which is at bottom probability logic, is consistently followed. This point needs stressing, for some interpretations of "ideal-typical method" (of which constructive typology is a closely related offshoot) do not hold the basically probable character of the "ideal type" clearly enough in view. It is for this reason, among many others, that "constructed type" is coming to be the preferred term.

Although not always constructed with sufficient care, and sometimes lacking possible empirical approximations (referents) and precise validation, constructed types abound in sociological research. Clans, castes, classes, nations, sects, cults, and like social structures are constructed types; individuation, superordination, accommodation, exploitation, and similar social processes are often in the same category. It should be pointed out, however, that the construct and the empirical approximation are not the same thing; no constructed caste will be exactly matched by a given empirical caste as it exists on a given day and hour. In this sense, therefore, nothing but "exceptions" to constructed types exist.

Moreover, constructed types are not necessarily averages, although every average, in the special technical sense of the mean (not the mode or the median) has some of the attributes of a constructed type. For example, the "average alumna" of a certain college, who reputedly bears .6 of a child during her entire reproductive period, does not exist in the flesh; she is not an empirical instance but is computed from empirical instances.

Constructed types usually include many more criteria than go to identify items capable of manipulation by present statistical techniques. Indeed, it is not at present feasible even to attempt numerical statement in the great majority of the problems dealt with by the constructive typologist. It follows, then, that although constructive typology is based on the logic of probability, it is not ordinarily "quantitative" unless every statement made in "more or less" terms can be so regarded.

H.B.

typology, sociological. Cf. typology, constructive.

tyranny. An arbitrary, despotic, and usually cruel exercise of power however gained; an exercise of power unlimited by law or constitution; "naked power"—the kind that involves no acquiescence on the part of the subject. It may be exercised by an individual or a group—Hitler's power being a perfect example of the former.

F.E.L.

U

ultimogeniture. The exclusive or preferential right in inheritance of the youngest son, child, or other heir. Cf. primogeniture.   G.P.M.

unadjustment. The situation-process of a person or a group faced with a difficulty as yet unsolved—whether the difficulty be defined as a problem by the persons most concerned or only by an outside observer. Unadjustment unsolved within the range of the normally available resources of the person becomes maladjustment, which if recognized as requiring outside aid, becomes a social problem, which may lead to disorganization. Cf. social pathology.
                                                                             T.D.E.

unaided recall technique. Research technique in which the informant is not given any clues to help him recall a given situation. Used widely in market and radio audience research. E.g., "What radio programs did you listen to yesterday?" Cf. aided recall for opposite technique.   M.PT.

underpopulation. A condition in society when the numerical population is too small to achieve or maintain a recognized and accepted social objective. The opposite of overpopulation (q.v.).

understanding, area of. Cf. area of understanding.

underworld. A semi-popular designation for the sub rosa existence of criminal activity, commercialized vice, gambling houses, places trafficking in contraband narcotics, and other interconnected illicit enterprises, such as bootlegging and "numbers racket." The criminal and pseudo-criminal elements constitute an underworld to the extent that association and activity take place outside the bounds of respectable society; hence, forming a sort of pariah caste. An underworld of crime and vice is likely to be a figment of the moral isolation of respectable from disreputable persons quite as much as a product of informal organization and association among the criminal and pseudo-criminal elements.   W.C.R.

unearned increment. An increase in value of property due primarily to the operation of social or economic forces rather than to the efforts or initiative of the owner.

unemployment. Enforced or involuntary separation from remunerative work on the part of a member of the normal working force, during normal working time, at normal wages, and under normal working conditions. The concept of normality, which may or may not be defined legally, is central to the concept of unemployment. "Normal working force," as used in this definition, ordinarily applies to wage earners, or by extension to salaried employees. It seldom is applied to self-employed, or business or professional, workers. Precision of definition acquires importance through the connection of this status with various social patterns such as social security legislation, trade union benefits, etc. When not defined legally, the normal expectation of any given society must be taken into account. For example, the term "unemployed" could not logically be applied to a three-year old child or to a bed-ridden octogenarian because neither is a member of the normal working force. Moreover, a competent worker could not be refused the status of unemployment because he refuses to take a job at ten cents a day or at sixteen hours a day, or under intolerable working conditions. The concept of "normal working time" presents serious difficulties, since it may be defined from the point of view either of the worker or of the industry. Obviously, the natural-ice-harvesting business cannot be expected to employ workers except in the winter nor the hop-picking industry for more than a few weeks in the summer. On the other hand, from the point of view of the worker, "normal working time" must be long enough to provide a decent livelihood (q.v.) for the worker and his dependents for a year. The conflict of interests represented in this situation is partially accountable for a considerable amount of disorganization and maladjustment within the capitalist system.

unemployment compensation. Money provided persons temporarily unemployed, usually through government. w.p.

uniform crime reports. Periodical statistical bulletins issued by the Bureau of Investigation, U. S. Department of Justice, containing data compiled from reports sent in regularly and according to a uniform plan by police agencies throughout the nation. These bulletins, first issued in 1930 on the basis of experiments made prior to that time by a committee of the International Association of Chiefs of Police, are the best source of information on criminality in the United States. t.s.

uniformity. A condition of observed likeness between or among objects in whatever attribute is under comparison; absence of differences, in any given respect, between persons or their behaviors. Absolute uniformity or identity in detail does not exist in nature, even in the "same" object from moment to moment, since change and uniqueness are universal. Uniformity is always relative to the purpose concerned. In social control, a policy of uniformity dislikes differentiation (q.v.) and seeks to increase the mode (q.v.) and reduce the number of variants and the range of variation. t.d.e.

unilinear. Reckoning descent (q.v.), inheritance (q.v.), or succession (q.v.) exclusively in either the male or the female line. Cf. bilateral. g.p.m.

unimprovability. A prognostic term designating an unfavorable outcome mainly used by German criminologists in clinical studies of prisoners. It is sometimes used by American prison psychiatrists to designate a likely failure to respond to treatment and a likely relapse into crime after release from prison. It is closely akin to the category of bad risk in studies by sociologists which predict outcome of offenders on parole and probation. The unimprovability can be due to a combination of constitutional and situational factors. As a level of prognosis, it is more easily observed than it is explained. Likewise as a condition akin to a prediction category such as bad risk for non-relapse into crime, it is measurable in an expectancy table but not readily explainable in terms of causes. w.c.r.

unincorporated village. Cf. village.

union, industrial. A trade union organization of all wage-earners in a given industry regardless of their craft or skill. The industrial union had its origin in the Knights of Labor of the 1870's but with the rise of craft consciousness in the American Federation of Labor industrial unions tended to disappear. Both the International Workers of the World (I.W.W.) and the Communist Party sought to foster industrial unionism to combat the conservative policies of the craft unions. Agitation for the organization of the unskilled workers on an industrial basis began in the A. F. of L. in the 1920's but the indifference of the craft unions and jurisdictional jealousies prevented active organization until 1936 when John L. Lewis, of the United Mine Workers, formed the Committee on Industrial Organization within the A. F. of L. Opposition to the Committee's activities forced the Committee to leave the ranks of the A. F. of L. and form the Congress of Industrial Organizations which now rivals the A. F. of L. in numbers and power. Bargaining power of an industrial union is secured by 100 per cent organization of workers rather than by the monopoly power over a few strategic skills. j.w.m'c.

union, labor. Cf. labor union.

union, ritual. Prescribed or compulsory sexual intercourse on ceremonial occasions, e.g., agricultural fertility rites, initiation or wedding ceremonies, or the termination of a period of ritual continence (q.v.) Cf. ceremonial license; defloration.   G.P.M.

union, trade. Cf. trade union.

union shop. Cf. shop, union.

union wage. Cf. wage, union.

U. S. S. R. Union of Soviet Socialist Republics.

unionism, trade. Cf. trade union.

uniqueness, marginal Cf. marginal uniqueness.

units, social. Cf. social units.

unity, collective. Cf. collective unity.

unity, group. Cf. group unity.

universal evolution. Cf. evolution, universal.

universal pattern. Cf. pattern, universal, of culture.

universal pattern of culture. Cf. pattern, universal, of culture.

universal principles. Cf. principles, universal.

universalism. A theory that society is a reality as well as a mental concept and is of supreme value. There are two varieties of universalism. (1) Extreme universalism which regards the individual as merely a part of the social whole and as of no value apart from the whole and that the whole is more valuable than the part. (2) Moderate universalism which concedes to the individual reality and some value apart from the social whole. Historically, universalism has alternated with singularism and integralism from 600 B. C. to 1900 A. D.   J.D.

universe, statistical. The total population from which a sample is selected; the aggregate of all possible cases of the group under consideration. Also called population, parent population, universe of discourse.   M.Pt.

universe of discourse. Cf. discourse, universe of.

unnatural. Not in conformity with nature. (q.v.). Affected by the application of human intelligence.

unrest. A feeling of restlessness or uneasiness resulting from long or varied frustration and unadjustment without acute crisis and without adequate problem-solving analysis, techniques, or social resources. When widespread it is called social unrest, and is indicated by increase in labor turnover, by hectic amusements and crazes, by high suicide and divorce rates, by anarchic tendencies in the arts, etc. It is fertile soil for exotic, revolutionary, criminal or morbid behavior patterns.   T.D.E.

unrest, social. Cf. social unrest.

unsocial. Lacking in the desire or inclination to participate in group activities.

unsocialized. Lacking in the traits necessary for successful adjustment to and participation in group life.

unsocialized drive. Cf. drive, unsocialized.

urban. Pertaining to a city or town. According to the United States Census reports between 1790 and 1900 inclusive, urban was applied to all incorporated places with a population of 8000 or more. Beginning with the census of 1910, urban has been applied to all incorporated places with a population of 2500 or more and to a few other political subdivisions which had densely populated areas. According to the census of 1940 the "other political subdivisions" constituted about 4 per cent of the total urban population of the United States.   O.W.

urban area. Cf. area, urban.

urban centralization. The concentration of population in urban areas. Less frequently, the term may refer to concentration of industry, commerce and cultural amenities in urban areas.   E.E.M.

urban decentralization. Population movement away from the densely settled urban areas to peripheral areas. Less frequently, the term may refer to outward movement of industrial or commercial enterprises.   E.E.M.

urban ecology. Cf. ecology, urban.

urban growth. Increase in area or population of a territory classified as urban.   O.W.

urban sociology. Cf. sociology, urban.

urban trends. Cf. trends, urban.

urban zone. Cf. zone, urban.

urbanization. The process of becoming urban; the movement of people or processes to urban areas; the increase of urban areas, population, or processes.

urn burial. Cf. burial, urn.

usury. A charge made since ancient times for the use of money lent to or deposited with an individual or institution, generally computed annually or for fractions of a year. This charge has always aroused resentment because of the high rates imposed and the heavy penalties for defection. It is difficult to determine the criteria of usury because it is fixed by the ethical norms prevailing in a given culture; this is especially true in a liberal economy where transactions are voluntary.   E.F.

utilitarian. Motivated by practical usefulness, pleasure or comfort, or by the avoidance of their opposites; cool blooded, as contrasted with sympathetic, affectional motivation in "primary" group contacts and relationships, or with idealistic, dogmatic or fanatic motivation in mass movements, war, etc.   T.D.E.

utilities. Services, such as water, light, heat, refrigeration energy, cooking fuel, and heating domestic hot water, which must be provided in order that a dwelling unit shall be "decent, safe, and sanitary."   S.S.

utility. The inherent and real capacity of an object to satisfy a human desire. It is intrinsic to the object itself, and may or may not be apprehended by the human observer. Belief in utility is the basis of value (q.v.), but the utility may be spurious or entirely lacking.

utility, marginal. Cf. marginal utility.

utility, public. Cf. public utility.

utilize. To make use of, to consume, to put to a useful purpose.   E.E.M.

utopia. Specifically the word refers to an epoch-making book of this title, describing an ideal commonwealth, by Sir Thomas More, published in Latin in 1516, and in English translation in 1551. The term has two general usages: (1) in the realm of the humanities and social sciences, any romantic or philosophic description, through the literary medium of the dialogue, the novel, or some similar form, of an imaginary and perhaps unrealizable state of society, free from human imperfections; (2) in common parlance, any supposedly impracticable or apparently fantastic scheme of social endeavor.   J.O.H.

utopianism. The construction of blueprints for the fulfillment of the dreams of men for a perfect society; conscious social improvement by ideas, ideals, and definite agencies of social modification.   J.O.H.

V

vagabond. An impecunious roamer, an itinerant musician or actor of the Middle Ages, a literary person living from hand to mouth. One who makes a show of living his life, disdaining his poverty. The term is also applied to certain types of wanderers who are better described as hobos, tramps or vagrants. Generally begging or mendicancy is associated with vagabondage. Sometimes the early scholars begged and wandered. In the class of vagabonds might be included certain soldiers of fortune of an earlier period. N.A.

vagrancy. Except where defined by statute, the behavior of a person without permanent social attachments; aimless wandering of an individual without visible means of legitimate self-support.   J.M.R.

At common law vagrancy means wandering about from place to place by an idle person who has no visible means of support, and who subsists on charity and does not work, though able to do so. But the connotations of vagrancy have been extended by statutory regulations so as to include other forms of behavior than that cited above. It would appear that vagrancy is the broadest of the categories of offense. To enumerate but a few of the types of conduct for which vagrancy charges have been sustained, the following may be cited: prostitution, gambling, fortune-telling, drunkenness, begging, and many other forms of behavior which are deemed socially undesirable, if not dangerous. Though the charge of vagrancy may not be sustained if the alleged offender has regular employment, or is wandering in search of it, it is to be noted that in times of business depression convictions for vagrancy manifest a sharp increase in industrial areas.   A.E.W.

vagrant. An unattached, itinerary, and indigent person. The several types are variously described on the basis of behavior or appearance. For example, "The hobo works and wanders; the tramp dreams and wanders; and the bum drinks and wanders." The hobo, an itinerant worker who may on occasion be a mendicant, is now practically non-existent. The homeless indigent types change from one period to another and are different in different localities. The vagrant is so identified because he presents a problem to the security of a community because he is homeless, voteless, without local interests and there is strong presumption that he is or may become a delinquent.   N.A.

validity of data. Extent to which data correspond with some criterion which is an acceptable measure of the phenomena being studied. The accuracy with which data represent what they purport to represent. To be distinguished from reliability of data.   M.Pt.

valley section. A theory which holds that a typical river valley will display examples of the fundamental forms of social organization through the influence of occupation. Near the source of the river, in the mountains, will be found miners, followed in turn, by shepherds, small farmers of the piedmont, planters of the coastal plains, city-dwelling commercial folk near the river mouth, and fisher folk and seamen on the ocean off shore. H.E.M.

valuation. The process of ascertaining the relative importance or worth of two or more goods or services, generally expressed in terms of money. Cf. value.   E.E.M.

value. The believed capacity of any object to satisfy a human desire. The quality of any object which causes it to be of interest to an individual or a group. Value

331

is strictly a psychological reality, and is not measurable by any means yet devised. It is to be sharply distinguished from utility (q.v.), because its reality is in the human mind, not in the external object itself. Value is strictly a matter of belief; an object, the utility of which is strictly spurious, will have the same value as if it were genuine until the deception is discovered. Ultimate values are axiomatic and are inherent in human nature (q.v.) itself. Their existence may be discovered by social or psychological research, but neither their validity nor their justifiability can be demonstrated. They are, at the same time, the final sources of the motivation of all conscious rational telic behavior.

value, objective. Standard or judgment of persons, groups or institutions constructed and proven by the consensus of competence.　　　　　　　　　　　　　　　J.H.B.

value, subjective. Standard of judgment accepted by persons, groups or institutions, stemming from and conditioned by their societal context.　　　　　　　J.H.B.

value, survival. The quality of any trait or characteristic that gives it, or its possessor, advantage in the struggle for existence. The concept is inherent in the Darwinian theory of evolution, particularly in association with the concept of "survival of the fittest." It is important to note that in this connection the term "value" has no significance except with respect to survival itself. Traits which are positively repugnant to human beings may be useful in promoting the persistence of non-human types, and in the social arena traits which are definitely at variance with social values may nevertheless conduce to the survival of their possessors.

values, scale of. Personal and/or social values ranged in order of relative importance in the attitudes of a given person or group of persons, and evidenced either by law, priorities, or other conscious formulae (e.g., "Women and children first," "Billions for defense but not one cent for New Deal"), or by observed consistency of behavior or statistical measurement of choices or outlays.　　　　　　　　T.D.E.

values, social. Cf. social values.

variable. Any trait, quality, or characteristic which can vary in magnitude in different individual cases. Also called variate. Used in contradistinction to attribute and to constant.　　　　　　　　M.Pt.

variable, dependent. Cf. variable, independent.

variable, independent. When two magnitudes are so connected that, when one takes on a set of definite values, the corresponding values of the other are defined, the former is called the independent variable; the latter, the dependent variable. It will be seen that the distinction between the two often depends on the point of view of the investigator. For example, one might consider men marrying at various specified ages and calculate for each age-group the mean age of the bride in which case age of husbands would be the independent variable, or one might reverse the process and make age of brides the independent variable.　　　　　　　P.H.F.

variables, societal. Cf. societal variables.

variation. Departure from established type. In organic evolution, the term applies to deviation in the interrelated germ plasm and somatoplasm as a result of which new varieties and species arise. In sociology, the term is valuable in an analogical sense.

variation, cultural. Cf. cultural variation.

vasectomy. A surgical operation in which there is a restriction, severing, or removal of a part of the vas deferens, the tube which conducts the sperm away from the testicle. It is usually a simple operation that can be performed in an hour or less with the aid of only a local anesthetic. A method of sterilization of the male.　　　　　　　　　　　O.W.

vendetta. An Italian term designating a blood feud, a custom that shows survivals in Corsica, the Kentucky mountains, and many more primitive areas of the globe.　　　　　　　　　　　　　　T.S.

venereal disease. A group of diseases located usually in the genital-urinary system. The two most prominent venereal diseases are syphilis and gonorrhea. The former is caused by a micro-organism which enters the blood stream and ultimately invades the bones, vital organs and nerve tissue causing deterioration of both mind and body. Gonorrhea is caused by a germ which attacks the urethra and on rare occasions the eye. While both syphilis and gonorrhea can be transmitted by other means than bodily contact, sexual intercourse is by far the most usual source of infection.   J.W.M'C.

vengeance, blood. Cf. blood vengeance.

verification. A situation-process by which the truth or actuality of an hypothesis or theory or doctrine or idea is demonstrated or disproved. Scholastic verification consists in showing logical derivation from, or consonance with, dogma. Scientific verification consists in testing a claim (by the same or other observers), by repetition of experiments or observations under similar or more refined conditions or with parallel control-experiments for isolation of specific differential factors, or by attempting to reach similar findings with different instruments or methods. Cf. scientific method; proof.   T.D.E.

vertical circularity. Social mobility between classes, or strata that are considered to have different status with respect to superiority or inferiority.

vertical group. Cf. group, vertical.

vertical mobility. Cf. mobility, vertical.

vested interest. Cf. interest, vested.

vicarious sacrifice. Cf. sacrifice, vicarious.

vice. Personal behavior of a sort disapproved by the moral code, particularly because of its tendency to injure the personality physically, mentally or socially, and because of its liability by contagion, either physical or social, to produce corresponding injuries in others. Vice takes many forms, but almost invariably it represents the use of some natural impulse or appetite for other than its intrinsic end or purpose, or the abuse of such an impulse by excessive gratification. The practice of vice tends to form habits, and to

lead to ever-increasing indulgence. Its evil effects may be confined strictly to the individual. Societal disapproval of vice rests upon the injury to society through the deterioration of any individual member, and upon the danger of communication to other individuals.

vice, commercialized. As customarily used in sociological studies, the business of prostitution. Prostitution shows varying degrees of commercialization, all the way from independent conduct of prostitution by girls themselves to exploitation of prostitutes in brothels or syndicated houses of prostitution. In some Oriental countries the business of prostitution has been accepted as an institution. In Western countries, either it has been tolerated as a part of police policy, or it has had illegal status, in which latter instance it has been the object of suppressive measures of law enforcement.   W.C.R.

vice areas. Cf. areas, vice.

vice squad. A special detail of American police, charged with raiding and closing houses of prostitution and gambling resorts. The vice squads are likely to become unusually active in law enforcement campaigns.   W.C.R.

village. An agricultural village is that form of association resulting from local contiguity of residence of people of various occupations whose homes are aggregated in a small area and whose economic and social organizations and institutions are largely dependent for their support on the farm families in the surrounding area which they serve. Fishing, mining, or industrial villages are characterized by their inhabitants being engaged chiefly in these occupations. According to the U. S. Census, incorporated villages are incorporated places of less than 2500 inhabitants. There is no established usage with regard to the size of population of unincorporated villages, some of the leading students of villages using 250 as the minimum (calling those with less than 250 hamlets), while others would accept the common usage of rural people and designate any aggregation of 100 or more people a village; but the Census usage of under 2500 as a maximum is generally recognized.   D.S.

village, farm. Cf. community, village.

village, incorporated. Cf. village.

village, line. A type of rural settlement. Cf. form of settlement.

village, unincorporated. Cf. village.

village community. Cf. community, village.

virgate. A measure of land used in medieval England to designate an area generally amounting to thirty acres. N.L.S.

vision quest. A purposive search for a personal guardian spirit, who is revealed through a dream or vision, usually after fasting and vigils, undertaken by the Indians of many North American tribes during childhood or adolescence. G.P.M.

visiting nurse. A public health nurse whose original function was only to give nursing care to the sick in their homes, but which has been broadened to include any or all parts of the public health nursing program for health promotion, prevention of illness, and correction of defects usually designated to public health nurses in an adequate community health program.

visiting teacher. A social worker who is employed to assist in adjusting behavior problems of the school child. To this end visiting teachers try to work out cooperative relationships between home and school in adjusting such problems and "visit" the child's parents in order to secure their assistance and to understand the child's background. M.A.E.

vital index. Cf. index, vital.

vital revolution. Cf. revolution, vital.

vital statistics. Cf. statistics, vital.

vitality. Constitutional conditions favorable to longevity, health or fecundity. *Note.* The term is sometimes applied to observed high fertility, as such, on the erroneous assumption that social conditions have a negligible influence on fertility. F.L.

vocation. The permanent activity which guarantees one a livelihood, and membership in his particular occupational group. E.F.

vocational guidance. Systematic efforts to assist young people in choosing their occupations wisely. It includes counseling children of high school age and older persons to discover their own abilities, to gain information about various fields of employment, to secure adequate preparation, to obtain suitable employment in their chosen field, and finally, to make successive adjustments looking toward a satisfying vocational and economic status. A.E.W.

vocational rehabilitation. A program of retraining persons with physical defects and handicaps for profitable employment. Although most states of the U. S. included some vocational training provisions in their laws relating to the care of the blind, and some made similar provisions for physically handicapped, vocational rehabilitation did not become general throughout the country until the passage of the Sheppard-Towner Act in 1920. By this Act the federal government granted subsidies to states which established a program of vocational rehabilitation. Many states now include vocational rehabilitation as an alternative to long term benefits under workmen's compensation laws. This has been made possible by the extension of federal subsidies through social security legislation of 1936 and 1939. J.W.M'C.

vocational training. Education for specific trades or occupations, usually consisting of a combination of classroom instruction and practical training in working with actual materials similar to those used on the job. Vocational training is distinguished from the more rudimentary type of practical instruction known as manual training by its more exact relationship to job requirements. It first developed on a large scale in the secondary schools of America under the impetus of Federal aid supplied through the provisions of the Smith-Hughes Act of 1917. The term also includes some college training, and out-of-school instruction for specialized types of work, of the sort developed on projects of the National Youth

Administration and in war industries.

S.C.M.

volition. (1) In a broad sense, the ability to perform foreseen acts, i.e., acts proceeding from an idea or representation of the act. In this sense, voluntary acts are distinguished from reflex acts; the acts may, however, be determined by the idea or representation. In repeated acts of this type (habit), the voluntary character may become lost. (2) In a strict sense, the ability to perform controlled, premeditated acts. These acts are not merely preceded by the idea of the act, but by a reflection on the idea, under the form of a discussion or deliberation. In this sense, voluntary acts are distinguished from spontaneous acts. (3) The ability to choose. (4) (*philosophy*) Tendency towards an object apprehended by the intellect as good. Cf. will.

B.M.

voluntary association. Cf. association, voluntary.

voluntary cooperation. Cf. cooperation, voluntary.

voluntary parenthood. Cf. parenthood, voluntary.

volunteer Negro. A person who by legal definition is a Negro, but because of physical appearance could pass as a member of the white racial group. Often referred to as a "Negro by election."

W.R.C.

votive offering. A sacrifice made in fulfilment of a vow.

G.P.M.

vow. A solemn promise made to a supernatural being by which a person binds himself, either absolutely or on condition of receiving some anticipated divine favor, to perform a particular service or act of devotion or to refrain from a particular type of behavior.

Vucetich method. A system of classification of fingerprints designed by the Argentinian, Juan Vucetich, in 1891 and still widely employed with modifications in various Latin-American and south European countries and in Norway.

T.S.

W

wage, living. The rate of remuneration for work which suffices to obtain the necessaries of livilihood. M.VK.

wage, minimum. A basic payment, established by law, by union agreement, or by action of an employer, which is not to be lowered for workers in a given classification or area. In recent legislative proposals, "minimum" has given place to "fair", as in the Federal Government's Fair Labor Standards Act. M.VK.

wage, prevailing. (1) On work other than public work of the United States Government: the wage paid the majority of workers in a specific class of occupation in a particular community. (2) On public works of the United States Government: the wage or rate for any specific class of labor as set by the Secretary of Labor under the Bacon-Davis Act, August 30, 1935.

wage, union. The rate of remuneration established by a union and applicable in all enterprises which have established industrial relations on the basis of collective bargaining. M.VK.

wage rate. Determination of wages on a specified time or unit basis; e.g., per hour, day, piece, etc. E.E.M.

wage scale. A series of rates of pay, applicable to an occupation or a group of occupations and to a given place of employment or over an entire area of employment. M.VK.

wages. Prices paid by business owners for the services of free (nonslave) human labor. E.E.M.

wages, nominal. An expression of wages, usually in money terms, without reference to purchasing power. E.E.M.

wages, real. Quantities and qualities of goods or services that money wages will buy at or over a period of time. E.E.M.

wakanda. The Siouan concept of impersonal supernatural power. Cf. mana. G.P.M.

wampum. Strings or belts of shell beads used as ornaments and as a standard of value by the North American Indians. G.P.M.

want. The absence or lack of necessaries; hence destitution, poverty. In economics, wants are goods or services beyond the absolute needs of life or efficiency, sought by man. E.E.M.

war. Armed extensive conflict between organized bodies of people, regarding themselves as politically sovereign and ethically entitled to assert by force their rights, which they claim to be blocked or invaded by their armed opponents. C.J.B.
Wars manifest two main types. The first is ordinarily called "international," although the parties involved may not be true nations (q.v.) in the strict sense of the word. They are always societies operating through the institution of the state (q.v.). Some of the greatest wars of history have been imperial wars, in which the armies on one side were composed of representatives of many different nationalities and ethnic groups. The second type of war is ordinarily called "civil", in which the conflict takes place between separate sections of a single political unit. Frequently, such wars take the form of rebellion, in which case the political sover-

eignty of one group is more a matter of conviction, aspiration, and theory, than of reality. The causation, methods, and consequences of these two types of war are likely to be quite different.

war, tong. Violent conflict between rival Chinese groups or tongs. Such groups or societies in the United States are a transfer from China where they are based upon kinship, district, or other forms of affiliation. They often serve useful purposes in business or social welfare. But through business rivalry, or efforts to control illicit forms of gain in relation to vice, gambling, or the opium traffic some of the tongs become involved in criminal violence. Membership in the tongs may consist in part of merchants who are forced to join in order to get protection from rival tongs who seek control over their business. Tong wars ensue. Cf. racketeer.   A.E.W.

warning. A promise or prediction of disagreeable consequences to follow from present practice. Whereas a threat always has a present reference, a warning always has a future reference.   F.E.L.

waste. The use of any object in such a way as to derive less than the maximum satisfaction from it. The wanton destruction of any valuable substance. Waste takes two main forms: (1) the destruction or misuse of irreplaceable materials, either natural resources, human capacities, or time; and (2) the use of any consumption good in such a manner as to derive less than the full satisfaction from it. (E.g., eating only the heart of a lamb chop and letting the rest go into the garbage pail.) In a price-and-profit system, under conditions where unemployment (q.v.) exists or threatens, the latter form of waste produces much less serious results than the former, and may have a certain paradoxical utility in keeping the system operating.

water burial. Cf. burial, water.

way, right of. Cf. right of way.

wealth. (1) In relation to self-maintenance, material objects owned by human beings and external to the bodies of the owners. The quality of value (q.v.), but not necessarily utility (q.v.), is implicit in the concept of wealth on the assumption that nothing is owned unless it has value. The source of all wealth is the land (q.v.), and the processes of creating wealth are comprehended in the general term "production" (q.v.). The phenomena arising in connection with the making and distribution of wealth form the subject matter of the special social science of economics. Wealth is of two main types, production goods (q.v.) and consumption goods (q.v.). (2) Material possessions of considerable amount. Riches. Abundance. Large accumulated stores of valuable objects.

we-feeling. Cf. feeling, we-.

we-group. Cf. group, we-.

weight. (*statistical*) The relative value or importance of items involved in a given computation. Multiplier used to modify the magnitude of an item in accordance with its relative importance.   M.Pt.

weighing. (*statistical*) The assignment of weights to various items in accordance with their assumed or estimated value.   M.Pt.

welfare. An interest directed to the well-being of persons or groups. "General welfare" as set forth in the Constitution is that responsibility for the common good which must be assumed by government.   N.A.

welfare, child; child care. A composite of, first, the social and economic forces in community life which make it possible for a child's own family to nurture it through the years of childhood, and second, the instrumentalities, both public and private, which supplement the capacities and resources of a child's natural family in such measure as may be necessary to insure wholesome growth and development.   W.P.

welfare, organic. Welfare which is neither individualistic nor socialistic, but mutually constituted; neither for men as producers merely nor for men merely as consumers, but for both. Process of production, if efficient, should be enjoyable and enriching to personality, not destructive of normality (q.v.); consumption should enhance efficiency. As a goal for social-economic community organization it is also a criterion by which the value and results of economic, social, and political processes and programs may be tested.   T.D.E.

welfare, public. That part of the activities of a community which deal with social problems of individuals and families including social planning; usually governmental programs.   W.P.

welfare, social. Cf. social welfare.

weltanschauung. (German, literal translation: view-of-the-universe.) A coherent, intuitional and rational conception of the totality of the world, comprising life, society and its institutions, as seen by a person or group from a given value system, and its application through appropriate behavior and attitudes.   J.H.B.

wergild. The worth of a man injured by another according to the man's station in society. The wergild was the amount of compensation the offender was compelled to pay the injured or his representative in order to compose the difficulty. If the wergild was not paid, private retaliation could then be exercised against the offender and his kin by the injured and his kin. Cf. blood vengeance; blood money.   J.L.G.

whipping post. A post to which criminals, often those who have committed relatively mild offenses, are tied for whipping as a means of legal punishment. Such a practice was once widespread in England and in the American colonies. Delaware still retains the whipping post for certain offenses.   M.A.E.

white-collar criminal. Cf. criminal, white-collar.

white man's Negro. A person discernibly Negroid who ingratiates himself with white people in order to gain what he believes are advantages. "Uncle Tom" is the epithet applied to such a Negro by the Negro intelligentsia.   W.R.C.

white slave traffic. The popular name in the United States given to the induction of girls into brothel prostitution. It is intended to dramatize the fact that pandering may enslave some girls into brothel prostitution. Actually, the so-called traffic was never found to be extensive in cities of the U. S. The claim is made that it is more extensive in European, Asiatic, and South American countries. The induction of girls into prostitution as slaves of the brothel system applies to girls of all races. Hence, white slave traffic is not a very accurate term. Indeed, it was coined during the anti-vice crusades of the former generation as part of the American public's recoil to rumors and exposures of the underworld.   W.C.R.

wholes, social. Cf. social wholes.

wholes, societal. Cf. societal wholes.

widow. A woman whose husband is deceased and who has not married again.   W.G.

widower. A man whose wife has died and who has not remarried.   W.G.

widowhood. The state of being a widow; the period during which a widow remains unmarried.   W.G.

wife. A woman united to a man in lawful marriage. A married woman.   W.G.

wife-capture. Marriage by capture.   G.P.M.

wife-purchase. Marriage by purchase.   G.P.M.

wigwam. A hut of the Indians of eastern North America, varying in shape from arched to conical, usually covered with mats or bark.   G.P.M.

will. The capacity to govern personal behavior by choice among two or more possibilities. The capacity to balance one stimulus or impulse against another, and to select the one which is believed to be preferable from the point of view of the major interest of the individual concerned. The concept of will carries the implication that human behavior is something more than the result of a mere parallelogram of forces and that the ego has the power to give arbitrary weight to one impulse in preference to others, producing a result different from that which would be expected if the human personality was a mere reacting mechanism governed by instincts, reflexes, or tropisms. There is no significant distinction between "will" and "free will." Both are believed to be exclusive human endowments. Will is logically associated with such concepts as volition, choice, reason, foresight, and decision. Perhaps the existence and operation of will is most clearly revealed in types of behavior where there is no imaginable advantage on the part of one alternative over the other. E.g., one may lay a lead pencil on the desk before him and decide by his will whether to move it to the right or to the left.

will, free. Cf. will.

will, group. Combined will of two or more participants possessing the implication that group will is different from the will of each participant and from the sum of the wills of the participants. A much disputed concept. Cf. will, individual; will, social.   M.S.

will, individual. Cf. individual will.

will, social. Cf. social will.

wish, dominant. Wish taking precedence over and controlling other wishes.   M.S.

wish, individual. Cf. individual wish.

wish, social. Cf. social wish.

wissenssoziologie. (German). The sociology of knowledge which holds that the "modes of thought" of all individuals are determined by, and therefore related to, the nature of the social groups to which the individuals belong—not merely economic classes but also "generations, status groups, sects, occupational groups, schools, etc."   J.S.R.

witchcraft. The practice or art of influencing the well-being of another, usually to his detriment, by magical means or with the aid of familiar spirits (q.v.). Cf. sorcery.   G.P.M.

withdrawal. A contraceptive method. Cf. coitus interruptus.

without-presence group. Cf. group without-presence.

with-presence group. Cf. group with-presence.

woman. In general, the feminine half of humanity. Specifically, a mature human being of the female sex. In the abstract, a generalized total of all feminine traits.

woman's rights movement. A social movement originating in the first half of the nineteenth century, led by women, to secure for themselves a higher social and legal status and larger property rights than they then enjoyed. Although a contemporary struggle was taking place in England, in which both men and women participated, the movement in the United States took a more organized form. The democratic views current at the time had already secured a larger measure of freedom and opportunity for children in the American family; but the subordinate status of wives remained unchanged. Not only did a woman lose personal independence at marriage but she lost the right of separate legal action and all personal control over her property so long as the marriage continued. It was this denial of legal personality and property rights to wives that was the primary source of the woman's rights movement in America. The concurrent demand for political emancipation received its chief impetus from the desire to free married women from financial dependence and legal subordination. Beginning in the eighteenforties, the woman's movement was led by a band of able and devoted women such as Lucy Stone Blackwell, Elizabeth Cady Stanton and others. Despite the gradual revision of the domestic relations laws of the various States after the Civil War, the struggle to free women from the injustices of English common law had not been wholly won at the end of the nineteenth century.   W.G.

woman's suffrage. The right of women to vote for public officials on the same basis as men. The demand for the right to vote was begun in the United States before the Civil War, and although overshadowed by the events of that war it continued to grow nationally and internationally, during the latter part of the 19th century. The movement in America made most rapid progress under the leadership of Carrie Chapman Catt, the successful conclusion of the reform coming in 1920 with the passage of the 19th Amendment to the Constitution of the United States forbidding the several states to exclude citizens from the privilege of voting because of sex. This action in America was soon followed by the passage of Act of Parliament extending suffrage to women over thirty; this was followed in 1928 by another act granting full suffrage on an equality with men.   J.W.M'C.

work relief. Cf. relief, work.

worker, migratory. A worker who finds casual employment in different places at various times of the year, so that he must travel from one job to another. The concept includes both essential farm workers and industrial workers such as those in the oil and construction industries, whose employment entails frequent migration from one place to another.   S.C.M.

worker, social. Cf. social worker.

workers' education. Cf. education, workers'.

workhouse. An English institution for the confinement of vagrants, beggars, and paupers. An American institution for short-term offenders. The same as jail.   J.P.S.

working class. The manual labor group in modern industrial society, occupying the lower ranks among the classes in point of income, status and surrounding conditions, and, by reason of the common concerns and problems arising out of its position, tending to form a more or less cohesive secondary group.   K.DP.L.

workmen's compensation. The right and system of payment to employees, and provision for medical or hospital care, for workers injured at work by accident or occupational disease, predetermined on the basis of specified injury and derived from a fund based on the principles of insurance.   M.VK.

World Court. Cf. Court, World.

worship, ancestor. The custom of worship of ancestors met with in almost every society as it emerges from barbarism. In China, Japan, and India the custom has persisted to modern times. Cf. ancestor cult.   W.G.

Y

yellow-dog contract. An agreement which an employer requires an applicant for employment to sign as a condition of employment, binding the employee not to join a union. M.VK.

youth. A person from the age of adolescence to full maturity. As a collective term, "youth" refers especially to young persons of high school and early college age. Persons aged 15 through 24 are usually considered the youth group by researchers dealing with census data. The National Youth Administration considered persons aged 16 through 25 as youth eligible for assistance. S.C.M.

youth correction authority. An administrative agency for the treatment of convicted youthful offenders. Designed by a committee of the American Law Institute and described in a model act approved by the Institute in 1940, the agency meets many of the demands for reform in penal treatment urged by social scientists and lawyers in recent times. The model act was, with modifications, adopted by California in 1941. T.S.

youth correction authority act. A proposed uniform act for the treatment of young offenders from sixteen to twenty-one years of age which the American Law Institute drew up in 1940 and recommended to the several states for adoption. With the exception of those cases in which he may impose the death penalty, life sentence, or fine, the act requires the judge to turn over all cases to the Youth Correction Authority in his state for study, after which a plan of rehabilitative treatment shall be followed. The Youth Correction Authority, consisting of three persons, is empowered to employ the assistance of educators, psychiatrists, psychologists, sociologists or other experts. The Authority may prescribe treatment in existing institutions or may recommend the creation of new institutions. In case young offenders seem to be incurable, they may be permanently incarcerated. Those who are deemed capable of benefiting from treatment are not to be released from the jurisdiction of the Authority until they are considered "safe risks." Cf. rehabilitation. M.A.E.

Z

zadruga. Slavic name for a joint family or communal household ruled over by the oldest man or woman of the group. Sometimes used today to designate a cooperative association. N.L.S.

zone, ecological. (1) Any encircling (or partially encircling) band or area, laid off on a radial axis, and characterized by some distinctive quality of man-environment adjustment. (2) Any area laid off along an ecological gradient, lying between maximum and minimum limits as expressed in terms of the variable factor of the gradient. J.A.Q.

zone, erogenous. Cf. erogenous zone.

zone, urban. An area of the city characterized by any particular phenomenon, such as business, manufacturing, residential, immigrant, wealth, poverty, crime. O.W.

zone of agreement. That area of discussion embracing matters about which there is no dispute as between persons or groups holding diverse views. It is sometimes said of certain public officials or social agencies, that they operate "within the zone of agreement." They do not venture beyond the limits of this area lest they invite criticism. N.A.

zone of deterioration. An urban area or zone in which a lower grade land use has more or less permanently succeeded a higher grade land use. For example, the rise of a slum district in a former cottage or apartment house area. E.E.M.

zone of transition. An urban area or zone in a temporary state of deterioration characterized by a lower grade land use than formerly, and not yet ripe for a succeeding more valuable land use. For example, a rooming house district arising in a once exclusive residential area, but in time destined to be wiped out by encroaching business uses. Cf. area of transition. E.E.M.

zoning. The marking off of the city in geographic areas or zones with definite restrictions upon the character of the buildings to be built and the use to which present and future buildings may be put. Zoning is a plan for guiding the growth of the city to gain maximum use from land, prevent haphazard growth, and to stabilize land values. Although first developed in Germany, zoning came into extensive use through the English Town Planning Act of 1909. Since 1910 zoning has been instituted by nearly every large city in the United States. J.W.M'C.

zygote. The cell produced by the fusion of the two gametes, sperm and egg; the fertilized egg. F.H.H.

Irmina Tamés

Phone: 392-2720

If you find me
Please, return me
To my owner
The book.